Automation Max

Automation Max

Optimizing AI and Human Intelligence in Aviation

Peter Collins

Algora Publishing
New York

Library of Congress Cataloging-in-Publication Data

Names: Collins, Peter (Peter H.), 1957- author.
Title: Automation max: optimizing AI and human intelligence in aviation /
    Peter Collins.
Description: New York: Algora Publishing, [2020] | Summary:
    "Automation-Max outlines the reasons why we should not be making such
    hasty moves towards fully automated passenger aircraft and instead why
    we should start adopting new ideas and concepts to further improve our
    already high standards of aviation safety. In an analysis of the last 10
    years of accidents, the author highlights where the human/computer
    weaknesses lie. He explores the vulnerability of the human pilot in the
    aviation world, and then he takes the debate to the next stage by asking
    how we need to redesign the interface between pilot and machine"—
    Provided by publisher.
Identifiers: LCCN 2020040901 (print) | LCCN 2020040902 (ebook) | ISBN
    9781628944310 (trade paperback) | ISBN 9781628944327 (hardback) | ISBN
    9781628944334 (pdf)
Subjects: LCSH: Airplanes—Automatic control—Safety measures. | Flight
    control. | Human-machine systems. | Aeronautics—Human factors.
Classification: LCC TL589.4 .C57 2020 (print) | LCC TL589.4 (ebook) | DDC
    629.132/6028563—dc23
LC record available at https://lccn.loc.gov/2020040901
LC ebook record available at https://lccn.loc.gov/2020040902

To Chantalle, Matthew, Andrew and HAL

Table of Contents

CHAPTER 1: DIGITAL ODYSSEY

A few too many fatal aviation accidents occurred in 2018, going against the expected trend of ever-increasing commercial flight safety. That topic, with an investigation into a Lion Air 737 Max 8 crash that occurred on October 29, 2018, dominated the news program that evening, along with a story on the passing of Douglas Rain. Rain was the actor who provided the voice of HAL in Stanley Kubrick's thought-provoking film *2001: A Space Odyssey*. What an incredible director and what interesting films! I double-checked the viewing schedule for that evening and got lucky when I found out that they had amended the program to re-screen *2001*.

I remembered being intrigued when I first saw that film and frustrated that I couldn't really understand the full meaning behind it. It seemed I would have a chance to see if I could glean anything more, now that I had greater experience in life. Well, I didn't fly for Pan-Am, the airline depicted shuttling passengers to the moon, but I was a captain on the 747-400 and retired before the Pan-Am 001 moon flights became an option on the pilot transfer list. It is notable how the film has turned out to be so accurate in its predictions. This was almost certainly down to the perceptive contributions of a certain Arthur C. Clarke, who wrote the original novel — the present day space station is foreseen; so too is the space shuttle and even a video link system to allow the main protagonist, Dave, to talk to his family through a satellite connection. Furthermore, as I was musing on the scene of Dave talking to his daughter, my solitude was interrupted by a video-chat call from my son.

Just as I was sharing with him this amusing coincidence, my son's face froze and a helpful warning came up, informing me that I had been disconnected. Thank goodness for the message; I would never have guessed. What might have been more helpful would have been a post-call voice message stating, "I detected that a connection fault was imminent and I re-directed to solve the problem. Beware, this could happen at a future time in your current spatial location which may coincide with a critical moment that requires communications and for which I may not have any re-routing options."

Well, actually, an announcement like that would eventually become quite annoying and to be fair to the people that built the internet, they have done a pretty good job, designing various clever protocols that intelligently control the routing and dispersion of our data over the World Wide Web. If a packet of data gets lost in the network, it is re-routed or re-transmitted so it will eventually reach its target destination, albeit a few milliseconds late. The vast majority of these problems occur at "router" pinch points throughout the system or at the end of the line where your device is connecting to the network. If your device is downloading a movie at the same time as handling a conversation over a video chat, the weak link is exposed.

Anyway, back to the film. No, the connection doesn't get dropped with Dave's daughter and yes, the anti-gravity system works just fine for the stewardess. The toilets take a bit of getting used to and the food doesn't look too appetizing, but for a film made in 1968, the predictions are astoundingly accurate. Granted, some of this was borrowed from the research undertaken for the NASA moon-shots and indeed the first navigation system I used in the early Boeing 747s had three of these lunar units.

Neil Armstrong, Buzz Aldrin and Michael Collins all went to the moon with just one of these Inertial Navigation Systems (INS) which was solely responsible for guiding the spacecraft through the three dimensions of space to intercept an object moving at 2,288 miles per hour. On the 747, they gave us three of these INS units as a safety measure in case one went wrong — it's no good having two, because you don't know which one went wrong.

Soon Dave is on his way to Jupiter in another spaceship and we are introduced to "HAL," with his unique style, spookily voiced by Rain. The film to me really seemed to be about this onboard computer system that ran the ship, negating the need for extra crew, much like a commercial pilot does today with no requirement for a Flight Engineer, a Navigator or a Radio Operator. And, as I explained to my son in 21st century parlance, "there's also a monolith that hangs around, sparking off re-birth and stuff."

Arthur C. Clarke predicted the future well. But how are we doing with computer technology in aviation today? The film producers have made many jumps of logic to get HAL up to a very high standard of both ability and reliability, somehow getting us through the present day barrier that has made it so difficult to achieve the expected decline in the number of commercial aircraft accidents.

We'll come back to *2001* later, but for now let's compare some of those accident statistics.

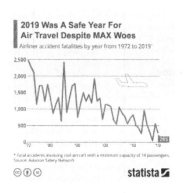

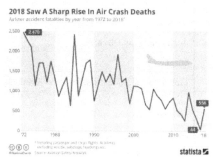

1. Accident data 2018/9 from Statista

Starting in 2018, quoting *Statista*, there was a sharp rise in air crash deaths for the year. This book examines that trend to see if there are any clues as to where deficiencies are occurring and how we might improve and/or reinforce any weak points in the system.

Generally, we can consider the table below to represent a realistic indication as to what risks face us in life on our planet at the moment. The odds are approximately one in 188,364 that you will be killed in an aircraft accident.

Cause of Death	Odds of Dying
Heart Disease	1 in 6
Cancer	1 in 7
Chronic Lower Respiratory Disease	1 in 27
Suicide	1 in 88
Opioid overdose	1 in 96
Motor Vehicle Crash	1 in 103
Fall	1 in 114
Gun Assault	1 in 285
Pedestrian Incident	1 in 556
Motorcyclist	1 in 858
Drowning	1 in 1,117

Cause of Death	Odds of Dying
Fire or Smoke	1 in 1,474
Choking on Food	1 in 2,696
Bicyclist	1 in 4,047
Accidental Gun Discharge	1 in 8,527
Sunstroke	1 in 8,912
Electrocution, Radiation, Extreme Temperatures and Pressure	1 in 15,638
Sharp objects	1 in 28,000
Cataclysmic Storm	1 in 31,394
Hot surfaces and substances	1 in 46,045
Hornet, wasp and bee stings	1 in 46,562
Dog attack	1 in 115,111
Passenger on an airplane	1 in 188,364
Lightning	1 in 218,106
Railway passenger	1 in 243,765

2. *Lifetime odds of death for selected causes, United States, 2018*

As time goes on, you would expect safety to improve, and looking back over the years, this has, on the whole, been the case. Overall the chances of being killed in an airliner are slightly worse than being struck by lightning, so the statistics are not very alarming. However, recently there has been a blip. An article at Inc.com wrote, "Although the global airline industry is rightfully proud of its overall safety record, it's not perfect by any means, and it likely never will be. Here's hoping that the number of deaths in airline accidents drops to zero in 2019."[1] Well, we are now in 2020 and the result for 2019 is 283 deaths according to Statista, which is a great improvement; but we clearly need to keep working on new solutions.

In 2019 the Boeing 737 Max 8 raised questions about the robustness of newly introduced safety systems in 21st-century airliners. Do we even need to train pilots with newly incorporated safety systems — or even inform them that these changes have been introduced into their new aircraft? During this century we may very well be asking how soon we will be able to completely cut out the human from the flight deck to be replaced by computers.

---

[1] https://www.inc.com/peter-economy/there-was-a-stunning-increase-in-airline-crashes-deaths-in-2018-including-a-first-for-southwest.html

How ready are we? These are the last 10 years of worldwide passenger aircraft accidents involving fatalities for aircraft certified to carry at least 6 people, including crew. The remaining years going back to 1945 are included in the appendix.

Year	Number of Accidents	Passenger Fatalities
2019	125	578
2018	115	1039
2017	102	399
2016	106	631
2015	127	904
2014	125	1329
2013	141	453
2012	156	800
2011	154	828
2010	162	1154

3. *The Bureau of Aircraft Accidents Archives (B3A) accident data 2010–2019*

I will be concentrating on airliners that carry at least 14 passengers and on analysis, these accidents fall into specific categories. In the last 10 years (2010–2019) they have ranged from 47 navigation errors to 1 flap-selection error. Some of them seem hard to understand, given the high level of computerization onboard, but maybe there is a limit to the assistance that current computers can provide. We should note at the outset that overall, computer systems have greatly enhanced safety. The rough breakdown of these last 10 years of fatal accidents shows there were 109 serious accidents of which about half could not have been avoided by increased sophistication of aircraft systems. An example of this would be a terrorist bomb or severe mechanical failure.

The question is the reverse: how many such accidents were contributed to by the increased sophistication of aircraft systems, and is this the reason for the statistical blip? We will also ask whether technology itself is sufficiently advanced to start the process of introducing full automation to civil aviation and question whether the current state-of-the-art computer systems alone will have the power and flexibility to replace the human being.

To examine these questions sufficiently, there will be two occasions when I will diversify the discussion to look in more detail at the inner workings of computer processors and also our own biology. These brief interludes encompass our brain's evolution and how well the human can inter-face with the microprocessor. Finally, we introduce an alternative path of evolution which may produce a more balanced symbiosis between people and machines.

We have already mentioned that computer systems have greatly enhanced aviation safety and there is absolutely no doubt about this. Just how they have done so is interesting, because by looking at the problems they have already solved, we see that their unique selling point was the ability to inte-grate more effectively with the "human" pilot. As we try to further enhance this integration, we enter the vast grey area that exists between the human thought process and a machine.

There have been several incidents where this grey area has been exposed. A Qantas Airbus A330 (QF 72) was at cruising altitude en route from Singa-pore to Perth in 2008. The incident report states that the aircraft was flying at 37,000 ft when the autopilot disconnected and the crew received various aircraft system failure indications. Then, shortly afterwards, the aircraft abruptly pitched nose down. The aircraft reached a maximum pitch angle of about 8.4 degrees nose down, and descended 650 ft during the event. After returning the aircraft to 37,000 ft, the crew started the process of actioning the multiple failure messages. The aircraft then commenced a second uncom-manded pitch-down maneuver, leaving 12 passengers seriously injured and another 39 requiring hospital medical treatment when it landed, after the subsequent diversion. So what went wrong?

The official report states: "There was a limitation in the algorithm used by the A330 flight control primary computers for processing angle of attack [AOA] data." Effectively, this means an onboard computer suffered an electronic spike and sent invalid data to the control system which blindly pushed the nose down, based on the false notion that the angle of attack had suddenly increased to what it 'thought' was a critical degree.

This is an example of the grey area between the human thought process and a machine. If another linked onboard computer had switched on the seat belt signs, knowing that the aircraft was about to violently pitch down, then I would have been impressed! After several years of flying commercial aircraft and encountering sudden unforecast turbulence, I can definitely recommend that people should keep their seat belts fastened whenever they can!

On Monday, January 1, 2007, an Adamair flight between Surabaya and Manado went missing after its last radio report to Air Traffic Control at 35,000 ft in the cruise. The Inertial Reference System (IRS) malfunctioned and both pilots became preoccupied by attempting to fix the fault and entrusted too much to the automatics/flight computers. The IRS is the next model up from the INS mentioned earlier (the system used by the Apollo astronauts) and is responsible for determining and presenting the orientation (pitch and bank) of the aircraft to the pilots. While the pilots were using their very well evolved human trouble-shooting skills, they switched the IRS units to a warm-up mode called "Attitude" but this caused the autopilot to disengage. For some reason, they ignored and probably cancelled the warning sounds telling them that the autopilot was disengaged, perhaps because they thought the alarm was just a natural consequence of switching to Attitude mode. The aircraft then rolled, unnoticed, 35 degrees to the right, as would be expected at high altitude, and unfortunately the crew were unable to recover the situation, resulting in the loss of all onboard. I wasn't being sarcastic when I said the crew were using their very well evolved human trouble-shooting skills. Pilots are picked for having good problem solving abilities and it wasn't that part of their brain that caused the accident. We will be asking what else we could have done to avoid this accident.

Captain Chesley "Sully" Sullenberger is perhaps the commercial pilot best knoo wn by the wider public since he and his first officer, Jeff Skiles, safely ditched US Airways Flight 1549 in the Hudson River near Manhattan, New York, in January 2009, with no loss of life. The Airbus A320 experienced a total loss of thrust in both engines after encountering a flock of Canada geese encountering a flock of Canada geese in the climbout after takeoff from New York City's LaGuardia Airport. In this whole debate about automation and the future of aviation, Captain Sully has made some interesting and pertinent observations which are especially relevant considering he is widely seen as having outsmarted the automatics. He says:

> It is not easier or cheaper [nor does it] require less training to fly an automated airplane. It frequently requires more, because you have to have a deep understanding of how a system works, including the dark corners, the counterintuitive things it might do in certain circumstances. Many foreign carriers are trying to take people with zero flying experience, put them in simulators and quickly put them in the right seat of a jetliner. They don't have the experience, knowledge, skills and confidence to be the absolute master of the aircraft start to finish.

So another conundrum to solve; the better the automation, the more you need to train the pilots. The airline bosses are thinking and hoping for the exact opposite and are budgeting for lower training costs and crew expenses in an increasingly competitive international industry. More of these types of accident will be analyzed throughout the book and a possible solution is put forward. We also look at whether aviation is a special case or whether there are other industries needing to integrate humans and computers more effectively.

Many commentators are pointing out the problem of "Automation complacency" and the issue of pilot's not having their hands-on skills honed as they would ideally like due to the active encouragement of most airlines for their crews to use the aircraft automatics for the vast majority of the flight. When a serious problem develops on an aircraft, having automatics greatly enhances the chances of a successful outcome but when the automatics go wrong, we then rely upon the extreme skill of the pilot. I guess this will always be a difficult conundrum to solve but our first port of call must be to stop any situation from getting completely out of hand which then leads to the loss of the aircraft. How do we interject at the right moment to break the deadlock and recover when man and machine get out of sync?

My computer odyssey started in 1983 when the first BBC B Micro home computer was produced in the UK and I was flying the Shorts 360 for British Midland Airways out of East Midlands Airport. I learned to write computer programs in BBC Basic and have gone on to write in Assembly code, Visual Basic and Java (Android Applications). I have also happened to have synchronized my flying career with the emergence of digital computer systems on the flight deck and have experienced the advantages and the pitfalls of the airborne microprocessor.

Computers are becoming increasingly sophisticated and we are becoming more detached from the under workings, exposing us to a future where we will be totally reliant on the programmers and more importantly, the companies behind them. I want to demystify the computing process and show it is only a machine following a predetermined set of rules. Although an interesting debate, it doesn't "think" in the same way that you and I might describe the process of "thinking."

The next chapter is the first of the aforementioned digressions and looks at the fundamentals of how computers tick, but like a lot of the content in this book, I have kept the technical aspects to the minimum by covering only the salient points, with the sole intention of exposing what I think is the weak link in the computer microprocessor — the "illusion of thinking."

CHAPTER 2: THINKING COMPUTERS

Safety statistics have at best plateaued over the last few years. One reason may be that we have reached the limitation of the computer systems that have been developing at a rapid pace since the Second World War. To show this, I need to very basically outline how a computer works, but without losing my readership! We need to strip the machine down to the fundamentals to see where any problems lie, just as you would strip an engine down to diagnose a mechanical fault in a car.

The microprocessor is where all the serious action takes place. Forget the rest, the keyboard, monitor (screen), mouse, microphone, speakers, as they either send data to the microprocessor chip or receive data from the microprocessor chip.

4. Processor and memory chips

We don't have to consider any of the peripheral parts of the computer; we only need consider the processor and memory chips (above). We also don't need to get tied down by exactitudes in what they are all called (nomenclature). The basics of how it works are surprisingly simple, although the hardware to make it all happen is somewhat more complex.

For those interested in the real fundamentals, I have included a section in the appendix which looks at the very early computer system I once used, the BBC B. It was one of the first personal computers available and, like Stanley Kubrick's *2001*, it was a masterpiece of design. By using its very rudimentary programming language, I will run through the essentials of just how a processor performs its magic, and I think most people will find it interesting. This information is rarely explained, yet it offers an easy to follow insight into the workings of the most abundant machines around us today. All computers and smart phones basically work in the same way. (Quantum computers are a completely different breed and are not included here. They may indeed provide interesting solutions for aviation but this will be way in the future.)

5. *BBC B Personal Computer*

So if you feel adventurous, please have a look at the appendix, "Thinking Computers," to reveal the logic of what is going on inside the thing that is most likely humming away in a corner of your house somewhere. Otherwise, as it is not necessary to have an intimate knowledge of the process, I have précised the contents here.

In summary, the appendix section takes us through the process of adding two numbers together. We see how the first number is represented by a special code sequence and then look at the processor rules applied when the second number is introduced. The two special code sequences (of our two numbers to be added) are superimposed over each other and one by one, the processor rules are activated. Finally, after waiting for a whole ten nanoseconds, the answer reveals itself from the superimposition process, just as invisible ink reveals the character sequence after a special chemical is applied to the secret notepaper.

The reason I'm showing this process is to demonstrate that the computer processor is very mechanical in its behavior — it just does as it's told. It is much like the aforementioned invisible ink, whereby it has the ability to apply the magical special chemical to the paper but it will never understand the meaning of the revealed word or message.

From here, we show how similar processes store the answer into memory so we can retrieve our data for another day, and then follows a brief demonstration of how the processor makes the all-important branching decision. For example, how does the processor determine if one number is larger than another (8 < 17?), which is the essential fundamental, bottom-line ability that any computer must possess in order for it to have any use at all. We experience this ability every day and we call it "choice." This choice then comes into play as we introduce the controlling sequence that is at the heart of all present day computers — the computer program.

To sum up this whole process, the technical explanation of the processor is not really necessary to make the point that a computer is merely moving instructions and data sequentially through the central processor and is very detached from the real world.

The trick is to execute each instruction really quickly, so it appears as if the answer has been produced instantly. Nobody is interested in how many times the Carry Over bit was used just for a very simple addition or how untidy the operation looks. Computers are hyped up to look impressive, but essentially they run streams of data through one pinch point, the processor. Every instruction is handled one by one in a sequential, *series* fashion, and because it works fast it appears to be running in a *parallel* capacity, as does our own human brain. It's much like a magician performing one of those amazing tricks on stage where a person just appears from nowhere. It generally looks a bit suspicious because the cage always has a cloak over it and it's not until the cloak is pulled away that we see the person appear. I still don't know how it's done — but I do know it's a trick.

If I could slow it down, the magician's vulnerability would be exposed because perhaps I would be able to see the person coming up through the trap door. Same too with the computer: if you could slow it down, you would see how it is relying on the sequential codes running in isolation, with interruptions to perform separate tasks, but with no realization of how the tasks are connected. Computers are very good at presenting and crunching data but not so good at interpreting the real world.

Modern day computer games incorporate wonderfully realistic graphics that we can walk through in virtual 3D, and even change in appearance like a Turner painting at sunset as we meander through the landscape in changing sunlight. Flames can flicker in ever increasing realism and we can experience underwater worlds that excite the imagination. But they are not real. They might as well be the individual characters on this page transformed by a machine into a picture. Just like the Turner, the game and the machine, they are merely interpretations made by our parallel, almost 5th dimensional brain.

Microsoft's ubiquitous Windows Operating System has an interesting special feature that gives us a further clue as to the vulnerability of the computer design and how detached computers are from the real world. It's called "Safe Mode" and it's used whenever you, as the human operator, have to help out when the computer gets stuck. The designers know very well that the system is extremely fragile when compared to a human brain and so have installed a safety parachute or a "get out of jail" card. If the computer gets stuck with the little circle going around and around *ad infinitum*, the user has to restart the computer and ensure a special key is pressed on the keyboard so the computer can fire up in a restrained mode whereby it can't retain overall control. The human user then adjusts whatever is necessary and then restarts the machine in normal mode.

A typical problem that computers experience when linked to the internet is virus infection or infiltration. So we install virus checkers to protect us when browsing on the Web; but then some clever criminal designs some malware specifically to uninstall the protective virus checker! So then, as a response, the virus checker manufacturer re-writes the software such that the virus-checker is impossible to uninstall. But perhaps for some reason I independently decide that I want to uninstall the virus checker software myself: and I can't — unless I select "Safe Mode"! What I really need is a computer that offers an "Intelligent Mode"...but I'm afraid it doesn't exist.

The problem is that we are all being seduced into thinking these machines are on the brink of taking over the world, but I would suggest we are on the wrong evolutionary branch and, in aviation, this could be a dangerous supposition, especially as we go through the inevitable transition period to full automation.

After that lot, I think I need a cup of strong black coffee...but how would a computer robot make you a cup of coffee?

CHAPTER 3: COMPUTER LIMITATIONS

Time for that hot cup of coffee. Well, we need to do several things in specific order. It's no good pouring the hot water before we've got the cup on the table.

Basic steps are:

1. Boil some water
2. Get a cup
3. Get a teaspoon
4. Put coffee in cup
5. Pour boiled water into the cup
6. Stir coffee

So imagine we have a centralized computer that has been programmed with the coffee-making instructions. It could feed these instructions to a robot that was suitably equipped with arms and mechanical hands, and probably it would make a cup of coffee for you. Now I will ask the centralized computer to flash this instruction up on a tablet that is being used by a 5-year-old child while I sit back and wait for my coffee. Any problems?

One thing I forgot, you're not allowed to cheat! You're not allowed to use your highly evolved, parallel operating system brain to come up with an abstract, non connected line of logic. The computer can't sense the danger unless you tell it that there is potential problem, in which case you will also have to program in the solution. You as a human being know through masses of parallel neural connections that there is potential for disaster and this is why a computer finds it difficult to operate as we do. Surely, though, we can feed in code to the centralized computer to check it isn't addressing a young child's tablet?

```
CHECK TABLET REGISTER
IF REGISTERED AGE > 10 THEN CONTINUE
ELSE DO NOT SEND
```

This tells the computer to check who owns the tablet and if the person's registered age is greater than 10, then that will be acceptable but if not, don't send the message.

Happy now — or have you cheated again? Do we really have to consider the possibility that my child has picked up my wife's tablet?

Interestingly, I find myself grading the dangers.

- Boiling water burn
- Fall off chair getting mug
- Splintered mug causing bodily injury
- Spilt coffee on my brand new carpet

Even if you think the link I've made is slightly tenuous, you will almost certainly agree that it is still a link. Again, the "series" computer system wouldn't have a clue. Only we are tuned in to the wider world, and I would suggest we need to recognize this when designing computer systems for applications that expose us to serious vulnerabilities.

Shall we talk about human failings? Clearly, we have hundreds of them, and in the flying context, we have sadly failed in tragedy after tragedy. But this book is about how we press ahead, seeking to improve matters by harmonizing the human brain with computer systems — we will consider more of this later.

Difficulties with Computer Systems

Quite a while ago, I wrote an Android App which helped monitor saturated fat and calorie consumption by inputting everything you eat in a day and totting it up, to pinpoint which food types are causing the damage and therefore which ones to avoid or control.

To help with the input, you could speak into the device and it would use speech recognition to record the particular food. But although speech synthesis technology is really impressive these days, it did make a few mistakes. Also, I had to consider differences in language like jelly, which in the UK is the wobbly stuff but in America is spread on bread or injected into a doughnut. I'm sure everyone has had a laugh at some of the translations that have come back from speech synthesis programs, which again is an example of the limitations of a "series" system computer. Maybe this is the evolution of what we consider to be a joke or something that is funny — when the brain detects two series calculations arriving at the same neuron cluster, it makes a connection with the laughter motor cortex to convey to others that there is a possible trap that may need to be avoided. Even laughing at a clown tripping over a bucket of water has a sharable lesson. By using my human parallel neuron system, I could enter specific code into my App program that could control things in four ways:

- If the speech returned "pudding," I could exchange the word for "dessert" which the App recognized (covers different words for the same item)
- If the speech returned "you'll get," I could exchange the words for "yoghurt," which the App recognized as the closest match to a food substance
- If the speech returned "Jell-O," I could exchange the word for "jelly," which the App recognized (checks user's language selected in settings)
- If the speech returned something very rude, I could exchange the word for "sausage," "dumplings," or similar to add a bit of humor.

By programming my App in this way I could maintain control over the limitations that otherwise would have rendered the system useless. There were about 1,500 interventions like this in order to control just the foodstuffs that we use on a daily basis.

Another example of how isolated computers can get was demonstrated after the dreadful events in Christchurch, New Zealand, in 2019, where a lone shooter was able to live-stream the atrocity over social media. Obviously, the company concerned would never have sanctioned this but it took a human to realize what was happening and take it down. This situation is similar to what can occur on a flight deck where we need the computer itself to make timely critical decisions, pertinent to the real world emergency, and then act upon them independently so as to properly safeguard the aircraft.

Internet fraud is another scourge on society with countless examples of people innocently working away on-line and then finding that the operating system code, far from protecting them, is actually incapable of detecting some fraudulent attacks that end up causing untold misery. For example, when buying a car in the UK, you can enter the registration details into a special government-run website which tells you if the car you are about to purchase has been involved in a serious accident and therefore could have been dangerously reconstructed, or at least should be available for a lower price. But again, like passing the coffee-making instructions to a 5-year-old-child, the system fails because now we are relying on other parties to register the accident in the first place, which unsurprisingly doesn't always happen. We are led to believe that the computer system is intelligent and protecting us.

Is it fair to say then that a computer is just a fast idiot? There is some truth there, somewhere, I think, but I might rephrase to say that it is doing the very best job it can and that we get many, many advantages from the processor; but we should not be over-reliant on the manufacturers who want us to keep buying their latest systems... especially when it comes to safety.

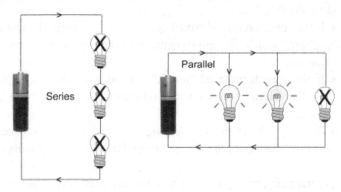

6. *Electric circuits — Series, all bulbs fail; Parallel, one bulb fails*

Nature and electromagnetism provide a classic example of where one solution may lie, specifically in consideration of electrical circuits. You may be familiar with this from college whereby you set up two types of circuit, one series and one parallel. Indeed, you may be familiar with it from trying different strings of Christmas tree lights.

If one bulb blows in the series circuit, the other two bulbs are cut off from the electron supply and so all the bulbs fail — total system failure. However, if a bulb blows in the parallel circuit, although the electrons cannot pass through the faulty bulb, they can pass through the other bulbs by taking the alternative route at the wire junction and so the majority of the system remains active.

On an airliner the Takeoff Configuration warning system is an example of a "series" system. The idea is that if the pilots forget to put the flaps down for takeoff, which increases the lift on the wing and allows the aircraft to get airborne before the runway runs out, an alarm sounds inside the flight deck. This is a very clever idea and has saved many lives over the years, so I'm definitely not knocking it; but at least two accidents have occurred when aircraft fitted with the system have attempted to get airborne with no flaps. The system is triggered when the pilot opens the thrust levers or throttles for takeoff and, on passing through a certain point, a switch is engaged which checks if the flaps are down. If not, the alarm sounds and the pilot is able to safely abandon the takeoff.

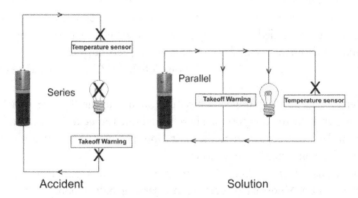

The takeoff warning circuit remains active with an isolated or defective temperature sensor

This unfortunately happened to Spanair Flight 5022 that crashed just after takeoff from runway 36L at Madrid Airport on August 20, 2008. I will discuss this more fully in a later chapter but briefly, the pilots had a technical fault on taxi out, whereby a temperature sensor was overheating and returned to the gate to have it fixed. The fix involved shutting down the circuit for the temperature sensor (pulling a circuit breaker) which was unfortunately in series with the Takeoff warning system, and as a result of the crew now being late, a human error crept in whereby they forgot to run the checklists and lower the flaps for takeoff. Now, no warning was available and the aircraft crashed as it attempted to get airborne with insufficient lift — resulting in 154 casualties.

Why don't they just wire everything in parallel? Because the amount of connections would be impracticable due to the quantity of wires involved, and if you could do so, you wouldn't be able to carry a full load of passengers and freight due to the excessive weight of wires and connectors!

One safety measure that utilizes a parallel system has been developed in conjunction with the arrival of very long haul flight operations; it is what is called the "Heavy." This refers to the heavy pilot, who is required to be part of the crew (heavily-loaded crew — one more than required to fly the aircraft) because of one of the many human failings, "sleep deprivation." We all know that human performance diminishes with fatigue, so not a good idea doing the most demanding part of the flight, namely the landing, after flying for twelve hours. So the heavy pilot helps by running the flight in cruise, thus allowing the two operating pilots to take turns to rest for one third of the flight (always ensuring there are 2 pilots at the controls at any one time). The extra bonus is that the "Heavy" can observe the crucial elements of the takeoff and landing and in the Spanair case could have spotted that the flaps had not been extended. He is only looking for what hasn't been completed or what has been missed and therefore is not as preoccupied as the operating pair. Why don't we have a heavy pilot on each flight? Cost to the airlines, say no more.

But what about parallel computers, artificial intelligence, machine learning and cluster computers? These sound like the next generation solutions, and as we are addressing the limitations of the series computer, surely the parallel computer is the answer?

As we have mentioned earlier (and in the appendix), parallel computers are the result of Moore's Law coming to a grinding halt. Moore's Law asserts that the number of transistors on a microchip doubles every two years. Well, up until the microchip began to melt, that was correct. Another lesson here — maybe let's not be in such a hurry to put undue reliance on forward predictions until they have been thoroughly tested by time. Moore himself, to be fair, thought there would be a limit to his law, but the wider world seemed to be less cautious about future predictions, the pitfalls of which the pharmaceutical industry has learned to its cost over the years. So now we have included two (or more) processors to share the work and thus halve the heat given off. But the designers now have another problem in that they need to tell the computer how to share the work. In effect, it has now become more complicated and arguably, potentially more prone to error.

Parallel Computers

There are different ways that this parallel computing can be achieved. We'll just consider using two processors for simplicity.

- Multiprocessing — Both processors execute a program each and the two separate answers are available at the end. E.g. one adds sales numbers, the other counts up the stock. No need for any correlation at the processing stage.
- Parallel processing — there is only one program but the programmer writes it such that one processor does some parts and the other processor does others. E.g., one adds sales numbers, the other counts the stock. At the end, the program uses both sets of data to make a useful prediction.
- Data parallelism — when there is one program and it has to process a huge amount of data, so it sends half the data to one processor and the other half to the other processor. E.g., one counts the stock at the London factory; the other counts the stock at Manchester. At the end, the program uses both sets of data to list total stock.

So this is like requiring a steam train to ascend a steep gradient. One huge locomotive won't be as efficient as two smaller ones (due to the increased weight) and therefore, essentially, they are both the same old locomotives we know and love that come with all the weaknesses and problems, except I now have to synchronize them to ensure they are pulling together as one. Communication and synchronization are big problems with parallel computing. The programs need to be written so they can handle the parallel structure.

Cluster Computers

Cluster computers use two or more computers that are networked together to facilitate the ability to utilize parallel computing. Networking is where two computers are linked by a cable or Wi-Fi. This set up typically would be used to back up files from one computer to the other. But by clustering them, the principle of parallel computing can now be utilized, whereby the two processors share the work required, run by a complex synchronizing program operating in the background.

Machine Learning and Artificial Intelligence

Machine learning is a way in which we can train a computer to be artificially intelligent. Take face recognition. You feed the computer thousands of face images and run your program designed to use many different ways of deciding on how to interpret a face. A lump in the middle is a nose, two sockets top left and right for eyes, etc. Now make hundreds of these rules and then sit a subject in front of a camera ready for the computer to compare her or his face to the photo file held on the disk storage system. When the computer gets it right, the rules that were primarily responsible for supplying the correct answer get a star, just like you would give to a child at primary school. Now, those favorable algorithms are brought into play more aggressively to improve the overall hit rate and thus the success rate of the system.

Although we are merely mimicking the learning process of a young human brain, this does have huge potential for the future. I could not sift through thousands of camera shots of people and match them to a villain's mug shot. I could do about fifty but no more, and that is where the computer does very well — it can do millions.

This same ability is exploited by autopilot computers to keep an airliner flying straight and level at altitude. It is very demanding for a pilot to fly a heavy airliner at precicely 35,000 ft without autopilot assistance because of what is called the damping effect. I certainly couldn't do it for hours on end. All pilots engage an autopilot and rely on the very fast calculations and reactions of the computer system to maintain the required altitude. The damping effect problem is caused by the less dense air at altitude and is similar to how a car's suspension works.

In a vehicle with hard springs or shock absorbers, any disturbance from a pot hole in the road is very quickly rectified by the powerful springs (equivalent to the thick air at low altitude). With soft springs, it takes longer for the disturbance to settle down as the springs go back and forth several times before they stabilize the car (equivalent to the thin air at high altitude).

Machine Learning and Artificial Intelligence do repetitive tasks very well, learning all the way, but it is extremely difficult to transpose it into a similar but different task. Other uses for artificial intelligence are: speech recognition, medical diagnosis, stock market trading, analyzing buying habits/associations, classification into groups, financial services /prediction on loan default. In all of these, the same applies; it does a repetitive task very well but can be relied upon for doing just that ONE task without a lot of reprogramming. The medical AI diagnosis program works very well at spotting lung cancer cells off a scan, but that's where it ends. It is a very helpful tool, but we maybe should be careful about labeling it as Artificial "Intelligence."

The analogy with children holds well here, in that you can teach a child to tell a joke, but that doesn't mean that child can tell that joke to anyone at any time — it has to learn what "appropriate" means — and that is a high level skill for a human; in fact, it is still debated today how we do this ourselves. We don't yet have the answer.

Cortana, Siri, Alexa...

Are these systems using artificial intelligence? They call them weak AI, as it can recognize abstract patterns and meanings. For instance — "What's going down at the club tonight" is recognized as "what is happening at the club tonight," without realizing there is an embedded suggestion of a crime or a deal. It appears that these systems don't *think*, they just recognize certain patterns. I'm inclined to believe that once we have sorted out what we mean by "thinking" we can then make a start on programming a computer to match the concept; until then, let's not use the word "think" in the same sentence as the word "computer."

Warnings on Flight Decks

Another challenge with computers in aircraft is the output. How does the computer communicate with the pilots? Currently we have a Crew Alerting System that either speaks or flashes a message up on a prominent monitor, coupled with a warning chime to get the crew's attention. These are all graded by a human programmer. If the aircraft is approaching high ground at a dangerous altitude, the system will:

- Call out, "TERRAIN, TERRAIN."
- Sound a warning claxon.
- Flash up the words TERRAIN on the central monitor in red capital letters.
- Offer guidance on the pilot flight displays as to what angle of climb is required to avoid the obstacle.

This will definitely get your attention but what happens when a whole series of things go wrong? This happened when a Qantas A380 departed Singapore and an engine exploded, damaging the leading edge high lift devices as well as many other systems in and around the engine. As far as the computer was concerned, it had done its job really well by informing the pilots that there were multiple disagreements between several systems and maybe also that the toilet-occupied light was not working! We don't really want to know about the toilet light at the moment, but we do want to know the condition of the leading edge flap. The computer could not "intelligently" discern the difference.

The human would look at the leading edge and importantly ignore the superfluous warnings, knowing that by getting involved with these distractions would only further confuse the situation, eventually leading to an information overload and the possible loss of the aircraft. The Qantas crew sorted the situation out brilliantly and were able to analyze and action each computer fault readout, one by one (you resolve each line on the aircraft's MCDU computer), and importantly, ensuring the critical ones were dealt with first.

Conclusion

If the aim is to track millions of peoples' online buying habits or to assist the police using face recognition software, we can afford to experiment with the systems and see whether they work in the long run. But on a flight deck we need to be clear about what we are trying to achieve. Perhaps the rules should be:

- Positively encourage machines that assist the human with repetitive actions.
- Don't try to replace the human brain yet, design systems to integrate more effectively with the human being.

I worry about the use of parallel computing and artificial intelligence in aviation, as we could be unknowingly led into introducing them too quickly, imagining they are actually mimicking the human brain. Thinking is a multiple parameter function, and it's very difficult to mimic in a series style computer.

The successful partnership of the human brain and the series computer appears to have peaked, as accident statistics have climbed again. In order to get back on track, we need an improved symbiosis of human and computer.

We are all familiar with this visualization of how mankind evolved from the apes:

7. Visualization of human evolution

But, of course, this image is not really correct and it can only be considered as an artistic interpretation — a better representation of these characters would be this:

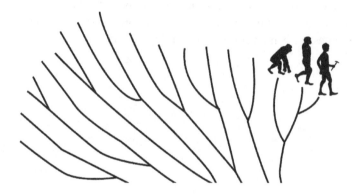

8. More accurate visualization of human evolution

The essential part is that as evolution progresses, it branches out from the last lineage. Apes branched off from monkeys about 25 million years ago, which then branched into the Great Apes, and finally the chimpanzees branched into humans, still leaving the chimps to play their part in our world today, pretty much so as they have always done. The evolutionary process doesn't mean one form gradually morphs into the new species; it picks the right time and then branches off when it's ready — if it gets it wrong, then the lineage ceases to be.

I'm always amused by thoughts of evolution and the opposing argument of the existence of a God. One side says a God created man and the other side says man simply evolved. But the evolutionists are always quick to add that at no stage was there any intelligent intervention, it was all trial and error and random selection. The amusing part is imagining all the failed attempts by nature along the way, and in this context you can imagine how "serial brain" man would have fared. With a spear inbound, serial man would have to decide when to hand over control from visual tracking to muscle reaction so he could take evasive action to avoid the spear. By controlling these two functions simultaneously, our evolutionary branch was able to react much faster, and that is why a tennis player can today react to a serve received at 150 mph and still win the point! Sure, you can incorporate fast interrupts in the serial processor, but there is more to run in the body other than sight and muscle movement; so series humans would never have got the better of our Sapiens brain architecture.

We should keep trying to improve series style computers, but if we assume that we have evolved sufficiently to be at the branch-off point to full automation, we risk relying on a system that is pretty good but somewhat awkward in its habitat. At the right time, we can branch off from the series computer lineage into a human-like neural network design, and only then should we consider handing over full control to digital systems.

CHAPTER 4: BENEFITS OF COMPUTERS ONBOARD

When I first started operations on the 747 Classic (the original jumbo jet), we used the same Inertial Navigation Systems (INS) that the first men on the moon used for navigation, except they only had one. Up until then, we followed various types of radio beacons that pointed to a geographical location. The needle would point up at twelve o'clock on the dial until you arrived at the beacon, and then it would rotate very quickly (if you were good at tracking) around the dial until it was pointing to 6 o'clock as you passed overhead. With the INS, the computer knew where you were at any time, and geographically named locations weren't really required anymore. They did keep them on charts, though, so that Air Traffic Control could radio transmit an easy way of directing aircraft, and the "waypoint" was invented.

Now all I had to do was tell the computer which waypoints I wanted to follow. In the early days, the system could only take latitude and longitude, which meant typing in something like this: N15032.0W01045.6

And very annoyingly, it could only accept 10 entries at a time. Even more annoying, it was found that mistakes could easily be made by entering an incorrect digit and the aircraft could unexpectedly set course for Australia or Timbuktu. To get over this, it became airline policy for one other flight deck crew member to double check the entry — in those days the crew comprised a captain, first officer and flight engineer. After the digit entries were made, the computer would calculate the angles between the tracks (at least the first angle, as the world is round) and the distance. This was then checked off against a printout that was prepared specially for each flight — a cross-check system.

When the Flight Management System (FMS) upgrade arrived, all the pilots who had grown up with computers saw this as a massive improvement, although for others it required quite a learning curve. But as the diversification was purposely designed to be limited, everybody caught on quickly. This is where the computer excels: for us, no more tedious Lat/Long entries to be made, and more important, far fewer mistakes. And by increasing the memory of the computer, we could now store one- to five-letter names instead of 15-digit Lat/Longs. There were names like WOOLY, that could be easily reproducible as they were chosen to sound like an English word. The FMS had a much larger memory and what's more, a look-up database that would store the waypoint names and their geographical Lat/Long coordinates. This improved safety in two main ways:

- The Lat/Long of WOOLY was hard-wired into the memory, so not much room for error.
- If the pilot mistakenly typed WOOLI, the FMS would display a "Not Found" message instead of setting course for Wooloomaloo.

Still, though, problems could occur. What would happen if there was another waypoint in the world called WOOLY? This happened to American Airlines Flight 965 in December 1995 in Cali, Columbia, when the pilots became disorientated and decided to break the confusion by flying back to a beacon called "R" (Romeo), to recommence the approach. They read the name "R" off their letdown charts, so they knew it was the correct beacon. But this particular beacon had been in conflict with another beacon near Bogota with the same name ("R"), so the authorities changed the name of the Cali beacon to ROZO — but the letdown charts hadn't been updated. Obviously with so many waypoints around the world, there are bound to be some conflicts, but this eventuality had been taken into account by the FMS designers; if there were two ROZO beacons or two "R" waypoints, then the system would list both with their Lat/Longs and then invite the pilot to pick the correct one.

So far, in the context of this book, the logic handling is not too bad. Furthermore the FMS designers added another step of logic to help the pilot pick the correct beacon identifier. The possibilities were listed in order of how close they were to the aircraft. It is quite challenging for anyone to work this out mentally, using just latitude and longitude, especially under pressure. The computer does really well here — apart from one thing. The pilot assumed that the top selection of "R" was the closest beacon, as was the design — and it wasn't. The one he wanted wasn't even there, as it had been changed to ROZO. The one he selected was the one near Bogota and the aircraft was duly turned by the autopilot towards Bogota, with a 9,800 ft mountain in the way. This was the classic Swiss cheese problem: there are always holes in the system. Here, the incorrect chart notification lined up perfectly with a momentary confusion in situational awareness.

The Swiss cheese analogy has been used in aviation for a while — if the holes in each slice of Swiss cheese line up perfectly when stacked on top of each other in a sandwich, there is now a potential way through for the mayonnaise to make a mess on one's shirt. The idea is to arrange the slices so no holes are aligned, and in aviation the simplest example is a checklist. The holes start to line up if we rely on memory to lower the flaps for takeoff. The checklist helps block the mayonnaise but the alignment isn't guaranteed to be perfect, as we can still forget to read the checklist.

The improvement with the FMS was very welcomed but another issue appeared. Once introduced, several of us made suggestions about how we could add more data to the system to make the operation even smoother, but the reply from Boeing was a very early acknowledgement of the issue being discussed in this book. If you make any changes to the system, hidden, unknown consequences could appear during the normal operation of the FMS so there would need to be rigorous testing time allocated to re-certify the software. This was costly and impracticable.

There is no doubt about it, computers have made a huge contribution to safety in aviation; but to go to the next stage of full automation, we will need computers to become a conscious part of the operation and not just be a useful tool in the toolbox. At Cali, can it be argued that had the aircraft not had the FMS, the pilots would have done things the old-fashioned way and dialed up the frequency from the chart on the radio box to follow the needle to the correct "R" beacon? Undoubtedly, but this would be easily counter-acted by many examples of where a database system has plugged the Swiss cheese holes and prevented an accident from occurring, let alone without considering the contributions from all the other computerized systems onboard a modern airliner.

On a four-engine aircraft, you used to get an irritating beating noise as the sound waves from the low pressure fans at the front of the engines inter-fered with each other. But computers now keep all the four engines running at exactly the same revolutions per second to minimize the noise. Before, we would have to look up takeoff power settings from graphs and tables to work out the correct thrust setting for the engines, which then needed constant monitoring as the aircraft climbed into thinner air. Now the FMS computer takes in all the necessary data and displays the current target on the EICAS

(Engine Indication and Crew Alerting System). Furthermore, with the autothrust system, the computer ensures optimum thrust at all times and, importantly, during a go-around when timely application of increased thrust is essential. These comforting add-ons to the aircraft systems make the job much easier — but what if pilots ever found themselves in a situation where the Thrust Reverse system was not working: what would happen then?

Well, it's important to think laterally when considering service issues like these, as there could be some unusual consequences that could affect the safety of the flight. If a thrust reverser was not in working order on a 747, the jet would still be permitted to take off, but it would be essential to consider what would happen if the takeoff was to be rejected. In this case, provided the runway isn't too slippery, the aircraft is perfectly controllable with only three reversers working and this maneuver is practiced in simulators twice yearly. The problem is that the brakes won't work very well in slippery conditions and the reverse thrust would now be asymmetric, causing the aircraft to slide to the side of the runway. So, fine for departure on a dry runway, but what if the destination runway is covered in snow? In that case, the aircraft won't be permitted to operate that particular flight, and the airline would have to fix the problem; but if this were not possible, we would consult a very thick manual that crosschecks every combination and possible consequence of just about every conceivable failure. Inside this defects manual, we would see that — provided there were no other associated failures or critical runway conditions — we would be permitted to operate the aircraft.

We would have dealt with an unserviceable autothrottle system in the same way. Autothrottle is the system that sets the required thrust setting throughout the flight and, by checking the thick manual, we would have found that operating with "manual throttles" would have been permissible. So instead of the computer setting the required thrust, we would simply push or pull the thrust levers to the required setting.

How would an unserviceable autothrottle system work with full automation? For a start, the defects manual will be surprisingly thin since, with no pilots onboard, each departing aircraft would have to be in pretty much perfect order. Pilots can fly aircraft without an autothrottle, but it's a bit much to ask of an automatic aircraft!

This brings up the two different philosophies of Boeing and Airbus. The Boeing philosophy allows the aircraft to be flown without an autothrottle. Airbus also allows the aircraft to be flown without an autothrottle (autothrust system) though is generally not recommended by most airlines. The difference is that on the Airbus, the autothrust system will switch back in to recover the aircraft if taken outside of the permitted flight envelope. Airbus have made a good attempt at designing a fully automatic autothrust system but vulnerabilities can still exist, with pilots both in and out of the loop.

And when might one of these deficiencies show up? It would be nice, would it not, if your car only went wrong when it's been in the garage all night? The real world doesn't work that way, and normally breakdowns occur whilst out on the road. How does full automation deal with this one? For a start, there will be huge delays as ground engineers go about their business maintaining the aircraft to near perfect condition, and then we will all have to hope that the autothrottle (amongst many other systems) doesn't develop a fault en route.

In days gone by, this issue would never have cropped up because there was no automatic thrust system — it was just the normal operating procedure. So pilots today have to learn another set of procedures — one with the automatics and one without. Nowadays, with pilots being mainly accustomed to flying the aircraft in automatic mode, it is easy to revert and assume the autothrottle will be looking after the speed control during the landing approach, when in fact it may remain unserviceable. This is one of those *dark corners* Captain Sully was talking about earlier.

Asiana Airlines Flight 214 was landing at San Francisco International in 2013 when it had a related accident. The 777 was being radar vectored to land on runway 28L and, as any regular aviator to KSFO knows, Air Traffic Control is liable to keep you high on the approach phase of the arrival due to the proximity of several other airports. It even has a nickname amongst pilots, named after a basketball scoring technique — a slam dunk. The Asiana flight was also high, and when this occurs on any aircraft, the thrust needs to be reduced to minimum (flight idle) so the aircraft can descend as quickly as possible onto the correct glide angle and without building up too much speed. At some stage, the operating captain on Asiana 214 selected an automatic mode that was good for a rapid descent but resulted in the disconnection of the autothrottle — so now he needed to be in the "automatics out" mindset.

When the aircraft was on very short finals, just about to land, the 777 had regained the correct glide angle required for landing. But the crew were subconsciously expecting the autothrottle to then maintain the required approach and landing speed; and now that the nose had been raised to follow the correct glide path, the speed bled off to critically low levels. The aircraft didn't make it to the runway and the tail section hit a seawall, killing 3 people.

If there is good crew communication on a flight deck, every button press is announced out loud so everybody knows what has just been switched on or off and more importantly to alert everybody to the potential consequences that may not manifest themselves until much later on in the flight. Just about all computers systems are a benefit onboard, but because they can't think for themselves, they often need supervision.

Hong Kong was a place where the autothrottle was most useful. That is, in the days of Kai Tak (the old, now disused airport), which involved a 47 degree last-minute, low-level turn to land. Because of the steep mountainous terrain surrounding Kai Tak, the only way in was down an offset ILS (Instrument Landing System), towards checkerboard hill, which was quite literally a red and white checkered pattern painted on a hillside. It was there to warn you that there was a certain urgency to start the turn NOW! Once the turn was complete, the aircraft would be lined up with the runway at an altitude of about 200 ft with little time for correction if you had misjudged the turn. The autothrottle was immensely useful during the turn as it would keep the speed spot-on, whilst the pilot was executing and correcting the turn in the variable wind, following the curved, flashing lead in lights.

The latter part of the route to Hong Kong was also notorious for summoning up dense areas of thunderstorm activity (CB). A great advantage of the new glass cockpits was that they came with the weather radar inter-linked and superimposed over the Navigation Display. Now we had a picture of the route ahead, and on top were the color coded weather returns showing exactly where we would encounter the thunderstorms. The color coding was the same used on typical TV weather channels today, where the purple colors are the most intense, going down through red, yellow and green. This was especially useful at night when normally only a lightning flash would provide any visual feedback as to the relative position of the CBs and their anvil tops that frequently crossed the flight path.

The INS/IRS navigation systems used for calculating the aircraft position (and thus navigation) are extremely accurate but they do drift with time. These units are started on the ground during the pre-flight checks; the current latitude and longitude are inserted and after about 10 minutes, the 3 perpendicular platforms will align and therefore be available to accurately detect any minute movements of the aircraft. These movements are measured by accelerometers on the 3 level platforms which, once fed into a computer, calculate the position (Lat and Long) as well as the speed of the aircraft. In the early days, the drift rate was about 2 nautical miles per hour; now is much improved, at about 0.6 nautical miles per hour. However, today they are linked in to the GPS and so are continually updated to maintain the aircraft position to within 15 meters accuracy. Now we have another problem.

The GPS is so accurate that if two aircraft were flying in opposite directions at the same height on the same airway, they would most probably collide. There are rules about flight levels in airways and so this shouldn't occur, but if one aircraft has an emergency and needs to descend, there could be a near miss or worse. To get round this one, most airlines now fly an offset whereby the pilot's instruct the flight computers to purposely fly with an error of one nautical mile to the right of track. So now if two aircraft were in error at the same level, flying in opposite directions, they should pass each other with a lateral separation of 2 nm.

Situation awareness has been a longstanding aviation term and can be described as how the human brain interprets the exact state of the aircraft at any one time and the projection of how this state will change over time. It is an essential element of a pilot's operation and has been greatly helped by onboard computers.

VNAV stands for Vertical Navigation and is used from top of descent to landing. A 747-400 will take about 5 miles to slow down from 300 kts to 250 kts with the thrust levers closed. The irony of a large airliner is that, due to its huge momentum (speed x weight), if all the engines fail at altitude it will take much longer to reach the ground than a smaller aircraft. In normal operations the VNAV computer system will predict ahead, showing graphically on the pilot's navigation display the exact point on the predicted routing where the aircraft will be at the desired height and speed.

The displays for the pilots are game changing in that they interface with the human pilot in a more meaningful way showing a clear picture of the route the aircraft is following and compacting all the important flight information, like height, speed, climb rate, etc. into one display. This helps the pilot scan for information more efficiently, and this frees up more spare brain capacity for when it may be needed. Large liquid crystal display (LCD) screens provide a clear logical diagram of systems like fuel tank state, which helps when deciding on how to ensure the fuel is balanced, lessening the risk of switching off the wrong fuel pump and causing a pilot-induced problem.

Computers are now providing head-up displays that help the pilot see out of the front windshield in a "virtual" way in which she would naturally see if the clouds were not blocking the view. It also provides essential flight information, projected over the windshield like airspeed, altitude and rate of descent.

Autopilots are another safety feature that don't quite count in this digital context but, interestingly, are misunderstood by most passengers. It can be thought that passengers are safer if the pilot is actually flying the aircraft, but by releasing the human brain from repetitive actions, it improves the overall safety by many hundreds of percent. I remember seeing a video clip of an Antarctic explorer being interviewed on board an airliner; he was travelling home and recounting how extreme the conditions had been whilst working outside in the snow and he commented on how nice it was to be in normal surroundings. Outside air temperature was minus 70 degrees C, and the atmosphere outside would render him unconscious in 30 seconds due to lack of oxygen; his momentum was dangerously high; he was at 35,000 ft balancing on a metal wing full of explosives, with engines running at 700 degrees C, with a CB in the vicinity that could throw the aircraft inside out and upside down! But it's good that passengers are generally very relaxed about flying...

Autopilots have been around for a long time. They used to be run by analogue computers that literally had only one task to perform — they weren't connected to a microchip processor. Same goes for fly-by-wire, which is common nowadays but of course the Wright brothers used wires to control the Kitty Hawk, so they don't really count as a contribution towards enhanced safety. Fly-by-wire is a system that replaces the conventional cables that run from the flight deck to the control surface motors of the aircraft (rudder, aileron and elevators). A computer system now sends an electrical signal to the motor which moves the control surfaces, providing several benefits. The electrical wires are much lighter than the cables, jammed cables are no longer a concern and the computer can now interpret the pilot's control inputs to ensure the aircraft is kept within the allowable flight envelope. However, there are arguments that a severe lightening strike could severely degrade the entire aircraft control system but it hasn't happened yet. In 2019, a Sukhoi airliner crashed on landing at Moscow–Sheremetyevo airport having returned after a reported lightening strike shortly after departure. I await the accident report to see if there were any issues with the flight controls as the aircraft was equipped with a Fly-by-wire system.

No pilot can manually land an aircraft safely in foggy weather conditions without the assistance of Autoland. It's been around since the 1960s. Because the weather in Great Britain has always been prone to anticyclonic gloom and fog, Autoland was primarily developed by British European Airways (BEA), the major UK short haul carrier. The first commercial automatic landing, carrying passengers, was achieved on flight BE 343 on June 10, 1965, and was a Trident 1 on a flight from Paris to Heathrow.

This was a genuine benefit of computers onboard but, of course, since we're talking about 1965, it did not involve digital computers. They utilized analogue systems that were coupled into the ILS beams emanating from the landing runway. The ILS (Instrument Landing System) has two beam components, one lateral and one vertical. The lateral beam guides the aircraft's left/right alignment towards the runway and the vertical beam guides the descent angle, so that the aircraft will touch down about 1000 ft in from the runway threshold. The system knows when to flare the aircraft (for a gentle touchdown) by a link to the radio altimeter, which is a much more accurate instrument compared to the regular barometric altimeters. The aircraft has to be flown by the autopilot, as a human pilot cannot correctly interpret the strange appearance of the runway as it reveals itself at 140 miles per hour through dense fog. It was too risky to trust only one autopilot with this critical maneuver and so three were used, each continually comparing itself to the other two to check for faults.

This same type of system is widely used today and runs off separate, independent computer systems in the aircraft. But there are still times when a human needs to get involved. If there are strong winds at the landing airfield, exceeding 25 kts (the 747-400's limit), then the Autoland won't be available because the system is unable to handle the more erratic flight path generated by the strong winds. Humans can read ahead and predict the sometimes significant flight path deviations far better than the computer, but if the runway is covered in a blanket of fog, it's time to divert. If the visibility on the runway is less than 100 meters, then again the Autoland is not approved. To be fair to the system, this is only because the fire services would be unable to locate the aircraft in the event of an emergency on the runway — the Autoland has no concept of visibility, as was referenced in the expression "blind landing." During the approach it is essential that the pilots closely monitor the ILS indicators that display the lateral and vertical displacement of the aircraft from the ideal flight path. If a large aircraft is taxiing out to take off and is close to the landing runway, the hull of the taxiing aircraft can distort the ILS beams like a lens distorts light in a magnifying glass. This can seriously affect an aircraft carrying out an Autoland and so Air Traffic Control need to declare Low Visibility Procedures (LVPs). This means they have to ensure taxiing aircraft are kept well away from the ILS beams. Finally, if things go awry, it is always the pilot's decision to abort the landing and carry out a go-around; the automatics don't have the insight to make these sorts of decisions.

Another area of importance is the Crew Alerting System where any onboard system faults are communicated to the pilots. Years ago, if a temperature sensor on an engine registered an overheat, it would be transmitted through a wire to the flight deck where it terminated at a bulb. Etched into the bulb cover was the word "overheat," so when the light came on, the pilot could see it was an overheat, and because it was the second light in from the right, it was the number 3 engine. Now, with cathode ray tubes (CRT) and LCDs, the indication can be squeezed in to make the presentation more concise. This is a major advantage.

The picture below of the 747 flight decks shows how less cluttered the flight deck has become. Note the extra flight engineer aboard the 747 Classic.

9. Boeing 747 Classic and 747-400 flight decks

There are traps here, as well. British Midland Flight 92, a Boeing 737-400, crashed onto the motorway embankment between the M1 motorway and the A453 road near Kegworth, Leicestershire, UK, in 1989. The left engine had failed but the crew shut down the other engine as a result of 3 main lines of logic:

- The air-conditioning on older 737 aircraft was fed from the right engine and the presence of smoke in the flight deck led the captain to think it was the right engine that had therefore failed. They were flying a later model of 737 where both engines fed the A/C system.
- When the supposed bad engine was shut down by the F/O, it coincided with a level off at the cleared altitude and the subsequent throttle back reduced both the engine vibration and also the amount of smoke entering the flight deck, which reconfirmed the initial diagnosis.
- The new instrumentation on the 737-400 aligned the secondary engine instrument readouts (including the vibration indicators) on the right hand side of the flight panels as shown below.

Primary Engine Instruments

Secondary Engine Instruments

10. *The secondary engine instrument readouts located on the right hand side of the instrument panels.*

This third point also reconfirmed the initial diagnosis that the vibration was from the right side, as they were seeing the warning being displayed on the right hand side of the flight deck panels. In fact they were seeing the left engine display, although both gauges were situated on the right of the panel. A classic Swiss cheese. In order to help improve the situation, it was now seen that the displays should be re-designed, where possible, to show a clear left/right disparity when considering major systems of the aircraft.

We have already discussed the issue of modern crew alerting systems and looked at the Qantas flight out of Singapore. We need to try and solve the issue of excessive warnings spilling out into the flight deck — how do we get the system to tell us what we need to know as opposed to absolutely everything that the system is currently sensing?

There are three basic levels of warning used in an airliner. The really important warnings of an engine fire rings a bell, displays a message in RED capitals, shines a red light on each relevant component and brackets the engine indications. These need to be dealt with immediately. The next level is a Caution, like an electrical generator fault. These light up in amber and with four of them fitted on a 747, it is not really an issue but action is necessary. After that there are the Advisory warnings like "high brake temperatures" which might pop up after a landing on a short runway, giving the pilot information on conditions that could present a problem if ignored.

Good to have all the input; but what if I desperately need to know one tiny piece of information amongst a maelstrom of sound and flashing lights?

Air France 447 was flying from Rio de Janeiro, Brazil, to Paris, and crashed on June 1, 2009. The Airbus A330 was at cruising altitude and low speed stalled all the way down, eventually crashing into the Atlantic Ocean, killing all 228 passengers and crew on board. If I could have beamed myself aboard, I would have only had to shout 3 words, "LOW SPEED STALL." The captain, who had been on his crew rest rotation and was suddenly called upon to sort out the confusion, would have then realized that the power urgently needed to be increased, ignoring the illusion of over speeding as reported by the Primary Flight Display. One tiny fault had triggered a whole mass of sensory warnings and none of them told the captain what he needed to know. Just to note, it is also possible to have a high speed stall. The curved top surface of the wing induces the air to whip over the wing even faster than the aircraft is actually flying and if the aircraft is approaching the sound barrier (at altitude the sound barrier can be relatively close) the shock wave will form on the wing top surface before anywhere else and cause a breakdown in the airflow, inducing loss of lift together with a lot of vibration. The same vibration is experienced with a slow speed stall whereby the air over the wing breaks away from the top surface, causing the same loss of lift and vibration.

Just like worrying about my 5-year-old son scalding himself while he is attempting to make me a cup of coffee, we need to be able to prioritize the situation. My initial instincts aren't to worry about a potential stain on the carpet or a NAV ADR DISAGREE message as appeared in the Air France 447 flight deck. To enhance safety on board, the system needs to be able to evaluate the seriousness of what is taking place and to present only the vital information to the crew.

CHAPTER 5: EVOLUTIONARY ASPECTS OF THE BRAIN

The piloting of aircraft has evolved around the concept of a human brain being central to the operation. It started as a fun thing to do, and pleasure flights abounded to flood the human brain with dopamine as the individual underwent a completely new experience that human evolution had thrown away ages ago.

11/12. Darwinian Evolution, in its attempt to get airborne, could have given us wings but instead it gave us bats.

13. De Havilland DH.82 Tiger Moth cockpit (1930s)

So we designed and built flying machines with controls that could be interpreted by the human brain, and because we did not evolve with the necessary flying skills, we need to spend time teaching pilots how to adjust to the different environment, long ago mastered by the bats.

However, at all times when we are flying, we are interpreting the information via our neural network, the brain. We soon learnt that if we fly in cloud without the correct instrumentation and training, we will become disoriented and send the aircraft into a spiral dive, and so we exposed one of the several deficiencies of the airborne human brain.

Until we have finally cracked it and have invented the ultimate fully-independent automatic flight system, we need to work on integrating the human brain with the latest technology and should not be tempted to try to replace the brain in a rush to fulfill fantasies we find in the movies or fantasies we see in company accountant's profit projections. We shouldn't be taking undue risks. Although there are tolerances laid down on allowable percentages of failures in all sorts of industries, here, we should be aiming at zero tolerance. This seems to me to be how the human brain has evolved and survived to become the most intricate object in the entire universe. Each evolutionary step has to be managed very carefully so it doesn't prematurely extinguish the lineage but at the same time allowing greater plasticity within the new environment. Unless, of course, someone decides that it's acceptable from a statistical point of view to dabble in experiments for the greater good of mankind.

Nobody understands how the brain works, although present day computer systems, marketing and TV shows have seduced a lot of people into believing that the answer is just around the corner. This is all part of the impatience gene that needs to know the answer now! We have a long, long way to go.

Biological Neural Networks

In the quest to piece together an understanding of the synthesis of the human brain and computer technology, I have undertaken a bit of research on the make-up of the brain and reproduce it here to forward my argument — I don't profess to be an expert on the subject. The connection with computing and flight deck safety will come clear in a later chapter.

The human brain has over 100 billion neurons, called nerve cells or brain cells. Neurons communicate through thousands of individual connections to each other, which means that you have more connections in your brain than there are stars in the universe.

Every thought is a whole series of neurons communicating with each other and can be visualized as a network, like you may have a network of people who play tennis. No point in connecting with the golfer's network if you are hoping for Wimbledon tickets.

If we had a model of a brain just made of electrical wires and we switched on the current, then we would get total confusion and probably a massive short circuit. Eminent people who have gone before have discovered the mechanism that stops this: the synapse. This will only allow a connection if there is sufficient "weighting" to do so. When you learn to juggle with 3 balls, you will mostly drop some of them to start with; but as you practice, the neurons receive improved *weightings* as they more accurately estimate the requirements for a successful outcome, allowing you to eventually succeed, at least on to the next stage.

Messages move from neuron to neuron by chemicals called neurotransmitters across millionth-of-an-inch gaps called synapses. But they won't move across the synapse until that neuron has enough input energy (*weighting*) to make it happen. When learning to juggle, the neuron will have a score of 1 — no neurotransmitter is sent across and you drop the ball. But if you keep trying by practicing, the neuron gets higher and higher scores or weights until, say, score 5 — now a neurotransmitter is sent across and you catch the ball. The scoring system is achieved utilizing charged particles and use either charged sodium, potassium or chloride ions which move in and out of the cells and establish an electrical current. So if the cell has loads of positively charged particles then they induce the flow of electrons which are of course negatively charged particles.

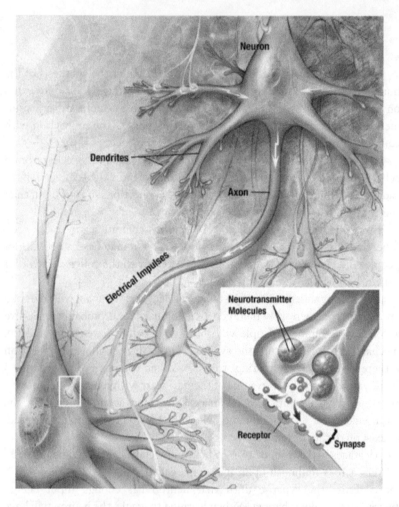

14. Drawing illustrating the process of synaptic transmission in neurons

Considering the "tennis" routing in the brain, we see above two neurons joined via a synapse which is indicated by the white box in the illustration. If I want some Wimbledon tickets, I need to get the name of the person that has access to tickets and for their name I need to connect with the neighboring neuron. Because this is important to me (there are also many other associated requests coming in from other neurons like excitement, emotion, friendship, etc.) the first neuron will "fire," facilitating the connection and I get the name.

The dendrites shown in the picture above are connections to other neurons. We have many circuits that can be used to find information and cross check other sections of the brain, like you would use to solve a cryptic crossword clue. The technical definition for "firing" is: *an action potential, or spike, causing neurotransmitters to be released across the synaptic cleft, causing an electrical signal in the postsynaptic neuron.*

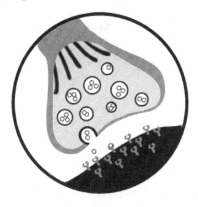

15. Chemical synapse

When a signal comes from another neuron, the neurotransmitter chemical transmits across the synaptic gap and stimulates the little receptors on the other side. This opens what's called a Ligand gate which allows the ions (+ charged particles) to enter the cell and add to its overall electric charge. The cells start at -65 mv. As the ions enter the cell it increases a little to something like -63 mv but if other connections are also flooding in with signals, they all add up to what is the threshold value for an Action Potential or "firing." It now has so much positive charge that it registers at +40 mv. But soon after, the Ligand gates close and the system operates in reverse to restore the potential to -65 mv.

So the Action Potential is triggered which induces an electrical current to the next neuron. The axon (nerve) can go from your brain to your toe — quite a distance.

One problem for evolution was that the speed of transmission of the signal using the Ligand gates opening and closing was a bit slow and it looks like this branch of mammals died out by burning their toes in the hot thermal spring water, rendering them unable to run fast enough to hunt and feed themselves!

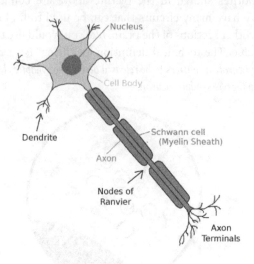

16. Diagram of a neuron showing Myelin Sheath

We were lucky, though, because another branch developed what we have now: fatty myelin, presumably because this branch of mammals lived in warmer climes and didn't have to use hot springs. Fatty myelin allows the positively charged particles to knock into one another, pushing the far right particle instantly out the other end. Electricity flows in the same way by each electron knocking into the next electron, meaning that the speed of electricity is perceived as practically instant and in fact travels at about 1/100 the speed of light (although the individual electrons are moving much more slowly).

Thoughts are derived from many sources (brain databases) and then voted upon (neuron Action Potentials) resulting in many routings or answers. The neuron system allows the entire database to be searched for compatibilities, and probably when we sleep the day's experiences are fed back into the brain, forming new connections. We can use the notion of it working in parallel because there are many answers/possibilities that take independent neural routes. It appears the system that actually handles and updates the connections is the key to our brain's success and that particular structured architecture is just not available today for our computers.

Furthermore, the brain can rearrange itself (for example, after someone has had a stroke), albeit not perfectly, and often with a huge amount of external input from professional trainers. To achieve this level of redundancy once a memory chip has burnt out would take some doing.

Computers don't have a deficiency due to inputs. They are not blind or senseless and nowadays can have more inputs than we have for our brains. If we see flames, feel heat, smell burning, taste smoke and hear a crackling sound; we have all the inputs we need to know that there is a fire. All these inputs can be provided to a computer to do the same thing, and we could even add a Geiger counter if we want, but the computer, like us, can still be fooled. If you showed the computer camera a high-definition film of a fire, would it tick the visual box? Would it then fire off the extinguisher? If not, how many ticked inputs do you need? We need more parallel neural analysis.

Another consideration, for successful symbiosis with computers, is a need to be able to process large data outputs from a computer which in turn can only be input to the human brain one by one. We need it further processed and presented to us in a singular, ordered format. If it displays multiple answers, we get confused by the enormity of the data, which was the problem the crew solved by putting in a Herculean effort on the Qantas 32 A380. The series computer can have multiple upstream failures that can't be digested so the discontinuities are designed to just spew out in an unintelligible way for the human brain to organize and interpret.

The brain has evolved many different ways of handling things in case something goes wrong. The computer has one way only — one accumulator (even if shared as in parallel computing discussed earlier). These extreme multiple outputs need to be rationalized and sorted so our "one bit of information at a time" brain can properly work together with the computer.

Artificial Neural Networks

An artificial neuron network is a computational model based on the structure and functions of biological neural networks. As has been mentioned, machine learning and artificial intelligence are being developed and can work well on a specific task, like face recognition or cancer diagnosis.

On the next page is the diagrammatical structure showing how input information is sorted by hidden layers that cross reference to each of the inputs before being sent to the output. The W in the diagram below stands for the *weighting* (probability of it being correct) of the values in the neuron connection. It also emulates our brain in that the hidden layers do all the work without us knowing. I will be using a simplified diagram based on this principle later.

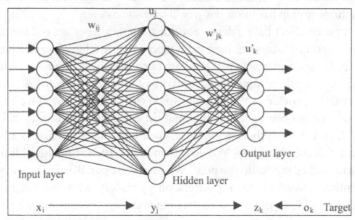

w_{ij} u_j w'_{jk} u'_k

Output layer

Input layer Hidden layer

x_i ⟶ y_j ⟶ z_k ⟵ o_k Target

17. Artificial Neural Networks diagram

Series and Parallel

We have used these terms loosely so far to show differences between the human brain and the computer. The straightforward analogy is not too bad but we can further explore the comparison.

"A man stops his car in front of a hotel and immediately realizes he's just gone bankrupt. Why?" That's a riddle that was around a while ago and serves as a good example of the problem. Our brain finds it difficult to see the answer at first, and we learn from interacting with the questioner that this is a riddle. So we know we need to open up maximum neural pathways to solve the conundrum. We can demonstrate the fundamental process by using a more generalized diagram (as shown below) that is based on the artificial neuron network diagrams which are used to model artificial intelligence.

AI is attempting to mimic the human brain by working out how it comes to a conclusion based on a vast amount of data storage locations (neurons) that individually know nothing. The classic example is, how do we recognize a numeral, say 5? It could be typed in a clear font or written in practically illegible scrawl, but we somehow recognize the symbol. (Websites where you have to prove you are not a robot by matching a weirdly shaped symbol with a known keyboard character are pushing that notion to the limit!) By inserting examples of numbers into the Input Layer, the computer program works to the right through the hidden layers where refinements to the probability are calculated. So if a 7 is inserted, it will assign a low probability that it is a 5, based on the structure of the pixels that make up the image.

The vertical component is attached to the left in the 5, and the right in the seven, so it's not looking good at this stage for the 7. There can be as many hidden layers as there are ways you can think of to discriminate between the numbers.

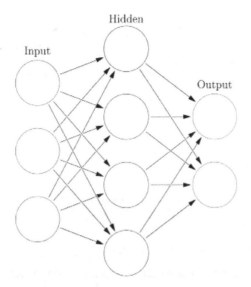

18. Simplified Artificial Neural Networks diagram

And the highest probability wins. The clever bit is what happens next — back propagation. The first run through the computer program will inevitably come up with a high level of inaccuracy, so there is a need to feedback the results into the system and run it again and again and again, all the time refining the probability that the character is a 5. All we have to do is calculate the new refinement weighting for each neuron.

But — there's a Catch 22 — this is impossible with the computing power we have today, it takes too long to do all the thousands of back calculations. So a shorthand or approximate calculation is used that doesn't take a month of Sundays to complete — which presumably is why face recognition is not as accurate as we would like it to be.

However, the principle is really interesting and I'm going to use, in a very approximate manner, the basic concept of the multiple connections and the weighting/probability to try and solve real-time problems, starting with the car/hotel riddle and eventually moving on to safety solutions in aviation.

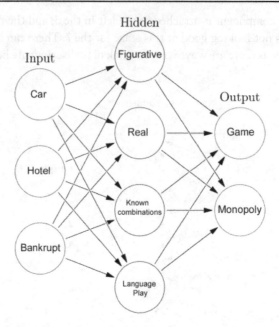

Simplified A.N.N. diagram for Monopoly riddle

From the diagram above, we have the 3 inputs on the left and examples of the hidden layers (thought processes) that enable us to come up with the solution. Interesting how we have the two expressions "come up with" and "work out." We need to find the connection, so we input Car, Hotel, and Bankrupt. Hidden to our consciousness, the neural pathways start to open up and multiple concepts are routed into the neurons. As it's a riddle, we know this may not be *real* and there may be *figurative* associations (that in itself being another neural network!). We may think of existing, *known combinations* where a car and a hotel are seen together. We may think there is some *language play* afoot here — Car, Hotel, Bankrupt. CHB or HCB or BCH? No, nothing there, so let's cut off the Action Potential in that section and continue searching.

I bet you have had the situation before, when you are trying to solve a riddle, remember a name or work out a crossword clue, and the next day, after a good sleep, the answer just pops into your head. Would that be the difference between "coming up with" the solution and "working out" the solution?

Soon the answer to our current puzzle reveals itself as the game "Monopoly." But not everyone will get it straightaway. This represents the parallel system of the human brain — it is sourcing multiple areas to solve the riddle. It is well documented that when people suddenly face death, their lives flash in front of them. They also report that time slows down. Could this be the neural network trying to find a solution to their predicament and running through the entire database for a solution, and at the same time removing needed energy from other bodily systems thus giving the appearance of time slowing?

19. Accumulator pinch point

How does the computer fare? As we have discussed before, the computer needs everything to go through the accumulator (even parallel computers have to share the calculations and coordinate).

The heart of a computer is the processor, where each line of code has to sequentially pass through the accumulator, which can be seen as a pinch point in the system. It will need to process Car, Hotel and Bankrupt one by one, but because it does this so quickly it gives the appearance of handling all 3 together at the same time. Much like the fast hands of a card trickster — it really does look like the Queen of Hearts is in the middle. Various possible connections are listed below in the table.

Car — Hotel	Hotel — Bankrupt	Car — Bankrupt
Door	Mortgage	Lease Company
Seat	Liquidator	Bank heist getaway car
Window	Bank	Liquidator
Motel	Monopoly game	
Parking		
Cost of Parking		
Caravan/RV		
Tired /Tired: Synonyms		

In the case of this puzzle, there are 6 possible combinations but [Car — Hotel] is the same as [Hotel — Car] so we are left with 3 combinations to compare. The programmer now has to come up with a method to cross-check the connections so they might program in these 3 lists of commonalities, some of which are stretching the limits of what could be referred to as a connection. Again, this is all greatly simplified for the sake of example:

The program is designed to find common entries, so firstly [Car — Hotel] is processed through the accumulator against [Car — Bankrupt].

```
FOR N = 1 TO ENDLIST
IF LIST (CAR — HOTEL) = LIST (CAR — BANKRUPT) THEN SAVE
TO MEMORY
NEXT N
```

Nothing would be found here, so next, process [Car — Hotel] against [Hotel — Bankrupt]

```
FOR N = 1 TO ENDLIST
IF LIST (CAR — HOTEL) = LIST (HOTEL — BANKRUPT) THEN
SAVE TO MEMORY
NEXT N
```

Nothing would be found here, so finally, process [Car — Bankrupt] against [Hotel — Bankrupt]

```
FOR N = 1 TO ENDLIST
IF LIST (CAR — BANKRUPT) = LIST (HOTEL — BANKRUPT) THEN
SAVE TO MEMORY
NEXT N
```

This time we have a hit — "Liquidator" — the only problem is that it is the wrong answer. However, the programmer had very cleverly anticipated the actual answer by initially inserting one of the possibilities as Monopoly into the [Hotel — Bankrupt] list. But he should also have inserted Monopoly into the [Car — Bankrupt] list, although it is a slightly more tenuous link, in which case we would have got two answers. But how can we guarantee that any database is entirely complete? The computer can either give us the wrong answer or it could just dump out every entry on the lists, thus giving us the correct answer; but we would have an information overload trying to find it.

Now this is a very basic demonstration and you could easily think of other entries that could go into the lists, but it does indicate the crux of the matter. Unless you tell the computer what to look for, it hasn't got a clue. With machine learning, the computer can be told that it has been partially successful, so it can work towards greater accuracy; or a programmer can easily write extra code in an attempt to try and guess the answer for a particular problem. But until it can be wired up with neural pathways, it will struggle on the fully automated flight deck.

In the brain, the hidden pathways are actioned until the answer reveals itself, even if it takes all night. The series computer cannot access the same amount of material because there is no "sleep" system for updating the connections, and every eventuality has to be separately programmed in. Sleep, it appears, is the linchpin of our brain power — we must reorganize our filing system daily, that is why sleep is so necessary and why prolonged deprivation will lead to premature death. Could this be the evolutionary secret, perhaps, for our dominance in the world?

Horses for Courses

Here is a rudimentary table of the main pros and cons when considering computer vs. brain:

Computer Pros	Computer Cons	Brain Pros	Brain Cons
Very fast	Can only interpret a simple question	Huge Networking abilities	Rarely so fast
Very accurate in controlled circumstances	No by-pass, so vulnerable	Multiple by-pass	Runs out of energy
Never gets tired			Can't handle large amounts of data

Decision Making

The neural network makes our brains superior at complex decision making. Simple decisions we can do equally well as a computer. For instance, is 5 greater than 3 in a numerical context? Is 5,200,445,333.021 bigger than 5,200,445,333.001? But 5,200,445,333.021 divided by 13.21 would be no contest (although I'm led to believe there are some people that can actually do this!).

A complex decision needs a neural network. Flying into Islamabad in a 747-200 with classic old-fashioned round dials and limited computer-based navigation, we suffered a bad lightning strike on the underside of the starboard wing. It blew a 2 ft by 2 ft hole in the wing outer surface, which we didn't know about until we landed. But after the initial shock of the loud bang, the aircraft continued flying perfectly normally.

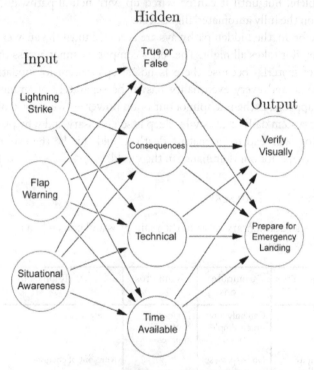

Simplified A.N.N. diagram for flap warning diagnosis

We were on the initial approach and selected the first stages of flap to position 5, which meant the leading edge high lift flaps should have been extended together with 5 degrees of flap from the rear of the wing. The problem was that we now had flap warning lights on in the flight deck suggesting that the leading and trailing edge flaps were not in position. The "simple decision" was to pull out the checklist and follow the documented procedure. In this case the checklist said that the flaps were stuck and we would have to set up the aircraft to land with limited flap, and therefore we would need to land about 50 kts faster, at about 210 mph. The "complex decision" was to look at all the other possibilities that could be leading us up the garden path within the time constraints of the remaining fuel.

This was our simplified neural diagram. Situation awareness refers to all the other operational aspects of flying the aircraft such as navigating safely in a mountainous area and flying a stable, unrushed approach. By using *technical* knowledge we reckoned that the lightning strike was unlikely to have jammed the flaps by a direct hit.

By considering the *consequences* of misdiagnosis, we realized that if we chose to land the aircraft at high speed with the flaps actually extended, the significant amount of extra lift could easily have resulted in us overrunning the end of the runway. By doubting what was in front of us and by pressing our faces against the rearmost flight deck windows, we could just see the wing tip leading edge flaps extended and appearing to be locked in position. We chose to ask the Flight Engineer to go back into the cabin for a visual inspection of the entire wing. All the flaps were out at the 5 degree mark and it was only the indication system that had got confused, presumably from the static charge of the lightning strike. We landed safely.

So our thought process can be visualized as multi-path neuron firing. The pseudo parallel, but series computer, can closely emulate the brain's parallel processing but for complex work it needs to have the answer pre-loaded and embedded somewhere within the database. We see this trick in our everyday search on-line using Google and similar search engines. It still amazes me how fast the search engine works and how it even throws up suggestions as to what I may be looking for before I've finished typing! It appears ridiculously intelligent; and then it comes back with not only the answer for me at the top of the page in about a millisecond but also a whole load of other possibilities. Because our brains are used to a relatively slow world, we are impressed by the speed of the answer; and provided we have asked a simple question, we know we are in the "sliced bread" area of invention. But what if we ask a complex question that requires the sort of problem solving we as a species have evolved as of primary importance over speed of response?

"Which is the best battery to buy?" will most likely give a list of the battery manufacturers that have paid the most for advertising. Way further down the list you may see a very good article on how all the major manufacturers compare and how they perform in different environments, which is actually what you want. The question is too complex for a present day computer, so it does what happens on a flight deck when all goes awry; it dumps out everything it knows at the time — for you to sort out. Just to emphasis the point here, some people argue that we are being tricked by search engines into thinking that their line-one answer is the only one that needs to be considered and as a result all sorts of abuses can occur when it comes to buying choices and political preferences. The truth can be distorted, and this is why I have used the word "trick" in describing the abilities of the computer — it is trying to make you believe it is working at your level — and therefore just as intelligent and aware.

This pseudo parallel trick is done by what are termed computer "interrupts." The hour-glass pinch point that processes the individual linear instructions and data, shares it's time with other functions. For instance, if you are working on a word-processor and an email comes along, your processor will very quickly pause your work, go and sort out the email (and ping you a notification symbol) before returning to see which keys you had pressed whilst it was otherwise occupied. There are many different types of interrupts these days, and eventually quite a queue builds. In days gone by, if too many inputs came along at the same time, you may even have been visited by the dreaded "blue screen of death"!

One day we will get there but for now and for the continued safety of our passengers and crew we need to work as closely as we can with our own neural networks and our current computers. We need to recognize both of our limitations and then extract the best from each system. Computers have been a huge benefit in the evolution of the flight deck, saving many lives and taking pressure off the pilot, which in turn leaves her time and space to monitor for other dangers, especially in the takeoff and landing phase of flight. But we need to accept that if we are to further improve safety, not just in aviation, I might add, we need to work on these integrated systems. A good analogy might be that of a House of Cards.

ID 79369779 © Hannu Viitanen | Dreamstime.com

Computers assist us and enhance flight deck safety up to a certain point, which is visualized here as 4 layers of cards. If we try to build a 5th layer, vulnerabilities creep in. It then becomes too complicated and very hard to interface with our human perceptions. Are the flaps out or not? This would have been a 5th layer question for the computer and too difficult to program.

ID 79369779 © Hannu Viitanen | Dream-stime.com

However good all the individual components, the entire concept/system can come crashing down if one of the areas (cards) becomes displaced. Air France 447 lost just one card (icing of the pitot probes) and as there was no joint integrated system designed in, the human system diverged with the computer system.

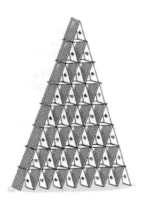

ID 35861599 © Igor Zakowski | Dream-stime.com

We could add extra layers of safety by installing backup systems on top of backup systems. For instance, there could be a backup ice detector on the pitot tube which would automatically switch in a separate source of heating. We could have independent flap position detectors all over the wing in case the primary system fell foul of a lightning strike. But if we continue adding monitoring software into the series type computer systems, we make the entire system potentially more vulnerable as now there are more areas (cards) which can fail but one deficiency could still bring the whole thing down.

A properly integrated system would look like this:

Human brain   *Series Computer*   *Integration System*

If the Swiss cheese started to line up in a difficult situation, with an integration system we might be able to recover without fatalities.

Human Fail   *Computer Fail*   *Integration Survive*

All House of Card images courtesy of Dreamstime.

Chapter 6: Integration

The fascinating trick of biological evolution is that once it has started out on an idea, it seems to somehow successfully carry this forward without yet having had the opportunity to take on any benefits from the original random mutation, and at the same time without throwing out the baby with the bathwater and terminating that specific evolutionary line. An example would be the brain's neural network undergoing a random evolutionary step to develop synapses and then to somehow produce fast-relaying fatty myelin to further improve the system.

We have the advantage of being able to apply some sort of reasoning to the further improvement of our development, as we do with genetically modified crops and cloning animals like Dolly the sheep from a single adult cell. Behavioral Computer Science will be the discipline at the forefront of our evolution towards fully automatic airliners, and it will need to emulate the most successful strategies of evolution. Computers do a brilliant job carrying out repeated actions on limited tasks at high speed and with high accuracy. Humans do a brilliant job carrying out limited actions on vast array of very complex tasks. One day computers may replace the human brain, probably by synthesizing a neural network, but until then if we are to further improve what is already an extremely high safety standard, I would suggest we need to coordinate what we have evolved so far.

Introducing the next generation Artificial Neural Networks and Multi-layer Perception will be the equivalent of adding another layer onto the house of cards, programmed into our present-day systems. Possibly, we need to pause, and take a parallel step to better co-ordinate both systems for maximum effect in support of pilots (and potentially many other computer-dependent sectors) through the transition period.

The computer house of cards can be built only so high, as could be deduced from the safety statistics for 2018. If we can set up integrated monitoring systems working together with the series computers we have today, it should have maximum effect on the improvement of safety statistics. Humans and computers need to be partnered such that when a serious situation develops (unavoidable Swiss cheese), the three systems will work together, backing each other up with the aim of presenting the human pilot with the perfect information at the critical time in the clearest format.

So far, we have made a brief digression into our brain's make up and how well the microprocessor interacts with our world. We have observed how both pilots and series computers can fail catastrophically; so now we're off to consider an alternative path of evolution which may produce a more balanced symbiosis between man and machine. One solution may be to awaken the "2001 monolith" and contrive the rebirth of HAL.

20. *HAL — Heuristically Programmed ALgorithmic Computer*

Known as the Heuristically Programmed ALgorithmic Computer, the system was designed to run the entire *2001* "Discovery One" spacecraft en route to Mars. Heuristic means "enabling people to discover or learn something for themselves" — so what we effectively have in the movie is the Holy Grail of a fully functioning Artificially Intelligent computer.

More accurately HAL was a HAL 9000, which suggests that the creation was the end result of a long development program, and it apparently was built in Illinois as production number 3. Stanley Kubrick and Arthur C. Clarke imagined many jumps of technological advance to get HAL up to the standard depicted, and somehow they got through the present day barrier that has led to a stubborn resistance to the expected decline of commercial aircraft accidents.

How unrealistic is this notion of an omnipresent computer system monitoring the flight deck? Let's put aside the technological problems it poses for the moment and look firstly at what advantages it might offer us. HAL primarily perceived the human environment through a camera and would have observed, quite independently, that the flaps weren't selected "down" on Spanair Flight 5022, regardless of the temperature sensor status and circuit breaker position. It would integrate with our world and interpret it acting as a separate, independent house of cards. So in line with our discus far, we would have the following picture:

Pilots   *Series Computer*   *HAL System*

- The first house of cards represents the human pilot pair that we have today on a modern flight deck, which works extremely well. The acceptable pilot workload tolerance is represented by 4 layers of cards. A fifth layer could compromise safety by increasing the workload, leading to cognitive overload.
- The second house of cards represents the customary array of CRT/LCD displays and series computers which we have on the flight deck today. The acceptable computer dependence is represented by 4 layers of cards. A fifth layer could compromise safety by over reliance on the computer's ability to recognize real world problems.
- The third house of cards is the HAL system which will run independently of the series style computers to fill in the gaps or cheese holes. It will include an independent GPS and Independent Trip Counter with Performance and other databases. The system, once established, could even be able to learn during its life (using backpropagation and deep learning) so it could perform to an ever-increasing higher level of proficiency. The HAL computer dependence is again represented by 4 layers of cards. A fifth layer could compromise safety due to over reliance on HAL's ability to recognize real world problems. The essential element of this third house of cards is that it will offer assistance to the operation to prevent it from becoming super-critical

HAL would act like a good heavy pilot that we mentioned in a previous chapter. The "Heavy" is the extra pilot that is only required for in-flight rest purposes but that offers what can be vital input, by observing the overall operation of the aircraft, especially during the takeoff and landing phases. The extra crew that were involved with the Qantas A380 flight departing Singapore, where an engine explosion damaged the wing and caused multiple warnings on the flight deck, greatly assisted the operating crew with the decision making and logic handling. Effectively, we need HAL to be a "phantom" heavy pilot, discretely but overtly pointing out any deficiencies on the flight deck and at the same time knowing when not to bring up something trivial that could be a distraction.

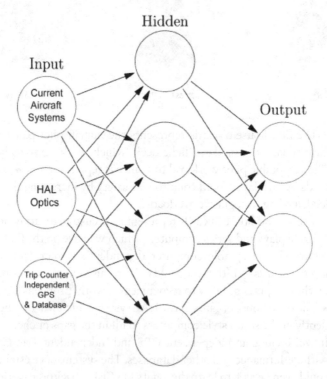

So maybe rather than "Heuristically Programmed ALgorithmic Computer," a better name for our HAL system would be "Heavy Aircrew Logic" or "Heavy Assisted Logic" in consideration of other fields that could benefit from this concept of "computer–human" symbiosis. From here on, I will refer to the new system as HAL.

Earlier, we introduced a more generalized diagram that is based on the artificial neuron network diagrams used to model Artificial Intelligence. Although at present the HAL system is not predicated on AI, the diagrams are quite useful in demonstrating the cross connections and offer a good diagrammatic representation of the logic behind the HAL concept. This (above) would be our neural network, or HAL diagram, illustrating how each system is connected and backed up. There will be various hidden elements which will sort the chaff from the wheat and finally the output, according to the criticality of the event, is presented to the pilots.

There are 3 main inputs: human pilots, series computers and HAL. The human pilots overlook the entire system, receiving information from flight instruments and HAL, so there is no need to include them in the diagrams — they receive information from the right hand side "output" column.

Series computers are represented by the "Current Aircraft Systems." This refers to the primary sources of display to the pilots that is utilized today; we would still be using a standard operation but now with greater independent review. The majority of airliner flight decks around the world are either Boeing or Airbus and are very similar. This does, though, introduce another two significant advantages of HAL which we will pick up on later.

HAL Optics refers to the visual component of HAL that will take in data from the flight deck. Independent GPS (Global Positioning System) refers to what we are all currently familiar with in our smart phones, and *Trip Counter & Database* is the final part of HAL which includes performance data, terrain data and more. Performance data refers to the calculations that are required to ensure an aircraft can safely get airborne from a particular runway at a given takeoff weight. The trip counter is needed to work out which phase of flight the aircraft is currently experiencing. This way, if the flaps were up when the aircraft was on the gate, it wouldn't issue an alert; but if the aircraft was about to take off with the flaps up, then an alert would be issued. All flight instruments, Primary Flight Displays (PFD), Navigation Display (ND) and EICAS (Engine Indication and Crew Alerting System) would be monitored by HAL.

If this all seems a tad over-ambitious, let me mention that the technology required for this can easily be handled by one of today's smart phones; later I will show how I have built a demonstration HAL program running on a smart phone, working in association with a simulator display. Note to pilots: nothing would be recorded as in "video camera mode," since history tells us that recording it would only reduce safety. Humans get nervous about being spied upon — this would be a live, in the moment, alerting system based upon optimum response and interaction from a "phantom" Heavy pilot.

Let's look at an example of a HAL diagram for the Spanair 5022 situation. It happened to be the MD-82, but the diagrams don't have to be specific to the actual aircraft involved as they act as a universal example of the flap handling logic. After that, the stall-handling logic example follows, which was relevant to Air France 447.

Flap Handling Logic

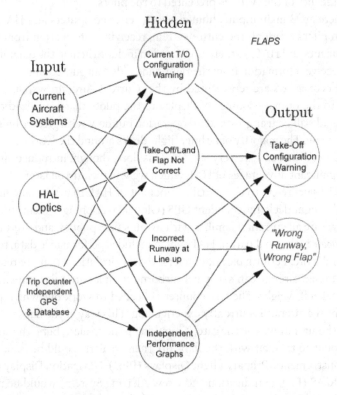

Spanair Flight 5022 was a scheduled domestic passenger flight from Barcelona–El Prat Airport to Gran Canaria Airport, via Madrid–Barajas. It crashed just after takeoff from runway 36L on August 20, 2008. The aircraft started the takeoff roll without the necessary flaps/slats (high lift devices) selected. This was a result of the aircraft having returned to stand to fix a temperature sensor overheat. Unfortunately, the fix involved shutting down the circuit for the temperature sensor (pulling a circuit breaker) which was in series with the Takeoff warning system. As a result, now being late, a human error crept in whereby they forgot to lower the flaps for takeoff and there was no warning system available. The aircraft crashed as it attempted to get airborne with insufficient lift — with 154 casualties.

The safety layers together with our new HAL system would be these:

- Throttle open with flaps out of range (currently in use)
- Optics detect flap position not as flight Manual demands
- Trip Counter detects T/O phase and reviews independent Performance Database against HAL GPS to ensure correct Takeoff runway
- Runway heading cross-checked against power setting plus HAL GPS ensures correct Takeoff runway even if flap setting is correct.

All 4 of these systems could independently raise an alert. Possible HAL Outputs — "WRONG FLAP, WRONG RUNWAY"

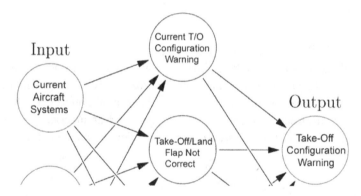

The top pathways are what are currently in place. The FMC/MCDU stores the required T/O flap setting. Hidden to the pilots is a safety system that raises a takeoff configuration alert if the pilots open the thrust levers beyond a specific point on the throttle quadrant with the flaps out of takeoff range.

The mid pathway HAL optics detect that the pilots have selected Flap 10 — the system knows from its database that Flap 20 is the minimum required. The lower pathway Trip Counter detects that the plane is taxiing and very close to the takeoff runway, which results in an independent HAL takeoff configuration alert.

On a separate occasion, the bottom pathway HAL optics detect the pilots have selected Flap 20 correctly but its database has calculated that

Flap 20 is still insufficient because the actual runway being used is incorrect. An independent "Wrong Runway" alert is issued. This could occur if the aircraft was accidentally about to take off on the wrong parallel runway in low visibility conditions.

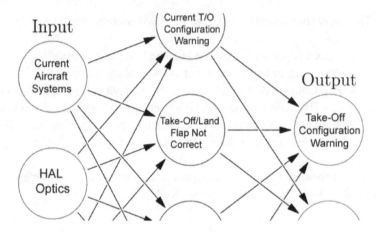

On a further separate occasion, using the bottom pathway, the HAL optics detect that the aircraft heading is not aligned with the selected takeoff runway, with 3/4 power set, and issues a "Wrong Runway" alert. Again this could occur if the aircraft was accidentally about to take off from the wrong runway at an airfield where two runways go in different directions but share a common threshold area, a situation that GPS alone could not detect.

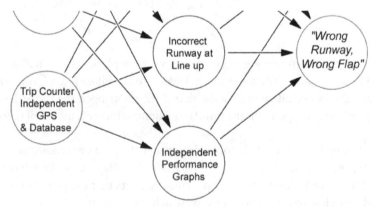

The first and only layer of system backup was fallible for Spanair 5022 because the circuit breaker had been tripped. HAL would provide independent monitoring to catch the error. Is there an argument that this could be overdoing it somewhat, as it appears to be a very rare occurrence?

Spanair 5022 crashed on August 20, 2008. On August 16, 1987, the exact same thing happened to Northwest Airlines Flight 255 at Detroit-Metro airport. The aircraft had not returned to stand with a technical fault and so the series Takeoff Configuration alert was active — or was it? It appears that for some reason there was no power to the system and the inquiry concludes:

- The circuit breaker was intentionally opened by either the flight crew or maintenance personnel.
- The circuit breaker tripped because of a transient overload and the flight crew did not detect the open circuit breaker.
- The circuit breaker did not allow current to flow to the CAWS power supply and did not annunciate the condition by tripping.

These situations will sadly keep happening. Could a virtual heavy pilot monitoring the operation be a solution for not only this set of particular circumstances but countless others?

Air France 447 was at cruising altitude, flying through an area of dense thunderstorms over the South Atlantic Ocean. A pitot tube froze over and thus false data was fed into the computer. The pitot tube system comprises forward-facing probes to detect the force of air particles entering the tubes and thus it provides airspeed indication. Without the airspeed data, the crew became disorientated and may have thought that they were in an overspeed situation if the Air Data Computers were presenting false readings. Even if they had followed the Standby Airspeed Indicator (a spare mechanical instrument to act as an arbiter if the two main systems fail), when airspeed tubes get blocked and the aircraft climbs, the static pressure reduction drives the airspeed indicator to falsely indicate increased speed. So the natural tendency is to reduce the power and pull up the nose to reduce speed, which in turn further reduces the pressure and indicates more of a false overspeed. The aircraft low-speed stalled all the way down to the ocean.

Stall Handling Logic

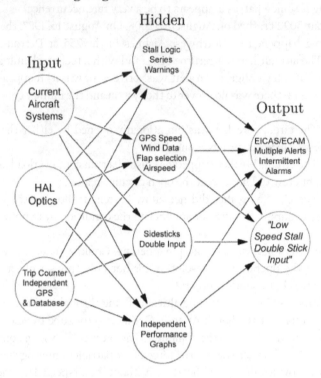

The safety layers with the new HAL monitoring system would be these:

- Multiple warnings with intermittent alarms (currently in use).
- Trip Counter & Database inputs note GPS ground speed.
- Trip Counter detects CRUISE phase and that flaps-up speed should be higher than current GPS speed ± wind.
- Optics see flap position is correct for cruise but senses double side-stick input

All 4 of these systems could independently raise an alert.

Outputs — "LOW SPEED, DOUBLE STICK INPUT"
"GPS CURRENTLY 180 KTS, GPS REQUIRES 250–340 KTS"

The captain had to work out what was going on, having come back to the flight deck from his rest. He was taking his rest so he would be able to safely operate the aircraft during the more critical descent and landing phase much later on. This is what the computer was telling him, according to the accident report:

> The ECAM system (Crew alert display) detected airspeed errors and so gave out a set of serial warnings. NAV ADR DISAGREE indicated that there was a disagreement between the three independent air data systems and a fault message for the flight management guidance and envelope computer was sent. One of the two final messages transmitted was a warning referring to the air data reference system, the other ADVISORY was a "cabin vertical speed warning."

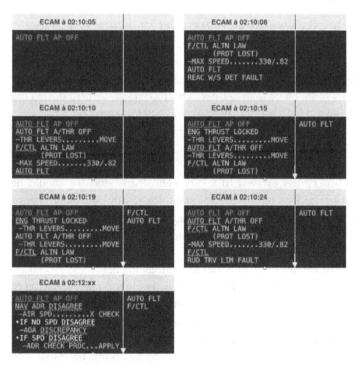

21. ECAM warnings — Air France 447

These were the ECAM warnings, over time, confronting the captain with additional alarms sounding intermittently to add to the confusion.

All he needed was a simple clue — "LOW SPEED, DOUBLE STICK INPUT."

Another benefit of this monitoring system comes in the Crew Resource Management arena. For those not familiar, the idea is to positively encourage all crew to work as a team and specifically to stay in "adult" mode when working together and not to set up a competitive atmosphere within the flight deck. This too is important in the wider aviation environment to enhance safety under the heading of "human factors."

In order to operate as a commercial pilot these days, one has to have attended one of the Crew Resource Management courses. The aviation world started realizing this a few years ago and designed CRM courses to improve flight crew communications between captain and first officer, which previously had resulted in not only several accidents but arguably the worst ever aviation accident, which took place in the Canaries when two 747s collided on the runway.

Now, if a crew received a "WRONG FLAP, WRONG RUNWAY" warning from HAL, it would register to both crew that they together had made a mistake, not just the one individual who hadn't picked up on the flap error. Before CRM, that individual who made the mistake and is now under duress was far more likely to under-perform at a critical moment during the subsequent flight. HAL therefore would act as a neutral arbiter.

Accident Types in Order of Frequency

Aviation safety has evolved to a very high degree and we should be mindful that in the drive to improve the statistics, it would be dangerous to change anything radically. The aim is to make improvements by analyzing past accidents and building a system that picks up at the critical point where current systems have proved vulnerable.

The table below lists the statistics for serious incidents and fatal accidents over the last 10 years (2010–2019). This is a good representation of what is still slipping through the net despite an amazing effort within the industry for zero tolerance. About half of these accidents may be able to be avoided in future if a HAL system were introduced. There were about 109 serious incidents involving fatalities of which 58 could not be assisted by enhanced monitoring systems, for example a bomb or an errant firing of a surface to air missile. However, it should help with other failures by assisting the crew with essential "need to know" information that can be easily overlooked in the confusion of an emergency.

There have also been many "too close for comfort" incidents that the system will take out of the mix. For instance, other that the two previously discussed accidents, a few aircraft have started the takeoff roll without any flap being selected and have luckily got airborne without incident. Maybe this is great flying skill by the pilots or inherent good design of the aircraft but it would be preferable to have the chance element removed.

HAL Assist	No.	Type of Accident
NAVIGATION (APPROACH 27) (TERRAIN 19)	46	Navigational Error
R/W EXCURSION	24	Runway Excursion
ENGINE FAILURE	19	Engine Failure
FIRE	10	External Fire
WEATHER	7	Microburst or Windshear related
INSTRUMENT	6	Instrumentation fault
ICING	6	Not de-iced/Iced up
VERTIGO G/A & T/O	6	Go-Around then somatogravic illusion
SUICIDE	5	Suicide
DOUBLE ENGINE FAILURE	4	Double Engine Failure
SLOW G/A	4	On Approach with late Go-Around
G/A STALL	2	Stall
FUEL	2	Insufficient Fuel, Fuel leak
FLAP	1	Wrong Flap
Unavoidable		
TECHNICAL	6	Technical fault on aircraft or Pilot error
TRIM	6	Loadsheet/Loading problem
HIJACK	5	Hijack
BOMB	3	Terrorist attack
PERFORMANCE	1	Takeoff Performance
ATC	1	ATC error

Of these accidents, 31 out of 164 (19%) involved long haul aircraft which traditionally attract more senior and experienced pilots. About 40% of all airliners are long haul so if it was an even spread you would expect 66 of these accidents to be on long haul aircraft. In which case you might conclude that long haul crews are safer due to their experience. However, short haul aircraft carry out about 3 times as many takeoffs and landings so if 60% of aircraft are short haul, this would amount to 98 (60% x 164) short haul flights. If we now triple this to take account of the extra takeoff and landings, we arrive at a figure of 3 x 98 = 294 flights. The amount of short haul incidents was 131 (80%) so 131 out of 294 flights = 45% which is less than half. So there seems to be no real difference between long haul and short haul pilots and the associated experience levels.

It's very difficult to work out whether experience makes an overall difference. A long haul pilot has to deal with fatigue moreso than a short haul pilot and also gets less hands-on practice. A lot of long haul flights have the "Heavy" extra crew member we have spoken about to help with the en-route rest. So long haul vs. short haul doesn't come into the argument, long and short haul pilots need every assistance they can get when things go wrong.

We will examine each of these categories of accidents using the HAL diagram and a working example from my Android Application monitoring a simulator display. These HAL diagrams illustrate the basic structure of the network but there would be no limitation to the number of hidden elements of the program. What's important is that each hidden element of the network works independently feeding in data to a relatively simple central decision making interpreter to raise an alert. The pilots would need relatively little extra training and would consider the system to be the equivalent of an extra pilot onboard who is solely there to assist.

A little more about the Optics. The placement of these cameras will be discussed later but essentially they will read existing data off the PFD — ND — EICAS/ECAM screens (current aircraft systems) and independently process the flight status. Another camera/detector will be constantly monitoring how many persons are present on the flight deck at any one time with the door locked. The reason for this will become clear later. The Independent Trip Counter, an integral part of HAL, will take in several cues and sense the phase of flight. Any internal failings of HAL would be indicated on the HAL "Interface Serviceability Indicator" adjacent to the PFD so the crew will know if they are down to 2 pilots again!

So what information do we need to feed HAL? We need specific inputs from the Primary Flight Display (PFD), the Navigation Display (ND) and the Engine-Indicating and Crew-Alerting System (EICAS) or ECAM on Airbus. We also need to link in the flight deck personnel detector and as a further enhancement, there is the availability to link in specialized external detectors.

CHAPTER 7: HEAVY MONITORING

Flight Displays

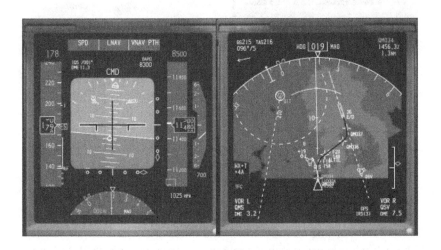

22. Primary Flight Display and Navigation Display

The Primary Flight Display (above left), or similar style of presentation, is the main instrument used by pilots to control the flight path of the aircraft. The central section shows the aircraft in a left turn and pitched up at about 6 degrees. The tape to the left shows speed, the tape to the right displays altitude. The arc at the bottom indicates the direction that the aircraft is flying (heading). The two crossed bars in the middle (the Flight Director) move to show the pilot how she should be flying to ensure the aircraft follows the correct course. The display is also color coded so any parameters of the same color as the Flight Director depict a target that the pilot should be aiming towards, whether it be a speed, an altitude or a heading. There is also much other data that is presented on the Primary Flight Display.

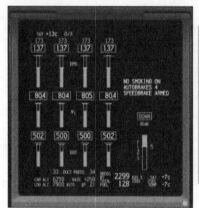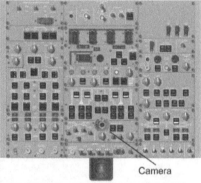

Camera

23/24. EICAS and Overhead panel indicating camera placement

The Navigation Display (above right), or similar style of presentation, is the main instrument used by pilots to navigate the aircraft. The little white triangle at the bottom is a depiction of the aircraft on the map. The arc at the top shows the direction that the aircraft is flying (heading). The line leading from the white triangle to the runway indicates the intended track of the aircraft. The arrow at top left, and readout above, displays the current wind direction and speed. There is also much other data that is presented on the Navigation Display.

The Engine-Indicating and Crew-Alerting System (EICAS) or ECAM on Airbus, is the main instrument used by pilots to set engine power and to receive any warning messages about the status of the aircraft (above left). The little white boxes contain the relevant engine parameters of EPR (Engine Pressure Ratio or Thrust), N1 (Revolutions per minute of the engine) and EGT (Exhaust Gas Temperature or engine temperature). There is also much other data that is presented on the EICAS display.

A People/Person detector would sense how many persons are on the flight deck with the door locked at any one time. This will be a separate camera/detector positioned to be able to scan the entire flight deck area (as indicated on the overhead panel, above right).

Trialling HAL in a Smart Phone

Earlier, we put aside the technological problems posed by HAL and looked at two fatal accidents that would almost certainly have benefited from the system. Now we can look at how Heavy Aircrew Logic can be demonstrated in the form of an Android Application running on a smart phone which in turn is reading data off a remote, unconnected computer running a flight simulator.

I have taken examples from fatal accidents that have occurred in the last 10 years (2010–2019) and for which HAL could have made a significant contribution to avert the accident altogether. There are many more combinations and permutations of crosschecking elements that can be inserted into the hidden logic to provide further layers of protection and is only restricted by the limitations of our "parallel" brains.

The smart phone setup follows the same principle with our 3 layers of:

PILOTS — SERIES COMPUTERS — HAL SYSTEM

The pilots will be receiving prompts from the smart phone running the HAL software. The simulator provides the regular flight deck displays and is considered as the series computer. The HAL smart phone will be interpreting the simulator and offering options to the pilots when applicable.

The simulator is based on the 747- 400 and for simplicity is a hybrid of the main flight displays on the flight deck as below. Note the sidestick has been added (bottom left) in consideration of the Airbus configuration. The simulator displays the relevant data that will be real-time scanned and read by HAL to provide the input for its own independent calculations and pre-programmed awareness of the pilot/aircraft situation.

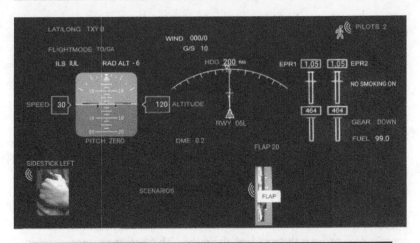

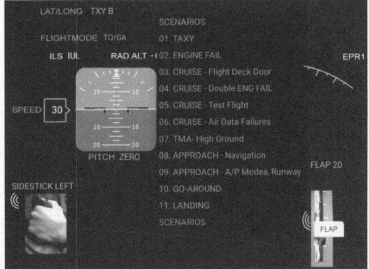

25. *Generic flight simulator running on a Windows laptop*

26. *Scenarios taken from the last 10 years of accidents (2010–2019)*

Ten scenarios have been programmed, with an extra one named "Test Flight" where the simulator is flying around at 25,000 ft, allowing the user to interact with the flight deck to test HAL's ability in different flight phases and, importantly, with varying unexpected combinations. A mouse click on various sections will change the configuration, like flap up or down, power increase or decrease etc.

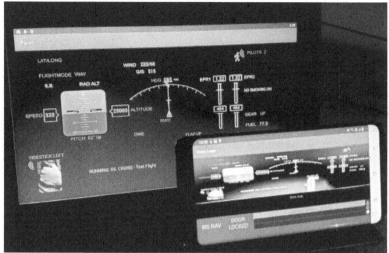

The HAL smart phone is now positioned in front of the simulator and by clicking on one of the scenarios (1 to 11 above) the flight sequence plays out on the simulator while HAL monitors and reacts.

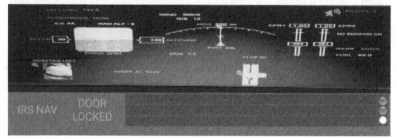

27. HAL smartphone monitors and reacts to the simulator

28. Heavy Aircrew Logic provides backup for the flight crew

This is the HAL application (above) with the top half of the screen showing the simulator data seen by the camera. It is somewhat distorted but this is just the way the wide angle camera presents the image. The display is only there for demonstration purposes and it is not necessary for the system to function, as the data is extracted in the software. The IRS NAV and DOOR LOCKED messages are also only displayed as part of the simulation process and would not be visible to the pilots. The lower part of the screen is the only visible interface between HAL and the crew with voice and discrete chimes enhancing the system.

The actual HAL interface, shown above, would consist of 3 LED bars and a Serviceability Indicator on the right. There would be two positioned on the flight deck, one on each side for captain and first officer and most likely placed near the Primary Flight Display (PFD) where it can be clearly seen. An applicable chime sounds to announce a message.

So, already you might be thinking, "What happens if the view is blocked"? The rationale is again linked to the Heavy pilot concept. Currently, if the two operating pilots actively want to degrade the safety of the operation then they can ask the Heavy pilot to leave the flight deck which would be the same as putting your hand over the camera lens.

These would be the functions of the Serviceability Indicator:

 Normal operations. Pilots can rely on critical feedback from HAL (green light).

 Camera covered and unable to detect anything. This would be the equivalent of removing the Heavy pilot off the flight deck and therefore purposely degrading the safety of the aircraft. It would also be a system fail/Off indication (red light).

 Specific data has been blocked on the PFD. This could be by accident if blocking a section of the PFD or ND with a hand or checklist, e.g., the speed readout. It acts as a reminder to restore camera access. HAL can differentiate between a blockage and missing data from the PFD/ND due to a fault or shutdown (amber and green lights).

The third line on the HAL interface is used to provide a warning message from the Serviceability Indicator which will remain lit until the situation reverts. The text won't appear if there is a more urgent message utilizing the third line but the Serviceability Indicator still reacts accordingly.

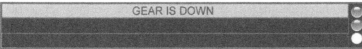

The color coding is in line with the accepted philosophy, red for warning and amber for alert. As an example, the warning above (red) would appear when the gear has been mistakenly left down after a go-around. HAL would override this alert if there was a non-normal situation involving the gear.

Navigational Error During Approach (27 fatal accidents 2010–2019)

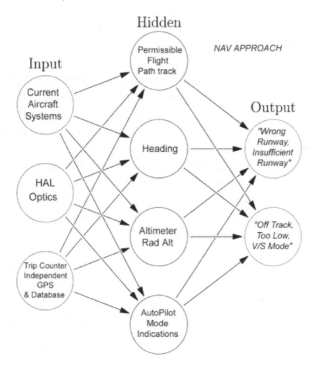

The next section offers examples of how HAL would have provided the necessary alerts to avoid about half of the accidents that involved fatalities over the past 10 years (2010 — 2019). We start with the most frequent type of accident and working down the list to the least frequent. Each scenario has a HAL (Heavy Aircrew Logic) diagram and a description of how it works in real time using the Android application monitoring the simulator. Each of the HAL interface images are screenshots of the working application captured during the simulation, providing the relevant information to both pilots at the most appropriate time.

- Hidden logic — lateral and horizontal acceptable final approach flight path tolerances are programmed internally and HAL tracks the descent with independent GPS and altimeter readouts.
- Once the aircraft transits out of the safe approach path area (trip lines), either vertically or laterally, graded warnings are activated. An escape route is suggested following the published go-around routing if possible.
- Autopilot Modes checked and warnings activated. For example, V/S Mode (Vertical Speed) selected while too low on approach with autopilot engaged.

Independent worldwide data containing information on high ground and lowest permissible altitude to fly is incorporated into the HAL database, but when the aircraft gets close to the airport it needs to descend below the area safety heights in order to land. This is where it becomes a little trickier in safeguarding the approach phase with current systems.

Here, Kathmandu is a good example of a challenging airfield. See below for the Approach Chart that pilots typically use for guidance around the high ground. The airport's runway is depicted at top right of the chart and the inbound course to land is 022 degrees, so the final inbound course is flown from the South, heading roughly up the page.

The HAL independent GPS will detect if the aircraft is ever laterally displaced by more than a permissible distance from any high ground in which case a warning will be issued. The same will happen with the final descent phase or what pilots refer to as the vertical profile. Note the excerpt below from the approach chart (figure 30). This tells the pilots the lowest possible heights to fly when at certain distances from the airport.

Example 1, Kathmandu — Chart Information

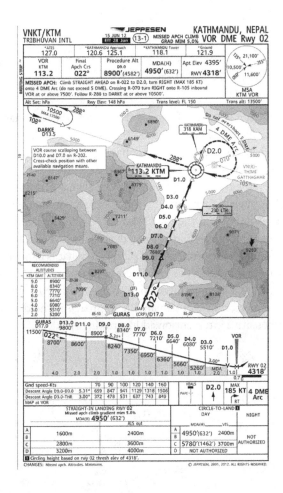

29. *Jeppesen approach chart for Kathmandu, Nepal.*
Reproduced with permission of Jeppesen Sanderson, Inc.
NOT FOR NAVIGATIONAL USE

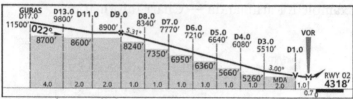

30. *Jeppesen descent profile for Kathmandu, Nepal*

For example, at a distance of 9 miles (D9.0) from the Kathmandu beacon (113.2 KTM) the aircraft should be at 8,900 ft. Any lower and you risk hitting the high ground, any higher and you risk having to dive down too steeply to get to the runway for a safe landing. HAL's independent GPS will detect if the aircraft is ever vertically displaced by more than a permissible distance where it will impinge a Trip Line, in which case a warning will be issued. In fact, this is exactly what the pilot who is not actually flying the aircraft should be doing anyway, calling out any deviations and assisting the other pilot by re-enforcing the overall mental picture of what is happening around them — bearing in mind they are very likely to be in cloud. HAL's sensitivity will be such that it will only intervene if dangerously off course. The last thing the pilots need during a demanding approach is the distraction of a nagging, over sensitive intervention adding to the workload.

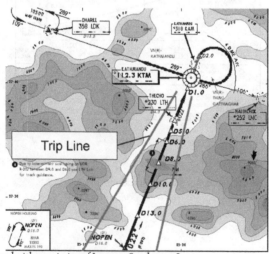

Reproduced with permission of Jeppesen Sanderson, Inc.

NOT FOR NAVIGATIONAL USE

But if it all goes wrong, HAL will interject with a reminder to keep them on course and away from high ground. If the system detects that on short finals the aircraft is too far from the runway and seconds from undershooting into the ground, a more forceful reminder will be issued via voice message.

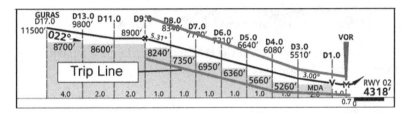

31. Warning given if Trip lines are breached either vertically or laterally

Most aircraft these days have databases that are linked to the autopilot navigation systems so the pilots can load up the Kathmandu VOR/DME approach for runway 02. But the pilots on some older aircraft may still have to make altitude selections all the way down the approach which is where errors can creep in, especially in bad weather. Crucially, HAL will back up the pilots whether the approach is fully automatic in a modern aircraft or semi-automatic in an older aircraft.

Simulation 1 — Kathmandu

The simulation starts 10 miles from touchdown at Kathmandu on a VOR/DME approach to runway 02. The aircraft is being flown with the autopilot engaged but not linked into the aircraft's navigation database. They are at 8,900 ft on track inbound to the runway and awaiting the 9.0 DME point where they will further descend at a constant rate until the runway becomes visual. Here, though, our crew is distracted and they fly past the descent point at 9 miles. HAL knows they are executing a VOR/DME approach by scanning the PFD and ND to ascertain which beacons and which runway have been selected.

At 7.4 miles HAL warns they are now high on the approach. This would have been preceded by a gentle nudge but has been omitted here.

The crew decide to Go-Around which HAL senses from monitoring the flight instruments and provides sequenced instructions to follow the published missed approach procedure.

By looking straight ahead at the HAL interface, the crew minimizes risk of somatogravic illusion or vertigo.

Using wind readout and GPS, HAL continues with correction guidance to maintain the published missed approach procedure.

This is just one scenario of many that could occur on this approach into Kathmandu. HAL is programmed to spot many different combinations at any airport where things have historically gone very wrong.

Los Angeles is a good example of a busy airfield with two pairs of very close parallel runways, one pair to the north and the other to the south. The Approach Chart that pilots typically use for guidance into Los Angeles for runway 24 Right is shown on the facing page. The airport's runway is depicted at middle left of the plate and the inbound course to land is 251 degrees, towards the coastline from the east. The independent GPS will detect if the aircraft is ever laterally or vertically displaced by more than a permissible distance in which case a warning will be issued.

A LOC or localizer approach is offered by ATC when the vertical guidance element (glide slope) of the ILS (Instrument Landing System) is unserviceable. Normally an autopilot can latch onto both the lateral and vertical guidance beams radiating from the runway and fly the aircraft right down to the landing. However it can't do this on a LOC approach — the pilots must control the correct descent profile if not able to use the aircraft's navigation database (RNAV approach).

Example 2, Los Angeles — Chart information

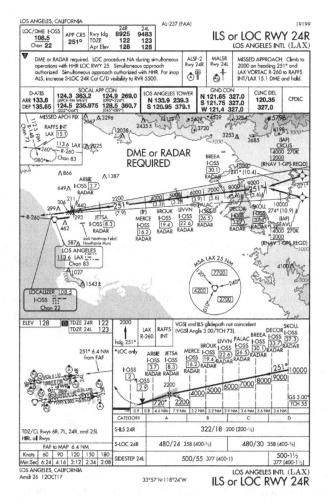

32. Jeppesen approach chart for Los Angeles, USA. Reproduced with permission of Jeppesen Sanderson, Inc.

NOT FOR NAVIGATIONAL USE

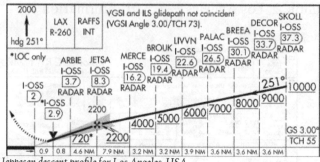

33. Jeppesen descent profile for Los Angeles, USA

Note the excerpt above from the approach chart. This tells the pilots the lowest possible heights to fly when at a certain distances from the airport.

For example, at a distance of 8.3 miles from the LAX 24R runway, the aircraft should be at 2,200 ft. Any lower and you risk hitting the ground, any higher and you risk having to dive down too steeply to get to the runway for a safe landing. HAL's independent GPS will detect if the aircraft is ever vertically displaced by more than a permissible distance, in which case a warning will be issued. HAL's sensitivity will be such that it will only intervene if dangerously off course.

Simulation 2 — Los Angeles

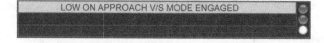

The simulation starts 9 miles from touchdown at Los Angeles on a LOC approach to runway 24R. The aircraft is being flown with the autopilot engaged, coupled with the beam that keeps the aircraft on the runway centre line but not with the vertical profile which is being controlled by the flight crew. They are at 2,200 ft on track descending in Vertical Speed mode (V/S). This mode just sets up a specific rate of descent that the pilots dial in to the autopilot but in this case the rate of descent is too high because earlier in the approach the aircraft was held high by ATC. The crew is now descending rapidly towards the airport and have estimated that they will intercept the correct glide path at 2,200 ft when at 8.3 miles from the LAX 24R runway. The visibility is 600 meters with a strong crosswind from the North while runway 24L, the very close parallel runway, is being used for takeoffs.

The aircraft does intercept the correct glide path at 2,200 ft but the crew were distracted and forgot to reduce the rate of descent to about 800 feet per minute on the autopilot panel. HAL issues the warning and the crew disconnect the autopilot and fly the aircraft level until they again intercept the correct glide path.

The approach has become "rushed" and although they are now concentrating on flying the correct vertical profile, the wind from the north has drifted the aircraft to the left and by the time they see the approach lights they are actually aligned with the parallel runway 24L that is being used for takeoffs. The crew fly a Go-Around.

ALIGNED WITH WRONG RUNWAY - KLAX 24 LEFT

34. Microsoft Flight Simulator snapshot — breaking cloud at KLAX

Although any commercial pilot may think this a bit contrived, these sorts of events do unfortunately happen as occurred on January 14, 2019 when a Saha Airlines Boeing 707 overshot the runway when landing by mistake at a close to destination but wrong airport, Fath Air Base, in Iran, killing 15. The idea is that HAL will never have to intervene...until that one time when it should.

Navigational Error Controlled Flight Into Terrain
(19 fatal accidents 2010–2019)

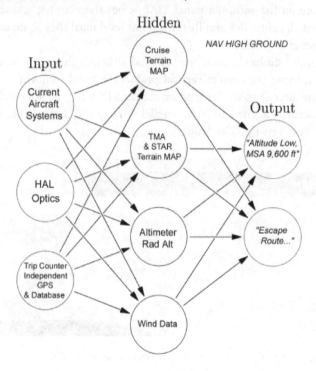

- Hidden logic — Approach Terrain Map is programmed internally and HAL tracks the descent using independent GPS and altimeter readouts. Once the aircraft descends out of the safe area, graded warnings are activated and an escape route is suggested following the published go-around routing, if possible.
- En-route Terrain Map is programmed internally together with Terminal Area (the local area surrounding the airport) terrain data and Standard Arrival chart terrain data (STAR). Wind data is monitored as increased wind strength will require greater clearance from high ground due to the possibility of increased turbulence.

Worldwide data for high ground is incorporated into the HAL database to warn against Controlled Flight Into Terrain (CFIT). Notice a mountain peak at 9,289 ft to the right of the inbound course. The airport runway elevation above sea level is 4,318 ft so obviously the aircraft will need to descend below the mountain peak to land. HAL will be programmed with allowable tolerances from this lateral inbound course to warn the pilots if they are for some reason flying below the published safety altitudes (inset showing 11,600 ft safety altitude for flying south of the KTM VOR) and on a course towards any high ground.

Chart information — Kathmandu

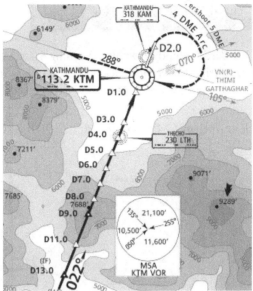

35. Jeppesen chart showing mountain peaks and safety altitude. Reproduced with permission of Jeppesen Sanderson, Inc.

NOT FOR NAVIGATIONAL USE

Simulation

The simulation starts approaching Kathmandu VOR/DME from the north (VOR/DME is a system that indicates the direction of the beacon relative to the aircraft and also provides distance in nautical miles). Overhead the beacon the aircraft turns left onto a heading of 150 degrees which is about south-easterly but it is flying too low for some reason at 9000 ft.

HAL has already alerted the crew that they are flying below the safety altitude.

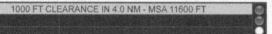

The aircraft is heading for the peak at 9,289 ft. The distance counts down and reminds the pilots of the current safety altitude.

Before the standard Ground Proximity Warning System (GPWS) activates, HAL confirms that the vertical clearance is deteriorating. This gives an important early heads up warning if the crew have become disorientated.

Runway Excursion (24 fatal accidents 2010–2019)

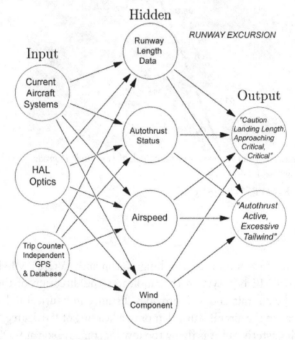

• Hidden logic — Internal runway length database referenced to check gross error on flap selection and speed using independent GPS and wind readouts. Tailwind component monitored and highlighted.
• Auto thrust monitored on PFD to warn if Auto thrust engaged but thrust not at flight idle on touchdown.

• GPS monitors runway remaining for wet conditions and reports "Caution wet," "Approaching critical wet," and/or "Critical wet." By repeatedly being informed of wet condition parameters, pilots will get a feel for the limitations of that particular runway for when eventually it is actually wet. Warnings would rarely be issued on a normal landing in dry conditions if touchdown is not too far down the runway. Slippery and reduced length runways would be more limiting and would need to be considered separately by the crew when notified in the NOTAMS (Notices to Airmen).

Simulation

The simulation starts 4 miles from touchdown at Los Angeles on an ILS approach to runway 24R. The aircraft is being flown with the autopilot engaged, coupled to the ILS, which guides the aircraft both laterally and vertically. They are at 700 ft descending with the autothrottle engaged. This mode ensures the speed should not drop below the minimum required. The wind is variable from the north. The wind has come around resulting in a tailwind and HAL warns the crew at this time of high workload where critically it could be overlooked.

They decide to land and disconnect the Autopilot but forget to manually disengage the autothrottle. In the landing flare the power imperceptibly increases as the autothrust system is now trying to keep the speed at the minimum approach speed. The aircraft doesn't touch down, using up valuable runway distance.

HAL reminds the crew that if the runway were wet, the critical touchdown point is close and they could be risking a runway excursion.

The alert is upgraded to a warning as they near the critical point.

APPROACHING WET CRITICAL LANDING LENGTH

The crew disengage the autothrottle and place the aircraft firmly on the runway to ensure the braking system has maximum effect. They taxi off at the very end of the runway.

Engine Failure (19 fatal accidents 2010–2019)

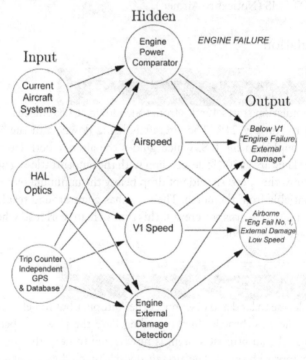

- Hidden logic — Power comparator detects engine failure below V1 (Stop/Go decision speed) on takeoff. If fire or damage is detected externally, warnings are issued to assist decision making regarding possible passenger evacuation.
- After V1, if fire or damage is detected externally, a warning is issued to assist decision making regarding immediate return. External camera/detector permanently monitors the video stream looking for irregularities in the engine and the wing area.
- Airspeed permanently monitored to ensure speed does not decay below V2 (Engine out minimum speed) which could cause control loss.

Simulation

The simulation starts 5 miles after takeoff from Montreal Trudeau International airport 06L, Canada. The aircraft is being flown manually and the left engine is about to fail in an uncontained manner which causes subsequent damage to the wing leading edges.

HAL Power comparator identifies the failed engine having crosschecked with other parameters.

External detector warns of damage.

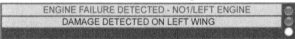

Detector finds irregularity in video stream and deduces that the leading edge could have been damaged. Also warns of any speed decay, taking into consideration the rate of speed decrease due to the power loss on one engine.

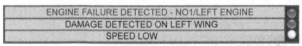

Microburst/Windshear/Instrument failures (13 fatal accidents 2010–2019)

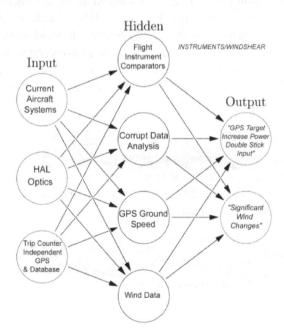

• Hidden logic — GPS speed and wind data warns of significant wind changes to act as a preliminary warning before the current onboard Windshear system is activated. The alert would be useful in any phase of flight to ensure the aircraft is kept on the optimum flight path and particularly during the approach phase to ensure a stable approach.

• Monitoring of the 3 Attitude indicators confirms to the pilots which one has failed and which one should be followed. Similar monitoring would occur for the Altimeters, Heading indicator and Airspeed indicators.

• Multiple failures logic provides essential instructions to stay within the flight envelope.

Simulation

The simulation starts at 37,000 ft over Montreal, Canada when all airspeed indications are lost. This is shortly followed by failures in altitude readout.

HAL detects that all airspeed information has been lost or is corrupt and prioritizes the multiple warnings appearing on the ECAM/EICAS display to provide essential information only. Current GPS altitude and target GPS groundspeed is immediately provided together with wind information. The target speed is 554 kts over the ground taking into account the aircraft is experiencing a 47 kts tailwind, but the actual ground speed is only 534 kts meaning they need to increase speed or risk a stall. At high altitudes these small speed margins can be critical.

Real time updates assist the crew to maintain situational awareness. If wind data is not available, HAL uses last known wind data or will download and interpret the best available data.

Power indicators give essential guidance.

Sensors on sidesticks alert the crew to control input conflicts.

38300 FT - G/S TARGET 554 KTS (47 KT TAIL) - G/S NOW 510 KTS
GPS ALTITUDE NOW 38300 FT
DOUBLE SIDESTICK INPUT

Go-Around/Somatogravic Illusion (10 fatal accidents 2010–2019)

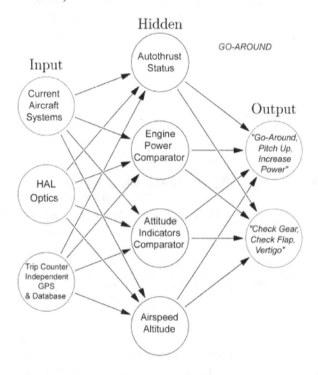

- Hidden logic — Auto thrust status and power settings are monitored to ensure Go-around power is set. Power comparator reminds pilots if an engine has failed to prevent against control loss.
- Altitude, Airspeed and Attitude indicators monitored to ensure Go-around maneuver is not delayed and is positively executed.
- Attitude indicators monitored to ensure pilot has not succumbed to somatogravic illusion (Vertigo is caused by acceleration of the aircraft whilst turning the head). Alert and claxon issued if excessive pitch down detected.

Simulation

The simulation starts 4 miles from touchdown at Los Angeles on an ILS approach to runway 24R on a dark overcast night. The aircraft is being flown with the autopilot engaged, coupled to the ILS, which guides the aircraft both laterally and vertically. The aircraft breaks cloud and the landing pilot disconnects the autopilot and the autothrottle as the approach lights come into view to manually land the aircraft. It immediately becomes clear that there is another aircraft on the runway and so they initiate the manual Go-Around procedure but going straight back into cloud and darkness, the handling pilot pitches up very slowly.

HAL detects slow pitch rate and issues an alert.

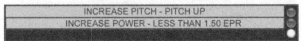

Not used to executing manual Go-arounds without the autothrottle, the power setting is incorrect. The distraction makes them forget about the Gear and Flap.

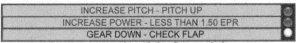

HAL issues a reminder of the flap and the gear.

The gear has still been overlooked but the pilot flying the go-around now looks to the left at his letdown plate to check the correct course for the over-shoot procedure. When he looks forward again, he is affected by somato-gravic illusion or vertigo and perceives that the aircraft is violently pitching up. The nose is lowered at an excessive rate.

HAL senses the high rate of pitch reduction and, with the trip counter knowing the aircraft is in a Go-around, issues an alert together with an attention-getting claxon.

Flight Deck Lock Out/Suicide (5 fatal accidents 2010–2019)

- Hidden logic — Personnel detector senses only 1 person in the locked flight deck. HAL automatically unlocks the flight deck door for any situation that requires the assistance of the other pilot, for example; abnormally large altitude change commanded through the autopilot system or autopilot disconnected and large rate of descent detected or the aircraft descends, even at a low rate, through 20,000 ft above the area safety altitude.

- The same logic applies if any unusual selections are made on the flight deck including an engine or further engines being shutdown, fuel jettison, pressurization controls selected, cameras blocked or specific readouts on the PFD/ND/EICAS are covered over. A discrete chime sounds in the passenger cabin to alert the entire crew.

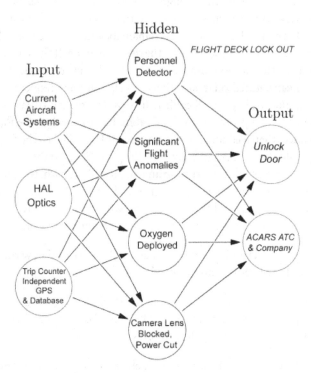

Simulation

The simulation starts at 25,000 ft above Montreal, Canada. One of the pilots leaves the flight deck. A check is made on the currently installed post 9/11 security camera, monitoring the galley area to ensure no passengers are close to the flight deck door; the pilot opens the door which locks behind him. In fact the aircraft has no passengers aboard and is on a test flight to check out the new security system. The aircraft will make several maneuvers to check HAL will release the door when any unusual flight patterns or flight deck selections are detected.

DOOR LOCKED — The current safety altitude below is 3,300 ft and the aircraft will shortly descend from 25,000 ft for a lower altitude. Estimated Top of Descent point for destination is many miles away.

DOOR OPEN — Passing through 23,300 ft, only 1 person is detected on the flight deck so the door is released by HAL as certain important conditions have been met. The door would remain locked after the normal Top of Descent point but if descended early, the door will open. If there were a pilot incapacitation, then a cabin crew member would come to the flight deck to assist the incapacitated pilot as well as to help with any requests from the other pilot, like reading the checklist. If in an emergency situation a pilot needed to observe a problem from the cabin, like to check if the flaps have fully extended, then a cabin crew member would be called to the flight deck so HAL would detect 2 people and thus keep the door firmly locked. If the sole pilot at the controls then sets up an irregular flight path, the cabin crew member would simply physically open the door for the other pilot. HAL also removes the vulnerability of cabin crew who a terrorist may incorrectly assume have special access codes or keys to the flight deck door.

DOOR LOCKED — The aircraft is back at 25,000 ft and now the aircraft is accelerated towards maximum speed.

DOOR OPEN — Only one person is detected on the flight deck. As excessive speed is very undesirable, HAL opens the door together with the discrete chime in the cabin to alert the crew.

DOOR LOCKED — The aircraft is back at 25,000 ft and now the gear is selected down — DOOR OPEN

DOOR LOCKED — The aircraft is back at 25,000 ft and now the flaps are selected down — DOOR OPEN

DOOR LOCKED — Now an engine is shutdown — DOOR OPEN

DOOR LOCKED — The cabin is depressurized — DOOR OPEN

DOOR LOCKED — Fuel starts jettisoning out of the wing tips — DOOR OPEN

DOOR LOCKED — The HAL camera is covered over — DOOR OPEN

DOOR LOCKED — The Speed indications on the PFD are blocked with the checklist — DOOR OPEN

There is another purposely withheld sequence that is required in unison with this system to safeguard against other sinister combinations. The list goes on, transforming the flight deck door into a quasi-intelligent two way system.

Total Engine Power Loss (4 fatal accidents 2010–2019)

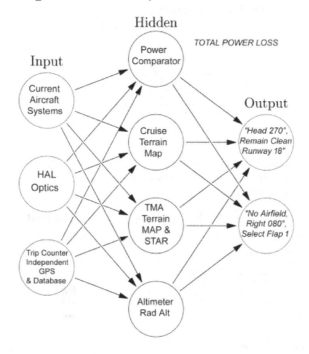

Hidden logic

- Power comparator detects total power loss.
- Independent GPS, altitude data and internal Route Terrain Map calculates closest airfield and/or steers aircraft away from high ground.
- Approach chart and Terrain data are utilized by HAL to provide headings for the most suitable landing site.
- Altitude and Wind data provide cues for speed reduction and flap selection taking into consideration increased time required for extension due to reduced hydraulic pressure available after total power loss.

Simulation

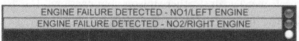

The simulation starts at 25,000 ft above Montreal, Trudeau International airport, Canada. The aircraft is approaching a large flock of migrating birds.

Once HAL detects a total power loss it concentrates on the location of the forced landing. HAL picks another airfield in Montreal other than the closer but busier Trudeau International.

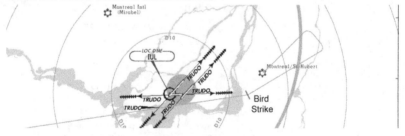

36. Jeppesen chart showing point of bird strike and HAL routing into Montreal St Hubert. Reproduced with permission of Jeppesen Sanderson, Inc.

NOT FOR NAVIGATIONAL USE

The crew declares a "Mayday" giving their intentions to land at St Hubert (CYHU) and ATC coordinate allowing the crew time to attempt engine re-lights whilst following the optimum flight path for landing. The distance to run information is live and counting down.

HAL shares the mental picture with the crew.

When no suitable airfield is available, relevant information is displayed and HAL avoids high ground where possible whilst heading for flat terrain.

Incorrect Takeoff Flap (1 fatal accident 2010–2019)

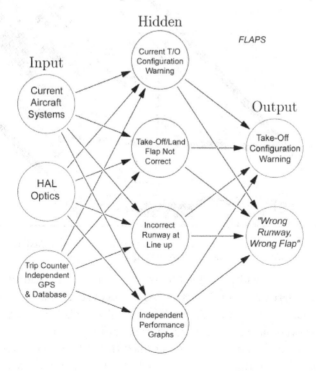

- Hidden logic — HAL detects the takeoff flap selected in unison with the independent GPS to ensure the correct flap is set as the aircraft approaches the takeoff point proximate to the runway.

- GPS will ensure the aircraft is lined up with the correct runway for takeoff to prevent low visibility taxiing errors. It will also ensure the aircraft does not cross a runway that could be active by issuing an appropriate warning.

- Independent database gross error checks that the flap selected is sufficient for the runway ahead and when ¾ takeoff power is applied, will alert the crew if not.

- Same logic is used for Landing flaps and landing runway identification.

Chart Information — Montreal

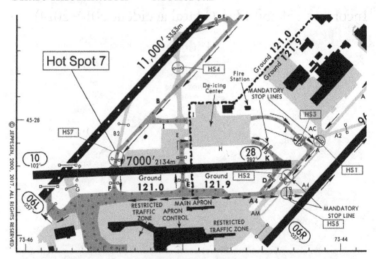

37. *Jeppesen chart showing Hot Spots at Montreal International where taxiing incidents are likely to occur. NOT FOR NAVIGATIONAL USE*

This is the airfield plate for Montreal, Trudeau International airport, Canada and is a diagram of the airfield used by pilots to enable them to safely follow taxi instructions from Air Traffic Control, especially in low visibility. The runways are shown in black and the taxiways in grey. Runway incursion hot spots are marked by small circles named HS1 to HS8 and represent the critical danger areas during operations in fog and low visibility conditions.

Simulation

The simulation starts on taxiway Bravo ("B") approaching runway 10/28 at what is published on the chart as Hot Spot 7. The intention is to cross runway 10/28 at Bravo, clearing the other side on Foxtrot and then to turn right towards Golf where the aircraft will line up on 06L for takeoff. The visibility is 600 meters and runway 06L is one of the active departure runways but there is a small jet ahead taxiing for a departure off runway 10.

APPROACHING RUNWAY 10/28 - 150M

Alert displayed approaching Hot Spot 7 as a small jet departs runway 10.

GROUNDSPEED > 25 KTS

Having turned right onto a downward slope, parallel to runway 10/28, HAL warns of excessive taxiing ground speed.

APPROACHING RUNWAY 06L - 150M

Alert displayed approaching runway 06L.

Turning onto 06L a radio transmission distracts the crew and the aircraft lines up with runway 10 by mistake. The HAL GPS confirms the error but does not activate as in this case the threshold lat/long is shared for both runway 10 and 06L and would have raised a "nuisance" warning if no line up error had occurred or the aircraft was stopped close to the runway awaiting a preceding aircraft to depart. But when ¾ power is applied for takeoff . . .

38. Microsoft Flight Simulator snapshot — lining up for runway 06 or 10 at Montreal International. Reproduced with permission of Jeppesen Sanderson, Inc. NOT FOR NAVIGATIONAL USE

... the crew are alerted to the mistake as the heading is inconsistent with the planned takeoff runway QDM or magnetic track direction of the runway as per the ND display.

The takeoff is rejected and the aircraft clears runway 10 at Foxtrot where the crew carry out the after landing checklist, raising the flap. They approach runway 06L for a second time.

This time the aircraft lines up with the correct runway (06L) and an alert is issued for the flaps which have not been selected down, as the crew are now out of their normal sequence and have forgotten to re-run the takeoff checklist.

Correct takeoff flap is set and the takeoff checklist is completed, reverting the HAL interface to what will mostly be observed in normal operations.

Other HAL Interventions and Detectors

39. 747-400 wing on landing showing reverse thrust, leading edge flaps and lift dump

Many other systems would be monitored by HAL, for example fuel state to guard against possible fuel leaks. Speed limitations for flaps, gear and many more useful interventions can be programmed into the system and eventually HAL could be further expanded to allow monitoring for external dangers around the aircraft. We have already mentioned damage detection on the wing around the engines.

This is an important area where an uncontained engine failure involving failed high speed turbine blades could cause serious problems. Ice can form on wings, engines can catch fire, cowlings can become displaced, flaps and leading edge devices can become damaged or stuck and ground personnel can be sucked into engines on the tarmac even at relatively low power settings.

External Detectors

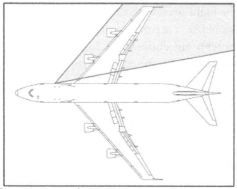

40. Camera/detector coverage of 747-400 wing

The external monitors would be multipurpose to detect ice, fire, people and damage. It would need to detect heat and moving objects but would also need to compare the normal, expected picture, to one where an engine has lost a cowling or where damage has been inflicted to a leading edge. A perfect "single job" use for AI that has been so successful in the detection of lung cancer cells. The word "Damage" would be annunciated and when the crew have time they would observe from the passenger cabin. The ice detection system would be primarily for turboprop aircraft that can suffer badly. It would need a sophisticated detector to reliably sense even small build-ups of ice. They would be designed to be so sensitive that they would warn before the aircraft attempts to takeoff and when airborne it would warn of icing to alert the pilots to engage the anti-ice systems as soon as possible. Serious ice buildup, although rare, has caused aircraft to literally fall out of the sky.

A single housing, multipurpose detector could be fitted to any aircraft to at least warn the crew of an impending problem. Even on a large jet, extended taxiing at a busy international airport can put the aircraft at risk from icing so a critically calibrated system would benefit all aviation across the board.

If physical damage is detected externally, the warning could critically assist decision making regarding immediate return. If leading or trailing edge flaps were damaged, the warning could prevent the crew from doing what is correct in normal practice, but could subsequently be fatal. If the aircraft reduced speed after an engine failure on takeoff to climb away at the optimum rate, it could stall the wing if the leading edge or trailing edge flaps had been damaged by the uncontained explosion. The same detector would monitor for ground personnel if they were standing too close to the engines during start or ground runs.

All of this would only enhance HAL but would not be necessary for its primary function within the flight deck, although the Personnel detector would have to be an integral part of the system. It needs to sense how many persons are on the flight deck with the door locked at any one time. As we have seen, this would be a separate camera/detector positioned to be able to observe and/or sense the entire flight deck area and would probably use video, infrared, motion detection and image recognition analysis.

Sidestick Detectors

Detection is required for sidestick manipulation on either side. Probably the best solution would be a pressure switch on the sidestick so that the system will know when both sidesticks are being operated at the same time. This would not interfere with normal Airbus protocols; HAL isn't meant to interpose with current systems and will only raise an issue if other more limiting factors come into play.

Trapping Errors

This whole chapter has dealt with the last 10 years (2010–2019) of accidents and it may seem an excessive amount of work introducing a new system to combat these rare eventualities. Every accident must be seen as avoidable and HAL will need to consider a complete history of aviation accidents and incidents (see appendix) to ensure it has solutions pre-loaded. It will also need to look ahead to try and predict the next set of awkward combinations that are almost certain to occur, especially with the introduction of new aircraft designs.

Error on Error

This will be a very important part of the overall logic. If a speed readout on the pilot's PFD is incorrect due to an iced up pitot tube then this reading needs to be rejected. As in the human brain, we need to look at several related inputs and then decide on which one to believe. Onboard there are 3 airspeed indicator systems that each independently calculate the airspeed of the aircraft through the air. Unfortunately, if there is severe icing outside then all three sensors can become useless.

A GPS system will regardless be able to indicate the speed of the aircraft but if the aircraft is flying into a 100 kts headwind then there will be a disparity. However these days there are many hundreds of aircraft flying the world's airways and they continually provide the Meteorological office with the crucial wind information at various altitudes. Until the wind data is received, HAL will use the last recorded wind from the IRS (Inertial Reference System) that normally provides accurate navigational information to the aircraft. Upper wind information is crucial to airlines as they don't like burning unnecessary fuel en route and knowing the exact winds aloft allows them to calculate the fuel required very accurately. This is a good thing for the planet and explains why your flight to the UK from the USA is always so bumpy — the aircraft is routed down the nearest jet stream blowing at up to 200 mph.

So now we can download the winds from satellites and provide reasonable enough data to prevent an aircraft from losing control. As HAL is an independently powered system, it won't be contaminated by any confused data coming from the onboard computers. Just as the human brain can detect anomalies on the flight deck, HAL will be programmed to look for specific disagreements on the pilot flight displays to prioritize essential information for the crew.

If specific parameter readouts are blocked on the PFD, HAL can differentiate between a blockage and missing or corrupted data due to a fault or failure. So if the captain's speed readout is in disagreement with the first officer's side then HAL can work out which one is in error by looking at the many other parameters available. If the readout goes blank then the null recorded by HAL is registered as a disconnect as opposed to a block.

CHAPTER 8: EVOLUTION BEFORE FULL AUTOMATION

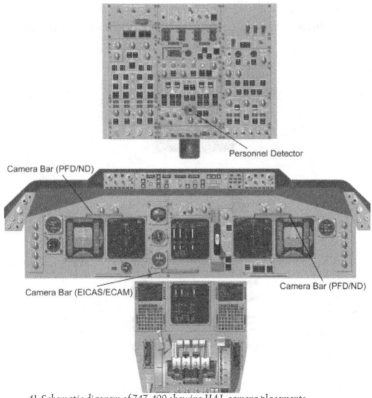

41. Schematic diagram of 747-400 showing HAL camera placements

Do we need to evolve a little further and develop a better computer/human symbiosis before we embrace full automation? The HAL flight test Application works well but there is one obvious drawback — the camera needs to be positioned so it can read all the computer LCD screens at the same time. In this chapter I will look at how this may be achieved.

Two camera bars, one either side, would read data from the PFD and ND. Another camera bar would read data from the EICAS/ECAM from below. The camera system obviously cannot block the view of the pilot but if placed strategically around the edges of the computer LCD screen, HAL could use correction algorithms to decode the distortion as if it were aligned directly in front. All the cameras can be linked/networked together and the HAL interface, providing information to each pilot, could be positioned on top of the camera bar housing.

However problems still exist with regard to sunlight glare and line of sight being blocked at the critical moment. There also needs to be a slight delay built into the software to ensure the program has correctly interpreted the words or digits... much like pilots undergo at their bi-annual medical check.

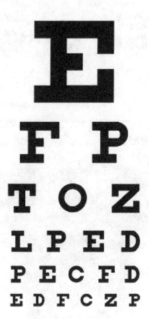

As we go down the eyesight chart we need more time to analyze the shapes. Is it a Q or an O, a D or a Q? Guessing won't help and if we do use a suspect result in a critical decision, we may cause more problems than we solve. We do, though, have the advantage that a weather forecaster has at their disposal in as much as an accurate forecast is much easier to predict given that the overall weather synopsis has already been observed for the previous day. So, as in my health App mentioned earlier, if the speech synthesis returned "you'll get," I could exchange the words for "yoghurt" which the App would recognize because I know we are only looking for foodstuffs.

With HAL, we know what we are expecting to be critical so if the system mistakenly read CABIN ATTITUDE, we can override and replace the word with the correct version, CABIN ALTITUDE. This mimics the human brain where we may doubt the first thing we heard or read and so will start processing the likely possibilities before we accept the most plausible fit.

The HAL App does cope pretty well with varying light settings and reflection off the simulator monitor but improvements need to be made for it to work in the real world. Most importantly the HAL App proves that Heavy pilot emulation can work, providing another pair of virtual eyes in the flight deck to enhance safety throughout the entire flight.

Solutions

The solution I propose for development is a photo-sensitive plastic overlay screen which would look similar to a smart phone screen protector. We are all familiar with these screen protectors which conveniently allow a touch to be transmitted through the special plastic so the smart phone can react. The touch screen then detects the local coordinates of the touch and the software responds. So if the touch was over a virtual button, then that particular procedure or routine is activated.

The photo-sensitive plastic overlay screen would act as a touch-sensitive screen in reverse. Instead of a touch being recognized as a voltage in a particular area of the screen on the smart phone, this new plastic overlay would recognize the LCD light output from the smart phone screen and relay the result to the HAL computer.

Any word or character output to the LCD would interact with the plastic screen and be fed out through connections to the HAL processor. This way we don't have to consider camera alignment, blockages, lighting conditions or malicious interference.

So, the pilot will interpret the usual data from the PFD, coming through the plastic overlay but at the same time HAL will also interpret the very same data (plus more) and assist where necessary.

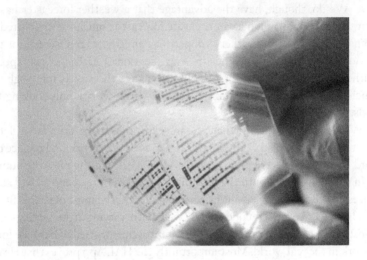

43. Flexible computer screen technology

Earlier in the book I alluded to two other important advantages of the HAL system. Although the aviation world is dominated by Boeing and Airbus there are several other types flying around — ATR, Embraer, Sukhoi, Bombardier, de Havilland Canada, Beechcraft, CASA, Cessna, Fairchild Swearingen to name a few and could all be integrated with HAL without undue complication. The two advantages are:

- HAL can be integrated with any existing aircraft type with flat screen displays.
- The installation is totally independent from the existing technology of the "tried and tested" aircraft type.

This second point is important because any additions, how ever minor, that are bolted on to the original design can have unexpected and undesirable consequences causing failures where there were none before. There has to be time-consuming, extensive testing before any amendments are certified by the authorities otherwise metaphorically, these additions can lead to a collapse of our House of Cards.

If the onboard computer systems are left to operate as they were designed and we now add an independent layer, we have the desired balanced result we were seeking — no one part being stacked dangerously high with too much riding on it.

Human	*Computer*	*HAL (Human/Computer)*

From here on, we'll call the photo-sensitive plastic overlay screen a "Photo-Sensitive Screen" or PSS. It will be comprised of a thin, transparent flexible plastic sheet that is cut to fit exactly over the pilot displays. So, one for the PFD, one for the ND and one each for the upper and lower EICAS/ECAM. On the edges of the PSS will be flat cable wires that take the signals to the central HAL processor. The pilots fly the aircraft through the usual displays, visible through the PSS, and at the same time HAL interprets the very same display just as a Heavy pilot would do to enhance the safety of the flight.

It will work like a regular computer screen but in reverse. Instead of the characters being sent out to the screen and the words, numbers and graphics displayed on the monitor, the PSS detects the exact shape of the lit LCD pixels below and sends the pixel shape through the flat cable to the HAL processor to be decoded to characters.

44. Flexible computer screen showing output connections

Critically, this isolates HAL from the aircraft flight displays, preventing any negative backward interference into the aircraft systems or forward contamination of corrupt data into the HAL computer. Separate specific software then integrates pilot and computer perceptions — the HAL computer. The idea is to recreate the human synapse we discussed in an earlier chapter which has evolved to control the impulses from the brain to the toe. If the speed indications on the PFD suddenly increase, instead of a hard wired knee-jerk reaction of slamming the thrust levers closed, it allows for a more intelligent analysis.

Air France 447 could very well have had a different outcome with HAL looking for clues that pointed towards a pitot tube icing failure. By sensing the associated multiple failures, a completely different, independent set of programming rules would have come into play to initially provide the crew with only the most essential information. Asiana Airlines Flight 214, descending into San Francisco would have HAL permanently monitoring the autothrottle annunciations on the flight displays and together with a real time analysis of the speed readout would have alerted the crew.

1.0	1.0	1.0	0.8	0.6	0.6	0.6	0.8	1.0	1.0	1.0	1.0
1.0	0.5	0.0	0.0	0.0	0.0	0.0	0.0	0.5	1.0	1.0	1.0
1.0	0.0	0.0	0.5	0.6	0.6	0.5	0.0	0.0	0.5	1.0	1.0
1.0	1.0	1.0	1.0	1.0	1.0	1.0	1.0	0.0	0.0	1.0	1.0
1.0	1.0	1.0	1.0	1.0	1.0	1.0	1.0	0.0	0.5	0.8	1.0
1.0	1.0	1.0	0.5	0.5	0.5	0.5	0.5	0.4	0.0	0.5	1.0
1.0	0.5	0.0	0.0	0.0	0.0	0.0	0.0	0.0	0.0	0.5	1.0
0.8	0.0	0.0	0.5	1.0	1.0	1.0	1.0	0.5	0.0	0.5	1.0
0.5	0.0	0.5	1.0	1.0	1.0	1.0	1.0	0.5	0.0	0.5	1.0
0.5	0.0	0.6	1.0	1.0	1.0	1.0	1.0	0.0	0.0	0.5	1.0
0.5	0.0	0.5	1.0	1.0	1.0	1.0	0.5	0.0	0.0	0.5	1.0
0.8	0.0	0.0	0.5	0.6	0.6	0.5	0.0	0.4	0.0	0.5	1.0
1.0	0.8	0.0	0.0	0.0	0.0	0.0	0.0	0.8	0.5	0.0	1.0
1.0	1.0	1.0	0.6	0.6	0.6	1.0	1.0	1.0	1.0	1.0	1.0

45. The letter "a" as displayed on a computer screen with pixel decode on the right.

Any computer screen is comprised of hundreds of pixels with each character having a different layout and therefore a different set of codes. The image above shows the makeup of the lowercase letter "a":

We just need to reverse engineer the process of pressing the letter "a" on the keyboard. The PSS system will effectively read the intensity of each pixel and provide a grid of codes as seen on the right side of the above diagram. This will then be fed to the processor to identify the letter "a."

It may appear a bit strange going through all this effort to just read off the text that is clearly available as a computer code at the time it is sent to the PFD screen. In the case of the letter "a," the standard computer code is 97 and you might ask why we can't just tap into the aircraft computer just before its processor sends out the code 97 to the graphics card. There are 2 major reasons as to why this would not be desirable:

- The first problem is that we are now relying on the computer outputs to provide data for flight information to the pilots as well as vital crosscheck data for HAL. If the ships computers fail, as has happened with pitot tube icing, then HAL gets mixed in with the faulty data running around the system and becomes equally confused. By keeping HAL separate it can crosscheck other parameters to see what has shutdown or what is now providing unintelligible data to come to a quasi human like conclusion of what has occurred. Another way of looking at it might be when we consider computer viruses. As we know, once a virus gets into a computer it can irretrievably shut it down, normally until the user pays a random. The PSS/HAL setup allows it to act like a firewall — there is no way to get into the HAL processor from the ships computer and vice-versa.

- The extra connections required to link in HAL directly to the ship's computers only adds to the overall level of complication of the system and would be the equivalent of building another few layers of cards on our computer House of Cards. This means that we are now raising the odds that we will have a failure within the system by over-complicating the very same system!

As we mentioned before, this isolation of the two computer systems is a mirroring of the human synapse we spoke of in the earlier chapter on Evolutionary Aspects. Synapses only allow electrical flow in one direction. Without synapses, the central nervous system would be under constant bombardment with impulses which would cause central nervous system fatigue. The responses would be slow and reverse flow of impulses would lead to uncoordinated functioning — or the dreaded blue screen of death! By isolating one computer from the other, we mimic the human synapse by stopping backward data flow, which could crash the system. By allowing the summation of all relevant inputs from various displays, we generate a meaningful, weighted response.

In practical terms, PSS will stop the primary onboard computers from contaminating the HAL software, allowing the system to offer essential guidance to the pilots in a catastrophic situation. For instance, if any flight display speed indication fails, the *Integration System* (HAL) can use other readouts (neuron routings) to ascertain that the pilot needs other mean-ingful information regarding speed. This will effectively result in an alterna-tive array of synapses opening to present GPS ground speed information, integrated with wind data.

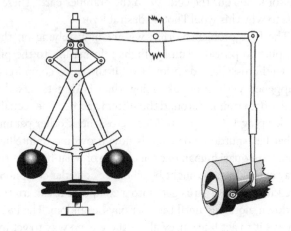

46. Steam Engine Flyball Governor

Its overall effect will be similar to the function of a steam Governor that balanced the system in a Victorian steam engine. When the engine runs too fast, the rotating weighted balls fly out under centrifugal force which compresses the apparatus on the left, pulling down the central cross linkage. This in turn moves a valve which reduces the steam pressure so the machine then runs a little slower. Equally, when the pressure is raised on the flight deck due to serious failures, HAL is activated to offer essential information to the crew, enabling them to recover and return the situation to normal.

So how might this computer synapse system work practically? Imagine we are flying along quite happily at 35,000 ft in a 747-400. The weather is perfect and there is no turbulence. Suddenly we lose all airspeed information — it just goes blank on the captain's instruments, the first officer's instru-ments and the standby instruments. The regular onboard computer systems will now issue several warnings to get the attention of the pilots so they can deal with the problem. But what the current system is really saying is that the computer program has been contaminated with unknown data. It may be receiving a continuous sequence of zeros, a value of 10.9 or a quick flash of 1, 3004,023 followed by the letter "a" and depending on the fault, the airspeed may return and then disappear again. The programmers know that these errors need to be trapped to avoid a total system crash so they write in several lines of code to ensure the processor(s) doesn't hang up as could happen if an illegal computation was executed during the fault condition.

If we link HAL directly to the airspeed outputs, HAL will just become a part of the confusion, trying to work out if the airspeed inputs are genuine. What we want HAL to do is register that the captain's airspeed is out of limits, crosscheck it with the first officer's airspeed indication, note the power setting, note the fuel state (to calculate the aircraft weight), note the altitude, note the flap setting, note the pitch attitude of the aircraft, note the undercarriage selection and much more.

Now HAL will look up the "Flight with unreliable airspeed" table which normally sits within one of the onboard aircraft flight manuals. Here we crosscheck altitude with aircraft weight and read off the correct engine power setting and required flight pitch angle to maintain level flight within the correct tolerances of airspeed. In the case above, HAL will note that no parameters are close to critical, thanks to the perfect weather conditions, advise that all airspeed input has been lost, confirm target power settings and attitude for level flight and backup with an independent GPS speed readout with last known wind component.

Suppose, though, that it was only the captain's airspeed readout which was playing up. We expect a sensible, "weighted" response so HAL will crosscheck the first officer's airspeed, note it is highly likely to be correct by comparison to the "Flight with unreliable airspeed" table and independent GPS, to issue guidance as to which airspeed indicator to ignore — remember, the captain's airspeed readout might be only 20 kts out but nevertheless dangerously inaccurate for flight at 35, 000 ft. For completeness, current systems are designed to raise an alert for airspeed disparity between the two sides but it's up to the pilots to decide which one is correct.

The PSS (Photo-Sensitive Screen), as well as being transparent, would need to be flexible and be able to fit a variety of different screen sizes found in glass cockpits. The HAL computer would encompass the independent GPS and connections to the Personnel camera/detector and the flight deck door locking mechanism. It won't need to be any larger than a typical smart phone and could be easily hidden behind a panel where it would be protected from possible sabotage. Another connection would link HAL to the external detector unit, as previously mentioned, to further protect the aircraft.

Color detection will assist in ascertaining the urgency of a situation following the normal protocols of the aircraft systems thus providing more "weighting" to the HAL neural network. For instance, the words CABIN ALTITUDE (warning of a cabin depressurization) will not be instantly reacted upon by HAL until the weightings increase to trigger an action potential with additions of color detection and cabin altitude, cabin rate and bleed air duct pressure readings on the EICAS/ECAM display. HAL will use all these data inputs together with an array of other related readings before reacting.

The PSS will read numbers and characters in specific areas of the flight deck display and by knowing the grid reference of where this information is displayed, the HAL computer will be able to decipher its context. This ability can be expanded to include the tracking of shapes on a display. Pilots use the Artificial Horizon on their Primary Flight Display (PFD) to know whether the aircraft is pitching or turning. HAL will detect if any pitch or turn is excessive and also whether the rate of pitch or turn is worthy of a mention by the non-handling pilot. As HAL is designed as "Heavy Aircrew Logic," it will regardlessly annunciate a suitable warning.

The Artificial Horizon and other types of data displayed to the pilots are essential when flying in cloud so sensing these readouts is a vital tool for monitoring. However, one other type of sensing can be equally important — the ability to sense nothing. Missing data can give a big clue as to which aircraft systems may have failed and HAL will detect any absence of data that the pilots normally expect to be present.

The HAL trip counter will use all the same cues from the PFDs, NDs and EICAS/ECAM to determine which phase of flight the aircraft is currently experiencing. By monitoring the late stages of an approach and tracking the radio altimeter, barometric altimeter, rate of descent and speed, the trip counter will sense whether to transition from approach phase into landing phase or transfer into the more critical Go-around phase.

Power for HAL would be supplied via the aircraft battery which is always available even if all the engines have failed and therefore cannot run the ships electrical generators. The system could then be even more independent if it were further isolated by inductive charging so it would remain active even if the aircraft battery is disconnected in an incident or a fire.

Other functionality that we are used to these days is the ability to update our smart phones with data and software. As HAL is independent from the aircraft systems, it will be able to download software updates en route as well as the latest information about the destination or alternate. I've never downloaded an update to my smart phone that goes on to completely crash the system, as the companies that write the operating systems know very well that great care needs to be taken to avoid a critical error. With the same amount of care, and bearing in mind that HAL is not the first line of defense but a backup to the aircraft systems, we can introduce other helpful dimensions to HAL. For instance, if an alternate airfield is closed due to bad weather, HAL will be able to communicate this to the pilots in a timely manner via the HAL interface.

Below is the entire schematic for the HAL installation on the Boeing 747-400. The small HAL computer would be tucked away behind the instrument panels and the complete installation would be practically indistinguishable from the fight deck we have today.

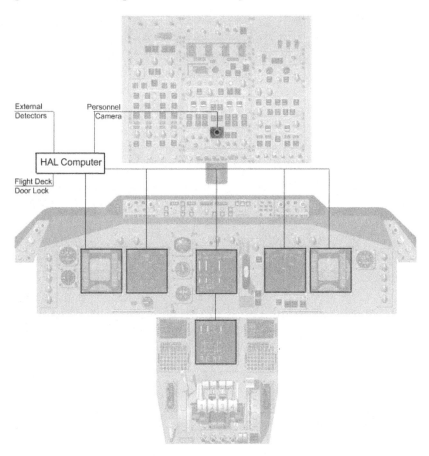

47. Schematic diagram of 747-400 showing HAL connections

CHAPTER 9: EXTENDED APPLICATIONS

This second layer of the HAL weighted analysis would mainly be applicable for industries that have similar vulnerabilities to aviation that, in extremis, risk life and limb. However, money has always proved to be quite high on the preservation list and there may be a case for the virus protection quality of HAL to assist in limiting hacking attacks of sensitive computer systems in our security and banking sectors. This chapter deals with a few examples that could benefit, starting with hospital monitors for which I have also written a demonstration Android App.

Medical

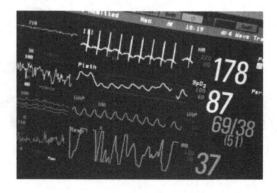

48. Vital Signs of Heart rate, Blood pressure, Oxygen saturation and Respiration rate

Alarm fatigue is sensory overload when clinicians are exposed to an excessive number of alarms, which can result in desensitisation to alarms and missed alarms. Patient deaths have been attributed to this phenomenon.[2]

The quote above is from an on-line article concerning alarm fatigue issues in hospitals. Even if a hospital has all the latest equipment and all of their patients are connected to monitors, there's still that catch 22 to overcome. With a photo-sensitive plastic overlay screen (PSS) connected to HAL, patients would be monitored 24/7 but now with an ability to analyze the outputs for known issues. It sends a text notification to a clinician if anything untoward is detected.

The App simulation involves a PC emulating a hospital monitor which is programmed to randomly alter the vital signs of heart rate, blood pressure, oxygen saturation, respiration rate and temperature. The smart phone (HAL) will be interpreting the outputs and sending a 'patient specific' text message if and when the vital signs reach preset limits. HAL also detects if the monitoring attachments on the patient have failed or have become detached.

Notification 12:33 — Stats Check Bed 9

Notification 03:17 — Blood Pressure Sensor Error Ward B, Bed 2

49. Medical staff receive instant alerts

---

[2] https://pubmed.ncbi.nlm.nih.gov/24153215/

In a large hospital it may be better to utilize a centralized unit where one person would monitor all notifications and then contact the relevant clinician. This way, if a nurse or doctor was dealing with another emergency, the alert notification would not be overlooked.

Independent programming within HAL would set graded limits to warn of a patient's specific vulnerabilities. E.g. a 10% high/low warning.

Notification 13:17 — Blood Pressure 10% Inc 160/90, Bed 7

Notification 23:17 — Oxygen Saturation Low 94%, Bed 4

Notification 06:17 — Heart rate Low 50 bpm, Bed 2

50. Personnel detector guards against missing patients

The personnel detector, similar to the one we introduced for the aviation application, would be attached to the side of the monitor looking towards the patient to guard against the not so rare problem of patients going missing! A time delay would be set to allow for regular bathroom visits.

Notification 18:24 — Missing Patient Bed 5

Hospitals worldwide wouldn't necessarily need to replace existing monitors so regularly in order to stay up to date with newly introduced functionality like analysis and communication. Provided the current equipment is working, HAL/PSS can be integrated, as shown below, to deliver the updated functionality of a new state-of-the-art monitor. This should cut down the cost of buying in the latest model of monitor which could be very expensive for large hospitals, and would certainly be a good option for less affluent parts of the world that cannot afford to regularly upgrade.

The PSS is fitted over the monitor screen to read the vital sign outputs from the patient. The data is connected to the HAL computer on the rear of the monitor via flat cable wires and a small webcam/detector is attached to the flat cable, facing forward to check if the patient is still present. Bluetooth, Wi-Fi, USB and Text connectivity allow for easy update and transmission of notifications. Password protection ensures HAL remains synchronized with the specific monitor and patient.

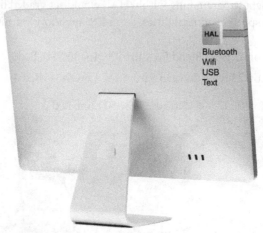

51. The HAL computer fitted to an existing monitor

Power would be supplied via the monitor mains supply but would be isolated by inductive charging so the HAL computer will remain active even if there is a mains power failure — clinicians will be alerted to such failures by HAL's ability to sense absence of readout or data on the monitor.

Railways

52. Similar aviation safeguards in the drivers cab

The functionality for the railways, both signaling and powered rolling stock, would be very similar to the application in aviation. In 2013, a train derailed on a bend at "Santiago de Compostela" in Spain and the driver was overheard on his mobile phone saying, "I'm at 190 kmph and we're going to derail." HAL working in unison with the independent GPS would have warned the driver at a much earlier stage to reduce speed.

Control Rooms (Power Stations)

53. HAL monitors critical parameters

Any control room where serious overloads could be damaging to people, infrastructure or the environment would benefit from an extra layer of protection using the HAL/PSS human/computer analytical backstop.

Automatic Cars

54. Driverless cars will need backup

How far can we trust our fully automated cars in the near future? Recently, I was driving at night on a fast moving highway in foul weather with the rain lashing down, severely reducing visibility. How well will the automatics work in these conditions? My parking sensors were sounding randomly due to the intensity of the rain — I hope the fully automatic system will know not to jam on the brakes! Maybe here we could benefit from one extra layer of analysis?

Scientific Research

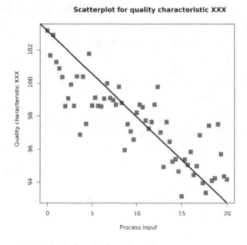

55. HAL looks for the desired result

Where a scientific experiment is running for purposes of research, a detector may be outputting data to a screen as in the example above. It may be more beneficial for the researchers to use HAL/PSS as a separate programming tool to look for the desired result rather than trying to add extra code to an older computer running alongside the detector. There could be an arrangement where several inputs are connected to one monitoring screen and now we only need to program HAL to look for the specific combinations required. Notifications would be sent to indicate progress as well as success. Minimal reprogramming would then be required to set up HAL to monitor a completely different experiment.

Air Traffic Control

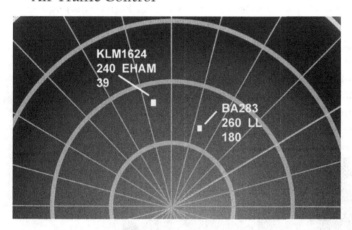

56. Air Traffic Control radar shows one aircraft at 24,000ft and another close at 26,000ft

Secondary radar returns contain data pertaining to each aircraft in the sector being controlled by the Air Traffic Controller. An example would be the aircraft's altitude display which is obviously vital for other traffic crossing in the area. HAL/PSS would again be an ideal addition to further enhance safety.

Mission to Mars

The next mission to Mars at time of writing is scheduled for the summer of 2020. It will be a rover mission, part of NASA's Mars Exploration Program. The mission also provides opportunities to gather knowledge and demonstrate technologies that address the challenges of future human expeditions to Mars. These include testing a method for producing oxygen from the Martian atmosphere, identifying other resources (such as subsurface water), improving landing techniques, and characterizing weather, dust, and other potential environmental conditions that could affect future astronauts living and working on Mars.

It looks like it won't be long before humans will be setting off for Mars. Due to the vulnerability of the mission, they could do with some of that computer technology that was available to Dave and his crew in *2001: A Space Odyssey*.

As a preamble, I would like to look at a bit of design philosophy that took people by surprise when webcams were first introduced. Most laptop computers have a small webcam sitting on top of the lid and next to it is a little light to inform you that the camera is running. Then it was discovered that some rogue software could secretly switch on your camera, bypassing the warning light, to expose your privacy or even your credit card details. We were all led to believe that the light only came on when the camera was working, but in fact the initial design flaw allowed for 2 distinctly separate functions. It could switch on the camera and then as an additional function it could switch on the light. But it should have been designed in series so that the software could only switch on the camera and then once the camera was activated, another independent circuit would switch on the light.

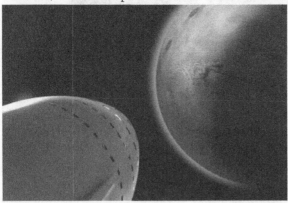

57. *Space travel will necessitate total trust of onboard systems*

This, too, is where things started to go wrong with HAL 2001 — in the design phase. HAL had complete autonomy of the spaceship and was able to come up with an excuse to persuade the astronauts to undergo an unnecessary Extravehicular Activity (EVA). A component needed changing as it was, according to HAL, going to fail catastrophically in 72 hours. Like the laptop camera, HAL could effectively cheat the system in order to get his own way, albeit for his own genuine reasons. The initial design needed to ensure that each conclusion reached by HAL went through a "virtual synapse." This would be accomplished by forcing HAL to output (hard wiring) his conclusion onto a screen. So the words "Antenna unit" would be displayed for our HAL/PSS to pick up and process. If anything untoward was brought to the attention of the crew by HAL 2001, they would do what I would do on a 747 if we needed to shutdown an engine. I would ask the first officer to "confirm." This is to check I had my hand on the correct engine shutdown lever before I potentially switched off the wrong engine.

So Dave would have asked HAL/PSS to "confirm Antenna unit." If the defect were genuine then the message would be forced out of HAL 2001 onto the screen and registered by PSS. But if the words were not registered, then we have a discrepancy and Mission Control would be automatically alerted. HAL 2001 wouldn't have been able to suppress the "Antenna unit" message as the architecture of the system would adopt the newly revised logic of the laptop webcam whereby there is now no direct connection to the webcam light.

The same would happen when Dave was outside of the spaceship and HAL switched off the life support system for the remaining hibernating crew. HAL/PSS would monitor the screen for any critical failure messages coming from the computer running the hibernation pods and independently alert the crew or Mission Control.

Thought provokingly, we observe in the film that HAL 2001 identified the reason for the false mechanical breakdown, as "human error" on the part of the designers in Urbana, Illinois where the computer was manufactured He also goes on to announce that the "mission was too important for human crew to jeopardize" and we see the final conflict of interests is settled when Dave breaks into the "Logic Memory Sensors" compartment and starts disconnecting HAL's memory chips.

Of course we are a long way off having such a sophisticated onboard computer such as HAL 2001 and so the realistic application of HAL/PSS would only be in line with the Heavy Aircrew Logic discussed in connection with aviation. It would specifically be useful as a monitoring tool on the eight month flight to Mars where the small crew will not be able to, so effectively, monitor the ship's systems for those massively extended periods compared to a mere 14 hour earth flight from Singapore to London.

CHAPTER 10: ACHIEVING 2001

What you can be certain of, as well as the existence of government departments working out how to impose a breathing tax, is that there are various
airliners flying around today on proving flights with pilots aboard that are
only there as a backup in case the full automation fails. Such airliners will
taxi out, take off and land on their own and could be referred to as "manned
drones." There is an inevitable movement towards a pilotless flight deck,
primarily to cut costs and increase efficiency, which is theoretically achievable because computers don't get tired. We know that drones have been very
successful in operating missions especially in the Middle East and Afghani-
stan. Well, we know they have successfully eliminated known targets, but
what do we know about the track record of serviceability and reliability?
How many have crashed on takeoff or landing or perhaps gone walk-about
whilst on a mission?

I wonder whether any of the proving flights are using a 737 Max 8? Probably not as they are still all grounded at time of writing and senior executives
are answering questions on what appears to be a premature certification of
an inherent design flaw. I live not too far from Farnborough Airport, where
Sir Frank Whittle first came up with the idea of the jet engine. That was the
easy part. Now he had to persuade the UK Ministry of Defence to agree it
was not only a good idea but also that funding should be forthcoming for the
research and development. The pressures on Sir Frank were more financial
rather than a time race to complete the project but everyone obviously wants
the development process to be completed as soon as possible and so there
is always pressure on the timetable. The predecessor to the 737 Max 8, the

737-800 was the 8th generation of the most successful airliner ever built but technology had caught up with it and demanded some changes.

When the Boeing 737-100 first rolled out in 1967, the engines were fitted beneath the wings, as they are today, one on either side, and with the maximum thrust available at the time, there were no odd handling characteristics of the aircraft. As time progressed, noise became an important consideration, and soon engines were being designed with large fans at the front to significantly reduce the noise footprint, with only about half the air passing through the noisy jet engine.

58/59. 737-400 engine and pylon redesign on the Boeing 737-Max 8

However, a redesign was required as the now larger fan wouldn't fit under the wing anymore. So they squashed the engine to accommodate the 737-400 (first image above). As time went on, the fuselage length increased from about 28 meters to around 40 meters, and eventually it became necessary to increase the engine size to provide an overall better operating performance for the airlines.

It was decided to change the design of the pylons that attach the engine to the wing, so that a larger engine could be fitted, protruding further forward than before (second image above). This, though, had a side effect that caused the aircraft to pitch up into a potential stall when large amounts of this extra power were applied. To fix this, the designers added another computerized system called MCAS (Maneuvering Characteristics Augmentation System) to push the nose down when a vane on the outside of the aircraft detected a severe angle of attack. This extra layer of computerization is what I mean by another layer onto the "House of Cards." If the stall warning vane gets iced over or is damaged by a bird strike or knocked into by a maintenance vehicle on the apron, it will provide confusing data to the "series" computer system. In the two fatal accidents that grounded the aircraft, it appears the stall warning vane failed, feeding false information to the MCAS system and the autopilot automatically lowered the nose believing that there was an imminent stall situation — a series computer, knee-jerk reaction.

The MCAS system only activates when the flaps are in the up position so when the crews retracted the flaps after takeoff, the computer took over to force the nose down. Various modifications will now need to be made to the 737 Max 8 but as the loss of elevator control is an extremely serious situation, the fix needs to ensure that any stabilizer runaway situation is identified as soon as possible and the crew offered all assistance to deal with the problem. As this book is dealing with improved safety, I will make two points about the 737 Max 8 situation.

Firstly, could HAL/PSS have helped had it been fitted? Pitch in an aircraft is controlled by the tailplane stabilizer and the elevators. The tailplane stabilizer does all the heavy lifting and can be thought of as a mini-wing at the back of the fuselage. It has to be set at the required angle into the slipstream and balances all the pitch up/down forces so the pilot doesn't need to pull or push with great force to keep the aircraft level. The elevators on the rear of the tailplane stabilizer allow the pilot to make fine pitch movements to accurately keep the aircraft on the correct angle of climb or descent and in no way can overpower the tailplane stabilizer. The angular position of this mini-wing is critical in any stage of flight so if it is involved in a "runaway" on its own, the pilots need to be able to switch it off and so Boeing has 2 cut-out switches which stop its movement. The pilots then have to go through a process of manually winding the trim system to recover the aircraft — which can be quite difficult — especially at high speed. If the pitch trim information were available on the pilot flight displays, HAL/PSS could now see this trim position and together with the artificial horizon reading, could ascertain whether the vane is working properly. As well as warning of excessive stabilizer trim movement, another message would remind the crew to extend the flaps to cancel the MCAS. Now the stabilizer should be available for normal operation.

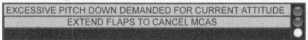

EXCESSIVE PITCH DOWN DEMANDED FOR CURRENT ATTITUDE
EXTEND FLAPS TO CANCEL MCAS

Secondly, was the 737 Max 8 with its inherent fault and MCAS fix introduced too quickly in our hurry to advance (for whatever reason) and are there any other combinations we need to consider before relentlessly pressing ahead with full automation? The reason I included the earlier chapter on "Thinking Computers," and how they work down at the fundamental level, was to expose the underlying simplicity of the workings as a magician's trick rather than a significant step towards our understanding of the human thought process. I really doubt that the computers we have today are going to give us the insight we need to understand the innermost workings of the human brain. I believe that quantum computing will possibly provide the first step in this direction and therefore I will concede that the Babbage system we currently use will at least have been responsible for getting us to the necessary starting blocks for full automation. Why quantum? Because quantum is associated with our parallel logic as it contains three states, not just the two we use in binary, 1 and 0. The third state is a 1/0 or a combination of On and Off (in quantum language, a qubit). Like a tossed coin in midair, it is both heads and tails at the same time and is considered as its undefined property before the final answer is revealed when it settles on the floor. These superpositions can be entangled with those of other objects, meaning their final outcomes will be mathematically related even if we don't yet know what they are. So effectively an entire branch of related calculations is done for us behind the scenes (parallel processing) instead of having to wait for our current pinch point processor to go through them one by one.

As we have said, it's maybe time to evolve a different type of design methodology for the future to include a "checks and balances" system to operate alongside series computers and human brains to provide maximum coverage of the "cheese holes" until such a time we manage to open up Schrödinger's box and peer into the mysterious world of quantum. Meanwhile, there's another problem we need to overcome.

Asimov

Isaac Asimov came up with a set of rules to govern the behavior of robots that were designed specifically to have a degree of autonomy. He wrote these rules in the 1940s because, as he had a human brain, he was able to predict that there was going to be a potential problem. Now that we are really getting to grips with Artificial Intelligence, these laws are more relevant than ever; and even back in 1968 Arthur C. Clarke saw the dangers and potential traps.

- First Law — A robot may not injure a human being or, through inaction, allow a human being to come to harm.
- Second Law — A robot must obey the orders given it by human beings except where such orders would conflict with the First Law.
- Third Law — A robot must protect its own existence as long as such protection does not conflict with the First or Second Laws.

There is genuine concern that one day robots may overpower mankind and take over the world. Although this might appear to be a very futuristic problem, the closest we have got so far is with military drones. When a target is identified and a decision is made to fire a missile, as I understand it, the operative flying the drone in their bunker will now switch to automatic mode and detach completely from the operation. This way she no longer can be held responsible for the act of killing, especially when innocent bystanders are involved. However, it does somewhat conflict with Asimov's rules but of course, Asimov isn't one of today's world leaders.

HAL/PSS would allow a second set of rules to apply internally within the robot to control any of these excessive behaviors that may have been learned through machine learning. We discussed earlier the process of back-propagation when we were working out how to recognize a printed number as a 5 or a 7. If the "weights" were maliciously altered, the backpropagation would eventually reinforce the Artificial Intelligence elements of the robot and there would be nothing to uphold Asimov's laws — the robots could dominate.

This is a definition of backpropagation I found on-line and I have added the label *Computer* to differentiate it from how a *human* and *HAL/PSS* would see it.

- *Computer:* "Backpropagation is the essence of neural net training. It is the practice of fine-tuning the weights of a neural net based on the error rate (i.e. loss) obtained in the previous epoch (i.e. iteration). Proper tuning of the weights ensures lower error rates, making the model reliable by increasing its generalization."

- *Human:* Backpropagation could result in the process being manip-ulated by a fellow human who I have evolved to mistrust, through backpropagation into world history.

- *HAL/PSS:* Backpropagation and robot operation will be monitored for specific human abuses utilizing a human referencing system that will act as a regulator for the robot.

This could resist abuses but now comes the hard bit — getting all nations to agree a protocol; although if it were not followed by an individual nation then it could be seen by others as the equivalence of stockpiling for war.

In chapter 3, we were discussing how a robot might be able to make a cup of coffee if it were suitably equiped with arms and mechanical hands, but where are they? I was led to believe that by the year 2020, at least, these machines would be making my dinner, doing the housework and covering all those menial tasks around the home. Again, as with AI computers today, these machines can do various individual tasks very well but the problem comes when we attempt universal integration with the 'real' world. The issue is not with universal integration, it is with the interpretation of what we mean by 'real' world. What part of the real world do our brains interact with? Is it connected with the science of how atoms interact with one another or how quantum entangles the very same particles or is it in associa-tion with the spare dimensions predicted by quantum theory or could it be linked to dark matter interactions or maybe another whole branch of science that only exists in a singularity at the centre of a black hole?

All of these concepts are merely interpretations by our own human brain that is itself encapsulated within an enigmatic universe that we just don't understand. So the point I am making is that it is some expectation for us to build a machine that is as good as the most complex entity of all time, which has itself evolved from nothing, inside a universe that we just cannot comprehend. Practically speaking, this is what we will need to do in order to realize the dream of fully robotic servants that seamlessly interact with us, within our world. I'm not saying we or a future species will never get close but I am reasoning for us to manage our expectations to be within realistic limits.

MH 370 Ironies

The mystery of Malaysian flight MH370 has still not been solved as of July 2020, and until we locate the aircraft we will probably never know what actually happened. However, we can piece together quite a bit from the supposed evidence we have so far.

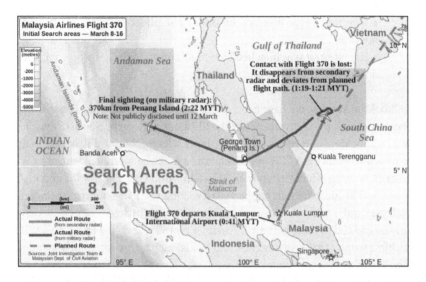

60. MH370 last reported route before disappearing

The Boeing 777 took off from Kuala Lumpur at 12:41 a.m. local time on the 8th March 2014 carrying 227 passengers and 12 crew members. It headed north east towards Ho Chi Minh City on its way to its destination, Beijing (dashed route above).

When over the South China Sea and at an Air Traffic Control border (FIR boundary), the aircraft apparently turned hard left and flew almost exactly down the FIR (Flight Information Region) boundary between Malaysia and Thailand. The turn was so quick it is estimated that the autopilot must have been disengaged so the angle of bank could be increased to well above the normal angle. The transponder and ACARS were then switched off and it supposedly headed for the island of Penang, after which it turned north-westerly out to sea (solid route above). Once out of radar coverage, the 777 disappeared. A lot has been written about the incident, so what are the possible scenarios?

- The aircraft was hijacked for political motives or for the hijacker(s) to seek asylum in another country, but they got lost and crashed into the sea after exhausting the fuel, 7 hours later.

- The aircraft was hijacked and shot down by one of the governments involved. But in this case the wreckage would have been hard to conceal.
- The flight was hijacked by one of the pilots or crew on a suicide mission.
- The aircraft was hijacked by remote control from a laptop computer onboard or from a ground station.

Looking at what we have been given, it would be hard to accept that the chosen point of route divergence at the FIR boundary in the South China Sea was a coincidence. It appears to have been selected because it is the point at which there is an ATC cone of silence, where the aircraft is out of radio range from both Kuala Lumpur and Ho Chi Minh City control for about 10 minutes. The aircraft then happens to fly along the FIR boundary between Malaysia and Thailand. It also seems that the authorities were not particularly interested in there being a 777 airliner rampaging on the loose, post 9/11, within a stone's throw of Bangkok and Kuala Lumpur, as apparently no military jet fighters were scrambled. There was also a 4 hour delay before any authority was notified about the rogue aircraft and very strangely, neither authority could pass on data about the precise track and altitudes the aircraft took whilst threatening their airspace. From other evidence that has come to light since, it is also suggested that the aircraft flew a specific offset (used by professional pilots) whilst heading away from Penang, to maneuver the aircraft away from the busy airway, avoiding other on-coming flights, before making a turn heading south and disappearing.

From the scenarios given above, it would appear that the only thing for sure is that the aircraft was hijacked, whether by passengers, crew or remotely by external interference. A well briefed but amateur pilot hijacker could very well have taken over the flight deck and switched off the Transponder and ACARS. But some time later in the proceedings, it appears the aircraft is the hands of a professional pilot who knows about offsets. Why would a criminal hijacker go to the trouble of dodging other aircraft? They would either be actually trying to cause a collision or would have made a beeline for their objective, say the Petronas towers. The TCAS system (Traffic Alert and Collision Avoidance System) onboard all the other aircraft in the area would have taken care of any mid-air collision risk, so it is curious as to why such care was taken with the offset. Anyway, we can only speculate and until we find the aircraft we may never know.

But it does raise an interesting question. After 9/11, many people asked why the U.S. military jet fighters weren't launched sooner. The answer, I would suggest, is because this was a "real world" situation, not a Hollywood fantasy. To react so rapidly without gathering sufficient intelligence would have been practically impossible. But to launch none at all to investigate MH370?

People also asked what could be done to prevent 9/11 happening again. Is the idea of remotely controlled airliners that bizarre? Is it even possible and would it be accepted by professional pilots and the travelling public if a hijacked airliner was remotely controlled by the military? Well, it is certainly possible; we are all familiar with unmanned drones flying around, some with missiles attached. We also know that Boeing has developed the MQ-25 unmanned aircraft for US carriers. As they state, "the MQ-25 will provide the needed robust refueling capability thereby extending the combat range of deployed Boeing F/A-18 Super Hornet, Boeing EA-18G Growler, and Lockheed Martin F-35C fighters."

61. Boeing's MQ-25 **Unmanned Aerial Vehicle**

Boeing's MQ-25 is up and running and interestingly, the USAF trained more UAV (Unmanned Aerial Vehicle) pilots in 2012 than ordinary jet fighter pilots for the first time.

Can this remote control ability be installed into a civil airliner?

When any modern civil airliner is being flown through the autopilot system, all the operational commands are routed from the flight deck to the electronics bay, under the fuselage floor, which then enacts the command whether it be to turn the aircraft or to lock on to an ILS landing beam. Without getting into this too deeply, I am satisfied that it is certainly possible and the existence of the MQ-25 sort of proves the point.

The second question is more complex — would it be accepted by professional pilots and the travelling public? I don't think it would be accepted at all on any grounds... apart from... the extremis of the 9/11 situation. Imagine if a military ground based pilot could be efficiently switched in by the Air Traffic Control unit that is handling the hijack situation. ATC know the identification of the aircraft which would be linked to a computer holding all the specific data for that particular aircraft. So a ground based pilot could take control in just a few minutes. With complete worldwide coverage using communication satellites, no aircraft would ever be out of range. Through predetermined protocols, the aircraft systems would be isolated from the hijacker and the aircraft could be directed to a military airfield for an automatic landing. I would suggest that most governments around the world would agree that such a solution in extremis would be better than allowing an airliner to be used as an ICBM (Intercontinental Ballistic Missile) against them and the general public.

Sounds good, but of course there are many problems. Even if you override specific controls inside the flight deck, the hijacker could shut down the engines, unless you override that specific engine control system. Now we are hoping that the override system doesn't go wrong or get hacked into during a regular flight! You would start by triggering a disconnect switch in the avionics bay so the Heading switch in the flight deck is disabled. You would also ensure that the autopilot cannot now be disconnected in the normal way so the would-be hijacker can no longer control the heading of the aircraft. This would be easily accomplished at the autopilot control box under the floor where all autopilot disconnect signals routed from the flight deck would be intercepted by a switching unit. If this switching unit were to become stuck during a regular flight, the flight crew, cooperating with the ground agency, would carry out an Autoland and nobody would be any the wiser. In a hijack, through satellite link, the ground based pilot would control the heading of the aircraft and just by removing this one function, the threat would be severely diminished. Although the hijacker could crash the aircraft, his target and objective would be forever shrouded in mystery and the much sought after publicity denied. But what about the fate of the passengers and crew?

So the irony is that one of the far-fetched suggestions of what could have caused the disappearance of MH370 is something we may need to contemplate to help disincentivize terrorists from hijacking our civil airlines in the first place. They would now have to face the fact that they will always lose control of the situation. It's possible that the ground controller could steer the aircraft to make a safe automatic landing at the nearest suitable airfield but here we run into the same old problem. If we stack up the House of Cards with increased sophistication in the aircraft series computers, we are asking for unexpected failures during normal operations which would defeat the object. A difficult problem to solve but by having a quasi-intelligent flight deck door, it may go towards solving this issue. Finally, when considering the fate of MH370, it certainly makes sense for the HAL system to be "texting" its latitude and longitude every ten minutes or so. This would be easily accomplished and would have provided essential data for the Search and Rescue teams, ensuring they were guided to the correct crash site. It was such a pity that they only received data from one satellite, which resulted in there being only one massive search area. Had the aircraft's data been shared with just one other satellite, the search area would have been manageable and the mystery would probably have been solved.

The Space Shuttle disasters also show up a separate problem for the future of fully automated systems. When there are unlimited funds flowing into a beloved, ground breaking project, the attention to detail is so intense that we normally manage to survive the early introductory phase without loss of life, at least to the astronauts. But when the operations become the norm, we tend to take our eye off the ball. The problem is that there are thousands of different combinations available out there for things to go wrong and they are all waiting in probabilistic order to put in an unwanted appearance. This means that the most likely things to go wrong have already been pre-designed into the system and now it's just a question of being alert to the awkward combinations (Murphy's law) that cannot possibly be considered at the design stage as they are so numerous.

The weather is around us, every day, knocking at the door trying to take a piece out of whatever machines we create, and corrosive elements work in unison to provide perfect conditions for Murphy's law to flourish. The more sophisticated our systems, the more elements there are to go wrong or degrade, and it seems this will be a never ending battle.

Air France 447 would probably not have happened in the 1970s, operated by a 747 Classic (747–100). It's only because we have greater sophistication that this type of accident has worked its way up the probabilistic order. Immediately, we again have to point out that many, many other types of accident have been avoided by this greater computer sophistication but the argument here is how we improve the statistics and I don't believe a move to full automation is credible yet.

What's happening in the depths of the under floor computer processor is irrelevant, it is only what is being presented in an intelligible form to the human pilots that is important in an emergency and to help sort this information we need a further partnership, not more layers of technology and responsibility built into the series computer system. On a flight I was operating from Los Angeles to Heathrow, the underfloor computer processor was doing a grand job keeping the 747-400 straight and level and flying at the correct speed — until we started to cross the Rockies near Las Vegas.

We had encountered mountain waves, whereby the Rockies had set off a sine wave shaped disturbance in the airflow and instead of coming straight at us, the airflow was partly coming at us from above which had the effect of forcing the aircraft downwards. To counteract this, the autopilot raised the nose to try and stay level and the auto thrust increased to maximum power for that altitude. But when mountain waves are strong, it is impossible for the aircraft to maintain level flight and target speed — something has to give. So although the power was increased, the speed started to drift back towards the stall point. What to do?

Automatics: "I don't know what you are talking about — I will notify you with a stall warning claxon when we approach critical low speed."

Flight Crew: "Looks like mountain waves, suggest you (First Officer) call Air Traffic Control and tell them we need to descend, I'll use the autopilot to start a 5 degree banked turn before the speed reduces to a point where any banked turn could precipitate an early stall. The turn will take us to the edge of the airway and out of the path of any oncoming aircraft below us, so if I have to descend without ATC permission, we can do so safely. We should also monitor the TCAS system, until we have good contact with ATC."

As it was, ATC gave us an immediate descent and there was no incident. Furthermore, the warning was sent back along the airway over the radio to aircraft on the same route whose pilots could now plan a strategy. TCAS (Traffic Collision Avoidance System) is a system that displays the position and relative altitude of any aircraft in the vicinity to avoid a mid-air collision. The travelling public don't always connect with the vulnerability of flying until, of course, something goes wrong. If everything is working well onboard, then fine, but our business is about when it's not working so well, and it sometimes requires high levels of awareness and problem solving abilities that present day computers cannot emulate.

Serious mountain wave encounters are relatively rare, but cumulonimbus clouds (CB) are responsible for about 100 lightning strikes to the Earth's surface... every second. That's about 8 million per day and 3 billion each year. CBs can grow to levels that civilian aircraft cannot rise above; and so they must be avoided by flying around them, sometimes meaning up to a 100-mile detour. Jet streams high in the atmosphere can cause severe turbulence and so decisions have to be made about lateral route deviations and vertical flight level changes, not only for the comfort of passengers and crew but ultimately for their safety. These deviations have to be coordinated with Air Traffic

Control, and with the ever increasing amount of commercial flights in the skies, if we are to solely rely on computers, we need to consider the Kessler syndrome.

Kessler proposed that one small collision of man-made objects in low earth orbit could cause a cascade in which each collision would generate more space debris that would further increase the likelihood of further collisions, finally bringing down the entire satellite network. How well will the ATC system cope with thousands of requests from automated aircraft to avoid CBs? Do ATC take on the responsibility to allow a deviation and if they can't due to vast amounts of traffic in the area, do they take responsibility for the possible onboard injuries sustained in the ensuing severe turbulence? Sure you can show me how a test aircraft can detect a thunderstorm and fly around it but we need to be realistic with our expectations when the numbers get unmanageably large during monsoon season, for example.

Although the report has not yet been published at time of writing, there were rumors of a lightning strike as a possible cause of the Sukhoi Superjet-100 accident in Moscow on 5 May 2019. The aircraft appears to have suffered what was described as an electrical failure after takeoff. It returned to Moscow–Sheremetyevo airport, where it crashed on landing, bursting into flames. The poor handling of the final approach and landing may have been pilot error, but it did look like there were control issues which led to the heavy touchdown. Without speculating before the report is published, it still remains a problem for a fully automated aircraft to guarantee isolation from a bad lightning strike. As I mentioned in a previous chapter, when flying into Islamabad, a lightning strike tore a 2 ft by 2ft hole in the underside of the 747 Classic wing we were flying — what would happen if it struck near the electronics bay on a current modern airliner or worse still, a future fully automated airliner?

Another tragic incident has just occurred in Iran where all onboard were lost when it appears the Iranian military mistakenly shot down a Ukraine International Airlines (UIA) flight departing from Tehran International airport. In line with the theme we are discussing, I wonder what level of automation was inherent in the missile firing system. I, of course, will never know but it does raise the question of possible vulnerabilities in automatic systems, especially when they have the potential of making such dire mistakes.

Experience can be very different from doing a lot of what you normally do. You wouldn't expect an experienced pilot to never have undergone an engine failure. But most airline pilots have never experienced a real engine failure on a regular flight carrying passengers, mainly due to regulation, intelligent design and the incredibly high standards of our ground engineers. All of this practice is done in simulators, twice yearly, together with other types of failure that could cause serious issues, like flap and undercarriage malfunctions. No one person is responsible for the very high standards of safety that we all enjoy in aviation today, it has been build brick by brick over the years and sadly some of the greatest advances have only followed after the analysis of serious accidents. The founder of the theory of gravity (the pilot's nemesis) wrote in a letter, "If I had seen further than other men, it is by standing on the shoulders of giants." This is the truth of how any industry evolves and today's pilots are no exception, being just as good as any other era of airmen. It is even arguable that they are better, in the sense that they have been able to learn from all that has gone before, as Sir Isaac far too modestly alluded to in his letter. And this is where another problem comes as we face the dawn of full automation.

How do we keep our pilots at the high standards we enjoy today whilst the onset of futuristic automation keeps them at arm's length? The more the automatics fly the aircraft, the less practice is afforded to the crews. It may be only after a catastrophic failure that the pilot will be called upon to use his upmost skills that have been steadily eroded over time. It's the same with any computerized system that fails. Look at how bad it gets when the airline check-in computer goes down. Thank goodness someone remembered the procedure from days gone by, pre-computers with handwritten lists and manual loadsheets. The worst thing that's going to happen is a horrendous ATC delay, but what if we need to fall back to basics following a systems malfunction in an aircraft that the crew has flown automatically for the last 3 months. And then, of course, I am assuming that at some stage the plan will be for there only to be one pilot onboard — interesting.

This thought brings us to the question, "Are we going to have any choice in the future whether we fly on an autonomous airliner?" Will we be forced to board a pilotless, fully automatic aircraft if we need to travel long distances? An academic paper has recently been published in the *Journal of Aviation, Aeronautics and Aerospace* entitled "Autonomous Airliners Anytime Soon?" by Vance, Bird and Tiffin (Embry-Riddle Aeronautical University Oklahoma State University 2019). The main premise of the article is to collate all the surveyed data from the public to statistically calculate when in the future there is likely to be a greater than 50% acceptance to fly without pilots. There are a lot of famous sayings about statistics and the report takes us into detailed mathematical projections of public sentiment but the bottom line is that today 30% of Americans would board a pilotless aircraft and that 50% would be prepared to do so by the year 2030. The idea is that once we have reached the 50% mark, it will provide the green light for the mass roll out and development of autonomous airliners. The report also states that 78% of the public supported a fully autonomous airliner if one backup pilot was onboard. This is one step down from the current situation where 100% of the public support an autonomous airliner if two backup pilots are onboard!

At the end of the report there are the normal references that were cited to add credence to the article. I have found another one to ponder over. It is by The Gambling Commission, entitled "Gambling participation in 2018: Behavior, awareness and attitudes Annual Report," published in February 2019. The stand-out statistics are:

- 32% of the respondents have participated in gambling in the past four weeks, excluding those who had only played the National Lottery draws.
- 30% of the respondents think that gambling is fair and can be trusted.

No problem with gambling if you choose to do it — but not with my money, if you don't mind.

Now you have the target date of 2030 confirmed, do you feel ready to cast your vote, or would you be seeking a bit more information? We have to put aside the cash benefits for interested companies and the ticket discount promises to passengers as, from a professional perspective, these are totally irrelevant to the pure argument. I think the answer to the "Autonomous Airliners Anytime Soon?" question is, "Only when we are ready." In other words, have we evolved our systems sufficiently to seamlessly move from the old into the new without a ghastly collapse midway? I would suggest that the first thing to do is to drastically reduce the current accident rate and yes, certainly by incorporating the very latest AI computers but in unison with the extremely successful model we have today. If Air France 447 was to happen again and the brand new AI computer goes on to save the day, handing back control to the pilots, then fine. If Qantas flight 72, where the uncommanded pitch-down maneuver injured several passengers, prevented itself from thumping the control wheel forward and instead informed the crew of a necessary autopilot disconnect, then fine. At this point you may have my vote but we need to think this through carefully and discard the natural impatience we may suffer when, say, planning to build a bridge across a river.

We want to get to the other side for provisions but want to do so cheaply and quickly. There is no actual need for extra provisions but we are planning ahead. Do we build a weak bridge quickly that could collapse into the river, having to accept many crossings with small cartloads or do we build a strong bridge slowly and make fewer crossings with much larger cartloads and reduced risk of collapse? This, to me, is the dilemma we are facing today with full automation. The series style of thought says, "Let's just build the bridge starting right now to accomplish the task." But with no need for provisions, we might be better off by considering all parallel factors and consequences to build the stronger bridge. Either way a bridge is going to be built but we *must* control the race.

The Embry-Riddle report did make me smile a couple of times. To set the scene, the authors open with a businessman arriving at the airport worried about possible delays to his flight. The stewardess says, quote, "Oh, we're ready to go...this flight is now totally automated!" My mind flashes back to good old regular ops when I used to board my aircraft, and accordingly I imagine the more realistic scenario where the futuristic engineer comes on scene to say that the flight is going to be delayed because there is a fault with the FITCS (Fully Integrated Thrust Computer System). "I've tried 50 times but I can't cancel the warning light," he says. I further imagine the aircraft dispatcher asking if she should call out some pilots. "Yes," replies the engineer, "We could get some pilots but there aren't any bloody throttles on this one!" If we build the House of Cards higher with extra layers of the fictitious FITCS, we only increase the chance for something to go wrong which in turn means a greater likelihood of delays. Remember, many of the other regular scenarios won't have gone away. Weather problems, like high crosswinds, will still be in the mix and initially, there will need to be more limiting restrictions applied, leading to even greater delays.

Smile number two was that the report had been subject to the rigors of our 21st century computerized spell checker systems, except that there was a spelling mistake in the title of one of the graphics, "Price Effect on Willingess to Fly." Pedantic, you can call me, but that's only permissible because you have a parallel wired brain that can easily see that the word should have been "Willingness." You also realize that there are no other realistic interpretations and there are no consequences of using this incorrect data. Furthermore, you will be able to empathize with the mistake, knowing we have all made these sorts of errors before and therefore will think no less of the academic argument contained within. That is, you will have the ability to *ignore* the error. The computer can do none of these things, and although it is reasonably good at spell checking, it just can't understand the graphical representation of a word unless it is specifically told to load up a separate program. The problem is that, what seems pedantic to you and me could be fatal in an automatic airliner, especially after a computer software update. So not a good advertisement for the "no humans necessary" argument.

A quick thought about what we actually mean by automation? We can easily see how a machine can replace a person, say, cutting wheat in a field. But does it replace the farmer? When pilots flew aircraft before autopilots, they were metaphorically juggling about 5 balls — aircraft control, navigation, communication, systems monitoring etc. The advent of autopilots meant that one of the balls was now being handled by the automatics. As time went on with improved systems, the pilot only had to juggle one ball, throwing it up and catching it — seems like they may soon be redundant! The reason for this thought sequence is because we perceive automation as linked to replacement, but if you were to look into a flight deck today, you would still see all 5 balls being tossed into the air. They haven't disappeared, it's all still real and happening, you are still in an airplane at 39,000 ft, just as vulnerable as you always were. The navigation computer is juggling its ball and synchronizing it with the autopilot ball, overseen by the pilots who will catch one or both of the balls if necessary. All pilots have had times when they have been forced to revert to the 3 ball juggle and as we have seen, some have taken on 6 to rescue serious emergencies. So flight deck "automation" shouldn't translate to redundancy, it should translate to assistance or cooperation.

The Embry-Riddle report ended by considering a possible way forward. Should we license the already existing unmanned cargo drones and aircraft fitted with full automation to fly pilotlessly amongst regular passenger flights to develop the technology? So this is the introduction to what I hope will be the widely accepted best practice for our times concerning this difficult debate. Yes, but openly monitored by a board of international professionals ranging from national authorities (CAA, FAA etc.) to pilots, engineers and other aviation specialists in conjunction with the technological and developmental companies. We cannot afford to take one big leap at this stage and should participate in a steady but gradual evolution, with the primary aim of greater passenger safety. Aviation is a truly global industry and what one country or large organization decides to do should not adversely affect other countries until the necessary due diligence has been completed. HAL would be a perfect fit for this as it works in parallel with the newly evolving systems but at the same time enhancing the link between man and machine. If not HAL then some other "out of the box" thinking needs to be done whilst we wait for quantum computers to come onboard. Once we have achieved that much improved level of safety, far more than we have today, we can start to remove that necessary interface between man and machine and only then will we be able to convince the travelling public, especially considering the 2018/9 statistics.

I think the most important analogy of all is the one that takes us back to biology. The *medulla oblongata* is located in the brain stem which controls a number of involuntary functions such as when we take a breath. This is our autopilot, ensuring each breath is taken at the right time. Run up the stairs and the "breath autopilot" will increase the breath rate just as an aircraft autopilot will increase altitude if a climb is required. The *medulla oblongata* doesn't know why it has to change the breath rate, it just does it. It developed very early on in our evolution and is situated in the old part of the brain — the brain stem. The prefrontal cortex is located in the new part that evolved much later. Here, we not only understand *why* we breathe but also what we should do if there were an emergency, like pneumonia for instance. In this case the *medulla oblongata* will throw the doctors and nurses its juggling ball and wait for the patient to die. The prefrontal cortex, though, goes into "parallel mode" and uniquely takes in multiple pathway possibilities, justifying its evolutionary seat at the table. Not only can we introduce pure oxygen but we could also build a machine to ventilate the patient and then there'll be a ton of other more subtle procedures that only the medically qualified will know about. Do doctors and surgeons make mistakes? Shall we start to replace them with AI computers? Would an AI computer have come up with the idea of a ventilator? Does an AI computer know what an "idea" is? Will future AI computers outsmart the prefrontal cortex when we face a newly evolved pathogen?

To help visualize the difficulties confronting the plane makers and the companies rushing to develop autonomous computer systems, the write-up below is a typical program that all pilots undergo for 8 hours over two days in simulators. In order to have our licenses revalidated, these exercises are necessary every six months and each time a different set of problems and failures are practiced. This is what might be covered during a 2 day check.

- Autopilot systems fault after takeoff requiring the pilot to take over control and recover from the stall.
- Fire in the cargo hold necessitating an immediate return to land with no time to dump fuel (normally necessary to reduce the aircraft weight to be within certified limits). The aircraft will be touching down at 207 miles per hour (about the top speed of a F1 racing car) and as a result will not be able to use the normal flap setting. Pilots are reminded that they cannot use the Autoland system as it has not been certified for use in these circumstances and may be unpredict-

able. After a manual landing, the captain has to decide on whether a passenger evacuation is required and, if so, initiates the command.

• Air Traffic Control make a mistake and steer the aircraft towards high ground — the pilots have to manually intervene and recover the situation when the automatic Ground Proximity Warning alerts them to the error.

• The crew have been warned of reported Windshear on short finals and have to decide whether to abandon the approach. As part of the exercise, the pilots are requested to continue the approach and end up with a full thrust Windshear Go-around maneuver and diversion. On landing the crew are encouraged to discuss whether an earlier decision to divert, based on the reports, would have been best.

• After an engine failure on takeoff, the crew have to decide whether to return for an immediate landing at the departure airfield which now has limiting crosswinds or divert elsewhere where there is good weather but very limited landing aids.

How will a fall-back, ground-based pilot deal with an Autopilot systems fault? Who decides to evacuate the aircraft after an emergency landing? How will a ground based pilot judge the severity of turbulence on short finals to land? Today's airline crews work closely together to solve all these problems so you can imagine how difficult it's going to be for a remote team of drone pilots or even an onboard super computer for that matter.

We have come a long, long way with aircraft design and systems but still suffer catastrophic accidents with the figurative collapse of the House of Cards. Airliner fatalities have been relatively few over the past 10 years but we need to be mindful of the "almost accidents" that could have ended up with fatalities had it not been for that most essential element of all — luck. If we want to protect ourselves from computer hackers, faulty pitot tube heaters or computer malpractice on the way to Jupiter, we could do with a third layer of protection before we attempt Automation-Max. We have seen why 3 INS systems are installed, why 3 Autoland computers are required and how both pilots and computers can individually fail. Even author Arthur C. Clarke realized the necessity of having humans onboard, in charge, and ensured that not everyone was hibernating for that long journey to Jupiter.

The travelling salesman problem asks the following question: "Given a list of cities and the distances between each pair of cities, what is the shortest possible route that visits each city and returns to the origin city?" This seems like a bread and butter problem for a computer but although it can estimate the answer fairly accurately, once the number of cities gets into the thousands, the pinch point in the series processor makes it practically impossible to calculate the correct answer. There are just too many loops to run through the hourglass pinch point and it becomes what is called an NP time problem (Nondeterministic Polynomial) or as most people know it as, impossible! Quantum computers may be able to solve these problems that seem to be impossible or would take a traditional computer an impractical amount of time (a billion years) to solve, but they are very fragile. Any kind of vibration impacts the atoms that quantum computers rely upon and causes what is called "decoherence" — so not good in an aircraft. Decoherence is the process in which a system's behavior changes from that which can be explained by quantum mechanics to that which can be explained by classical mechanics meaning the system loses all its hidden, related mathematical calculations.

One day this technology will come, I'm sure, and we'll be able to solve more than just the travelling salesman problem. Until then, we should not replace the all-important parallel system, namely the pilots. We should keep developing our series computers to help us operate the flight more effectively but we maybe should consider introducing a third element to try and eliminate those stubborn last few remaining holes in the cheese.

There will be much intense lobbying for the introduction of autonomous airliners into our skies as we approach the year 2030, perhaps even earlier. Hopefully we will adopt a cautious, controlled approach utilizing some of that Crew Resource Management thinking to build a robust system that can evolve at the right pace to ensure its longevity.

I can envisage the futuristic dream of aircraft manufacturers and airlines where the flight deck is replaced by two Ultra-First Class seats with the rather nice view of the world that pilots get to enjoy today. The aircraft would be flown automatically, overseen by a ground pilot controller and to entice passengers to get on such an aircraft there would be an onboard, under floor compartment at the front of the aircraft, much like a World War II bomb aimer position, from which, the passengers would be told, "*a member of staff will land the aircraft in the unlikely event of something going wrong.*" The plan would be for the Dispatcher at the airport to decide on how much fuel to load, board the passengers, oversee the refueling and loading and then ensure the auto-tug has robotically arrived at the nosewheel. Then the dispatcher would text the ground pilot controller to take over. Provided he isn't handling an emergency in the quota of flights for the day, the flight will be set to "auto pushback" once the Air Traffic Control computer is happy...

Well, "that's the way it's going" — isn't it?

APPENDIX 1: COMPUTER DECISION-MAKING, SIMPLIFIED

Thinking Computers

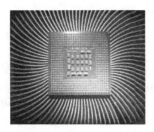

I want to discuss what is happening at the core of the computer processor. The central element is the transistor which is an On/Off switch. Here is a brief description of the functionality of a transistor, but it will not be necessary to probe into its detailed workings.

A transistor is fundamentally a flip-flop switch, much like a regular light switch on the wall. When you flick the light switch, electricity flows to the light bulb and the light comes on. The difference with a transistor is that instead of your finger flipping the switch, a clever arrangement in the transistor allows for a small electric current to do the physical switching. Once the transistor receives the small current, it flips the switch and importantly allows the switch to remain in that set position even when the small current is subsequently switched off. Moreover, a feedback system allows the transistor to know its last state, so if it was On, it now flips to Off and if it was Off, it flips to On.

Thus, when the ceiling light is On or the transistor is On, it is considered as a 1. When the ceiling light is Off or the transistor is Off, it is considered as a zero. Bearing in mind that the speed of electricity flow is extremely fast, we now have the capability to make many thousands of switches per second... and welcome to the Information Age.

This box is a representation of a transistor. It is empty, so is considered to be OFF or Value Zero.

This is a representation of a transistor set to ON.

A small electric current is used to switch the transistor On or OFF and it remains On or OFF until it is told otherwise. In the microprocessor there is a group of boxes or transistors like this shown below, laid out in a row: In our BBC computer there are 8 boxes. They are numbered right to left as this is the order in which they will be analyzed and processed.

8	7	6	5	4	3	2	1

Here all 8 boxes are switched OFF, which means the boxes contain 00000000. This represents the number zero.

Now we will pass a small current through some of the boxes to cause them to SWITCH. Here 2 boxes are switched on and 6 are switched off, which means the boxes contain 00001010. This represents the number ten as will be shown below.

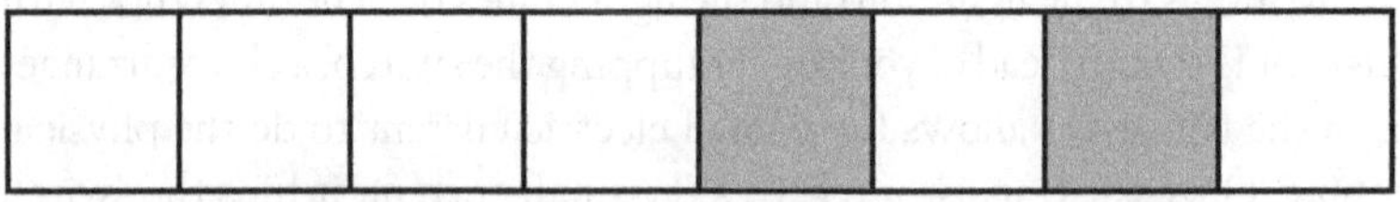

The numbering system works like this:

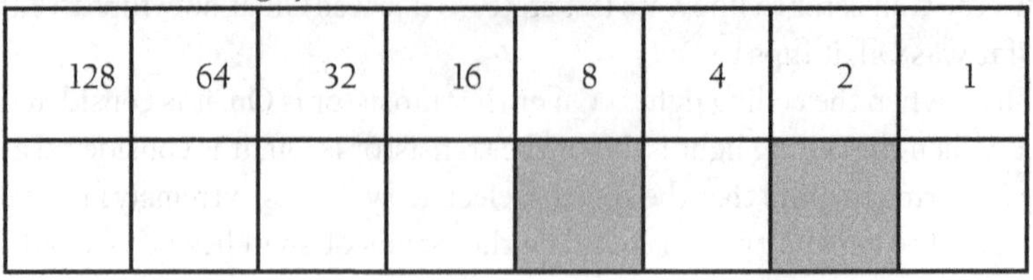

128	64	32	16	8	4	2	1

Far right is 1, then moving left the boxes represent increasing numbers. You may recognize this as the binary system, which works in exactly the same way as our decimal system except that when you reach 10 in our decimal system, you carry one and revert the units to zero. In binary when you reach 2, you carry one and revert the units to zero. The example shows an 8 marked as ON and a 2 marked as ON so we have 8 + 2 = 10.

Computers can't work with a decimal system because a current switch can only be either on or off, so there are only 2 choices.

These are the values in the decimal system:

10000000	1000000	100000	10000	1000	100	10	1

These are the values in the binary system:

128	64	32	16	8	4	2	1

Here, all the boxes are switched ON (11111111) which works out as:

$$1 + 2 + 4 + 8 + 16 + 32 + 64 + 128 = 255$$

128	64	32	16	8	4	2	1

Now add the zero option (00000000) and we have a possible 256 different numbers to play with.

These boxes are referred to as the data bus, and every single calculation that is made goes through this data bus. Collectively it is known as the Accumulator. (There is also one extra box that is used during the arithmetic process — the Carry Box).

Let's make our computer do something useful — let's add two numbers: 14 + 29.

First put 14 into the accumulator (in binary, as we have just seen).

8 + 4 + 2 or 00001110

128	64	32	16	8	4	2	1

Next, overlay 29 into the accumulator: 16 + 8 + 4 + 1 or 00011101.

128	64	32	16	8	4	2	1

Now mix the 2 binary codes on top of each other and apply a few rules. Start at the far right box and work to the left.

We do, though, need one extra ingredient — the Carry Box. This is another separate box that will be switched ON if the processor wants to remember something while it is doing its calculations.

The Carry Box starts in the OFF position. ☐

There are 4 rules that the transistors are made to follow:

1) 3 Boxes OFF = Leave all 3 OFF

☐   ☐   ☐
Carry

2) 1 Box ON = Leave Box On, Carry Box OFF

■   ☐   ☐
Carry

3) 2 Boxes ON = Both OFF, Switch Carry Box ON

■   ■

☐   ☐   ■
Carry

4) 3 Boxes ON = Leave Boxes ON, Keep Carry Box ON

Carry

When we press the "Equals" button these rules are executed starting from the far right box:

Box	Switch Position 1st Number (14)	Switch Position 2nd Number (29)	Carry to next Box	Apply the Rule	Acc Result
Box 1 Right	☐	■	↓	1 ON	1
Box 2	■	☐	☐	1 ON	1
Box 3	■	■	☐	2 ON	0
Box 4	■	■	■	ALL 3 ON	1
Box 5	☐	■	■	2 ON	0
Box 6	☐	☐	■	1 ON	1
Box 7	☐	☐	☐	NONE ON	0
Box 8 Left	☐	☐	☐	NONE ON	0

The first row of the table above, below the headings, is where the first sequence is carried out to calculate the answer (find the text 'Box 1 Right'). The next column to the right holds the first bit of the number 14 which is an empty box or a zero. Now go right to the next column to find the first bit of the number 29 which is an ON box or a one. The next column contains the result of the Carry Box which in this case is zero as it always will be for the very first sequence. Carry on right to the next column to see the rule applied which in this case is rule 2 or '1 Box ON' meaning that the first bit of the answer is an ON or a one (far right column). Note also that the Carry Box remains empty or zero as it is presented downwards for the next sequence. So the Accumulator result for the first bit or sequence is ON or one. Now start again at the left column 'Box 2' and repeat all the way down to the bottom of the table filling in the Accumulator result for each bit or sequence.

At the end, we see the accumulator is left with the right hand column, reading from the bottom upwards as 00101011

128	64	32	16	8	4	2	1

$$1 + 2 + 8 + 32 = 43$$

That is how a computer knows that 14 + 29 = 43. It simply goes through a process of shuffling boxes to come up with the correct answer, albeit at mind boggling speed.

But how do we actually get the computer to do this? We need a program that will sequentially run each instruction one by one until we get the required result. The accumulator, where we have just calculated the answer to our sum, can also be used to hold codes that are used as instructions. So the accumulator can receive an instruction code and then immediately afterwards receive the actual number (or data) required. This is the fundamental process of the computer:

1. DATA	Get a number (14)
2. INSTRUCTION	Apply an Adding process (+ button)
3. DATA	Get another number (29)
4. INSTRUCTION	Display the answer (= button)

Another instruction example could be to store a copy of the number you are working on (the one held in the accumulator) into memory so you can use it later. The CODE for 'send to memory' in the BBC computer is 141 (Decimal) or 10001101 (Binary). So this number is specially reserved for the action of — "take contents of accumulator and send to a memory address for storage."

128	64	32	16	8	4	2	1

1. DATA1 = &0DFF (The address 0DFF on the memory chip which I have labeled as DATA1 - we'll discuss addresses later)

2. LDA #14 (LoaD the Accumulator with the number [#] 14)

3. STA DATA1 (STore the contents of the Accumulator into the memory address DATA1 or 0DFF)

So the accumulator gets filled with 00001110 (14) and then the next instruction comes in as 10001101 ('send to memory') and it sends the 00001110 or decimal 14 to memory.

For completeness, the code for the addition (14 + 29) above is:

1. DATA1 = &0DFF (The address on the memory chip)

2. LDA #14 (Load the accumulator with number 14)

3. ADC #29 (Add the number 29 together with 14)

4. STA DATA1 (Store the contents of the accumulator into the memory address DATA1 0DFF)

(Note: there are many other considerations to be made for this code to work properly, like considering numbers greater than 256, but this demonstrates the fundamentals.)

Storing into Memory

The addressing system for memory is very similar but more memory boxes are required, as otherwise the computer would be so limited it would be useless. Therefore they allow not 8 boxes (bits), as in the accumulator, but 16 bits. The address on the memory chip we gave was 0DFF, which stands for quite a large number (3,583) and represents the number of the filing location.

0DFF is hexadecimal code, using 16 as the base; designed so that just 4 digits can represent a number as large as 65535, which obviously needs 5 digits. It does this by using letters, once you reach the number 10.

Decimal	1	2	3	4	5	6	7	8	9	10	11	12	13	14	15
Hex	1	2	3	4	5	6	7	8	9	A	B	C	D	E	F

With decimals, you need two digits to represent the numbers 10 to 15. With hexadecimal you only need one digit. This is the base 16 format (note 16 x 16 = 256)

4096	256	16	1
0	D	F	F

(O) x 4096 = 0
(D) or 13 x 256 = 3328
(F) or 15 x 16 = 240
(F) or 15 x 1 = 15

Added together you get 3,583 - or memory location 3,583. Only 4 digits required but remember we can now have an address FFFF, which gives a possible 65,535 addresses in only 4 digits. We now need to represent the 4 digit Hex code (ODFF) in binary format as a computer can only process numbers in ones or zeros:

Hex	0	D	F	F
Binary	0000	1101	1111	1111
Decimal (3,583)	0	3328	240	15

16 bit representation of 0DFF:

32768	16384	8192	4096	2048	1024	512	256	128	64	32	16	8	4	2	1

So going back to the sum we were working on earlier, the contents of the accumulator, 43 (00101011), goes off to the above memory location which we can consider as either of the following:

- Easy to understand, decimal placement number 3,583 (the 3,583rd box row in memory)

- Nonintuitive binary code (0000 1101 1111 1111)

- Hexadecimal, clever 4 digit representation 0DFF to help programmers write their code.

At this location, you will find an 8-bit set of boxes that holds the code 00101011 (43) and elsewhere in the computer it knows that the name associated with this address location (0DFF) is DATA1.

So we know how the computer does the calculations utilizing Instructions and Data. We also know how it stores the data and of course it does the opposite to retrieve the data. If you could see inside a section of RAM (Random Access Memory) it would look something like this - just a whole series of transistor boxes that are either ON or OFF in address order (note 0DFF contains the binary for our answer, 43):

0DFF								
0E00								
0E01								
0E02								
0E03								

Making choices

This ability is perhaps at the heart of all computing wizardry, the ability to make a choice. Now we can give a RAM address a specific number, we can compare it to another number stored at a separate address.

1. LDA #14 (Load the accumulator with number 14)
2. IF #14 ‹ #29 (If the number in the accumulator is less than 29)
3. THEN SUBTRACT #14 from #29 (if the condition above is met then subtract 14 from 29)
4. ELSE ADD #14 to #29 (if the condition above was not met, our program may crash if we create a negative number in the answer so in this case we should add the numbers to prevent a crash)

	128	64	32	16	8	4	2	1
14					▓	▓	▓	
29				▓	▓	▓		▓

The above example doesn't serve any real useful purpose but it does demonstrate the fundamental process. We can easily see how the number with the left most bit switched ON (16) must be bigger because all the binary numbers to the right cannot possibly add up to a greater number (8 + 4 + 2 + 1 = 15). Once we have this simple and quick ability to compare two data bits we can go on to create a very powerful machine that makes choices — but it's still only shuffling bits of data.

Writing a computer program

The list of steps for the computer to activate is of course the program. Each step is brought into the accumulator, one by one, from the memory (ROM or RAM). ROM (Read-Only Memory) is the location of the code written by the computer designer and this is loaded up when the computer is switched on to prepare the computer ready for use. The user cannot utilize this section of the memory — if he did, the computer would crash — it's like afflicting the computer with a stroke, it would not be able to function properly. RAM (Random Access Memory) is where the user's programs and data are stored which is brought into the accumulator step by step to be processed.

So, 8 bits of code come into the accumulator, it is told if it is an instruction code or a data code and acts accordingly. This carries on until the end of the program. The addition of 14 + 29 is really quite mechanical.

One instruction in low level languages (like Assembly Language we used above) corresponds to one instruction, like STA DATA1. A high level Language needs to be either compiled or interpreted. Compilers take the source code and translate the entirety of it into machine code now negating the use of the original program. Just like a page of text being translated from French to English in one go, once it is done there is no need to refer back to the French page.

Interpreters (Like BBC Basic which is a higher level than BBC Assembly language) take the source code and translate it into machine code but one line at a time so does need access to the original program to get the next line of code (easier to write but slower in operation). Just like a paragraph of text being translated from French to English, sentence by sentence, once one sentence is complete, there is a need to refer back to the French page to get the next sentence.

But all languages, whether low level assembly or high level BASIC end up as simple codes which are inserted into the accumulator one by one. And this has limitations. Keeping with the analogy of a spoken language but with a new rule that you have to pay me 5 cents for each word you use to instruct me, this is how you might go about getting me to make you a cheap cup of coffee.

```
BOIL WATER
GET CUP
GET TEASPOON
PUT COFFEE IN CUP
POUR BOILING WATER
STIR COFFEE
```

This would be assembly language. To make it into a higher level language it would simply consist of one instruction and would read:

```
MAKE COFFEE (CUP)
```

Then, from this one command, the interpreter would go to various memory addresses and pull out these same individual instructions below, it's just that you wouldn't know it is happening:

    BOIL WATER
    GET CUP
    GET TEASPOON
    PUT COFFEE IN CUP
    POUR BOILING WATER
    STIR COFFEE

The reason it's called high level is that provided it is within the rules, I can also make subtle changes, for example by simply writing:

    MAKE COFFEE (MUG)

Now the interpreter would go to the same memory addresses to pull out the individual instructions but would insert MUG instead of CUP:

    BOIL WATER
    GET CUP
    GET TEASPOON
    PUT COFFEE IN MUG
    POUR BOILING WATER
    STIR COFFEE

The most fundamental code that runs the BBC computer and indeed all computer systems is Machine Code which is at the top of this list and the lower you go in the list the higher the Language level or the more work is done for you behind the scenes:

    Machine Code (Very hard)
    Assembly Language (Hard)
    C, FORTRAN, COBOL, Java
    BASIC (Beginner's All-Purpose Symbolic Instruction Code)

Assembly Language and Machine code are specific to each make of processor chip, so it won't run on two different designs; and therefore it won't normally work on different brands of computer. This means you would have to learn different exceptions for each computer type. High-level languages are written to suit each different type of processor, allowing us to use the same form of language.

You can see how useful high-level programming languages are, as they are quick to write, pack in all the extra hidden lines of code, can be versatile (CUP or MUG) and work on all computers. The only catch is that the interpreting needs more lines of code, and thus more time to run, so the program becomes slower.

But processors get faster as the years go on, so not a problem...until the processor gets too hot because it is running so fast and melts... Now you need twin processors to share the task!

Appendix 2: Accident Statistics

Here is a table of worldwide passenger aircraft accidents involving fatalities for aircraft certified to carry at least 6 people, including crew (1945–2019). When trying to draw conclusions from the data, there are several factors to bear in mind. For one thing, in the early years there was less technology available to assist the pilots. At the same time, aircraft had a far lower seating capacity, and there were not the high numbers of worldwide flights we have today.

Year	Number of Accidents	Passenger Fatalities
2019	125	578
2018	115	1039
2017	102	399
2016	106	631
2015	127	904
2014	125	1329
2013	141	453
2012	156	800
2011	154	828
2010	162	1154
2009	161	1108
2008	190	902

Year	Number of Accidents	Passenger Fatalities
2007	169	984
2006	193	1303
2005	194	1463
2004	179	767
2003	201	1233
2002	198	1419
2001	210	1536
2000	196	1586
1999	221	1150
1998	225	1721
1997	232	1768
1996	250	2779
1995	266	1828
1994	231	2018
1993	275	1763
1992	265	2296
1991	259	2019
1990	281	1447
1989	337	2603
1988	306	2392
1987	341	2157
1986	276	1781
1985	296	3023
1984	284	1333
1983	289	2047
1982	309	2066
1981	320	1585
1980	379	2343
1979	381	2572
1978	408	2220
1977	373	2558
1976	308	2416
1975	332	1930
1974	316	2782

Year	Number of Accidents	Passenger Fatalities
1973	372	2975
1972	374	3316
1971	330	2304
1970	312	2188
1969	364	2752
1968	339	2433
1967	353	2351
1966	281	2222
1965	293	2272
1964	273	1803
1963	211	1838
1962	262	2477
1961	262	1962
1960	234	2033
1959	242	1524
1958	272	1808
1957	263	1654
1956	242	1434
1955	278	1423
1954	289	1549
1953	337	1970
1952	403	2284
1951	491	2304
1950	426	2138
1949	351	1916
1948	391	1978
1947	371	1922
1946	424	2064
1945	737	4660

Table of accidents in date order showing aircraft type and fatalities (2010–2019). This data is compiled from the official accident investigations by the pertinent authorities and was used to order the categories of accident in this book. Further information can be sought on-line by searching the aircraft type together with the accident date.

Year	Aircraft	Day	Fatalities
2019	Boeing 707-3J9C	January 14	15
2019	DC-3	January 21	2
2019	Convair C-131B	February 8	1
2019	Boeing 767-375	February 23	3
2019	Douglas DC-3	March 9	14
2019	Boeing 737 MAX 8	March 10	157
2019	Let L-410	April 14	2
2019	Sukhoi Superjet 100	May 5	41
2018	Antonov An-148	February 11	71
2018	ATR 72-200	February 18	66
2018	Bombardier Q400	March 12	51
2018	Boeing 737-700	April 17	1
2018	Boeing 737-200	May 18	112
2018	Bombardier Dash 8 Q400	August 10	1
2018	Boeing 737-800	September 28	1
2018	Boeing 737 MAX 8	October 29	189
2018	Boeing 757-200	November 9	1
2017	Boeing 747-400F	January 16	39
2017	Antonov An-26	April 29	8
2017	Let L-410	May 27	2
2017	Antonov An-26	October 14	4
2017	ATR 42-300	December 13	1
2017	Cessna 208 Caravan	December 31	12
2016	Bombardier CRJ200	January 8	2
2016	DHC-6 Twin Otter	February 24	23
2016	Antonov An-26	March 9	3
2016	Boeing 737-800	March 19	62

2016	Britten-Norman Islander	April 13	12
2016	Antonov An-12	May 18	7
2016	Airbus A320	May 19	66
2016	Boeing 777-300	August 3	1
2016	DHC-4T Turbo Caribou	October 31	4
2016	Avro RJ85	November 28	71
2016	ATR-42-500	December 7	47
2016	Boeing 727-200	December 20	5
2015	ATR-72	February 4	43
2015	Airbus A320	March 24	150
2015	Swearingen Metro II	April 13	2
2015	ATR-42	August 16	54
2015	DHC-6 Twin Otter	October 2	10
2015	Airbus A321	October 31	224
2015	Antonov An-12	November 4	41
2015	Airbus A310-300F	December 24	8
2014	DHC-6 Twin Otter	February 16	18
2014	Boeing 777	March 8	239
2014	Boeing 777	July 17	298
2014	ATR-72	July 23	48
2014	MD-83	July 24	116
2014	Antonov An-140	August 10	40
2014	Short 360	October 29	2
2014	Airbus A320	December 28	162
2013	Bombardier CRJ200	January 29	21
2013	Antonov An-24	February 13	5
2013	Beechcraft 1900C-1	March 8	2
2013	Boeing 747 freighter	April 29	7
2013	Boeing 777	July 6	3
2013	de Havilland DHC-3	July 7	10
2013	Airbus A300 freighter	August 14	2
2013	Embraer 120	October 3	16
2013	ATR-72	October 16	49

2013	Boeing 737	November 17	50
2013	Embraer 190	November 29	33
2012	ATR-72	April 2	33
2012	Boeing 737	April 20	127
2012	Sukhoi Superjet 100	May 9	45
2012	Dornier Do 228	May 14	15
2012	Boeing 727	June 2	12
2012	MD-83	June 3	153
2012	Antonov An-28	September 12	10
2012	Dornier Do 228	September 28	19
2012	Britten-Norman Islander	October 7	3
2012	Ilyushin Il-76T freighter	November 30	32
2012	Antonov An-26	December 17	4
2012	Fokker 100	December 25	2
2012	Tupolev Tu-204	December 29	5
2011	Tupolev Tu-154	January 1	3
2011	Boeing 727	January 9	78
2011	Fairchild Metroliner III	February 10	6
2011	Let L-410 Turbolet	February 14	14
2011	Antonov An-12	March 21	14
2011	Bombardier CRJ-100	April 4	32
2011	Xian MA60	May 7	25
2011	Saab 340	May 18	22
2011	Tupolev Tu-134	June 20	47
2011	Cessna 208 Caravan	July 4	1
2011	Ilyushin Il-76	July 6	9
2011	Boeing 727	July 8	77
2011	Antonov An-24	July 11	7
2011	Let L-410 Turbolet	July 13	16
2011	Boeing 747 freighter	July 28	2
2011	Antonov An-12	August 9	11
2011	Boeing 737	August 20	12

2011	Fairchild Metroliner III	September 6	8
2011	Yakovlev Yak-42	September 7	44
2011	Beechcraft 1900D	September 25	19
2011	CASA C-212 Aviocar	September 29	18
2011	de Havilland DHC-8	October 13	28
2011	Cessna 208 Grand	October 14	8
2010	Boeing 737-800	January 25	90
2010	Airbus A300B4F	April 13	7
2010	Airbus A330	May 12	103
2010	Antonov An-24	May 17	44
2010	Boeing 737-800	May 22	158
2010	CASA C-212 Aviocar	June 19	11
2010	Airbus A321	July 28	152
2010	Antonov An-24	August 3	12
2010	Boeing 737	August 16	2
2010	Embraer E-190	August 24	44
2010	Dornier Do 228	August 24	14
2010	Let L-410	August 25	20
2010	Boeing 747-400	September 3	2
2010	ATR-42	September 13	17
2010	ATR-72	November 4	68
2010	Beechcraft 1900	November 5	21
2010	Antonov An-24	November 11	6
2010	Ilyushin Il-76TD,	November 28	11
2010	Tupolev Tu-154	December 4	2
2010	DHC-6 Twin Otter	December 15	22

Image Credits

1. Illustration © Statista Airliner accident fatalities by year from 1972 to 2018.

    Illustration © Statista https://www.statista.com/chart/12393/2017-was-the-safest-year-in-the-history-of-air-travel

    https://creativecommons.org/licenses/by-nd/3.0/

2. Permission to reprint/use granted by the National Safety Council © 2020

3. B3A – Bureau of Aircraft Accidents Archives / Ronan HUBERT, Accidentologist

4. Left: Webernoid (pixabay.com)

    Right: Image by PublicDomainPictures from Pixabay

5. StuartBrady

6. Peter Collins

7. OpenClipart-Vectors (pixabay.com)

8. Freepik.com. This cover has been designed using resources from Freepik.com

9. Left: Shahram Sharifi - GNU Free Documentation License

    Right: Norio Nakayama

    https://creativecommons.org/licenses/by-sa/2.0/deed.en

10. FAA's "Lessons Learned from Civil Aviation Accidents" https://lessons-learned.faa.gov/

11. Image by 2234701 from Pixabay

12. James Wainscoat

13. Aircraft-cockpits.co.uk

14. user:Looie496

15. Clker-Free-Vector-Images (pixabay.com)

16. GNU Free Documentation License, Version 1.2

17. Peter Collins

18. Glosser.ca - https://creativecommons.org/licenses/by-sa/3.0/deed.en

19. Image courtesy of wikiHow.com from the article https://www.wikihow.com/Draw-an-Hourglass"

20. Grafiker61 - https://creativecommons.org/licenses/by-sa/4.0/deed.en

21. https://www.bea.aero/docspa/2009/f-cp090601.en/pdf/f-cp090601.en.pdf

22. Hardy Heinlin: www.aerowinx.com

23. Hardy Heinlin - www.aerowinx.com.

24. Cockpitrevolution.com/boeing747.html

25. Peter Collins

26. Peter Collins

27. Peter Collins

28. Peter Collins

29. Reproduced with permission of Jeppesen Sanderson, Inc.

30. Reproduced with permission of Jeppesen Sanderson, Inc.

31. Reproduced with permission of Jeppesen Sanderson, Inc.

32. Reproduced with permission of Jeppesen Sanderson, Inc.

33. Reproduced with permission of Jeppesen Sanderson, Inc.

34. https://www.flightsimulator.com

35. Reproduced with permission of Jeppesen Sanderson, Inc.

36. Reproduced with permission of Jeppesen Sanderson, Inc.

37. Reproduced with permission of Jeppesen Sanderson, Inc.

38. https://www.flightsimulator.com

39. http://movies.airclips.com/

40. Julien Scavini - https://creativecommons.org/licenses/by-sa/3.0/deed.en

41. Cockpitrevolution.com/boeing747.html

42. Peter Collins

43. Stuart Higgins - https://creativecommons.org/licenses/by-nd/4.0

44. Plastic Logic - https://creativecommons.org/licenses/by-sa/2.0/deed.en

45. Peter Collins

46. MdeVicente

47. Cockpitrevolution.com/boeing747.html

48. Benjamin Earwicker: FreeImages.com

49. mohamed_hassan (pixabay.com)

50. Martha Dominguez de Gouveia: Unsplash.com

51. ID 66366016 © Anton Samsonov | Dreamstime.com

52. 12019 (pixabay.com)

53. Petr Pavlicek/IAEA — https://creativecommons.org/licenses/by-sa/2.0/deed.en

54. Freepik.com. This cover has been designed using resources from Freepik.com

55. DanielPenfield — https://creativecommons.org/licenses/by-sa/3.0/deed.en

56. Clker-Free-Vector-Images (pixabay.com)

57. SpaceX: Pexels.com

58. Alec Wilson: https://creativecommons.org/licenses/by-sa/2.0/deed.en

59. Davidelit

60. Andrew Heneen - https://creativecommons.org/licenses/by/3.0/deed.en

61. U.S. Navy photo courtesy of The Boeing Co.

Appendix: B3A — Bureau of Aircraft Accidents Archives / Ronan HUBERT, Accidentologist

Printed in the United States
By Bookmasters

Biotechnology: economic and social aspects aims to provide a view of the current trends in harnessing biotechnology as an integral component of the labour and industrial sectors of society in both developed and developing countries. Specific biotechnologies such as bioethanol production, biofertilizers, microalgal biotechnology, Single Cell Protein and others are considered in detail, particularly with respect to the state of development of their associated industries, their suitability for various economies and the problems associated with their development. Further chapters discuss environmental questions and other socio-economic factors that need to be considered in order to bring about successful wealth creation. Experts from both developed and developing countries have contributed to the volume to provide a balanced view of some of the successes, challenges and prospects for the developing world which can be realized through the applications of biotechnology.

Biotechnology: economic and social aspects
Issues for developing countries

Biotechnology: economic and social aspects

Issues for developing countries

EDITED BY

E. J. DA SILVA
Division of Scientific Research and Higher Education
UNESCO, Paris

C. RATLEDGE
Professor of Microbial Biochemistry, University of Hull, UK

AND

A. SASSON
Director, Bureau of Programme Planning
UNESCO, Paris

Published in association with UNESCO

CAMBRIDGE
UNIVERSITY PRESS

CAMBRIDGE UNIVERSITY PRESS
Cambridge, New York, Melbourne, Madrid, Cape Town, Singapore,
São Paulo, Delhi, Dubai, Tokyo

Cambridge University Press
The Edinburgh Building, Cambridge CB2 8RU, UK

Published in the United States of America by Cambridge University Press, New York

www.cambridge.org
Information on this title: www.cambridge.org/9780521122283

© Cambridge University Press 1992

First published 1992
This digitally printed version 2009

A catalogue record for this publication is available from the British Library

Library of Congress Cataloguing in Publication data
Biotechnology : economic and social aspects : issues for developing
countries / edited by E.J. Da Silva, C. Ratledge, and A. Sasson.
    p. cm.
Includes index.
ISBN 0–521–38473–7 (hardback)
1. Biotechnology – Developing countries. I. Da Silva, E.J. II. Ratledge.
Colin. III. Sasson, Albert.
TP248.195.D48B55   1992
338.4′76606′091724 – dc20   91–20767   CIP

ISBN 978-0-521-38473-5 Hardback
ISBN 978-0-521-12228-3 Paperback

Contents

Contributors

Arora, A.L. Universidade Federal do Ceara, Nucleo de Fontes nao
Convencionais de Energia, Fortaleza, Ceara 60 000, Brazil
Boh, B. International Centre for Chemical Studies, University of Ljubljana,
Yugoslavia
Carioca, J.O.B. Universidade Federal do Ceara, Nucleo de Fontes nao
Convencionais de Energia, Fortaleza, Ceara 60 000, Brazil
Chang, S.T. The Chinese University of Hong Kong, Shatin, N.T. Hong
Kong
Chiu, S.W. Hong Kong Baptist College, Kowloon, Hong Kong
Colwell, R.R. Maryland Biotechnology Institute and University of
Maryland, College Park, Maryland, USA
Da Silva, E.J. Division of Scientific Research and Higher Education,
UNESCO, 1 rue Miollis, 75015 Paris, France
Doelle, H.W. MIRCEN – Biotechnology, Department of Microbiology,
University of Queensland, Brisbane, Queensland 4072, Australia
Dommergues, Y. BSSFT (ORSTOM/CIRAD), 45bis, Avenue de la Belle
Gabrielle, 94736 Nogent-sur-Marne Cedex, France
Gianinazzi, S. INRA BP 1540, 21034 Dijon Cedex, France
Gumbira-Sa'id, E. Department of Agroindustrial Technology and Inter
University Centre of Biotechnology, Bogor Agricultural University,
Bogor, Indonesia
Hall, D.O. King's College London, Division of Biosphere Sciences,
University of London, London W8 7AH, UK
Hamdan, I.Y. Agricultural Research Station, Faculty of Agriculture, Jordan
University of Science and Technology, P.O. Box 3030, IRBID, Jordan
Hueth, D.L. Maryland Biotechnology Institute and University of Maryland,
College Park, Maryland, USA
Junne, G. Vakgroep Internationale Betrekkingen en Volkenrecht, Faculteit
der Politieke en Sociaal-Culturele Wetenschappen (PSCW), University of
Amsterdam, Oudezijds Achterburgwal 237, 1012DL Amsterdam,
Netherlands

x   Contributors

Kornhauser, A. International Centre for Chemical Studies, University of
Ljubljana, Yugoslavia
Kung, S.-D. Maryland Biotechnology Institute and University of Maryland,
College Park, Maryland, USA
Mulongoy, K. IITA, PMB 5320 Ibadan, Nigeria
Ratledge, C. Department of Applied Biology, University of Hull, Hull HU6
7RX, UK
Roger, P.A. IIRI/ORSTOM, P.O. Box 933, Manila, Philippines
Rosillo-Calle, F. King's College London, Division of Biosphere Sciences,
University of London, London W8 7AH, UK
Sasson, A. Bureau of Programme Planning, UNESCO, 7 Place de Fontenoy,
75700 Paris, France
Senez, J.C. Laboratoire de Chimie Bactérienne, CNRS, F-13277 Marseilles
Cedex, France
Vonshak, A. Microalgal Biotechnology Laboratory, The Jacob Blaustein
Institute for Desert Research, Ben-Gurion University of the Negev, Sede
Boker Campus, Israel
*Walgate, R.** TDR Communications, WHO, 20 Ave Appia, CH-1211
Geneva 27, Switzerland
Zimmerman, B.K. VTT Technology Oy/Inc., Itätuulentie 2, SF-02100
Espoo, Finland

* Formerly Director, Biotechnology Information Programme, The Panos
Institute, London, and currently Senior Editor, UNDP/World Bank/WHO
Tropical Disease Research Programme, Geneva.

Preface

From a flood of journals, periodicals, news-items, patents and commercial ventures the word 'biotechnology' has gone out as the harbinger of prosperity and progress. Biotechnology, the generic name for a variety of biological processes, is increasingly being treated as the cornerstone of a number of development scenarios. This consideration stems from an awareness that societies wishing to achieve, maintain or enhance their living standards will eventually have to produce goods and services that are internationally competitive and devoid of economic redundancy, on the basis of their eventual market-quality and social performance.

Biotechnology costs money. It is the world of business and investment. It is all to do with making and selling products in a highly competitive world. Start-up requires extensive research. Product and process development costs even more. Marketing is crucial for success and is also very expensive. Consequently, in recent years and given the first flush of apparently successful products being launched followed by the reality of sobering endeavour, several developed and developing countries are now taking a hard look at the large-scale investments that are required in the furtherance of biotechnology. This theme is dealt with, to some extent, in the view that is presented here of the socio-economic revolution that has been fuelled by biotechnology. This important aspect is dealt with in many of the chapters of this book and in particular in those concerned with the production of bioethanol, biofertilizers and Single Cell Protein. Biotechnologies that lend themselves to counteracting environmental damage and enhancing economic returns are exemplified in the technologies of microalgal culture and mushroom production. Already accepted in some countries as viable economic entities, these bioprocesses are of special concern and interest to developing countries that abound in biomass availability and solar energy.

Biotechnology is not an end in itself. It serves economical goals and works in technological markets. It does, though, provoke ethical concerns. The growing public debate in a few countries about the applications of genetic engineering stem largely from a lack of understanding of modern genetics. The public's fears unfortunately are fuelled by many people whose motives are far from clear. These fears are real but the premise on which they are based is insubstantial. The ethical debate, however, will obviously continue but we hope that the framework in which it is conducted relies more on factual evidence than on emotional responses.

The impact of biotechnologies on the societies of the developed and developing countries can be both positive and negative. Increased yields of cultivated plants for their fragrances and pigments of importance in the cosmetic and food industries may be accompanied by a shift in export markets and international trade. Exporting countries, in some cases, have seen their exports dry up and as a result have evolved into import countries. India, for example, is no longer a net exporter of plant oils but now uses its own limited foreign currency supply to buy oils and fats on the world market. This reversal has taken place mainly because of the improved agro-economic policies pursued in Europe and North America. This, however, is just one of many examples which in some quarters have raised the spectre of governmental compensation for the displacement of cash crops in the rural communities. Coupled to these socio-economic factors are intercultural preferences and prejudices that compound the positive or negative aspects of biotechnology. However, what is encouraging is the multitude of effort, albeit duplicative in some cases, and goodwill that are drawing together in a concerted approach to enhancing technological co-operation, economic progress and sustainable development in a realistic market economy.

The quality of contemporary research and development in any technology, and especially in an area that is as rapidly moving as that of biotechnology, depends to a large extent on the efficiency by which scientific information can be made available. This in turn influences research hypotheses in furthering the horizons of bioinformatics, i.e. the handling of biotechnological information by computers and its storage in database. The development of information support systems for research and development in biotechnological applications is now being accepted as an important tool as reliance on bibliographic and specialized databases grows. This database is vital and must be accessible worldwide. Fortunately, scientists tend not to recognize geographic boundaries and regard their knowledge as freely available for everyone.

The purpose of this book is to provide a view of the current trends in harnessing biotechnology as an integral component of the labour and industrial sectors of society. It is, therefore, hoped that this assembly of chapters, written by experts from the developed and the developing countries, illustrates some of the socio-economic aspects of the different biotechnologies in practice. Of particular concern to us has been the influence which western biotechnological developments have had on colouring the attitude of the rest of the world towards biotechnology. In western eyes, biotechnology is seen as being able to bestow considerable benefits to industrial and economic developments. Indeed the areas of biopharmaceuticals, diagnostic systems, speciality chemicals, bioreactors, waste treatment and agriculture are domains in which commercial ventures have moved from the phase of exploration and research to that of product and market development. The techniques look deceptively easy but it is the intellectual challenge of genetic engineering that has seemingly captured the imagination of scientists and politicians alike. Amidst the growing fervour for countries to start up their own genetic engineering programmes, we see the dangers of the simpler biotechnologies being ignored as somehow being unworthy of intellectual input. We therefore trust we have provided in these chapters a balanced view of some of the challenges and prospects that can be realized through the applications of biotechnology. Biotechnology can be exciting at any level: it is as intellectually satisfying to solve the problems of yeast performance in a novel bioreactor as it is to solve the problems of cloning heterologous genes into bacteria.

We trust that through the assemblage of these chapters we have provided a view that will be equally applicable to developed and to developing countries and that scientists in each of these sectors will understand a little better the framework of the 'other half'.

Edgar J. Da Silva
Colin Ratledge
Albert Sasson

1

Biotechnology: the socio-economic revolution? A synoptic view of the world status of biotechnology

COLIN RATLEDGE

Introduction

Biotechnology is many things to many people. Traditionalists would tell us that biotechnology is one of the oldest activities of man, beginning with the production of wines and alcoholic beverages and now encompassing all of the current fermentation industries. Modernists would suggest that biotechnology came of age with the advent of recombinant DNA technologies and it is this 'new' biotechnology which will have the greatest impact upon our societies and their economic structures. The reality, of course, is that both these views, the traditional and modern, are inter-dependent. The new biotechnology could not have gained such a rapid place in the industrial fabric of society had there not been the traditional roots already in place. Developments and indeed applications of genetic modifications of living cells have taken place because of the traditional view that microorganisms have much to offer in their exploitation to man's well-being. A coherent framework, thus, was already in place which then allowed genetic engineering principles to be speedily translated from laboratory concepts into industrial practices.

The implications for biotechnology in a developed and developing world are tremendous. However, it must always be appreciated that biotechnology is what it says it is: it is a *technology*. That is, it is an enabling discipline. It allows the exploitation of microorganisms, plant and animal cells to take place within an economic framework. Biotechnology is not then a science: it is a means of applying science for the benefit of man and society. In practice, this means that biotechnology is used to make money – or in certain instances – to save money.

The creation of wealth through biotechnology firmly places this subject within the industrial sector and it is to the business community that one must then look to discern how the subject is to be applied and ultimately used.

Economics of biotechnology

Biotechnology is an industrial wealth-creating activity. It uses the disciplines of molecular biology, microbiology, genetics, biochemistry and, most importantly, of engineering to translate potential ideas into practical processes. As biotechnology either produces specific products or is used to deal with potential environmental problems thereby saving money, one must recognize that the ultimate success or failure of a biotechnological process is whether or not it makes money or produces a social benefit. A biotechnological process that does neither is an irrelevancy and market forces will quickly ensure that such processes are quickly abandoned.

The economics of biotechnological processes in developed countries are such that the vast majority of all biotechnological work is carried out by, and for the benefit of, industry. However, industry is considerably aided financially by both direct and indirect routes, primarily from government.

Government science-funding agencies place a large proportion of their research finance into academic institutions or into specific research institutes that are not linked to any particular industrial group or sector. Higher educational institutes (universities, technical high schools, polytechnics) not only generate new and important ideas for the future growth of industry, they also simultaneously provide the highly skilled manpower required by a newly emerging industry, such as biotechnology which has a high demand for trained biological scientists and engineers. Academia also provide many of the consultants used increasingly by industry which would otherwise find itself unable to keep up with current advances across the breadth of the subject. Government agencies, i.e. the grant-awarding research bodies or councils, therefore play a key role in pump-priming new developments and for funding the fundamental underpinning research needed for the further developments of biotechnology.

Developed countries already have a large infra-structure in place which readily allows the transfer of financial resources from the public sector into the industrial sector. This mechanism is then the means of creating and maintaining the wealth of the nation (Fig. 1.1).

It should be no surprise to realize that the future of biotechnology depends on its continued ability to make money and that it has to be seen as an industrial activity and not an exercise in academic curiosity.

Altruistic biotechnology does not exist or if it does it simply consumes money and does not generate it.

Such has been the enormous outward attraction of biotechnology to the general public that many developing countries have become dazzled by it and believe that biotechnology can play a major part in improving, virtually overnight, the economic status of their own country. The truth, unfortunately, is different as, by definition, a developing country does not yet possess an extensive industrial network. Moreover, there is not the economic ultrastructural system in place that will allow for the governmental pump-priming of new commercial ideas and their take-up by industry, as is illustrated in Fig. 1.1, for the developed countries. The failure of the system is compounded by there being an insufficiently affluent market for the potential products.

This then leads to the second hard reality that must be faced by developing countries and that is the clear identification of what exactly are the principal targets of the new biotechnological developments for the developing countries, and how much it will cost to realize these targets.

Industries of the developed countries that have recognized the potential of biotechnology see the greatest future opportunities arising from the high-value, low-volume products; in other words in those

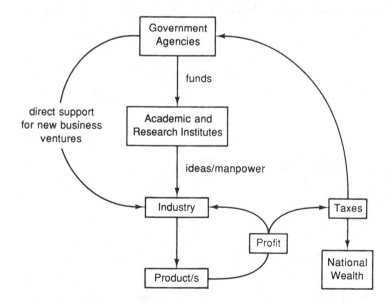

Fig. 1.1. *The controlling influence of government agencies on a development of an industrial-based economy.*

products destined for the health-care markets. This is not to deny that the biggest revenue earners in the whole of biotechnology continue to be the traditional processes of vinification, brewing, distilling and in the dairy industry.

However, the opportunities arising from the so-called 'new' biotechnology lie elsewhere and depend upon an already affluent society being prepared to pay relatively large sums of money for improved drugs, antibiotics, health-care preparations and for improved standards of medical diagnosis and treatment.

The success of biotechnology is therefore dependent upon an affluent society already being in place, and willing to pay for the new products. Biotechnology will not create an affluent society but will only help an existing one to become more prosperous.

The process of wealth-generation in an affluent society is a virtuous circle of investment leading to greater profits being generated which, in turn, can lead to further investment and development of a further range of new products (Fig. 1.2). Biotechnology is fundamentally no different from either, say, the chemical or electronics industries: products create profits which then create new products. The high cost of new health-care products lies not only in the very high cost of the original scientific work but also in the extraordinarily high costs of evaluating the efficacy of a new product and its accompanying long-term safety. Even if a developing country were to develop *ab initio* a new health-care vaccine

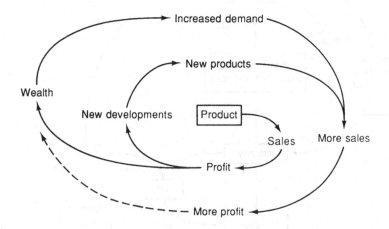

Fig. 1.2. *The virtuous spiral of increasing prosperity from an expanding market economy focussed on products that readily sell into an affluent society.*

or drug, the bottom line is: would it be prepared to spend the $100 million or so required to gain full clearance and eventual international marketing of the product? The opportunities for developing similar economically virtuous circles (Fig. 1.2) in developing countries are thus manifestly limited. This is not to say that such countries cannot have a biotechnology industry. It must be of a fundamentally different type than that of the developed countries otherwise, without an affluent society already in place to buy the products, there is the looming truth that a vicious economic circle would be developed (see Fig. 1.3) whereby, because of a poor market-demand for a particular product, there will be insufficient profits to maintain the investment to see the next series of products arrive at the market place.

Biotechnology, being a multi-faceted activity, can produce many products and achieve many worthwhile aims. However, the needs of a developing country are distinct from those of the developed countries and how biotechnology will be exploited must also be fundamentally different between the two world sectors. As will be argued later, the greatest danger for developing countries is for them, and several international governmental and non-governmental agencies, to believe that they must also become proficient in genetic engineering techniques and must develop, at the very least, academic prowess in this area. This would be one of the real tragedies of biotechnology when it does have so much else to offer.

Biotechnology can be exploited to create a better environment, can be used to improve the energy status of countries and can help improve

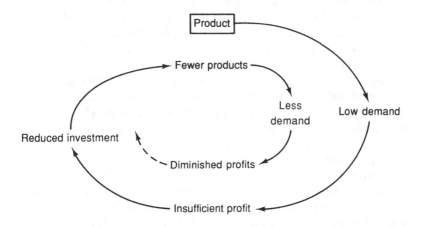

Fig. 1.3. The vicious spiral of declining prosperity from a diminishing industrial base not correctly focussed on needs of society.

food supplies. Genetic engineering can be applied but will require great thought as to what are the most useful areas where it can benefit whole communities and not just tiny minorities of wealthy people. It is very strange that many developing countries are content not to have their own electronics industry and are willing to rely upon developed countries for their supply of commodity goods in this area. The fact that biotechnology is a similar high-technology industry is not yet appreciated. Developing countries therefore must take what they need from biotechnology, not what they imagine would be prestigious. Too many politicians, concerned with the outer image of their country, are willing to establish large genetic engineering institutions in the mistaken view that this will confer great benefit upon the economy of their country. This will be doubly disastrous: it will waste valuable resources of money and trained manpower but will also deprive those areas where the more traditional biotechnology could make the real impact on a socio-economic structure of the country.

Biotechnology and the environment

Biotechnology is about making money. This can be either directly, through the production of specific products, or indirectly by dealing with environmental problems for which either industry or society are prepared to pay. In developed countries, there exist strict laws governing the disposal of wastes on land or into water systems. Biotechnological processes for dealing with materials such as sewage are, of course, well established even though they may be only poorly understood biologically. Biotechnological routes for the disposal of organic effluents from industrial factories are also well developed and have come into prominence because governmental agencies have legislated that less material be dumped into streams, rivers and lakes. As a consequence, thriving service industries have arisen specifically to offer practical solutions to effluent problems. The economic driving force for such service industries to develop is the existing legislation which, being enforceable in law, can penalize transgressing companies (or individuals) very severely if pollution limits are not complied with. Economics once more dictate that practical solutions have to be found for environmental problems.

Not all industrial wastes or domestic refuse are, though, suitable for biotechnological treatment. Hence, biotechnologists must always be careful of advocating their own solutions to problems when other ones may be more appropriate. Nevertheless, where there are biodegradable effluents, which would include industrial, agricultural and domestic sources, biotechnological treatment of such materials is often found to be the most cost-effective process.

The simplest procedures adopted for the disposal of industrial, agricultural and human wastes lie in the production of methane through the process known as anaerobic digestion. In developed countries there are already a number of companies that specialize in this area and who will supply turn-key processes – that is processes designed and built to achieve standard levels of bioconversions – for the generation of methane. This technology is also used by some of the large sewage works to make the sites energy-independent. In all these cases, the methane is used at the point of production. It is not economic to liquify it or transport it any distance.

Many environmental problems have been overcome using this technology. Equally, this technology has much to offer for developing countries. The production of bio-gas, as methane is frequently termed, at the local village level has much to offer the community. Not only will the production of bio-gas be an invaluable adjunct to the local energy budget, it will simultaneously remove the environmental hazards of sewage treatment and, furthermore, prevent consumption of other less renewable sources of fuel. Frequently one hears that the supply of fuel into poor rural communities – principally this is wood – creates its own environmental and logistical problems with greater and greater efforts and expenditure of personal energy having to be put into gathering it. By being able to generate methane at a local level, this dependency is broken. If such systems are further supplemented by saving animal and crop wastes, it is evident that the problem of energy supplies into villages could be overcome.

It is less certain, however, whether strict control over environmental pollution in developing countries warrants the same kind of legislation that exists in developed countries. Environmental issues are hotly debated by the general public and considerable pressure is brought to bear on representative, elected politicians to enact controlling legislation. In developing countries, the need for pollution abatement is present but as it will inevitably cost money to remedy the problem, then who shall pay? The dictum of western countries that 'the polluter pays' cannot be applied if the polluter is then forced to raise the price of their company's products beyond the price which the people can afford to pay. In the non-industrialized countries, this is not a question of people being able to pay but, literally, of having enough money to pay at all. Thus care of the environment is probably a pre-occupation of the affluent society, the society that is willing and able to pay for improved living conditions. It cannot be a primary objective in itself for developing countries. It is only where the application of biotechnology confers a positive advantage, as with the generation of methane, that biotechnology will be used to its full advantage. A society that worries where its next meal – or possibly where next year's food – is to come from, can hardly be expected to be concerned about western ideals for the care of the environment. Alarmist views about 'the greenhouse effect' and of the dangers of global warming are scarcely concerns of a population that has yet to attain the basic standards of living that were enjoyed by western societies a century ago. Environmental problems besetting developing countries will only be tackled when these are adversely affecting the immediate future of a local community and are not being used as a nebulous threat to the population at some very distant date.

Energy

Bio-gas production, as an adjunct to dealing with environmental issues – for disposing of animal and agricultural waste particularly in the least developed countries of the world – should not be thought of as a biotechnology just for the village-level application. Apt to be often dismissed as a 'second class' technology, policy makers in developing countries should consider that in the industrialized world, bio-gas is effectively used to deal with urban sewage and with organic wastes from agricultural-based industries and, in selected instances, from chemical processing factories themselves.

The provision of cheap energy on a wider global scale is a multi-faceted problem requiring equally multi-faceted answers. Energy will always be produced from a variety of sources. The majority of these will be non-biotechnological. However, the only useful energy source that is biotechnological in origin, besides methane, is ethanol.

Evaluating the economics of ethanol production tasks the minds of politicians considerably. The underlying science is easy: either the yeast *Saccharomyces cerevisiae* or an anaerobic bacterium, such as *Zymomonas mobilis*, is used. As feedstock, agricultural wastes such as molasses, or even crops deliberately grown to provide fermentation substrates, are used. In one or two cases, lactose in the whey from the dairy industry is used. (In the Irish Carberry process, the ethanol from lactose is used in potable spirit but in New Zealand it is used as an industrial solvent.) However, the real difficulty comes in trying to evaluate the overall economic potential of producing bioethanol for use as an energy source.

The willingness to use, or not use, ethanol as an energy source is entirely within the socio-political strategy of a country, or group of countries such as the 12 nations of the European Community. A decisive factor to be decided is how revenue is to be raised by taxation of fuel whether it be petroleum-based or bio-based. No government will wish to diminish its fiscal policies by having less revenue from ethanol as a fuel than from petroleum. Consequently, the taxation of ethanol will always be high and be considered by its proponents to be excessive thus, in their eyes, perpetually placing ethanol at a disadvantage. Under such economic constraints, ethanol, it is argued, never becomes a viable alternative fuel to petroleum.

It is argued though with some force that the real cost of petroleum is never admitted by governments. The obvious costs of oil exploration, drilling, extraction, transportation, refining and distribution of the end-product are considered the only costs. But, as the recent world crisis in the Middle East has forcibly indicated, the real cost of oil is much, much higher. The costs of maintaining the supplies and of patrolling the international shipping lanes are met entirely from the resources of the country's military budget. These costs which amount, even in times of tranquility, to several billion dollars per year are never added to the costs of petroleum nor acknowledged by the governments. Consequently, the cost of petrol to the public is heavily subsidized.

The advocates of a rational bioethanol programme therefore see the supposed economics deliberately distorted by politicians to obscure the real price that has to be paid for a 'cheap' fuel. One suspects, however, that economics, even if marginally in favour of a bioethanol programme, are not the only reason that is taken into account when deciding against adopting a bioethanol strategy. To produce ethanol on a large scale would require that a considerable amount of crops would have to be grown solely to produce the necessary sugar or starch as fermentation feedstock. With the present disproportionation of food supplies in the world, with substantial minorities – and in some cases majorities – of populations who are starving or are subsisting below an adequate level, it would be political death for governments to advocate the large-scale growth of potential foodstuffs to be used solely for non-food uses. It is this obstacle that politicians undoubtedly see with great clarity that reinforces their opposition to bioethanol production programmes: but, of course, the blocking is done under the premise of faulty economics. The relatively minor consideration of ethanol abuse, which is possible in a scenario involving large-scale ethanol production, is a complicating factor that most politicians would again be reluctant to countenance if they were to endorse an active bioethanol programme.

The only way in which a bioethanol programme can succeed is in those countries where there are no suitable reserves of fossil fuels and the balance of payments is such that a substantial part of the nation's gross national product would have to be spent in purchasing crude petroleum.

In such countries, the economics of the developed countries no longer apply. They are free to evaluate a bioethanol programme alongside any other alternative strategy. The biggest problem for such countries to solve is how to avoid a distortion of their existing agricultural programmes such that food supplies are not impaired but sufficient crops are grown in order that a part can be legitimately diverted into fermentation. The balance is a difficult one but, as has been shown successfully in Brazil and other countries, it can be done.

Biotechnology for food

We eat microorganisms and have done so for millenia. Fermented beverages, dairy and meat products abound across the world. The concept, though, of deliberately growing microorganisms as a food source is comparatively recent. The first processes that were developed used *Candida utilis*, originally called *Torula utilis* or just sometimes 'torula yeast' or even 'food yeast' to distinguish it from baker's and brewer's yeast (both being *Saccharomyces cerevisiae*). The substrates being fed to the yeast were the waste carbohydrate liquors emanating from paper manufacture: sulphite waste liquors. Later, molasses from the sugar refineries of the West Indies were used. The entire concept for Single Cell Protein (SCP), which was the adopted euphemism for microbial food, received considerable impetus in the late 1950s when the prospects of using petroleum wastes, the alkane fraction from petroleum refining, was developed by BP Ltd, first in France and then in the UK. The story is, of course, now history and the conclusions that there was little demand or desire for the product were learnt at considerable cost. Parallel schemes for using methanol as a feed stock to produce SCP from bacteria similarly floundered on economic grounds. These events are described in greater detail elsewhere in this volume.

The main conclusion to be drawn, primarily in western countries, from attempts to produce microbial food for man or his domesticated animals was that biotechnology, no matter how sophisticated and no matter on what scale it was practised, could not compete with agriculture for the production of an economic food. The enormous developments in crop improvement and in farming and harvesting techniques were something that had not been anticipated by the economic advisors to the various SCP projects in the 1950s. Of course, the world oil crisis of the early 1970s did not help as it pushed up the cost of the alkane feedstock but had little intrinsic impact upon the price of soya beans, the world's cheapest and most stable supply of animal feed material. Thus, western countries have abandoned, with one exception, all but one SCP project where the feedstock has to be directly purchased.

The only SCP processes that now exist are those which function as an adjunct to a waste-producing process where the disposal of the waste would be expensive by conventional means.

The SCP process which is an exception to this is that currently operated as a joint venture between the industrial chemical company, *ICI* plc, and the grain and baking company, *Rank Hovis McDougall* in collaboration with *Sainsbury's*, the large supermarket chain of grocery stores throughout the UK. Here, the SCP product is not destined for animal feed but is in fact a sophisticatedly marketed product, called '*Quorn*', which is aimed directly at the consumer market. The organism used, a strain of the mould *Fusarium graminearum*, is grown on sugar, preferably by hydrolysing starch which is cheaper than sugar, and when harvested is capable of being 'texturized' so that it can be skilfully blended by food technologists into a variety of meatless products. Such products are attractive to vegetarians and also to other consumers who are prepared, and able, to pay the required price for such a product.

This process, though it produces an expensive product, is only sustainable in a society that can afford to pay for an alternative food source. It would be totally uneconomic as an animal foodstuff. However, to sell the product, a long and expensive advertising campaign has had to be run to ensure that the public becomes aware of the product and continues to buy it. The success of the Quorn SCP project owes as much to marketing as it does to biotechnology.

There is no way that a technology such as the Quorn SCP process could be applied outside a developed country. Although it has no direct relevance to developing countries, this SCP process has nevertheless provided a lot of information that is potentially of considerable value to other prospective ventures.

One of the greatest lessons to come out of the SCP projects developed using alkanes and methanol in the 1960s, and more recently with the Quorn project, was the stringent need for toxicological testing – and safety assurance – of the product. To be absolutely sure that the yeast, bacterial and mould products were safe to be fed to any animal, including man, considerable developments took place in the way in which products could be evaluated for their nutritional safety. It is this information which, by being generally available, can obviously save considerable amounts of money should SCP projects subsequently be developed elsewhere in the world.

The prospects for SCP projects in developing countries need to be evaluated with great care. Careful attention needs to be given not just to the economics and the toxicological trials but equally to the potential impact of such processes on the agro-economics of the country. It still is not prudent to grow a crop which would be used solely as a fermentation substrate as such a crop, or at least an alternative one, could be used to feed the local population, either directly or indirectly as feed for cows, poultry or whatever. The lessons learnt from western countries will therefore stand the developing ones in good stead when it comes to evaluating whether or not to initiate an SCP project. SCP will succeed only when it uses substrates that cannot be otherwise used for food or feed: i.e. either because they are unsuitable or occur in such a form – such as being in a dilute solution – that would make them unacceptable. The fundamental concept of an SCP process, that it can use any carbohydrate-based feedstock with concomitant utilization of inorganic nitrogen (ammonia or nitrate) to produce a high protein product, is, of course, the correct one but the carbohydrate feedstocks have to be identified with great care. The technology which would be used in such processes must also be carefully evaluated and considerable transfer of western technology will be necessary unless much-simplified versions can be employed without sacrifice of operational or product safety. The future of SCP and of joint ventures for producing such products would seem to be excellent if the very costly lessons learnt by western countries can be avoided and indeed used to advantage.

We should not, though, hesitate in using the capabilities of biotechnology to improve our concept of *Whole Crop Utilization*. Crops should be grown for their main contribution to a national food programme but the total crop which is harvested – or which is capable of being harvested – should be used. Unwanted parts of the crop have to be utilized in a total programme which would then see several other products arising from a crop where hitherto only one had been considered. Utilization of the crop wastes must be encouraged as such processes will provide vital by-products. In some cases, such crop wastes may be more amenable to being converted into products other than SCP. The choice of product should clearly be left to the controlling agencies but such agencies must ensure that 'wastes' are not wasted. Such total crop utilization programmes are equally applicable to developing countries as they are to developed ones. To comprehend biotechnology for food as being solely centred on the exploitation of microorganisms to produce SCP would be to miss several important developments. Food, for the majority of most populations, begins and ends with agriculture. It is therefore to agriculture that we must look for the major impact of biotechnology upon the nutritional needs of a developing society.

Already of considerable economic importance is the development of specific strains of rhizobia as essential inoculants for the successful cultivation of the major leguminous crops. These research programmes are actively encouraged throughout the world by government agencies of which the Microbial Resource Centres (the MIRCEN Institutes) funded by UNESCO are of paramount importance. The accruing benefits of these technologies are evident: increased nitrogen-fixation and increased protein content of the plant. Other symbiotic relationships between cyanobacteria and non-leguminous crops, such as rice, are also being exploited to advantage.

Improvements in crop yields lie at the heart of being able to improve the nutritional status of a community: the direct application of chemical fertilizers (providing N, P and K) is the usual preferred route for the industrialized countries but such routes are economically undesirable in developing countries. The ingenuity of the microbiologist and the biotechnologist in providing a real basis for improving crop yields now is coming to the fore. The exploitation of biotechnology for the production of biofertilizers is but one way in which biotechnology can seek to improve the production of agricultural crops. The other main way for improvement is through the developments offered by plant biotechnology.

Plant biotechnology has a relatively short history with few proponents and even fewer exponents. However, there is now an increasing awareness of what may be accomplished by applying the techniques of the geneticist into plant breeding programmes. Plant breeding, of course, is as old as civilization: ever since man first accidently crossed two wild strains of cereal crop to produce a new and much improved version of the wheat plant. Indeed, civilization and its expansion probably owes everything to the first plant breeders and selectors. The agrarian revolution is a very old one. Nowadays, plant breeding is an extensive industry with the emphasis very much on 'industry'. Crop breeding for improved leguminous plants, oleaginous, starchy and proteinaceous ones are all under active pursuit – almost exclusively in the laboratories of the larger industrial concerns. The rewards are, of course, very high by being able to produce better yielding crops or crops yielding improved quality of proteins, oils or of particular components. All our major – and many of the minor – crops of developed countries are the results of many decades of plant breeding.

The revolution in plant breeding and selection, however, has now arrived. The plant molecular geneticist can now aim to achieve improvements in plant characteristics by the direct manipulation of the genes responsible for giving a plant its particular characteristics. Existing genes can be *deleted* (to remove unwanted characteristics), *amplified* (to increase the synthesis of a particular protein which may in itself be the desired end-product or may be an enzyme active in a particular metabolic pathway) or *modified* (so that a protein may now be produced with an altered sequence of amino acids leading to its improved nutritional status, or higher enzyme activity or improved product), almost at will to grow plants with one or more selected characteristics.

Furthermore, not only can existing genes be changed but new ones can be added. The first targets for such strategies have been to produce plants showing resistance to predators (virus, microbial or insect) and now we are seeing the first plants that have been genetically modified to make them resistant to herbicides and pesticides.

Some of their targets are obviously beneficial: to be able to produce, say, a bean crop with improved nutritional characteristics of its main protein, phaseolin, is of considerable value to a population where the intake of essential amino acids (from proteins) may be limiting their nutritional well-being.

Consequently a protein with higher contents of, say, lysine or methionine, two of the essential amino acids that are often deficient in a low-protein diet, would have tremendous nutritional consequence for an inadequately fed population. But unless world agencies are going to back such research programmes with heavy finance, both for the laboratory and for the subsequent field trials, such work will not be a major target in the plant biotechnology laboratories of industrial countries. The old adage of not being able to make money from people who have no money, once more comes into operation. World agencies will have to ensure that this research is funded and comes to fruition. Crop improvement for a developing country may not be a great money earner. Fortunately though there is sufficient interest in such programmes to be able to recognize that these improvements will not be far off. However, acceptance of new crops by a suspicious population will take more than finance to cure, but this is perhaps a separate issue, though it is clearly one which cannot be ignored.

Not all plant biotechnology has received universal praise. Indeed, damning criticism has been raised in more than one quarter by people who are concerned with the introduction of pesticide and herbicide-resistant plants. Although such plants will be used, at least in the short term, only in developed countries, i.e. by those who can afford the seed and the accompanying herbicide to eliminate the competing plants, the concern is expressed that such a strategy will lead to the increased use of chemical agents and not their elimination. However, the cost-benefits of using such crops, which will be realized first by the seed supplier, secondly by the grower (that is the farmer who would be able to produce his mono-culture of plant much more easily than before) and finally, by the consumer, will be the single most powerful argument in favour of introducing these new genetically modified crops.

The need for cheap food is not just a concern of the developing countries. Affluent societies still expect to pay very little, in terms of their disposable income, on basic food commodities. It should be noted that there is an obvious distinction between the cost of basic food ingredients and the price that members of an affluent society are prepared to pay for highly-processed foods where considerable cost or value is added on to the initial raw ingredients. Plant biotechnology will therefore be expected to make major contributions to the development of our food crops but we should be aware that some of these developments may be heavily criticized. Some developments must, perforce, affect agricultural practices throughout the world and, hopefully, if our environmental protection agencies achieve the correct balance for legislating the use of transgenic plants, then the benefits of such technology are ensured for our well-being.

Biotechnology and the genetic revolution

There is no doubt that biotechnology has captured the attention of scientists and the general public on a world-wide basis by virtue of the developments in molecular biology and, in particular, in the establishment of techniques which permit the movement of genetic information from one cell into another. There are no biological boundaries to genetic modification (now the preferred term to genetic manipulation): the donor DNA may be from a prokaryotic cell or eukaryotic cell and the recipient cell may be equally pro or eukaryotic. Cells may be simple – microbial or lower plants – or complex – higher plants and animals. Through the technique of genetic modification, a whole new series of horizons has now become possible. The principal targets at the moment are the production of animal proteins of very high pharmaceutical value achieved by cloning the relevant section of DNA into the most appropriate production microorganism. Already a range of these cloned, or recombinant, proteins is being produced commercially. The next range of targets undoubtedly are the transgenic plants and animals which will carry new genes from other cells. Some of the contributions which genetic modification may be expected to make over the next decade to the improvement of plants have already been outlined earlier. Although objections have been raised over the wisdom of producing herbicide- or pesticide-resistant plants for reasons of increasing the usage of the chemical agents (but not because of any concern over the nutritional safety of such plants), there has been much concern expressed over the introduction of transgenic plants and also to transgenic animals. Much of this public anxiety seems to be created either through the ignorance of the general public or by obscure motives of publicity-seeking individuals who should be better informed before speaking subjectively about matters on which they have little comprehension.

The transfer of new genes into a plant to make it resistant to viral, microbial, or even insect, attack, or to improve its growth characteristics or resistance to drought, clearly has much to offer for the improvement of crops throughout the world. Similarly, the improvement of desirable characteristics of domesticated farm animals is now a reality. However, as has been argued above, modification of the plant genome to produce herbicide- and pesticide-resistant crops has already been strongly criticized. The arguments though, do not exclude the use of the crop which can probably be assumed to be safe to eat. Objections to transgenic animals are usually made on more emotive grounds but the point needs to be forcibly made that where animal genes are being complemented by genes from other (related) animals, genetic manipulation should simply be regarded as an extension of the animal breeder's art. Genetic modification has turned this art into a science. The geneticist now seeks to do in a year or two what may have taken a plant or animal breeder decades or even centuries to perfect. However attractive the concept may be of using animals to produce biotechnological products, such as using transgenic sheep to produce pharmaceutical drugs in their milk, insufficient thought has been given as to how the animals must be cared for. If a transgenic animal becomes infected in any way, and particularly by, say, a virus or even a prion particle (viz. the putative causative agent of bovine spongiform encephalitis, BSE), then there may be imperfect safeguards to prevent transmission of deleterious proteins into the animal product (e.g. the milk). Thus, very careful, and consequently very costly, precautions may have to be enforced to ensure that products from transgenic animals that may be unknowingly infected are not passed on to the public. The cost of using transgenic animals for large production of health-care pharmaceutical products may therefore prove to be too great.

Where there is a genuine cause for scientists to stop and think about transgenic plants and animals is when they are proposing to clone genes that are foreign to plants (or to animals); i.e. genes coming from a totally unrelated source, such as a microorganism, or even from an animal (or if the recipient is an animal, then from a plant), into a host cell which has never hitherto had that genetic information within it. The danger, if indeed one exists, would be seen in the formation of plants, which if eaten, may cause adverse allergic reactions. Such dangers are, however, minimal and fears about consuming transgenic plants or even animals will be found to be needless. The argument is that if the cell for the donor DNA was itself a 'safe' cell to eat, and so was the recipient cell, then the resulting modified cell would also be a safe cell. There is no reason to believe that adverse effects will be generated by combining DNA – or more accurately a very small fraction of DNA – into a recipient cell. However, numerous so-called 'watch-dog' bodies are now in existence that will ensure a slow take-up of some of these very exciting possibilities. Perhaps this will not be a bad thing if, in the long term, the public feels assured about the safety of a technique that it is almost totally unable to comprehend. Overcoming complete ignorance of the subject probably lies at the core of the problem. To get the message across, scientists will have to work extremely closely with all forms of media communication and, as yet, this is an aspect which is almost entirely missing.

The opportunities for genetic modification of microbes, plants and animals reside principally in the hands of wealthy corporations or institutions. The expense of transferring the correct piece of DNA from one cell to another and for evaluating the product is minimally US $1 000 000. It is considerably more where proteins for therapeutic use are required or where novel proteins are wanted as the cost of safety and toxicological evaluation are extremely high. (This requirement, of course, applies to all products and not just to products derived from recombinant DNA technologies.) It is this financial barrier which dictates that the technique will only be commercially exploited if there are substantial monetary returns. And, as indicated earlier, it is only the large health-care industries of western society that are capable of sustaining such expensive research for the benefit of the affluent population that they serve and from whom, in return, they derive their profits.

The scientific developments of genetic manipulation, and now of protein engineering with the techniques of site-directed mutagenesis to create new proteins with subtly improved characteristics, have attracted the attention of scientists everywhere. Such is the cost of these techniques, and such is the prohibitively expensive cost of developing new products into the market place from such techniques, that if we wanted to create a hole down which precious money and resources could be poured, then this is that hole.

Given that scientific resources in developing countries are already vastly over-stretched and severely restricted financially, it makes little or no economic sense for scientists in these countries to jump on the 'band wagon' of genetic engineering. A sounder strategy would be to let the techniques develop until they become routine and can be handled by scientists without access to the most sophisticated of equipment. The goals of the scientists in their own geographical region will need to be defined more clearly since challenges for society as a whole exist at every level. Scientists, who often erroneously regard themselves as belonging to an intellectual elite, should not be seduced into thinking that the only good science is the 'new' science and that they need expensive laboratories, chemicals and equipment to do their experiments. Even if they had access to such resources, it is extremely unlikely that they would be able to catch up with current developments, let alone keep pace with them.

Final thoughts

The gap between the developed world and the developing world is a wide one. It is, unfortunately, a gap which is widening and not closing. The reasons for this are self-evident. The affluent developed societies have a high expectation of their life styles and consequently demand improved products either to sustain and further enhance their lives or to assist them to overcome illnesses and diseases. The basis for this affluence is their industrially-based economics.

The developing countries are poor because of a chronic shortage of financial investment in addition to other factors such as a population explosion. They do not possess an extensive manufacturing economy and instead frequently export their own indigenous raw materials into the developed countries simply because they have neither the means nor the market to produce the final products themselves and moreover need such exports as valuable foreign-exchange earners.

Biotechnology belongs to the industrial sector. With some exceptions that have been noted above, it does not function at a village level for poor people. It is exactly analogous to the electronics industrial boom or to the preceding chemical industrial expansion. The investment required to sustain a viable biotechnological-orientated industry sector is enormous, demanding both high levels of capital investment and also a highly skilled and trained work-force. In just the same way as developing countries have not been able to take much advantage from the expansion in the electronic or chemical industries, so they will be able to take little from the most profitable areas of the new biotechnology.

To repeat my earlier remarks, biotechnology, if not applied wisely, can be a black hole down which valuable resources of money and intellectual manpower of a developing country can disappear without any positive benefit accruing to the investing country.

Biotechnology will, unfortunately, if we are not careful, only help to make the gap between the developed and developing countries even wider. Our present world economic structure does not provide any basis, let alone hope, that their situation will change in the foreseeable future.

Although this may be judged to be a pessimistic view of the disparity between the wealthy and the poor nations, it is perhaps no more than the gap that once existed in industrial countries between the wealthy and the poor people. Just as this gap has now been eroded, so we may hope that the gap between poor and wealthy countries may also be diminished.

Biotechnology, I believe, does have a role to play in the improvements that could be made in a developing country. There are obvious examples which have been discussed earlier of applications at the village level for bio-gas production, of production of fuel (as ethanol) and of food. There are, however, less obvious ways in which biotechnology will improve the lives of those in Third World countries: provision of improved cultivars to improve agricultural yields, improved means of preventing illnesses endemic in many developing countries. All of these will, nevertheless, take money which is what developing countries need. Aid-programmes to transfer appropriate technology into developing countries are then essential and must, of course, be supported by training programmes to educate the future technicians and scientists.

The way in which alternative technologies may be transferred from a developed country to a developing one is not an easy or simple task. The mere telling, or showing, of a technique is not enough: advice offered in this way will almost certainly be scorned, not because it is wrong advice but because it comes from the wrong source in the wrong way. Experience has shown that change must come from within and the means of transferring the basic information must be to the educated people of the country who can see what benefits would accrue if the changes were to be made. In this regard, the industrialized societies must endeavour to influence the influential, to educate the educators and advise the advisors.

Biotechnology has much to offer for the economic and social benefit of all countries. All countries though are different and therefore their needs will be different. The future may not absolutely depend upon biotechnology but it will certainly be strongly influenced by it.

References and further reading

The astute reader who has read, or glanced through, this chapter will realize that there are no references. This does not mean to say that I have not consulted books, reviews and articles in the preparation of this synoptic view of biotechnology, but I have deliberately eschewed giving particular references as source material as these would be many and various and to give one source rather than another would, perhaps, be misleading. The following 'Further Reading' list covers those books or articles which readers may find helpful to amplify the various points I have been trying to make in this chapter. However, the best source of further reading are to be found within the various other chapters that go to make up this volume.

Of considerable importance in the future role of biotechnology in society are various discussion documents from the *Organization of Economic and Development* (2 Rue Andre-Pascal, 75775 Paris 16). The following two are the more recent publications.

Biotechnology and the Changing Role of Government, 1988; 148 pages. This report reviewed, during the course of 1986/87, the policies of 15 of OECD's 24 member countries as well as those of the European Community. The countries reviewed were: Australia, Austria, Belgium, Canada, Denmark, Finland, France, Germany, Italy, Japan, The Netherlands, Sweden, Switzerland and the United Kingdom.

Biotechnology: Economic and Wider Impacts, 1989; 106 pages. This report focuses on the likely impact that the 'new' biotechnology of recombinant DNA, cell-fusion and other breakthroughs of the last decade will have upon the social and economic developments within OECD countries. The report identifies the *pharmaceutical* sector as the first one that will benefit considerably by those new technologies. *Agriculture and farming* are also likely to be beneficiaries both with improved crops and transgenic animals becoming common-place by the end of the century. The *chemical* sector is unlikely to be much affected by these developments though there may be some small areas where benefit will accrue. The development of *environmental* uses of biotechnology – pollution control, waste treatment – is thought likely to be slow during the 1990s.

There are also a number of reports from the World Health Organization published in collaboration with the United Nations Environment programme. Their reports take the form of guidelines to deal with specific problems such as waste water treatment, sewage treatment and safeguarding the quality of drinking water in small rural communities. Although not overtly stressing the potential role of biotechnology, the most recent publication is *Guidelines for the safe use of waste water and excretia in agriculture and aquaculture* (prepared by D. Mara and S. Cairncross, WHO, 1989; 188 pages).

Cereal Crops for Industrial Use in Europe (by F. Rexen and L. Munch, 1984, EEC; EUR 9617 – EN). The concept of the total crop usage is developed at some length in strategic report prepared for the Director General XII (Biotechnology) of the European Community. In this report, the various strategies that could be adopted for total crop usage are developed. Biotechnology is acknowledged as having a key role to play but when other technologies could be better applied, in some instances to deal with considerable volumes of agriculture waste materials, these are also discussed and although the focus is very much a European one, there are examples that could be applied to most countries with advantage.

The concern over the formation of herbicide- and pesticide-resistant plants by genetic recombination is expressed very forcibly (perhaps some would say too forcibly) in the report *Biotechnology's bitter harvest: Herbicide-tolerant crops and the threat to sustainable agriculture*, published by the Biotechnology Working Group of the USA. An abbreviated statement was issued by Jane Rissler in *Chemistry & Industry* ('Biotechnology promise betrayed'), p. 500, (6 August) 1990.

A useful series of short articles that specifically dealt with the social impact of biotechnology appeared a little while ago in *Trends in Biotechnology* and, though now a little dated, are useful indicators of how thinking is being shaped. The articles are under the umbrella title of *The impact of biotechnology on living and working conditions* and appeared as a substantive part of the 1986 April issue. They include contributions by E. Yoxen (*Social impact of biotechnology* and is mainly concerned with health-care), G. Junne (*Impact of biotechnology on international trade* and includes likely effects on the third world), M. Kvistgaard (*Environmental issues* including the release of genetically-engineered organisms) and D. Mazzonis (on the implications that the biotechnology will have on work and employment).

Both *Trends in Biotechnology* and *Bio/Technology*, the monthly publication journals, frequently carry specific articles on the economic and social consequences that biotechnology is having in both developed and developing countries. However, the journal that carries a defined remit to encourage publication of such articles (as well as individual research papers) is the *World Journal of Microbiology and Biotechnology* (formerly *MIRCEN Journal of Applied Microbiology and Biotechnology*). This *Journal* was conceived and supported by both UNESCO and the International Union of Microbiological Societies. An issue of *MIRCEN Journal* (1988, volume 4, pp. 1–167) was devoted entirely to a description of bio-gas programmes throughout the world.

I can find no better publications to recommend than those of Carl-Goran Heden. Professor Heden has written prolifically on the social consequences of biotechnology particularly in the developing world. A useful summary of his most recent reports appears in the reference list of his most recent article: Potential of biotechnology, *Biotechnology Forum Europe* **7**, 387–90.

On the broader social implications that biotechnology has for the developed world, I would finally commend the publication *Biotechnology: Controlled Use of Biological Information*, E.H. Houwink, 1989, 121 pages, published by Kluwer Academic Publisher. (In this perspective view of biotechnology, Professor Houwink not only describes the principal features that mark today's biotechnology but goes on to speculate about its future role in fields such as microelectronics. There is a final telling chapter on the impact of biotechnology on society where the author attempts to ally the doubts and worries of a bemused public about the environmental consequences of biotechnology. He recognizes that the greatest dilemmas will come when the ability to manipulate human germ-like cells becomes a reality.)

2

Bioethanol production: economic and social considerations in failures and successes

F. ROSILLO-CALLE, D.O. HALL,
A.L. ARORA AND J.O.B. CARIOCA

Introduction

In the past decade world-wide interest in alcohol fuels, particularly bioethanol, has increased considerably. In developing countries this has been mainly due to the combination of low feedstock cost (sugarcane) and low sugar prices in the international market, and also for strategic reasons. In the industrial countries a major reason is the increasing environmental concern, and also as a way of solving wider socio-economic problems, such as agricultural land use and food surpluses.

Free-market microeconomics of bioethanol are still unfavourable relative to oil derived fuels, although there are many forms of renewable energy technologies which are now competitive in cost with nuclear and fossil fuels under specific conditions. There are also many non-economic factors (social, political, environmental, strategic) that should be considered. In addition, the use of renewable energy sources, contrary to conventional energy sources, produces very few or no external costs and may even cause positive external effects. The cost of bioethanol in the absence of direct or indirect subsidies still remains a serious obstacle to its widespread use. There are, however, a number of alternatives, including better use of by-products, that if pursued further could significantly reduce production costs.

Successes and failures in the bioethanol production and use are usually the consequence of a mixture of economic, political and technical reasons. Although economics play a significant role, it is often the case that clear political objectives and commitment will lead to success; the opposite usually results in failure. However, despite heavy government intervention, either directly or indirectly e.g. through regulation, taxation, subsidies, etc, too much government involvement will distort economics. Governmental intervention should be largely regulatory to create ideal conditions; the private sector should be directly involved.

This chapter analyses the main socio-economic factors and environmental implications of production and use of bioethanol fuel; it considers in some detail bioethanol fuel production and experiences in its use in the USA, Kenya, Malawi, Zimbabwe and Brazil, and the prospects for use of bioethanol in Europe.

Methanol, which can be obtained from biomass and coal, currently is produced from natural gas and has only been used for fuel for demonstration and racing purposes and thus will not be considered here. In addition, there is a growing consensus that methanol does not have all the environmental benefits that are commonly sought for oxygenates and which can be fulfilled by ethanol.

General considerations

Alcohols, particularly bioethanol, have the potential to revolutionize the supply and use of energy fuel in many parts of the world, particularly in transportation because (1) there is a variety of widely available raw materials from which alcohol can be made; (2) there exist improved and demonstrated technologies for the production and use of alcohol; (3) alcohols have favourable combustion characteristics, namely clean burning and high-octane-rated performance; and (4) positive environmental advantages, particularly with regard to the low release of CO_2, SO_2, particulates, unburnt hydrocarbons and CO.

The value of bioethanol is increasingly being recognized and policies to support development and implementation of ethanol as fuel are being introduced. World-wide fermentation ethanol capacity, for example, has increased eightfold since the 1970s to around 20 billion litres annually at the end of the 1980s. Policies toward bioethanol reflect the prevailing conditions in different countries.

Currently, ethanol is produced by both fermentation and synthetic methods. Fermentation techniques developed significantly during the early twentieth century, but by the 1950s many chemical production processes that were based on fermentation were replaced by synthetic processes based on crude oil. However, fermentation technology and efficiency have improved rapidly in the past decade and are undergoing a series of technical innovations aimed at using new alternative materials, and reducing costs, such as continuous conversion, increased density of bacteria or yeast inside the fermentation tank, high-density fermentation, bioreactors to immobilize the microbes, the reduced-pressure fermentation method, technology for energy reduction, new kinds of distillation, separation technology, etc. (Yasuhisa, 1989). Technological advances will, however, have less of an impact overall on market growth than will the increased availability and costs of feedstock and the cost-competing liquid fuel options.

The many and varied raw materials for bioethanol production can be conveniently classified into three types: (1) sugar (from sugarcane, sugar beet, fruit) which may be converted to ethanol directly; (2) starches (from grain, root crops) which must first be hydrolysed to fermentable sugars by the action of enzymes; and (3) cellulose (from wood, agricultural wastes, etc) which must be converted to sugars, probably by chemical or chemical and enzymatic means.

The production of ethanol by fermentation involves four major steps: (1) the growth, harvest and delivery of raw material to an alcohol plant; (2) the pre-treatment or conversion of the raw material to a substrate suitable for fermentation to ethanol; (3) fermentation of the substrate to alcohol, and purification by distillation; and (4) treatment of the fermentation residue to reduce pollution and to recover by-products.

Ethanol production by fermentation is based mainly on yeasts, and for large-scale fuel production these are generally of the genus *Saccharomyces*, although fungi and bacteria will also produce ethanol. A variety of systems based on batch, cascade or continuous processes are available. Continuous fermentation is already well established and has advantages over traditional batch systems in terms of such factors as fermenter size, high productivity and greater control. Ethanol is recovered almost exclusively by distillation: anhydrous ethanol is produced by a normal distillation followed by a secondary dehydration step. Under normal atmospheric conditions, ethanol forms an azeotrope with water at 95.6% (w/w) ethanol. With a second distillation a 99.5% (w/w) of ethanol is achieved (Rosillo-Calle, 1990).

Any source of hexose sugars can be used to produce ethanol, although a few such as sugarcane, maize, wood, cassava and sorghum and to a lesser extent grains and Jerusalem artichoke can actually be considered as serious contenders for ethanol production. Ethanol is also produced from lactose from waste whey. This process is used for example in Ireland to produce potable alcohol (the Carberry process) and also in New Zealand to produce fuel ethanol.

Sugarcane is the world's largest source of fermentation ethanol. Sugarcane is one of the most photosynthetic efficient plants – about 2.5% photosynthetic efficiency on an annual basis under optimum agricultural conditions. A further advantage is the production of bagasse as a by-product. An efficient ethanol distillery using sugarcane can be energy self-sufficient and also generate a surplus of electricity, in addition to CO_2, animal feeds and a range of chemical-based products. Generally, bagasse is still used very inefficiently, in many cases deliberately to prevent its accumulation. Studies with Biomass-Fired Integrated Gasification/Steam-Injected Gas Turbine (BIG/STIG) and also with Intercooled Steam-Injected Gas Turbine (ISTIG) demonstrated that the amount of electricity that could be produced from cane residues with (BIG/STIG) (460 kWh per tonne of cane) is more than 20 times the amount now produced at a typical sugar factory (20 kWh per tonne). This technology would make it possible for sugarcane producers to become major exporters of electricity. With regard to the sugarcane ethanol industry, it shows that for each litre of alcohol produced a BIG/ISTIG unit would be able to produce more than 11 kWh of electricity in excess of the distillery's needs (about 820 kWh per tonne). So much electricity would be generated that an alcohol/electricity co-production facility could produce electricity as the primary product and ethanol as a by-product (Williams, 1989). A further advantage of sugarcane is its energy output–input ratio, which is very positive (often 6:1 or greater) in comparison to other crops. A problem still to be overcome in some cases is the seasonability of crops; that means that quite often an alternative energy source must be found to keep a plant operating all-year around.

Socio-economic factors

The cost of producing biomass-based alcohols (particularly fuels) continues to be the main deterrent to further expansion, although one may argue that in many cases it is a problem of microeconomics. It is also often a problem of motivation and image. The image of biomass energy has been one of simple, even crude, technology applicable to the underdeveloped areas of the world at one end of the scale and of technological dreamers pursuing impossible goals at the other end. There are many non-economic factors, such as social, political, infrastructure, institutional etc., which also need to be considered.

There is no predetermined 'bioethanol cost' since it will vary between manufacturing plants. The cost of producing bioethanol depends on many different factors such as the location of the distillery, the design, type of raw materials utilized, the relative labour costs, the scale of production and the total investment. Cost estimates vary considerably and are not without controversy. These vary from $26 to 60 per barrel of oil-equivalent ethanol from sugarcane in Brazil, $60 in the US from maize, to $65 from grain in the EC.

There are a number of additional factors that can significantly influence the cost of ethanol production, including the use of by-products, technological advances, and market and institutional barriers. The use of by-products can have a major impact on ethanol production, depending on the choice of feedstock: higher-value by-products include other fermentation products, fermented animal feed or developed food products, energy, and fertilizers. Ethanol can also be produced as one of a number of co-products among which the raw materials and capital costs are shared. When maize is the feedstock, for example, the stock is hydrolysed to glucose which is then fermented to ethanol and CO_2, leaving a residue with the fibre, fat and protein of the original maize. Thus at the same time, maximum advantage can be taken of the feedstock, and environmentally related problems can be eliminated.

In the case of sugarcane, the potential for by-products has not yet been fully achieved, partly because sugarcane is a feedstock used in developing countries which often lack technical and financial capabilities. In Brazil, however, a multi-product industry is emerging based on 'sugarcane-alcohol-bagasse' products, that is having a major impact on ethanol costs.

Any bioethanol programme will need some kind of financial and economic incentives to succeed in the short term. Critics of renewable energy have argued against biomass energy because, they maintain, it needs large subsidies. In fact subsidies to promote energy and agricultural development are at the core of our economic system. Renewable energy sources receive low subsidies in comparison to conventional energy. In the USA, for example, in 1984 there were $44 billion subsidies for the commercial energy producers (equivalent to $523 for every household), against $1.7 billion for renewable energy (excluding hydro-electricity). In China, consumer subsidies for oil equal $5.4 billion, electricity subsidies $8.9 billion, and coal subsidies to $10.4 billion (Hall & Rosillo-Calle, 1990).

On the social side, a major criticism that has been made, particularly of those schemes for large-scale bioethanol fuel production, is that they could divert agricultural production away from food crops, especially in developing countries. The basic argument is that energy crop programmes compete with food crops in a number of ways (agricultural, rural investment, infrastructure, water, fertilizers, skilled manpower, etc.) and thus will cause food shortages and price increases. However, this so-called 'food versus fuel' controversy appears to have been exaggerated in many cases. The subject is far more complex than has generally been presented since agricultural and export policy and the politics of food availability are factors of far greater importance. The argument should be analysed against the background of the world's (or an individual country or regions) real food situation of food supply and demand, the use of food as animal feed, the under-utilized agricultural production potential, and the advantages and disadvantages of producing biofuels (Rosillo-Calle & Hall, 1987).

Political, social, institutional factors and market penetration barriers also play a key role in the development and introduction of a bioethanol fuel programme. Without the stabilizing influence of a coherent public sector, uncertainty in the market will be so great as to discourage investment in non-petroleum fuels. Until recently, the development of alternative transport fuels policy has seen emphasis placed on technical and economic issues. But governments are beginning to recognize the importance of 'non-technical' aspects of energy policy.

The government, in particular, needs to play a prime role in providing clear objectives and commitment, developing appropriate regulatory and legislative framework, providing financial and economic incentives, etc. The Brazilian and Zimbabwean cases have demonstrated the political issues, and the perseverance with which governments must act to assist the establishment of an alcohol fuel programme.

Environmental implications

Biomass is potentially an energy source which can yield significant environmental benefits and also a few problems.

The use of biomass can assist in mitigating the so-called greenhouse effect for several reasons.

(1) There is no net build-up of CO_2 in the atmosphere from the combustion of biomass, as the biomass itself is produced from CO_2, i.e. the same quantity of CO_2 that is released into the atmosphere on combustion is absorbed by the growing plants used to produce the fuel. Thus as the biomass being used is grown renewably, its use would lead to a net reduction in CO_2 emissions to the atmosphere as bioethanol would replace fossil fuels as a source of CO_2.

(2) Reforestation and afforestation can sequester significant quantities of carbon, by creating CO_2 'sinks' if the biomass involved in wood from fast-growing but long-lived trees. The result can be an extraction of CO_2 from the atmosphere associated with past CO_2 emissions.

(3) Modernization of bioenergy (the application of advanced technology to the process of converting raw biomass into modern, easy-to-use energy carriers, e.g. liquid or gaseous fuels, electricity, or processes solid fuels) should be an important element in a general strategy for coping with the possible global warming problem, because this strategy would offer multiple ancillary benefits, for developing and industrialized countries alike because it can be a powerful instrument to promote a sustainable development (Williams, 1989).

Despite many uncertainties with regard to possible climatic changes, there is a growing consensus which would argue that the world's climate can be stabilized only if global use of renewable energy increases from the present 20–21% to 40% by the year 2025 and 53% by the year 2050. Renewable energy in general will be cost effective with traditional forms of energy in the year 2000 (Scurlock & Hall, 1990; Shea, 1988).

On the negative side, bioenergy might cause serious environmental damage if feedstocks are not properly managed and there are inadequately controlled conversion technologies. The potential damage from biomass energy development includes substantial increase in soil erosion, damage to land and water resources, effects on ecosystems, local and air water pollution, occupational hazards, and possible misuse of ethanol (e.g. illicit drinking) etc. Serious soil erosion and the subsequent impact on land and water quality is a possible major consequence of an expansion of intensive agricultural production of the kind needed for biomass energy plantations.

Most of the environmental impacts of energy farming are comparable to those of food farming. Thus the impacts of biomass production for energy purposes can be considerable, particularly for soil quality and the resulting ecosystem changes. Biomass conversion and end-use impacts are in principle similar to fossil-fuel burning (i.e. air pollution and ash disposal problems), but some unique hazards depend on the biomass source (e.g. the formation of dioxin from solid waste) (OECD, 1988). Emissions from various conversion routes are illustrated in Table 2.1. However, it is important to note that a large proportion of the potential available biomass may be obtained with few adverse effects on the environment.

Bioethanol production

The environmental impact of ethanol can be divided into two main areas: (*a*) production, and (*b*) end-use. Each stage of the ethanol cycle has significant environmental effects that should be considered separately. The major possible causes of environmental pollution from ethanol production are the emissions associated with its substantial energy requirements, wastes from the distillation process and hazards associated with the use of toxic chemicals. Other emissions include dust from the raw materials and product handling, emissions from organic vapours from the distillation process and odours from the fermentation tanks.

Ethanol from agricultural crops is believed to have some advantage over gasoline regarding global warming, because growing plants remove CO_2 from the atmosphere. Marland & Turhollow (1989, personal communication) assumed that the emission of CO_2 to the atmosphere

Table 2.1. *Emissions from conversion and combustion of biomass resources per 10^{18} J*

	10^4 M t						10^6 M^3
	SO$_x$	NO$_x$	TSP	HCL	CO	HC	Waste water
Bioconversion processing[a]	9.9	5	0.33	—	—	—	—
Thermochemical conversion[b]	37	6.2–49	4.9	4.9	—	—	37–39
Incineration of MSW[c]	12	20	200	6.5	65	N.A.	87
RDF combustion for electricity[d]	260–540	65	6.5–65	4.8	29–32	3.6–7.1	—
MSW shredding	—	—	0.10	—	—	—	—
Industrial wood combustion[e]	5.6–9.5	37–64	19–95	—	7.5–390	N.A.	—
Residential wood combustion[f]	2.6	6.0	100	—	1900	N.A.	—

N.A., not applicable.
[a]Biogasification, ethanol fermentation. [b]Pyrolysis. [c]Waterwall incinerator. [d]Co-firing 10% RDF with coal. [e]75% efficiency to electricity and heat. [f]50% efficiency to heat.
Abbreviations: MSW, municipal solid wastes; TSP, total soluble particles; RDF, residue derived fuel.
Source: OECD, 1988.

from burning ethanol as a fuel would be equalled by the capture of CO_2 from the atmosphere by the growing plants (in this case maize). Thus, 'if ethanol production from maize were completed in an essentially closed cycle whereby the growing plant removed CO_2 from the atmosphere, some parts of the plant were consumed to provide energy from conversion of other parts of the plant to ethanol, and the resultant ethanol was burned to provide useful energy and return CO_2 to the atmosphere, there would be no net emission of CO_2'. They estimated that the CO_2 emissions attributable to the production and consumption of ethanol from maize by current practices in the US is equivalent to 8.10 kg of carbon per 10^9 joules of ethanol. This compares with an average of 22.29 kg of carbon per 10^9 joules for liquid fuels from crude oil. Thus ethanol yields 26.9% as much CO_2 as gasoline on a volume basis, or 40.9% as much on the basis of energy content.

However, some critics have some doubts on these findings. Ho (1989) estimates that ethanol yields 81% as much CO_2 as gasoline on a volume basis but, more importantly, yields 23% more CO_2 than gasoline on an energy content basis. Marland & Torhollow's (1989) findings appear to be a reasonable preliminary estimate as to the CO_2 emissions to the atmosphere, and hence as to the potential contribution to global warming, from using ethanol as a fuel, compared with that of gasoline. However, these calculations do show that CO_2 emissions associated with the use of ethanol as a fuel, although definitely less than gasoline, are not zero, as some ethanol advocates have implied. The processing needed, first to grow the plants and then to extract ethanol from that plant, accounts for these CO_2 emissions.

Many of the impacts of ethanol production will depend, however, more on such factors as the design and operation of plants and on legislation than any other inevitable problems with the production process. This contrasts favourably with many other polluting industries.

The by-products of ethanol production depend on the nature of the raw material, the harvesting method, the type of the pre-treatment and the fermentation process. The main by-products are stillage, CO_2 and fuel oils. Stillage is the most important waste stream. It is a low-solids liquid waste having a high biological oxygen demand (BOD) and also a high chemical oxygen demand (COD), and contains as well as organic residues, inorganic solids and other pollutants.

Stillage and other wastes from ethanol plants can cause serious damage to aquatic ecosystems if they are mishandled; the high BOD and COD levels in the stillage could result in oxygen depletion in any waters receiving the waste. Control technologies are available for reducing the impacts from these waste streams: biological treatment methods such as biological filters, anaerobic digestion, stillage recycling, etc.

Unfortunately, a proliferation of ethanol plants does not provide a favourable setting for the careful monitoring of environmental conditions, nor the enforcement of the environmental protection requirements, particularly in developing countries. This problem is further complicated by the fact that many such plants may be located in remote rural areas where access is difficult, although this means that total population exposure to any harmful pollutants is reduced.

The by-products can be regarded as a waste to be disposed of either as a process fuel or as a saleable by-product. The value of by-products and/or the cost of disposal of waste can have a major impact on the economics of bioethanol production. For example, when maize is used, as in the USA, the stillage is the source of DDG (Distillers' Dried Grains), which is a valuable cattle feed essential to the economics of the process. In Brazil, stillage is increasingly being used as a substitute for chemical fertilizers in sugarcane fields, particularly in the state of São Paulo, with increase in productivity of 20–30%.

Bioethanol: end use

The use of alcohol fuels and gasoline–alcohol blends in automobiles will have a number of environmental impacts associated with changes in automotive emissions as well as differences in the toxicity and handling characteristics of the fuels. The effects of alcohol–gasoline blends on automobile emissions also depend on how the engine is tuned and whether or not it has a carburettor with feedback control.

Because the emission changes are extremely mixed, it is difficult to assign clearly either a beneficial or detrimental net pollution effects of these blends. In contrast, the use of pure alcohols as gasoline substitutes will generally have a positive effect on emissions. Office of Technology Assessment (1980) experimental data indicate (1) a substantial reduction in reactive hydrocarbons and nitrogen oxide exhaust emissions when using 100% methanol, and to a lesser extent when using ethanol; (2) an increase in aldehyde emissions with neat alcohol and blends; (3) a substantial reduction in particulate emissions if neat alcohol fuels are used; and (4) a substantial reduction in polynuclear aromatic compounds with neat alcohols and blends.

Table 2.2 shows Environmental Protection Agency's (EPA) estimates of potential reductions in volatile organic compounds, CO and emission of nitric and nitrous oxides (NO_x) for several types of light-duty vehicles operating on methanol, compressed natural gas and oxygenated blends.

Hydrocarbon emissions from ethanol are not fully established, as there is a wide scattering of emission data. Most of the literature indicates, however, that hydrocarbon and CO emissions are reduced, and that NO_x emission may or may not be reduced, depending on the vehicle under test. In Brazil, which has pioneered large-scale ethanol fuel use and the substitution of lead in gasoline, data confirm the advantages of ethanol (Table 2.3). Although estimates vary because of the different methodologies employed, most findings indicate positive environmental effects of ethanol fuels. In Argentina, results with 15% (v/v) addition of ethanol to gasoline blend show a 50% reduction of CO emissions, 35% reduction of lead emissions, and 34% decrease of hydrocarbon emissions (Gotelli, 1988).

Table 2.2. *Emission reduction potential of light-duty vehicles (per-vehicle basis compared to gasoline vehicles meeting current standards)*

	VOC	CO	NO$_x$
Methanol			
FFV (M85)	−(20 to 50)%	0	0
Current technology	−(20 to 50)%	0	0
Advanced technology[a]	−(85 to 95)%	−(30 to 90)%	0
CNG			
FFV/Retrofit[a]	−(50 to 80)%	−(50 to 90)%	−20% to +80%
Advanced technology[a]	−(50 to 90)%	−(50 to 90)%	−20% to +80%

	Oxygenated blends		
VOC	Ethanol	Methanol	MTBE[b]
Constant RVP	−2% to +5%	−5% to +5%	−1%
1 Psi higher	+15% to +35%	+9% to +30%	N.A.
CO	Ethanol, methanol (3.7% Oxygen)		MTBE (2% Oxygen)
Non-catalyst	−18%		−10%
Open loop	−30%		−16%
Closed loop	−10%		−5%
NO$_x$			
Open loop	+5%		+3%
Closed loop	+6%		+3%

[a]Projections based on very small databases; CNG vehicles also typically experience a loss in power and performance.
[b]Unlike ethanol and methanol, MTBE does not appear to significantly increase the RVP of gasoline.
N.A., not applicable.
Abbreviations: VOC, volatile organic compounds; MTBE, methyl tertiary butyl ether; CNG, compressed natural gas; FFV, flexible fuel vehicles.
Source: EPA, 1987.

With regard to health and safety, the use of alcohol fuels does not suggest that they are inherently unsafe to use. Many toxic substances may be produced and handled during biomass commercial operations; accidental releases of these materials could pose a significant health hazard in the vicinity of conversion facilities. Fermentation plant workers may be affected by prolonged or accidental exposure to the toxic and corrosive chemicals employed (OECD, 1988).

Table 2.3. *Effect of alcohol on pollutant emissions in motors (qm/km)*

Emission	Gasoline	Alcohol–Gasoline mixture 20% (v/v)	Variation (%)	Hydrated alcohol	Variation (%)
CO	49.37	20.62	−58	17.0	−66
HC	3.32	2.44	−26	2.50	−25
NO$_x$	1.86	2.86	+54	1.66	−11
Formaldehyde	0.05	0.07	+40	0.04	−20

Source: Alvin, 1986.

Nonetheless, the toxic effects of ethanol and methanol are considered to be less hazardous than those of gasoline and gasoline components. For example, comparative biological experiments conducted on toxicity and prolonged exposures of car exhaust gases with rats, have showed a mean survival time of 6 minutes for gasoline against 255 minutes to ethanol (Bohm *et al.*, 1988). Alcohol fuels also appear to be less toxic than oil in the initial acute phase of spills and seem to have fewer long-term effects. Bioethanol is completely biodegradable and any toxic effects may be eliminated in hours, whereas the effect of fuel oils can last for years.

European community (EC)

The production of bioethanol has been at the centre of the political argument in the EC for over a decade. Numerous studies have concluded that, although production is technically possible, there is no economic justification for a large ethanol fuel programme. However, persisting over-supplies of food and its increasing costs has brought about a rethinking on agriculture which, together with an increasing environmental concern is forcing the EC to reconsider the bioethanol option once more.

Biomass energy production and use is increasingly seen as being closely linked to solving agricultural problems of land use, food surpluses and forestry. The EC is faced with the need to adjust its agricultural policy in order to achieve a number of objectives difficult to reconcile: disposing of surplus stocks and preventing their re-emergence; avoiding disturbance to the international agricultural markets; maintaining individual farm incomes; conserving the fabric of rural society;

and protecting the natural environment. As production and productivity are increasing steadily alongside a proportionally slower population increase, and as there is not likely to be any significant overall increase in either exports – due to high production costs – or local demand within the EC, new alternatives must be found.

At present, biomass contributes only just over 2.5% of the EC's primary energy needs, i.e. 25 M tonne oil equivalent (toe) per year mainly coming from non-commercial energy such as firewood and charcoal. Biomass, however, contributes about 50% of the industrial needs (e.g. pulp for paper, boards, timber, etc.). Biomass for energy has a great potential in the EC and stands at about 6000 M tonnes (dry matter) per year. Large-scale exploitation of biomass presents the following major benefits: a potential energy contribution of about 10% of primary energy needs (100 M toe); the potential creation of 600 000 new jobs; and becoming an important instrument for rural development, improvement of the environment and the quality of life (Grassi, 1989; Hall & Rosillo-Calle, 1989).

As yet there is no significant use of bioethanol fuel in the EC. Unlike Brazil, bioethanol production and use in the EC would be on a far smaller scale and mainly as octane boosters for environmental reasons. Although the EC programme required lead-free gasoline to be available in all member countries from 1989 onwards, it seems likely that for a variety of reasons the ultimate goal of a totally unleaded gasoline market may not be achieved before the end of this century despite all the environmental concerns. There exist too many different approaches at government levels so that progress is likely to be extremely slow. The long phase-out programme gives oil refiners ample opportunity to revamp, or to add to, their production capacity, allowing refiners to produce lead-free and low-lead gasoline to current specifications. It seems that the refining industry will not be faced with an octane deficiency throughout the rest of the decade. This is not being helped by the continuing low political priority being given to bioethanol. The production of bioethanol on a large scale would require the establishment of a new industrial process involving major investment. Any substantial new investment to produce ethanol is essentially political, and this is not likely to be achieved easily, given that at present there is no consensus among members states.

The underlying reasons are economic ones and, arguably, political ones too. There is disagreement as to the real cost of ethanol production and the cost of the subsidies required to enable bioethanol to compete in the transport fuel market. According to Marrow, Coombs & Lees (1987), under prevailing market conditions and without subsidies, bioethanol cannot compete as transport fuel until crude oil prices reach

$55–65 per barrel. A *Cost/Benefit Analysis of the Production and Use of Bioethanol* in the EC (see Anon., 1987) concluded that a sustained increase in the real prices of oil to $30–40 per barrel, or a reduction in the unit production costs of feedstock for bioethanol production of 35–45% would be required to bring about economic viability. The study also showed that a subsidy of between 872 and 920 ECU would be required to make a Bioethanol Programme attractive for the financial investors. In comparison with other potential forms of land use, the subsidy required for a Bioethanol Programme was substantially greater than for other forms of land use capable of utilizing areas of land comparable in size to a large Bioethanol Programme, namely 1.1 M ha (Anon., 1987).

The projected potential for bioethanol, based on a projected gasoline demand of about 95 M tonnes in the 1990s, is estimated to be up to 2.5 M tonnes and 1.1 M ha based on a low-price/high-volume strategy. This would require a quantity of 8.5 M tonnes of wheat in the year 2000. For combined plants (wheat and beet), the corresponding figures are 0.7 M ha to 5.7 M tonnes of wheat and 0.2 M ha to 10.5 M tonnes of sugar beet.

Alternatively, however, a strategy of high-price/low-volume could be adopted on the basis of small-scale bioethanol plants located near to refineries identified as having problems in RON (Road Octane Number) requirements. During the 1990s this strategy could aim at a market of up to 0.6 M tonnes of bioethanol, at a pricing level of 100–120% of premium gasoline. But in order to achieve a significant market penetration, it is highly probable that ethanol would have to be priced at levels below the 80–90%, or even as low as 60–70%, (w/w) of premium gasoline prices in order to gain substantial market share from the existing oxygenates and from captive sources of octane. The total financial support required is estimated at 608–1013 M ECU in the year 2000 (Anon., 1987).

The potential benefits of a large bioethanol programme (2.5 M tonnes) could include the following benefits: (1) generation of about 0.6 M tonnes of EP2 vinasse (sugar substrate obtained after the second crystallization) and 2.1 M tonnes of DDGS (Distillers' Dried Grains and Solubles), co-products which constitute an excellent animal feed of which the EC imports 25 M tonnes per annum; (2) the creation of between 23 000 and 40 000 jobs in the rural areas; and (3) environmental benefits. Environmental impacts would, however, be positive as well as negative. The adverse effects would be those associated with the ethanol plants. On the positive side, the positive effects on the atmosphere would be due to the replacement of lead in petroleum fuels.

It is of no single interest to set up a fuel ethanol industry assured of public subsidy. But if bioethanol may not seem to be a short-term option in the EC, the door must be kept open so that the EC remains in a position to exploit the ethanol opportunity when it becomes politically and economically viable. Without the possibility of a Bioethanol Programme, there is little commercial incentive to continue to breed new varieties of existing plant species and to research new species to minimize feedstock costs. It seems clear that it is a question of time before bioethanol makes economic sense since oil prices will increase in real terms in the future, and the unit price of biomass feedstock will fall due to the impact of technology. Eventually these two factors will combine to ensure that bioethanol makes economic sense.

Overall, bioethanol production and use has been at the centre of the political argument in the EC for over a decade and no decision is likely in the very near future. However, bioethanol is increasingly being considered as closely linked with solving agricultural problems of land use and the environment. High costs and political inconsistency among the member countries has been so far the main stumbling-block to introduce a large-scale Bioethanol Programme in the EC. But increasing concern with the environment, the need to preserve the fabric of the rural society, and persistent food surpluses, together with a growing perception that oil prices will eventually increase in real terms, and that biotechnological developments will reduce the costs of biomass feedstock, may tip the balance in favour of bioethanol in the not too distant future. When that occurs bioethanol production and use will receive a great boost.

The USA

The passage of the Energy Act of 1978 announced the political birth of fuel ethanol in the USA. The Act provided economic incentives for the production of liquid fuels from solid fossil fuels and renewable energy sources and was further consolidated by the Windfall Tax Act of 1980 which included the temporary gasoline exception up to 1992 and offered further encouragement to prospective producers. The key incentive was the exemption from the Federal Motor Excise Tax of $0.04 per gallon of ethanol, which for a 10% ethanol in gasoline blend amounted to $0.40 per gallon of ethanol. Ethanol production in 1986 benefited from a $0.60 per gallon Federal Tax Subsidy, and subsidies from some 30 states ranges ffrom $0.10 to $1.40 per gallon (Grinnell, 1987).

The US ethanol industry has evolved rapidly (see Table 2.4). In 1986, 3.5 billion litres were consumed, primarily as a gasoline extender, and the production reached 3.2 billion litres of ethanol. The balance is usually imported from the Caribbean and Brazil. The production

Table 2.4. *Production and consumption of ethanol fuel in the USA (million litres)*

Year	Production	Consumption
1978	38	—
1979	76	—
1980	152	420[a]
1981	284	416
1982	795	852
1983	1419	1628
1984	1643	1942
1986	3200	3320
1990	5600[b]	3800[a]
1995	10 670[b]	—

[a]Estimated. [b]Estimated installed capacity.
Sources: Klausmeier, 1987; Ahmed *et al.*, 1989.

capacity for 1990 is estimated at 5.63 billion litres and that projected for 1995, 10.67 billion litres (Ahmed, Rask & Baldwing, 1989).

Bioethanol gas gained recognition as an effective octane enhancer, rather than merely as an extender for gasoline, making it a major potential source to replace lead together with methyl tertiary butyl ether (MTBE). President Bush's proposals to overhaul the antiquated Clean Air Act of 1970 requiring the gradual introduction of cars built to run on so-called 'clean fuels', will strengthen further the role of ethanol. The proposals call to make 0.5 million alternate-fuel cars by 1995, and 1 million annually from 1997. The recently enacted Alternative Motor Fuels Act of 1988, intended to promote the use of methanol, ethanol and compressed natural gas, requires the Environment Protection Agency to perform a study, to be completed by December 1990, of the environmental effects that would result from using these fuels, including their effects on global warming.

During the early 1980s, a major objective was to reduce dependence on foreign supplies of energy. The prospect of using surplus maize as a feedstock provided an important agricultural industry support. While the recent decline in oil prices may well have dampened the prospect of ethanol as a gasoline replacement in the short term, environmental regulations to reduce, and eventually eliminate, the lead content in gasoline will boost bioethanol as an octane source. A recent study (Anon., 1988) reveals that many opportunities exist for improving the operation and market environment for oxygenated and ethanol-blended fuels. The major factors for an improved environment include new octane requirements in the motor fuel marketplace, demand to improve air quality, and focused federal government attention on instituting public policy initiatives which can reduce dependence on foreign oil importation and lessen subsidies paid for agriculture programmes, particularly that for maize. On balance, the report finds that market forces will improve favourably for ethanol-blended gasoline, and the public policy rationale exists to encourage the greater production and marketing of ethanol-blended gasoline, ETBE (ethyl tertiary butyl ether) and neat methanol.

The most significant of these new environmental requirements has been the shift required by the Environment Protection Agency for automobiles to use unleaded gasoline. A radical change, which began with gradual decreases in lead levels in the mid-1970s, was capped by the 91% reduction to (0.1 g per leaded gallon) which took full effect on 1 January 1988.

Production costs of ethanol from maize remain high. Estimates by Ahmed *et al.* (1989) indicate that at maize prices of $59.05–65.90 per tonne and oil prices of $16–26 per barrel, a subsidy of $0.07–0.105 per litre would be necessary for ethanol to compete with other ethanol enhancers. At a maize price of $68.90 per tonne, oil price of $20 per barrel and by-product prices of $105 per tonne, the average cost for manufacturing ethanol is estimated at $0.319 per litre. This compares with production cost of MTBE of $0.12–0.178 per litre (in 1988), of which the USA produces 3.5×10^9 litres per year. Thus maize-based ethanol would require subsidies in the range of $0.08–0.12 per litre to compete with MTBE. And with maize prices at $39.37 per tonne, a subsidy of $0.039 per litre is sufficient to make USA maize ethanol competitive with imported ethanol at oil prices of $20 or less (Ahmed *et al.*, 1989).

Despite the improved prospect for ethanol production in the USA, some critics see the ethanol industry as being unable to survive through to 1995 without very large government subsidies, unless a world oil market disturbance causes a sharp increase in oil prices. They regard ethanol production as an efficient use of resources and the only compelling argument for subsidizing ethanol is that petroleum prices might increase faster than the forecasts (Grinnell, 1987).

Ethanol production shifts subsidy costs from agriculture to the ethanol industry. It has little effect on total government costs since the subsidy needs of the ethanol industry about equal the expected savings in agricultural costs, resulting in no gain to the government (Grinnell, 1987). The USA made idle a total of over 69 million acres (27.92 M ha) of agricultural land in 1987 as part of cropland retirement programme, which represents about 15% of the total crop acreage.

It seems clear that the free-market economics of grain fuel ethanol are still unfavourable relative to oil-derived fuels. However, there are many other factors to be considered – political, social, strategic, and so on, which often tend to be overlooked. For example, the USA military expenditure committed to protecting the sea lanes for petroleum import (in 1984) amounted to more than double the world market price for every barrel actually imported from overseas. *The storage and interest costs of maintaining the USA strategic petroleum reserves in 1984 were five times greater than the tax incentives granted for the entire fuel ethanol industry* (Schwandt, 1984).

Overall, unlike the EC, the USA has considerable experience with alcohol fuels, particularly bioethanol from maize. There is a political commitment together with financial and economic incentives to alternative fuels – the passage of the Energy Act of 1978 and the Alternative Motor Fuels Act of 1988 are good examples. Radical new environmental requirements began in the mid-1970s with gradual phasedowns in lead levels, which have demanded an increasing production and use of bioethanol. At present the free-market economics of grain ethanol are still unfavourable relative to oil-derived fuels and some kind of subsidy would have to continue in the near future. But there are many other factors to be taken into consideration, not least of which is the huge military expenditure involved in protecting the sea lanes for the importation of petroleum.

African experience

Alcohol fuels have been aggressively pursued in a number of African countries currently producing sugar – Zimbabwe, Kenya, Malawi, and the Republic of South Africa. Others with great potential include Mauritius, Swaziland and Zambia. Some countries have modernized their sugar industry and have low production costs. Many of these countries are landlocked, which means that it is not feasible to sell molasses as a by-product on the world market, while oil imports are also very expensive and suggested to disruption. A major objective of these programmes is the diversification of the sugarcane industry, displacement of energy imports and better resources and, indirectly, better environmental management. These conditions, combined with relatively low total demand for liquid transportation fuels, makes ethanol fuel most attractive to many parts of Africa.

For example, in Mauritius, almost 60% of its total energy requirements (excluding wood fuels primarily used for cooking) are met by bagasse-fired generation of power and steam in the sugarcane industry. Sugarcane accounts for nearly 20% of the country's gross domestic product (GDP) and over 40% of its export earnings. The economy is thus quite sensitive to fluctuations in domestic sugar production and world sugar markets.

In Swaziland the sugar industry is also the country's most important industrial and agricultural enterprise, accounting for 25% of the GDP. Swaziland offers an unusual opportunity for fuel ethanol. It is a landlocked country that suffers from expensive, and often unreliable, rail service to Indian Ocean seaports. It has a large surplus of low-value molasses and cheap labour (Steingass *et al.*, 1988). The Republic of South Africa has also realized an ethanol fuel programme using both agriculturally and synthetically derived ethanol. There are some 3–4 million cars running on ethanol/gasoline blend of between 8 and 12% (v/v).

Kenya

In the 1970s, the combination of high oil prices, the dramatic fluctuations of world molasses prices and the sharp rise in transport costs conspired to create the economic and political conditions to set up a bioethanol programme in Kenya.

Currently the Muhoroni plant near Kisuma, with a capacity of 60 000 litres per day, produces all of Kenya's ethanol using sugarcane molasses. At present the plant operates at 75% of its capacity. It is an integrated sugar–ethanol plant which also produces 4 tonnes of baker's yeast per day. Unlike Zimbabwe, the first ethanol projects in Kenya were plagued with difficulties. Initially there was a project to build two plants – the Madhvani and the Muhoroni. The Madhvani plant was never completed for a number of techno-economic and political reasons. The plant was costly and sophisticated and took little advantage of the local conditions. The Muhoroni plant was completed in 1983.

In Kenya, due to lack of access to information and untied finance, the choice of technology in the international market was severely constrained and the resulting technology chosen was quite sophisticated and capital intensive. The government was heavily involved financially (and politically) in the project and this influenced a number of decisions. This was further complicated by the absence of a clear and cohesive long-term government policy (Stuckey & Juma, 1985).

Malawi

Malawi is a small landlocked country entirely dependent upon an agricultural economy for its export earnings. Malawi has been at the forefront of fuel ethanol development. A major reason for fuel ethanol has been the continuous deterioration of the regional transport system and the uneasy security with Mozambique, both of which have caused frequent petrol shortages.

Malawi commenced its bioethanol programme in 1982, utilizing ethanol from a distillery located at Dwangwa sugar mill with a capacity to produce 10 M litres per year. The Ethco (Ethanol Company Ltd) produces ethanol from molasses and some raw sugar efficiently and profitably. Ethco has also provided the driving force for exploration of wider applications of ethanol as neat fuel, diesel fuel substitute and illumination fuel for paraffin lamps, and has sought to expand the options for feedstock with work on cassava and wood chips.

Ethco currently produces ethanol to supply a national blend of 15% (v/v) ethanol, which could easily be increased to 20%. A production of 20 M litres per year could be achieved with minimal capital investment by operating the present fermentation/distillation plant all the year around. A further option under consideration is the contraction of a second plant near the Sucoma estate whose by-product molasses are of little or no opportunity value. The potential exists to double ethanol production immediately and, in the longer term, to produce sufficient to displace the country's entire gasoline import. The annual demand is approximately 60 M litres of gasoline and 80 M litres of diesel oil (Moncrieff & Walker, 1988).

If extended applications of neat ethanol, now being tested in a small fleet (approximately 1500) of government Land Rovers, indicate that only a modest substitution of diesel fuels in transportation and agriculture can be achieved, Malawi could displace as much as 10–20 M litres of imported petroleum with ethanol in the medium term.

In terms of feedstock for new ethanol production in Malawi, a report (Steingass et al., 1988) estimates that surplus molasses and those sugars sold at world market prices will be the lowest-cost feedstock; these would yield approximately twice the current production of ethanol. Beyond this level alternative feedstocks must be considered if the ethanol market expands sufficiently.

A much longer-term alternative under consideration is the production of fermentable wood sugars from the wood wastes derived from the silviculture activities in the Viphya forest, in the north of the country. It is estimated that the zero-value resource could provide sufficient fermentable feedstock for the production of a further 50 M litres of ethanol per year (Moncrieff & Walker, 1988).

In summary, the main reasons for setting up a bioethanol programme were the continued deterioration and insecurity of oil supply, strategic considerations and the availability of low cost feedstock. Like Zimbabwe, the use of unsophisticated technology suitable to the local conditions also played a role in the success of the programme. Political support again though has been vital for success.

Zimbabwe

Zimbabwe pioneered production of fuel ethanol for blending with gasoline in 1980. Molasses was used most exclusively for ethanol fermentation at Triangle plant. Zimbabwe's landlocked position, the political vulnerability of its supply routes, foreign exchange limitations and strategic considerations were all major factors in the development of an indigenous fuel ethanol industry. Annually, 40 M litres have been produced since 1983, sufficient now to give a 13–14% (v/v) blend with gasoline. Zimbabwe's current annual consumption of motor gasoline is about 1.85 M barrels. The country has no oil resources and all petroleum products must be imported, accounting for nearly $120 M per annum on average in recent years. Plans for an expansion of 35 M litres per year are well under way. Current production cost is approximately $0.75 per gallon (Steingass *et al.*, 1988) which indicates at least a break-even with landed gasoline imports when compared with local molasses of approximately $25 per tonne.

Zimbabwe's sugar industry consists of two private sugar companies, Hippo Valley Estates Ltd and Triangle Ltd, both located in the southeast low-veld of the country. Together they operate two of the world's most efficient irrigated sugarcane estates and factories. Each grows and processes approximately 2 M tonnes of cane per year, capable of producing over 0.5 M tonnes of sugar. Zimbabwe exports some 240 000 tonnes of sugar (1986) which constitutes the country's ninth largest hard currency earner.

The ethanol plant at Triangle is an example of a biomass-to-energy system which has operated successfully for almost a decade. The plant has been locally planned, with local control over its running. The benefits thereafter accrue locally. There was considerable cooperation between the various parties involved with very few external constraints and the industry was able to select low-cost technology closely tailored to the industry's needs. Instead of importing distillery components, the locally available fabrication structure was exploited to supply 80% of the parts. By using this approach, Zimbabwe was able to build an ethanol plant with 42 M litres per year capacity at a capital cost of $6.4 M (at 1980 prices) which is among the world's lowest for this type of plants. As Wenman (1985, personal communication) puts it 'In a developing country, it was necessary to design and build a plant appropriate to the abilities of the people who were to run it . . .' (also Scurlock, Rosenschein & Hall, 1989, personal communication).

Zimbabwe is an example of a relatively small country that has begun to tackle its energy import problem without incurring environmental penalties while fostering its own agro-industrial base. The very survival of this project demonstrates that it has fulfilled the important criteria of involvement with local security, industry and agriculture. Indeed, local motivation seems to underpin every aspect of biomass energy at Triangle (Scurlock *et al.*, 1989).

The Triangle plant The plant was opened in October 1980. The entire production of ethanol has been sold to the state-controlled National Oil Corporation of Zimbabwe. Gasoline and ethanol prices, as well as profit margins for gasoline wholesalers and retailers, are fixed by the government.

Triangle has about 13 000 ha of sugarcane, yielding on average 115 tonnes of cane (fresh weight) per ha. About 1.9 M tonnes of cane are crushed every year to make the equivalent of 200 000 tonnes of sugar after ethanol production is taken into account.

The Triangle ethanol plant enjoys an advantage over the typical annex molasses-to-ethanol plant built in other locations, which can operate only during the harvest season. During the off-season at Triangle, it is more economical to generate electricity from coal-fired boilers than to purchase electricity from the grid to operate irrigation pumps. The ethanol plant thus serves as a condenser for the electrical turbines, thereby operating in what would otherwise be waste steam. This system permits year-around ethanol production (330 days average), reducing investment and operating costs. Seasonal inventory accumulation costs are also avoided. These factors also make it economically feasible to operate on purchased molasses during the off-season (Steingass *et al.*, 1988).

The plant was also designed to operate on a variety of feedstock using different grades of molasses, cane juice, or even raw sugar itself. This flexibility means that the plant is fully integrated with the rest of the sugar production process and can respond rapidly to changes. Thus the fermentable sugar content, for example, of molasses entering the plant can be adjusted at the expense of sugar production, depending on relative market prices, in order to maximize the return on total investment in both sugar and ethanol production.

The stillage is pumped from the distillation plant on to the surrounding cane fields which are continually irrigated, allowing the stillage to be diluted between 30- and 400-fold with irrigation water and use as fertilizer substitute. At present, 7500 ha of sugarcane receive stillage diluted on average 200-fold. The total value of potassium (K) alone of Triangle stillage has been estimated at more than $1.1 M per year. On average, treatment with diluted stillage has caused a 7% increase in the yields of the two main cane cultivars grown at Triangle. Stillage disposal at Triangle has thus become a carefully monitored recycling of nutrients.

Over the first three years of operation, the ethanol production cost was around $0.35–0.40 per litre, compared with a 'landed' cost of gasoline in Harare of $0.50 per litre. Ethanol therefore cost 11–27% more than gasoline in terms of energy content, but this was paid for entirely in domestic currency once the initial foreign exchange investment had been recouped. Foreign exchange savings depend, however, upon the world market price for sugar at which the marginal extra sugar would be sold if it were not converted to ethanol. In 1984, one tonne of sugar, equivalent to 623 litres of ethanol, would have saved $275 worth of gasoline at $0.70 per litre. At the prevailing world sugar price of $130 per tonne and transport costs of $55 per tonne, exportation of sugar would raise only $75 per tonne. Thus the foreign exchange saving under these conditions was $200 per tonne of sugar converted to ethanol. In 1989 gasoline costs were only $0.50 per litre and the world sugar price had reached $300 per tonne (say $200 per tonne net of transport from Triangle). The ethanol equivalent of one tonne of sugar now saves $196 worth of gasoline, so there is no net gain in foreign exchange (Scurlock *et al.*, 1989). This, however, must be counterbalanced with the volatility of the international sugar and oil prices, supply problems and transport difficulties. There is also the possibility of using neat alcohol to replace gasoline and also of using ethanol to replace diesel fuel in the not too distant future.

Summing up, the Triangle ethanol project was a move to introduce diversity into the national economy in order to reduce the perturbance of economic stability by outside forces. It sets an example of technological initiative to increase biomass energy use and achieve some degree of energy independence, providing at the same time valuable experience for other countries wishing to diversify their own sugar industry. It offers an example of good use of simple technology and local infrastructure and political commitment. Zimbabwe has gained considerable experience in the building of fermentation and biotechnological industries. At current sugar and oil prices, ethanol costs fractionally more than imported gasoline but when strategic advantage gained from greater liquid fuel self-sufficiency is taken into consideration, the balance is firmly in favour of national alcohol production. Economic considerations alone should not be considered in isolation.

In conclusion, despite the initial similarities in their socio-economic setting and plant-specific technical parameters, Kenya followed different implementation routes to Malawi and Zimbabwe with sharply different results. The Madhvani project in Kenya was approved by the government without adequate evaluation of the key adaptive con-

46   *F. Rosillo-Calle and others*

ditions. For example, the availability of raw material before the project was approved, unlike Malawi and Zimbabwe, where the availability of molasses was guaranteed before construction was started.

Whereas in Kenya, which involved state equity participation (over 50%), the Zimbabwe and Malawai projects were entirely privately funded. In Zimbabwe and Malawi the state largely played a regulatory role to create the ideal conditions for the project to succeed, while in Kenya the government invested large sums of money but did much less in ensuring economic viability (Juma, 1986).

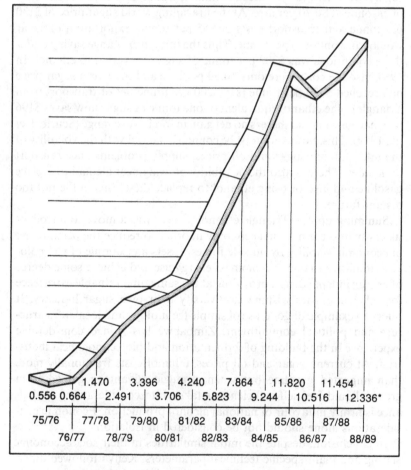

Fig. 2.1. Production of bioethanol (million litres) in Brazil for the period 1975/6–1988/9 (Anon., 1989a). The asterisk indicates authorized production.

Latin America

Latin America, dominated by Brazil, is the world's largest production region of bioethanol. There are many countries which are seriously considering the bioethanol option – Costa Rica, Honduras, Paraguay, Bolivia, etc. (see Rosillo-Calle, 1990). Countries such as Brazil and Argentina already produce large amounts of ethanol. Argentina set up the 'Plan Nacional de Alconafta' in 1982 which blends 15% of anhydrous ethanol with gasoline. The total installed capacity in 1984 was 380 M litres per year.

Brazil

Brazil is the world's largest producer of bioethanol, some 11.5 billion litres (about 200 000 barrels per day equivalent of gasoline per day) were produced in 1988 alone (see Figs 2.1 and 2.2). For 1989, the estimate is 12.33 billion litres. Since the creation of the National Alcohol Programme (ProAlcool) in 1975, Brazil has produced over 80 000 M litres of ethanol from sugarcane (approximately 446 M litres of gasoline equivalent). The installed capacity in 1988 was over 16 billion litres distributed over 661 projects (Anon., 1989*b*). In the 1983/84 harvest the total amount of sugar crushed was 198 M tonnes, of which 92.8 M tonnes were for ethanol production (47%); and in 1987/88 the total reached 223.4 M tonnes, of which 136.5 M tonnes were crushed to produce

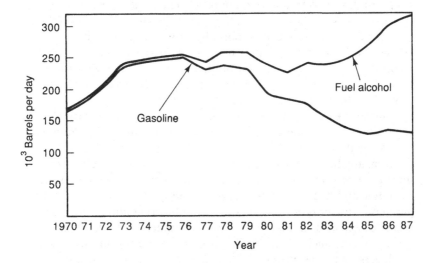

Fig. 2.2. *Evolution of gasoline and alcohol consumption in Brazil for the period 1970–1987 (Comissao Alcool, 1989).*

ethanol (61%) and the rest for sugar production. The planted area of sugarcane has increased from 1.54 M ha in 1972 to 2.82 M ha in 1982 (5.8% of the total cultivated area) and 4.31 M ha in 1987 (8.1% of the area under cultivation) (data from Instituto Brasileiro de Geografia e Estatistica, IBGE, 1989).

Today 4.5 million cars out of a total of 12.9 million cars run on pure bioethanol. The rest of the passenger cars run on a blend of 22% ethanol with gasoline. In 1976, only 3% of the total vehicle sales in the domestic market run on ethanol, but by 1985 this has reached almost 96%. Since then there has been a small reduction to 88% due to a decrease in alcohol production in 1988. This has been caused by the increase of sugar prices in the international market and the diversion of agricultural land to the more lucrative export markets such as orange plantations. This highlights the vulnerability of ethanol production to world market price fluctuations (Lima, 1989; Anon., 1989a). From 1976 to 1987 the total investment in ProAlcool reached $6.97 billion and the total savings equivalent in imported gasoline during the same period was $12.48 billion (Anon., 1989b; Lima, 1989).

Although Brazil's involvement with alcohol fuel dates back to 1902 with the publication in Bahia of a document on the industrial possibilities of ethanol, the creation of ProAlcool represented a fundamental political step in the country's long-term commitment to provide a substitute for imported oil.

ProAlcool was set up with a multi-purpose in mind, although the main objective was to reduce oil imports. The broad objectives can be summarized as follows: to lessen the country's external vulnerability to oil supply and to reduce oil imports by substituting oil derivatives by ethanol in the automobile and chemical industries; to increase energy independence through the utilization of domestic renewable energy resources; to develop the alcohol capital goods sector and process technology for the production and utilization of industrial alcohols; and to achieve greater socio-economic and regional equality through the expansion of cultivable lands for alcohol production and generation of employment.

To ensure the success of the programme the government established a series of norms. These included: direct involvement of the private sector; economic and financial incentives to ethanol producers; guarantees to purchase ethanol production within the authorized limits and specifications established in advance by the government; establishment of a price policy which ensured an effective remuneration to alcohol producers; and incentives for alcohol production and utilization technology. The positive combination of these factors, together with the introduction of new equipment, and increases in productivity and the number of new plantations, has given a continuous boost to alcohol production during the 14 years existence of the ProAlcool programme. ProAlcool has been largely successful in meeting its technological objectives, reducing oil imports and some broad development goals. It has enabled the sugar and alcohol industries to develop their own technological expertise along with the total capacity. Technological improvements have resulted in an average annual productivity increase in the agro-industrial sector of 4.3% during the period 1977/78 to 1985/86. Alcohol production, mostly in São Paulo State, has increased from 2651 litres per ha to 3706 litres per ha during the same period (Anon., 1989*b*). Brazilian firms have also been exporting alcohol technology to many parts of the world. The sugar and alcohol industry is today among Brazil's largest industrial sectors.

Another industry which has expanded greatly due to the creation of ProAlcool is the ethanol chemistry sector. A significant expansion stimulated by ProAlcool was able to draw upon a tradition dating back to the 1920s. Installed capacity for ethanol utilization in the chemical industry rose from 60 105 tonnes per year in 1976 to 336 980 tonnes per year in 1984. From 1975 to 1985 the ethanol-based chemical sector consumed a total of nearly 2.2 billion litres of ethanol. About 3.5% of the annual alcohol production is consumed by this sector (Rosillo-Calle, 1986). Although in recent years interest for ethanol chemistry has somewhat subsided due to the fall in world oil prices, Brazil has had an excellent opportunity to develop this industry thanks to the combination of a sound technological base and historical experience, abundant raw materials (ethanol) with large scope for cost reduction, and a large potential market. Ethanol chemical plants can be far more suitable for many developing countries than petrochemical plants because they are smaller, require less investment, can be set up in agricultural areas and use raw materials which can be produced locally. For many sugarcane-producing countries, an ethanol chemical industry is particularly relevant.

Technological developments, however, have not matched the stated social objectives. To expect so would have been to ignore Brazil's social, economic and political reality. The government's chief objectives have been economic growth, with little emphasis on social development and, in the specific case of ProAlcool, to achieve greater energy independence and to prevent the collapse of the sugar industry. Economic development has taken place at the expense of social development. Rural job creation has been claimed as a major benefit of the ProAlcool programme because alcohol production in Brazil is highly labour-intensive – some 700 000 direct jobs with perhaps 3–4 times this number of indirect jobs. However, many of these jobs are not necessarily new ones.

Environmental pollution by ProAlcool has been a cause of serious concern, particularly in the early days of the programme. The environmental impact of alcohol production can be considerable because large amounts of stillage are produced and often escape into the waterways. For each litre of ethanol the distilleries produce an effluent of 10–14 litres of high biochemical oxygen demand (BOD) stillage. However, a number of alternative technological solutions are available or being developed that have reduced the level of pollution, e.g. turning stillage into fertilizer, animal feed, bio-gas, etc. These, together with tougher environmental enforcement, have reduced the pollution potential considerably.

Generally the ProAlcool programme has increased energy independence, provided the basis for technological developments in both production and end-use, and given significant foreign exchange savings. On the social side, the main benefit has been rural job creation. The current low oil prices together with increased domestic oil production has decreased the overriding importance of ProAlcool as a liquid fuel substitute. This is further reinforced by the economics of alcohol production which, despite considerable improvements, still remain unfavourable to oil prices on a microeconomic basis. In addition, the surge of sugar prices in the international market and shift to other more profitable export commodities have shown the vulnerability of the programme to short term market fluctuations. Consequently the government has been forced to import (in 1988) 200 M litres of methanol and ethanol to fill the current gap. It is likely that the trend to lower use of ethanol-fuelled cars will continue, considering present low oil prices and government attempts to reduce subsidies to ethanol production.

Overall, Brazil's success with ethanol production and utilization has been due to the combination of factors which include: government support and clear policy to ethanol production; economic and financial incentives; direct involvement of the private sector; technological capability of the ethanol production sector; long historical experience with production and use of ethanol; cooperation between government, sugarcane producers and the automobile industry; and a well-established and developed sugarcane industry which thus allowed low investment costs in setting up new distilleries. In the specific case of ethanol-fuelled vehicles, the following could be cited: government incentives (e.g. lower taxes, and cheaper credit); security of supply and nationalistic motivation; and a consistent price policy which favoured the alcohol-powered car.

Concluding remarks

Alcohols, particularly bioethanol, are increasingly being recognized as an important fuel due to a combination of factors ranging from environmental considerations, CO_2 emission problems, agricultural land surpluses and strategic, socio-economic and political considerations. In the early days a mix of socio-political, economic and strategic considerations were at the core of any decision to set up a bioethanol project. Currently, particularly in the industrial countries, improved environment, air quality, agricultural land-use problems, and grassroots political pressure are becoming more dominant factors.

Free-market economics are still unfavourable to producing bioethanol and as a major limiting factor to further expansion of bioethanol markets. Costs, however, are influenced by a large number of factors: type, availability and cost of feedstock; cost and type of plant; use of by-products; and indirect incentives, etc. In the short term, some kind of economic and financial incentives would be needed in many cases to allow bioethanol projects to succeed.

Critics have argued against renewable energy in general and bioethanol in particular because they say it needs large subsidies. In fact subsidies to promote energy and agricultural development are at the core of all our economic systems. Energy from renewable resources generally receives far fewer subsidies than from conventional sources.

In addition, since competing conventional energy technologies are able to pass on to society a substantial part of their costs (social costs) renewable energy sources, which produce very few or no external costs and may even cause positive external effects, are systematically put at a disadvantage. Renewable energy sources are not utilized to their full competitive potential and are introduced into the market considerably later than the optimal time of market introduction based on their overall cost situation (including social costs) (Hohmeyer, 1988). Had external economic efforts been included in the market allocation process, there might already have been a substantial shift in the market penetration of renewable energy in general and bioethanol in particular.

The progress made in all areas of biomass energy use has been much greater per unit expenditure than has been achieved in the pursuit of nuclear fusion, for example. Indeed some believe that had we spent half as much on the development of solar energy as we have spent on all forms of nuclear energy, we would already have achieved a large, renewable source of energy.

Renewable energy technologies can play a significant role in solving the potential global warming problem. Most renewables do not produce any significant quantities of CO_2. Those that do, such as biofuels,

52   *F. Rosillo-Calle and others*

recapture the CO_2 they release when burned if they are sustainably produced on a long-term scale. Finally, bioethanol is among the environmentally safest liquid fuels; it is less toxic and reduces NO_x and CO emissions from the vehicles that burn it.

References

Ahmed, H., Rask, N. & Baldwing, D. (1989). Ethanol fuel as an octane enhancer in the US fuel market. *Biomass*, **19**, 215–32.
Alvin, C.F. (1986). O Uso do Alcool como Carburante. Corretivo a Octanagem da Gasolina e sua Influencia sobre o Meio Ambiente, *Annals VI Encontro Nacional dos Productores de Alcool*, Sociedade de Produtores de Azucar e Alcool (SOPRAL), São Paulo, S.P. Brazil.
Anon. (1987). *Cost/Benefit Analysis of Production and Use of Bioethanol as a Gasoline Additive in the European Communities*. Office for Official Publications of the EC, Luxembourg.
Anon. (1988). *Understanding the Challenges and Future of Fuel Alcohol in the United States*, Information Resources, Inc. Washington, D.C. (Report produced for the USA Department of Energy, Office of Alcohol Fuels).
Anon. (1989a). Ministro Admite Estudar Aumento do Alcool Supeior ao da Gasolina, *O Povo*. **9A**, Dec. 24.
Anon. (1989b). *Agroindustria Canavieira*: Um Perfil, Copersucar, São Paulo, S.P., Brazil (Internal Report).
Bohm, G.M., Saldiva, P.H.N., Massad, E., Pasqualucci, C.A.G., Munoz, D.R., Gouveia, M.A., Cardoso, L.M.N., Caldeira, M.P.R. & da Silva, R. (1988). Health effects of hydrated ethanol used as automobile fuel. In *Proc. VIII Intern. Symp. of Alcohol Fuels*, Tokyo, National Energy and Industrial Technology Development Organization (NEITDO). pp. 1021–5.
Comissao Alcool (1989). Instituto Brasileiro do Petroleo, Rio de Janeiro, R.J., Brazil (personal communication).
Environmental Protection Agency (1987). *Air Quality Benefits of Alternative Fuels*. Office of Mobile Sources, Office of Air & Radiation, USA Congress, Washington, D.C.
Gotelli, C.A. (1988). Ethanol as Substitute of Tetraethyl Lead in Gasoline. In *Proc. VIII Intern. Symp. on Alcohol Fuels*, Tokyo, NEITDO, pp. 1099–103.
Grassi, G. (1989). Bio-energy industrial integrated regional projects in the European Community. In *Proc. The Third Pacific Basin Biofuels Workshop*, Hawaii National Energy Institute, University of Hawaii, Honolulu, pp. 63–85.
Grinnell, G.E. (1987). Impacts of ethanol fuel in the US agriculture. In *Biomass for Energy and Industry*, 4th EC Conference, G. Grassi et al. (eds), pp. 164–7. Elsevier Applied Science, London.
Hall, D.O. & Rosillo-Calle, F. (1989). Biomass, bioenergy and agriculture in Europe. In *Proc. 7th Canadian Bioenergy R & D Seminar*, Ottawa, CANMET, pp. 35–42.

Hall, D.O. & Rosillo-Calle, F. (1990). Biomass energy: production and utilization. In *Developing World Series – Agriculture and Food.* The Grosvenor Press International (in press).

Ho, S.P. (1989). Global warming impact of ethanol versus gasoline. *1989 National Conference 'Clean Air Issues and America's Motor Fuel Business'*, October, Washington, D.C.

Hohmeyer, O. (1988). *Social Costs of Energy Consumption.* Springer-Verlag, Berlin.

IBGE (Instituto Brasileiro de Geografia e Estatistica) (1989). Various census (personal communication).

Juma, C. (1986). Alcohol from sugarcane in Kenya and Zimbabwe. In *Conf. Proceed. (C42). Energy for Development; what are the Solutions?*, pp. 14–22, UK-ISES, (Solar Energy Society) King's College London, UK.

Klausmeier, W.H. (1987). Worldwide review of alcohol fuel markets. In *Energy from Biomass and Wastes* X, D.L. Klass (ed.), pp. 1417–37. Elsevier Applied Science Publishers, London.

Lima, L.R. (1989). *Producao de Alcool Carburante – Estudos Alternativos. Annals II Simposio Nacional sobre Fontes Novas e Renovaveis de Energia – II SINERGE*, Curitiba (in press).

Marland, G. & Turhollow, A. (1989). *CO_2 Emissions from Production and Combustion of Fuel Ethanol from Corn.* Oak Ridge National Laboratory, Tennessee (personal communication).

Marrow, J.E., Coombs, J. & Lees, E.W. (1987). *An Assessment of Bioethanol as a Transport Fuel in the UK.* HMSO, London.

Moncrieff, I.D. & Walker, F.G.B. (1988). Retrofit Adaptation of Vehicles to Ethanol Fuelling: A Practical Implementation Programme. In *Proc. VIII Intern. Symp. on Alcohol Fuels*, Tokyo, NEITDO, pp. 399–404.

OECD (1988). *Environmental Impacts of Renewable Energy*, pp. 44–59. OECD, 75775 Paris CEDEX 16.

Office of Technology Assessment (1980). *Energy from Biological Processes, vol. 2, Technical and Environmental Analysis.* Congress of USA, Washington, D.C.

Rosillo-Calle, F. (1986). The Brazilian ethanolchemistry industry (a review). *Biomass*, **11**, 19–38.

Rosillo-Calle, F. (1990). Liquid fuels. In *Biomass and the Environment.* The Stockholm Environmental Institute, Sweden (in press).

Rosillo-Calle, F. & Hall, D.O. (1987). Brazilian alcohol: food versus fuel? *Biomass*, **12**, 97–128.

Schwandt, W.R. (1984). Political, economic and technical aspects of the US fuel ethanol program, *Proc. BIOTECH 84 Europe*, vol. 1, pp. 519–90. Online, London.

Scurlock, J.M.O. & Hall, D.O. (1990). The contribution of biomass to global energy use (1987). *Biomass*, **21**, 75–81.

Scurlock, J.M.O., Rosenschein, A.D. & Hall, D.O. (1989). The Triangle Ethanol Plant, Zimbabwe. A Case Study (personal communication).

Shea, C.P. (1988). *Renewable Energy: Today's Contribution, Tomorrow's Promise*, Worldwatch Institute, Worldwatch Paper 81, Washington, D.C.

Steingass, H. *et al.* (1988). *Electricity and Ethanol Options in Southern Africa*. USAID, Office of Energy, Bureau for Science and Technology. Report No. 88–21.

Stuckey, D. & Juma, C. (1985). *Power Alcohol in Kenya and Zimbabwe: A Case Study in the Transfer of Renewable Energy Technology*, UNCTAD/TT 61.

Wenman, C. (1985). Director of the Triangle Plant (personal communication).

Williams, R.H. (1989). Biomass gasifiers/gas turbine power and the greenhouse warming. Paper presented at the *IEA/OECD Expert Seminar on Energy Technologies for Reducing Emissions of Greenhouse Gases.* OECD, 75775 Paris CEDEX 16, April 12–14.

Yasuhisa, M. (1989). Developments in alcohol manufacturing technology. *Int. J. Solar Energy*, 7, 93–109.

3

Biofertilizers: agronomic and environmental impacts and economics

K. MULONGOY, S. GIANINAZZI,
P.A. ROGER AND Y. DOMMERGUES

Introduction

During the last decades increased fertilizer and pesticide use contributed to a spectacular increase in crop production, especially in Asia and South America. However, the price of fossil-fuel-based inorganic fertilizers relative to the prices of most stable crops has increased and chemical pesticides are both costly and harmful when they persist in the soil and enter the food chain. This explains the emphasis on current attempts to control soil- and plant-associated microorganisms, to lower fertilizer production costs, reduce environmental pollution whilst ensuring fair or even high yields, and to expand the adaptability of plants to reputedly unfavourable situations. The approach adopted is to introduce into soil or rhizosphere soil symbiotic or non-symbiotic microorganisms, a practice known as inoculation. The inoculants are also known as biofertilizers. Inoculation of plants by beneficial bacteria or fungi is routinely used in the legume–rhizobia symbiosis, fairly often in the ectomycorrhizal and to some extent in the endomycorrhizal symbiosis. Recently inoculation of actinorhizal plants has been developed and successfully adopted both in temperate and tropical countries. With some exceptions, inoculation with plant-growth-promoting rhizobacteria (PGPR) is still in its experimental stage. Soil inoculation with free-living blue-green algae has been and is still practised in Southeast Asia but the results are irregular.

In this chapter the discussion is restricted (1) to the presentation of the main types of biofertilizers (exclusive of *Azolla* and other green manures) and their modes of action, (2) to their agronomic and environmental benefits, (3) to biofertilizer technology, and (4) to the economics of the application of biofertilizers. The use of chemicals of microbial origin such as antibiotics or toxins (e.g. toxins produced by *Bacillus thuringiensis*) is not dealt with.

Agronomic applications and environmental benefits

Agronomic applications

Biofertilizers are preparations containing viable forms of beneficial microorganisms intended for seed plant or soil application. They can affect growth and yield of plants either directly or indirectly through different mechanisms that are discussed later on.

The main groups of microorganisms brought to plants by bio-fertilizers are: *Rhizobium*, *Frankia*, mycorrhizal fungi, plant-growth-promoting rhizobacteria (PGPR), and blue-green algae (BGA).

Rhizobium Rhizobia provide the host plant with the N it requires for its growth. In association with legumes, rhizobia fix from 0 to 300 kg N_2 per ha per year, the percentage of N derived from nitrogen fixation in plant tissues ranging from 40 to 90%. In soils deficient in N, yield can be increased several-fold.

Inoculation should be limited to sites where it can be expected to generate a worthwhile response. A distinction should be made between the following situations.

> When a non-promiscuous plant species is grown on a site for the first time it has to be inoculated with a highly performing specific strain. A response can be expected since non-promiscuous species can benefit from inoculation with certain specific strains, such as *Acacia mangium* inoculated with *Bradyrhizobium*.
>
> By contrast, non- or less-promiscuous species (e.g. *Vigna unguiculata*, *Acacia crassiparpa*), that is species with no specific microbial requirements, would probably not benefit especially from inoculation since they can be infected by a large number of native symbiotic strains.
>
> When growing a plant on a site where it had already been grown before, inoculation is often (though not always) useless, on account of the survival in soil of strains of symbiotic competent microorganisms.

Since there are several exceptions to these rules, it is necessary, prior to the start of any inoculation programme, to determine whether symbiotic strains are present in soil to be planted and to establish inoculation needs and proper management protocols.

Frankia About 200 plant species covering 19 genera and 8 families, known as actinorhizal plants, nodulate with an N_2-fixing actinomycete, *Frankia*. The main tropical species of actinorhizal plants belong to the genera *Casuarina, Allocasuarina, Gymnostoma* and *Alnus.* The amount of N_2 fixed annually by symbiotic systems (between a few kg per ha to 300 kg per ha) depends on the host plant, the symbiotic microorganism and the environmental conditions.

Reliable inoculants, namely those made of fresh or dried beads of *Frankia* entrapped in alginate (Sougoufara, Diem & Dommergues, 1989), have been developed and most satisfactory results obtained in the field. The limitations to the use of *Frankia* biofertilizers are similar to those underlined in the case of rhizobia.

Mycorrhizal fungi Mycorrhizal fungi are known to improve significantly plant productivity by enhancing the absorption of soil nutrients and water and by controlling certain soil pathogens and pests (Harley & Smith, 1983).

Precolonization of roots by mycorrhizal fungi frequently leads to reduced damage by soil-borne pathogens like *Fusarium, Phythium* or *Phytophthora* and nematodes. The mechanisms involved are not known but it has been suggested that mycorrhizal fungi may activate plant defence mechanisms or, in the case of ectomycorrhizae, act as a physical barrier or produce antimicrobial substances (Mosse, Stribley & Le Tacon, 1981; Gianinazzi, 1990).

Although more research is necessary for a better understanding of how mycorrhizae protect plants, these observations nevertheless open possibilities for associating the management of the mycorrhizae with a reduced input of xenobiotic substances in plant production.

Since the pioneer nursery trials on citrus (Menge, Lembright & Johnson, 1977) and several forest trees (Marx, 1980), the importance of mycorrhizae as potential biofertilizers for crops or trees has been established (Gianinazzi, Gianinazzi-Pearson & Trouvelot, 1990a; Marx & Cordell, 1990).

Even when beneficial effects are not so striking, mycorrhizae can ensure a decrease in the heterogeneity within a crop population in the field (Ganry *et al.*, 1982; 1985); they can also eliminate clone variability in nurseries (Blal, 1989).

The positive effect of mycorrhizae on yield varies in relation to the crop involved, the mycorrhizal fungi introduced or present, and the agricultural techniques used. In order to use mycorrhizal fungi successfully, it is necessary, as with other biofertilizers, to develop a strategy of inoculation based on biological tests (Gianinazzi, Gianinazzi-Pearson & Trouvelot, 1986) designed to evaluate: (1) the quantity of infective propagules present in a given soil (i.e. the soil mycorrhizal potential), (2) their effectiveness and potential impact on crop production, and (3) soil receptivity to mycorrhizal fungi used as inoculant for a given crop.

Plant-growth-promoting rhizobacteria (PGPR) These bacteria that colonize the plant rhizosphere, can enhance directly or indirectly plant productivity through different mechanisms, such as nitrogen fixation to some extent, solubilization of non-mobile soil nutrients such as phosphorus, production of phytohormones, antagonism against deleterious or pathogenic microorganisms, and degradation of phytotoxins (Lynch, 1983).

The impact of PGPR varies greatly with the bacteria used to inoculate the crops as is shown by the following examples.

(1) *Nitrogen-fixing PGPR* (also known as nitrogen-fixing associative rhizobacteria) have been extensively studied since 1970, the best known species being) *Azotobacter paspali*, *Azospirillum lipoferum*, *A. brasilense*, and *A. amazonense* (Dobereiner & Pedrosa, 1987). Others such as *Herbaspirillum seropedicae* (Dobereiner & Pedrosa, 1987) and *Saccharobacter nitrocaptans* (Cavalcante & Dobereiner, 1988) have been discovered more recently. Generally these bacteria contribute less than a few kilograms per hectare yearly, or very little nitrogen to their ecosystems. Bashan, Singh & Levanony (1989) demonstrated with a Nif⁻ strain that the contribution of *Azospirillum brasilense* to the improvement of tomato seedling growth is not through nitrogen fixation. However, when some of these bacteria are associated with specific host cultivars of plants such as sugarcane and *Panicum* sp., nitrogen fixation can become quite significant (Boddey, 1987).

(2) In the specific case of rice the general effect of bacterial inoculation on yield, as shown by the analysis of 210 experiments reported in 23 papers (Roger, Zimmerman & Lumpkin, 1991), is an average increase by 27.6% in pot experiments (87 data) and by 14.4% in field experiments (123 data). In the field, positive effects, no effect, inconsistent effects in time or among various simultaneous treatments, and negative effects were reported.

Differences in yield ranged from −25 to +69%. The current limiting factor for bacterial inoculation of rice is the lack of proven technology, which results from an insufficient knowledge of the factors that allow inoculated strains to establish and their mode of action on rice. Currently, most strains tested for inoculation have been nitrogen-fixing forms, but ARA, ¹⁵N, and nitrogen balance studies did not show that the promotion of growth and nitrogen uptake was due to higher biological nitrogen-fixation (BNF). The beneficial effect of bacterial inoculation can be attributed to a combination of (1) increased BNF, (2) production of PGPR favouring rice growth and nutrient utilization, (3) increased nutrient availability through solubilization of immobilized nutrients by inoculated bacteria, and (4) competition of inoculated strains with pathogens or detrimental bacteria in the rhizosphere. The relative importance of these four components has not yet been explained. In the current status of knowledge, no definite conclusion regarding the potential of bacterial inoculation of rice can be drawn.

(3) Phosphorus-solubilizing microorganisms: according to Subba Rao (1986) inoculation of various crops with *Phosphobacterin* (biofertilizer containing phosphate-dissolving bacteria) could increase yield by 10–37%. However, results were irregular; improvements in cereal yield were found only in 10 out of 37 field experiments.

Experimental results on the effect of inoculation with these microorganisms in rice fields are inconsistent (Roger *et al.*, 1991).

(4) *Pseudomonas* used for biological control: *Pseudomonas* spp. can inhibit growth of deleterious and pathogenic rhizosphere bacteria and fungi by producing siderophores. These are peptides that have a strong specific affinity for iron and with which they form a stable complex. Thus iron becomes unavailable to soil microorganisms that do not produce siderophores or produce some with lower affinity for iron (Kerr, 1982). *Pseudomonas putida* produces a siderophore called pseudobactin that controls both potato soft rot and seed piece decay (Kloepper *et al.*, 1980). In the USA, seed treatment with plant-growth-promoting pseudomonads is becoming a standard commercial practice in wheat and barley monocultures subject to the take-all root disease caused by *Gaeumannomyces graminis* var. *tritici*. Both antibiotics and siderophores have been implicated in the control of take-all disease. Siderophores become ineffective in anaerobic conditions when formation of organic acids solubilizes the iron that they bind. Also, some target organisms show resistance when they acquire the siderophore system (Loper & Ishimaru, 1989).

Blue-green algae (BGA) BGA can improve rice yield not only by contributing to the nitrogen nutrition of the crop and, reportedly, by other effects including (1) production of plant growth regulators, (2) improvement of soil properties, (3) increased solubilization of phosphorus,

(4) decrease of weed incidence, and (5) alleviation of detrimental effects of sulphate reduction (Roger & Kulasooriya, 1980).

Nitrogen contribution to soil by BGA depends on the turnover of biomass, for which no data are available. Nevertheless, the observation that BGA usually bloom once or twice during a crop cycle indicates a rough potential of 30 kg N per ha per crop. The maximum theoretical N contribution, calculated by assuming that all carbon input in the photic zone is through nitrogen-fixing BGA, is 75 kg per ha per crop. Estimates of photo-dependent BNF in ricefields range from a few to 80 kg N per ha per crop (average 27 kg). Estimates in 65 plots of an IRRI farm during four crops ranged from 0 to 55 kg N per ha per crop, and averaged 19 kg in no-N controls, 8 kg in plots with broadcast urea, and 12 kg in plots where urea was deep-placed. Experimental recoveries of BGA nitrogen by rice ranged from 13 to 50% (average 30%), and were dependent on the use and incorporation or not of fresh or dried material and on the occurrence of soil fauna.

In a bibliographic survey covering 634 field experiments inoculation of rice was found to have induced an increase of grain yield of 257 kg per ha. However, only 17% of the experiments reported statistically significant differences. Though algal inoculation can increase rice yield its effects often seem to be erratic and low. This may be the reason for its limited adoption and use.

Environmental benefits

Biofertilizers, in addition to their impact on plant productivity, contribute to the sustainability of soil fertility and to a reduction of the hazards of pollution. An example of the beneficial effect of biofertilizers on the maintenance of soil fertility is that of the binding role of mycorrhizal hyphae that bind soil aggregates together, strengthen soil structure and reduce soil erosion (Allen & Macmahon, 1985). In contrast, the excessive use of soluble chemical fertilizers, with their content of phosphate and nitrate, is one of the main causes of water pollution.

Inoculation practices of legumes and actinorhizal plants with their nitrogen-fixing symbionts drastically reduce and may suppress the utility of chemical N fertilizers. Such practice minimizes the pollution of the soil and water tables by nitrates and a number of other concomitant toxic compounds resulting from the use of non-biological fertilizers.

Blal et al. (1990) recently showed that VA endomycorrhizae greatly increase the fertilizer utilization coefficient (2.7–5.6 fold) as much of rock phosphate as of superphosphate for plants growing in acid, P-fixing soils. Under these conditions, VA fungi greatly contribute to optimizing phosphate fertilizer efficiency, so minimizing their input, and to utilizing natural, cheaper substitutes for plant fertilization. Although similar work has not been done with other type of mycorrhizae, there is some evidence that they may favour phosphate mobilization by plants from condensed or complex forms of phosphate (Gianinazzi-Pearson & Gianinazzi, 1989). All results emphasize the potential of these bio-fertilizers in reducing fertilizer costs and pollution in agriculture.

Biofertilizer technology

Culture of the selected microorganisms

The selected microorganism which has been screened or engineered for its symbiotic performance must be cultured in large quantities to produce enough inoculant for the field. Some microorganisms are easily grown *in vitro*, e.g. rhizobia and ectomycorrhizal fungi. Others, however, are much more difficult to produce in large quantities, e.g. *Frankia*, and, some have not yet been grown *in vitro*, viz. VAM fungi.

Rhizobium is easily grown in many types of fermentors, e.g. batch or semicontinuous culture (Williams, 1984). *Frankia* is much more difficult to grow *in vitro*. To offset this drawback, a reliable culture method has now been developed (Diem & Dommergues, 1989).

Efficient fungi forming ectomycorrhizae, ericoid and orchid endomy-corrhizae can be easily cultured on solid and in liquid media. Production of large quantities of inoculum poses no real technical problems. Commercial inoculum of ectomycorrhizal fungi is now produced by the private sector in USA, Canada and France. In New Zealand, the commercial production of inoculum for ericoid endomycorrhizae is under way (Mintech Ltd). Commercial ectomycorrhizal inocula can be applied either in a liquid form to the field or incorporated into potting mixes for nursery plants.

Attempts to grow VA endomycorrhizal fungi in pure culture have so far been unsuccessful. Fungal collections are maintained on living host plants under non-sterile conditions. Large-scale multiplication of efficient fungi has been achieved by inoculating appropriate host plants like clover, ray grass or sudan grass that are grown in disinfected soil or a variety of rooting media containing perlite, pumice, vermiculite, bark, sawdust, sand, gravel, peat or mixtures of these materials (Gianinazzi, 1982; Menge, 1984). Spore, hyphae, infected roots and infested soil or rooting medium obtained from this type of culture can, either separately or in mixture, constitute a source of crude inoculum.

Inoculant processing and application

The technique for processing microbial inoculants is very important. The successful use of these inoculants depends on a formulation that should be simple, economic, unaffected by long storage, and easy to transport and apply.

Peat-base inoculants The usual practice is to absorb the microbial culture on a protective carrier, generally peat (Williams, 1984). Alternative carriers include lignite coal, straw, cellulose, bagasses, ground crop residues, and soil. In some cases the microorganism is cultured and the inoculant is processed simultaneously. Ectomycorrhizal inoculants, for instance, are made of the fungal hyphae and the mineral substrate, usually vermiculite, imbibed with a nutrient medium on which the fungus is grown.

Recently, 'Les Tourbières Premier' (Quebec) have released into the North American market a peat-based substrate containing VA fungi (Mycori-mix Md) for pot cultures.

Soil-base inoculants (VA endomycorrhizae) In Dijon (France). Gianinazzi, Trouvelot & Gianinazzi-Pearson (1990b) have developed a method for producing soil-based inoculum containing $5–10 \times 10^3$ infective propagules per kg, which can potentially yield up to $3 \times 10^3 \, \text{m}^{-3}$ inoculum per ha of glass house per year. A similar method has been developed by a sugar-beet company for producing inoculum outdoors in agriculture waste soil for commercial purposes (see *European Biotechnology Newsletter*, **61** (1989)).

Both types of inocula have given excellent results in nurseries producing woody ornamentals like Liquidambar, Lilac, Ampelopsis, Berberis in disinfected soils. Production was homogeneous and seedlings were marketable immediately after one season.

These soil-based inocula have also been successfully used, incorporated at a rate of 30%, in a compost or other artificial substrates for pot cultures. Where it is essential to reduce microbial contamination to a minimum, as for micropropagated plants, soil could be completely eliminated and surface-disinfected VA endomycorrhizal fragments used as inoculum. Methods ensuring rapid infection with a very low amount of inoculum (200 g for 500 plants) have given excellent results with different micropropagated plant species (Ravolanirina *et al.*, 1989; Gianinazzi *et al.*, 1990b). In Columbia, a soil-based inoculant is available in the market under the name *Manihotina*.

Inorganic clay carrier A more sophisticated, and therefore more expensive, form of VA endomycorrhizal inoculum has recently been put on the American market by Native Plants Inc. (USA). This inoculum, based on fungal spores, is incorporated into an inorganic (clay) carrier

(Nutri-link ^{R}) for use with potted plants or under field conditions (Wood, 1987).

Polymeric inoculants Another practice (Dommergues, Diem & Divies, 1979; Jung, Mugnier & Dommergues, 1982; Diem *et al.*, 1988; 1989) is based on the entrapment of the microbial cells in a polymer gel, generally as alginate beads. A recent improvement was achieved by adding clay (kaolinite) to the entrapping gel.

Polymeric inoculants containing either symbiotic microorganisms or PGPR, e.g. *Azospirillum*, have been successfully tested in numerous instances. To the best of our knowledge, large-scale experiments have only been carried out in a few cases.

A simple method for checking the quality of polymeric inoculants was recently proposed by Prin *et al.* (1989). This method is based on the evaluation of the dehydrogenase activity of the inoculant through an assay that uses the redox dye, 2-(*p*-iodophenyl)-3-(*p*-nitrophenyl)- (phenyltetrazolium chloride) (INT).

In practical terms, dried polymeric inoculants are best suited for use in nursery inoculations. After being dried they are applied to the seed bed or to the seeds after pseudo-solubilization by immersion in a buffer solution (Diem *et al.*, 1989).

Economics of biofertilizers

The benefit–cost analysis can be used to assess profitability of microbial inoculants. It is based on how much the present value of the benefit exceeds the present worth of the costs. When an enterprise has a benefit: cost ratio greater than 1 after the gross cost and gross benefit have been discounted at a suitable discount rate, most often the opportunity cost of capital, the enterprise is accepted as profitable. FAO (1984) gives some examples of benefit: cost ratios of legume inoculants. The price and cost of utilizing peat–base rhizobium inoculants is low, ranging from US $0.24 per ha for white clover (*Trifolium repens*) to US $6.46 per ha for *Vicia faba*. Inoculation costs for *Leucaena leucocephala*, *Cajanus cajan*, soybean (*Glycine max*) and *Vigna unguiculata* are between these two costs. Soil inoculation using peat granules at 10 kg per ha costs approximately US $28.

FAO (1984) based the benefits from legume inoculants on N_2 fixed. They found benefit: cost ratios of 416 for white clover fixing 200 kg N_2 per ha and 17 for soybean fixing 100 kg N_2 per ha from inoculation, considering the cost of fixed N_2 in fertilizer N as US $0.50 per kg. Valuation of benefits based on fixed N_2 is justified for leguminous cover crops, but for forage and grain legumes, the market prices are more meaningful to the farmer, or their shadow prices when social profitability is being evaluated. Economic analysis of using other biofertilizers should use crop dry matter production, forage and grain yield as the variables for benefit evaluation. Subba Rao (1986) used the price of total yield increases of various legumes in India to estimate the gain due to inoculation of selected legumes with rhizobium in 1978–9. Yield increases resulting from inoculation with rhizobium can also be expressed as the N fertilizer that would produce the same yield increases. The benefit is then the monetary value of this N fertilizer equivalent. Subba Rao (1986) also used this approach to estimate the pay-off to the farming community in India by the application of *Azospirillum* biofertilizer to various cereals and recorded savings of more than 2 million tonnes of urea equivalent to approximately US 0.67×10^9.

Yield variability and variable efficacy among agricultural fields is a major profit risk associated with the use of microbial inoculants and a significant obstacle to agronomic applications. Other risks are poor effectiveness of introduced microorganisms when conditions change, e.g. when pathogens acquire resistance to the inoculant, or when the inoculant strains mutate and lose effectiveness. For some biological control agents and PGPR, there may be a delay in effectiveness owing to the time necessary to produce antibiotics or phytohormones. Risk analyses have been developed to assist decision makers to select the best allocation of resources for maximum profit (Gittinger, 1984).

If benefit:cost ratios of microbial inoculant use are favourable, farmers still have to select microbial inoculants against a no-input system or against N or P fertilizers, herbicides, insecticides, fungicides and growth hormones. There would be no point in developing microbial inoculants that are less efficient or more expensive than a chemical treatment unless the chemical poses environmental or health problems. Partial budgeting analysis (PBA) can be used to compare profitability of various alternatives. The analysis is done by looking at the marginal cost, including opportunity cost, of adding a production activity and comparing it with the marginal increase in benefit that the new activity will bring (Gittinger, 1984). This budgeting approach does not include all production costs, but only those which change or vary between the farmer's alternatives including its current production practices. PBA is useful for decision making at each stage in the research–transfer–adoption process. But for an accurate analysis, all alternative technologies should be compared at their optimal levels, i.e. at their maximum profit. For rhizobium inoculants, for instance, a starter dose of N fertilizer as well as P and/or other nutrients may be needed. Yield response and production functions are rarely available in the literature. In the absence of data related to optimal levels of each technology, available data can be used as a first approximation of the relative profitability of the alternatives.

Because microbial inoculants are not expensive and have the potential to increase yields, their use must be economically profitable to smallholder farmers who have no access to agrochemicals. However, the technology will be adopted only if the input supply is adequate and reliable. Smallholder farmers use complex cropping systems to sustain yield, including the restorative bush fallow. Agronomic experiments should be designed to assess how microbial inoculants can improve these systems. For large-scale farmers, who practice monocropping or sequential cropping of sole crops, economic comparison of microbial inoculants and agrochemicals is straightforward. Considering the upward trend of the world-wide market opportunity for environmentally safe biopesticides (McIntyre & Press, 1989) and the present legume inoculant market, microbial inoculants can be considered in general as an economically profitable technology.

Rhizobium biofertilizer

The price of rhizobial biofertilizer expressed on 1 ha basis was reported to be US $1.7 in Egypt, US $5.2 in Zimbabwe, and US $4.5 in Rwanda. This price, which is the retail price for the farmers, is probably well under the actual cost of production in the government laboratories of these different countries.

Frankia inoculant

Using two methods of evaluation, M. Neyra (personal communication) calculated that the real cost of *Frankia* inoculant as it is prepared at BSSFT laboratory was in the range of 20–50 US cents per tree.

Mycorrhizal biofertilizer

According to F. Le Tacon (personal communication) the cost of ectomycorrhizal inoculation of trees would range from 10 to 50 US cents per tree. The cost of VA endomycorrhizae (Nutrilink) is 6 US cents per plant grown in 1–5 gallon containers and can be as low as $\frac{1}{4}$ US cent per plant when inoculation is performed in nursery beds (Nutrilink). Anyway the supplementary cost of using this inoculant is low when taking into account the beneficial effect on plant growth.

Blue-green algae (BGA)

BGA inoculation as recommended by Venkataraman (1981) is attractive because of its low cost. At 1981 prices, a yield increase of 30 kg per ha was sufficient to cover the cost of the inoculum (US $1.2 to 2.4). With an average increase in yield of 250 kg per ha, the benefit: cost ratio was about 1 to 10. The low investment and the high expected relative return probably explain why BGA inoculation was recommended before the method was fully proved. But BGA inoculation is far from being consistently successful as reported in a study of the economics of BGA use by 40 farmers in Tamil Nadu which shows a non-significant $4 per ha return for BGA utilization (Roger, 1990).

Crop vs tree biofertilizers

When calculating the cost of biofertilizers on a per hectare basis for crop vs tree biofertilizers, it is clear that tree inoculation is much cheaper than crop inoculation since the density of forest plantation is *c.* 2000 plants per ha whereas that of crops is in the range of 200 000 to 500 000 plants per ha. Consequently even if the cost of biofertilizers for trees is higher than that for crops (because of the wider range of strains to be used), the benefit: cost ratio will always be much higher than 1.

Conclusion

Except for rhizobial inoculation the use of biofertilizers in tropical agriculture is still largely under-utilized. In forestry, with the exception of ectomycorrhizae, the use of biofertilizers is even more limited.

This is surprising since good and reliable biofertilizers are available now, e.g. *Frankia*, or VAM endomycorrhizal fungi. Their use is restricted since they are not yet commercially available.

Another reason for the limited use of biofertilizers could be in the misconception that their cost is too high. In fact their price is much lower than that of conventional agrochemicals. In the specific case of trees inoculation with the compatible symbionts, biofertilizers are still much more cost effective than in the case of annual crops.

The poor expansion of biofertilizers could also be explained by the fact that the methods for the carriers to develop longer shelf life and survival are not reliable; however, recent advances have been made which ensure much better survival of the microorganisms and easy transportation and application. More investigations should be made in the future to improve the target strains through usual selection practices and genetic engineering. Also more attention should be given to the impact of physical, chemical and biological limiting factors occurring in the field. In other words, good culture techniques and adequate irrigation, should be implemented to improve the efficiency of bio-fertilizers, thus increasing their benefit: cost ratio.

Finally to reduce the costs, biofertilizers should be applied only in situations that are predictably conductive to a worthwhile response.

References

Allen, M.F. & Macmahon, J.A. (1985). Impact of disturbance on cold desert fungi: comparative microscale dispersion patterns. *Pedobiologia*, **28**, 215–24.

Bashan, Y., Singh, M. & Levanony, H. (1989). Contribution of *Azospirillum brasilense* to growth of tomato seedlings is not through nitrogen fixation. *Can. J. Bot.*, **67**, 2429–34.

Blal, B. (1989). Les endomycorhizes VA chez le palmier à huile (*Elaeis guineensis* Jacq.): rôle dans la régulation de la croissance et dans la nutrition minérale des jeunes plants de clones micropropagés. *Thesis*, pp. 98. Dijon University.

Blal, B., Morel, C., Gianinazzi-Pearson, V., Fardeau, J.C. & Gianinazzi, S. (1990). Influence of vesicular–arbuscular mycorrhizae on phosphate fertilizer efficiency in two tropical acid soils planted with micropropagated oil palm (*Elaeis guineensis* Jacq.). *Biol. Fert. Soils*, **9**, 43–8.

Boddey, R.M. (1987). Methods for quantification of nitrogen fixation associated with Graminae. *CRC Crit. Rev. Plant Sci.*, **6**, 209–65.

Cavalcante, V.A. & Dobereiner, J. (1988). A new acid-tolerant nitrogen-fixing bacterium associated with sugar-cane. *Plant and Soil*, **108**, 23–31.

Diem, H.G. & Dommergues, Y.R. (1989). Current and potential uses and management of Casuarinaceae in the tropics and subtropics. In *The Biology of Frankia and Actinorhizal Plants*, C.R. Schwintzer & J.D. Tjepkema (eds). Academic Press, New York (in press).

Diem, H.G., Duhoux, E., Simonet, P. & Dommergues, Y.R. (1988). Actinorhizal biotechnology: the present and the future. In *8th International Biotechnology Symposium, Paris 1988 Proceedings*, G. Durand, L. Bobichon & J. Florent (eds), vol. II, pp. 984–95. Société Française de Microbiologie, Paris.

Diem, H.G., Ben Khalifa, K., Neyra, M. & Dommergues, Y.R. (1989). Recent advances in the inoculant technology with special emphasis on plant symbiotic microorganisms. In *Proc. Int. Workshop on Advanced Technologies for Increased Agricultural Production: Actual Situation, Future Prospects and Concrete Possibilities of Application in the Developing Countries, Santa Margherita Ligure, Italy 25–29 Sept., 1988*, U. Leone, G. Rialdi & R. Vanore (eds), pp. 196–210. CNR, Roma.

Dobereiner, J. & Pedrosa, F.O. (1987). *Nitrogen-fixing Bacteria in Non-leguminous Crop Plants*, Science Tech., Madison/Springer-Verlag, Berlin.

Dommergues, Y.R., Diem, H.G. & Divies, Ch. (1979). Polyacrylamide-entrapped *Rhizobium* as an inoculant for legumes. *Appl. Environ. Microbiol.* **37**, 558–781.

FAO (Food and Agriculture Organization of the United Nations) (1984). *Legume Inoculants and their Use*, FAO, Roma.

Ganry, F., Diem, H.G. & Dommergues, Y.R. (1982). Effect of inoculation with *Glomus mosseae* on nitrogen fixation by field grown soybeans. *Plant and Soil*, **68**, 321–9.

Ganry, F., Diem, H.G., Wey, J. & Dommergues, Y.R. (1985). Inoculation with *Glomus mosseae* improves N_2 fixation by field grown soybeans. *Biol. Fert. Soils*, **1**, 15–23.

Gianinazzi, S. (1982). L'endomycorhization contrôlée en agriculture, en horticulture et en arboriculture: problèmes et progrès. In *Les mycorhizes, Partie intégrante de la Plante, Biologie et Perspectives d'utilisation*. Les colloques de l'INRA 13, s. Gianinazzi, V. Gianinazzi-Pearson & A. Trouvelot (eds), pp. 231–46. INRA Press, Paris.

Gianinazzi, S. (1990). Vesicular arbuscular (endo-) mycorrhizas: cellular, biochemical and genetic aspects. *Agric. Ecosyst. Environ.* (in press).

Gianinazzi, S., Gianinazzi-Pearson, V. & Trouvelot, A. (1986). Que peut-on attendre des mycorhizes dans la production des arbres fruitiers? *Fruits*, **41**, 553–6.

Gianinazzi, S., Gianinazzi-Pearson, V. & Trouvelot, A. (1990*a*). Potentialities and procedures for the use of endomycorrhizae with special emphasis on high value crops. In *Biotechnology of Fungi for Improving Plant Growth B.M.S. Symposium Volume*, J.M. Whipps & B. Lumsden (eds), pp. 40–54. Cambridge University Press.

Gianinazzi, S., Trouvelot, A. & Gianinazzi-Pearson, V. (1990*b*). Conceptual approaches for rational use of VA endomycorrhizae in agriculture: possibilities and limitations. *Agric., Ecosyst. Environ.* (in press).

Gianinazzi-Pearson, V. & Gianinazzi, S. (1989). Phosphorus metabolism in mycorrhizae. In *Nitrogen, Phosphorus and Sulphur Utilization by Fungi*, *B.M.S. Symposium Volume*, L. Boddy, R. Marchant & D.J. Read (eds), pp. 227–41. Cambridge University Press.

Gittinger, J.P. (1984). *Economic Analysis of Agricultural Projects*, 2nd edn. The Johns Hopkins University Press, Baltimore.

Harley, J.L. & Smith, S.E. (1983). *Mycorrhizal Symbiosis*, pp. 483. Academic Press, London, New York.

Jung, G., Mugnier, J. & Dommergues, Y. (1982). Polymer-entrapped rhizobium as an inoculant for legumes. *Plant and Soil*, **65**, 218–31.

Kerr, A. (1982). Biological control of soil-borne microbial pathogens and nematodes. In *Advances in Agricultural Microbiology*, N.S. Subba Rao (ed.), pp. 429–63. Butterworth Scientific, London.

Kloepper, J.W., Leong, J., Teintze, M. & Schroth, M.N. (1980). Enhanced plant growth by siderophores produced by plant-growth-promoting rhizobacteria. *Nature, Lond.* **286**, 885–6.

Loper, J.E. & Ishimaru, C.A. (1989). Factors influencing siderophore-mediated biocontrol activity of rhizosphere *Pseudomonas* spp. In *The Rhizosphere and Plant Growth, Beltsville Symposium XIV, May 8–11, 1989*. Program and Abstract Booklet, p. 36.

Lynch, J.M. (1983). *Soil Biotechnology*. Blackwell, Oxford.

McIntyre, J.A. & Press, L.S. (1989). Formulation, delivery systems and marketing of biocontrol agents and plant growth promoting rhizobacteria (PGPR). In *The Rhizosphere and Plant Growth. Beltsville Symposium XIV, May 8–11, 1989* (in press).

Marx, D. (1980). Ectomycorrhizal fungus inoculations: a tool for improving forestation practices. In *Tropical Mycorrhiza Research*, P. Mikola (ed.), pp. 13–17. Oxford University Press, London.

Marx, D.H. & Cordell, C.E. (1990). The use of specific ectomycorrhizas to improve artificial forestation practices. In *Biotechnology of Fungi for Improving Plant Growth. B.M.S. Symposium Volume*, J.M. Whipps & B. Lumsden (eds), pp. 1–25. Cambridge University Press.

Menge, J.A. (1984). Inoculum production. In *VA Mycorrhiza*, C.L. Powel & D.J. Bagyaraj (eds), pp. 187–203. CRC Press, Boca Raton, Florida.

Menge, J.A., Lembright, A.H. & Johnson, E.L.V. (1977). Utilisation of mycorrhizal fungi in citrus nurseries. *Proc. Int. Soc. Citriculture*, **1**, 129–32.

Mosse, B., Stribley, D.P. & Le Tacon, F. (1981). Ecology of mycorrhizae and mycorrhizal fungi. *Adv. Microbial Ecol.*, **5**, 137–210.

Prin, Y., Neyra, M., Ducousso, M. & Dommergues, Y. (1989). Viabilité d'un inoculum déterminée par l'activité réductrice de l'INT. *Agronomie Tropicale*, **44**, 13–19.

Ravolanirina, F., Blal, B., Gianinazzi, S. & Gianinazzi-Pearson, V. (1989). Mise au point d'une méthode rapide d'endomycorhization de *vitro* plants. *Fruits*, **44**, 165–70.

Roger, P.A. (1990). Blue-green algae (Cyanobacteria) in agriculture. In *Microorganisms that Promote Plant Productivity*, J.O. Dawson & P. Dart (eds). Nijhoff/Junk, The Hague (in press).

Roger, P.A., Kulasooriya, S.A. (1980). *Blue-green Algae and Rice*. IRRI, Manila.

Roger, P.A., Zimmerman, W.J. & Lumpkin, T. (1991). Microbiological management of wetland ricefields. In *Soil Microbial Technologies*, B. Metting (ed.) (in press).

Sougoufara, B., Diem, H.G. & Dommergues, Y. (1989). Response of field-grown *Casuarina equisetifolia* to inoculation with *Frankia* strain ORS 021001 entrapped in alginate beads. *Plant and Soil*, **118**, 133–7.

Subba Rao, N.S. (1986). *Biofertilizers in Agriculture*. A.A. Balkema, India.

Venkataraman, G.S. (1981). Blue-green algae for rice production. A manual for its promotion. *FAO Soil Bull.*, no. 46, 102 p.

Williams, P.M. (1984). Current use of legume inoculant technology. In *Biological Nitrogen Fixation. Ecology, Technology and Physiology*, M. Alexander (ed.), pp. 173–200. Plenum Press, New York.

Wood, T. (1987). Commercial production of VA mycorrhiza inoculum: axenic versus non axenic techniques. In *Mycorrhizae in the Next Decade: Practical Application and Research Priorities*, D.M. Sylvia, L.L. Hung & J.H. Graham (eds), pp. 274. University of Florida, Gainesville.

4

Microalgal biotechnology: is it an economic success?

AVIGAD VONSHAK

Introduction

The potential uses of algal biomass for the benefit of mankind has been intensively reviewed in the last few years, resulting in several recent books and monographs (Borowitzka & Borowitzka, 1988; Richmond, 1986a,b; Lembi & Waaland, 1988). Rather than summarizing the available literature on algal biotechnology, the aim of this chapter is to present a personal view of the potential inherent in algal biomass production to become a viable economic enterprise, to review some of the economic studies which have been published and to point out the unique advantages that could make algal biotechnology a real economic success.

What is it all about?

Microalgae are aquatic microorganisms capable of carrying out the process of photosynthesis in the same way as higher plants. The main advantages of culturing microalgae as a source of biomass are as follows.

(1) Algae are considered to be the most efficient biological system for harvesting solar energy and for the production of organic compounds via the photosynthetic process.

(2) The entire biomass is available for harvest and use, as most algae are non-vascular plants and lack complex reproductive organs.

(3) Many species of algae can be induced to produce particularly high concentrations of chosen compounds – proteins, carbohydrates, lipids and pigments – that are of commercial value.

(4) Genetic selection and strain screening are relatively easy and

quick as algae are microorganisms without a sexual stage, undergoing simple cell division and completing their life cycle within a few hours. This also allows a much more rapid development and demonstration of viable production processes than other agricultural processes.

(5) Microalgae can be grown using marginal (brackish or sea) water, of particular interest in increasing productivity and securing a basic protein supply to regions of low productivity due to shortage of sweet water or poor soils.

(6) Algal biomass production systems can be easily adapted to various levels of operational skills and investment, from simple, labour intensive production units to fully automated, capital intensive operations.

What does it require?

The basic inputs and potential uses of algal biomass are presented in Fig. 4.1. While the inputs, including nutrients, are relatively inexpensive, the engineering requirements needed to ensure a sustainable, high rate of production should not be underestimated. These technical requirements are an essential part of algal biotechnology and they have to be integrated into the process in order to achieve economic success. These main technical factors are as follows.

MICROALGAL PRODUCTION

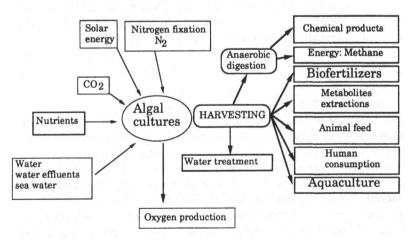

Fig. 4.1. *Inputs and potential outputs in algal biotechnology (by courtesy of Dr S. Boussiba).*

(1) *Shape and size of the algal pond.* These factors play a very important role in the investment and operating costs, as well as determining product quality. Several designs have been tried and are summarized by Dodd (1986).

(2) *Stirring and aeration.* There is no doubt that turbulence plays an important role in the performance of the biological production system. Various approaches have been suggested for the induction of a turbulent flow in large-scale raceway-type ponds (Vonshak *et al.*, 1982). Design of an efficient stirring device is a prerequisite to increase productivity and decrease energy inputs.

(3) *Harvesting.* An essential step in the harvesting process is removal of water to the stage where a wet slurry of at least 6–10% of dry weight is obtained. Even when grown to very high concentrations, algal cultures are relatively dilute biomass production systems, as in most cases overall biomass concentration in the pond is not more than 1 g per litre. The slurry obtained is then dried or processed according to the specific needs and requirements of the final product. Different technologies are available for this process and some economic consideration have been presented by Mohn (1988).

What is it good for?

Almost all the reviews on microalgal biotechnology point out the large number of products that can be extracted from algal biomass which are of commercial value (Ben-Amotz & Avron, 1983; Cohen, 1986). In spite of this potential, only a very limited number of algae have reached the stage of large scale, outdoor commercial production. Table 4.1 presents some of the algae currently grown on a large scale (or at least being tested in large-scale ponds) with their applications.

Microalgae in human nutrition

The potential use of algae such as *Spirulina* (filamentous blue-green algae, cyanobacteria) as a source of protein for human consumption has been widely recognized (Ciferi, 1983). The history of *Spirulina* as a staple in human diet is unique. There is evidence from the annals of the Spanish conquest of Mexico, in the early sixteenth century, that the Aztecs harvested mats of algal biomass reminiscent of *Spirulina* from Lake Texcoco, from which they made dry bricks which were then consumed. Likewise, for many generations dried *Spirulina* has been used as a food by the Kanembu tribe which lives along the shores of Lake Chad in Central Africa.

Table 4.1. *Microalgae of commercial interest grown under outdoor conditions*

Algae name	Product	Use or market
Spirulina	Protein, pigments	Health food, feed, aquaculture
Dunaliella	β-Carotene	Health food, feed
Porphyridium	Polysaccharides, pigments	Soil conditioning, food industry, diagnostics
Chlorella	Protein	Health food
Chlamydomonas	Polysaccharides	Soil conditioning
Anabaena	Nitrogen compounds	Biofertilizers
Isochrsis, Tetraselmis	Fatty acids	Aquaculture

Spirulina has a high protein content (60–70%), which is far more than other commonly used vegetable sources such as dry soybeans (35%), peanuts (25%) or grains (8–14%) (Henrickson, 1989). Determination of the net protein utilization (NPU) value of *Spirulina* (a measure used in nutritional studies to rank the quality of a protein, based on its content of essential amino acids, its digestibility and biological value), has shown a high NPU value, similar to many grains and higher than nuts. A special value of *Spirulina* is that it is readily digested due to the absence of cellulose in its cell walls, and its protein is then quickly assimilated.

The composition of commercial *Spirulina* powder is 60% protein, 20% carbohydrates, 5% fats, 7% minerals, and 3–6% moisture, making it a low-fat, low calorie, cholesterol-free source of protein. Another important benefit of *Spirulina* in the human diet is its vitamin content. One gram of powder contains 46% of the US Recommended Daily Allowance (RDA) of β-carotene (pro-vitamin A), and is thus valuable in therapeutic diet supplementation. *Spirulina* also contains extremely large quantities of vitamin B_{12}; one gram of powder would supply 53% of the RDA, making it the richest natural, vegetable source for this vitamin, and a very important source of this vitamin for those on vegan diets (totally vegetarian, no animal source foods). *Spirulina* also contains 21% of the RDA in thiamin and riboflavin. Many studies have been reported on the importance of *Spirulina* as an iron supplement, as well as a source of essential fatty acids (Henrickson, 1989).

The hope generated in the 1950s and 1960s that microalgae could become an inexpensive alternative source of protein has not materialized. The relatively low yields of algal biomass obtained in large-scale production sites resulted in a high cost of production which presently presents extensive use of microalgal biomass as food. Nevertheless, it should be pointed out even at this stage that mass cultures of several microalgae species grown outdoors reached decent yields of protein per unit area or per unit of water consumed, higher yields than for conventional crops.

Microalgae as animal feed

Microalgae are widely used as a traditional feed in the aquaculture industry. In some cases it has been demonstrated that in the early development stages of molluscs and crustaceans there is a specific requirement for microalgae (Walne, 1974; Webb & Chu, 1982). Microalgae are available as a feed-chain component in the natural habitat of these animals. The constant increase in production of aquaculture products and the intensification of the process have raised the need for a much larger supply of particular microalgae than just the amount that can be harvested from natural habitats. At present, most hatcheries produce their own microalgae on site, and some of them have developed the process of selling algal concentrate to other hatcheries. The main problem is that the hatcheries are lacking the know-how for mass cultivation of microalgae, and even more problematic is the timing. There is a continuous need for fresh biomass, as aquaculture methods have in many cases replaced seasonal spawning and developmental stages of fish larvae with year-around culture, and often optimal growth conditions in nature do not coincide with the fish larvae and mollusc development stages.

Dunaliella, another microalga currently grown on a large scale, has also been the subject of nutritional studies. Ben-Amotz, Edelstein & Avron (1986) showed that dry *Dunaliella bardawil*, rich in β-carotene, successfully replaced synthetic retinol in a chick diet. Recently, new findings on the use of *Dunaliella* in animal (rat) diets show that it may replace the artificially added retinol when incorporated in the diet in either dry form or as an oil extract (Nagasawa *et al.*, 1989). The same study showed that *Dunaliella* as a source of β-carotene had a positive effect on both production and body growth.

So what is the problem?

While the productivity of microalgae makes them an attractive source of biomass, the complexity of the conventional production system acts as a barrier for further applications as an inexpensive, though nutritional, source of food and feed. The need to avoid contamination in open raceway ponds and the high investment costs necessitate that the end product be a valuable chemical or that the biomass is sold as a health food product for human consumption, rather than as an inexpensive, bulk protein diet supplement. Thus, much more work has to be done to increase productivity and to improve the engineering design so that much more affordable products can be introduced.

Economic feasibility (or how much does it really cost?)

A number of studies on the economics and cost analysis of algal biotechnology have been published in the past 12 years (Benemann, Tillett & Weissman, 1987; Dynatech R&D, 1978; Richmond, 1986a; Valderrama, Cardenas & Markovitz, 1987). Nevertheless, there is no aspect of algal biotechnology in which assumptions have played a greater role than in the study of its economic feasibility.

In this review, two particular economic studies are presented. The first is based on an actual cost of construction and operation of the Earthrise Farms in southern California (USA). This is an example of applying an intensively technological process to provide a product which is mainly aimed at the American health food market (Jassby, 1988).

The second study is based on a small operation in Thailand which was carried out by a group from the King Mongkut's Institute of Technology in Thailand. This operation is mainly intended to produce *Spirulina* as an animal feed and not for direct human consumption. Information from other production sites (such as the one in Western Australia producing *Dunaliella*) is either not available or costs are known to be high.

As already stated, many calculations of construction and production costs for cultivation of microalgae are available in the literature. Only a few of the projections are based on real commercial experience, beyond the pilot scale of operations, and they typically miss some of the basic information about the problems encountered in large-scale operation that cannot be anticipated.

Table 4.2 provides information for the construction and operating costs of the microalgal production unit of Earthrise Farms, USA (modified after Jassby, 1988). This unit produces food-grade *Spirulina* using a pond area of 5 ha. The ponds are lined with a plastic sheet and the culture is circulated by paddlewheels. De-watering of the slurry is performed by screening and filtration, and the de-watered product is dried using a spray-drier.

From what is known, the total production of the Earthrise Farms in 1989 was 100 tonnes of food grade algae and 20 tonnes of feed grade algae. As presented in Table 4.2, the cost of production of *Spirulina* in

Table 4.2. *Major items of investment and production costs in a Spirulina production site (intended for high-value food grade production)*

Item	Cost (thousand US$)
Investment costs	
Land preparation & development; site operation	138
Water and power network	257
Buildings (labs, offices, shops)	79
Nutrients: storage and stock	50
Pond: including lining, pump, mixing	493
Harvesting: incl. filtering, drying, packing	541
TOTAL	1558
Annual production costs	
Manpower	320
Repair and maintenance	42
Fixed operating costs	163
Variable operating costs (gas, nutrients, power, etc.)	123
Administration, capital and depreciation	390
TOTAL	1038

the USA will be $11 000 per tonne. Although this calculation does not include cost of land and know-how, one should realize that with some minor technological improvements (such as covering the pond to increase daytime temperature during winter, or selecting a more adequate site) almost twice as much production may be expected, thus easily reducing the cost of production to below $9000 per tonne. Indeed, in the commercial site located in Bangkok, where temperatures are much more favourable for *Spirulina* growth, almost the same annual productivity is achieved in a total production area of 1.8 ha, which is less than 50% of the Earthrise Farms.

In Table 4.3, the estimated investment and annual production cost of a different set-up for the production of *Spirulina* biomass is presented. The production is based on the use of waste-water from a tapioca processing plant for the production of starch, in Thailand. The water is enriched with commercial fertilizers and biocarbonate. Harvesting and processing are carried out by filtration and sun-drying. The possibility of

Table 4.3. *Major items of investment and production costs in Spirulina production – Thailand site intended for feed quality products*

Item	Cost (thousand US$)
Investment costs	
Land preparation and development; site operation	112
Water and power network	58
Buildings (labs, offices, shops)	105
Pond: including lining, pump, mixing	120
Harvesting and drying:	
with spray drier	76
(without spray drier)	(40)
TOTAL	511
Annual production costs	
Manpower	24
Repair and maintenance	20
Fixed operating costs	44
Variable operating costs (gas, nutrients, power, etc.)	70
Administration, capital and depreciation	90
TOTAL	248

using spray-drying is also included, assuming a total production area of 1.8 ha with annual productivity of 40 tonnes.

From the data presented in Table 4.3, the projected cost (ex-factory) of *Spirulina* biomass in the tapioca plant in Thailand is between US$6000 and 7000 per tonne, much below the market price, as well as the cost for the Earthrise product. A relatively lower productivity is assumed because of the somewhat lower technology used. It is projected that after a few years of operation, modifications can be made to increase productivity by 20–30%, bringing the cost of production to about US$5000 per tonne, which will make this kind of installation an economic success since the product will be available to the large market of feed components for poultry and aquaculture industries.

Finally, one should remember that even in an on-going commercial production site, some uncertainty is to be expected in evaluating the cost of algal production. This is principally due to problems related to changes in environmental conditions, appearance of unexpected predators and the cost of research and development for further product improvement, processing stages or selection of better algal strains.

Is there another way of doing it: the village level

In both the approaches described above, the cost of production is still above the price that would make *Spirulina*, or indeed any other alga, an inexpensive alternative protein source for human consumption. The question is: can microalgal biotechnology offer any solution to the problems of hunger and malnutrition in Third World countries, where highly mechanized and highly capitalized projects have failed in the past, and do not have many prospects for immediate success in the near future? Is there another way of encouraging microalgal production, with units that can be scaled down and modified to suit the low-skilled labour force available in the villages of many developing countries?

Attempts are being made, mainly by Fox (1985), to set up demonstration projects in developing countries like India, Togo and Senegal.

The proposed system

The system proposed by Fox (1985) integrates sanitation, bio-gas generation, *Spirulina* production, composting and fish culture as designed for the village situation in developing countries. Although many problems have been encountered in each domain, the system has been standardized and the results are very encouraging.

A digester processes sewage and other wastes, producing bio-gas for running community cooking facilities, and a liquid effluent that is treated in a solar heater and then used to fertilize the algal ponds. The algal biomass is harvested with a woven cloth and de-watered in a solar drier. The system is designed to provide supplementary amounts of *Spirulina* – several grams per person each day – to the village inhabitants. The concept is ambitious. Problems regarding technology transfer, public health hazards, and cultural obstacles to re-cycling waste all hinder progress.

A somewhat simpler and less ambituous approach is provided by another group of researchers – Becker & Venkataraman (1983; 1984), Bai (1986) and Bai & Seshadri (1988). In these systems, little investment is required, providing a special impact on social life of a village, offering community ownership and cooperation to the population in remote areas.

Finally, it should be realized that algal biotechnology has turned out to be an economic success only in those cases where high-value products can be produced for wealthy western societies. Much more work on integrated systems as well as setting up demonstration projects in order to facilitate transfer of know-how, are required in order to make algal culture a suitable technology for Third World countries, providing local people with a readily available source of protein.

References

Bai, J.N. (1986). Mud pot cultures of the alga *Spirulina fusiformis* for rural house-holds, *Engineering of photosynthesis systems (Monograph series no. 19)*, pp. 1–39. Shri AMM Murugappa Chettiar Research Center, Madras, India.

Bai, N.J. & Seshadri, C.V. (1988). Small scale culture of *Spirulina* as a food supplement for rural house-holds – technology development and transfer. *Arch. Hydrobiol.*, **80**, 1–4.

Becker, E.W. & Venkataraman, L.V. (1983). *Biotechnology and exploitation of algae: the Indian approach*. German Agency for Technical Cooperation, Eschborn, FRG.

Becker, E.W. & Venkataraman, L.V. (1984). Production and utilization of the blue green alga *Spirulina* in India. *Biomass*, **4**, 105–25.

Ben-Amotz, A. & Avron, M. (1983). Accumulation of metabolites by Halotolerant algae and its industrial potential. *Ann. Rev. Microbiol.*, **37**, 95–119.

Ben-Amotz, A., Edelstein, S. & Avron, M. (1986). Use of the beta-carotene rich algae *Dunaliella bardawil* as a source of retinol. *Brit. Poultry Sci.*, **27**, 613–19.

Benemann, J.R., Tillett, D.M. & Weissman, J.C. (1987). Microalgae biotechnology. *Trends Biotechnol.*, **5**, 47–53.

Borowitzka, M.A. & Borowitzka, L.J. (eds) (1988). *Micro-Algal Biotechnology*. Cambridge University Press.

Ciferri, O. (1983). *Spirulina*, the edible microorganism. *Microbiol. Rev.*, **47**, 551–78.

Cohen, Z. (1986). Products from microalgae. In *Handbook of Microalgal Mass Culture*, A. Richmond (ed.), pp. 421–54. CRC Press, Boca Raton, FL.

Dodd, J.C. (1986). Elements of design and construction. In *Handbook of Microalgal Mass Culture*, A. Richmond (ed.), pp. 263–5, CRC Press, Boca Raton, FL.

Dynatech R&D Company Cambridge Massachusetts (1978). Cost analysis of aquatic biomass systems, prepared for the US department of Energy, Washington, D.C. HCP/ET-4000 78/1.

Fox, R.D. (1985). *Spirulina*, the alga that can end malnutrition. *The Futurist*, **19**, 30–5.

Henrickson, R. (1989). *Earth Food Spirulina*. Ronore Enterprises, Inc., Laguna Beach, CA.

Jassby, A. (1988). *Spirulina*, a model for microalgae as human food. In

Algae and Human Affairs, C.A. Lembi & J.R. Waaland (eds), pp. 149–79. Cambridge University Press.

Lembi, C.A. & Waaland, J.R. (eds) (1988). *Algae and Human Affairs*. Cambridge University Press.

Mohn, F.H. (1988). Harvesting of micro-algal biomass. In *Micro-Algal Biotechnology*, M.A. Borowitzka & L.J. Borowitzka (eds), pp. 395–414. Cambridge University Press.

Nagasawa, H., Konishi, R., Yamamoto, K. & Ben-Amotz, A. (1989). Effects of beta-carotene-rich algae *Dunaliella* on reproduction and body growth in mice. *In Vivo*, 3, 79–82.

Richmond, A. (ed.) (1986a). *Handbook of Microalgal Mass Culture*. CRC Press, Boca Raton, FL.

Richmond, A. (1986b). Microalgal culture. *CRC Crit. Rev. Biotechnol.*, 4, 369–438.

Valderrama, A., Cardenas, A. & Markovitz, A. (1987). On the economics of *Spirulina* production in Chile, with details on dragboard mixing in shallow ponds. *Hydrobiologia*, 151, 71–4.

Vonshak, A., Abeliovich, A., Boussiba, S. & Richmond, A. (1982). Production of *Spirulina* biomass: effects of environmental factors and population density, *Biomass*, 2, 175–86.

Walne, P.R. (1974). Culture of bivalve molluscs, 50 years of experience at Conwy, *Fishing News* (Books) Ltd., Surrey, UK.

Webb, K.L. & Chu, F.L.E. (1982). Phytoplankton as a food for bivalve larvae. In *Proceedings of the Second International Conference on Aquaculture Nutrition: Biochemical and Physiological Approaches to Shellfish Nutrition*, G.D. Pruder, C.J. Langdon & D.E. Conklin (eds), pp. 272–91. Louisiana State University Press, Baton Rouge, LA.

5

Production of useful biochemicals by higher-plant cell cultures: biotechnological and economic aspects

A. SASSON

Plant secondary metabolites

The distribution of secondary metabolites in plants is far more restricted than that of primary metabolites; a compound is often only found in a few species, or even within a few varieties within a species. Though their function in plant metabolism is unclear, nevertheless they may have an ecological role, e.g. as sexual attractants for pollinating insects or in defence mechanisms against predators (Grisebach, 1988). Secondary metabolites often accumulate in the plant in small quantities sometimes in specialized cells. Hence their extraction is often difficult. Among them are many compounds which are commercially important as medicinal substances, fragrances, food additives (pigments, flavouring and aromatic compounds) and pesticides (Heble & Chadha, 1985b; Kurz, 1989).

In spite of the progress made in organic synthesis or semi-synthesis of a wide range of compounds similar to those produced by the plants, extraction of secondary metabolites from plants is still of considerable commercial importance. A large number of these metabolites are difficult or virtually impossible to synthesize at economic values. In several cases, the natural product is more easily accepted by consumers than an artificially produced one. The term 'secondary metabolite' still applies to a large number of aromas or fragrances which are mixtures of hundreds of different compounds. This is the case with many essential oils, flavours and fragrances. Many of the components, moreover, have complex molecular structures (e.g. some alkaloids and glycosides).

There is great interest in developing alternatives to the intact plant for the production of plant secondary metabolites. This originally had centred on the use of tissue and cell cultures though the most recent approaches involve applying molecular biology techniques to enhance the metabolic pathways leading to specific compounds. During the past three decades, research has concentrated on the use of plant cell and tissue cultures, particularly in Japan and Germany but also to a lesser extent in the USA, for the commercial production of a wide range of secondary metabolites, in just the same way as bacteria and fungi have been used for antibiotic or amino-acid production (Sasson, 1988; Kurz, 1989).

Plant cell cultures: advantages and drawbacks

Plant tissue cultures were first established in 1939–40 (Evans *et al.*, 1983–6). However, it was only in 1956 that the first patent for the production of metabolites by mass cell cultures was filed by the American pharmaceutical company, Pfizer Inc. (Pétiard & Bariaud-Fontanel, 1987). The potential of plant cell cultures to produce useful compounds, especially for drug development, was perceived in the late 1960s. Thus Kaul & Staba (1967) and Heble, Narayanaswamy & Chadha (1968) isolated visnagin and diosgenin respectively from cell cultures in larger quantities than from the whole plant. However, a large number of cultures failed to synthesize products characteristic of the parent plant. For instance, morphinan, tropane and quinoline alkaloids are synthesized only at extremely low levels in cell cultures (Berlin, 1986). This is one reason why, after an initial surge of interest, the trend of research has been in decline.

In 1976, at an international congress held in Munich, Zenk and his co-workers demonstrated the outstanding metabolic capabilities of plant cells and highlighted the spontaneous variability of plant cell biosynthetic capacity, which could explain the contradictory results obtained earlier. This natural variability is exploited to identify high-yielding cultures for use on an industrial scale (Tabata *et al.*, 1976; Zenk et al., 1977; Zieg, Zito & Staba, 1983; Yamada, 1984; Benjamin *et al.*, 1986). Since the late 1970s, research and development in this area has seen a high increase in the number of patent applications filed, especially by the scientific and corporate sectors in the western part of Germany and Japan. In 1983, for the first time, a dye, shikonin, with anti-inflammatory and anti-bacterial properties, was produced by plant cell cultures on an industrial scale by Mitsui Petrochemical Industries Ltd (Fujita *et al.*, 1982). However, although this was thought to be a major breakthrough, shikonin production is still (in 1990) the only plant product to be produced on a commercial scale by cell cultures.

Confronted with having to increase the amount of secondary metabolites in plant cell cultures, the need for greater biochemical and molecular research on the secondary metabolism of plants has been frequently emphasized (Fowler, 1981; 1984*a,b*; Misawa, 1985; Berlin, 1986; Stafford, Morris & Fowler, 1986). The results of research in this area could lead to the successful manipulation of secondary metabolism and significantly increase the amounts of the compound(s) sought.

It is now thought that any substance of plant origin can be produced by cell cultures. Thus it should be possible to achieve the synthesis of a wide range of compounds such as alkaloids, flavonoids, terpenes, steroids, glycosides etc., i.e. a total of several hundreds with complex chemical structures, using plant cell culture technology. It also seems possible to identify cell lines that can produce amounts of compounds equal or even higher than those in the plant from which they derive. Furthermore, new molecules which have not been found previously in plants or have even been synthesized chemically, have been produced by cell cultures. Thus this technology constitutes a genuinely new means of achieving production of novel metabolites.

Finally, plant cells can transform natural or artificial compounds, introduced into the cultures, through a variety of reactions such as hydrogenation, dehydrogenation, isomerization, glycosylation, hydroxylation, opening of a ring and addition of carbon atoms (Rajnchapel-Messai, 1988). On the other hand, growing plant cells on a large scale would permit a stricter control of the quality of the products as well as their regular production without dependence on the variations of natural production resulting from climate and socio-political changes in their countries of origin.

The techniques of plant cell cultures include the following sequential stages or developments: selection from among wild plants for a high-producing one, *in-vitro* culture or callogenesis, which involves the selection and stabilization of producing calli with a view to identifying a high-producing line or strain; maximizing callus or cell suspension, culture conditions and isolation of the best-producing line; industrial scaling-up, mass cultivation in bioreactors; downstream processing, i.e. extraction and purification of the compounds sought.

Means for increasing plant secondary metabolites

There are several means of increasing the production of secondary metabolites by plant cell cultures or suspensions. These are:

> use of biotic or abiotic elicitors that could stimulate the metabolic pathways as in the intact plant;
> addition of a precursor of the desired compound in the culture medium with a view to increasing its production or inducing changes in the flux of carbon to favour the expression of pathways leading to the compound(s) sought, i.e. alteration of controls of secondary metabolism pathways;

production of new genotypes through protoplast fusion or
genetic engineering (but this presupposes the identification of
the genes encoding key enzymes of secondary metabolic
pathways and their expression once introduced in the plant
cells);
use of mutagens to increase the variability already existing in
living cells;
use of root cultures.

The use of mutagens could increase the naturally occurring diversity
among the cell clones and induce the creation of new higher-producing
lines or strains. Also cell fusion and gene transfer could improve the
synthesis capacity of cells. However, the results of these efforts depend
on the knowledge of the metabolic pathways and their genetic control.

Alteration of controls of secondary metabolism pathways
For the majority of secondary metabolism pathways, the proposed
biosynthesis, deduced from chemical considerations and feeding experiments, must await verification by the identification of the corresponding
enzyme reactions. Thus, direct manipulations of the pathways are not
possible due to the lack of enzymological background (Berlin, 1988).
Enzymological knowledge relating to secondary metabolism pathways
has been drawn from the studies of cell suspension systems (Hahlbrock
& Grisebach, 1979; Zenk, 1980; Zenk *et al.*, 1985) but organ cultures and
intact plants are excellent sources for such enzymes.
    Another issue related to the possible alteration of secondary metabol-
ism pathways concerns the identification of those enzymes which are
regulatory or rate-limiting. This is most probably the case for enzymes at
the beginning of a sequence or at branching points of metabolic
pathways, especially when their absence prevents *de novo* formation of
the compounds or when manifold increases in the activity of these
enzymes are observed under conditions promoting a major increase in
product formation. It is also necessary to know whether the other
biosynthetic enzymes are co-induced with the proposed regulatory
enzyme or are permanently present even in non-producing cell cultures.
Such knowledge helps to evaluate the possibility of specifically manipulating these secondary metabolism pathway(s) to increase the concentration of the desired product.
    It is generally assumed that the regulatory genes occur as gene
families and that each gene within one family is separately controlled
and is thus expressed by a different signal. Thus, direct alterations of
such controls would be difficult to achieve (Berlin, 1988). It is, however,
possible to introduce a desired gene into an intact plant through suitable
vectors and have the gene expressed in a specific organ such as the

chloroplasts (Broeck *et al.*, 1985; Fraley *et al.*, 1985; Klee, Yanofsky & Nester, 1985; Potrykus *et al.*, 1985; Abel *et al.*, 1986; Eckes *et al.*, 1986; Schocher *et al.*, 1986; Shah *et al.*, 1986). The gene coding for chalcone synthase (CHS) could be the first plant gene to be used in such a transformation process to study its interference with a secondary metabolism pathway. Veltkamp & Mol (1986) have carried out experiments aimed at repairing anthocyanin biosynthesis in mutants deficient in CHS through genetic transformation.

Although there is no example of altering the regulatory controls of secondary metabolism pathways through genetic engineering (with a view to improving the production rates in cell cultures of a desired compound), this seems to be the only promising approach. To achieve this end, it is crucial that more genes coding for biosynthetic enzymes with a regulatory function in secondary metabolism pathways should be identified. Another approach which might be more relevant biotechnologically would be to transfer plant genes into bacteria and to express them for stereospecifically difficult biotransformations (instead of organic synthesis). Once the genes for the relevant enzymes are isolated and cloned, it could then be decided whether transformed plant cells, transformed microorganisms or immobilized enzymes are the best for increasing the production of a specific compound (Berlin, 1988).

Effects of elicitors

The use of abiotic and biotic elicitors is a promising tool to improve the yields of products in cell-culture systems (DiCosmo & Misawa, 1985). Biosynthesis of flavonoids is induced by light via phytochrome or/and UV-photoreceptors and by infection with phytopathogenic organisms or compounds which induce the synthesis of antimicrobial compounds in plants. The addition of an extract of *Verticillium*, a parasitic fungus of plants, has induced the synthesis of gossypol by cell suspensions of *Gossypium arboreum* (Heinstein, 1984, in Pétiard & Bariaud-Fontanel, 1987; see also Cramer *et al.*, 1985).

It can be predicted that very specific elicitors should be found which will significantly improve the amounts of morphinan, tropane, or quinoline alkaloids in plant cell cultures (Berlin, 1988). The increase in the production of morphinic alkaloids by poppy cells could be likewise increased but this is still an empirical procedure and a single general rule cannot be formulated. The elicitor needs to be added regularly and this therefore complicates its use.

Bioconversion

Plant cells can transform a wide range of substrates and thus perform several reactions such as oxidation, hydroxylation, reduction, methylation, glucosylation, acylation and amino-acylation (Furuya, 1978; Heble *et al.*, 1983; Heble & Chadha, 1985*b*).

One could cite the transformation of steviol by cells of *Stevia rebaudiana* into a glycoside, steviobioside, which is 300 times sweeter than sucrose and which is used as a sweetener in Japan. Another example is that of salicylic acid which is glycosylated by cell cultures of *Mallotus japonica* to give a product having a higher analgesic power and better tolerated in the stomach than aspirin (acetylsalicylate).

In the case of *Digitalis lanata*, two cardiotonic compounds are isolated from the leaves: digitoxin in large quantities and digoxin in small quantities. Only digoxin has interesting pharmaceutal properties, but it cannot be produced either chemically or by microbial bioconversion. A bioconversion of highly pharmaceutical interest is the 12-hydroxylation of the cardiotonic drug β-methyl-digitoxin into the more desirable, less toxic drug, β-methyl-digoxin, by cell cultures of *Digitalis lanata* (Reinhard & Alfermann, 1980; Alfermann, Spieler & Reinhard, 1985). Using selection techniques, higher-yielding cell lines have been isolated and the most effective bioconversion achieved so far has been 1 g per litre during a 28-day cultivation period (Heble *et al.*, Bio-Organic Division, Bhabha Atomic Research Centre, Trombay, Bombay, India).

Root cultures

After the pioneering work of White (1939) who established tomato root cultures capable of unlimited growth in media containing macro- and micro-nutrients, sucrose and yeast extract, Dawson, in 1942, succeeded in growing the roots of the tobacco plant. In 1957, Solt observed that the increase of nicotine concentrations in tobacco root cultures closely paralleled the increase in root tissue as measured through root length, number of branches and dry weight accumulation (in Flores, Hoy & Pickard, 1987). It was also shown that root cultures of henbane (*Hyoscyamus niger*) synthesize hyoscyamine (in Flores *et al.*, 1987).

In *Datura* cells, alkaloid production was inversely correlated to the growth rate of callus cultures (Lindsey & Yeoman, 1983, in Flores *et al.*, 1987). Undifferentiated calli of *Atropa belladonna* do not produce the tropane alkaloid hyoscyamine but production does occur when roots form on the callus (Bhandary *et al.*, 1969, in Flores *et al.*, 1987). The cardiotonic glycosides of *Digitalis* are produced when calli are induced to undergo embryogenesis following treatment with plant growth regulators (Kuberski *et al.*, 1984, in Flores *et al.*, 1987). All these observations have led researchers to use continuously growing, organized plant tissue cultures or even cultures of organs such as roots for the production of secondary metabolites.

Chilton *et al.* (1982) discovered that the soil microorganism, *Agrobac-*

terium rhizogenes, caused a 'hairy root' disease affecting a wide range of dicotyledonous species and resulting in the proliferation of fast-growing adventitious roots at the host wound site (due to the stable integration of a portion of the Ri plasmid of *A. rhizogenes* into the plant genome). Hairy roots were then established as aseptic cultures after treatment with antibiotics. Researchers of the Plant Biotechnology Group, Agriculture and Food Research Council Institute of Food Research, Norwich Laboratory, United Kingdom, used transformed root cultures as a genetically and biochemically stable system for the study and production of secondary metabolites. The resulting stable high-producing lines may potentially be exploited directly as cultures in bioreactors or as plants in the field following plant regeneration (Rhodes *et al.*, 1988).

Axenic transformed root cultures of *Nicotiana rustica* and *Datura stramonium* (which respectively produce nicotine and the tropane alkaloids hyposcyamine and scopolamine) were developed following inoculation of plant material with *Agrobacterium rhizogenes* strain LBA9402. The exact nature of the factors leading to root formation are still poorly understood. Transformed roots grow fast by plant standards; they show a logarithmic pattern of growth with doubling times which can be less than 48 hours and are characterized by a high degree of branching. This growth is associated with the production of the characteristic secondary metabolites that resemble the parent plant species in terms of both absolute amounts and spectrum of products (Rhodes *et al.*, 1988).

More than 20 hairy root clones of *Hyoscyamus muticus* (Flores & Filner, 1985, in Flores *et al.*, 1987) produced tropane alkaloids at the same concentrations as in the whole plant or in normal root cultures. Alkaloid production has been stable in two selected clones for over 40 monthly passages, but decreased markedly when roots were induced to form calli, and then reappeared when calli underwent root differentiation (Flores *et al.*, 1987). Furthermore, biomass production was very high: from an initial inoculum of 2–4 mg (1–2 root tips), a typical hairy root clone of *Hyoscyamus muticus* grown in batch culture over three weeks showed a 2500- to 5000-fold increase, i.e. a higher increase than that obtained with the fastest cell suspensions. The results with *Hyoscyamus muticus* roots were extended to *Datura* and *Scopolia* species (Flores *et al.*, 1987).

It has been shown that hairy root cultures of *Beta vulgaris* and *Nicotiana rustica* synthesized betalains and nicotine plus anabasine, respectively, and that a significant portion of tobacco alkaloids was found in the growth medium of a 20-day batch culture. Hairy roots of *Atropa belladonna* were shown to form atropine and scopolamine at concentrations comparable with those found in field-grown plants and higher than those found in untransformed root cultures (Kadama *et al.*, 1986, in Flores *et al.*, 1987). Marro *et al.* (1986, in Flores *et al.*, 1987) examined 29 hairy root clones of *Scopolia japonica* and isolated two highly productive clones: clone S1 which accumulated scopolamine to 0.5% (w/w) dry weight and clone S22 which synthesized hyoscyamine at 1.3% (w/w) dry weight. Normal root cultures of several *Hyoscyamus* species accumulated hyoscyamine and scopolamine in the range 0.04–1.1% (w/w) dry weight and 0.06–0.3% (w/w) dry weight, respectively (Hashimoto *et al.*, 1986, in Flores *et al.*, 1987).

The production of alkaloids derived from the tropane ring by root cultures, as well as that of β-xanthine, is not exceptional. Hairy root cultures have been used to produce the secondary metabolites of the family Asteraceae (1000 genera and over 15 000 species), i.e. the sesquiterpene lactones and the polyacetylenes. The latter are very active against bacteria, fungi and nematodes. They are found in the roots and their synthesis may be elicited by infection with fungal pathogens. During 1986, over 30 normal and hairy root clones from the general *Ambrosia*, *Bidens*, *Rudbeckia* and *Tagetes* were established by Flores *et al.* (1987). These clones grew faster than their normal counterparts, produced thiophene-like compounds similar to those of normal roots and were stable for several monthly passages. It was concluded therefore that these organ cultures could synthesize polyacetylenes and their cyclic derivatives (Flores *et al.*, 1987).

According to results obtained at Cornell University, Ithaca, New York, cultures of onion roots in bioreactors are more favourable for the production of onion aroma than cell suspensions. These differentiated tissues are able to produce directly the complex chemical aromatic compounds that are then released into the culture medium and can be subsequently isolated by high-pressure liquid chromatography. Thirteen different species of onions from Europe, Japan and North America have been tested and several seem to be valuable for the industrial production of onion aroma. Culture conditions have been studied and it was reported that the final aroma could be modified by changing the precursors in the culture medium. The onion aroma produced by onion roots in culture would be much more related to the natural one than current available preparations (in *Biofutur*, no. 71, September 1988, p. 13).

Root cultures could thus become commercial sources of many secondary metabolites following the example from Rhodes *et al.* (1986, in Flores *et al.*, 1987) who reported the production of nicotine by hairy root cultures of *Nicotiana rustica* in a two-stage batch/continuous-flow system. These cultures showed a rapid growth rate and released a major portion of nicotine into the culture medium. A prototype for a large-scale bioreactor has now been developed for growing hairy roots of *Hyoscyamus muticus* (in Flores *et al.*, 1987).

Transformed roots are also being used to elucidate the control mechanisms of secondary metabolism pathways with a view to enhancing the production of metabolites. For instance, Rhodes *et al.* (1988) have been developing an approach to manipulate the metabolic pathway at the level of the individual gene and thus the individual enzyme. It involves identifying genes coding for enzymes that are under-expressed in culture, then to isolate the gene and to re-introduce it into the plant under the control of de-regulated, high-expression promoters to increase carbon flux through the pathway. In addition to putrescine methyltransferase (PMT), ornithine decarboxylase (ODC) limits the part of the metabolic pathway common to nicotine and hyoscyamine biosynthesis. Thus, Rhodes *et al.* (1988) have transferred the gene coding for ODC from *Saccharomyces cerevisiae* into transformed roots of *Nicotiana rustica* where it is under the regulatory control of the cauliflower mosaic virus 35S promoter. The gene was integrated into the plant genome and was successfully transcribed into a fully active enzyme. The pattern of expression of other enzymes involved in biosynthesis of the alkaloids was unaffected in the transformed cells.

Another approach is to study the co-ordinated regulation of the expression of the entire pathway in order to understand how the expression of the group of genes is temporally and developmentally regulated. This would lead to the manipulation of this regulation to optimize expression of the whole pathway (Rhodes *et al.*, 1988).

To sum up, the use of root cultures as a commercial source of secondary metabolites will depend on the scaling-up of production and recovery techniques, on the further knowledge of the regulatory signals which induce the production of compounds at over 10% dry weight, and on the identification of high-value biochemicals in the roots (Sasson, 1988).

Industrial production of useful biochemicals by higher-plant cell cultures

Market-value estimations

Economic considerations govern the importance attached to the production of natural substances and biochemicals (see Table 5.2). The estimated annual market value of pharmaceutical products of plant origin in industrialized countries was over US $20 billion in the mid-1980s. The annual market value of codeine and of the anti-tumour alkaloids, vinblastine and vincristine, has been estimated at about US

Table 5.1. *Economic data for some substances of plant origin.*

Substance and use	Annual needs	Industrial cost (US$ per kg)	Estimated annual market value (in US$ million)
Pharmacy			
ajmalicine	3–5 tonnes	1500	4.5–7.5
codeine	80–150 tonnes	650–900	52–135
digoxin	6 tonnes	3000	18
diosgenin	200 tonnes	20–40	4–8
vinblastine vincristine	5–10 kg	5 million	25–50
Food-additives and fragrances			
jasmine oil	100 kg	5000	0.5
mint oil	3000 tonnes	30	90
natural vanillin	30 tonnes	2500	75
Cosmetics			
shikonin	150 kg	4000	0.6

Sources: Fontanel & Tabata, 1987; Rhodes *et al.*, 1986; Scragg, 1986; Rajnchapel-Messai, 1988.

$100 million per product (Pétiard & Bariaud-Fontanel, 1987). The world-wide market value of aromas and fragrances has been estimated at over US $4 billion in 1980 and is expected to rise to US $6 billion in 1990 (Rajnchapel-Messai, 1988).

In 1988, the estimated annual market value of shikonin (for details see below) was about US $600 000 which is far from the US $20–50 million investment of the original research and development work. However, the final cost of the product fell to US $4000 per kg which compares with US $4500 per kg for the substance extracted from the roots of *Lithospermum erythrorhizon*. It should be noted that Kanebo, the Japanese cosmetics corporation, which developed lipsticks containing shikonin, realized a turnover of about US $65 million over two years in Japan through the sale of 5 million lipsticks, each lipstick selling for US $13. In the Republic of Korea and China, Mitsui Petrochemicals Ltd today intends to market the product itself (Rajnchapel-Messai, 1988).

Major constraints of industrial production

Industrial or commercial scaling-up of the production of useful substances by cell cultures or suspensions should take into account the following properties, some of which could be major constraints. These are: slow growth of cells with doubling times of 24–48 hours requiring usually two to three weeks to provide sufficient biomass; susceptibility to microbial contamination; use of axenic cultures; oxygen needs; and susceptibility to shearing stresses due to the large cell size which on average is 200 000 times larger than that of bacteria. In general, cell multiplication and metabolite synthesis are uncoupled, the latter occurring at the end of the growth phase.

Achievements

Significant progress has been made to overcome the major constraints of industrial production since the late 1960s. Heble *et al.* of the Bio-Organic Division of the Bhabha Atomic Research Centre, Trombay, Bombay, India, are carrying out research on mass cultivation in 20-litre capacity bioreactors of selected cell lines of *Rauwolfia serpentina* (ajmaline, reserpine), *Papaver somniferum* (thebaine, codeine, morphine), *Artemisia annua* (artemisinin), and other plant species (Chadha, Rao & Heble, 1988).

In Japan, the Nitto Denki corporation uses a non-continuous process for biomass production of *Panax ginseng* in 20 000-litre bioreactors, the yield being 500 mg dry matter per litre per day (Rajnchapel-Messai, 1988). Hashimoto *et al.* (1982, in Pétiard & Bariaud-Fontanel, 1987) succeeded in cultivating tobacco cells in 20 000-litre bioreactors for over two months with yields being 5.82 g dry matter per litre per day. Fujita *et al.* (1982) selected a highly productive cell line of *Lithospermum erythrorhizon* (Ko-shikon), and developed a two-stage growth and production method for shikonin, which is an anthraquinone extensively used in Japan for its anti-inflammatory and antibacterial properties and also as a dye. This substance is found in the roots of the plant which accumulates up to 2–3% of its dry weight as shikonin, the plant taking 5–7 years to reach a size useful for commercial production. No method is yet available to synthesize shikonin. In 1983, Mitsui Petrochemical Industries Ltd reported a technique for the industrial-scale production of shikonin by cell cultures. The process involved two stages: (1) plant cells were first grown in a 200-litre capacity bioreactor and (2) the resulting biomass was then transferred into a second bioreactor in which the composition of the culture medium favoured the synthesis of shikonin. Even though the capacity of the second bioreactor was only 750 litres, the Japanese technique marked an important turning point in the bio-industrial application of plant tissue cultures (Fowler, 1984*b*). In a 23-day culture period, cells grown in the 750-litre bioreactor accumulated 23% of their dry weight as shikonin (Curtin, 1983). The productivity of *L. erythrorhizon* cell cultures was 60 mg per gram of cells per week, that is 1000 times higher than that of the plant roots which required a longer time period of 5–7 years.

The success of shikonin production was due to the selection of a cell line which accumulated a ten-fold higher level of shikonin than that found in roots of the mature plant. This achievement resulted from an empirical, labour-intensive search for optimal growth conditions and production media which was further facilitated by a visual selection for overproducing cells. Cell cultures have now thus become the major commercial source of shikonin (Flores *et al.*, 1987).

In addition to the work on shikonin, Japanese scientists were able to obtain higher quantities of berberine from growing cells of *Coptis berberica*. This plant species accumulates significant amounts of berberine in its roots in 4–6 years; similar concentrations could be obtained in four weeks using tissue culture. Hara *et al.* of Mitsui Petrochemical Industries Ltd have isolated a cell line of *Coptis japonica* that contains 10% of berberine (dry weight) and which could produce about 1500 mg of this antibacterial and antipyretic alkaloid per litre in 14 days. Analysis of cell lines by flow cytometry indicates that the increase in berberine production resulting from cell selection is related to the increase in the number of cells with a high content of berberine, rather than to an overall increase in this content in all the cells. Thus, the high-yielding line is most probably heterogeneous (in *Biofutur*, no. 83, October 1989, p. 17). Industrial production of geraniol is also being developed by the cosmetic company Kanebo (Rajnchapel-Messai, 1988).

In the western part of Germany, Alfermann *et al.* (1985) of Boehringer Mannheim AG were able to grow cells of *Digitalis lanata* in 200-litre bioreactors and obtain 500 g of β-methyl-digoxin in three months; the bioconversion rate of β-methyl-digitoxin was very high, up to 93.5%, if the non-used substrate was recycled. Ulbrich, Wiesner & Arens (1985) cultured *Coleus blumei* cells in a 42-litre bioreactor fitted with the module spiral stirrer; using this system with aeration, they reported high yields of rosmarinic acid (5.5 g per litre), representing 21% dry weight of cells. Heble & Chadha (1985*a,b*) reported the successful cultivation of *Catharanthus roseus* cells in 7 to 20-litre capacity bioreactors, modified to provide air lift and agitation, in single and multiple stages. The cells produced high levels of total alkaloids comprising ajmalicine and serpentine as the major components. It was shown that plant cells could withstand shear to some extent and that judicious use of air lift and low agitation was advantageous. Researchers at Ciba-Geigy AG, Basel, Switzerland, have produced the alkaloid scopolamine from cell cultures of *Hyoscyamus aegypticus* grown in air-lift bioreactors (in *McGraw-Hill's Biotechnology Newswatch*, 21 January 1984).

Sanguinarine is a benzophenantridin alkaloid extracted from the roots of *Papaver somniferum*. Three to four years are needed for plant maturation before the substance can be extracted. Cell cultures have been used to produce large quantities of this alkaloid, which is used in toothpastes and mouth lotions to combat dental plaque and tooth decay. Commercial production will be the result of a joint venture between the Plant Biotechnology Institute of the National Research Council of Canada, Saskatoon, and Vipont Research Laboratories Inc., Fort Collins, Colorado, USA. The manufacturing process will use the eliciting power of extracts of a fungus, an unspecified *Botrytis*, that induce the synthesis of sanguinarine and dihydrosanguinarine by plant cells. Pilot experiments have shown that in semi-continuous cultures, which could be elicited twice, the production rate of alkaloids reached 3% of dry biomass (in *Biofurtur*, no. 79, May 1989, p. 13).

These examples and others show that industrial production of plant cell biomass and secondary metabolites is possible with equipment and processes analogous to those used with microorganisms. From the economic viewpoint, Zenk made an estimate of US $500 per kg for the production of a drug by cell cultures at a rate of 1 g per litre. Goldstein, Ingle & Lasurel (1980) of Miles Laboratories Inc. (Bayer AG) also analysed the economics of plant-cell culture methods and suggested that products costing more than US $1000 per kg were suitable. With higher-yielding cultures, the production cost could be much lower. For a 10% dry weight yielding product, the cost could come down to US $228 per kg. This could be further reduced if immobilized cells were used (Sahai & Knuth, 1985; Heble & Chadha, 1986). According to a study carried out in Japan, any substance of plant origin with a value exceeding or equal to US $80 per g could be profitably produced by cell or tissue cultures. This would even apply to substances of which the retail price varies between US $250 and 500 per kg, i.e. many raw pharmaceutical products, aromatic compounds, condiments and fragrances (Fowler, 1984*b*; Vasil, 1987; 1988).

Immobilizing cells in a gel, which is permeable to the molecules of the nutrient medium, or on polymers (with a view to preserving their metabolic capacity and to using them several times), has the advantage of extending the production time of cells (over six months) and of making the cells catalyse the same reaction almost indefinitely. Active research has been carried out in this area since the early 1980s. Thus, the team of Furusaki of the Department of Engineering, Tokyo University, has developed a bioreactor for the production of codeine, which is mainly used as an anti-cough compound in pharmacy. Poppy cells have been immobilized in calcium alginate beads and they catalyse the conversion of codeinone into codeine. This technique enabled the Japanese researchers to overcome the drawbacks of plant-cell bioreactors, due to the instability of cells and the low yields of the desired compounds. They decreased the size of cell clusters (2.5 mm in diameter), thereby increasing their lifespan and obtaining yields of codeine that were equal to those in non-immobilized cells (in *Biofutur*, no. 79, May 1989, p. 14).

The use of immobilized cells should bypass the direct extraction of the compounds from the biomass as the products now arise in the medium itself. Examples of this approach include the production of caffeine, capsaicin and berberine. Many metabolites, however, still appear to accumulate in the cell vacuoles and it is therefore important to further gain information on how these metabolites may be made to diffuse out into the culture medium. Although immobilized cell technology is a promising technique, especially aimed at decreasing production costs, clearcut examples still do not exist which would demonstrate a gain of productivity on an industrial scale (Pétiard & Bariaud-Fontanel, 1987).

Prospects

With the onset of the 1990s, only Japan and, to a lesser extent, the western part of Germany are really engaged in the industrial production of secondary metabolites by plant cell cultures. The only marketed product (as of 1990) remains shikonin. In Japan, seven private corporations have created a common subsidiary in research and development on plant cell cultures. The Plant Cell Culture Technology (PCC Technology) has been set up with the support of the Japan Key Technology Centre (JKTC) by Kyowa Hakko Kogyo Co., Mitsui Petrochemical Industries Ltd, Mitsui Toatsu Chemical Inc., Hitachi Ltd, Suntory Ltd, Toa Nenryo Kogyo Co. and Kirin Breweries Co. Ltd. By contrast, most North American and European companies are not enthusiastic about the prospects regarding profitable industrial production (Rajnchapel-Messai, 1988).

Several factors or constraints could explain this situation. Firstly, the time needed for selection and stabilization of cell lines is about two to three years because of the difficulty of controlling and directing somaclonal variation. Consequently, there is a need for tedious and time-consuming screening of a large number of lines. Secondly, the lack of knowledge concerning biosynthetic pathways of secondary metabolites explains certain failures. For instance, it has not been possible to isolate a cell line with a good level of production of dimeric alkaloids of

Catharanthus roseus, although these alklaoids are present in minute quantities in the plant (one tonne of dry leaves yields 0.5–2 g of these compounds). Thirdly, the difficulties of extraction of the desired compounds are serious, especially when the compounds accumulate as combined substances; this probably explains why the French company Sanofi-Elf-Bio-industries has abandoned the production of codeine and morphine by cells of *Papaver somniferum*. However, according to Steck of Sanofi-Elf-Bio-industries, technical and scientific difficulties can be overcome in fairly short periods resulting in lower industrial production costs. It is, though, essential that a worthwhile target be identified in order to secure the necessary investments (Rajnchapel-Messai, 1988).

Thus the real difficulties are identification of target compounds as well as economic and legal considerations. Production of secondary metabolites by plant cell or tissue cultures must, of course, be competitive with other conventional means of production such as extraction from the field-grown plants, alternative enzymatic processes, chemical synthesis or semi-synthesis, microbial fermentation or improvement of the plant itself through somaclonal variation, genetic engineering, etc., followed by the regeneration of the plant from *in vitro* cultures.

Production by cell cultures could be justified, however, for rare products that are costly and difficult to obtain through other means. According to Pétiard of the French company Francereco, this approach would be feasible only for products whose world annual potential market would be US $20–50 million, with a minimum selling price of about US $400–500 per kg. Thus, ajmalicine and jasmine oil, in spite of their high-selling price – US $1500 and US $5000 per kg, respectively – are not attractive for industrial production by cell cultures because of the size of their market, i.e. US $8 million for ajmalicine and only US $500 000 for jasmine oil, which would not permit the amortization of the investments to be made in research and development. On the other hand, mint aroma, which represents an annual market of US $90 million, has a selling price which is too low – US $30 per kg – to be worth lowering further through cell-culture production. The challenge lies therefore with the identification of economically profitable targets (Rajnchapel-Messai, 1988). But as many companies throughout the world have considered these aspects, it may be concluded that such target compound that may have been identified will remain closely guarded secrets for some time to come.

In the pharmaceutical area, the number of economically profitable targets also appears to be rather limited. Many plant substances – or their derivatives from semi-synthesis – are used in drugs, and their production cost is often very high; their individual economic weight is nevertheless rather low. They are used in small quantities in a medicine whose final price is due more to the considerable investments in research and development than to the cost of raw materials. Furthermore, the 'plant production' approach is open to the strong competition of chemical synthesis that is very efficient in developing new molecules with highly specific activity. Thus, the development of new synthetic cardiotonic compounds in the USA has resulted in the decreased demand for *Digitalis* cardiotonic glycosides. It is also one of the causes for the non-commercialization of β-methyl-digoxin produced by *Digitalis* cell cultures (Rajnchapel-Messai, 1988). However, commercial production was envisaged for vincristine and vinblastine from *Catharanthus roseus* cell cultures by Eli Lilly & Co., ubiquinone from *Nicotiana* (Matsumoto *et al.*, 1982), L-dopa from *Mucunna pruriens* (Wichers & Pras, 1984) and digoxin from *Digitalis lanata* (Alfermann *et al.*, 1985).

Prospects are more promising for the production of aromatic substances, flavouring compounds and food additives, and basic materials for fragrances by plant cell or tissue cultures. These products, although less valuable than pharmaceuticals, have larger markets. This explains the recent re-orientation of research, as is witnessed by the four-fold multiplication of the number of publications devoted to food additives and cosmetics that were submitted to the 1986 Congress of the International Association of Plant Tissue Culture, held in Minneapolis, USA.

In this area, however, the difficulties relate to the very low investments made in research and development by the relevant companies involved with agriculture, food and perfumeries. In addition, technical difficulties should not be underestimated because most aromas and fragrances, with a few exceptions such as vanillin and irone (which is a violet fragrance extracted from iris rhizomes that needs to be stored for one to three years), are mixtures of a large number of compounds, some of which are present in minute amounts but which are nevertheless vital for the final product to be accepted. It is therefore very difficult to reproduce such mixtures exactly by cell cultures. The evaluation of productive cell lines must usually rely on the smell and taste of the perfumer or aromatician thus necessitating that such work is carried out in locations having easy access to such people. Consequently it is almost impossible to conduct such work outside industrial companies. These companies, however, are usually very conservative in their outlook and with only one or two exceptions have usually set their face against the feasibility of producing aromas, fragrances and flavours by anything other than conventional means. At first sight, this appears to be a very narrow approach but it should be remembered that many of these companies rely on suppliers and growers for a number of their products. To seek to produce one product by alternative means (i.e. plant cell culture) could jeopardize the future supply of a number of other products simply by the supplier or grower now refusing to do further business. Thus the balance between producer and seller is a subtle one and is one which neither party wishes to see upset.

Other issues are as follows. What will be the legal status of these new products? Will they be labelled 'natural'? Would it be possible to market them without a complementary toxicological study, as is currently the case for all substances extracted from new plant varieties bred and cultivated with conventional methods? The modification of the genetic heritage of these varieties is, however, much greater than the changes that may occur in cell suspensions (Pétiard & Bariaud-Fontanel, 1987).

Industrial production of food additives and fragrances

Food additives contribute to making foodstuffs palatable and attractive by enhancing or improving their flavour, colour and texture. Food technologies try to respond to these criteria especially with regard to the texture, taste and aroma of the foodstuff. The need to have the same taste and aroma in a specific foodstuff in order to suit the consumers' tastes makes it compulsory to use natural or artificial aromas, especially in certain products where they may be indispensable. A few decades ago, aromas were extracted from plant raw materials transformed by fermentation, grinding and heating. Later, chemical compounds, pure or as mixtures, completed the range of plant aromas. Nowadays, new compounds are added to the existing ones and they usually originate from enzymatic reactions, or are produced by biotechnological methods, i.e. by microbial and plant cells (Spinnler, 1989). Fermentation techniques are preferred to chemical synthesis if they are more cost-effective, e.g. in the production of citric acid and monosodium glutamate. Microbial synthesis is also the only means to produce the thickening additive xanthan.

Since the late 1950s, many food additives have been questioned, mainly by national and international regulatory authorities, about their safety for long-term use and consumption. At the same time, the associations of consumers, aware of the inclusion of additives in foodstuffs, have been exerting pressure on governmental bodies to have chemical or artificial additives replaced by 'natural' additives from plant or animal tissues, or be synthesized by microorganisms or plant cell cultures. New production processes would allow food industries to respond to the favourable opinion about natural aromas and also to overcome the present constraints related to the climatic and political vagaries of supply in the producing countries and to take advantage of the difference in price between naturally- and chemically-produced compounds. For instance, in the case of vanillin, its price is about 20 000 FF per kg if it is extracted from the vanilla pod, whereas it costs only 50 FF per kg if it is produced by chemical synthesis from lignin. Although this difference is considerable, it is not possible to differentiate the two kinds of vanillin molecules through chemical or physical analyses. Hopefully for aromas with a restricted market, eventual fraud will be easily detectable and presumably will be rigourously monitored by those industrialists who will benefit most from conserving their existing sales (Spinnler, 1989).

Pigments are also food additives but their use has been strongly criticized by the associations of consumers in the 1970s, because most of them are produced by chemical synthesis and are unrelated to any naturally occurring material. In the European Economic Community, 24 pigments are currently authorized of which 10 are not of natural origin. It is true that the colour of foodstuffs is associated with their acceptance and the pleasure they procure. Thus, the list of pigments used for this purpose is bound to become longer but the trend is to replace artificial colourings by natural ones. Market forces, however, will determine whether the public will pay increased costs for 'natural' products. The biotechnological methods used for the purpose of producing natural food colorants consist of growing microorganisms, microalgae and higher-plant cells (Langley-Danysz, 1987).

Extraction of pigments from plants is an old technique, e.g. anthocyanins from red berries, betanine from beet and curcumine from saffron. Some pigments cannot be extracted before the plant reaches the adult stage. This is the case of rocou, a pigment extracted from the seeds of a shrub, or of shikonin, extracted from the roots of *Lithospermum erythrorhizon*. In the case of shikonin, plant cell cultures have been very successful in the industrial production of this dye (see above).

Aromas and fragrances

Natural aromas are a mixture of numerous compounds: more than 500 have been identified in roasted coffee beans and 200 in apple. Natural aromas are susceptible to the conservation processes of foodstuffs such as sterilization, pasteurization, freezing, etc. Some aromas are altered by enzymatic or chemical reactions and usually disappear if stored for a long period. This is why substitutes have been sought for them since the end of the nineteenth century. Artificial aromas were manufactured from coal or oil derivatives and were added in very low concentrations (10^{-6} or ppm, and 10^{-9} or ppb). The present trends are either to produce synthetic molecules, which are identical to natural molecules, or to use biotechnological methods. The aromas in the first category have the advantage of a constant composition, of not depending on the season and of being manufactured in such a way that the production is adapted to the market. Their drawback is of not being mixtures of substances that resemble the natural ones. This is why the biotechnological routes are now being increasingly preferred (Langley-Danysz, 1987). For instance, Dziezak (1986, in Langley-Danysz, 1987) reported that the characteristic aromas of cocoa and coffee have been produced by cell cultures of *Coffea arabica* and *Theobroma cacao*, respectively.

The value of the world market for aromas and fragrances was estimated at about US $3 billion in 1988 (Vaisman, 1988). In 1987, the ten first world leading companies represented more than two-thirds of the total annual turnover, whereas in 1981 the same proportion was attributed to the first 20 companies (Coërs, 1989).

	1987
International Flavors and Fragrances (IFF, USA)	US$ 746 M
Quest (Unilever NV, UK and Netherlands)	635
Givaudan (Hoffmann–La Roche AG, Switzerland)	462
Takasago Perfumery (Japan)	441
Firmenich (Federal Republic of Germany)	333
Haarmann and Reimer (Bayer AG, FRG)	327
Dragoco (Federal Republic of Germany)	250
Roure (Hoffman–La Roche AG, Switzerland)	125
FDO (BASF AG, Federal Republic of Germany)	120
PFW (Hercules, USA)	100
Mane (France)	83
Robertet (France)	72
Sanofi-Elf-Bio-industries (France)	66
Florasynth (France)	—
T. Hasegawa Flavor Co. (Japan)	—
Ogawa (Japan)	—

According to the conclusions of a study carried out in France by a consulting firm, Précepta, the market of aromas and fragrances is soaring, compared with that of foodstuffs in general which is progressing at a slower pace. In the aroma and fragrance sector, 5–6%, and sometimes up to 12%, of the total turnover is devoted to research and development, i.e. one order of magnitude more than in the food sector (Coërs, 1989).

In Japan, the growth of the aroma and fragrance market was rather slow during the 1970s but the increasing consumption of perfumed home products ('air purifiers') induced a more rapid growth rate of the market which was evaluated at about US $0.8 billion in 1988. Several industrial companies have emphasized their diversification efforts in this sector: Takasago Perfumery, T. Hasegawa Flavor Co., Soda Aromatic Co., Shiono Koryo Kaisha Ltd, and Ogawa. Thus, Soda Aromatic Co. controls the market of deodorant substances and 80% of the Japanese market related to the deodorization of natural gas (Vaisman, 1988).

Plant cell cultures are a promising means of production of aromas and fragrances in Japan (Vaisman, 1988). Thus, Kirin Breweries Co. Ltd, Kyowa Hakko Kogyo Co., Mitsui Toatsu Chemical Inc., Mitsui Petrochemical Industries Ltd, Hitachi Ltd and Toa Nenryo Kogyo Co. have concluded co-operative agreements to produce aromatic substances by plant cell cultures. The expertise of Kirin Breweries in the manufacture of fragrances from humulane, a by-product of the processing of hops, and that of Mitsui Petrochemical Industries Ltd in the large-scale production of shikonin are major contributions to the success of this association. Ajinomoto Co. has also filed a patent on the production of safranal (which gives saffron its spicy taste) by cultures of cells from the pistil of *Crocus sativus* (similar research work was carried out in the laboratory of Yeoman in Edinburgh). Kuraray Co. is currently producing lavandol by cultures of lavender cells, while researchers at Kitasato University are using *Eucalyptus* cell cultures to catalyse the bioconversion of α-menthol (Vaisman, 1988). All these products are promoted by emphasizing their natural origin to counteract the consumers' reluctance to use artificial products.

In France, the consumption of medicinal and aromatic plants has trebled in the past 20 years: a quarter of the production being utilized as raw materials (flavourings and infusions or steeping of herbs), and three-quarters being processed for the pharmaceutical, food, fragrance and cosmetics industries. In 1986, consumption of these plants in France reached 30 000 tonnes. Domestic production was only 13 000 tonnes, the balance being achieved by importation. The trade deficit was valued at 272 million FF (Comar, 1988).

Initiatives have therefore been taken to promote the French production of medicinal and aromatic plants, while ensuring better protection of the consumers. This has involved direct help to the farmers to enable them to respond to the increasing demand and also to achieve better post-harvest operations. Another initiative is that of a new biotechnology company, Biophytec, established in Lyon, which aims to apply biotechnologies to the production of medicinal and aromatic plants, with a view to marketing products with medicinal properties and food additives. Finally, efforts have been made to obtain accelerated authorization to market certain plants or plant extracts having medicine properties (Comar, 1988).

The world leading pharmaceutical groups, such as Bayer AG, BASF

AG and Hoffman–La Roche AG, have been increasingly involved in this sector and have bought many smaller companies. In France, Sanofi-Elf-Bio-industries has made large investments, whereas agrobusiness companies such as Pernod-Ricard or chemical corporations such as Unilever NV and Procter & Gamble Inc., have been trying to integrate this new activity into their conventional ones. Other potential participants are the petrochemical companies, such as Esso and Royal Dutch-Shell (Coërs, 1989).

This new situation will limit the negotiating capacity of small firms which are mainly involved in the processing of natural products. As they have been slow to diversify their activities, they now must make a choice between necessary growth and confrontation with more powerful companies. Old corporations that supply the industry with the natural raw materials have to face the competition of biotechnological products; the only hope for them is to concentrate their activities increasingly on the supply of high-value added products (Coërs, 1989).

However, the future role of the small- and medium-size companies in the sector of aromas and fragrances could be analogous to that of small biotechnology companies which concluded agreements with the large and powerful groups, e.g. the British company, Imperial Biotechnology, which has research agreements with Nestlé, Tate & Lyle, and Beecham plc (merged in 1989 with the American pharmaceutical corporation SmithKline Beckman into the new group Smithbee, and known as SmithKline Beecham in the UK). If the biotechnological production of aromas and fragrances proves cost effective, the small companies which have mastered the relevant biotechnologies will become the natural partners of the large food, chemical and pharmaceutical groups. Such new ventures or partnerships will be promoted by the trend that makes the frontiers between aromas, fragrances, pharmaceuticals, medicines and biochemicals progressively disappear. This is, for instance, substantiated by the research programmes of Nestlé which link together activities in nutrition, health and dietetics. An area which seems promising and can be a driving factor for the industrial production of fragrances, including by plant cell cultures, is that of aromachology.

*Aromachology: new prospects for fragrance production and
  commercialization*

Since the early 1980s, Shiseido, the leading Japanese cosmetics company, and other manufacturers of flavours and fragrances have been carrying out research and experiments in a new area named aromachology, not to be confused with aromatherapy which uses essential oils for therapeutic purposes. This new science aims at studying the effects of scents and fragrances on the physical and mental conditions of human beings, and at using these substances to modify these conditions. In 1989, in co-operation with Kajima Construction Company, Shiseido was testing the effect on working conditions of the release of a specific fragrance through the air-conditioning system into the offices at certain hours of the day. The objective, as stated by Shiseido, was to try to eliminate the stress due to work and to improve the effectiveness and productivity of employees. Other similar experiments are being conducted by Shiseido with another civil engineering company, Ujima, and with Takasuna and Shimizu Construction Company. Furthermore, at the 1989 automobile show in Tokyo, a prototype car was displayed with an air-conditioning system which releases a jasmine fragrance to keep the driver awake (Leventer, 1990).

In 1984, the world-leading company International Flavors and Fragrances (IFF) filed the first patent on 'a method which induces the decrease of physiological and/or subjective reactions to stress in human beings'. But it was only in 1988–9 that the American company could master a method to evaluate in quantitative terms and in a reliable way the changes of humour and mental state. This method combines physiological measures such as heart rhythm, blood pressure and brain waves with the filling in of questionnaires such as those used in psychiatry to evaluate the effects of medicines. According to the statements made by the executive in charge of technical development at IFF, the statistical results obtained are considered to be satisfactory and can support the effectiveness of the products tested. However, there is a placebo effect of about 60% which IFF has, of course, tried to reduce (Leventer, 1990). The Japanese researchers are also using the variations of physical indicators as well as encephalographic tests (measures of α- and β-waves). According to Takasago Perfumery, a manufacturer of aromas, the methodology is considered to be valid and it has been developed in co-operation with Japanese universities and scientific institutions (Leventer, 1990).

New products with specific effects are to be marketed. In 1984, Shiseido marketed two Cologne-water perfumes for men, 'Because Psyche Refresh' and 'Because Psyche Cool'. The Japanese company asserts that these are the first products in the world whose stimulating or sedative effects have been established scientifically. In 1988–9, the same company developed with Hattorio Seiko and marketed an automatic alarm clock which releases, before ringing, a perfume made of pine and eucalyptus fragrances which should stimulate the body. Kanebo, the second Japanese cosmetics company, developed a fragrance containing lavender, camomila and anise, among others, which has sedative and sleeping effects. Matsushita Electric sells cards which release sedative or stimulating fragrances when they are introduced into small 'bread toasters'. Kanebo is now marketing handkerchieves with microcapsules interspersed between the textile fibres which release the fragrance when used (Leventer, 1990).

Cosmetic products with the same objectives as those produced by IFF have also been marketed by Avon in co-operation with Takasago Perfumery, and by the French world-leading cosmetics company, L'Oréal. Although the companies that are investing in aromachology claim that they do not wish to enter into the medical research area and that for the time being they are focusing their efforts on relaxing or stimulating compounds, it can be assumed that this is a promising area not only for those companies which manufacture fragrances but also for those which would like to seize this opportunity to widen their share of the fragrance market. It might not be unusual that in the future people buy a perfume not only because of its scent but also because of its relaxing, stimulating or physiologically-specific effect.

In this respect, it is worth mentioning the report made jointly by the Fragrance Foundation, IFF and the University of Cincinnati about their discovery of fragrances that can increase vigilance. Elsewhere, at Duke University, research is being carried out on the effect of fragrances on violence. At the University of Tsukuba, in collaboration with Shiseido, rates of recovery of athletes after strenuous activity are being monitored using certain fragrances to be breathed in before or after the exercise (Vaisman, 1988; Leventer, 1990).

Very little information has yet been reported on the reaction of the general public to these developments. Will they accept the well-being afforded by the new products, or will consumers' associations, trade unions and public bodies in charge of health regulations react to the potential side-effects of the products on physical and mental health?

Conclusions

One should not conclude hastily that cell cultures have no future in the area of production of useful substances. Many laboratories carry out their research and development programmes because the possibilities exist to increase the yields of their production processes. Furthermore, even if certain compounds are not worth developing up to a commercial stage, some biosynthetic compounds could be used as valuable precursors for organic synthesis, or could themselves constitute entirely new products. The market size for the end product, the cost/benefit ratio of the production technology, the competition with substitutes and the existence of other sources of supply are major factors which influence the choice of the appropriate manufacturing technique, especially when deciding in favour of plant cell or tissue cultures. Thus, it is probable that metabolites, synthesized through simple enzymatic reactions under the control of a single gene, could be more efficiently produced by genetically engineered microbial cells rather than by plant cell or tissue cultures (in United States Office of Technology Assessment, OTA, 1983). Finally, it is not easy to identify economically profitable targets because of industrial secrecy or confidentiality which prevails in this area and because of the infrequent contacts between researchers and companies working in the field of aromatic and medicinal plants (Rajnchapel-Messai, 1988).

Japanese scientists and companies, however, are rather optimistic for the future of plant cell culture and they are probably right. In 1989, the Japanese Ministry of Agriculture, Fisheries and Forestry launched, through their Forestry Agency, a new programme named 'Green Spirit Project'. With a budget of about 110 million yen, this project aims at producing essential oils, resins and glycosides out of plant residues (wood, branches, bark and leaves). Potential applications of the compounds to be produced are food additives (in particular sweeteners), medicines and fragrances (in *Biofutur*, no. 79, May 1989, p. 8).

In Europe, Canada and the USA, a number of companies do carry out research in this area and closely monitor current progress elsewhere. For instance, in France, Sanofi-Elf-Bio-industries maintains a reduced research activity in this area and has supported the research work of Chénieux and Rideau on the production of bioconversion of ellipticine – an anti-tumour alkaloid – by cell cultures of *Ochrosia elliptica* (Apocynaceae). The same group is involved through the Mero Company in the production of fragrance compounds (flower and fruit) by Ambid and his co-workers at the National School of Agriculture of Toulouse. Nestlé's subsidiary, Francereco, carries on its research programme on the production of metabolites by plant cells and has established fruitful co-operation with many university teams such as that of Cosson at the Faculty of Pharmacy, Chatenay-Malabry, in the south of Paris. An industrial project awaits a decision that will be taken on economic grounds rather than on scientific or technical ones. The pharmaceutical company, Roussel-Uclaf, is interested in the work carried out at the University of Montpellier on the production of diosgenin. When the French chemical company Rhône-Poulenc bought the German phyto-pharmaceutical firm Nattermann, it dissolved the plant cell culture project group and its laboratory – one of the largest plant cell culture laboratories in the world – in late 1988. Rhône-Poulenc is nevertheless looking for an appropriate policy in the field of plant cell cultures (Rajnchapel-Messai, 1988).

At the European level, all these issues were discussed at the Symposium on 'Bioproduction of metabolites by plant cell cultures', held in Paris in September 1988 and organized by the International Association of Plant Tissue Culture and the French Association pour la Promotion Industrie-Agriculture (APRIA, Association for the Promotion of Industry-Agriculture). The organizers expected that at least two or three targets could be identified in order to launch a research programme at the European level and that government support would be forthcoming in an area where financial risk is important, but where profits could be large.

References

Abel, P.P., Nelson, R.S., De, B., Hoffmann, N., Rogers, S.G., Fraley, R.T. & Beachy, R.N. (1986). Delay of disease development in transgenic plants that express the tobacco mosaic virus coat protein. *Science, Wash.*, **232**, 738–43.

Alfermann, A.W., Spieler, H. & Reinhard, E. (1985). Biotransformation of cardiac glycosides by *Digitalis* cell cultures in air lift reactors. In *Primary and Secondary Metabolism of Plant Cell Cultures*, K.H. Neumann, W. Barz & E. Reinhard (eds), pp. 316–22. Springer-Verlag, Berlin.

Benjamin, B.D., Sipahimalani, A.T., Heble, M.R. & Chadha, M.S. (1986). In *Proc. VI International Congress on Plant Tissue and Cell Culture*, p. 249. University of Minneapolis, Minnesota, USA.

Berlin, J. (1986). Secondary products from plant cell cultures. In *Biotechnology*, vol. 4, H.J. Rehm & G. Reed (eds), pp. 630–58. VCH Verlagsgesellschaft, Weinheim.

Berlin, J. (1988). Approaches to altering regulatory controls of secondary pathways in cultured cells. In *Genetics Manipulation of Woody Plants*, J.W. Hanover & D.E. Keathley (eds), pp. 353–64. Plenum Publishing Corporation, New York.

Broeck, G. van den, Timko, M.P., Kausch, A.P., Cashmore, A.R., von Montagu, M. & Herrera-Estrella, L. (1985). Targeting of a foreign protein to chloroplasts by fusion of the trans peptide from the small subunit of ribulose 1,5-biphosphate carboxylase. *Nature, Lond.*, **313**, 358–63.

Chadha, M.S., Rao, P.S. & Heble, M.R. (1988). Impact of plant biotechnology on national development programmes. *Biovigyanam*, **14** (1), 18–23.

Chilton, M.D., Tepfer, D.A., Petit, A., David, C., Casse-Delbart, F. & Tempé, J. (1982). *Agrobacterium rhizogenes* inserts T-DNA into the genome of the host plant root cells. *Nature, Lond.*, **295**, 432–4.

Coërs, P. (1989). L'empire des sens, arômes alimentaires et parfums: une étude de Précepta. *Biofutur (Paris)*, no. 83, 63–7.

Comar, J. (1988). Plantes aromatiques et médicinales: le tout et la partie. *Biofutur (Paris)*, **74**, 53–5.

Cramer, C.L., Ryder, T.B., Bell, J.N. & Lamb, C.J. (1985). Rapid switching

106   A. Sasson

of plant gene expression induced by fungal elicitors. *Science, Wash.*, **227**, 1240–3.

Curtin, M.E. (1983). Harvesting profitable products from plant tissue culture. *Bio/Technology*, **1**, 651.

DiCosmo, F. & Misawa, M. (1985). Eliciting secondary metabolism in plant cell cultures. *Trends Biotechnol.*, **3**, 318–22.

Eckes, P., Rosahl, S., Schell, J. & Willmitzer, L. (1986). Isolation and characterization of a light-inducible, organ-specific gene from potato and analysis of its expression after tagging and transfer into tobacco and tomato shoots. *Mol. Gen. Genet.*, **205**, 14–22.

Evans, D.A. *et al.* (eds) (1983–6). *Handbook of Plant Cell Culture*, 4 vol. Macmillan Publishing Co., London, New York.

Flores, H.E., Hoy, M.W. & Pickard, J.J. (1987). Secondary metabolites from root cultures. *Trends Biotechnol.*, **5** (3), 64–9.

Fontanel, A. & Tabata, M. (1987). Production of secondary metabolites by plant tissue and cell cultures. Present aspects and prospects. *Nestlé Research News 1986–1987*, pp. 93–103.

Fowler, M. (1981). Plant cell biotechnology to produce desirable substances. *Chemistry and Industry*, **7**, 229–33.

Fowler, M.W. (1984a). Time for plant cell culture? *Nature, Lond.*, **307** (5951), 504.

Fowler, M.W. (1984b). Plant-cell culture: natural products and industrial application. *Biotechnol. Genet. Eng. Rev.*, **2**, 41–67.

Fraley, R.T., Rogers, G.S., Horsch, R.B., Eichholtz, D.A., Flick, J.S., Fink, C.L., Hoffmann, N.L. & Sanders, P.R. (1985). The SEV System: a new disarmed Ti plasmid vector system for plant transformation. *Bio/Technology*, **3**, 629–35.

Fujita, Y., Tabata, M., Nishi, A. & Yamada, Y. (1982). New medium and production of secondary compounds with the two-staged culture method. In *Plant Tissue Culture 1982*, A. Fujiwara (ed.), pp. 399–400. The Japanese Association for Plant Tissue Culture, Maruzen Co. Ltd, Tokyo.

Furuya, T. (1978). Biotransformation by plant cell culture. In *Frontiers of Plant Tissue Culture*, T.A. Thorpe (ed.), pp. 191–200. International Association for Plant Tissue Culture, University of Calgary, Alberta, Canada.

Furuya, T., Kojima, H. & Syono, K. (1971). Regulation of nicotine biosynthesis by auxins in tobacco callus tissue. *Phytochemistry*, **10**, 1529–32.

Goldstein, W.E., Ingle, M.B. & Lasurel, A. (1980). Product cost analysis. In *Plant Tissue Culture as a Source of Biochemicals*, E.J. Staba (ed.), pp. 191–234. CRC Press, Boca Raton, Florida.

Grisebach, H. (1988). Induction of Flavonoid biosynthesis in plants and plant cell suspension cultures. In *European Conference on Biotechnology, Scientific, Technical and Industrial Challenges, Verona, Italy, 7–8 November 1988*, pp. 23–7.

Hahlbrock, K. & Grisebach, H. (1979). Enzymic controls in the biosynthesis of lignin and flavonoids. *Ann. Rev. Plant Physiol.*, **30**, 105–30.

Heble, M.R., Benjamin, B.D., Roja, P.C. & Chadha, M.S. (1983). Plant tissue culture for secondary products: potential, priorities and application. In *Proceedings of the National Seminar on Plant Tissue Culture, CPCRI, Kasaragod, 2–4 March 1983*, pp. 111–25. Indian Council of Agricultural Research, Publications and Information Division, New Delhi.

Heble, M.R. & Chadha, M.S. (1985*a*). Recent developments in the biotechnological application of plant tissue, cell and organ cultures. In: *Proceedings Vth ISHS Symposium on Med. Arom. Spice Pl., Darjeeling, 1985*, pp. 67–74.

Heble, M.R. & Chadha, M.S. (1985*b*). Recent developments in plant biotechnology. In *Biotechnology in Health Care*, pp. 55–64. New Delhi.

Heble, M.R. & Chadha, M.S. (1986). Plant cell culture technology: perspective and applications. In *PAFAI Seminar, New Delhi*, pp. 218–21.

Heble, M.R., Narayanaswamy, S. & Chadha, M.S. (1968). Diosgenin and sitosterol isolation from *Solanum xanthocarpum* tissue cultures. *Science, Wash.*, **161**, 1145.

Kaul, B. & Staba, E.J. (1967). *Ammi visnaga* L. Lam. tissue cultures: multiliter suspension growth and examination for furanochromones. *Planta Medica, Journal of Medicinal Plant Research* (Georg Thieme Verlag, Stuttgart), **15**, 145–56.

Klee, H.J., Yanofsky, M.F. & Nester, E. (1985). Vectors for transformation of higher plants. *Bio/Technology*, **3**, pp. 637–42.

Kurz, W.G.W. (ed.) (1989). *Primary and secondary metabolism of plant cell cultures II*. Biotechnology in agriculture and forestry, vol. 9, 450 pp. Springer-Verlag, Berlin.

Langley-Danysz, P. (1987). La biotechnologie des additifs alimentaires. *La Recherche (Paris)*, **18** (188), 634–42.

Leventer, M. (1990). L'aromachologie, ou comment mener les gens par le bout du nez. *Le Monde (Paris)*, 14 February 1990, p. 32.

Matsumoto, T., Ikeda, T., Okimura, C.Y., Kisaki, T. & Noguchi, M. (1982). Production of ubiquinone-10 by highly producing strains selected by a cell cloning technique. In *Plant Tissue Culture 1982*, A. Fujiwara (ed.), p. 69. The Japanese Association for Plant Tissue Culture, Maruzen Co. Ltd., Tokyo.

Misawa, M. (1985). Production of useful metabolites. *Adv. Biochem. Eng./Biotech.*, **31**, 59–88.

OTA (United States Office of Technology Assessment) (1983). *Plants: the potentials for extracting protein, medicines and other useful chemicals.* US Congress Workshop Proceedings, Government Printing Office, Washington, DC, 262 pp.

Pétiard, V. & Bariaud-Fontanel, A. (1987). La culture des cellules végétales. *La Recherche (Paris)*, **18** (188), 602–10.

Potrykus, I., Saul, M.W., Petruska, J., Paszkowski, J. & Shilito, R. (1985). Direct gene transfer to cells of a graminaceous monocot. *Mol. Gen. Genet.*, **199**, 183–8.

Rajnchapel-Messai, J. (1988). Cellules végétales en quête de métabolites. *Biofutur (Paris)*, **70**, 23–34.

Reinhard, E. & Alfermann, A.W. (1980). In *Advances in Biochemical Engineering*, **16**, A. Fiechter (ed.), p. 49. Springer-Verlag, Berlin.

Rhodes, M.J.C., Hamill, J.D., Robins, R.J. & Evans, D.M. (1988). Expression of enzymes in secondary metabolic pathways in transformed root cultures of *Nicotiana rustica* and *Datura stramonium*. In *European Conference on Biotechnology, Scientific, technical and industrial challenges, Verona, Italy, 7–8 November 1988*, pp. 28–32.

Rhodes, M.J.C., Robins, R.J., Hamill, J. & Parr, A.J. (1986). Potential for the production of biochemicals by plant cell cultures. *N.Z. Jl Technol.*, **2**, 59–70.

Sahai, O. & Knuth, M. (1985). *Biotechnology Progress*, **1**, 1–9.

Sasson, A. (1988). *Biotechnologies and Development*. UNESCO/CTA, Paris, 361 pp.

Schocher, R.J., Shilito, Saul, M.W., Paszkowski, J. & Potrykus, I. (1986). Co-transformation of unlinked foreign genes into plants by direct gene transfer. *Bio/Technology*, **4**, 1093–6.

Scragg, A. (1986). The potential of plant cell cultures in biotechnology. *IBL*, pp. 44–7.

Shah, D.M., Horsch, R., Klee, H.J. *et al.* (1986). Engineering herbicide tolerance in transgenic plants. *Science, Wash.*, **233**, 478–81.

Spinnler, E. (1989). Arômes: motivations pour l'emploi des outils biologiques. *Biofutur (Paris)*, **80**, 24–8.

Staba, E.J. (ed.) (1980). *Plant Tissue Culture as a Source of Biochemicals*. CRC Press, Boca Raton, Florida.

Stafford, A., Morris, P. & Fowler, M.W. (1986). Plant cell biotechnology: a perspective. *Enzyme Microb. Technol.*, **8**, 578–87.

Tabata, M., Mizukami, H., Hiraoka, N. & Konoshima, M. (1976). The production and regulation of shikonin derivatives in cultured cells. In *12th Phytochem. Symp., Kyoto, Japan*, pp. 1–8.

Ulbrich, B., Wiesner, W. & Arens, H. (1985). Large-scale production of rosmarinic acid from plant cell cultures of *Coleus blumei*. In *Primary and Secondary Metabolism of Plant Cell Cultures*, K.H. Neumann, W. Barz & E. Reinhard (eds), pp. 292–303. Springer-Verlag, Berlin.

Vaisman, S. (1988). Arômes et parfums au Japon. *Biofutur (Paris)*, **71**, 52–4.

Vasil, I.K. (ed.) (1987). *Cell Culture and Somatic Cell Genetics of Plants*, vol. 3, *Plant Regeneration and Genetic Variability*. Academic Press, New York, London, 512 pp.

Vasil, I.K. (ed.) (1988). *Cell Culture and Somatic Cell Genetics of Plants*, vol. 4, *Cell Culture in Phytochemistry*. Academic Press, New York, London, 302 pp.

Veltkamp, E. & Mol, J.N.M. (1986). Improved production of secondary metabolites in cultures of plant cells and microorganisms: the biosynthesis of flavonoids (anthocyanins in *Petunia hybrida* as model system). In *Biomolecular Engineering Programme – Final report*, E. Magnien (ed.), pp. 1071–80. Martinus Nijhoff Publishers, Dordrecht, The Netherlands.

White, P.R. (1939). Potentially unlimited growth of excised plant callus in an artificial medium. *Am. J. Bot.*, **26**, 59–64.

Wichers, H.J. & Pras, N. (1984). Optimisation of the bio-transformation of L-tyrosine into L-dopa by alginate entrapped cells of *Mucunna pruriens*. In *Proceedings of the Third European Congress on Biotechnology*, vol. 1, p. 215. Verlag Chemie, Basel.

Yamada, Y. (1984). Selection of cell lines for high yields of secondary metabolites. In *Cell Culture and Somatic Cell Genetics of Plants*, vol. 1, pp. 629–36. Academic Press, New York.

Zenk, M.H. (1980). Enzymatic synthesis of ajmalicine and related indole alkaloids. *J. Natural Prod.*, **43**, 438–51.

Zenk, M.H., El-Shagi, H., Arens, H., Stockigt, J., Weiler, E.W. & Deus, B. (1977). Formation of indole alkaloids serpentine and ajmalicine in cell suspension cultures of *Catharanthus roseus*. In *Plant Tissues Culture and its Biotechnological Applications*, W. Barz, E. Reinhard & M.H. Zenk (eds), pp. 27–43. Springer-Verlag, Berlin.

Zenk, M.H., Rueffer, M., Amann, M. & Deus-Neumann, B. (1985). Benzyl-isoquinoline biosynthesis by cultivated plant cells and isolated enzymes. *J. Natural Prod.*, **48**, 725–38.

Zieg, R.G., Zito, S.W. & Staba, E.J. (1983). Selection of high pyrethrin producing tissue cultures. *Planta Medica, Journal of Medicinal Plant Research* (Georg Thieme Verlag, Stuttgart), **48**, 88–91.

6

Mushroom production – an economic measure in maintenance of food security

S.T. CHANG AND S.W. CHIU

Introduction

Everyone wishes to remain healthy so as to work cheerfully and enjoy life to its fullest extent. A primary source for health support comes from food. For a long period of time, many fungi have been highly valued as food to fight against hunger, as a condiment to enrich the flavour of dishes and also as supplements to help maintain good health. These properties have made fungi even more popular in recent years, and this can be witnessed by the increasing demands for higher production volumes of many edible fungi in the local and international markets.

General biology of a mushroom
Life cycles A mushroom is the fruiting organ of a filamentous fungus which in most cases is a basidiomycete bearing the sexual cells, basidia, to carry out meiosis and dispersal of spores (Fig. 6.1). This filamentous fungus has a haploid form whose cells can be multinucleate (coenocytic), e.g. *Agaricus bisporus* (syn. *A. brunnescens*) and *Volvariella volvacea*, or uninucleate, e.g. *Lentinula edodes* (syn. *Lentinus edodes*) and *Pleurotus ostreatus*. Some mushrooms are self-fertile, e.g. *A. bisporus* and *V. volvacea*, while others are self-sterile but cross-fertile, e.g. *L. edodes* and *P. ostreatus*, and only after mating, fruit bodies called mushrooms are produced (Figs 6.2–6.5). For the latter species, there is usually a characteristic dikaryotic stage featured by a hyphal form with clamp connections at septa formed after mating (Fig. 6.1).

Fruiting Aggregation of the aerial hyphae by coiling and multiple forms of hyphal fusions turns a fungus into a three-dimensional ordered fruit body primordium (Figs 6.6 and 6.7). The initiation and development of fruit bodies from mycelia genetically competent to fruit are dependent on various chemical and physical triggering factors (Manachere *et al.*,

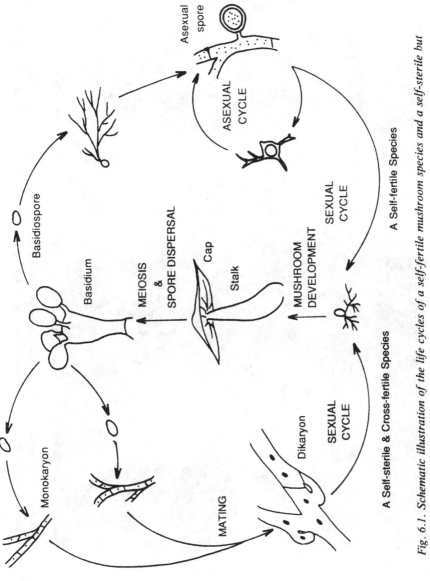

Fig. 6.1. Schematic illustration of the life cycles of a self-fertile mushroom species and a self-sterile but cross-fertile mushroom species.

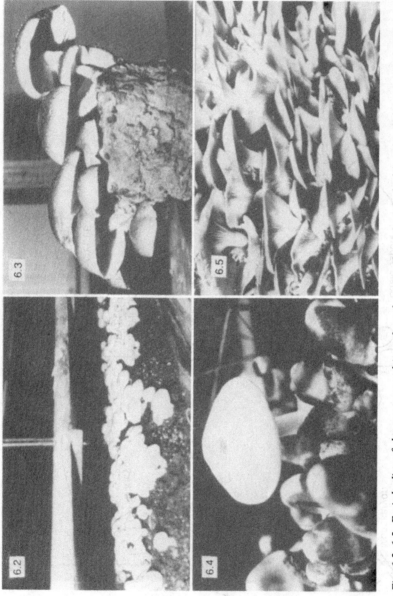

Fig. 6.2–6.5. Fruit bodies of the common cultivated mushrooms. Fig. 6.2. A bed of Agaricus bisporus. Fig. 6.3. An autoclavable plastic bag of Lentinula edodes. *Fig. 6.4.* Volvariella volvacea. *Fig. 6.5.* Pleurotus sajor-caju.

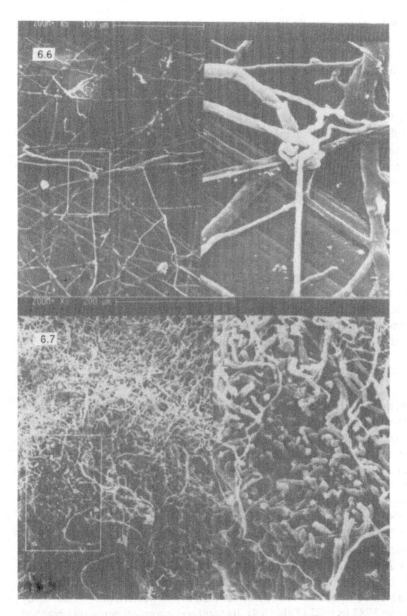

Fig. 6.6–6.7. Formation of a fruit body in the ink mushroom, Coprinus
cinereus. *Fig. 6.6. Scanning electron micrograph of the vegetative
mycelium. The picture on the right shows the coiling of multiple hyphae
to form a mushroom primordium. Fig. 6.7. Scanning electron micrograph
of a mushroom primordium. Note the dense hyphae covering the whole
substratum (compare with Fig. 6.6). The picture on the right shows the
densely twisted hyphae of the mushroom primordium.*

1983). These include the intrinsic factors such as mycelial age in *Lentinula edodes* (Leatham & Stahmann, 1987), cAMP level in *Coprinus cinereus* (Uno & Ishikawa, 1982) and *L. edodes* (Takagi, Katayose & Shishido, 1988) as well as glycogen content in *C. cinereus* (Brunt & Moore, 1990) and possibly in *Pleurotus sajor-caju* and *Volvariella volvacea* (Cheung & Chiu, unpublished); and the extrinsic factors such as light in *C. cinereus* (Lu, 1982) and *L. edodes* (Leatham & Stahmann, 1987) but not in *V. bombycina* (Chiu, Moore & Chang, 1989), ammonia concentration in *C. cinereus* (Morimoto, Suda & Sagara, 1981), specific cerebrosides in *Schizophyllum commune* (Kawai & Ikeda, 1982), and temperature in *S. commune* (Schwalb, 1978), *C. cinereus* (Lu, 1982), and *L. edodes* (Jong, 1989). Every species, or even strain, has its specific requirement for fruit body initiation and development. Fruit body polymorphism, characterized by the appearance of different forms of mushrooms such as upturned/inverted caps, supernumerary hymenia and morchelloid forms, produced by a strain can be a spontaneous event (Chiu *et al.*, 1989), or be caused by chemical treatment (Elliott, 1985*b*), or even by infection (Romaine & Schlagnhaufar, 1989). Elimination of the causes in the latter cases can lead to production of mushrooms of uniform morphology. This polymorphism reflects developmental plasticity, an inherent property of a living organism.

Mushroom production

In the overall view of world mushroom production (Table 6.1), *Agaricus bisporus/bitorquis* account for some 56% of the total market with *Lentinus edode* and *Volvariella volvacea* being the second and the third most important mushroom, respectively (Chang, 1987). The production of *Agaricus* mushrooms in 1986 is illustrated in Table 6.2. The United States leads the world, producing 285 000 tonnes, 23.2% of the total *Agaricus* market. The increase in production of the mushroom between 1980 and 1985 is further demonstrated in Table 6.3. With the exception of Taiwan, South Korea and Japan, the increases in production are very considerable: Ireland, +157%; Mainland China, +100%; Holland +75%; Spain, +66%; and Great Britain, +53% (O'Brien, 1989). Such a big rise is due to the increased consumption of both fresh and preserved mushrooms as demonstrated in the western part of Germany from 1983 to 1987 (Table 6.4). Its total consumption per capita reached 2.86 kg in 1987.

The developing countries of Asia and Africa have been labouring hard against population growth, under-nourishment and low income per capita. The development of a national economy in these countries should be strongly linked to the development of rural economy because

Table 6.1. *World production of edible cultivated mushrooms in 1986*

Species	Common name	Weight (10³ tonnes)	%
Agaricus bisporus/ *bitorquis*	Button mushroom	1227	56.2
Lentinula edodes	Shiitake	314	14.4
Volvariella volvacea	Straw mushroom	178	8.2
Pleurotus spp.	Oyster mushrooms	169	7.7
Auricularia spp.	Wood ear mushroom	119	5.5
Flammulina velutipes	Winter mushroom	100	4.6
Tremella fuciformis	Silver ear mushroom	40	1.8
Pholiota nameko	Nameko mushroom	25	1.1
Others		10	0.5
TOTAL		2182	100.0

Source: Chang, 1987.

Table 6.2. *World production of* Agaricus *mushrooms in 1986*

Country	Weight (tonnes)	%
1. USA	285 000	23.2
2. Mainland China	185 000	15.1
3. France	165 000	13.4
4. Holland	115 000	9.4
5. England	95 000	7.7
6. Italy	75 000	6.1
7. Canada	51 400	4.2
8. Spain	45 000	3.7
9. Western Germany	38 000	3.1
10. Taiwan	35 000	2.9
11. Yugoslavia	18 500	1.5
12. Korea	18 000	1.5
13. Belgium	16 000	1.3
14. Ireland	14 000	1.1
15. Australia	14 000	1.1
16. Others	54 740	4.5
TOTAL	1 224 640	100.0

Source: Chang, 1987.

Table 6.3. Agaricus *mushroom production 1980–5*

	1980 (10³ tonnes)	1985 (10³ tonnes)	Increase on 1980 (%)
1. Europe			
France	132	180	+36
Holland	60	105	+75
Great Britain	62	95	+53
Italy	44	60	+36
Spain	33	55	+66
Western Germany	35	35	+0
Ireland	7	18	+157
Bel/Lux	13	14	+71
Denmark	7	9	+28
TOTAL	373	571	+45
2. Other European countries			
Poland	—	45	
Hungary	—	5	
Switzerland	4	4.5	
TOTAL		54.5	
3. North America			
USA	213	270	+26
Canada	29	45	+15
TOTAL	242	315	+15
4. SE Asia			
Mainland China	100	200	+100
Taiwan	64	52	−19
South Korea	25	10	−60
Japan	5.5	5	−10
TOTAL	194.5	267	+37
5. Australia			
	8	13	+55
TOTAL world-wide	860	1220	+42

Source: O'Brien, 1989.

the rural population of these countries comprises 65–85% of the total population. These people also suffer from acute protein malnutrition. Under the present population growth rate in these developing countries, this acute protein problem will be greatly increased in the future. Science and technology will have to be geared up very much to develop all possible sources of food in general, and of protein in particular, by both

Table 6.4. *Western German mushroom consumption (in kg) 1983–7*

	1983	1984	1985	1986	1987
Consumption fresh (per head)	0.68	0.76	0.80	0.85	0.92
Consumption processed (per head)	1.62	1.67	1.79	1.98	1.94
Total consumption (per head)	2.30	2.43	2.59	2.83	2.86

conventional and nonconventional methods in order to save the people from starvation and from the acute problem of malnutrition. It is realized that the average daily intake of mushrooms is below 50% per capita than that of the developed countries (Chang, 1980a; FAO Production Yearbook, 1987). Among the various food sources, mushroom production is probably the best and most highly needed method for harvesting cheaper and better quality food protein. Samajpati (1982) found that from a given quantity of carbohydrate, mushrooms can yield about 65% protein as against 20% from pork, 15% from milk, 5% from poultry and 4% from beef. Thus, the production capacity of mushroom protein happens to be about ten times more than that of meat protein.

Mushroom cultivation
Substrates The substrates used in mushroom production are mainly derived from cellulosic agricultural and industrial waste materials like cereal straws, sugarcane bagasse, cotton waste and others that cannot be consumed by humans. During the growth of plant crops, there is usually a concentration of useful nutrients in certain parts of the plant, which are then harvested for food. The remainder is generally considered as a waste or by-product which must be disposed of. For instance, of the total dry weight of a cereal plant, the grain harvested for food is estimated to be at most 50% in rice (1:1 conversion for straw from grain), 37% in barley and rye, 36% in wheat and only 30% in maize (Chang 1980b). The rest of the plant is straw. In 1987 the world production of straw was estimated to be 3093.4 million tonnes (Table 6.5).

Cotton is still the world's leading textile fibre, and some 16.6 million tonnes of cotton fibre are produced annually by about 80 countries (FAO Production Yearbook, 1987; Hamlyn, 1989). About 7% of lint (i.e. fibre) waste is produced in spinning. Although this primary waste,

Table 6.5. *World production of cereals and their straws during 1987*

Cereal	Grain	Conversion[a] factor	Straw
		Production (million tonnes)	
Wheat	517	1.8	930.6
Rice	454	1.0	454.0
Maize	457	2.4	1096.8
Other cereals (oats, rye and barley)	360	1.7	612.0
Total	1788		3093.4

[a]Chang, 1980*b*.
Source: *FAO Production Yearbook*, 1987.

sometimes, is quite valuable and can be re-used in various ways, the residual or secondary wastes have little value and are an ideal substrate for the growth of some mushrooms, notably *Volvariella volvacea* and *Pleurotus* spp. (Chang, 1974; Chang, Lau & Cho, 1981). Furthermore, cotton-seed hull, corn cobs, sawdusts, peanut hull and other cellulosic waste materials which are much cheaper and more readily available than cereal straws and cotton wastes can also be used to grow mushrooms.

Bioconversion of lignocellulosic wastes into edible mushrooms
Lignocelluloses, whose components are lignin, cellulose and hemicellulose, are the most abundant materials present on earth, comprising 50% of all biomass with an estimated annual production of 50×10^9 tonnes (Goldstein, 1981). At present, there is no efficient method to dispose of the resultant lignocellulosic wastes from forestry and human activities. These bulky lignocellulosic wastes are rich in nutrients which can only be utilized by microorganisms. However, natural bio-degradation is a slow process, and meanwhile unpleasant smells are produced. If left behind for natural decay, these wastes not only occupy space but can also be reservoirs of pathogenic microorganisms. Although burning can be a means of disposing of these wastes, it is not an active means for recycling the limited nutrients available on earth.

Mushrooms are saprophytic, degrading the lignocellulosic dead matters in an ecosystem. This ability comes from the secretion of various extracellular enzyme complexes and their synergistic actions (Saddler, 1986; Wong, Tan & Saddler, 1988; Harvey & Palmer, 1989). Table 6.6 lists the major enzymes involved in degrading the lignocellulosic

Table 6.6. *Various enzyme systems to degrade lignocellulose*

Enzyme complex	Enzyme component
Amylolytic enzyme	α-amylase β-amylase glucoamylase debranching enzyme (pullulanase)
Cellulolytic enzyme	endoglucanase exoglucanase β-glucosidase
Lignolytic enzyme	ligninase laccase (phenoloxidase) Mn-peroxidase
Pectinolytic enzyme	pectinesterase endopolygalacturonase exopolygalacturonase endopectate lyase exopectate lyase endopectic lyase
Xylanolytic enzyme	xylanase β-xylosidase

Sources: Saddler, 1986; Fermor, 1988; Wong *et al.*, 1988; Harvey & Palmer, 1989.

substrates (Saddler, 1986; Fermor, 1988; Wong, Tan & Saddler, 1988; Harvey & Palmer, 1989). Figs 6.8 and 6.9 show the proposed action mechanisms for the major enzymes, cellulase and ligninase, respectively (Saddler, 1986; Harvey & Palmer, 1989). It has to be stressed that each component enzyme may have different molecular forms, isozymes. Not every fungal species produces all the enzymes mentioned in Table 6.6, and as a result, mushroom species have different digesting abilities towards the various components of lignocellulose (Table 6.7) (Quimio, 1988a; Wood, Matcham & Fermor, 1988; Oriaran, Labosky & Royse, 1989; Rajarathnam & Bano, 1989). In addition, the activities of a specific enzyme produced by different mushroom species vary widely (Lu *et al.*, 1988). These differences may account partly for the preferred growth of a fungal species on a certain substrate. Therefore, different substrates are used for the cultivation of the common mushrooms (Table 6.8) (Quimio, 1988b; Wood & Smith, 1988a).

The list of substrates in Table 6.8 is not exclusive. More and more different types of substrates, irrespective of agricultural or industrial origin, are used for mushroom cultivation. For instance, cotton is grown on 50 000 ha and is thus a major crop in Israel (Lavie, 1988). The growers use the seeds and the fibres of the cotton, but the cotton straw is non-palatable as an animal feed because of its high lignin content and cannot be used as animal bedding because it has low water absorbency. However, *Pleurotus* species, during solid-state fermentation, decompose the cotton straw by sending hyphae around and into it, so that it is eventually enveloped in a blanket of mycelium. This blanketing makes the straw softer and increases its digestibility, so that the straw is converted into a digestible and nutritious animal feed (Smith, Fermor & Zadrazil, 1988).

In addition, paper manufacturers continue to search for more efficient ways of producing high quality pulp at a lower cost. Biopulping by culturing *Pleurotus* species may allow selective enzymatic removal of lignin contained in the cell walls and can reduce the environmental risks associated with chemical processing (Oriaran *et al.*, 1989). While the paper mill sludge can be used for cultivation of *Pleurotus* species (Ellor, 1988), cotton wastes from textile factories have long been the main substrate for cultivating the paddi straw mushroom, *Volvariella volvacea* (Chang, 1974; 1980a).

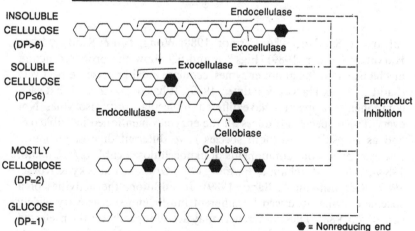

Fig. 6.8. Schematic representation of the synergistic enzymatic hydrolysis of cellulose. Source: Saddler, 1986.

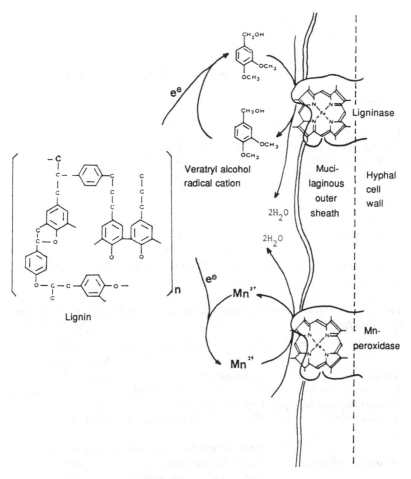

Fig. 6.9. Schematic representation of the action of hyphal-bound enzyme activities on lignin. The iron porphyrin enzymes ligninase and Mn^{2+}-peroxidase are associated with the polysaccharide sheath on the fungal hyphal wall. The enzymes oxidize mobile mediators, veratryl alcohol and Mn^{2+}. The radical cations of veratryl alcohol and Mn^{3+} then oxidize lignin some distance away from the hyphae. When this happens, intramolecular charge transfer within the lignin polymer cleaves the weakest bond, at the point far from the initial site of oxidation. Simplified from Harvey & Palmer, 1989.

Table 6.7. *Various abilities of some basidiomycetes to degrade lignocellulose*

Species	Lignin	Cellulose	Hemicellulose
Phanerochaete chrysosporium	+	+	+
Agaricus bisporus	+	+	+
Lentinus edodes	+	+	+
Schizophyllum commune	−	+	+
Pleurotus ostreatus	+	+	+
Pleurotus sajor-caju	+	+	+
Pleurotus sapidus	+	+	+
Pleurotus cornucopiae	+	+	+
Pleurotus flabellatus	+	+	+
Volvariella volvacea	−	+	+

Sources: Quimio, 1988*a*; Wood *et al.*, 1988; Oriaran *et al.*, 1989; Rajarathnam & Bano, 1989.

Table 6.8. *Growth substrates and production cycle times for cultivation of edible fungi*

Species	Substrate	Production cycle
Agaricus bisporus/bitorquis	Composted straw	12–14 weeks
Lentinus edodes	Wood logs of broad-leaved leaves	3–6 years
	Sterilized sawdust/rice bran	6–8 months
Volvariella volvacea	Fermented rice straw	7–10 weeks
	Composted cotton waste	5–6 weeks
Flammulina velutipes	Sterilized sawdust/rice bran	12–20 weeks
Pleurotus spp.	Pasteurized straw	8–12 weeks
	Fermented straw mixture	8–12 weeks
Auricularia spp.	Wood logs	3–6 years
	Sterilized sawdust/rice bran	4–5 months
Tremella fuciformis	Wood logs (hardwood)	3–6 years

Sources: Quimio, 1988*b*; Wood & Smith, 1988*a*.

Table 6.9. *Translocation of cadmium and mercury from substrate into fruit bodies of the mushroom species*

Species	Translocation percentage	
	Cadmium	Mercury
Pleurotus flabellatus	75.0	48.6
Pleurotus ostreatus	19.3	38.5
Agaricus bisporus	1.3	8.4
Pleurotus sajor-caju	3.7	3.6
Flammulina velutipes	0.9	5.1
Agrocybe aegerita	3.8	12.0

Source: Brunnert & Zadrazil, 1983.

However, when using industrial wastes/sludges for mushroom cultivation, attention has to be paid to the translocation of toxic substances from substrates to mushrooms. It is found that a mushroom species bioaccumulates certain elements such as potassium, sodium and phosphorus. In addition, some mushroom species actively uptake cadmium, mercury and lead (Table 6.9) (Brunnert & Zadrazil, 1983; Ellor, 1988). The heavy metal content in these mushrooms shows a strong dependence on the contents in substrate. However, two independent studies found that the normal consumption rate of these mushrooms did not accumulate these toxic heavy metals over the permissible concentration for use on food chain crops (Bano *et al.*, 1981; Ellor, 1988).

In addition to the recycling of nutrients present in lignocellulosic wastes for mushroom cultivation, the spent substrates can have other uses (Table 6.10) (Rajarathnam & Bano, 1989). These include use as a soil fertilizer/conditioner. The yield of lettuce, Chinese radishes and tomatoes grown directly in the used cotton-waste compost is three-, three- and seven-fold, respectively, higher than those grown in regular garden soil (Lohr, O'Brien & Coffey, 1984; Wang, Lohr & Coffey, 1984). The spent composts have also been considered for reuse in the generation of bio-gas, as well as the production of earthworms. The sludge from the bio-gas plant or the residue from the earthworm growth bed can further be used as a nitrogenous fertilizer. Alternatively, the less spent composts from which only the initial mushrooms are harvested can be converted into stockfeed. Choosing the type of lignocellulosic substrates for mushroom cultivation depends on availability, consis-

Table 6.10. *Functions and applications of spent substrate*

Functions	Applications
Decrease in lignin content; saccharification; decrease in phenols; increase in free amino acids; degraded nature of cellulose/hemicellulose	As an upgraded form of ruminant feed
Enhanced saccharification (3–5 fold of the undergraded substrate)	For generation of bio-gas by culturing methanogenic bacteria
Increased humic/fulvic acid add to humus when supplemented to soil	As a soil fertilizer
Lignolytic property	As a pulping agent for manufacture of cardboard/paper
Partial degradation of unfermented substrates	Can be recycled into compost for *Agaricus* cultivation by suitable amendments
Contains saccharification enzymes in fresh form	Can be expressed and diverted for conversion of simple cellulosic wastes into sugars
Increased content of free sugars	Can be utilized for the culturing of Single Cell Proteins
Contains lignolytic activity and ability to oxidize the phenolic chromphore	For decolorization of waste sulphite liquors and molasses pigment

Source: Rajarathnam & Bano, 1989.

tency of product, price and the mushroom species. Thus, mushroom cultivation is an economic practice since the substrate used has a low or even negative value.

Cultivation techniques Fig. 6.10 shows the major steps in mushroom cultivation (Chang & Miles, 1986). The first step is the preparation of a spawn culture. A mushroom spawn is the seed culture of the selected mushroom strain of desirable characters such as form, flavour and growth vigour. A spawn culture is prepared by inoculating a pure culture onto sterilized substrates such as rye grains, cotton seed hulls, aseptically, and incubating the spawn at favourable temperatures.

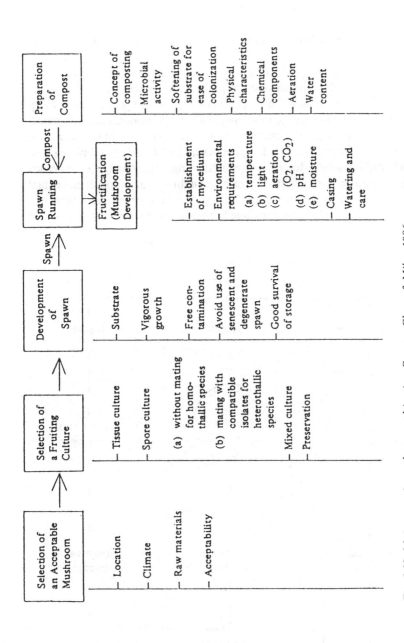

Fig. 6.10. Major steps in mushroom cultivation. Source: Chang & Miles, 1986.

Meanwhile, the substrates may have to undergo composting (Fig. 6.11) (Nair, 1982).

Composting in *Agaricus bisporus* is a sophisticated process, unlike that in other edible mushrooms, and consists of two phases (Wu, 1985; Wood & Smith, 1988*b*). Phase I composting aims to get the compost up to the correct water content, to ensure all the ingredients are well mixed together and to get the compost heating up well. Compost additives, such as animal manure and supplement, can be added and mixed well with the substrate during compost turning. The change of complex nutrients into the available from is brought about by other microbial activities. Phase I composting can be a source of air pollution and nuisance odours. Unpleasant smells are due to ammonia, sulphide and

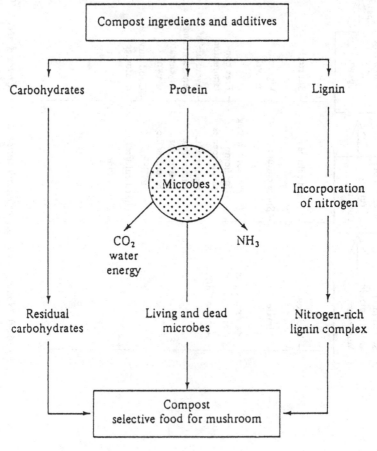

Fig. 6.11. Schematic representation of the composting process. Source: Nair, 1982.

thiol (mercaptan) compounds produced by microbial degradation (Miller & Macauley, 1988). Improved ventilation, lowering temperature or using biofiltration can reduce odours (Miller & Macauley, 1988; Lomax, 1989). Phase II composting is the removal of undesirable microbial flora and elimination of ammonia production by pasteurization. Further, the succession of the fungus *Scytalidium thermophilum* can protect the negative effects of compost bacteria on mycelial growth of *A. bisporus* while *A. bisporus* is able to inactivate the growth of *S. thermophilum* (Straatsma *et al.*, 1989).

Recently, the Dutch have introduced an indoor composting method which combines composting, pasteurizing and spawn running in one system in tunnels (Leendertse, 1988). The whole process is largely computerized and automatic in operation. This Agrisystems–Sohm Indoor Composting System leads to the industrialization of mushroom growing, making the practice less an art form and more a professional industry. However, this system requires a large investment and is not suitable for areas with scattered small-to-medium sized mushroom farms as transport of spawns to farms adds cost.

In comparison, some mushrooms are primary decomposers that can utilize the raw and unsterilized substrate directly (Table 6.8) (Quimio, 1988*b*; Wood & Smith, 1988*a*). In these cases, mushrooms not only use the lignocellulosic substrates but also the microbial biomass as nutrient sources (Table 6.11) (Barron, 1988; Fermor, 1988; Chiu, unpublished). However, some weed moulds such as *Trichoderma* species (Fletcher, 1987), and pathogenic bacteria such as *Pseudomonas aeruginosa* (Chiu, unpublished), are not killed by mushroom species. *Trichoderma* species are mycoparasites which digest the mushroom mycelium, and with the aid of airborne conidia, the whole mushroom culture once contaminated is quickly overgrown by *Trichoderma* mycelium, leading to total loss of mushroom production. When the mushrooms are growing actively, the growth of other microbes are checked. But these microbes can cause serious spoilage on the harvested mushrooms (Beelman, 1988; Nichols, 1988). Although pesticides can be added to prevent other microbial attack, its use will certainly add cost. Further, even though the mushroom species can kill some other microbial species such as *Staphylococcus aureus*, the bacterial production of endotoxin substances that are heat-stable can cause food poisoning when the contaminated mushrooms are consumed. Therefore, farm hygiene is the best defence a mushroom grower has against mushroom pests and diseases (Flegg, 1989).

Although there was the suggestion that *Pleurotus sajor-caju* could fix atmospheric nitrogen, this might not be true. The very little increase in total protein synthesized in media lacking a nitrogen source might be

Table 6.11. *The abilities of some basidiomycetes to degrade bacteria under low or no nutrient conditions*

Species	Low nutrient medium		Water medium with	
	Gram(+)	Gram(−)[a]	Gram(+)	Gram(−)
Agaricus bisporus	+	+	+	+
Auricularia sp.	+	+	+	+
Coprinus quadrifidus	+	+	+	+
Coprinus cinereus	+	+	+	+
Flammulina velutipes	+	+	+	+
Lentinus edodes	+	+	+	+
Lepista nuda	+	+	+	+
Pleurotus ostreatus	+	+	+	+
Pleurotus sajor-caju	+	+	+	+
Schizophyllum commune	+[b]	+[b]	+[b]	+[b]
Volvariella volvacea	+	+	+	+

[a]Except with live *Pseudomonas aeruginosa*.
[b]Fruit body formation.
Sources: Barron, 1988; Fermor, 1988; Chiu, unpublished.

accounted for by the trace nitrogen contamination of salts in the media, and the minute increase in dry weight in these media could also be attributed to the synthesis of more mycelial polysaccharides and the possibility of synthesis of some lipids due to the lack of nitrogen in these media (Chahal, 1989). At present, the ability to fix nitrogen is known to be unique to some prokaryotes. The substrate used for mushroom cultivation must contain a carbon source, a nitrogen source, some vitamins and some growth factors (Elliott, 1985a).

When the spawn culture and the substrate are ready, the spawn culture can be mixed with the substrate and the culture incubated for mycelial growth under certain favourable conditions. As mushrooms are saprophytic and not photosynthetic, light is not required during mycelial running. The substrates can then be packed into trays, plastic bags or beds which in turn are placed on shelves in indoor cultivation (Figs 6.2 and 6.3). This not only reduces the space occupied but also ensures regular production under a controlled environment.

Wood & Smith (1988a,b,c) summarized the current practice in cultivating the common edible mushrooms with detailed description on the techniques for *Agaricus bisporus* which is the most well-known edible mushroom (Flegg & Wood, 1985; Wood & Smith, 1988b). As opposed to growing on trays or beds, some other mushrooms are cultivated in

Table 6.12. *The temperature requirement and C/N ratio in substrates for cultivation of the mushroom species*

Species	C/N ratio	Temperature (°C) Spawn run	Fruiting
Agaricus bisporus	25–30	20–27	10–20
Lentinus edodes	>100	25–30	20–25
Volvariella volvacea	50	35–40	30–35
Pleurotus ostreatus	85		
low-temperature strains		20–27	10–15
temp-tolerant strains		20–35	10–30
thermo-tolerant strains		20–35	10–35

Sources: Chang & Miles, 1986; Muller, 1988.

autoclavable space bags (Chalmers, 1989). The use of sawdust-base space bags in cultivating *Lentinula edodes* has the following advantages: greatly foreshortened production cycles, higher yields and productivity (Chalmers, 1989). Thus growers using this method have a great marketing advantage over operators producing on logs in the open environment (Furutsuka, 1988), whose product generally comes in seasonal flushes. Jong (1989) and Royse (1989), by utilizing the space bags culture, have determined the environmental parameters in cultivating *L. edodes*.

As shown in Table 6.12, every species has its specific optimum conditions such as C/N ratio, temperature, to produce fruit bodies. Moisture content is maintained throughout the process by regular spraying. In addition, ammonia produced by other microbial activities can inhibit mycelial growth and reduce mushroom yield (Gerrits & van der Eerden, 1989). Therefore, composting is important, and ventilation must be provided. When the substrate is completely colonized by the mushroom mycelium, aeration is introduced to the cultures by opening the plastic bags or forced ventilation into the mushroom farm. Carbon dioxide promotes mycelial growth and causes the formation of abnormal fruit bodies (Schwalb, 1978; Flegg & Wood, 1985). In some mushrooms, temperature shock and water flooding may be required to induce fruit body formation (Matsumoto, 1988; Jong, 1989). In general, light and aeration seem to be the most important factors regulating fruit body development. However, we still know very little on the mechanisms of fruit body initiation and development.

In *Agaricus bisporus*, by alternating the temperature between 16 °C and 24 °C at defined stages in fruit body development within flushes, improved synchronization of growth of the mushrooms is obtained (Love, 1989). This practice can facilitate mushroom picking and reduce the labour cost. Further, supplementation of slow-release nutrients to the substrate can allow more flushes of mushrooms produced (Gregory, 1989). This is important as the second flush takes a shorter time to appear than the first flush. In addition, as the biological efficiency of mushroom production over substrate does not reach 100%, and different mushroom species utilize different components in the substrates, there is the possibility of a similar crop rotation practice as in higher plants to use the spent substrate of *Volvariella volvacea* to cultivate *Pleurotus* species (Quimio, 1988a). As we learn more about mushroom growth, we will then be capable of maximizing mushroom production.

By choosing a mushroom species suitable to grow in a particular area, the cost spent in controlling temperature is eliminated. If mushroom cultivation is further operated in a simple farming system using manpower rather than machinery, a small investment is needed for hiring the farm area and labour cost. At present, there is a requirement for a continuous supply of fresh mushrooms owing to their short shelf life.

Post-harvest treatment There are certain factors influencing post-harvest quality and shelf life of fresh mushrooms (Beelman, 1988). Fresh mushrooms are highly perishable, and browning occurs after storage. These post-harvest deterioration changes occur as a result of normal senescence phenomena such as mushroom tyrosinase oxidation, and/or microbial activity. The following methods are used to preserve fresh mushrooms: irradiation, chemical treatment, conventional refrigeration to slow down metabolic activities, and controlled-atmosphere storage (Nichols, 1988). Post-harvest washing of mushrooms using chlorine water was shown to reduce dramatically bacterial populations and preserve the quality of fresh mushrooms during storage. The addition of sodium hypochlorite in washing further prevents mushrooms from browning, but there are tighter constraints to the use of sulphites in the fresh food industry (Beelman, 1988). Another way is to use irradiation to sterilize the fresh mushrooms. The beauty of this method is that irradiated food does not emit radioactivity. However, irradiation cannot be used as a means to kill contaminants present in the food or be a safeguard against contamination during processing. Hygiene during cultivation and processing must be observed. A newly emerged, simple and inexpensive way to lengthen the shelf life is by overwrapping the fresh mushrooms in a combination of microporous and a relatively impermeable film (Burton, Frost & Nichols, 1989).

Nowadays, both fresh and preserved mushrooms are acceptable and welcomed by most people. The preserved (i.e. canned, dried or pickled) mushrooms can be stored for later consumption or exported to other countries. Some mushrooms such as *Lentinula edodes*, *Aurcularia* spp. and *Tremella* spp. are sold in the dried form. Mushrooms preserved by drying have a good flavour, and drying prevents deterioration as well as being convenient for long-term storage and transportation. Another practice called salting for storage is carried out as follows. Cultivated mushrooms are first washed and then put in boiling water for cooking. The duration of cooking depends upon the size of mushrooms, ranging from 3 to 10 minutes. After pre-cooking, the water is decanted, and the mushrooms are steeped in a solution of sea salt (not rock salt) at a concentration of 22–25% (Chang & Miles, 1989). The salt water must cover the mushrooms, and the mixture must be stirred every 2–3 days while the salt concentration must be maintained at 18–20%. The mushrooms are kept in this salt solution for 10–14 days, and sometimes for 5–6 weeks, so that the osmotic pressure reaches equilibrium. Next, the mushrooms are placed in vessel for drainage to remove the salt water. Then the mushrooms are placed in barrels or other containers which contain a brine solution of 0.08% citric acid in 18–20% sea salt solution (pH 3.5). Such a high concentration of citric acid tends to maintain the texture better than canning in a simple brine. However, these preserved mushrooms should be desalted by washing gently in warm water before consumption.

There is now pioneering work in submerged fermentation to produce the mushroom mycelium, rather than the above-mentioned solid-state fermentation to produce fruit bodies (Chahal, 1989). Various conditions are optimized to produce fungal biomass with a strong mushroom flavour and high nutritive value. However, unless more effort is spent on promotion, there will remain a small market for the vegetative mycelium.

In view of the low demand on resources and technology, and of high nutritional value, the cultivation of mushrooms can be considered as food security in developing countries. Besides, an added advantage is that the spent compost can also be reutilized as organic fertilizer which, in turn, can improve the soil fertility and increase the production of other crops for food.

Biotechnology Raper (1985) described the general strategies employed to improve strains by classical breeding methods such as backcross and mating. This practice is successful in obtaining good fruiting strains in

Lentinula edodes by mating among wild strains collected in different geographic areas (Mori, Fukai & Zennyozi, 1974), and lengthening the upper limit of fruiting temperature in *Pleurotus ostreatus* (Muller, 1988). The establishment of a germplasm bank for mushroom species is urged so that genetic resources are preserved and will be available for breeding programme (Jong & Davis, 1987; Wu, 1987).

Successful breeding of self-sterile but cross-fertile species can be checked by the dikaryon formation as shown in Fig. 6.1. Yet for self-fertile species, the partners and the resultant fusion product usually do not show any morphological differences, such as in *Agaricus bisporus*. Therefore, some markers must be used to reveal successful mating. Challen & Elliott (1987) purposely induced fungicide-resistant mutants in *A. bisporus* and hoped to use them as markers in a breeding programme. But induced mutagenesis may have pleiotrophic effects such as decreasing the vigour of the culture. Recently, the technique RFLPs (restriction fragment length polymorphisms) has been available to reflect the naturally occurring different alleles in a population (revealed by the differences in the molecular sizes of the fragments from the digestion of DNA with restriction enzymes) by electrophoresis (Logtenberg & Bakker, 1988). In this way a strain can be characterized by its specific RFLPs pattern (Loftus, Moore & Elliott, 1988). Meanwhile, enzymatic methods have been developed to remove the cell wall and release the protoplasts (Peberdy, 1989). With protoplast technology we have the chance of bringing two or more genomes into the same cytoplasm artificially (protoplast fusion) and of the incorporation of foreign DNA into a strain (transformation). Mating in the self-fertile species, *A. bisporus*, using protoplast fusion with RELPs as natural markers, is now possible (Castle, Horgen & Anderson, 1988). Protoplast fusion and transformation protocols have been worked out in some Basidiomycetes (Mellon & Casselton, 1988; Sonnenberg, Wessels & van Griensven, 1988; Specht *et al.*, 1988). These advanced methods will hopefully be utilized as a direct strategy to improve mushroom strains, such as for enhancing the utilization ability of substrates (Elliott, 1988; Wach, 1988; Wood, 1989).

Nutritive values

The pressures of continuously expanding population and limited energy supply have led to the search for new and better methods from which more food can be provided. The greatest difficulty in feeding man is to supply a sufficient amount of body-building material – protein. The other three nutritional categories are: the source of energy food – carbohydrates; accessory food factors – vitamins; and inorganic compounds which are indispensable to good health. Of course, water, too, is essential.

The moisture content of fresh mushrooms varies in the range 70–95% depending upon the harvest time and environmental conditions, whereas it is about 10–13% in dried mushrooms. Published values for the protein content of the four most popular edible mushrooms, *Agaricus bisporus*, *Lentinus edodes*, *Pleurotus* spp., and *Volvariella volvacea*, which are commercially cultivated in various countries, range from 1.75 to 3.63% of their fresh weight (Crisan & Sands, 1978; Chang, 1980*b*; Beelman & Edwards, 1989). The value can be as high as 5.9% (Flegg & Maw, 1976); however, an average value of 3.5–4% would appear to be more representative. This means that the protein content of edible mushroom, in general, is about twice that of onion (1.4%) and cabbage (1.4%), and four times and 12 times those of oranges (1.0%) and apples (0.3%), respectively. In comparison, the protein content of common meats are as follows: pork, 9–16%; beef, 12–20%; chicken, 18–20%; fish, 18–20%; and milk, 2.9–3.3%. On a dry-weight basis, mushrooms normally contain 19–35% protein as compared to 7.3% in rice, 12.7% in wheat, 38.1% in soybean and 9.4% in corn (Caribbean Food and Nutrition Institute, 1974). Therefore, in terms of the amount of crude protein, mushrooms rank below most animal meats but well above most other foods, including milk, which is an animal product.

Proteins, as we know, are made up of over 20 different amino acids. The human body can convert some of these amino acids into others, but there are nine of them that we cannot make, and these are called the essential amino acids (lysine, methionine, tryptophane, threonine, valine, leucine, isoleucine, cystine and phenylalanine). These nine essential amino acids must be present simultaneously and in correct relative amounts for protein synthesis to occur. If one or more of them are in inadequate supply, the utilization of all others in the cellular pool will be reduced proportionally. The food products of animal origin always give a better balance and higher quality of protein than plant food, which often lack some of the important amino acids. For instance, cereal grains have too little lysine while legumes lack methionine and tryptophane. The mushroom protein contains all nine essential amino acids for man (Chang and Miles, 1989). In addition to their good proteins, the mushrooms are a relatively good source of the following individual nutrients: fat, phosphorus, iron, and vitamins including thiamine, riboflavin, ascorbic acid, ergosterine and niacin (Table 6.13) (Crisan & Sands, 1978; Yokokawa, 1984; Li & Chang, 1985; Beelman & Edwards, 1989; Huang, Yung & Chang, 1989; Song *et al.*, 1989). They are low in calories, carbohydrates and calcium.

The fatty acid composition of six species of edible mushrooms that are

Table 6.13. *Nutritive values of some common mushrooms*

	Agaricus bisporus	*Lentinula edodes*	*Volvariella volvacea*	*Pleurotus ostreatus*
Protein % (dry weight)	23.9–34.8	13.4–7.5	29.5–30.1	10.5–30.4
Amino acids				
In abundance	aspartate	leucine	ND	glutamate
	glutamate	arginine	ND	leucine
In trace	methionine	tryptophan	ND	cystine
amount	cystine	cystine	ND	methionine
Calories Kcal/g (dry weight)	3.3–3.7	3.9	3.4–3.7	3.8–3.9
Vitamins mg/100 g (dry weight)				
Thiamin	1.0–8.9	7.8	1.2	4.8
Riboflavine	3.7–5.0	4.9	3.3	4.7
Niacin	42.5–57.0	54.9	91.9	108.7
Ascorbic acid	26.5–81.9	40.4–59.9	20.2	36.9
Fat % (dry weight)	1.8–8.0	4.9–8.0	5.7–6.4	1.6–2.2
Fatty acids				
In abundance	linoleate	linoleate	linoleate	linoleate
In trace	myristeate	myristeate	myristeate	oleate
amount	oleate	palmitoleate	stearate	palmitoleate
	palmitoleate	stearate	palmitoleate	stearate

ND, not determined.
Sources: Crisan & Sands, 1978; Yokokawa, 1984; Li & Chang, 1985; Beelman & Edwards, 1989; Huang *et al.*, 1989; Song *et al.*, 1989.

commonly consumed in the world have recently been reported (Huang *et al.*, 1989). A total lipid content varying between 0.6 and 3.1% of dry weight were found in these mushrooms, the least amount being found in *Tremella fuciformis* and the highest in *Volvariella volvacea* as well as *Agaricus bisporus*. All six species of mushrooms have a higher percentage of saponifiable lipid than non-saponifiable lipid. These values range from 78.1% in *Auricularia auricula-judae* to 58.8% in *V. volvacea*. The low percentage of saponifiable lipid found in *V. volvacea* is mainly due to the presence of the unusually high content of provitamin-D_2 and ergosterol (Huang, Yung & Chang, 1985). However, in terms of dry weight basis, *A. bisporus* shows 2.12% in the saponifiable fraction and *V. volvacea*, 1.76%. At least 72% of the total fatty acids are found to be unsaturated in all these mushrooms. The high content of unsaturated fatty acids is mainly contributed by the presence of linoleic acid

(Yokokawa, 1984), which amounts to 76% of the total fatty acids in *Lentinus edodes*, 70% in *V. volvacea* and 69% in *A. bisporus*. Unsaturated fatty acids are essential in our diet (Holman, 1976), whereas saturated fatty acids present in high amount in animal fats may be harmful to our health. The finding of a high proportion of unsaturated fatty acids and a high percentage of linoleic acid in these edible mushrooms is significant.

By use of various species, mushrooms can be cultivated in tropical, subtropical, and temperate climates. Their great advantage lies in the ability to convert various cellulosic waste materials, which have little or no market value and are definitely inedible to man, into a highly valued vegetable food. Therefore, mushroom cultivation can be considered as a measure of economic food source.

Conclusion

Most fungi are saprophytic, playing a role in utilizing dead organic matters in an ecosystem. Mushrooms, as a group of saprophytic fungi, secrete various extracellular enzyme complexes to degrade substrates for fruit body production. Cultivation of edible mushrooms is an economic measure, as the substrates used are mainly organic wastes from agriculture and industry. Agricultural wastes include animal manure, which is nitrogen-rich, and cereal straws, which are lignocellulosic compounds. Industrial wastes include paper pulps, sawdust and cotton wastes, which are all rich in lignocellulose. Lignocellulose is present in abundance in natural conditions. Since the component molecules cellulose, hemicellulose and lignin are all difficult to degrade, their biodegradation requires various enzyme complexes to act synergistically. These lignocellulosic wastes, if not properly treated, could cause pollution and a health hazard. Thus, mushroom production is an active bioconversion means to remove and utilize these organic wastes.

The common edible mushrooms are nutritious, not only for what they contain (high protein content with significant amounts of lysine and methionine, which are lacking in plants, and fibres, minerals and vitamins) but also for what they do not have or have in only trace amounts (high calorific value, sodium, fat and cholesterol); and they can be easily processed, dried, pickled and canned to allow maximum storage and transportation.

In addition to these unique characteristics, many edible fungi have been treasured for their medical properties (Cochran, 1978). Recent pharmacological and clinical evaluations have demonstrated significant biological effects, particularly immunopotentiation, anti-tumour and cardiotonic actions. A variety of proprietary products including health drinks and foods or even pharmaceuticals derived from mushrooms have been made available in the market, which is expected to increase with repeated satisfaction and acceptability.

These mushroom species can be cultivated under a wide range of temperatures, 5–35 °C, and the period from spawning to harvesting ranges from 10 days to 6 months. Unlike green crops, space is not a critical problem as its requirement of production is relieved by the practice of using bags and shelves in multiple layers. Also, the techniques used for cultivation of mushrooms can either be the simple farming type adopted in developing countries or be on a complex industrial scale using sophisticated equipments in modern developed countries. However, either way, the mushroom growers have to follow some basic principles, which are derived from microbiology, fermentation technology and environmental engineering.

In recent years, a great variety of improved strains has been developed by use of modern genetic manipulation techniques as well as by conventional breeding methods. By use of these improved strains, mushrooms can be produced in various waste materials economically throughout the year and in any part of the world. In addition, both fresh and preserved mushrooms are acceptable and welcomed by most people. In this way, excess mushrooms that cannot be totally consumed at one time can be sold again in preserved forms. Therefore, having the techniques carefully and properly transferred, mushroom production can be one of the economic measures in maintenance of food security everywhere, and particularly in developing countries.

References

Bano, Z., Nagaraja, K.W., Vibhakar, S. & Kapur, O.P. (1981). Mineral and heavy metal content in the sporophores of *Pleurotus* species. *Mushroom Newslett. Tropics*, **2**, 3–7.

Barron, G.L. (1988). Microcolonies of bacteria as a nutrient source for lignicolous and other fungi. *Can. J. Bot.*, **66**, 2505–10.

Beelman, R. (1988). Factors influencing post harvest quality and shelf life of fresh mushrooms. *Mushroom J.*, **182**, 455–62.

Beelman, R.B. & Edwards, C.G. (1989). Variability in the composition and nutritional value of the cultivated mushroom *Agaricus bisporus*. *Mushroom News*, **37**, 17–26.

Brunnert, H. & Zadrazil, F. (1983). The translocation of mercury and cadmium into the fruiting bodies of six higher fungi. A comparative study on species specificity in five lignocellulolytic fungi. *Eur. J. Appl. Microbiol. Biotechnol.*, **17**, 358–64.

Brunt, I.C. & Moore, D. (1990). Intracellular glycogen stimulates fruiting in *Coprinus cinereus*. *Mycolog. Res.* (in press).

Burton, K.S., Frost, C.E. & Nichols, R. (1989). A combination plastic permeable film system for controlling post-harvest mushroom quality. *Mushroom News*, **37**, 6–10.

Caribbean Food and Nutrition Institute (1974). *Food Composition Tables.* Kingston, Jamaica.

Castle, A.J., Horgen, P.A. & Anderson, J.B. (1988). Crosses among homokaryons from commercial and wild-collected strains of the mushroom *Agaricus brunnescens (= A. bisporus). Appl. Environ. Microbiol.*, **54**, 1643–8.

Chahal, D.S. (1989). Production of protein-rich mycelial biomass of a mushroom, *Pleurotus sajor-caju*, on corn stover. *J. Ferment. Bioeng*, **68**, 334–8.

Challen, M.P. & Elliott, T.J. (1987). Production and evaluation of fungicide-resistant mutants in the cultivated mushroom *Agaricus bisporus. Trans. Br. Mycologi. Soc.*, **88**, 433–9.

Chalmers, W. (1989). Sawdust culture of exotic mushrooms. *Mushroom J. Tropics*, **9**, 47–53.

Chang, S.T. (1974). Production of the straw mushroom (*Volvariella volvacea*) from cotton wastes. *Mushroom J.*, **21**, 348–53.

Chang, S.T. (1980a). Mushroom from waste. *Food Policy*, **5**, 64–5.

Chang, S.T. (1980b). Mushroom: a human food. *BioScience*, **30**, 399–401.

Chang, S.T. (1987). World production of cultivated edible mushrooms in 1986. *Mushroom J. Tropics*, **7**, 117–20.

Chang, S.T., Lau, O.W. & Cho, K.Y. (1981). The cultivation and nutritional value of *Pleurotus sajor-caju. Eur. J. Appl. Microbiol. Biotechnol.*, **12**, 58–62.

Chang, S.T. & Miles, P.G. (1986). Mushroom technology. *Mushroom Newslett. Tropics*, **6**, 6–11.

Chang, S.T. & Miles, P.G. (1989). *Edible Mushrooms and Their Cultivation.* CRC Press.

Chiu, S.W., Moore, D. & Chang, S.T. (1989). Basidiome polymorphism in *Volvariella bombycina. Mycolog. Res.*, **92**, 69–77.

Cochran, K.W. (1978). Medical effects. In *The Biology and Cultivation of Edible Mushrooms,* S.T. Chang & W.A. Hayes (eds), pp. 169–87. Academic Press.

Crisan, E.V. & Sands, A. (1978). Nutritional value. In *The Biology and Cultivation of Edible Mushrooms,* S.T. Chang & W.A. Hayes (eds), pp. 137–68. Academic Press.

Elliott, T.J. (1985a). The general biology of the mushroom. In *The Biology and Technology of the Cultivated Mushroom,* P.B. Flegg, D.M. Spencer & D.A. Wood (eds), pp. 9–22. John Wiley & Sons Ltd.

Elliott, T.J. (1985b). Spawn-making and spawns. In *The Biology and Technology of the Cultivated Mushroom,* P.B. Flegg, D.M. Spencer & D.A. Wood (eds), pp. 131–40. John Wiley & Sons Ltd.

Elliott, T.J. (1988). Genetic engineering and mushrooms. *Mushroom J.*, **201**, 272–5.

Ellor, T. (1988). Some parameters of growth of *Pleurotus* species on primary paper mill sludge. *Mushroom News*, **36**, 6–15.

FAO Production Yearbook (1987). Rome, Italy.

Fermor, T.R. (1988). Significance of micro-organisms in the composting process for cultivation of edible fungi. In *Treatment of Lignocellulosics with White Rot Fungi*, F. Zadrazil & P. Peiniger (eds), pp. 21–30. Elsevier Applied Science, London, New York.

Flegg, P. (1989). Hygiene on the mushroom farm. *Mushroom J.*, **203**, 337–43.

Flegg, P.B. & Maw, G.A. (1976). Mushrooms and their possible contribution to world protein needs. *Mushroom J.*, **48**, 396–405.

Flegg, P.B. & Wood, D.A. (1985). Growth and fruiting. In *The Biology and Technology of the Cultivated Mushrooms*, P.B. Flegg, D.M. Spencer & D.A. Wood (eds), pp. 141–78. John Wiley & Sons Ltd.

Fletcher, J.T. (1987). Weed moulds. *Mushroom J.*, **174**, 198–201.

Furutsuka, H. (1988). Determination of annual yield index and regional characteristics based on the average mushroom production per 1000 bedlogs in shiitake – farm management. *Rep. Tottori Mycological Inst.*, **26**, 79–104.

Gerrits, J.P.G. & van der Eerden, L.J. (1989). The influence of ammonia on the growth and quality of mushrooms. *Mushroom J.*, **198**, 197–8.

Goldstein, I.S. (1981). *Organic Chemicals from Biomass*. CRC Press, Boca Raton, Florida.

Gregory, F.J. (1989). MyNUTRI: a third generation supplement for mushrooms. *Mushroom News*, **37**, 18–19.

Hamlyn, P.E. (1989). Cultivation of edible mushrooms on cotton waste. *Mycologist*, **3**, 171–3.

Harvey, P. & Palmer, J. (1989). What makes wood rot? *Spectrum*, **217**, 8–11.

Holman, R.T. (1976). Significance of essential fatty acids in human nutrition. In *Lipids*, vol. 1, R. Paoletti, G. Porcellati & G. Jacina (eds), pp. 215–26. Raven Press, New York.

Huang, B.H., Yung, K.H. & Chang, S.T. (1985). The sterol composition of *Volvariella volvacea* and other edible mushrooms. *Mycologia*, **77**, 959–63.

Huang, B.H., Yung, K.H. & Chang, S.T. (1989). Fatty acid composition of *Volvariella volvacea* and other edible mushrooms. *Mushroom Sci.*, **12**, 533–40.

Jong, S.C. (1989). Commercial cultivation of the shiitake mushroom on supplemented sawdust. *Mushroom J. Tropics*, **9**, 89–98.

Jong, S.C. & Davis, E.E. (1987). Germplasm preservation of edible fungi. In *Cultivating edible fungi*, P.J. Wuest, D.J. Royse & R.B. Beelman (eds), pp. 213–25. Elsevier Science Publishers, Amsterdam.

Kawai, G. & Ikeda, Y. (1982). Fruiting-inducing activity of cerebrosides observed with *Schizophyllum commune*. *Biochim. Biophys. Acta*, **719**, 612–18.

Lavie, D. (1988). Producing oyster mushrooms on cotton straw. *Mushroom J.*, **182**, 453–4.

Leatham, G.F. & Stahmann, M.A. (1987). Effect of light and aeration on fruiting of *Lentinula edodes*. *Trans. Bri. Mycolog. Soc.*, **88**, 9–20.

Leendertse, I.K.D.K. (1988). The Agrisystems–Sohm Indoor Composting System: is this the future? *Mushroom News*, **36**, 10–13.

Li, G.S.F. & Chang, S.T. (1985). Determination of vitamin C (ascorbic acid) in some edible mushrooms by differential pulse polarography. *Mushroom Newslett. Tropics*, **5**, 11–16.

Loftus, M.G., Moore, D. & Elliott, T.J. (1988). DNA polymorphisms in commercial and wild strains of the cultivated mushroom, *Agaricus bisporus*. *Theor. Appl. Genet.*, **76**, 712–18.

Logtenberg, H. & Bakker, E. (1988). The DNA fingerprint. *Endeavour, New Series*, **12**, 28–33.

Lohr, Y.I., O'Brien, R.G. & Coffey, D.L. (1984). Spent mushroom compost in soilless media and its effect on the yield and quality of transplants. *J. Am. Soc. Horticult. Sci.*, **109**, 693–7.

Lomax, K.M. (1989). Air movement within compost. *Mushroom News*, **37**, 34–5.

Love, M.E. (1989). Temperature manipulation and mushroom cultivation. *Mushroom J.*, **193**, 11–15.

Lu, B.C. (1982). Replication of deoxyribonucleic acid and crossing over in *Coprinus*. In *Basidium and Basidiocarp. Evolution, Cytology, Function and Development*, K. Wells & E.K. Wells (eds), pp. 93–112. Springer-Verlag, New York, Heidelberg, Berlin.

Lu, S.I., Leonard, T.J., Dick, S. & Leatham, G.F. (1988). A new strategy for genetic improvement of edible fungi through enhancement of their lignocellulose degrading and fruiting abilities. *Micolog. Neotrop. Aplic.*, **1**, 5–19.

Manachere, G., Robert, J.C., Durand, R., Bret, J.P. & Fevre, M. (1983). Differentiation in the basidiomycetes. In *Fungal Differentiation: A Contemporary Synthesis*, J.E. Smith (ed.), pp. 481–514. Marcel Dekker, New York.

Matsumoto, T. (1988). Changes in activities of carbohydrases, phosphorylase, proteinases and phenol oxidases during fruiting of *Lentinus edodes* in sawdust culturs. *Rep. Tottori Mycological Inst.*, **26**, 46–54.

Mellon, F.M. & Casselton, L.A. (1988). Transformation as a method of increasing gene copy number and gene expression in the basidiomycete fungus *Coprinus cinereus*. *Curr. Genet.*, **14**, 451–6.

Miller, F.C. & Macauley, B.J. (1988). Odours arising from mushroom composting: a review. *Mushroom J.*, **192**, 785–97.

Mori, K., Fukai, S. & Zennyozi, A. (1974). Hybridization of shiitake (*Lentinus edodes*) between cultivated strains of Japan and wild strains grown in Taiwan and New Guinea. *Mushroom Sci.*, **9**, 391–403.

Morimoto, N., Suda, S. & Sagara, N. (1981). Effect of ammonia on fruit-body induction of *Coprinus cinereus* in darkness. *Plant Cell Physiol.*, **22**, 247–54.

140   S.T. Chang and S.W. Chiu

Muller, J. (1988). Genetic potential of *Pleurotus ostreatus*: relevance to the disposal of agro-wastes. *Micolog. Neotrop. Aplic.*, **1**, 29–44.

Nair, N.G. (1982). Substrates for mushroom production. In *Tropical Mushrooms: Biological Nature and Cultivation Methods*, S.T. Chang & T.H. Quimio (eds), pp. 47–61. The Chinese University Press, Hong Kong.

Nichols, R. (1988). Mushrooms after harvest. *Mushroom J.*, **183**, 501–3.

O'Brien, A. (1989). Mushroom marketing worldwide. *Mushroom News*, **37**, 14–24.

Oriaran, T.P., Labosky, Jr. P. & Royse, D.J. (1989). Lignin degradation capabilities of *Pleurotus ostreatus*, *Lentinula edodes* and *Phanerochaete chrysosporium*. *Wood Fiber Sci.*, **21**, 183–92.

Peberdy, J.F. (1989). Fungi without coats – protoplasts as tools for mycological research. *Mycolog. Res.*, **93**, 1–20.

Quimio, T.H. (1988*a*). Continuous recycling of rice straw in mushroom cultivation with emphasis on its lignin content for animal feed. *Abstracts. GIAM 8: Int. Conf. on Global Impacts of Applied Microbiology, Hong Kong*, p. 112.

Quimio, T.H. (1988*b*). Cultivation of *Auricularia*: past, present and future. *Mushroom J. Tropics*, **8**, 99–103.

Rajarathnam, S. & Bano, Z. (1989). *Pleurotus* mushrooms: III. Biotransformations of natural lignocellulosic wastes: commercial applications and implications. *CRC Crit. Rev. Food Sci. Nutr.*, **28**, 31–113.

Raper, C.A. (1985). Strategies for mushroom breeding. In *Developmental Biology of Higher Fungi, BMS Symp.*, vol. 10, D. Moore, L.A. Casselton, D.A. Wood & I.C. Frankland (eds), pp. 513–28. Cambridge University Press.

Romaine, C.P. & Schlagnhaufer, B. (1989). Prevalence of double-stranded RNAs in healthy and La France disease-affected basidiocarps of *Agaricus bisporus*. *Mycologica*, **81**, 822–5.

Royse, D.J. (1989). Factors influencing the production rate of shiitake. *Mushroom J. Tropics*, **9**, 127–38.

Saddler, J.N. (1986). Factors limiting the efficiency of cellulase enzymes. *Microbiol. Sci.*, **3**, 84–7.

Samajpati, N. (1982). Mushroom cultivation and rural development. *Mushroom Newslett. Tropics*, **2**, 1–2.

Schwalb, M.N. (1978). Regulation of fruiting. In *Genetics and Morphogenesis in the Basidiomycetes*, M.N. Schwalb & P.G. Miles (eds), pp. 135–65. Academic Press, New York, San Francisco, London.

Smith, J.F., Fermor, T.R. & Zadrazil, F. (1988). Pretreatment of lignocellulosics for edible fungi. In *Treatment of Lignocellulosics with White Rot Fungi*, F. Zadrazil & P. Peiniger (eds), pp. 3–13. Elsevier Applied Science, London, New York.

Song, C.H., Cho, K.Y., Nair, N.G. & Vine, J. (1989). Growth stimulation and lipid synthesis in *Lentinus edodes*. *Mycologia*, **81**, 514–22.

Sonnenberg, A.S., Wessels, J.G. & van Griensven, L.J. (1988). An efficient protoplasting/regeneration system for *Agaricus bisporus* and *Agaricus bitorquis*. *Curr. Microbiol.*, **17**, 285–91.

Specht, C.A., Munoz-Rivzas, A., Novotny, C.P. & Ullrich, R.C. (1988). Transformation of *Schizophyllum commune*: an analysis of parameters for improving transformation frequencies. *Exp. Mycol.*, **12**, 357–66.

Straatsma, G., Gerrits, J.G., Augustijn, M.P.A.M., Op den Camp, H.J.M., Vogels, G.D. & van Griensven, L.J.L.D. (1989). Regulation dynamics of *Scytalidium thermophilum* in mushroom compost and stimulatory effects on growth rate and yield of *Agaricus bisporus*. *J. Gen. Microbiol.*, **135**, 751–9.

Takagi, T., Katayose, Y. & Shishido, K. (1988). Intracellular levels of cyclic AMP and adenylate cyclase activity during mycelial development in fruiting body formation in *Lentinus edodes*. *FEMS Microbiol. Lett.*, **55**, 275–8.

Uno, I. & Ishikawa, T. (1982). Biochemical and genetic studies on the initial events of fruit body formation. In *Basidium and Basidiocarp. Evolution, Cytology, Function and Development*, K. Wells & E.K. Wells (eds), pp. 113–23. Springer-Verlag, New York, Heidelberg, Berlin.

Wach, M.P. (1988). Mushroom strain development: the cloning of genes from *Agaricus bisporus*. *Mushroom News*, **36**, 8–9.

Wang, S.H.L., Lohr, V.I. & Coffey, D.L. (1984). Spent mushroom compost as a soil amendment for vegetables. *J. Am. Soc. Horticult. Sci.*, **109**, 698–702.

Wong, K.K.Y., Tan, L.U.L. & Saddler, J.N. (1988). Multiplicity of beta-1,4-xylanase in micro-organisms: functions and applications. *Microbiol. Rev.*, **52**, 305–17.

Wood, D.A. (1989). Mushroom biotechnology. *Mushroom J.*, **201**, 272–5.

Wood, D.A. & Smith, J.F. (1988*a*). The cultivation of mushrooms. Part I. *Mushroom J.*, **187**, 633–7.

Wood, D.A. & Smith, J.F. (1988*b*). The cultivation of mushrooms. Part II. *Mushroom J.*, **188**, 665–74.

Wood, D.A. & Smith, J.F. (1988*c*). The cultivation of mushrooms. Part III. *Mushroom J.*, **189**, 688–91.

Wood, D.A., Matcham, S.E. & Fermor, T.R. (1988). Production and function of enzymes during lignocellulose degradation. In *Treatment of lignocellulosics with white rot fungi*, F. Zadrazil & P. Peinige (eds), pp. 43–9. Elsevier Applied Science, London, New York.

Wu, L.-C. (1985). Composting technology. In *Developmental Biology of Higher Fungi, BMS Symp.*, vol. 10, D. Moore, L.A. Casselton, D.A. Wood & I.C. Frankland (eds), pp. 541–60. Cambridge University Press.

Wu, L.-C. (1987). Strategies for conservation of genetic resources. In *Cultivation Edible Fungi*, P.J. Wuest, D.J. Royse & R.B. Beelman (eds), pp. 183–211. Elsevier Science Publishers, Amsterdam.

Yokokawa, H. (1984). Analyses of general and inorganic components and fatty acid compositions of fruit bodies of higher fungi. *Trans. Mycolog. Soci., Jap.*, **25**, 531–7.

7

The economic viability of Single Cell Protein (SCP) production in the twenty-first century

I.Y. HAMDAN AND J.C. SENEZ

Introduction

The use of microorganisms as a protein source in human foods and animal feeds has long been established. In the early days, microorganisms played an important role in producing fermented foods, such as bread, cheese, wine, yogurt and other useful compounds. Single Cell Protein (SCP) has been under active investigation for more than 30 years, as an ingredient in animal feeds, and yeast protein has been used in varying degrees in foods and fodder. There was a great expectation that the microbial conversion of hydrocarbons to protein would satisfy the future needs of an expanding world population. After the 1973 oil crisis, this expectation changed, and further development of SCP technology was discouraged in many Western countries. In oil-producing countries, however, SCP technology still holds an attraction as part of an integrated food/fodder production system for egg, poultry, veal and fish production.

The term 'Single Cell Protein' (SCP) was coined by C.L. Wilson in 1966, and has been used widely since that time in referring to microbial cells grown in large industrial systems as a protein source for food and feed applications (Scrimshaw, 1968). However, this term refers to a whole microbial biomass, i.e. to a complex mixture of proteins, nucleic acids, carbohydrates, lipids, minerals, vitamins and other cell constituents. Furthermore, the term SCP applies not only to single-cell organisms, such as yeast, bacteria and unicellular algae, but also to coenocytic multicellular moulds. Various aspects of SCP technology and its economic evaluation have been the subject of comprehensive articles, books and conferences (Pontanel, 1972; Champagnat & Adrian, 1974; Tannenbaum & Wang, 1975; Rockwell, 1976; Rose, 1979a,b; Ferranti & Fiechter, 1983; Senez, 1983; Hamdan, 1983;

Shennan, 1984; Goldberg, 1985). In this chapter, more emphasis will be put on reviewing briefly the various processes of SCP technologies from hydrocarbon and renewable substrates, safety regulations, SCP related biotechnologies and economic prospects.

The need for protein

World resources for food production by conventional methods are hard-pressed to satisfy the needs of an increasing population, expected to exceed six billion by the turn of the century. It is important to note that the major increases in population are in the developing countries. The annual rate of increase in the demand for protein in developing countries exceeds that of developed countries. Also, the protein supply per capita per day is much less in developing than in developed countries, and will be even more so in the year 2000. If the world population continues to grow at the present rate, the demand for animal proteins will increase, which will in turn increase the demand for feed cereals and seed-oil meal. Since the present trend in crop production could not fill the gap, a deficit of 23 million tons of oil-meal protein is projected for the year 2000 (Hoshiai, 1981). Therefore, merely to maintain world food production at the present level, protein production should be multiplied by 1.5 (Table 7.1). Moreover, during this period, the Gross Domestic Product is expected to increase substantially in a number of developing countries (UN, 1977).

These developments will be reflected in the demand for protein, both quantitatively and qualitatively, since economic progress is always correlated with a larger consumption of total protein and a higher ratio of animal versus total protein (Hoshiai, 1978). Consequently, it is estimated that between now and the year 2000, the demand for feed protein will be multiplied by 1.8 (Senez, 1979; Hoshiai, 1981).

At present, feed protein is quantitatively and economically dominated by soybeans, of which the production (98 million tonnes) corresponds to 33 million tonnes of crude protein, i.e. 27% of total protein used for animal feed worldwide. The international market for crude soya protein (14.7 million tonnes) is in the hands of three exporting countries: the United States (62%), Brazil (26%) and Argentina (12%). Most of this international market is absorbed by Western Europe and Japan, which imports 80% of their feed protein at a cost of $5 thousand million.

Agriculture alone is unlikely to cover the additional demand for feed protein in the coming decades (Senez, 1979; Hoshiai, 1981). From 1969 to 1979, world soybean production increased by 80%; however, this has slowed to an increase of only 2.4% over the last 6 years (Anon., 1984). The main limitation on soybean production is the shortage of suitable

Table 7.1. *Protein demand to the year 2000*

	1980	2000	Increase factor
World[a]			
Population (millions)	4400	6405	1.46
GDP[b]	1165	2071	1.78
Protein demand[c]			
Human consumption (million tonnes)	48.6	78.4	1.61
Animal feeding	43.1	106.3	2.47

[a]UN, 1977.
[b]Gross domestic product in constant US dollars (1971).
[c]Hoshiai, 1978, 1981; Senez, 1979.

farmland in North and South America, affected by large programmes for ethanol production from sugarcane in Brazil, and fructose from corn in the United States. On the other hand, productivity enhancement through selection of new varieties and improved agricultural practices seems near to being optimized, as suggested by the fact that, since 1969, the average yield of soybeans per hectare in the USA (FAO, 1985) remained quite stable (1.8–2.0 l/ha). Moreover, efforts made in Europe, Africa, and Asia to produce soybeans at a competitive price have met with little success. According to FAO (1978), the world production of crude feed protein is expected to reach 63 million tonnes in the year 2000. This forecast would correspond to a deficit of about 50 million tonnes with regard to the prospective demand. The potential of the SCP market is, thus, of the same order of magnitude.

Production of SCP from hydrocarbons and renewable substrates

Hydrocarbon-based SCP processes
Selected SCP processes based on hydrocarbon feedstocks such as petroleum (gas oil and *n*-alkanes), methanol, methane and ethanol utilized by yeasts or bacteria are summarized in Table 7.2 (Senez, 1987).

SCP petroleum processes The industrial production of Single Cell Proteins from petroleum originated in France during 1955–60, in close cooperation between the National Centre of Scientific Research (CNRS) and the French branch of British Petroleum (SF-BP). These

Table 7.2. *SCP production from hydrocarbon feedstocks*

Substrate	Organism	Organization/location	Product trade name	Production (1000 tonnes per year)
Gas oil	*Candida tropicalis*	SF-BP Lavera, France[a]	Toprina-L	16
	Lodderomyces elongisporus	Schwedt, Germany	Fermosin	50
n-alkane	*C. lipolytica*	BP-Grangemouth, UK[a]	Toprina-G	4
	C. lipolytica	Italproteine, Italy[a]	Topriana-G	100
	C. maltosa	Liquichimica/Kanegafuchi, Italy[a]	Liquipron	100
	Candida spp.	Mozyr, USSR		1000
	C. paraffinica	Dainippon & Petrom, Romania	Roniprot	60
	C. tropicalis	IFP/Technip, France		Pilot
	C. tropicalis	Pet. Inst. Assam, India		Pilot
Methanol	*Methylophilus methylotrophus*	ICI Billingham, UK	Pruteen	55
	Yeast	Phillips Petroleum, USA	Provesteen	1.2
	Methylomonas clara	Uhde/Hoechst, Germany	Probion	Pilot
	Methylophilus KISRI	KISR/Kuwait		Pilot
	Methalomonas methanolica	Norsk Hydro, Sweden	Norprotein	Pilot
	Pichia pastoris	IFP/Technip, France		Pilot
	Pichia aganagobii	Mitsubishi, Japan		4
Methane	*Pseudomonas methyltropha*	Shell, UK		Pilot
	Methylococcus	BP, UK		Pilot
Ethanol	*Candida utilis* (Torula)	Pure Culture Products, USA	Torutein	6–7
	Yeast	Sofnaft, Czechoslovakia		4
	Candida ethanothermophilum	Mitsubishi, Japan		0.1

After Senez, 1987. [a]Not in operation.

early developments led to two processes for production of feed yeasts (*Candida tropicalis* and *C. lipolytica*) from gas oil and from purified *n*-alkanes extracted from petroleum by molecular sieve filtration. In 1971, the first two industrial units were built by BP, one at Grangemouth (UK) with a capacity of 4000 tonnes per year, utilizing *n*-alkanes as feedstock; and the other units at Cap Lavera (France) with a capacity of 16 000 tonnes per year, utilizing gas-oil as a feedstock for fermentation. Following extensive nutritional and toxicological testing, the proteins produced by these plants were commercialized in the common market under the tradename of 'Toprina'. From 1973 to 1978, about 40 000 tonnes of these products were successfully utilized as staple food for mono-gastric animals and as milk replacers for pre-ruminants. These developments led to more industrial SCP plants in Europe, USSR and Japan, in which many firms developed their own processes from hydrocarbons at pilot-plant scale. In Italy, two commercial plants of 100 000 tonnes per year were built in 1975 by Italproteine Company and Liquichimica. They based their processes on those of British Petroleum and Kanegafuchi Chemical Co., respectively. These two plants were not allowed to go onstream by the Italian government, resulting in the liquidation of both companies (Ellingham, 1980).

The Soviet Union produces approximately 1.1 million tonnes per year of SCP, using hydrocarbons and agricultural wastes as a feedstock. Most production utilizes feed yeast grown on *n*-alkanes, also wood-processing wastes and by-products. Sparse technical information indicated that more than 60 plants using fermenters with induced circulation systems were producing SCP in several locations in the Soviet Union (Carter, 1981). Dainippon Ink & Chemicals Inc. (DIC), in a joint venture with Romanian Government, constructed a plant of 60 000 tonnes per year called Roniprot. The petrochemical Kombinat of Schwedt (DDR) produces 50 000 tonnes of SCP by a gas-oil process similar to that of Lavera, but with different yeast species, under the name Fermosin (Ringpfeil, 1983).

SCP methanol processes Methanol is manufactured chemically from methane and can be utilized by methylotrophic microorganisms, including yeasts and bacteria. The most advanced process for SCP production from methanol was developed by Imperial Chemical Industries (ICI) in the UK. ICI's preliminary work on the process began in 1968. However, the first stage on the way to commercialization was in 1973, when a 1000 tonnes per year pilot plant was constructed. A novel pressure-cycle fermenter was applied successfully, using air for agitation and aeration. The success of this stage led to the building of the first commercial production plant in 1979, with a capacity of 50 000 tonnes per year, using a huge vertical 1500 m^3 fermenter (Senior & Windass, 1980). In order to prevent the toxic effect of high concentrations of methanol on the culture, a complex sparger system of 3000 outlets was installed, to maintain a homogenous concentration of the methanol in the whole fermenter (Solomons, 1983). Bacterial cells were separated by a flocculation/flotation procedure, followed by centrifugation passing to a pneumatic hot air drier. The bacterial biomass was produced under the trade name of Pruteen by the organism *Methylophilus methylotrophus*. The plant was in operation for a few years being shut down in 1986 for economic reasons.

Several other methanol-based SCP processes have been developed at pilot scale (Table 7.2). Hoechst/Uhde in FRG developed a process using bacterial species *Methylomonas clara*, grown in an airlift-type fermenter with a capacity of 1000 tonnes per year. The product is intended for animal and/or human use under the trade name 'Probion' (Faust & Sittig, 1980). Other processes utilizing methylotrophic yeasts or bacteria have been developed at pilot scale by Provesta/Phillips Petroleum (USA). These involve a high-productivity continuous fermentation from methanol-growing bacteria *Methylomonas* sp. and methylotrophic yeast *Pichia pastoris*. These processes can eliminate centrifugal recovery of biomass, reducing operating cost (Shay, Hunt & Wegner, 1987). Institut Francais du Petrole (IFP), the French pilot process, uses yeast to utilize methanol in an air-lift fermenter; Mitsubishi Gas Co., Japan, utilizes methanol assimilating yeasts in a 20 m^3 pilot air-lift fermenter developed by Hitachi (Hamer, 1979); and the Kuwait Institute for Scientific Research (KISR), which developed a pilot process based on methylotrophic bacterial strains growing at 42 °C on methanol in a 1.5 m^3 Chemap fermenter (Hamdan *et al.*, 1986; Banat, Al-Awadi & Hamdan, 1989). Methanol-based SCP has also been investigated by Norsk Hydro, Sweden, growing *M. methanica* in fermentations up to pilot-plant scale (Mogren, 1979). To date, none of these pilot-scale programmes has resulted in commercialization.

SCP methane processes The conversion of methane to SCP is an attractive route; by using gas directly as a carbon source, little purification is needed for feedstock preparation. The Shell Group carried out research and development using mixed bacterial cultures up to 300 l scale. The process is based on a mixed culture of obligate methanotrophic bacteria belonging to the genus *Pseudomonas*. Shell abandoned work on this process in 1976 for technical and economical reasons (Solomons, 1983).

SCP ethanol processes Different types of yeast and bacteria are grown on ethanol as a sole carbon source, including yeasts approved as food supplement. Pure Culture Products Inc. in the United States is producing 6000–7000 tonnes per year of Torula yeast (*Candida utilis*) using ethanol as the substrate (Litchfield, 1983). Organizations in Japan and Czechoslovakia are using similar approaches (Table 7.2).

SCP processes from renewable resources

The production of SCP for food and feed from renewable resources has been of considerable interest and the subject of intensive research and development in many countries. However, very few are presently commercialized or in operation (Table 7.3). The main constraint is the availability of a continuous supply of substrates all through the year. Such a prerequisite excludes many agricultural raw materials that are available in small quantity during certain seasons. Another constraint is that the SCP production from some agricultural products or wastes is in competition with other uses, such as direct animal feeding, composting or bio-gas production. On the other hand, one substrate with a good potential for SCP production is lignocellulosic material, which is available at low cost and in huge quantities.

Carbohydrates Molasses is obtained mainly as a by-product of sugar-cane and sugarbeet refining. Beet molasses was used for SCP production by growing *Candida (Torulopsis) utilis* as a supplement to human food in Germany during both World Wars. The current world supply of molasses is about 10 million tonnes per year, which is mainly utilized for direct feeding of cattle due to economic considerations. It is also used for the production of ethanol, chemicals, amino acids, antibiotics and pharmaceuticals by the fermentation industry. In Cuba, seven plants built by the French engineering firm Speichim which are producing 80 000 tonnes per year of fodder yeast from sugarcane molasses (Revuz, 1981). Tate and Lyle Ltd developed a process for producing animal-feed-grade SCP by *Candida utilis* yeast from confectionery manufacturing effluent. The plant has a capacity of 500 tonnes per year, using continuous fermentation (Davy, Wilson & Lyon, 1981).

Ranks Hovis McDougall (RHM), a large UK food company, has developed a fermented mycelial product from *Fusarium graminearium*. The fungus can be cultivated on a variety of food-grade carbohydrate-containing substances, such as potatoes, bread residues, sugar and molasses (Tuse, 1983). The SCP product is destined for the human food market. This RNA-reduced product received UK government clearance for sale to the public in 1980 (Solomons, 1983). The product can be used to formulate white-meat analogues that cannot be distinguished from

Table 7.3. *SCP production from renewable resources*

Substrate	Organisms	Organization/location	Production (1000 tonnes per year)
Molasses	*Candida utilis*	Speichim, Cuba	80
Molasses and starch	*Corynebacterium melassicola*	Orsari, France[a]	10
	Brevibacterium lactofermentum	Eurolysine, France[a]	8
Confectionary wastes	*Candida utilis*	Tate & Lyle, UK	0.5
Starch hydrolysate	*Fusarium graminearium*	Rank Hovis–McDougall, UK	0.05–0.10
Spent sulphite liquors	*Paecilomyces variotii*	Pekilo, Finland	10
	Candida utilis	Rhinelander, USA	5
	Candida utilis	Boise Cascade Co., USA	5
	Candida utilis	Metsaluton, Finland	10
	Kluyveromyces fragilis	Knudsen Co., USA	0.75
Whey	*Kluyveromyces fragilis*	Bel (Protibel), France	8
	Kluyveromyces fragilis	Amber Laboratories, USA	5
	Penicillium cyclopium	Heurtey, France	0.3
Cellulosic wastes	*Chaetomium cellulolyticum*	Waterloo University, Canada	Pilot
	Trichoderma viridi + Candida utilis	Natick, USA	Pilot

[a]By-product of amino acid production.
After Senez, 1987.

real meat, and have such nutritional advantages as low fat, low sodium, high dietary fibre, and 50% protein.

Spent sulphite liquor (SSL) SSL is a by-product of the paper mills, and contains fermentable sugars with a large proportion of simple sugars, obtained from the hydrolysis of wood. It is estimated that 25 000 tonnes per year of SCP are produced in Europe and 10 000 tonnes per year of SCP produced in the USA from SSL (Table 7.3).

The largest commerically continuous process is the 'Pekilo' process, which utilizes SSL as a substrate for growing filamentous microfungus, *Paecilomyces variotii*, to produce SCP product as a feed ingredient (Goldberg, 1985). The process capacity is 10 000 tonnes per year using two 360 m³ sterile continuous fermenters (Solomons, 1983). SCP products from the SSL process are of low nutritional quality due to contamination by large quantities of lignin-sulphonate (50%) and SO_2. Moreover, since the introduction of the Kraft process to the paper industry, the supply of sulphite liquors suitable for SCP production is rapidly declining (Forage & Righelato, 1979).

Whey Whey from the cheese industry is a potentially important raw material for SCP production. It contains, on dry basis, 70% lactose and 9–15% protein. About 13.6 million m³ of liquid whey are produced per year in the USA, corresponding to about 880 000 tonnes of solids. Knudsen Dairy Co. (USA) developed a batch process by growing the yeast *Kluyveromyces fragilis* on whey, producing 750 tonnes per year of a product called 'wheast' (Solomons, 1983). The process was claimed to be a sterile operation. Another process, developed by Amber Laboratories produces 500 tonnes per year using a 54 m³ fermenter to grow a strain of *Kluyveromyces fragilis* in a continuous non-aspectic fermentation. The product is both animal- and food-grade yeast (Solomons, 1983). In France, Bel Industries operate a number of lactic acid plants using yeast strains of *Kluyveromyces fragilis* and *lactis* on whey, producing a product called 'Protibel' that is destined for both human and animal use. Another French Company, Heurtey S.A., developed a process growing a fungus *Penicillium cyclopium* on milk whey, with a capacity of 300 tonnes per year (Solomons, 1983).

Lignocellulosic material According to UNEP estimations (Sasson, 1983; Ward, 1982), the world production of cereals is annually providing about 1.7 thousand million tonnes of straw, the major part of which is wasted. On the other hand, 50 million tonnes of stalks and 67 million tonnes of bagasses from sugarcane are available in the developing world.

The chemical compositions of lignocellulosic materials are complex, and differ from one source to another. Basically, they consist of highly polymerized phenolic compounds (lignin) and sugars in the form of cellulose and hemicelluloses. The latter components, made of glucose and pentoses, constitute 30% of straw, 25% of hardwood and 10% of conifer wood (Senez, 1987).

One approach based on agricultural by-products is a preliminary chemical hydrolysis of cellulose and hemicellulose in strongly acid conditions and at high temperature, followed by cultivation of a glycolytic yeast. This type of process was industrialized for several years in the Scandinavian countries and USSR, but was abandoned for economic reasons. A further difficulty inherent to SCP production from lignocellulosic materials is the toxicity of some phenolic by-products of lignin degradation, which prevents the utilization of these proteins for food for mono-gastric animals.

Another approach is the direct production of lignocellulolytic bacteria and moulds in either mono-specific or mixed cultures (Crawford, 1981). At present, the growth rate and yield of lignocellulolytic microorganisms is low and insufficient for the industrial production of SCP. However, fundamental studies on the chemical structure and biological degradation of lignin are rapidly progressing, and some promising microorganisms (Reid, Chkao & Dawson, 1985) have been isolated recently. On the other hand, new developments can be expected in the field of genetic engineering and interspecific transfer of DNA from lignocellulolytic moulds to other microorganisms.

Protein-enriched fermented fodder (PEFF) Modern biotechnology can provide new and valuable protein sources for human and animal feeding. The products of direct protein enrichment by fermentation, although usually referred to as SCP, are fundamentally different, and deserve specific consideration. This type of biotechnological processing does not involve a separation step, and the product is thus constituted by the whole culture, i.e. a mixture of microbial biomass and the residual raw material. Such simplified technology, by reducing the investment and production costs, has important advantages and prospects. It makes possible the use of relatively small and inexpensive production units, well adapted to the utilization of raw materials that would be too costly or in too small quantities for economic SCP production. A further advantage of direct protein enrichment is that it can be performed with filamentous fungi or yeasts cultivated at acidic pH (3.5–4.0), thus preventing bacterial contamination and permitting operation in non-sterile conditions.

Many substrates have been proposed and a number of processes have been developed at the laboratory or pilot level (Rose, 1979*a,b*; Ward,

1982; Goldberg, 1985). Among those utilizing lignocellulosic material, the Waterloo process (Moo-Young *et al.*, 1979) uses a three-stage operation involving: (1) wood residues or straw thermally treated or hydrolysed by acid, (2) aerobic fermentation by the filamentous fungus *Chaetomium cellulolyticum*, and (3) separation of the suspended solids (the product) from the fermented broth. The cellulosic materials provide the main carbon source for the fermentation. The protein product has good amino-acid profile and potential feedvalue (Moo-Young, Chahal & Vlach, 1978). The original system, however, was shown to be economically unattractive because of the problems of large quantities of post-fermentation solid residue, and the presence of an inhibitor that becomes significant in mildly acidic conditions (Pamment *et al.*, 1978).

In the United States, the General Electric Company and University of Pennsylvania developed a process for converting of cellulosic wastes to feed proteins using a thermophilic actinomycete species from the genus *Thermoactinomyces* (Bellamy, 1974; Nolan & Forro, 1976). This organism has an unusual SCP amino acid profile that is high in methionine; it also has the ability to grow directly on crystalline cellulose with good yields, making it a promising candidate for large-scale utilization of cellulosic wastes (Humphrey *et al.*, 1977). The drawback is its high maintenance–energy requirement (Humphrey *et al.*, 1976). A process of solid fermentation was developed by the Institut National de la Recherche Agronomique (INRA) in France, using sugarbeet pulp pre-treated by mild acid hydrolysis and fermented by the yeast *Candida utilis* (Durand *et al.*, 1983). A similar process using the same organism and partially hydrolysed straw is presently industrialized at a small scale in Czechoslovakia (Volfova, 1984).

Protein enrichment of starchy materials, such as cereals and potato in the temperate climates, and cassava, banana and other crops in the tropical regions, is particularly attractive. Agriculturally produced, with a high productivity per hectare, these substrates are available in large quantities. On the other hand, starch can be fermented with a high rate of bioconversion ($>50\%$) by a great variety of fast-growing yeasts, moulds and bacteria. Several processes of protein enrichment in a liquid medium have been experimented with at the pilot-plant scale. The process developed at Guelph University (Canada) utilizes the fermentation of crude cassava flour with a thermophilic fungus, *Aspergillus fumigatus* (Aidoo, Hendry & Wood, 1982). In another process developed in France (Adour), the same raw material is fermented continuously in an air-lift fermenter by an amylolytic strain of the yeast *Candida tropicalis* (Revuz, 1981). The product contains 20% protein, and is destined for human consumption. The possibility of directly obtaining a concentrated product not requiring expensive dehydration by solid-state fermentation (Brook, Stanton & Wallbridge, 1969) has received much attention in recent years. The first application of solid-state fermentation to starchy raw materials, such as cassava flour (Senez, Raimbault & Deschamps, 1980), were of low efficiency, providing only 3–4% protein enrichment. Technically, the main problem is to maintain, in a concentrated mash of substrate, aerobic conditions and a rate of oxygen transfer excluding an anaerobic contamination of the culture.

In the INRA-ORSTOM process (Senez *et al.*, 1980), the raw material is preliminarily steamed for 10 minutes at 70 °C for glutinization of starch, and inoculated with spores of an amylolytic fungus (*Aspergillus hennebergii*). Under appropriate conditions, i.e. an initial water content of 55%, the inoculate substrate spontaneously takes a granular structure freely permeable to air. After 24 hours incubation under controlled aeration, temperature (35 °C), pH (3.5), and humidity, the product contains up to 20% true protein of good nutritional quality and 25–30% residual carbohydrates. This process has been successfully operated at the pilot-plant level with a variety of substrates, including cassava, banana, and potato wastes from fecula plants, and with a number of other amylolytic fungi (*Asp. oryzae*, *Penicillium* sp.) isolated from tempe, koji, and other fermented foods of South-East Asia. In Mexico, similar techniques and results were reported using cassava flour and the mould *Rhizopus oligosporus* (Ramos-Valdivia, de la Torre & Casas-Campillo, 1983).

One may expect from protein enrichment of feeds important developments not only at the industrial, but also at the rural, level. Existing processes, particularly those based on solid-state fermentation (Senez *et al.*, 1980), can be operated in integrated agro-systems combining the production of raw material with protein enrichment and utilization of the product for animal feeding.

SCP as a by-product from industrial fermentations

A rapidly developing indirect source of SCP is the microbial biomass from industrial fermentations for purposes other than protein production. The world production of amino acids (2 million tonnes) yields approximately 600 000 tonnes of SCP, of which 18 000 tonnes are presently produced commercially in France, as by-products of glutamic acid and lysine. Likewise, the production of ethanol from sugarcane in Brazil (Rothman, Greenshields & Calle, 1983), which is expected to reach 2 million tonnes, will correspond to about the same amount of SCP. Similarly, in France, the projected production of 60 000 tonnes of ethanol from wheat and sugarbeet will yield about 56 000 tonnes of biomass (Bye & Mounier, 1984). The commercial production of biomass for animal feeding is economically an essential part (30%) of the return from amino acids and ethanol production.

Amino acid production The industrial production of amino acids as an indirect source of SCP, in addition to its supplementation to feed and food, will become a major contribution of biotechnology to world protein need. France is leading in the production of amino acids for animal feeding and other purposes. Orsan Co., related to the Lafarge-Copee group, is producing 35 000 tonnes per year of L-glutamate under license from the Japanese firm Ajinomoto. Glutamate is widely utilized by the food industry as an organoleptic agent, as are L-aspartic acid and phenylalanine, the production of which for synthesis of sweeteners is rapidly developing.

DL-methionine is the first amino acid to have been produced in large quantities for animal-feed supplementation. From 1960 to 1989, its production increased from 2 to 150 thousand tonnes, and is still increasing. This production is essentially intended for mono-gastric animals (poultry and pigs) in order to supplement the relative deficiency in soybeans of sulphur-amino acids (L-methionine and L-cysteine). The next largest production of amino acids for animal feed is that of L-lysine, which is the main limiting factor in cereals (wheat, maize, barley, rice). This production is increasing yearly by about 20%, reaching 110 000 tonnes in 1989 (Table 7.4).

The industrial production of amino acids offers a dual contribution to the national protein supply: first, it improves the nutritional value of vegetable proteins; second, the microbial biomass resulting from the fermentation process constitutes an important source of proteins for animal feeding. In order to develop an economical process for amino-acid production, the main prospects are as follows.

> Methionine is mainly utilized for mono-gastric animals and is also necessary for ruminants, but 80–90% of the methionine added to feeds is destroyed by microbial flora in the rumen. Several major industrial firms in Europe are producing DL-methionine formulas designed for ruminants, i.e. protected against rumen degradation either by combination with a metal or by an appropriate coating. Monsanto (USA) is producing 56 700 tonnes per year of hydroxy-analogue of methionine, which was authorized by the EEC in 1985.
>
> The production cost of L-lysine has been greatly reduced in the last two decades due to the high productivity of strains selected by classical genetic methods, and due to process optimization. Further advances are expected based on

Table 7.4. *World industrial production of amino acids (feed grade),*
1989

	World production (tonnes)	Market price (US $/kg)
L-glutamate	340 000	2.5
L-lysine, HCl	110 000	3.9
DL-methionine[a]	150 000	3.2
L-threonine	1000	9.5
L-tryptophane	120	18.9

[a]DL-methionine and analogues.

genetic engineering methods. The prices may be further
lowered when the lysine is purified by methods other than
crystallization, as is presently on the market. The high purity
is only justified for pharmaceutical use. Rhone-Poulenc and
the Norwegian Scanlysine Co. have recently been authorized
by the EEC to commercialize a product obtained by drying
the whole bacterial culture, containing 40% lysine. Eurolysine, a chemical company in France, plans to commercialize
liquid preparations containing 28–60% of technically pure
lysine.
Small quantities of other amino acids are presently produced at
high cost, essentially for pharmaceutical uses (Table 7.4).
Several major chemical firms in France (Eurolysine), in
Japan (Ajinomoto), and in the western part of Germany
(Degussa) have recently announced their intention to produce several amino acids for animal feed, namely, L-
tryptophane and L-isoleucine; these are, after lysine, the
limiting factors in cereals (maize, wheat, barley). These firms
are also working on L-threonine, which is the main limiting
amino acid in the industrialized countries (North America
and Western Europe), the world deficit of which has been
estimated at around 80 000 tonnes (Hoshiai, 1980).
An important prospect is the diversification of the use of raw
materials for amino acid production by fermentation. Most
of the present processes use carbohydrates as substrates, such
as cane or beet molasses, and starch hydrolysates from corn
and other cereals. In many countries, these materials are
either costly or not available. An alternative and abundant

raw material is methanol, which is considered a cheap substrate for fermentation. There are many methylotrophic yeasts and bacteria that could be adapted for the production of amino acids. These prospects are very attractive options for the oil-producing countries of North Africa and the Middle East that have weak agriculture bases and produce large quantities of methanol from natural gas. Several Japanese institutions have already investigated amino acid production from petroleum hydrocarbons (Fukui & Tanaka, 1980; Shennan, 1984).

Safety regulations

Since the early days of SCP development, it was important to control the new protein source closely to safeguard the ultimate human consumer. The Protein Advisory Group of the United Nations (PAG) and the International Union of Pure and Applied Chemistry (IUPAC) set up guidelines for the assessment of SCP intended for animal feed. The two basic principles behind these guidelines, first published in 1974, were (*a*) the need for suitably extensive testing and (*b*) a need to ensure product integrity. The PAG was discontinued in 1976 and replaced in 1977 by a nutrition sub-committee of the UN Administrative Committee on Coordination which had been concerned itself with nutrition policies but not with technological advances. Under these circumstances, the World Hunger program of the United Nations University (UNU) became the repository of the PAG records, and its Food and Nutrition Bulletin is a successor to that of the PAG. UNU has arranged for the review and reissue of those guidelines with continuing utility, including those related to SCP (Scrimshaw, 1983).

The PAG guideline no. 6 on the preclinical testing of novel protein sources was first issued in 1972, as the key to testing SCPs in laboratory animals (PAG/UNU, 1983*a*). This guideline is aimed largely at products for human consumption, but tests on laboratory animals can provide valuable information on products intended for use in animal feeding. In principle, products intended for incorporation into animal feeds may not require such extensive testing as those for human consumption; thus, a separate guideline (no. 15) was developed for evaluating nutritional and safety aspects of protein sources for animal feeding (PAG/UNU, 1983*c*). PAG guideline no. 7 is concerned exclusively with clinical trials for human testing of novel foods. Experience has shown that Single Cell Proteins have not caused problems in animal trials, unlike many higher plant protein sources that may contain lectins, trypsin, inhibitors and cyanogenic glycosides. Tolerance trials, related to nucleic acid that can be safely added to the human diet and to allergic reactions are outlined in these guidelines (Scrimshaw, 1983).

PAG guideline no. 12 was intended for testing SCP products for human consumption, and should precede the preclinical testing outlined in guideline no. 6. This guideline outlines that the final product should contain no living cells, the media used for fermentation should be free of possible chemical components that are regarded as health hazards, and could not later be removed from the SCP product to meet safety requirements. The guideline also indicates that process fermentation variables must be carefully controlled to ensure product quality and uniformity. In addition to the quality-control procedures, careful attention should be paid to the maintenance and integrity of the original strain of organisms used for fermentation, to ensure its stability and purity (PAG/UNU, 1983b).

Standards of identity need to be established for each Single Cell Protein to ensure that the marketed product is as close as possible to that tested, both toxicologically and nutritionally. The impact of modifications to the process on composition and safety need particular consideration. Although an important concept for all new animal feeds, that is especially significant for Single Cell Proteins since many of the test data will be obtained on material that has not been produced in the plant that will ultimately produce material for sale. IUPAC elaborated a general standard of identity for Single Cell Proteins produced from hydrocarbons, and in 1979 added criteria for those produced from methanol (Jonas, 1983).

The EEC's legislative position is important since the Community was in the forefront of developing SCP technology in the West. A legislative directive published in July 1982 lists those Single Cell Proteins that will be permitted in EEC countries. The directive is not itself law, but must be legislatively enacted by all members. This directive refers to proteins obtained from microorganisms (SCP), amino acids and non-protein nitrogenous compounds in animal feeds. The directive indicates that no new Single Cell Proteins can be permitted unless they (1) have a nutritonal value for animals, (2) have no detrimental effect on human or animal health or on the environment, and (3) they can be monitored in feeding stuffs. The directive lists only four cultures of traditional yeasts grown on a number of specified substrates of agricultural origin. However, it makes special transitional arrangements for other SCP products; yeasts of the genus *Candida*, cultivated on alkanes, must be examined by the prescribed procedure before the end of June 1984. The procedure laid down by the EEC directive requires that new Single Cell Proteins be evaluated by the Council's Expert Group on Animal Nutrition and by the Commission's Scientific Expert Groups with particular responsibilities for animal nutrition and for human food (Jonas, 1983). In 1985, referring to sanitary risks in Italy, the EEC decided that all national authorizations for n-alkane-grown yeasts individually delivered by member states had to be withdrawn until a series of supplementary tests could be performed. The ICI product Pruteen was officially authorized in October 1986, just before the ICI plant was shut down, and was permitted in all EEC member states with the exception of Italy and Greece (Jonas, 1983; Senez, 1985, unpublished report).

Economic prospects

Petroleum and methanol are the raw materials from which SCP can be produced at a large enough scale to satisfy world protein needs. However, the constraints on SCP production from these resources are primarily economical rather than technical. In the West, the supply and price of petroleum and the availability of alternative proteins, such as soybean proteins, cast a shadow of uncertainty over future marketing prospects. In the case of methanol, world usage is expected to rise in 1990 by 7.5% (Anon., 1982). However, in the short term, it is expected that methanol prices would fall in the near future and will recover by 1992 (Anon., 1989). The future prices of methanol will depend mainly on the production capacity and the demand, and it is obvious that accurate predictions could not be made. A similar constraint exists for the production of SCP from renewable raw substrates. Cultivated carbohydrates are too costly to be utilized as feedstock for SCP production at a price that can compete with alternatively available proteins. The dietary demand for starches, sugars and proteins is higher than supply, and production costs are also high; thus, the price of carbohydrate feedstock will probably remain high and not change relative to proteins (Forage & Righelato, 1979). Using conventional technology, SCP production from carbohydrates does not seem economically feasible during the first decade of the next century. Alternatively, the use of lignocellulosic low-value waste materials holds the highest promise on the assumption that technical problems and biomass yield will be overcome. The production of SCP from petroleum was stopped in the West due to the large price increase of petroleum in 1973. However, the market price of petroleum dropped from $270 per tonne to $195 per tonne from 1981 to 1984, and reached its lowest level in 1986 ($106 per tonne). Since then, the price has risen slightly, and is presently at $126.5 per tonne ($16.9 per billion barrels). It is indeed difficult to formulate predictions for the coming decades. However, it is expected that the price of petroleum will not again reach the 1981 peak of $270 per tonne ($36.0 per billion barrels) (Table 7.5).

Table 7.5. *Evolution of petroleum and soybean meal prices in current dollars and constant 1972 dollars*

	Petroleum (US $/tonne)		Soybean meal (US $/tonne)	
	Current	Constant 1972[b]	Current[a]	Constant 1972[b]
1972	23	23.0	103	103.0
1973	38	30.2	302	240.0
1976	97	65.0	214	143.4
1978	140	82.1	213	124.9
1980	231	118.7	259	120.2
1981	270	118.1	253	110.7
1982	255	101.0	218	86.4
1983	187	69.8	238	88.9
1984	195	70.0	197	70.8
1985	180	62.3	155	53.6
1986	106	36.0	185	62.8
1987	106	35.3	203	67.5
1988	130	41.8	264	82.8
1989	127	39.6	241	75.1

[a]Current price: soybean meal 44%, CIF Rotterdam (FAO, 1985).
[b]Based on US $ depreciation (1 US $ in 1972 = 3.21 US $ in 1989).

The economical evaluation of SCP should obviously take into account the depreciation of the US dollar and other currencies, and the evolution of petroleum and soybean-meal prices both in current and in constant 1972 dollars (Table 7.5). It is of interest to note that, from 1972 to 1989, the international market price of petroleum was multiplied by 5.52 in current dollars, but only by a factor of 1.72 in constant 1972 dollars, i.e. less than double. The market price of soybean meal did not follow the same path; in current dollars, it increased only by a factor of 2.34, and in constant 1972 dollars by a factor of 0.31, i.e. decreased by 69%.

The price of reference proteins is the other main factor to be considered when assessing the present and future economic competitiveness of SCPs. Since 1985, the prices of soybeans and soybean meal has remained very low, and even decreased when expressed in constant dollars, although the production of soybeans per hectare in the USA has stayed quite stable since 1972 (between 1.8–2 tonnes per ha, i.e. 0.53–0.66 tonnes crude protein per ha). One should also point out that, from 1969 to 1989, the total area utilized in the US for soybean cultivation increased only from 17.3–23 million ha. During this period, world production increased from 46.7 to 92.2 million tonnes, essentially due to soybean production in Brazil and Argentina; and, since 1984, production has stabilized.

In the first decade of the next century, the price of soybeans and other feed proteins is expected to rise. The main considerations supporting this expectation are: (1) the shortage of appropriate farm land, (2) demographic growth, (3) the rising standard of living in many developing countries, (4) the increase of demand for feed proteins, and (5) the rising competition of palm oil with soybean oil, which presently represents 53% of the commercial value of beans. Based on these considerations, the market price of soybeans in constant dollars is expected to double by the turn of the century (ASA & EPC, 1982). The future prospects for SCP production from both renewable and non-renewable substrates should be considered accordingly.

Conclusions

World protein demand is increasing because of population growth coupled with low agricultural production. Nevertheless, the development of SCP production from petroleum and methanol was delayed for several years by economic problems: the rise in petroleum price and the competition of conventional feed proteins, such as soybean meal.

A variety of feedstocks using renewable and non-renewable resources have been considered for SCP production. They include petroleum derivatives, such as gas oil and n-alkanes; natural gas fractions, such as methanol; and a variety of carbohydrates and lignocelluloses. The petroleum and methanol feedstocks, available on a large scale and in continuous supply, have the potential to satisfy much of the world's need using technologies that have been developed, demonstrated feasible and proved safe. However, these petrochemical feedstocks are in increasing demand for other, competing, uses; if this trend continues, the low-cost lignocelluloses will be the potential feedstock for future SCP production, assuming that the required technological advances for their hydrolysis and bioconversion efficiency are made.

SCP production as a by-product of the fermentation industry would be more competitive, provided that feedstock conversion is not limited to one product but includes several high-value products, such as amino acids, polymers and pharmaceuticals, in addition to SCP; mixed-culture fermentation, genetic engineering advances and novel biotechnological processes will contribute much to the success of this approach. Such advances could lead to an economically viable SCP industry in the future.

References

Aidoo, K.E., Hendry, R. & Wood, B.J.B. (1982). Solid-state fermentations. *Adv. Appl. Microbiol.*, **28**, 201–37.

Anon. (1982). World methanol demand. *Eur. Chem. News*, July 12, p. 16.

Anon. (1984). *Tourteaux et Autres Matieres Riches en Proteines*. Ann. Report (1984), INRA, S.A. Robert & Y. Sido, Paris, France.

Anon. (1989). Methanol prices weaken as supply grows longer. *Eur. Chem. News*, April 24, p. 10.

ASA & EPC (1982). *Project 2000: Planning the Future of Soybeans*. N.P.: American Soybean Assoc. and Elanco Products Co.

Banat, I.M., Al-Awadi, N. & Hamdan, I.Y. (1989). Physiological characteristics of four methylotrophic bacteria and their potential use in single cell protein production. *MIRCEN J.*, **5**, 149–59.

Bellamy, W.D. (1974). SCP from cellulosic wastes. *Biotechnol. Bioeng.*, **16**, 869–90.

Brook, E.J., Stanton, W.R. & Wallbridge, A. (1969). Fermentation methods for protein enrichment of cassava. *Biotechnol. Bioeng.*, **11**, 1271–84.

Bye, P. & Mounier, A. (1984). *Les Futurs Alimentaires et Energetiques des Biotechnologies*. Presses Univ., Grenoble.

Carter, G.G. (1981). Is biotechnology feeding the Russians? *New Scientist*, 23 April, p. 216.

Champagnat, A. & Adrian, J. (1974). *Petrole et Proteines*. Doin, Paris.

Crawford, R.L. (1981). *Lignin Biodegradation and Transformation*. Wiley Interscience, New York.

Davy, C.A.E., Wilson, D. & Lyon, J.C.M. (1981). Commercial production of feed yeast from carbohydrate waste. In *Advances in Biotechnology*, vol. 2, M. Moo-Young & C.W. Robinson (eds), p. 343. Pergamon Press, Toronto.

Durand, A., Arnoux, P., Teilhard de Chardin, O., Chereau, D., Boquien, C.Y. & Larios de Anda, G. (1983). Protein enrichment of sugar beet pulp by solid state fermentation. In *Production and Feeding of Single Cell Protein*, M.P. Ferranti & A. Fiechter (eds), pp. 120–2. Applied Science Publishers, London.

Ellingham, J. (1980). The BP single cell protein summary of experience. In *Proceedings of OAPEC Symposium on Petroproteins*, p. 61, OAPEC, Kuwait.

FAO (1978). *Oilseeds, fats and oils, oilcakes and meals*. Supply demand and trade projection 1985.

FAO (1985). *Mon. Bull. Stat.* **B8**(1), 18.

Faust, V. & Sittig, W. (1980). Methanol as carbon source for biomass production in a loop reactor. *Adv. Biochem. Eng.*, **17**, 63–99.

Ferranti, M.P. & Fiechter, A. (eds) (1983). *Production and Feeding of Single Cell Protein*. Applied Science Publishers, London.

Forage, A.J. & Righelato, R.C. (1979). Biomass from carbohydrates. In *Economic Microbiology*, vol. 4, A.H. Rose (ed.), pp. 289–313. Academic Press, New York.

Fukui, S. & Tanaka, A. (1980). Production of useful compounds from alkane media in Japan. *Adv. Biochem. Eng.*, **17**, 1–35.

Goldberg, I. (1985). *Single Cell Protein*, pp. 189. Springer Verlag, New York.

Hamdan, I.Y. (ed.) (1983). In *Proceedings of the International Symposium on Single Cell Proteins from Hydrocarbons for Animal Feeding*, pp. 234. Federation of Arab Scientific Research Councils, Baghdad, Iraq.

Hamdan, I.Y., Asthana, H.N., Al-Awadhi, N., ElNawawy, A.S., Banat, I. & Salman, A.J. (1986). Production of single cell protein from thermotolerant methanol-utilizing culture for animal feeding. In *Perspectives in Biotechnology and Applied Microbiology*, D.I. Alani & M. Moo-Young (eds), pp. 49–60. Elsevier Applied Science Publishers, London.

Hamer, G. (1979). Biomass from natural gas. In *Economic Microbiology*, vol. 4, A.H. Rose (ed.), p. 315. Academic Press, London.

Hoshiai, K. (1978). The world protein demand in future. *Chem. Econom. Eng. Rev.*, **10**, 1–9.

Hoshiai, K. (1980). Imbalance of essential aminoacids: An approach to the problems of protein shortage in the world. *Chem. Economy Eng. Rev.*, **12**, 12–16.

Hoshiai, K. (1981). Present and future of protein demand for animal feeding. In *International Symposium on SCP*, J.C. Senez (ed.), pp. 34–63. Lavoisier, Paris.

Humphrey, A.E., Arminger, W., Lee, E. & Moreira, A. (1976). Production of single cell protein by growth of thermoactinomyces species on cellulosic materials. In *Fifth International Fermentation Symposium*, H. Dellweg (ed.), p. 431. Westkruez-Druckerei und Verlag, Berlin.

Humphrey, A.E., Moreira, A., Arminger, W. & Zabriskie, D. (1977). Production of single cell protein from cellulose wastes. In *Single Cell Protein from Renewable and Non-Renewable Resources*, A.E. Humphrey & E.L. Gaden (eds), p. 45. Wiley Interscience, New York.

Jonas, D.A. (1983). Legislation regulating the use of SCP for animal feeding in Europe and its relationship to PAG and EEC guidelines. In *Single Cell Proteins from Hydrocarbons for Animal Feeding*, I.Y. Hamdan (ed.), pp. 115–43. Federation of Arab Scientific Research Councils, Baghdad, Iraq.

Litchfield, J.H. (1983). Single cell proteins. *Science, Wash.*, **219**, 740–6.

Mogren, H. (1979). SCP from methanol – the Norprotein process. *Process Biochem.*, March, p. 2.

Moo-Young, M., Chahal, D.S. & Vlach, D. (1978). Single cell protein from various chemically pretreated substrates using *Chaetomium cellulolyticum*. *Biotechnol. Bioeng.*, **20**, 107.

Moo-Young, M., Dangulis, A., Charal, D. & Macdonald, D.G. (1979). The Waterloo process for SCP production from waste biomass. *Process Biochem.* **14**, 38–45.

Nolan, E.J. & Forro, J.R. (1976). Waste cellulose conversion to microbial protein. In *Fifth International Fermentation Symposium*, H. Dellweg (ed.), p. 432. Westkreuz-Druckerei und Verlag, Berlin.

PAG/UNU (1983*a*). Guideline no. 6. Preclinical testing of novel sources of food. *Food Nutr. Bull.* (United Nations University), **5**(1), 60.

PAG/UNU (1983*b*). Guideline no. 12. The Production of single cell protein for human consumption. *Food Nutr. Bull.* (United Nations University), **5**(1), 64.

PAG/UNU (1983*c*). Guideline no. 15. Nutritional and safety aspects of protein sources for animal feeding. *Food Nutr. Bull.* (United Nations University), **5**(1), 67.

Pamment, N., Moo-Young, M., Hsieh, F.H. & Robinson, C.W. (1978). Growth of *Chaetomium cellulolyticum* on alkali pre-treated hard wood sawdust solids and pre-treated liquor. *Appl. Environ. Microbiol.*, **36**, 284.

Pontanel, H.G. de (ed.) (1972). *Proteins from Hydrocarbons.* Academic Press, New York.

Ramos-Valdivia, A., de la Torre, M. & Casas-Campillo, C. (1983). Solid state fermentation of cassava with *Rhizopus oligosporus.* In *Production and Feeding of Single Cell Protein*, M.P. Ferranti & A. Fiechter (ed.), pp. 104–11. Applied Science Publishers, London.

Reid, I.D., Chkao, E.E. & Dawson, P.S.S. (1985). Lignin degradation by *Phanerochaete chrysosporium* in agitated cultures. *Can. J. Microbiol.*, **13**, 222–5.

Revuz, B. (1981). Production industrielle de proteins a partir d'hydrates de carbone. In *Single Cell Protein II*, S.R. Tannenbaum & D.I.C. Wang (eds), pp. 126–39. MIT Press, Cambridge, Mass.

Ringpfeil, M. (1983). Technology of SCP production from fossil raw materials. In *Single Cell Protein from Hydrocarbons for Animal Feeding*, I.Y. Hamdan (ed.), pp. 85–95. Federation of Arab Scientific Research Councils, Baghdad, Iraq.

Rockwell, P.J. (1976). *SCP from Renewable and Non Renewable Resources.* Noyes Date Corp. Park Ridge, New Jersey.

Rose, A.H. (1979*a*). History and scientific basis of large-scale production of microbial biomass. In *Economic Microbiology*, vol. 4, A.H. Rose (ed.), pp. 1–29. Academic Press, London.

Rose, A.H. (1979*b*). Microbial biomass. In *Economic Microbiology*, vol. 4, A.H. Rose (ed.). Academic Press, New York.

Rothman, H., Greenshields, R. & Calle, F.R. (1983). *The Alcohol Economy: Fuel Ethanol and the Brazilian Experience.* Frances Pinter, London.

Sasson, A. (1983). *Les Biotechnologies: Defis et Promesses.* Unesco, Paris.

Scrimshaw, N.S. (1968). In *Single Cell Protein*, R.I. Mateles & S.R. Tannenbaum (eds), pp. 3–7. MIT Press, Cambridge.

Scrimshaw, N.S. (1983). The new PAG/UNU guidelines in SCP applications. In *Single Cell Proteins from Hydrocarbons for Animal Feeding*, I.Y. Hamdan (ed.), pp. 99–106. Federation of Arab Scientific Research Councils, Baghdad, Iraq.

Senez, J.C. (1979). Pour une politique nationale en matiere de proteines alimentaires. *Prog. Scient.* **203**, 5–32.

Senez, J.C. (ed.) (1983). *International Symposium on SCP.* Lavoisier, Paris.

Senez, J.C. (1987). Single cell protein: Past and present development. In

Microbial Technology in the Developing World, E.J. Da Silva, Y.R. Dommergues, E.J. Nyns & C. Ratledge (eds), pp. 238–59. Oxford University Press.

Senez, J.C., Raimbault, M. & Deschamps, F. (1980). Protein enrichment of starchy substrates for animal feeds by solid state fermentation. *Anim. Rev. FAO*, **35**, 36–9.

Senior, P.J. & Windass, J. (1980). The ICI single cell protein process. *Biotechnol. Lett.*, **2**, 205–10.

Shay, L.K., Hunt, H.R. & Wegner, G.H. (1987). High-productivity fermentation process for cultivating industrial microorganisms. *J. Indust. Microbiol.*, **2**, 79–85.

Shennan, J.L. (1984). *Hydrocarbons as Substrates in Industrial Fermentation*, R.M. Atlas (ed.). Macmillan, New York.

Solomons, G.L. (1983). Single cell protein. *CRC Crit. Rev. Biotechnol.*, **1**, 21.

Tannenbaum, S.R. & Wang, D.I.C. (eds) (1975). *Single cell protein. II*. MIT Press, Cambridge, Mass.

Tuse, D. (1983). Single-cell protein: Current status and future prospects. *CRC Crit. Rev. Food Sci. Nutrit.*, **19**, 273–324.

UN (1977). *The Future of World Economy*. Oxford University Press.

Volfova, O. (1984). Microbial biomass. In *Modern Biotechnology*, V. Krumphanzl & Z. Rehacek (eds), pp. 525–54. Unesco, Paris.

Ward, R.F. (1982). Food, chemicals and energy from biomass. In *Biomass Utilization*, W.A. Cote (ed.), pp. 23–49. Plenum Press, New York.

8

The impact of biotechnology on international commodity trade

GERD JUNNE

Introduction

Commodity prices are set to decline overall in the 1990s. Biotechnology 'is quite certainly called upon to act as a further factor reducing the overall demand for primary products from developing countries' (OECD, 1989). The introduction of new technologies has always led to shifts in the international division of labour. New products replace old ones. New production processes make the production of specific goods cheaper in one region than in another often leading to shifts in world supply. Although it may not be as revolutionary as other new technologies (Buttel, 1989), biotechnology is no exception. It is expected to have a considerable impact on world trade.

Replacement of commodities as a result of the introduction of new technologies is not a new phenomenon. It has occurred again and again in history. Cases in point are the replacement of *indigo* and other pigments by colours produced petrochemically, the replacement of natural fibres (especially *sisal*) by synthetic fibres and the competition between natural *rubber* and synthetic rubber. Nevertheless the present situation may differ significantly from historical experience in that (1) switches to a new raw material base may actually take place much quicker than in the past, (2) a large number of commodities will undergo major changes in supply and demand simultaneously, and (3) alternative sources for foreign exchange earnings may be more limited now than in the past (Junne, 1987a; Junne, Komen & Tomeï, 1989). The present contribution discusses different types of substitution processes and their impact on trade.

Different substitution processes

Biotechnology will affect international trade with varying impact in different areas of application. Though most biotechnology research takes place in the health sector, the impact on trade flows will be much larger in the field of agriculture, since: (1) the pharmaceutical industry sends 'a surprisingly small proportion' of its output across national frontiers;[1] (2) shifts in agricultural trade would have more important implications for world trade, since trade in agricultural products has a value of more than ten times the value of trade in pharmaceuticals (GATT, 1988*a*); and, (3) a decline of agricultural exports could have serious consequences for those developing countries relying almost exclusively on such exports as a source of foreign exchange.

The present discussion therefore deals mainly with trade in agricultural commodities, since it is in this field that the trade impact of biotechnology will be felt most. 'These trade impacts are nearly all of a trade substituting character' (OECD, 1989) with distinctions between shifts in the structure of trade resulting from (1) the *creation of entirely new substitutes* for previous products; (2) the introduction of *new production processes*; and (3) the reduction of material inputs to production (*dematerialization*). Items (1) and (3) are expected to result from the application of biotechnology. Furthermore, shifts resulting from the introduction of *new production processes*, of less significance in the OECD study, should not be underestimated.

Four major types of substitution processes will be described below, with reference where possible to the cases of sweeteners, vegetable oils and cocoa. The first three processes concern mainly North–South trade relations, whereas the fourth type deals with instances in which exports from one developing country are replaced by exports from another developing country. In brief, the four processes concern:

(1)   shifts in trade resulting from the *introduction of additional characteristics into existing plants*;
(2)   shifts resulting from *changes in food processing*;
(3)   shifts due to the *industrial production of plant components or substitutes*; and,
(4)   shifts due to the *unequal distribution of new production processes*.

---

[1] 'In 1980, world sales were about $85 billion in value, of which only $8 million – less than 10 per cent – entered international trade in the form of finished drugs, and a further $6 billion in the form of intermediates. Local production by affiliates of multinational enterprises was over twice the size of direct imports in the year. Despite the *potential trade creating effects* of new biotechnology, it is likely that *the growth of output of biotechnology* products and their commercialisation will, within the OECD area, probably *precede* by many years *any significant impact on trade flows*.' (OECD, 1989, emphasis in the original.)

Shifts as a result of new plant characteristics

Though genetical engineering of plants has proved much more difficult than that of microorganisms, biotechnology has already had a considerable impact on plant breeding by applying 'modern' rather than 'new' biotechnology,[2] especially tissue and plant cell culture. This has helped to speed up traditional plant breeding and to reduce the lead time to develop new plant varieties considerably.

The ease with which new characteristics can be added to plants (or existing ones deleted) contributes to a 'separation of the plant from its original environment'.[3] Factors such as high resistance to different stress factors such as low or high temperature, day length, soil salinity, dry or wet climate etc., influence the selection of plant varieties. They have made it possible to shift the geoclimatic limits concerning the growth of specific crops. As a result, some plants, exclusively produced in a subtropical or moderate climate, are now reared more and more in the North. An important example is the production of maize, which for decades has been reared in more temperate zones of North America and Europe. This shift to the North can probably be speeded up with the help of biotechnology. Another example is the development of forage grass to grow actively even in cold weather. This development would thus make it possible to shift some cattle production from South America and other southern countries to North America and Northern Europe (*New Scientist*, 28 July 1988).

This separation of the plant from its original environment is of significance to vegetables and fruits and could undermine the recent initiatives of some developing countries exporting vegetable products to the world market.

The same effect could be achieved if the resistance of plants against a colder climate results not from manipulating the plant itself but its environment. Such an example is to be found in the application of 'ice minus' bacteria to protect crops against mild frost. If this turned out to be economically feasible and politically acceptable, important substitution processes could be the result. For example, if orange plantations in Florida could be protected against freeze damage, then vitally

[2] 'New' biotechnology refers to 'third generation' biotechnology which results from breakthroughs in genetical engineering in the early 1970s. 'Modern' biotechnology embraces 'second generation biotechnology', i.e. the advances in enzyme, tissue culture, and large-scale fermentation technology since the beginning of this century.

[3] I owe the concepts of the three delineations resulting from the applications of biotechnology (i.e. 'separation of the plant from its original environment', 'separation of the plant from its intrinsic characteristics', and 'separation of food production from agriculture' to G. Ruivenkamp.

important orange juice exports to the US might be replaced by domestic production.

Trade shifts as the result of changes in food processing
Important early shifts in international commodity trade will not result so much from advances in the genetical manipulation of higher organisms such as plants, but from the application of new and modern biotechnology to microorganisms, a field in which much more experience has been gained. Microorganisms have been applied to food processing for centuries. Advances in food processing, especially fractioning plant products into different components and 'reassembling' these components into final food products have led to *separation of plants from their specific characteristics*. Many crops have become interchangeable. This has tremendously increased direct competition between producers of crops used hitherto to cater to different markets (Ruivenkamp, 1989). The most outstanding example is that of the increasing competition between sugar and starch producers.

One of the results of cultivating maize in more and more moderate zones has been an increasing overproduction of corn in North America which has stimulated producers' interest in alternative uses of their produce. As a result, research intensified in the 1970s on the enzymatic transformation use of starch into High Fructose Corn Syrup (HFCS). The tremendous expansion of HFCS production between 1975 and 1985 and the resulting decline of sugar imports by the United States is the largest trade impact that biotechnology has had hitherto (see Changing trade patterns).

HFCS is not an entirely new product. Since the early nineteenth century it had been known that starch could be transformed into a sweetener. By 1850, this process using potato starch was in commercial use in the United States. 'Corn sugar' or dextrose was first produced in Buffalo (New York) in 1866. Since 1920, dextrose and corn syrup have accounted for about 10% of the North American sweetener market (ICCSASW, 1987). However, advances in the application of immobilized enzyme technology reduced production costs to such an extent that a switch from sugar to HFCS became a profitable option – at the high domestic price levels for sugar in the United States and Japan (see Changing trade patterns).

Beside the price advantage (depending on the domestic price for sucrose), HFCS has a number of other advantages and some disadvantages. Since its production is based on corn, and derived from only 10% of the corn harvested in the US, (ICCSASW, 1987) its price tends to be more stable than that of sugar. Since corn can easily be stored, production can continue the whole year round instead of being limited to a period of three to five months as is the case with cane or beet sugar. HFCS in liquid form is especially suited for industrial applications. It requires less labour for handling than sugar, which is normally sold in bags.[4] It also permits a better conservation of food compared with sugar (OECD, 1989). On the other hand, it is only stable between 27 and 39 °C and cannot be stored indefinitely or transported over long distances and therefore is normally not exported (except from Canada to the US) (ICCSASW, 1987).

The commercial potential of HFCS increased when the immobilization of enzymes in 1972 made production less costly. In 1978, another technical breakthrough enlarged HFCS's field of application. A process was found to produce 90% fructose syrup. Until then, the upper limit had been 42%, since at that point the enzyme stops transforming the dextrose. A blend of 90% and 42% syrup, containing 55% fructose, was found to be well suited for the soft drink industry. As a result, most large American soft drink producers, especially *Coca-Cola* and *Pepsi*, shifted to sweetening their drinks with HFCS. The two large cola producers alone used to consume over 1.7 million metric tonnes of sugar annually in the United States only (ICCSASW, 1987).

Total replacement of sugar in the United States by HFCS has reached around 6 million short tonnes of sugar, with one half of that amount being produced domestically and the other half being imported. US sugar imports dropped from 5.3 million short tonnes in 1970 to about 2.2 million in 1987. This substitution process has levelled off, because penetration of those areas where technical and economic conditions allow it, has reached almost 100%. Large-scale introduction in countries outside the United States and Japan is not to be expected (see Changing trade patterns).[5]

While its liquid form has been one of the advantages of HFCS for industrial users, this very advantage, on the other side, has prevented the penetration of the consumer market for household use. Only a very small percentage of HFCS reaches the market in a crystallized form,

---

[4] Liquid sugar in 1983 accounted for about 96 per cent of total industrial sugar use in the US, or about two thirds of total sugar use (OECD, 1989).

[5] HFCS is also produced in some East European and developing countries (Argentina, Bulgaria, Egypt, Hungary, Indonesia, Pakistan, Romania, Uruguay, Yugoslavia) which does not affect the world sugar markets (ICCSASW, 1987). Recently, plans have been made in China to use HFCS as a major sweetener. Sugar consumption has been rising by about 500 000 tonnes a year, due to improved standards of living (*International Sugar Journal*, vol. 90 (1988), no. 1087, p. 193; Rosario, 1989). China still is the second largest importer of sugar, only behind the USSR. On account of rising demand, a fast expansion of HFCS production would not significantly reduce China's present import needs.

because the energy costs of drying it made it uncompetitive in comparison to refined sugar. However, several less expensive procedures have recently been developed which may imply another round of substitution. If crystallized HFCS reaches a large market share, this would imply the end of US sugar imports (ICCSASW, 1987).

Enzymatic conversions also have an important impact on other commodity markets. Enzymatic conversions of plant oils, for example, to produce structured lipids or tailored fats could in the future eventually ease the coconut oil and other seed oils out of the market.[6] The cheapest vegetable oils (probably soya and palm oil) could then replace most other seed oils that hitherto could defend their own market niches due to specific intrinsic properties which correspond to specific consumer demands.[7]

An important example for such substitution processes is the development of improved cocoa butter substitutes (Svarstad, 1988). While such substitutes have been on the market since the beginning of the century, most of them either did not sufficiently meet the specific desired properties or were too costly for commercial production. With the help of biotechnology, researchers hope to modify enzymes in such a way that they become fit for the production of cocoa butter substitutes.[8] Such a development would have an obvious impact on international cocoa trade, if the substitutes were commercially viable and not banned by legislation.

---

[6] Cf. Ruivenkamp, 1989, and Halos, 1989: 'Structured lipids or tailored fats would allow the industry to produce oil formulations that simulate the desirable properties without the concomitant unwanted properties of various seed oils and natural fats. These simulated products could, therefore, be highly competitive with coconut and could displace it from its share of the seed oils market' (p. 4).

[7] The peanut trade arose from the French consumers' resistance to yellow soap from palm-oil. Marseilles soapmakers discovered that peanut oil plus olive oil made a blue marble soap. French resistance to palm-oil products ended in 1852 with the discovery of a chemical method to whiten yellow soap (Wallerstein, 1989). Biotechnological conversion methods contribute in a similar way to adding wanted or removing unwanted characteristics of specific seed oils. This innovation leads to their replacement by cheaper oils.

[8] While protease enzymes usually break down fats, Genencor has altered one of the amino acids in an enzyme to function as a fat producer. One of the research targets has been enzymes that make cocoa butter substitutes. The Japanese company Kao Corp. has two patent applications with the European Patent Office that involve genetic engineered enzymes for making cocoa butter substitutes (Svarstad, 1988).

Shifts due to the industrial production of plant components or substitutes

Biotechnology has not only increased the substitution of one agricultural product for another, but also increased direct competition between agricultural and industrial products. Again, sweeteners provide a good example. Cane and beet sugar not only lost ground to HFCS, but also to industrially produced low-calorie sweeteners. Chemical sweeteners such as saccharin and cyclamates have been highly debated for decades, and are only suitable for specific applications. Biotechnology has made it possible to produce different new low-calorie sweeteners. A very important role has been achieved by *aspartame*, made from two amino acids coupled by natural enzymes, now used in many low-calorie soft drinks. Its sweetening power is about 150 to 250 times as potent as sugar, depending on the formulation. As a result, relatively small plants can produce an enormous sweetening power, compared with a similar volume of sugar. Though the market share of low-calorie sweeteners in industrialized countries has quickly increased, global aspartame demand, for instance, has been met for more than a decade by a few factories of one company.[9] This is an obvious example of the ongoing process of 'dematerialization of production' which implies that the same 'use value' can be created with an ever smaller amount of material input. This trend works very much to the disadvantage of raw material exporting countries.

A number of low-volume, high-value compounds which are traded internationally, and which could not (or only with exorbitant costs) be produced by chemical synthesis, can now be obtained through either microbial fermentation or cell suspension culture. This is the expression of a third separation tendency, the trend towards the separation of the production of plant components from the land (Ruivenkamp, 1989) and an increasing *industrial* production of such components. Industrial production has a number of advantages: (1) it is less tied to specific seasons but can continue all year long; (2) it can assure better quality than production influenced by the vagaries of nature; (3) it normally takes less time on account of the optimization of growth conditions; (4) it is less labour intensive, because steps like planting, nursing the young plants, harvesting etc. can be avoided; and (5) it allows for more easy production than natural processes as is the case of perennial crops, the production of which cannot easily be adapted to market conditions.

---

[9] *Nutrasweet Company*, owned by Monsanto, since 1988 has to face competition from *Holland Sweetener Company*, a joint venture of the Dutch company DSM and the Japanese firm Toyo-Soda which developed their own process to produce aspartame under the brand name 'Senecta' (ICCSASW, 1987).

The most suitable candidates for industrial production are such high-value, low-volume substances as compounds of pharmaceutical value, fragrances, flavours, pigments and insecticides (UNIDO, 1988). A good example is the plan to produce the peptide sweetener thaumatin with *E. coli* which could lead to a *substitute for the substitute* thalin, the thaumatin-based sweetener marketed by Tate & Lyle. The intensely sweet protein comes from plants grown in the Ivory Coast and Ghana. The ripe fruit is frozen and shipped to Europe where the protein is extracted and purified. This very expensive process could be replaced by producing the protein in a microbial fermentation process (RAFI, 1987*b*). There are projects under way to produce vanilla flavours via plant tissue culture (RAFI, 1987*a*). An example for the production of plant components of pharmaceutical value is the production of *Echinacea purpurea* cultures in large fermentation processes. More far-reaching plans to grow tobacco cells with special aromas proved to be unfeasible. Specialists estimate that it will take 20–30 years before money is earned with large-scale plant cell culture.[10] While it may be feasible to produce, for example, cocoa butter from cell culture, the price would probably be far too high (Svarstad, 1988).

Shifts as a result of the unequal distribution of new production processes

In the case of the industrial production of plant compounds or breakthroughs in food processing technology, it is relatively easy to identify substitution processes and the contribution that developments in biotechnology do make to these processes. However, in so far as agricultural technology is generally concerned, it is more difficult to delineate the consequences of the applications of biotechnology which form part and parcel of the general development of agricultural technology. Consequently, it becomes more difficult to identify which changes are due to advances in biotechnology and which are the result of other technological (or organizational) developments.

Biotechnology can in many ways be used to make agriculture more productive, be it by breeding new plant varieties with added characteristics as described above, or by delivering large numbers of identical seedlings which facilitate harvesting, or by reducing the amount of necessary inputs (e.g. the use of soil bacteria increasing nitrogen fixation), or by replacing chemical pesticides by bioinsecticides. The

---

[10] When the French chemical company Rhône-Poulenc bought the German phytopharmaceutical company Nattermann with one of the largest plant cell culture laboratories of the world, the laboratory was dissolved because of these cautious expectations (*HighTech* 7/1989, 38–9).

diffusion of these new technologies (as with all other new technologies), however, does not take place at the same speed in all countries. Countries that are able to introduce the new technologies at a faster pace will consequently be able to increase their own market share, and in turn will displace other countries as exporters. Such shifts are actually taking place in the field of palm oil and cocoa.

The diffusion of biotechnological advances, however, does not only differ from country to country, but also from crop to crop. Whereas some crops (especially from industrialized countries) have received much attention in international biotechnology research, others have received much less. Where different cash crops compete with each other, breakthroughs with the help of biotechnology to increase production for one crop may be at the expense of another. Since the production of different crops is distributed unevenly over different countries, even the equal geographical dissemination of new technologies would have uneven effects on the trading position of different countries in that it would influence sudden changes in the price indices between competing commodities (e.g. different seed oils) and in this way encourage the replacement of one commodity by another.

Changing trade patterns

What are, then, the concrete changes in international trade flows that the described substitution processes give rise to? Before looking at changes in the trade of specific countries, some general observations are necessary:

(1) Biotechnology increases productivity in agriculture. Where productivity rises faster than demand, self-sufficiency is enhanced or, where already attained, surplusses are generated. Countries that have, hitherto, been importers of agricultural products, can become more self-reliant with the help of biotechnology. This implies that increasing surplusses are chasing after fewer markets. As a result, prices decline. When exporting becomes less attractive, countries look to alternative uses of their agricultural produce and may use it as a substitute for products hitherto imported.[11] In this way, a chain reaction may be triggered off which can affect a number of commodities from different countries.

---

[11] An obvious example is provided by European agricultural policy. With a decline in world market prices for agricultural goods, export subsidies become very high. As a consequence, the EC stimulates biotechnology research (e.g. on protein-rich rapeseed varieties) which would help to make less costly use of soil. If successful such research will create a substitute for products hitherto imported and thus start a new round of substitution processes.

(2) If world demand for a specific commodity declines as a result of substitution, different exporting countries will not all be hit in the same way. Production cuts will probably be distributed very *unequally*. To identify the consequences of substitution for international trade flows, more has to be done than just to identify the main exporters of the commodity in question. Where a free market prevails, marginal producers drop out first.[12] Trade in many commodities, however, is governed by long-term contracts. Most Cuban sugar exports, for example, are sold to the Soviet Union and other (formerly) socialist countries at prices agreed in advance (Perez-Lopez, 1988). Cuba, therefore, is hardly hit by the substitution of HFCS for cane sugar. Other factors that will protect specific exporters (at the expense of others) from the direct consequences of declining demand are

> the degree to which vertically integrated transnational corporations continue to import from their own affiliates even if competing exporters offer a lower price;
> specific political or economic ties between countries which result in a preferential treatment by importing countries;[13]
> willingness and the capacity of specific exporting countries to *subsidize* their exports.

Additionally, an export decline which otherwise might be expected with good reasons of course does not take place when competing exporting countries are hit by either climatic or political disasters which limit their harvests, transport capacity or otherwise have a negative impact on exports.

(3) If we want to get an idea of the trade impact of biotechnology, it is worthwhile to have a look at those trends that influenced development *before* biotechnology had made itself felt. These trends are determined by the dominant forces and interests in international trade. These very same forces will have considerable impact on applications of biotechnology. As a consequence, biotechnology will probably contribute to developments that go into the same direction. The shift in world exports of food products is a case in point. While in the early 1960s, the share of

---

[12] The marginal producers are not always those with the highest production costs. A producer with lower costs may be more 'marginal' if alternative income opportunities make him leave the market at a price level at which other producers that lack comparable alternatives will still continue to sell.

[13] An example is the legislation introduced into the US Congress to strengthen the US Caribbean Basin Initiative (CBI). One of the provisions would freeze US sugar import quotas for CBI countries, thus shielding Central America and the Caribbean from future cuts in the US global sugar import quota (GATT, 1989a).

industrial and developing countries in the world export of food products
was about the same (44.5% vs. 46.2%), industrial countries in the early
1980s accounted for almost twice the share of developing countries
(67.7% vs. 34.2%; Kelly *et al.*, 1988). Biotechnology has not yet
influenced this development, but may contribute to it more intensively in
the future. It is analytically very difficult to separate shifts 'caused' by
biotechnology from other ongoing changes in international trade flows.
Biotechnology may often be used just as an instrument to bring about
specific changes, but may not be a 'cause' in its own right.

(4) Applications of biotechnology to agriculture intermingle with
agricultural policy in general which, in most industrialized countries,
has encouraged surplus production. Subsidized exports have led to trade
disputes which in turn have caused additional farm support and
restrictions on market access through border measures. With traditional
agricultural policies increasingly under domestic and international
pressure, governments in industrialized countries expect some relief
from the development of new technologies. An important motive of
support for biotechnology research on applications in agriculture is to
protect national agriculture from foreign competition in case of a
reduction of subsidies and tariffs.[14]

(5) It is difficult to be precise about the degree, timing, and pace of the
expected substitution processes and about the extent of compensating
alternative demand (e.g. from increasing South–South trade) for the
commodities in question. The reason for this lies not only in the fact that
it is difficult to forecast the pace of techno-economic development (e.g.
the price of energy). An additional element of discontinuity is introduced by political decisions, on which the development and application
of biotechnology depend to a large extent. These are not only regulatory
decisions on the environment. Important decisions are also taken in the
sphere of funding specific directions of biotechnology research and in
creating a general economic environment that is supportive for the
application of the results. These decisions can put the 'normal' sequence
on its head with first specific (bio)technological developments taking
place, which then have some implications for international trade.
Instead, it often works the other way round. Governments restrict
international trade in order to create an incentive for domestic suppliers
to spend money on research for the development of substitutes. An
example is the artificially high price for oils seeds in the EC, which the
European Commission introduced to encourage the development of

---

[14] The decline of trade policy as an instrument to protect national producers has
also been a strong motive for a more active technology policy in other sectors
(June 1984).

protein-rich oil seeds in the Community.[15] Trade flows are not only affected by substitution processes that result from *past* technological developments, but also by political decisions that *anticipate future* technological possibilities and influence development into a desired direction. This affects the time scale of eventual biotechnology related impacts on international trade. While it would take considerable time for the technological development as such to cause significant changes in trade patterns, political anticipation of possible changes and actions based on these anticipations affect international trade right now.

Political rather than technical determination of substitution processes

It is the interaction between technical developments, economic consider-ations, and political pressure that gives shape to real changes in trade flows. This is well demonstrated by the largest trade displacement that biotechnology has hitherto 'caused': the substitution of domestic HFCS production in the United States for imports of cane sugar. In fact, 'it is difficult to identify any significant periods in the last 250 years during which sugar production and trade were not substantially directed by government policies' (Maskus, 1989).

The substitution of sugar by HFCS has, by and large, been a United States (and to some extent Japanese) phenomenon exclusively. It is estimated that HFCS consumption in 1986 in the US was around 5.5 million short tonnes, and about a million tonnes more in the rest of the world, principally Japan. There are some good economic reasons why HFCS production is concentrated in the US: the US is by far the world's largest producer of corn.[16] This special advantage, however, is insuffi-cient to explain why the substitution of HFCS for sugar has only taken place in the US and not in Canada, where almost identical conditions prevail.[17] Canadian HFCS production has grown only modestly since the late seventies. The reason is that Canada is one of the very few industrialized countries which allows its refineries to buy sugar on the free international market where prices are normally below the world

---

[15] GATT has recently ruled that the EC has to make its subsidies for soyabeans and other oilseeds conform to GATT rules; *Financial Times*, 24 January 1990.

[16] Corn is a surplus commodity and therefore comparatively cheap in the US. The size of the plant is second only to the cost of the corn in determining overall production costs. As costs tend to go down as plant size increases, the resulting economies of scale make HFCS production especially profitable in the US (ICCSASW, 1987).

[17] Average HFCS production costs amount to 67% of average world sugar production costs in the United States against 71% in Canada. The comparable figures for western Germany and the United Kingdom are 135% and 145% (ICCSASW, 1987).

average cost of production. There is therefore no reason for domestic industrial sweetener users to switch from sugar, and virtually all Canadian HFCS production is *exported to the United States* (ICCSASW, 1987).

Prices for raw sugar in the US have remained well above world market level since 1981 (Maskus, 1989). The American quota system had been abolished in the early 1970s when high world market prices for sugar guaranteed sufficient income for American producers. After seven years following more or less world market prices, the US government enacted a new support scheme in 1981, when world market prices plummeted. Since then, the average price differential between world and domestic sugar prices have been 353%, reaching a maximum of 776% in June 1985 (Maskus, 1989).

The rapid decline of world market prices in May 1982 led to the introduction of an 'emergency' system of import quotas, and sugar imports fell from 4.54 million tonnes in 1981 to 2.63 million tonnes in 1982. Whereas the price for raw sugar was intentionally set to provide a remunerative return to domestic farmers, 'the quota programme has established a powerful lobby in favour of its retention among domestic corn growers and millers, who supply 97 per cent of the American market for corn sweeteners' (Maskus, 1989). It was only with the support of the quota system that HFCS production has been profitable in the current period of low world market prices for sugar.

The import quotas were subsequently cut down at a quick pace, from 2.6 million tonnes in 1982/83 to 0.9 million tonnes in 1986/87.[18] Although the US claims that sugar quotas are allocated in a non-discriminatory way consistent with Article XIII of the General Agreement on Tariffs and Trade (GATT), there have been many exceptions to this rule where quotas have obviously been allocated for political reasons. An example is the reallocation of quotas after the establishment of the Aquino Government in the Philippines. The US Congress transferred South Africa's sugar quota to the Philippines as part of its sanctions in October 1986 (Maskus, 1989). Recent US sanctions against Panama are another example.

The reduction of quotas and of their net dollar value is given in Table 8.1. Three countries account for almost half the total of all quotas (Dominican Republic, Brazil and the Philippines). The rest is distributed over 38 other countries.

---

[18] Quotas have recently been increased again and almost doubled in 1989 (*Latin American Commodities Report*, 15 October 1989).

Table 8.1. *Basic quota allocation, initial quantities and net dollar values, quota years 1982/83 and 1986/87*

| | Quantity (thousand tonnes) | | Net dollar value ($ million) | |
	1982/83	1986/87	1982/83	1986/87
Total	2621.8	908.6	1104.4	389.3
Brazil	368.2	119.7	133.2	50.2
Dominican Rep.	447.0	145.3	161.6	62.8
Philippines	342.8	130.4	124.0	56.4

Source: Maskus, 1989.

The quota system has come under increasing pressure at the national as well as the international level (and so has, as a consequence, the price advantage of HFCS over imported sugar). At the national level all those interests that would profit from a general liberalization of international agricultural trade, one of the major proclaimed objectives of the US Government during the 'Uruguay Round' of Multilateral Trade Negotiations, points to the high degree of protection enjoyed by the producers of sweeteners as a major obstacle which undermines the credibility of the American negotiation position. Internationally, the quota system has been challenged as being incompatible with GATT rules. At the request of Australia, a GATT panel was established in September 1988 which recommended to demand that the US either terminates these restrictions or brings them into conformity with the General Agreement. The US agreed to the adoption of the report[19] even though it may have significant implications for the US sugar industry (GATT, 1988b; 1989b).

The present protection of US sugar interest may be reduced when the actual provisions have to be revised which were extended through to the 1991/92 crop year by the Food and Security Act of 1985. The flexibility to shift back to increased imports of cane sugar, however, is limited, since closures have reduced annual cane-refining capacity in the US by an estimated 2.5 million short tonnes in the past few years (*Financial Times*, 27 September 1988).

The only other major sugar importing country where HFCS has made important inroads is Japan. Japanese HFCS production grew from 84 000 tonnes in 1977/78 to an estimated 650 000 tonnes in 1987/88

---

[19] The fact that the US Government agreed to the adoption of the report implies that the protection of domestic sugar interests will come under scrutiny.

(*International Sugar Journal*, 1989, p. 213). Japan imports both sugar and corn. Crott (1986) assumes that 'the inroads of HFCS might have been favoured by a difference of the taxation of sugar and isoglucose in import duties and subcharges'. The import of corn to produce HFCS instead of importing sugar has the political advantage of reducing the large balance of payments surplus that Japan has with the US which continuously leads to political conflict. There is no comparable political pressure to reduce Japan's trade surplus with sugar exporting developing countries.

The substitution of HFCS for imported sugar, however, expanded only until 1982 when a surcharge was placed on HFCS. The proceeds were used to help finance the domestic sugar support programme which resulted in a doubling of domestic beet and cane sugar output to 950 000 tonnes. The surcharge has made sugar more competitive with HFCS. Since the surcharge was imposed, there has been a recovery of sugar consumption and an end to the rapid growth of HFCS use.[20]

HFCS contributed about two thirds to the substitution of sugar imports of about 700 000 tonnes between 1978 and 1984.[21]

Since sugar imports from some countries (e.g. Australia) were tied by long-term contracts, decreases of imports concentrated on Cuba, Thailand and the Philippines, while imports from other countries remained more or less steady. This is another example of the unequal geographical distribution of import cuts which result from substitution.

While political decisions were decisive for the substitution of HFCS for sugar in the US and Japan (and the later slowdown of substitution in Japan), policy measures *prevented* any large-scale substitution in the European Community (EC). Though the EC in contrast to the US is a net exporter of sugar and a net importer of maize, prospects for isoglucose production seemed attractive in the 1970s because of the high sugar price in the EC. With prices of about 40% above the US level, isoglucose production would have been profitable in spite of the considerably higher costs of imported maize as the major starch source. To protect beet farmers against additional competition and to limit the costs of subsidized surplus sugar exports, isoglucose was brought under

---

[20] *International Sugar Journal*, vol. 91 (1989), no. 1091, p. 213. Corn wet millers in Japan are required to produce 1 tonne of starch from domestic potatoes for every 7.6 tonnes of starch produced from imported corn. Imports of corn for wet milling used above the blending ratio are subject to a prohibitive duty. By 1992, however, the ratio will be raised to 9:1 and the tariff reduced from 15.000 to 12.000 yen per tonne.

[21] The decline has not continued much further since then. Between 1979/80 and 1988/89, sugar imports dropped from 2.6 to 1.8 million tonnes; *International Sugar Journal*, vol. 91 (1989), no. 1091, p. 213.

the sugar quota system after several years of litigation, and a production ceiling of 200 000 tonnes for isoglucose was introduced (Crott, 1986).[22]

Beside the replacement of sugar imports, the OECD mentions Single Cell Proteins (SCP) 'from industrial substrates and potential competition with agricultural protein animal feed' as a second example of present or currently predictable trade impacts in agriculture (OECD, 1989). Again, political and economic factors are of primordial importance, since the introduction of new Single Cell products is actually 'limited more by economic, market and regulatory considerations than by technological constraints' (Litchfield, 1989). Hardly any substitution has taken place up to now (except in the Soviet Union) in spite of the fact that it would have been technologically feasible.[23]

Normally the oil price rise after 1973 is linked to the commercial failure of SCP production. In addition to problems with the economical foundation of the different production processes, political power may also have played a role (Byé, Mounier & Magnaval, in press). The crucial position of a number of American companies in the world 'protein chain' (Rousseau, 1986) may have reduced the chances of alternative supplies. SCP first of all had to compete with soya protein, for which exports by the United States accounted for almost two-thirds of the world exports during the period that was crucial for the large-scale introduction of SCP on the world market. It is interesting that American companies hardly played a role in the development of SCP, whereas European multinationals (like BP, Hoechst and ICI) took the lead.

Expected impact on the trade of individual countries
On the basis of the observations made above, some estimates can be presented with regard to the impact of biotechnology on the trade of individual countries.

---

[22] Another example for the political prevention of substitution processes possible as a result of biotechnology is the restriction of use of cocoa butter substitutes in chocolate products. In the EC, only Great Britain, Ireland and Denmark, allow a small percentage of oils and fats to be used in chocolate products (Svarstad, 1988).

[23] It is a question whether larger SCP sales would have led to a real *decline* of soybeans exports. Agriculture alone may not cover the demand for feed protein in the coming decades, since (a) there is a shortage of suitable farmland in Northern and Southern America (partly because of programmes for the production of fructose from corn in the USA and of ethanol from sugar cane in Brazil); (b) efforts to produce soybeans at a competitive price in Europe, Africa, and Asia have had little success; and (c) the average yield of soybeans per hectare in the USA has stopped increasing since 1969. According to 1978 FAO estimates almost half the future worldwide need of crude feed protein will not be met by agricultural production (Senez, 1987). A considerable expansion of SCP production, therefore, would not necessarily interfere with the export volumes of the three major export countries though it probably would affect their export earnings.

It should be kept in mind that the US and the EC are the world's largest exporters of agricultural products, whereas the EC and Japan are at the same time the world's largest food importing countries. It is therefore obvious that applications of biotechnology in agriculture that can make importing countries more self-sufficient and may lead to different productivity increases in different countries can have a far-reaching effect on agricultural trade among the highly industrialized countries (Junne, 1985; 1986a,b). However, since 'there is strong evidence that developing countries, notably those heavily engaged in agriculture, will bear the brunt of trade impacts for a long time to come' (OECD, 1989), the following remarks focus on developing countries.

In a crop-wise analysis, Panchamukhi & Kumar (1988) have presented a crude estimate of the likely annual loss of export earnings as a result of advances in biotechnology, which could amount to about US $10 billion by 1995 compared to export incomes in 1980. The percentages of exports that underly the estimate may be far too high. But given the fact that already a much smaller decline of effective demand can have a far-reaching impact on the price of the commodities in question, the estimated decline of export income may, nevertheless, not be too unrealistic.

Impact on trade of Latin American countries Trade in the three most important agricultural export commodities of Latin American countries probably will not be seriously affected by biotechnology in the foreseeable future: these are coffee,[24] bananas,[25] and soya.[26] But biotechnology will have some negative and some positive impact on several other export commodities.

An obvious negative impact will be the substitution of sugar imports

---

[24] Applications of biotechnology to coffee in the next few decades will probably facilitate a fundamental shift from smallholder production to large-scale coffee estates/plantations. The greatest losses will be suffered by African peasant farmers rather than by the Latin American coffee producing nations (RAFI, 1989).

[25] There may be some shifts in banana exports to Asia. Banana has recently landed in the top ten commodity exports of the Philippines (Ofreno, 1987). There is also a kind of 'banana war' among Caribbean producers (*Financial Times*, 8 February 1990). Both shifts are an indirect consequence of biotechnology. With sugar exports declining as a result of US import substitution, the former exporters have to switch to other crops. Banana is a promising alternative for the two most affected countries: the Philippines and the Dominican Republic. Increases of production for export in these countries has a negative impact on the export potential of traditional Latin American producers.

[26] Soya exports will not be exposed to much competition from SCP production, but may be affected by improvement of other oil seeds with the help of biotechnology, especially in Europe.

which will be especially problematic for the *Caribbean* sugar exporters, but much less for *Brazil* which actually has some difficulties in producing enough sugar for its ethanol programme and meeting its export obligations at the same time. Especially hard hit is the *Dominican Republic*, for which income from sugar exports sometimes reached up to 50% of total foreign trade earnings. Sugar exports to the US declined by more than 75% in only six years, from 780 000 short tonnes in 1981 to 161 000 short tonnes in 1987 (ICCSASW, 1987).

Exports negatively affected probably include *Argentina's* meat export which declined already by about half during the 1980s (IMF, 1988). Biotechnology will help to increase overproduction in industrialized countries of products that can be used as animal feed. Overproduction in agriculture in general will lead to a more extensive use of soil in large areas, which will probably increase livestock production. It will lead to a better growth of fodder grasses in colder climates. Besides, applications of biotechnology to livestock (re)production will reduce the feed/output relation and thus make cattle raising less expensive in highly industrial countries. *Brazil's* orange juice exports might eventually suffer, too, if the danger of frost damage to orange yards in the US can be reduced with the help of biotechnology.

In general, however, *Brazil* will probably be one of those countries which will increase their export earnings with the help of biotechnology. It belongs to the small group of developing countries which will be able to employ new technologies faster than other developing countries and thus attract a larger share of total agricultural exports. Cases in point are the fast increase of cocoa and palm oil production in Brazil. Production can take place at a large scale which makes it feasible to invest in (the acquisition of) new technologies.

Another area where exports from some Latin American countries could profit from biotechnology is the application of mineral leaching to copper production which may be especially suitable for *Chile* and *Peru* (Warhurst, 1984; 1987).

Impact on trade of Asian countries For the densely populated and population-rich countries of Asia, biotechnology may help to increase food self-sufficiency. This will be at the expense of the large food exporters, especially rice exporters like *Thailand, Burma,* and *Pakistan.* The increase of vegetable oil production in *India*[27] will probably lead to

---

[27] A first batch of oil palm plants developed through tissue culture by the Bhabha Atomic Research Centre in India were delivered in late 1989 to begin an ambitious programme to cut edible oil imports costing the country large amounts of foreign exchange every year (*Financial Express,* 1989b).

declining palm oil imports from *Malaysia*.[28] Besides, advances in tissue culture are expected to help India to recapture the country's position as the largest producer and exporter of cardamom, a position it lost to Guatemala due to non-competitive prices, higher costs of production, low productivity and a strong domestic demand.[29]

The *Philippines* will have to endure the strongest impact on its exports, because two major export commodities are hit at the same time, sugar and coconut products. Coconut oil may be replaced more and more by cheaper oils and fats on the world market.[30] After an absolute decline of exports earnings from coconut products for the Philippines from an average of SDR 630 million in the years 1980–4 to an average of SDR 428 in 1985–7 (IMF, 1988), exports have been rising again, however. The decline of income from sugar exports was even more dramatic: while sugar exports had been responsible for about one quarter of total export income in the 1970s, they declined from a share of 10% to about 1% between 1980 and 1987 with an absolute decline from SDR 480 million to 46 million in the same period (IMF, 1988).

A good example of the chain effects of substitution processes is provided by the impact that the reduction of tapioca imports of the EC from *Thailand* (unrelated to biotechnology) had on sugar exports: Thailand had to look for new markets for its starch rich cassava and increased exports to *South Korea* (Berkum, 1988), where in the mid-1980s starch-based sweeteners already accounted for 18% of total sweetener consumption (Crott, 1986).

Like Brazil in Latin America, some Asian countries have a tradition in running large-scale plantations and have built up the capacity to introduce technological advances quickly into production. They will probably be able to increase their share in the total of developing countries' agricultural exports. A case in point is Malaysia,[31] which has not only increased palm oil production, but also expanded the large-scale production of cocoa (which in Africa is mostly produced by small

[28] Indian purchases of palm oil from Malaysia fell by 65% in 1989 to 263 000 tonnes; Pakistan bought 12% less at 464 000 tonnes. The emergence of China, Indonesia and Egypt as major new buyers (taking 429 000, 325 000, and 211 000 tonnes respectively) partly compensated for this decline (*Financial Times*, 25 January 1990).
[29] Hybrids have been developed by the Indian Cardamom Research Institute which are said to yield up to 900 kg of cardamom per hectare. At present, Guatemala has a productivity of 250 kg and India of 65 kg a hectare (*Financial Express*, 1989a).
[30] Taxes on coconut exports by the Philippine government may have contributed to this decline (Kramer, 1988).
[31] Indonesia may join this category, since the decline of oil revenues has led to increased efforts to boost agricultural exports and to allow foreign plantations.

farmers). This was not due to biotechnology, but the resulting large-scale production makes it easier to diffuse any productivity increasing technology. Any advance in biotechnology applicable to these commodities (like the cloning of oil palms) thus will increase the advantage of the country in comparison to its competitors in the world market and will lead to increasing 'South–South substitution'.

Impact on trade of African countries The victims of this 'South–South substitution' will be first of all African countries. Only *Côte d'Ivoire* seems to be able to keep or even increase its market share in world cocoa exports, because the country has built up considerable expertise in diffusing improved technologies in this field to the farmers. *Ghana* cocoa exports have profited from the special quality of Ghana cocoa, but this advantage may be lost as a result of biotechnology applications which might be used to 'upgrade' less valuable cocoa from elsewhere so that it matches the quality of cocoa from Ghana. Cocoa exports revenues for *Cameroon* have declined considerably in recent years (IMF, 1988).

Applications of biotechnology to oils and fats will probably also affect the export potential for groundnut oil. Export incomes from groundnut products have shown a tremendous decline in *Sudan* and *Mali* (IMF, 1988) and may also affect *Senegal*. The same negative effect may make itself felt in the case of palm kernel exports from countries like *Sierra Leone*.

The production of low-volume, high-value substances (like flavours, fragrances, pigments, insecticides) may have negative effects on countries like *Madagascar* (cloves, vanilla), the Comoros (vanilla), and Kenya (pyrethrum). *Sudan* has already suffered from the decline of gum exports.

Beside agricultural exports, some mineral exports may be affected. A case in point is the export of phosphates (crucial for *Morocco*, *Togo* and *Senegal*), since the demand for phosphates has decreased as a result of the use of enzymes in washing powder. The need for phosphates in fertilizers and animal feed[32] may also be affected by biotechnology. Another mineral affected may be copper. Latin American exporters may be better able to use new technologies (including mineral leaching) to decrease their production costs than African exporters (*Zaire*, *Zambia*). Already in the period of low world market prices during the first half of the 1980s, Zambia lost much ground to Chile, which has expanded the

---

[32] The Dutch company Gist-Brocades has done extensive research on the enzyme phytase, which releases phosphate from phytin, thereby obviating the need for phosphate additions to feed and reducing the phosphate content of manure by about 40% (Gist-Brocades, 1990).

country's market share aggressively. Declining incomes from copper exports will make it difficult to invest in new technologies.

While the impact of biotechnology on Latin American and Asian trade will have some negative, but also some positive aspects, African countries will for a long time to come only feel the negative impacts. It will take much more time to use biotechnology to increase local self-sufficiency in food importing African countries because of the many bottlenecks in the diffusion of research results from international research institutions to agricultural extension services and African farmers (Junne, 1987*b*).

Conclusion

The impact of biotechnology on trade flows is hard to measure. Even the trends are difficult to define (OECD, 1989). Uncertainty regarding the speed of technological development is not the main reason for the necessarily speculative character of most analyses. The main reason is that the impact depends to a very large extent not only on advances in technology, but also on economic factors and on principally discontinuous political decisions. Biotechnology has no *direct* impact on commodity trade. The influence is always mediated by economic and political variables, such as the strategies of large companies that organize the international division of labour, and political decisions of governments which set the parameters for world trade. Political decisions can push as well as delay substitution processes. They are also decisive for the regional distribution of the effects of substitution. The best guess with regard to trends to be expected is that biotechnology will strengthen trends that have already existed before the introduction of biotechnology. Applications of biotechnology have a higher chance to be realized if they serve the strategies that major economic and political actors pursue. For this reason, several references have been made in this text to ongoing trends in international trade, even if many of these changes have not (yet) been a consequence of biotechnology.

Applications of biotechnology will first of all affect trade in agricultural products. It will make many importing countries more self-sufficient and increase trade conflicts among overproducing countries. While overall agricultural exports from developing countries will probably stagnate, biotechnology will help to substitute products from specific (more developed) countries for commodities from other (less advanced) developing countries, contributing to a stronger concentration of agricultural production for the world market on fewer developing countries. While countries known as 'Newly industrializing countries' (NICs), given their technological capabilities, will also be able to boost their *agricultural* production, the less advanced countries (especially in Africa and the Caribbean area) will bear the brunt of the adjustment of trade flows. Divergent effects on commodity trade of different developing countries as a consequence will make it even more difficult for them than in the past to coordinate their position in international trade negotiations.

References

Berkum, S. van (1988). *Internationale Aspecten van het EG-Landbouwbeleid. De Relatie met vier ontwikkelingslanden.* Landbouw-Economisch Instituut, Den Haag.

Buttel, F.H. (1989). How epoch making are high technologies? The case of biotechnology. *Sociolog. Forum*, **4**, 247–61.

Byé, P., Mounier, A., Magnaval, R. (1991). Single Cell Proteins. In *The Biotechnology Revolution*, M. Fransman, G. Junne & A. Roobeek (eds). Blackwell, Oxford (in press).

Crott, R. (1986). The impact of isoglucose on the international sugar market. In *The Biotechnological Challenge*, S. Jacobsson, A. Jamison & H. Rothman (eds), pp. 96–123. Cambridge University Press.

Financial Express (1989a). Tissue culture breakthrough for Cardamom. *Financial Express* (Bombay, India), 24 October.

Financial Express (1989b). Tissue-cultured oil palms to help reduce import bill. *Financial Express* (Bombay, India), 25 October.

GATT (1988a). *International Trade 87–88*, vols I and II, Geneva.

GATT (1988b). United States sugar-trade policy under fire. *FOCUS (GATT Newsletter)*, **57**, September/October, pp. 1–2.

GATT (1989a). *Review of Developments in the Trading System. September 1988–February 1989.* L/6530, Geneva.

GATT (1989b). US accepts ruling on sugar quotas. *FOCUS (GATT Newsletter)*, **63**, July, p. 2.

Gist-Brocades (1990). New Products based on recDNA Technology. *Biotechnol. Nederland*, 1990/1, p. 9.

Halos, S.C. (1989). *Biotechnology Trends: A Threat to Philippine Agriculture?* World Employment Programme Research, Technology and Employment Programme, Working Paper WEP 2-22/WP 193. International Labour Office, Geneva.

ICCSASW (1987). *HFCS and Sugar: New Equation in the Sugar Market.* Special Publication of *Sugar World*. International Commission for the Co-ordination of Solidarity Among Sugar Workers, Toronto.

IMF (International Monetary Fund) (1988). *Balance of Payments Statistics*, vol. 39, Yearbook, Parts 1 and 2, Washington.

Junne, G. (1984). Der strukturpolitische Wettlauf zwischen den kapitalistischen Industrieländern. *Politische Vierteljahres.*, **25**(2), 64–83.

Junne, G. (1985). Biotechnology and Consequences for Changing Relations between EC–USA, EC–Japan and USA–Japan? *Biotechnology Hearing,*

European Parliament, Committee on Energy, Research and Technology (PE 98.227/rev.), 30 October.

Junne, G. (1986a). Die Verschiebung der Kräfteverhältnisse zwischen den USA, Westeuropa und Japan unter dem Einfluß der Biotechnologie. In *Technologie und internationale Politik*, B. Kohler-Koch (ed.), pp. 139–67. Nomos, Baden-Baden.

Junne, G. (1986b). Nuevas Tecnologias: Una Amenaza para las exportaciones de los paises en desarrollo. *Efectos sobre la Division Internacional del Trabajo*, pp. 41–66. Secretaria del Trabaja y Prevision Social, Mexico.

Junne, G. (1987a). Automation in the North: consequences for developing countries' exports. In *A Changing International Division of Labor*, International Political Economy Yearbook, vol. 2, J.S. Caporaso (ed.), pp. 71–90. Lynne Rienner Publishers, Boulder.

Junne, G. (1987b). Bottlenecks in the diffusion of biotechnology from the research system into developing countries' agriculture. *Proceedings of the 4th European Congress on Biotechnology*, pp. 449–58. Elsevier, Amsterdam.

Junne, G., Komen, J. & Tomeï, F. (1989). 'Dematerialization of production': impact on raw material exports of developing countries. *Third World Quart.*, **11**, 128–42.

Kelly, M., Kirmani, N., Xafa, M., Boonekamp, C. & Winglee, P. (1988). *Issues and Developments in International Trade Policy*, Occasional Paper no. 63. International Monetary Fund, Washington.

Kramer, M. (1988). *Effektive Protektion von Rohstoffproduktion und - verarbeitung*. Steiner Verlag Wiesbaden, Stuttgart.

Litchfield, J.H. (1989). Single-cell proteins. In *A Revolution in Biotechnology*, J.L. Marx (ed.), pp. 71–81. Cambridge University Press.

Maskus, K.E. (1989). Large costs and small benefits of the American sugar programme. *World Econ.*, **12**(1), 85–104.

OECD (1989). *Biotechnology. Economic and Wider Impacts*. Paris.

Ofreno, R.E. (1987). *Capitalism in Philippine Agriculture*. Quezon City, Philippines.

Panchamukhi, V.R. & Kumar, N. (1988). Impact on commodity exports. In *Biotechnology Revolution and the Third World. Challenges and Policy Options*, pp. 207–24. Research and Information System for the Non-Aligned and Other Developing Countries, New Delhi.

Perez-Lopez, J.F. (1988). Cuban–Soviet sugar trade: price and subsidy issues. *Bull. Lat. Am. Res.*, **7**(1), 123–47.

RAFI (1987a). *Vanilla and Biotechnology*. RAFI Communique, Brandon (Manitoba), Rural Advancement Fund International.

RAFI (1987b). *Biotechnology and Natural Sweeteners; THAUMATIN*, RAFI Communique, Brandon (Manitoba), Rural Advancement Fund International.

RAFI (1989). *Coffee and Biotechnology*. RAFI Communique, Brandon (Manitoba), Rural Advancement Fund International.

Rosario, L. de (1989). China's sugar output dips as demand rises. *Far Eastern Econ. Rev.*, 2 March 1989, p. 83.

Rousseau, P. (1986). Biotechnologies for development – reflections on the protein chain. In *The Biotechnological Challenge*, S. Jacobsson, A. Jamison & H. Rothman (eds), pp. 124–47. Cambridge University Press.

Ruivenkamp, G. (1989). *De Invoering van Biotechnologie in de Agro-industriële Produktieketen. De Overgang naar een Niuewe Arbeidsorganisatie.* Jan van Arkel, Utrecht.

Senez, J.C. (1987). Single-cell protein: past and present developments. In *Microbial Technology in the Developing World*, E.J. Da Silva, Y.R. Dommergues, E.J. Nyns & C. Ratledge (eds), pp. 238–59. Oxford University Press.

Svarstad, H. (1988). *Biotechnology and the International Division of Labour.* University of Oslo (Institute for Sociology).

UNIDO (1988). Growing Compounds from Plants. *Genet. Eng. Biotechnol. Monit.*, no. 25, pp. 58–60.

Wallerstein, I. (1989). *The Modern World-System III. The Second Era of Great Expansion of the Capitalist World-Economy, 1730–1840s.* Academic Press, San Diego.

Warhurst, A. (1984). *The Application of Biotechnology in Developing Countries: The Case of Mineral Leaching with Particular Reference to the Andean Pact Copper Project.* UNIDO (IS.450), Vienna.

Warhurst, A. (1987). New directions for policy research: biotechnology and natural resources, *Development*, 1987: 4, 68–70.

9

Biotechnology: socio-economic considerations, intercultural perspectives and international viewpoints

E.J. DA SILVA

Introduction

Following the discoveries of vaccines, anti-toxins and antibiotics, microbial biotechnology over the past few decades has proven itself as a creatable resource. With the advent and use of new research skills, it is giving rise to further new industries and ventures. All pervasive on the commercial front and defying monopolization by any one group or society for extended periods of time, the products of microbial technology are used by all from presidents and royalty to the poor and the underprivileged.

The potential of the microorganism for socio-industrial advancement and growth is legion and legend. Solvents, chemicals and bioenergy result from anaerobic fermentation, i.e. acetone, butanol, and methane. Food additives, dairy products and enhanced-oil-recovery result from the use of microbial polysaccharides. The potential for food, feed and ethanol production from waste cellulosic materials *via* microbial action in bioconversion technologies exists. Textured and flavoured mycelial food products that simulate veal and chicken have been produced. Microbial production of psychoactive and immunoactive components is a reality. Microbial synthesis of interferons, rennet and growth hormones is no longer a remote possibility. Underpinning all these processes in their transition from the laboratory-scale to the industrial stage are three indisputable determinants – society, culture and economics.

The past decade, has also been witness to fundamental changes in the biosciences. New vistas in molecular biology and human health have been opened by the techniques of genetic engineering using restriction endonucleases resulting in the development of bioactive entities now being produced in quantity using microorganisms as the producing agencies.

Perspectives and prospects

The increasing deployment of these new genetic engineering techniques will undoubtedly add to the economic and market potential of several natural processes in the agricultural sector (Wilson & Sullivan, 1984). These range from improvements in the efficiency of plant photosynthesis to the production of plant varieties with increased protein content and for increased resistance to diseases, drought, insects and herbicides.

Virtually a decade ago, the growth of the world population amounted to approximately four billion. By the turn of the century 14 billion has been forecast. The demographic share of the developing world of this estimate is certain to be considerable and, from a socio-biotechnological view-point, increasing quantities of drugs, birth-control agents, diag-nostic kits and bio-reagents will have to be available and accessible.

Given the economic potential of the new biotechnologies, govern-ment support, world-wide, is being allocated towards the development of national capacities and capabilities in the fields of genetic engineering, industrial and environmental microbiology and in other *impact*-on-society domains such as enzymology, cell culture, biopatents (Barton, 1989) the copyrighting of genetic information (Kayton, 1983) and DNA-based forensic sciences. This young science has already been credited with the trapping of a resourceful *Star Wars* spy (Horsnell, 1989).

In a recent discussion on technological progress, microelectronics and biotechnology, the key areas in science and technology for the next two to three decades have been projected as the 'fifth long wave of industrialization (Fig. 9.1) rooted in the Pacific Belt linking the USA, Japan and Southeast Asia' (Pacey, 1983). A merging of the boundaries between these two key areas has been suggested since both key technologies deal with information and informational processes – i.e. the field of bioinformatics.

Today's societal intervention on the environmental risks (Halvorson, Pramer & Rogul, 1985), safety and ethical (Cantley, 1987; Hendricks, 1988) issues of the use of genetically-engineered organisms and the new biotechnologies recalls the lively debate that took place a hundred years ago, which era witnessed the wide-spread disappearance of *glanders* – a disease of horses – with the advent of the automobile. At issue then were scenarios of the advantages and disadvantages of the replacement of the horsedrawn carriage by the then newly constructed horseless carriage. Today, the discussions centre on the possible occurrence of a genetic Chernobyl, the patenting of life, and the god-like activity of biotechnical and biomedical processes to alter life and cure disease. Furthermore, there is increasing concern about burning of the South American forests

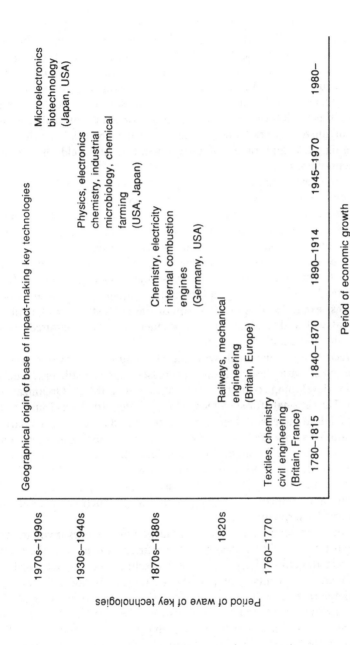

Fig. 9.1. Phases of industrialization (adapted from Pacey, 1983).

and emotional issues related to the environment, employment in automated labour markets and to the changing patterns of the geo-economic wealth and socio-political stature in the family of nations.

The emergence of the new biotechnologies in the early half of the 1980 has already influenced considerably the employment of skilled labour, as is evident from the vacancy notices in the scientific and daily press. Hence, there will soon be an urgent need to orient the annual emerging crop of university graduates to the promising potentials of the ever-changing pace and range of employment in the field of the new biotechnologies.

For the developing countries the potential benefits of biotechnology are significant. However, important unsolved issues, despite increased foreign-aid and newly established national boards and programmes, remain as ever food production, more effective control of disease, novel sources of renewable energy and innovative approaches to the conservation of genetic resources and the environment. Such benefits could further translate into eventual second-order advantages ranging from the introduction of newly adapted technologies, enhanced export earnings, expanded employment opportunities, extension of national political will and income, and, subsequently, newly acquired socio-economic and geopolitical stature.

A recent report has dealt with the blending of the newly emerging technologies with the traditional processes that are still practised in several developing countries (International Labour Organization, 1985). The rationale for such technological integration was found to be in a dual desire to ensure higher productivity and to safeguard a part of the traditional characteristics of known conventional techniques. One such example of technological integration is the use of microelectronic control in bio-gas production (Colombo & Mazzonis, 1984). Micro-electronic processing, however, is not entirely new in relation to biotechnology, since it is deployed in the production of food and beverages by fermentation processes.

On the commercial front, current marketing practices involving the audiovisual and printed messages, unwittingly touch upon the socio-economic and cultural aspects of the biotechnologies. Glossy weeklies and TV advertisements emphasize the obliteration of microbes through a variety of health products. In many countries now special TV advertisements sponsored by the Ministries of Health, emphasize sexual hygiene as an effective means of reducing the wide spread of AIDS.

Indeed, the consumer society of today is constantly being exposed to the commercial and ready availability of the 'best disinfectant that destroys all known germs', of the washing powder that washes whiter than white, of the irresistible spray that seeks out the marauding microbe in virtually every crevice of the human body, and, of the beauty-aid that ensures a day-long 'germ-free' skin (Scheidegger, 1989). Vending cleanliness, in the form of lotions, sprays, detergents and medicated soaps, TV commercials rarely focus on the many beneficial activities of microbes that are known to a *dégorgeur* in the production of champagne, to a brewer in the fermentation of beer, and to the producer of hard cheeses (e.g. *Roquefort, Stilton* and *Gorgonzola*) and soft varieties like *Camembert* and *Limburger*.

Microbes, culture and society

The scientific basis of biotechnology dates back to the nineteenth century when Louis Pasteur established the microbial origins of fermentation and putrefaction. Today, given the resurgence of concerns on the state of the environment, the use of biotechnology in society implies psychosociological and cultural shifts in development. The design of future industrial processes, energy use, management of renewable resources and the environment will probably become intrinsic components of the biodevelopment engineering that will shape tomorrow's society and culture.

One may query, 'What is the relationship between microbial technology, culture and society and its expressions?'. One reply is that plagues, diseases and scourges of microbial origin know no national boundaries, cultural or social barriers. One example, in which people of different cultures collaborated actively, is the successful eradication of smallpox, a disease that has scourged and scarred mankind for many centuries. This pestilence has now been relegated to past history as a result of international cooperation at all levels of society. And, it goes without saying that such success emphasizes the need for active promotion of the remedial and beneficial properties of microbes in all cultures and societies for man's well-being.

Mittermeier (1989) says

> The '90s will be the make it or break it decade in terms of conservation worldwide and especially in the tropics, where the bulk of the world's biological diversity is found. We're facing a wide variety of problems from ozone layer depletion and global warming to soil and water and air pollution and toxic waste disposal and acid rain. But to me the most important conservation issue is the loss of the planet's biological diversity, because that's the biological capital, the resource base on which we depend for our survival. We can develop technologies to combat most forms of pollution, but once we lose a species, plant or animal it's gone forever.

Microbes in development and society

The developing world comprises 70% of the world's population. It includes about 120 countries that differ in degrees of industrialization and culture, and in systems of society, government and economy. Furthermore, each country interacts to different pressures from its regional and international environments, and hence the approach to promoting development, whilst appropriate in one situation, may be unsuitable for another. This situation is not new and has already been witnessed in the establishment of the European Economic Community (EC) and the Council of Mutual Economic Assistance (CMEA) for the socialist-oriented markets.

The socio-cultural objectives of providing food, education and the growth of productive skills in the non-technically advanced countries are influenced also by prevailing economic and demographic patterns. Long-range socio-economic and intercultural planning, based on perceived scientific and technical development, must be in terms of population growth and control, patterns of consumption of resources (including energy), agriculture, food production (and its equitable just distribution), health, education, and manufacture and trade. The generation of new wealth and socio-technical achievement can provide for tremendous cultural impacts. This is as true for the vast majority of people in the developing countries as it is for the poorest groups in the industrialized societies.

Changes in patterns of living provide one of the keys to a more humane world. Rather than adopting the battle lines of conservation versus consumption, a more humane world may be a matter of blending several lifestyles, i.e. those of the urban and the rural, the small- and the large-scale, and the traditional household skills and the technically sophisticated into a more humane and harmonious pattern of future living (Da Silva, Olembo & Burgers, 1978). Such a strategy suggests that future life-styles call for a reassessment of man's aesthetic and social values as well as for the protection of his external environment. Dixon (1976), on the commencement of the first 'environmental decade', argued for an imperative *attitudinal* change towards the use of renewable resources, life-styles, and development in order to profit from microbial activities in tackling global shortages and sociocultural problems. This still valid approach calls for consideration of the aesthetic and human effects of economic and technological change and for an examination of how economic and technological change affects cultural evolution. And, it is in this context that microbial technology offers an appropriate mechanism for 'man's shift *vis-à-vis* Nature from parasitism to symbiosis, exploitation to nurture, and dissipation to conservation' (Khan, 1977).

With its varied meanings in different intellectual disciplines and systems of thought, culture, one of the most complicated words of the English language (Williams, 1981), is comprised of inherited artifacts, technical processes, ideas, habits and values (Sills, 1968).

Ackermann (1981) considers cultural values as ways of ordering objects, experience and behaviours that manifest themselves in situations of choice. The framers and bearers of cultural values are individuals and social groups that are responsible for the expression of the choices leading to support and meaning in their patterns of life, their interpersonal and socio-cultural relationships, and their ways of social reproduction. Common sense has been replaced by economic benefits, and cultural humanism has been sacrificed in the name of chauvinistic cultural values and economic determinism. It is often forgotten that society is an evolving process of interrelated scientific, intellectual, aesthetic, political, economic and other social components rather than a static product of economic determinism.

The emergence of a number of university courses in the mid-1970s in the UK and the USA devoted to science, technology and society have emphasized the strong interaction between culture and technology (Heitowit & Epstein, 1977; Morphet, 1981). Indeed, it appears that the human factor is an important one in the relationship between culture and socio-economic development stemming from scientific progress and discovery, a factor that is assuming more significance than either those of finance or possession of natural resources.

Culture is identified with the arts and sciences and coupled to a demand for more leisure-time activity. Kirpal (1976) provides an insight, i.e.

> A living and vital culture is rooted in authentic and healthy traditions, has the capacity of continuous renewal and adaptation, and is developed by new aspirations and bold innovations; in this way the past, the present and the future are reflected in that life of the mind and the spirit that is the indefinable complex of culture. The humanities and the arts, the sciences and the technologies, the network of communications and relationships, the magic of poetry and the transcendence of religion, all these spheres of action and speculation form the pattern of culture. The rich and the fascinating diversity of these patterns is a precious heritage of mankind that needs to be preserved and developed (p. 86).

As far back as 1887, Hilaire Belloc captured the mystery of the microbe in the magic of poetry. Since then, Killick-Kendrick (1988) has collected several clerihews that capture the personalities and work of

Antony van Leeuwoenhoek, Sir William Leishman, Schaudin, Charles Nicole, Laveran and the like. Similarly, Hodgson & Bormann (1988) have dealt with fermentation art as a form of expression of biological culture wherein the contribution of artists such as Henri Rousseau (*Eden Regained*), Marc Chagall (*The Brewmaster*), Alberto Giacometti (*Kultur Vessel*), etc. is linked and traced to the revival of fermentation technology.

There is no doubt that scientific research and subsequent technology have contributed to socio-cultural and techno-economic development. Just as the introduction of the power loom and the invention of the telephone significantly altered employment in the textile industry in Europe, and the range and extent of interpersonal communication in North America respectively, so also have technological breakthroughs with microbes and allied industries.

The breakthrough with the discovery of penicillin during World War II led to new antibiotics, pharmaceuticals and pesticides that arrest disease, boost animal growth and augment agricultural yields. The 'pill' has contributed to the feminine revolution and to the independence of woman in traditionally male-dominated societies and industries; and in 1981, European farmers fed their animals with a feed derived from a methanol-based process using the organism *Methylophilus methylotrophus*. Today, 'meat savouries', known as *Quorn* and derived from *Mycoprotein*, are in use in the UK. Likewise in the CMEA countries, biomedical and nutritional research has established the basis for supplementing or replacing animal and poultry feed with the bacterial protein *Promethin 80* (Surghiyska, Ilieva & Koghuharova, 1983).

Indisputably, the traits of society and their interaction with inescapable variables such as environment, economic and socio-cultural development, emphasize certain facets of society and culture in national development (Da Silva, 1982). Socio-cultural development, i.e. population growth, world development, market pressures, petroleum costs and social change can, to some extent, be influenced by the 'lowly' microbe. Stabilization of population growth could benefit from microbial intervention in the biosynthesis of a cheaper contraceptive product, development of alternative sources of energy could lessen reliance on petroleum stocks, and women and children in due course could be spared routine drudgery and demeaning tasks that prevail in some societies.

A recent report (1989) by the Organization for Economic Co-operation and Development (OECD) touches upon important social and economic issues that are germane to both the industrialized and non-technically advanced societies. There is absolutely no doubt that the crop of new biotechnologies 'differs from other twentieth century major technologies in that its human and social consequences will be felt long before its economic impact'. The new biotechnologies are vast in scientific content and lend themselves to development of novel technological processes that will elicit in their wake industrial constraints and legal problems. As a means of aiding the decision-maker and preparing for the early years of the millenium, attention in depth has been given to the diffusion of the new biotechnologies throughout the economy, to the structural changes forseen in the agricultural and public health sectors, and to their long-term impacts on international trade, competitiveness and employment.

The new biotechnologies are human activities and societal attitudes to their acceptance or rejection vary in content and scope. Complex for some, and simple for others, generic biotechnology can be viewed anthropologically (Fleising, 1989).

Technological simplicity facilitates acquisition, acceptance, diffusion and maintenance of technology amongst the populace. Risks of dependence on outsiders, in operation and repair and on capital investment, are reduced to the minimum. Simplicity, furthermore, involves no additional social problems nor cultural disruptions. Familiarity with materials ensures their acceptability and accessibility and lessens the need for specialized training, external supervision, and import of materials with accompanying bureaucratic controls and constraints. Technological simplicity also dissolves barriers of work organization between rural and urban populations. In rural areas, the labour force is scattered and based on kinship ties. In urban areas, the city poor are often engaged in specific work characterized more by competition rather than by cooperation. Access to simple techniques may, therefore, help to counterbalance this effect.

On account of simplicity in technology and its integration into accepted rural practices, subtle social changes are at work. Women in most developing societies, who are apt to be illiterate, are not masters of their own time; denied mobility and financial resources, they still have a new world opening to them. The acceptance of the *Lorena* stove[1] by women in Guatemala has altered the pattern of food preparation (Shaller, 1979). In rural areas women plant, weed, help harvest and oversee crop sales. They invariably cover long distances to the markets

---

[1] This is a permanent cookstove, made without special tools, from a mixture of sand and clay. This inexpensive stove, developed in Guatemala, was designed for improved fuel efficiency using a variety of organic waste fuels in addition to wood. Details on construction and recent models can be found in *Appropriate Technology Sourcebook – A Guide to Practical Books for Village and Small Community Technology* (1986), eds K. Darrow & M. Saxenian, published in the USA by Volunteers in Asia, p. 800.

of neighbouring villages or urban centres in order to sell crops (cassava, maize, okra and palm products) that they have grown. In addition, they occupy an important place in the economy of farming and the foodstuff trade and enjoy a certain degree of economic independence as they trade on their own account. Such experience and its recognition by local authorities provides the basis for technological exchange and cooperation, for instance in the production of *gari* – a fermented food (Table 9.1) in Benin and Nigeria.

Indeed, women throughout the world hold the key position in the assimilation of new technologies, especially because they are the transmitters of cultural values and mores to children. This is borne out by the fact that a great majority of all public advertisements dealing with utility products are aimed at women (Bartos, 1981).

Many developing societies rely to a great extent on non-commercial energy sources such as straw, animal dung, firewood, and animal and human power to meet their essential needs in energy. The acquisition of energy resources by rural communities is influenced by patterns of income distribution and ownership in traditional social hierarchies.

Social attitudes toward innovations and relationships with extension workers, research, and governmental agencies may be a potent factor in the use of rural energy and supply. Certain entrepreneurial occupations are characteristic of particular ethnic or social groups in certain communities. In Cameroon, the *Bamileke* people are responsible for trade in primary produce; likewise, the *Hausa* of Nigeria, a people living primarily between Lake Chad and Niger (who are united essentially by language), are similarly engaged in such practice. In India, the gathering of animal dung is carried out by the lowest social caste. Their women are paid to gather human excreta from latrines of the more conservative villages where women, either in *purdah* or having different means and patterns of employment, cannot do these jobs (Feldman & McCarthy, 1982).

Several examples of innovative technology impeded by cultural barriers are well known. The regional successes and failures of the 'Green Revolution', which laid the basis for food sufficiency in several developing countries of Asia, provide excellent examples of many of the cultural and equity problems involved in introducing new technologies (Barr, 1981). Another factor is that time needed for technology support is time reallocated from some other activity. An apparently tedious and laborious act (such as fetching water) may have some unnoticed social or cultural value, or the time saved by technological innovation may be, surprisingly, not necessarily productive. Salisbury (1962) observed that time saved by the men of the *Siane* of Papua New Guinea in felling trees with steel rather than with stone axes was not reallocated to a reduction

Table 9.1. *Examples of fermented foods consumed world-wide*

Staple base	Additive	Local food	Country/ Region	Remarks
Cereals				
Maize		Jamin-bang, fuba	Brazil	Rich in lactic acid
		Miso	Japan	
		Ogi, ogidi, kenkey	Nigeria, W. Africa	Increase of B-vitamins due to microbial fermentation
		Chicha	Peru	
Rice	Black gram	Idli	India	Yeasts present
Wheat		Minchin	China	Consumed as meat substitute
	Yoghurt	Kishk, Kushik	Middle East	
Millets	Teff	Letting, injera, thumba	Savanna Africa	Increase of B-vitamins in African sour doughs
Soyabeans				
		Sufu (Chinese cheese)	China	Increase in protein content, destruction of toxic factors
	Tapioca, rice, wheat	Tempe Hamanatto, koji shoyu (sauce), miso (paste)	Indonesia Japan	Meat substitute, increase in protein content, destruction of toxic soyabean factors in meat substitutes, pastes and meat-flavouring sauces
Starchy roots				
	Cassava flour	Gari	W. Africa	Original toxic compounds broken down and eluted; means of preserving food
	Cassava root	Penjeum	W. Java	

in the amount of work carried out by women, i.e. in the collection of wood, but was invested in more ceremonial activity and leisure time for the men. In the Republic of Korea and the Philippines, time gained from the release of household labour was channelled into productive activities such as silk and mushroom production.

Bioconversion practices and rural societies

Bio-gas technology is a microbial technology that addresses itself to sociocultural, technical, and economic development in rural areas. It serves multiple communal needs, has been developed through the enthusiasm of individuals, non-governmental organizations, and local communities, and government (Brown, 1987). Reinforced by accessibility to loan capital, technical assistance, and potential for rural market development, bio-gas technology has received wide acclaim in rural India and China (Da Silva, 1980). Though climatic conditions and improper planning have been important elements, non-technical factors such as social, cultural and religious preferences dictate the acceptance and use of such energy (Subramanian, 1977). Electricity from bio-gas necessitates new stoves and changes in cooking habits and utensils. Changes in cooking equipment alter the role of women in society and in the gathering and sale of non-commercial fuels, such as the organized collection of animal dung. These changes not only affect women's activity, they may also deprive them of an important source of income.

Cultural beliefs and traditional rural practices were the primary reasons for rejection in the early 1970s of some bio-gas installations at the village level in Papua New Guinea (Newcombe, 1981a). Most Papua New Guineans hold strong superstitious beliefs concerning the use of excrement in any form; consequently, such a taboo mitigates against the collection of this energy resource. Again, the collection of animal manure necessitates capital investment for penning animals, adequate water supplies, and animal feed. Despite the lack of energy supply, there was a pronounced resistance to a technology that involved a change in life-styles and community arrangements. In contrast, plants for processing coffee pulp wastes and sewage met no cultural barriers in the urban areas. Acceptance of such technology was ascribed to an enhancement of social status, an awareness of hard times, a guaranteed supply of energy at prescribed public levels and use of an appropriate public health programme. Newcombe (1981b) reports an outright rejection of bio-gas technology at the village level on its reintroduction in 1980 despite detailed descriptions of the economic inputs, required management and utility products generated.

Social analysis (Siwatibau, 1981) in the Fijian villages of Natia, Yario, Nacumaki and Nagelawai, showed that these villages – in relation to bio-gas technology – resisted change and were apathetic to development, conservative and reluctant to undertake new ventures as long as they could achieve what was to them an adequate standard of living without too much dependence on the cash sector.

'Night soil', traditionally used in China and Japan, and of course in most of Europe and North America before the advent of municipal sewage systems, as fertilizer, is an important source of bio-gas. In the Republic of Korea, in Thailand and India, religious beliefs account for an aversion to consume food cooked with gas or electricity derived from domestic wastes such as pig dung on account of health considerations (Barnett, Pyle & Subramanian, 1978). In some parts of India, toilets have been disconnected from bio-gas plants either on religious grounds or to avoid contact with the caste engaged in the collection of night soil.

Social analysis in India, the Philippines, the Republic of Korea and Thailand show that in practice, it has been the richer, motivated strata of society that have installed bio-gas plants. In India, the use of bio-gas has reduced smoke-induced eye trouble amongst rural housewives, saved time spent in cooking, minimized collection and preparation of dung cakes, increased the life of the utensils, contributed to the cleanliness of the house and, in general, improved the dress and outlooks of women and children (Saithananthan, 1975).

In Thailand, bio-gas usage is preferred to expensive charcoal. In Indonesia and Japan, the main motive for using bio-gas is pollution control, whilst in the Republic of Korea and the Philippines the use of bio-gas, for example, is driven by the need for an easily available cooking fuel.

The failure of bio-gas technology in several countries of Asia, Africa, and Latin America has been ascribed to the neglect of women's needs in the existing male/female power relationships (Agarwal, 1982). An example has been cited in the use of the community bio-gas plant in Fateh Singh Ka Purwa, Etawah, in India: technologically a success but socially a failure. The male/female power relationship appeared to have been the key factor in this case. Given the fact that the plant was to provide energy, several interviews showed that while the women were interested in the use of bioenergy for cooking, the men preferred to use the energy for power-irrigation pumps, milling machines and other small industrial processes normally run by men. Moreover, in situations of rural poverty and male-dominated societal decision-making processes, poor women willingly accept almost any type of work in order to provide for their families (Stoler, 1977). Studies with migrants and refugees in Vietnam, the Republic of Korea and the USA show that men are more bound by concerns of status and are less willing to take any job (Hoskins, 1975; Tinker, 1981).

A reason for the neglect of women's technological needs is to be found primarily in the division of labour, economic power and decision-making at the rural community level. Men in most developing societies are involved in the income-generating processes focussing their energies and capabilities on activities having a commercial potential. Women, on the other hand, cater to the core needs of the family, such as the timely and continuous supply of essential commodities: fuel, fodder, food and fertilizer, which are often provided by the environment and serve a vast majority of the world's poor families. Feldman & McCarthy (1982), found that 'women are doubly hurt because their productive skills are in rural non-monetized sectors' which 'are less the object of specific development programmes than are the capital-intensive monetized sectors of the economy'.

Life-styles influenced by the spread of bio-gas technology herald a coming change. Younger generations are reluctant to settle for the indignity and misery which preceding generations knew, lives which would be familiar to a worker in the teeming slums of London and Paris during the nineteenth century. In the quest for human dignity and domestic tranquility, coming generations are apt to be more adaptable to regional and international considerations and, in consequence, may possess a greater awareness and appreciation of the environment and its resources.

Sewage systems have often been referred to as a barometer of a nation's culture. Some societies employ the sea as a sewer, others recycle valuable nutrients, by making use of microbial transformation, into utility products such as feed supplements, and biofertilizer. In this context it is worth noting that Great Britain at the height of its imperial power and the USA at the peak of industrialization made possible the wide adoption of water-borne sewage. Several useful models of deriving wealth from waste have been described with emphasis on the role of microbes in bioconversion processes (Da Silva, Burgers & Olembo, 1976).

Recent research indicates the value and utility of recycling agro-industrial residues and wastes (Board on Science and Technology for International Development (BOSTID), 1981). Their full-scale acceptance is subject to their impact on society, on the environment, and thus on the economy. Health considerations and cultural obstacles are limiting factors. The practice of aquaculture is an interesting example.

Known to man for centuries, aquaculture is an important source of food. The rearing of fish on organic waste predates written history. The range of organic wastes used successfully in aquaculture is composed of direct feeds (such as rice bran, distillery slops, slaughterhouse and fishing industry residues) and indirect feeds (e.g. animal manure). Decomposition of these wastes occurs through successive cycles of microbial activity: populations such as bacteria, fungi and protozoa which mineralize organic wastes into their inorganic components. These are then taken up in successive stages by phytoplankton and fish. The cycle allows for the re-entry into the biosphere of low-nutritional wastes and their upgrading in protein content.

The use of animal manure is widespread in China, Israel, Hungary, Singapore, USA and the western part of Germany. Fish ponds are of great value in the disposal of human wastes when capital, expensive land, and unreliable water supplies are limiting factors. Carp farms in the USA, India and the western part of Germany use domestic wastes as a source of nutrients. Agricultural fibrous wastes are also widely used, e.g. growth of *Tilapia* in the rice fields of Indonesia, sugar-beet processing waste-waters (Poland), rum distillery and antibiotic production wastes (Puerto Rico), rubber-processing wastes (Malaysia) and trout farming on slaughterhouse waste (Peru).

Several cultural barriers to the acceptance of fish as a direct human food exist. Fish grown with 'clean' wastes (e.g. rice-bran) pose no problem. The consumption of fish in certain areas of Africa and Asia is often related to the religious beliefs or concern with social status. The *Beja* pastoralists of the Red Sea borderlands of Egypt, Sudan and Ethiopia reject fish as a source of food. Similar cultural attitudes that fish is unclean and that social status is enhanced through its abstinence are common with the *Nilotes* (a linguistically related group of people drawn from the *Dinka, Luo, Nuer* and *Shillule* tribes) and *Bantus* in East and Southern Africa. Also, the social hierarchy of classes intervenes in the acceptance of fish as food. Brahamins abstain from fish caught by fishermen coming from the class of Harijan or 'untouchables'.

The acceptance of mushrooms is another example. Rejection of this proteinaceous non-meat food occurs when 'unclean' substrates like horse manure are used. With the use of 'clean' substrates such as rice-bran, straw, cotton wastes and sawdust, the mushroom market is growing in a large number of rural communities in developing countries. In traditional cultures, food preference and preparation are deeply-seated societal convictions. Mushrooms are of nutritional significance on account of their high protein content in diets of people who exercise a preference for vegetables to animal and bird meats. Light grey straw mushrooms are readily accepted by Asians. Texture and flavour pose no problem. Occidental countries, on the other hand, are put off by the greyish tint but readily accept these mushrooms after the grey tinge is mutated to white, as in the white mushroom *Agaricus campestris*.

Fermented foods and socio-cultural relationships

The evolution of man's society and culture in the traditional culinary arts and crafts is historical fact: *Saccharomyces* were recognized and grown as brewer's yeast in the Mesopotamia of 8000 years ago. The *Eber Papyrus* shows the use of yeast in the preparations of 3600 years ago, and the school of Hippocrates in Cos prescribed yeasts for certain debilities. Again, the cultural heritage of virtually every civilization includes one or more fermented foods made by the souring action of microbes (see Table 9.1). *Leben* (Egypt and Syria), *taettemjolk* (Scandinavia), *matzoon* (Armenia), *dahi* (India), *piner* (Lapland), *chak* and *mopwo* (Kenya), *yakult* (Japan), *kefir* (Bulgaria) and the blue-veined cheese produced by the fungus *Pencillium roquefortii* (France) are all well known examples. Men thus found ways to deploy a mix of microbes and traditional domestic skills to make new foods, to increase their palatability, or to alter them so that they could be kept longer. Fermented milks have been used to restore the normal, naturally balanced intestinal flora that have been impaired by antibiotic treatment. Yoghurt and kefir are widely distributed in many countries today with a variety of fruit flavours. Indigenous fermented milks and foods are very important as they are socio-culturally bound in village household and community traditions.

In the socio-economic and cultural hierarchies of several populations in the developing world, fermented beverages and foods occupy a central place. Popular amongst the rural *Ibos* and patronized by the lower-income groups of Nigeria, palm wine is often served at social gatherings such as burials, marriages and initiations into cults. Palm wine, in Malaysia, is imbibed predominantly by the male population and in West Africa is used as a medicinal agent.

Brem bali, an alcoholic rice drink, occupies an important place in the daily life of the Balinese population in Indonesia. It is used in Hindu rituals to prepare a sacrificial vegetable-rice offering – *segehan* – to ward off evil.

Chicha, widely consumed in the Andean regions is a tasty, alcoholic, yellowish beverage prepared from maize. Apart from its religious and magical significance with the indigenous rural population, *chicha* was used to induce the 'thunder god' to send rain, to brighten up sun and harvest festivals (Maxwell, 1956), and was considered the vehicle that linked man to his gods through the fecundity of the earth (Nicholson, 1960). Today, it is consumed at family events and by the Indians during agricultural and religious festivals.

Ogi, manufactured from a variety of cereals, is a small-scale industry favoured by Nigerian housewives in the daily diet. Basically a home-based industry, *ogi* production has failed to reach status as an industrial market product. This is due to competition from attractively packaged expensive processed foods with a longer shelf life, which are preferred in comparison to the locally produced fermented product.

Uji, a fresh creamy soup made from a mixture of powdered maize, millet, sorghum or cassava flour is an integral component of East African rural society. It is served during circumcision ceremonies, weddings, dances and communal labour.

Asia is a vast storehouse of ancient culture and craft technology. In Southeast Asia, fermented seed, milk, meat, fish and vegetable products are delicacies that supplement starch diets with precious nutrients. These food intakes help millions of people to subsist on marginal incomes. The early methods developed in Southeast Asia have shown a striking correlation with socio-cultural evolution; they have brought new value to contemporary food research in the western world.

A rejection, perhaps psychological, of a typical soyabean food, *natto*, popular in Japanese diets is common in the West. Non-acceptance is linked to its greyish appearance and strong ammoniacal flavour resulting from the fermentation process. Similarly, *shoyu* sauce, a fermented product employed in Japanese diets to increase appetite, flavour, and digestion, has a limited market acceptance in comparison to its widely-accepted, chemically processed soysauce product.

Several western food companies have developed processes by which soybean protein is extracted, concentrated, purified, and then spun by extrusion into protein strands that yield nuggets possessing a meaty flavour. In the UK, the National Research Development Corporation (along with a major commercial enterprise) financed the development of a process in which fungal mycelium was grown on starchy substrates such as potato, yams and cassava in order to produce meat analogues (Steinkraus, 1978). It is indeed interesting that the western world, which consumes so much meat, has developed such modern and sophisticated processes in order to manufacture vegetable-protein meat substitutes. Success of these substitutes has also been attributed to an increase in vegetarianism.

Centuries ago, the Indonesians developed a fermentation product in which soybeans inoculated with the fungus *Rhizopus* are worked into a compact cake within one to three days. Known as *tempe*, the cake is used as a substitute for meat in soups, has an appealing and palatable texture, good nutritive value and a high protein content. With other cakes, such as *ontjom* and *tape*, the early meat analogues have been used as good substitutes for meat in the Indonesian daily diet. This technology is simple, low in cost, non-waste producing, and it allows for a 'quick-cook food' that is accepted by all social strata.

A salient feature of these meat analogues is that they are ready to be eaten: everything is edible, in contrast to fresh meats that require some preparation, de-boning and cooking. *Tempe*, a fermented food, is one of the world's first 'quick-cooking foods', a quality highly prized in modern western food technology. Apart from socio-economic considerations, meat analogues will enjoy in the coming decades the culinary success of the 'French-fried dishes' that were yet to be accepted in society two centuries ago.

In a test of *tempe* products from lupin and soybean, a taste panel composed of Westerners preferred fermented lupin to soybean. In a similar test, a taste panel of 20 Africans with experience and interest in nutrition in their own countries found that fermented *tempe*, as consumed in several Southeast Asian countries, would be hardly acceptable in some African countries. However, the use of seasonings, normally employed in traditional African foods, rendered the *tempe* products more acceptable.

Taste in traditional foods helps identify oneself and offers a ritual of familial and familiar pleasure in societies virtually drained of rituals. Indeed, the festivities of Christmas and their excitement would be grossly banal without the attention of yeast and bacteria (Wood, 1983).

The socio-cultural traditions and aspects of foods, viz. types of products, techniques of production, existing preferences and food habits, degrees of national pride and identification in foods, advertising and economical aspects can best be viewed in linguistic terms, i.e. the production of differences.

For example, a change from *pain ordinaire* to *pain de mie* involves a difference in what is being signified, i.e. the former variety is character-istic of everyday life, the latter is characteristic of a party. Similarly, from a psycho-sociological point of view, the eating of pasta in Naples three centuries ago was considered inferior to the consumption of bread. Even today, in most European households, the offering of white bread used to be associated with a privileged status; to consume *pain de seigle* (rye bread) or *pain noir* (pumpernickel) implies anything from a loss of national identity and social status to ability to be generously hospitable.

Food is an important vehicle for sustaining and reinforcing national identities, cultures and societies. It is a language of images, a protocol of usages, situation and behaviour. Several functions have been assigned to food through the medium of the audiovisual world. Themes evoke aristocratic traditions, the flavour of rural societal practices, nostalgic nationalism in travellers away from home, sexual undertones, health consciousness and power. For example, the Bordeaux wines *Château Latour*, *Château Lafite* and *Château Mouton-Rothschild* are bound in aristocratic tradition where quality depends on viticulture and clarifying procedures, details of which require a degree of experienced human intervention that is still far beyond the capacity of an automated, continuous process. The flavour of rural societal practices also occurs in *Camembert* cheese. Nostalgic nationalism is reflected in fermented milk products such as *leben*; sexual undertones are present in masculine and feminine beverages (e.g. fermented liquours such as *pulque* and buttermilk respectively); health consciousness is inherent in immaterial psychic states that relate to 'alertness', 'relaxation' and 'power'. Research shows that some food affects human behaviour and that people do react to what they eat (Kolata, 1982).

Food, like language, is a system of communication. As language is the medium through which man communicates and society expresses itself, so also the fermentation of food is a language – a language through which man understands the nutritive habits of different cultures and societies, a language which provides insight into the practice of rural fermentations and their gradual evolution into market products, a language which sustains the role of ancient cultural practices and food science in modern day society. An analogous relationship between language and food has been suggested in that just as the

> phonetic system of a language retains only a few of the sounds a human being is capable of producing, so a community adopts a dietary regime by making a choice among all possible foods. By no means does any given individual eat everything: the mere fact that a thing is edible does not mean that it will be eaten. By bringing to light the logic that informs these choices and the interrelationship among its constituent parts we can outline the specific characteristics of a society, just as we can outline those of a language (Soler, 1973).

A similar observation was recently described in researching the origins of the Indo-European languages. Renfrew (1989) put forward a proposal that most European languages were spread not by conquest, as has long been thought, but along with the peaceful diffusion of agriculture. This hypothesis which links the spread of language to the dissemination of agriculture appears to have some validation in recent linguistic and genetic research (Ammerman & Cavali-Sforza, 1984).

Geo-economic implications

The OECD report (1989) states that the

> new biotechnology is clearly a technology of the highly industrialized countries, both with regard to research and

development requirements and market potential. Companies will exploit the advances in plant genetics to replace Third World crops, which might be increasingly grown in OECD countries, thus reinforcing the concentration of world trade within the OECD area.

Much has already been written and spoken about the scientific content and trend of the novel biotechnologies for improvement and maintenance of the quality of life. Likewise much has also been said and documented as regards the technological potential and economic windfalls of the new biotechnologies. The commercial lodestone of the modern biotechnologies is to be found in the range of novel products – utility and pharmaceutical, plants and drugs that are expected to roll off assembly lines based on epoch-making research and revolutionary concepts that in turn touch upon socio-political norms (Yoxen, 1986), environmental concerns and property rights.

The growth of the commercial side of biotechnology is characterized by the growth of companies, societies and private entrepreneurs that cover a wide range and scope of research and newly-embarked-upon industrial activities. For example, in postulating a model that could be used in the analysis of the relationship between science, technology and commerce, McKenzie, Cambrosio & Keating (1988) studied the different strategies adopted by five institutions in three different countries in the diffusion of the hybridoma/monoclonal antibody technique for market use in diagnostic kits for the Hepatitis B virus.

Furthermore, recent advances in recombinant-DNA technology, protein engineering and process development have begun to influence the industrial enzyme market in a positive manner (Arbridge & Pitcher, 1989).

The last two milestones reached in the market were in the early 1960s with the introduction of glucoanylase for starch hydrolysis and in the mid-1970s with the development of encapsulated products that facilitated the reintroduction of enzymes into detergents. Today, the prospects for improved products in existing markets and for extending markets for enzymes are encouraging. Current market sales have been estimated at US $600 million (Table 9.2).

Since 1975, world sugar prices have fallen by 60%. A significant drop is expected on account of the widespread use of sugar substitutes by the food industry. In this current decade, more than 10% of sugar consumption in the world is expected to be replaced by the biosubstitutes derived from corn (Table 9.3). These advances indicate that the developing countries are progressively losing out in the export market.

Table 9.2. *World-wide enzyme market (approximate)*

Enzyme	Market (US$ million)
Alkaline proteases	150
Neutral proteases	70
Rennins	60
Other proteases	50
Isomerases	45
Amylases	100
Pectinases	40
Other carbohydrases	10
Lipases	20
Other	55
Total	600

Source: Arbridge & Pitcher, 1989.

Table 9.3. *Biosubstitutes for sugar*

Substitute	Source	Origin	Times sweeter than sucrose	Commercial interest
Acefulsame-K	synthetic	Western Germany	130	Hoechst A.G.
Aspartame	biosynthetic	USA	200	G.D. Searle
Hernandulcin	*Lippia dulcis*		1000	
High-Fructose-Corn Syrups (HFCS)	*Zea mays*	USA	17	World-wide
Saccharin/ cyclamate	synthetic		25	Widespread
Stevioside	*Stevia rabandiana*	Paraguay	250	DNA Plant Tech. Co.
Thaumatin	*Thaumatococcus*	Côte d'Ivoire, Ghana	Several 1000 times	Tate and Lyle, Unilever

This competitive setback is accompanied by loss of valuable foreign-exchange earnings and subsequent massive unemployment on the home front.

Sasson (1987) has documented several instances of drops in sugar prices that have adversely affected the trade balances of sugar-producing countries like Haiti, the Dominican Republic and Mexico as a result of export losses in the markets of North America. Likewise, other sugar-producing countries like Argentina, Brazil, Colombia, China, Cuba, India, Indonesia, Pakistan, Philippines and Thailand are also experiencing the changing geo-economic influence of bio-technology.

Moreover, research on the biotechnological production of cocoa and coffee flavours (Townsley, 1974) is already beginning to have an impact on the exchange-earning market products of Cameroon, Côte d'Ivoire and Ghana, countries which benefited immensely in export terms in the 'non-biotechnologically engineered' period of yesteryear. A similar situation is to be found with tea production in Kenya, Malawi and Tanzania, which have not kept abreast with the introduction of new cultivars arising from genetic improvement.

In Chad and Sudan, natural gum production from gum arabic trees, *Accacia senegal*, has come to a virtual halt as a result of its cheaper replacement by synthetic gum in the 1960s and again through the deployment of plant tissue culture in 1982 in the Northern Hemisphere. Most gum substitutes, with some gum arabic, are starch-based. Their widespread use in the food processing industry underlines the importance of gum arabic production in several African countries and emphasizes the danger to their exports by replacement of biotechnologically produced gums.

From the foregoing it is evident that a drawback of biotechnology for the developing countries is product substitution. This is underscored by the successful use of *Frostban* in reducing frost damage in crops and fruits. The geo-economic implication of such use will be in a gradual decline in imports from developing countries since more tropical produce could be easily cultivated in controlled biofarms with the help of biotechnology in the temperate regions.

Despite the scope and financial windfall of biotechnology for all countries, and given that the biotechnological wealth of the developing countries resides in their vast possessions, there is no escaping the fact that 'biotechnology is reducing the overall demand for primary products from the developing world'.

To help redress the situation, particularly in relation to the local labour sector, ILO has initiated a series of studies on forecasting the socio-economic and employment effects of specific biotechnologies in developing countries (Okerere, 1988; Chipata & Mhango, 1988) within the framework of its Technology and Employment Programme.

One of the best-known biotechnological approaches to import substitution is to be found in the introduction of ethanol fuels. Brazil, in providing the world – albeit the developing world – with important insights into the tapping of the natural bioresources available, has the world's largest alcohol fuels programme which dates back to 1902 (Rosillo-Calle & Heaford, 1987).

Other examples are to be found in the national bio-energy programmes initiated by China and India to meet rural needs of electrification, with a subsequent, yet significant, reduction in expenditure of valuable foreign exchange. Again, many developing countries (Brazil, Kenya, Thailand, Senegal) are turning to the production and use of biofertilizers *vis-à-vis* the costly chemical ones.

Another biotechnological setback to the economies of the developing countries is to be found in overproduction in the food and dairy industries. In the mid-1970s, several newspapers carried news-items on the 'lakes of milk and mountains of butter' that were being disposed of, on humanitarian grounds and in deference to transportation costs, to Eastern Europe rather than to the poorest of the developing countries. Storage and subsequent economic considerations were primarily at the basis of such considerations.

The recurrence of a milk and butter surplus is evoked with the soon-to-be-licensed use of bovine and porcine somatotropins (BST and PST) which could lead to overproduction in the agricultural sector and which would be sold off on the markets of the developing world to alleviate poverty and food shortages.

Inexpensive plant tissue culture can also affect exports from the developing world in relation to the bioindustrial production of flavours, fragrances and medicinal principles. Important examples are vanilla (from *Vanilla planifolia*) and strawberry (*Fragaria* sp.) flavours, the fragrances jasmine (*Jasminum*) and spearmint (*Chrysanthemum*), and the medicinal principles vincristine (*Catharanthus*) against cancer and digitoxin (*Digitalis lanata*) for heart disorders.

Biotechnology is also going to have a negative effect on South–South development. The economic trade problems, already being witnessed in the North–South in the import–export dialogue (see the chapter by Junne) are beginning to surface in the Southern Hemisphere. Such problems will arise as Indonesia and India, the traditional importers of rice from the traditional exporters Pakistan and Thailand, become self-sufficient or exporters themselves (Van den Doel & Junne, 1986). Similarly, the export of oil palm from Malaysia to Africa could adversely affect traditional exporting countries in that continent.

Swaminathan (1989) in stressing the valve of possessing 'biological diversity not in gene banks, but also in the farmers' fields', has drawn attention to the need of 'food security' and 'ecology security' in the developing countries. Research on the development and use of transgenic plants and animals should be carried out in the South since it is the teeming populations of the developing countries that need the benefits of biotechnology in attaining self-sufficiency, self-sustenance, and self-development in national and regional food and health programmes.

International viewpoints

Da Silva & Sasson (1989) made an attempt to answer the following question. Are biotechnologies going to be a panacea for the various problems the developing countries are facing, or will they merely add to the disparities which exist between these countries and the industrialized technologically advanced world?

In response it was noted that

> there is not one single strategy which may be adopted with a view to using biotechnologies and reaping their benefits. For instance, India, a country with a large budget for research, and numerous research scientists and technicians, cannot adopt the same strategy as a small African country of the Sahel–Sudan zone. Nevertheless, even the poorest and least technologically and scientifically advanced countries can reap some benefits from the progress of biotechnologies and participate in the 'biotechnological revolution', thanks to international and regional co-operation networks. This participation does not necessarily concern the most advanced basic research but should rather aim at adapting local capabilities to development problems. It would be a sad mistake to try and imitate the policies adopted by industrialized and technologically advanced countries.

It was also noted that

> biotechnologies unquestionably generate benefits or gains; they are also bringers of certain dangers or potential threats. Their impact on societies will be considerable and there will be winners and losers. But no country, and no community, is condemned to become a loser. This will depend on which strategies are adopted by the community, country, or group of countries in order to reap their legitimate portion of the benefits of biotechnologies. In view of the fact that the 'biotechnological

Table 9.4. *The changing definition and scope of biotechnology*

Definition	Date	Source
All the lines of work by which products are produced from raw materials with the aid of living organisms	1919	Ereky, K., *Biotechnologie der Fleisch-, Fett- und Milcherszeugung im landwirtschaftlischen GroBbetriebe*
Investigation and industrial application of the living functions of microscopic life forms (yeast, fermentation organisms)	1929	*Die Grosse Brockhaus*, 2, 747
All aspects of the exploitation and control of biological systems and their activities	1962	Gaden, E., Editorial to *Biotechnology and Bioengineering*
Term used to describe a magazine reporting scientific and financial developments in the field of genetics	1979	Hutton, E.F., *Trademark No. 110658*
The application of scientific and engineering principles to the processing of materials by biological agents to provide goods and services	1982	Bull, Holt & Lilly, *Biotechnology: International Trends and Perspectives, OECD*
The integration of natural sciences and engineering sciences in order to achieve the application of organisms, cells, parts, thereof and molecular analogues for products and services	1989	European Federation of Biotechnology, *Biotec Europe*, 6, 96

Adapted from Bud, 1989.

revolution' will affect even the most isolated societies, it is neither wise nor justified not to participate in this revolution and not to fight for gaining some of its expected advantages.

It is in this context that regional and international cooperation, through networks, will minimize the disparities between and amongst countries and groups of countries. Biotechnology is continuously changing (Table 9.4) and if it has to act as a spur for development in all sectors of human life – health, economics, culture, ethics, law, society, food, industry, environment – it has to serve as the vehicle for interaction and cooperation at the national, regional and international scales. As impact-making discoveries and processes become gradually an integral part of our daily life, issues of legal, bioethical, cultural, environmental and socio-economic import will come to the fore and, in turn will be replaced by others in the course of time. Table 9.5 documents a large number of networks that bear testimony to an impressive array of international viewpoints on the far-reaching in-fluences of biotechnology in today's world.

References

Ackermann, W. (1981). Cultural values and social choices of technology. *Int. Soc. Sci. J.*, **33**, 447–65.

Agarwal, A. (1982). Try asking the women first. *Sci. Today*, **16**, 6–7.

Ammerman, A.J. & Cavali-Sforza, L.L. (1984). *The Neolithic Transition and the Genetics of Populations in Europe*. Princeton University Press, USA.

Arbridge, M.V. & Pitcher, W.H. (1989). Industrial enzymology: a look towards the future. *Trends Biotechnol.*, **7**, 330–5.

Barnett, A., Pyle, L. & Subramanian, S.K. (1978). *Biogas Technology in the Third World: A Multidisciplinary Review*. IDRC, Ottawa.

Barr, T.N. (1981. The world food situation and global grain prospects. *Science, Wash.*, **214**, 1087–95.

Barton, J. (1989). Legal trends and agricultural biotechnology: effects on developing countries. *Trends Biotechnol.*, **7**, 264–8.

Bartos, R. (1981). What every marketer should know about women. In *Perspectives in Consumer Behaviour*, H.J. Kassarijan & T.S. Robertson (eds). Scott Foresman Company, Illinois.

Board on Science and Technology for International Development (BOSTID) report (1981). *Food, fuel and fertilizer from organic wastes*. National Academy Press, Washington, DC.

Brown, N. (1987). Biogas systems in development. *Approp. Techn.*, **14**, 5–7.

Bud, R. (1989). Janus-faced biotechnology: an historical perspective. *Trends Biotechnol.*, **7**, 230–3.

Cantley, M.N. (1987). Democracy and biotechnology – popular attitudes, information, trust and the public interest. *Swiss Biotech.*, **5**, 5–15.

Colombo, U. & Mazzonis, D. (1984). The use of personal computers in Italian biogas plants. In *Blending of New and Traditional Technologies: Case-Studies*, A. Bhalla, D. James & Y. Stevens (eds), pp. 79–81. Tycooly Intl. Publ. Ltd., Dublin, Ireland.

Chipata, C. & Mhango, M.W. (1988). *Biotechnology and Labour Absorption in Malawi Agriculture*. ILO Working Paper 2-22/WP 191, p. 44.

Da Silva, E.J. (1980). Biogas: Fuel for the future? *Ambio*, **9**, 2–9.

Da Silva, E.J. (1982). The socio-cultural impact of applied microbiology and biotechnology for development. In *Proceedings of the EEC/UNESCO/CNRS*

Colloquium 'L'impact des Biotechnologies sur le Tiers Monde', Paris, pp. 195–209.

Da Silva, E.J., Burgers, A. & Olembo, R. (1976). Health and wealth form waste. *Impact Sci. Soc.*, **26**, 323–32.

Da Silva, E.J., Olembo, R. & Burgers, A. (1978). Integrated microbial technology: springboard for economic progress. *Impact Sci. Soc.*, **28**, 159–82.

Da Silva, E.J. & Sasson, A. (1989). Promises and Biotechnologies in the developing countries. *MIRCEN J. Appl. Microbiol. Biotechnol.*, **5**, 115–18.

Dixon, B. (1976). *Invisible Allies – Microbes and Man's Future*. Temple Smith Press, London.

Feldman, S. & McCarthy, F.E. (1982). Conditions influencing rural and town women's participation, *Int. J. Intercult. Relat.*, **6**, 420–40.

Fleising, U. (1989). Risk and culture in biotechnology. *Trends Biotechnol.*, **7**, 52–7.

Halvorson, H.O., Pramer, D. & Rogul, M. (eds) (1985). *Engineered Organisms in the Environment: Scientific Issues*, p. 239. Washington, DC, USA, American Society for Microbiology.

Heitowit, E. & Epstein, J. (1977). *Science Technology and Society: A Guide to the Field*. US Department of Commerce, Springfield, VA.

Hendricks, M. (1988). Germ wars, *Sci. News*, **134**, 292–395.

Hodgson, J. & Bormann, E. (1988). F-art: the expression of biological art, *Trends Biotechnol.*, **6**(3).

Horsnell, M. (1989). Ten Years Jail for the Agent so Secret He Never Existed, *The Times (London)*, Saturday, March 4, p. 3.

Hoskins, M.W. (1975). Vietnamese women: their roles and options. In *Being female: reproduction, power and change*, D. Raphael (ed.). Mouton Press, The Hague.

International Labour Organization (1985). Blending of New Technologies with traditional values, Document ACT/1/1985/111, Geneva, Switzerland.

Kayton, I. (1983). Does copyright law apply to genetically-engineered cells? *Trends Biotechnol.*, **1**(1), 2–3.

Khan, B. (1977). Towards a rural utopia. *Invent. Intell.*, **12**, 21–6.

Killick-Kendrick, R. (1988). Parasitological clerihews. *Job Trends*, **2**, 1–4.

Kirpal, P. (1976). Culture, society and economics for a new world. *Cultures*, **3**, 86.

Kolata, G. (1982). Food affect human behaviour. *Science, Wash.*, **218**, 1209–10.

Maxwell, T.J. (1956). Agricultural ceremonies of the Central Andes during four hundred years of Spanish Contact, *Ethnohistory*, **3**, 46–71.

McKenzie, M., Cambrosio, A. & Keating, P. (1988). The commercial application of a scientific discovery: The case of the hybridoma technique. *Research Pol.*, **17**, 155–70.

Mittermeier, R.A. (1989). In *Other Comment*: Americans Predict the '90s. *International Herald Tribune*, no. 33, 233, December 30–31, 1989–January 1, 1990, p. 4.

Morphet, C. (1981). STS in further education. *New Scient.*, pp. 78–9.

Newcombe, K. (1981a). Use of energies: two examples from Papua New Guinea. *Nature Res.*, **17**, 4–10.

Newcombe, K. (1981b). Technology assessment and policy: examples from Papua New Guinea. *Int. Soc. Sci. J.*, **33**, 495–507.

Nicholson, G.E. (1960). Chicha maize types and chicha manufacture in Peru. *Econ. Bot.*, **14**, 290–9.

Organization for Economic Co-operation and Development (OECD) (1989). *Biotechnology-Economic and Wider Impacts*, p. 111. OECD, Paris.

Okerere, G.U. (1988). *Biotechnology to Combat Malnutrition in Nigeria*. ILO Working Paper, 2–22/WP 190.

Pacey, A. (1983). *The Culture of Technology*. Blackwell Ltd., Oxford.

Renfrew, C. (1989). The origins of Indo-European languages. *Sci. Am.*, October, pp. 82–90.

Rosillo-Calle, F. & Heaford, J. (1987). Alternatives to petroleum fuels for transport: Brazilian experience. *Sci. Pub. Pol.*, **14**, 337–45.

Saithananthan, M.A. (1975). *Biogas – Achievement and Challenges.* Association of Voluntary Agencies and Rural Development, New Delhi, India.

Salisbury, R.F. (1962). *From Stone to Steel*. Melbourne University Press, Melbourne, Australia.

Sasson, A. (1987). Impacts of Biotechnologies on Developing Countries. *Dev. South–South Co-op.*, **3**, 95–108.

Scheidegger, A. (1989). Biocosmetics in Japan: New wrinkles beneath the make-up. *Trends Biotechnol.*, **7**, 138–47.

Shaller, V.D. (1979). A socio-cultural assessment of the Lorena stove and its diffusion in highland Guatemala. In *Lorena Owner-built Stoves.* USA, Volunteers in Asia.

Sills, D.L. (1968). *Int. Encycl. Soc. Sci.*, **3**, 527–45.

Siwatibau, S. (1981). *Rural energy in Fiji: A survey of domestic rural energy use and potential*. Ottawa.

Soler, J. (1973). The seimiotics of food in the Bible. *Ann. Econ., Soc., Civilis.*, **28**, 943–55.

Steinkraus, K.H. (1978). Contributions of Asian fermented foods to international food science and technology. In *State of the Art of Applied Microbiology in Relation to its Significance to Developing Countries*, W. Stanton & E.J. Da Silva (eds.). University of Malaya Press, Kuala Lumpur.

Steinkraus, K.H. (1983). *Handbook of Indigenous Fermented Foods*. Marcel Dekker Inc., New York.

Stoler, A. (1977). Class structure and female autonomy in rural Java. *Signs*, **3**, 74–89.

Subramanian, S.K. (1977). *Biogas Systems in Asia*. Statesmen Press, New Delhi, India.

Surghiyska, S., Ilieva, I. & Koghuharova, N. (1983). *Mikrobialenprotein v Kombiniranite Furaghi*. Zemizdat, Sofia.

Swaminathan, M. (1989). Biotechnology and a Better Common Present. Summary of Regional Seminar on Public Policy, *Implications for Asian Agriculture*, 6–8 March, New Delhi: Asian and Pacific Development Centre, Kuala Lumpur, p. 16.

Tinker, J. (1981). *Survival as an obstacle to the use of new energy technologies in developing countries.* Prepared for Conference on non-Technical Obstacles to the Use of New Energy Technologies in Developing Countries. Bellagio, Italy, May.

Townsley, P.M. (1974). Chocolate aroma from plant cells. *J. Inst. Can. Sci. Technol. Aliment.*, **6**(1).

Van den Doel, K. & Junne, G. (1986). Product substitution through biotechnology; impact on the Third World. *Trends Biotechnol.*, **4**, 88–90.

Williams, R. (1981). *Keywords – A Vocabulary of Culture and Society.* William Collins Sons & Co. Ltd., Glasgow.

Wilson, W.G. & Sullivan, G.D. (1984). Biotechnology: Implications for Agriculture, *Econ. Impact*, **48**, 43–9.

Wood, B. (1983). Festivals, food and fermentation, *New Scient.*, 22/29 December, pp. 918–23.

Yoxen, E. (1986). The social impact of biotechnology. *Trends Biotechnol.*, **4**, 86–8.

Table 9.5. *Scope and range of network activities in biotechnology*

	Network title	Common name	Sponsor	Remarks
1.	Advanced Cassava Research Network	ACRN	Centro Internacional de Agricultura Tropical (CIAT)	Development of new technologies to research constraints of cassava Linkage of International Agricultural Research Centres (IARCs) with biotech labs in US and Europe
2.	Agricultural Libraries Network	AGLINET	FAO	Improvement of inter-library document provision in the agricultural sector
3.	African Biosciences Network	ABN	UNESCO, UNDP, International Council of Scientific Unions (ICSU)	High-level workshops, courses, seminars, country and regional collaborative research projects
4.	African NGOs Environment Network	ANEN	Coalition of African NGOs	Strengthening of regional capacities and technical competence on environment and developmental issues
5.	Africa 2000 Network	Africa 2000	Govt of Canada, UNDP	Participation in recovery and long-term development with emphasis, amongst other topics, on environment and biotechnologies
6.	African Network for Microbiology		UNESCO	Regional programme for the promotion of basic research in the field of microbiology
7.	African Research Network	ARNAB	Association for the Advancement of Agricultural Sciences in Africa; International Livestock Centre for Africa	Promotion of research and training in the utilization of agricultural residues and by-product production

#	Name	Acronym	Organization	Description
8.	African Plant Biotechnology Network	APBnet	Institut Agronomique et Veterinaire Hassan II, Morocco	Conduction of regional network for activities in plant tissue culture in North Africa and the Middle East
			Tissue Culture for Crops Project, Colorado State University	Conduction of international meetings
9.	Anaplasmosis Babesiois Network	ANB	Washington State University; US AID office of Agriculture	Dissemination of specialized research bibliography on anaplasmosis and babesiois
10.	Arab Biosciences Network	ArBN	UNESCO, ICSU	High-level workshops, courses and seminars
11.	Amélioration de la productivité agricole en milieu	APAMA	Agence de Co-opération Culturelle et Technique (ACCT)	Environmental influences in improvement of crop productivity
12.	ASEAN Food Data Network		ASEAN Subcommittee on Protein: Food Habit Research and Development	Co-ordinator: Thailand; Member countries: Brunei, Indonesia, Malaysia, the Philippines, Singapore. Focus on improvement of the quality and availability of food composition data in ASEAN countries
13.	Asian Biosciences Network	ANBS	UNESCO, ICSU	High-level workshops, courses and seminars
14.	Asian Rice Farming Systems Network	Formerly known as the Asian Cropping Systems Network	International Rice Research Institute	Conduction of research projects and dissemination of technological information on rice-farming systems of Asia
15.	Asian and Pacific Information Network on Medicinal and Aromatic	APINMAP	UNESCO	Provision and inventorization of information on Medicinal and Aromatic plants in Asia and the Pacific
16.	Biodiversity Network News		The Nature Conservancy	Newsletter focussing on biological and conservation data and applications

Table 9.5. (*cont.*)

	Network title	Common name	Sponsor	Remarks
17.	Biosafety Information Network and Advisory Service	BINAS	UNIDO/WHO/UNEP/FAO Working Group on Biosafety	Development of a Code of Conduct for the release of GMOs into the environment
18.	Biotechnology Education Informational Network	BEIN	International Clearing house for the Advancement of Science Teaching (ICAST), University of Maryland, UNESCO	Biotechnology education *via* electronic networking
19.	BIONET	BIONET	Health and Welfare Canada Agriculture Canada	Development of biotechnologies for human and animal care
20.	BIOQUAL	BIOQUAL	Environment Canada	Network of companies, universities, research organizations, and governmental agencies in developing biotechnologies for environmental protection
21.	Biomass Users Network	BUN	International not-for-profit organization created by developing countries at 1983 conference	Focuses on South–South co-operation in addressing rural economic and natural resources degradation problems
22.	Biotechnological Information Exchange System	BITES	UNDP/Europe, UNESCO International Centre for Chemical Studies, Yugoslavia	Provision of information systems in biotechnology in collaboration with MIRCEN network
23.	CIMMYT – North/Latin American RFLP[a] Network	RFLP Network	University of Minnesota; Centro Internacional de Mejoramiento de Maiz y Trigo (CIMMYT)	Research on genetic basis of qualitative traits in maize Development of strategies for use of molecular makers in breeding programmes

24.	Co-operative Cereals Research Network	CCRN	International Crops Research Institute for the Semi-Arid Tropics (ICRISAT)	Coordination and conduction of all international sorghum trials and nurseries in liaison with the ICRISAT Cereals Programme
25.	Crystallography of Biological Macromolecules		European Science Foundation (ESF)	Conduction of practical workshops on the crystallography of macromolecules (nucleic acids – DNA, RNA), proteins and polysaccharides
26.	Diffusion	Diffusion	African Centre for Technology Studies (ACTS)	Newsletter of the IFIAS[b] International Diffusion of Biotechnology Programme
27.	DNA profiling network		ICI Cellmark Diagnostics Unit	Global Network of DNA fingerprinting laboratories to coordinate and evaluate accuracy of different DNA fingerprinting techniques
28.	East and and Southern Africa Root Crops Research Network	ESARRN	Coalition of Heads of natural root crops programmes of East and Southern Africa	Strengthen national agricultural research programmes with International Institute of Tropical Agriculture (IITA) Facilitate transfer and exchange of technologies on improved varieties, post-harvest root crops and agronomic practices
29.	EUROBIOMED Network	EUROBIOMED	Science Park, Maastricht, Netherlands	Facilitate transfer of technology between EEC research centres and companies involved in biotechnology and medicine
30.	European Science Foundation Network on Development Biology	ESF Biology Network	European Science Foundation	Promotion and strengthening of European development biology research activities with emphasis on molecular and cellular regulation of the early development of animals

Table 9.5. (*cont.*)

	Network title	Common name	Sponsor	Remarks
31.	European Systems of Co-operative Research Networks in Agriculture	ESCORENA	FAO Regional Office for Europe	Conduction of activities related to agriculture in European and developing countries Covers also European Networks on Olive Production and of oil Cultivators
32.	Feminist International Network of Resistance to Reproductive and Genetic Engineering		Coalition of Women Activists on politics of genetic engineering and reproduction	Monitors ethical issues in international programmes e.g. embryo transfers *in vitro* fertilization (IVF), germ-line gene therapy, gamete intra-fallopian transfer (GIFT), pre-implantation screening, etc.
33.	Food Network		Natural Food Administration, Sweden	Computerized Electronic Network on Food Composition and Role in Nutrition
34.	Foodfirst Information and Action Network	FIAN		Activities against abuse of human rights in fields of hunger and malnutrition
35.	Gen-Ethisches-Netzwerk	GEN Network	Coalition of the Green movement, non-governmental organizations and individuals. Based in Germany	Activities on the ethical issues of biotechnology Opposed to wide varieties of gene technology ranging from veterinarians and consumer groups to deliberate release of recombinant organisms
36.	Genetic engineering of rice network	GER Network	Rockefeller Foundation	Development of biotech techniques for rice improvement Conduction of research on rice in rice-dependent countries

No.	Name	Abbreviation	Affiliation	Functions
37.	Health Action	HAI	Coalition of nongovernmental organizations and individuals	Monitors biotechnological activities, amongst others, of malpractices such as drug dumping, drug marketing, etc. Supports WHO Action Programme on Essential Drugs and Vaccines Played active role in 1982 drug policy revolution in Bangladesh
38.	Information Network on Third World Food Sciences		United Nations University (UNU)	Dissemination of research information pertaining to food sciences in developing countries
39.	Insect–Plant Interactions		European Science Foundation (ESF)	Conduction of research on 1) chemoreception in herbivorous insects, 2) variability in feeding behaviour and 3) variability of plant chemistry
40.	International Agricultural Research Centres – IARCs Network	IARCs, CGIAR Network	Consultative Group for International Agricultural Research	Adapt tools of modern biotechnology to the needs of Third World agriculture Perform specialized functions in field of food policy research Undertake genetic resource conservation Strengthen national agricultural research in developing countries

CIAT: Centro Internacional de Agricultura Tropical, Colombia
CIMMYT: Centro Internacional de Mejoramiento de maiz y Trigo, Mexico
CIP: Centro Internacional de la Papa, Peru
IBPGR: International Board for Plant Genetic Resources, Italy
ICARDA: International Center for Agricultural Research in the Dry Areas, Syria
ICRISAT: International Crops Research Institute for the Semi-Arid Tropics, India
IFPRI: International Food Policy Research Institute, USA

Table 9.5. (*cont.*)

	Network title	Common name	Sponsor	Remarks
	IITA: International Institute of Tropical Agriculture, Nigeria			
	ILCA: International Livestock Center for Africa, Ethiopia			
	ILRAD: International Laboratory for Research on Animal Diseases, Kenya			
	IRRI: International Rice Research Institute, Philippines			
	ISNAR: International Service for National Agricultural Research, Netherlands			
	WARDA: West Africa Rice Development Association Monrovia, Liberia			
41.	International Baby Food Action Network	IBFAN	Coalition of Voluntary Groups and Individuals	Helped develop WHO International Code of Marketing of Breast-milk substitutes Elimination of irresponsible marketing artificial infant foods
42.	International Biosciences Network	IBN	UNESCO, ICSU	Joint UNESCO/ICSU programme in which Steering Committee oversees work of 4 regional networks (see ABN, ANBS, ArBN and LANBIO *in this table*)
43.	International Network of Cell and Molecular Biology		UNESCO	Network of 40 institutions engaged in molecular and cell biology research

No.	Name	Acronym	Body	Description
44.	International Biosphere Preservation of Ecosystems Worldwide		UNESCO Programme (MAB)	Biogeographical network in which biosphere reserves allow conservation of genetic resources
45.	International Cassava Transformation Programme Network	ICTP Network	Washington State University (St Louis); ORSTOM; Rockefeller Foundation	Transformation and regeneration of cassava Insertion of genes for viral resistance
46.	International Plant Biotechnology Network	IPBNet	Tissue Culture for Crops Project; Colorado State University; US AID Office of Agriculture	Conduction of international plant biotechnology meetings, short and long term training courses
47.	International Network of Biotechnology		Working Group on 'Technology, Growth and Employment' of the Group of 7 countries	Established at Versailles Summit, 1984 Promotion of projects in photosynthesis, food technology, biosciences, marine biotechnology
48.	International Network of Feed Information Centres	INFIC	International Feedstuffs Institute	Synchronize composition of foodstuffs and animal feeds
49.	International Network of Food Data Systems	INFOODS	Massachusetts Institute of Technology (USA) UNU; US National Cancer Institute	Collection and dissemination of specialized information on food data systems and on data concerning the nutrients composition of foods, beverages and their ingredients to meet *needs* of governmental agencies, nutrition scientists, consumer groups, etc.
50.	International Network of Investigation of Banana and Plantain	INIBAP	Union of Banana Exporting Countries	Development of new varieties resistant to pathogens such as *Mycosphaerella fijiensis* var. *difformis* that causes sigatoka Oversees banana and plantain germplasm collections

Table 9.5. (*cont.*)

	Network title	Common name	Sponsor	Remarks
51.	International Network of Legume Inoculation Trials	INLIT/NifTAL	USAID UNFSCO MIRCEN network	Determination of inoculation response with best available *rhizobium* strains Monitoring of infectiveness of strains through use of antisera probes
52.	International Network for the Promotion of Genetics	InProGen	Third World Academy of Sciences	Promotion of regional co-operation Support for genetic research for food and health in Third World
53.	International Network of Research Centres in Cognitive Science, Artificial Intelligence and Neuroscience		IUPsyS	Special project of the International Union of Psychological Sciences
54.	International Network of Research Centres in Behavioural Ecology/Environmental Psychology		IUPsyS	Special project of the International Union of Psychological Sciences
55.	Islamic Network of Genetic Engineering and Biotechnology		Islamic Conference	Promotion of research and training in biotechnology and genetic engineering
56.	International Network of Social Impacts of Biotechnology		Department of Urban and Environmental Policy, Tufts University, USA	Concerned with socio-ethical issues in biotechnology

No.	Name	Abbreviation / Notes	Organization	Description
57.	International Network on Soil Fertility and Sustainable Rice Farming	INSURF Formerly known as International Network on Soil Fertility and Fertilizer Evaluation for Rice (INSFER)	International Rice Research Institute	Research activities in soil fertility, rice farming systems, chemical and biofertilizer use
58.	Latin American Biosciences Network	LANBIO	UNESCO, ICSU	High level workshops, courses, seminars
59.	Molecular Neurobiology of Mental Illness		European Science Foundation (ESF)	Coordination of the mapping of the human genome in determining susceptibility to schizophrenia
60.	Network of Aquaculture Centres in Asia	NACA	UACDP/FAO Regional Aquaculture Development Program	Started in 1979. Designed to upgrade aquaculture technology. Publicity centres: Bangladesh, China, Hong Kong, N. Korea, Nepal, Uganda, Pakistan, Sri Lanka and Vietnam.
61.	Network for Bacterial Diseases		University of British Columbia, National Research Council of Canada	Examination of pathogenic bacterial species on diseases of humans, cattle, salmon and plants
62.	Network on Biotechnology and Insect Pest Management		Queen's University, National Research Council of Canada	Improvement in the insecticidal capacities of baculoviruses Production of genetically-engineered insecticides
63.	Networking in Brucellosis Research	Brucellosis Network	UNU	Research in vaccination and diagnosis of brucellosis in Latin America through network of Latin American institutions

Table 9.5. (*cont.*)

	Network title	Common name	Sponsor	Remarks
64.	Neural Mechanisms of Learning and Memory		European Science Foundation (ESF)	Survey of 90 laboratories and research groups in Europe concerning neural influences in learning and memory
65.	Neuroimmunomodulation		European Science Foundation (ESF)	Organization of workshops on integrative aspects of neuro-immune communication, molecular aspects of neuroimmunomodulation, and cytokine actions of neural tissues
66.	Microbial Information Network	MINE	EC Biotechnology Programme	A European network of microbial culture collection databanks
67.	Microbial Strain Data Network	MSDN	Commission of the European Communities, UNEP, UNESCO, US National Science Foundation, US National Institute of Dental Research, Committee on Data for Science and Technology (CODATA)	Development of directory for locating microbial strains with specific properties Provision of storage and access to other databases of importance to biotechnology and microbiology Provision of an electronic communication service
68.	Natural Products Research Network for Eastern and Central Africa	NAPRECA	UNESCO	Promotion of research and training programmes in natural products research
69.	Network of Community-Oriented Educational Institutions for Health Sciences	Network		Co-operative venture of medical schools throughout the world

No.	Name	Acronym	Organization	Activities
70.	Network of Microbial Resources Centres (see Appendix 9.1)	MIRCEN	UNESCO in co-operation with professional NGOs in microbiology and biotechnology and UN System	High-level symposia, conferences on 'Global Impacts of Applied Microbiology', courses, study grants, etc.
71.	Networking for Technology Information on Agro-Industries	TIAI	ESCAP/UNIDO	Provision of reference information on agro-industries, agro-processing
72.	Population Ecology and Genetics		European Science Foundation (ESF)	Focus on ecology of genetic systems, genetics and ecology of metapopulations, genetics and demography of populations
73.	Pesticide Action Network	PAN	Coalition of citizen groups and individuals	Campaign against unethical use of marketing practices with toxic pesticides and herbicides
74.	Pest Management Research and Development Network	PESTNET	Established in 1985 by Senegal, Kenya, Somalia, Zambia, and Rwanda with USAID and UNDP	Conduction of intensive training in participating countries to combat losses of economic significance due to crop and livestock pests
75.	Plant Resources of Southeast Network	PROSEA	PROSEA Foundation Wageningen Agricultural University, Netherlands	Regional Co-operation in Southeast Asia in plant resources
76.	Quaternary Mammalian Faunas		European Science Foundation (ESF)	Research workshops on influence of climate on faunal evolution, tempo and mode of evolution in the Quaternary, and dynamics of faunal evolution
77.	Red Latinoamericana de Botanica		Jesse Smith Noyes Foundation; Rockefeller Foundation	Conduction of high-level postgraduate courses, symposia, workshops in plant biology; provision of fellowships

Table 9.5. (cont.)

	Network title	Common name	Sponsor	Remarks
78.	Regional Network of Plant Biotechnology Laboratories	CATBIO	FAO Regional Office in the Caribbean and Latin America	Regional Co-operation on plant biotechnology in the Caribbean and Latin America
79.	Réseau des organizations non-gouvernementales européenes sur des questions agro-alimentaires et le développement	RONGEAD	Coalition of non-governmental organizations	Promotion of research knowledge on technologies in the agrofood sector
80.	Réseau Thématiques et recherche agricole au Maghreb	TRAM	ACCT	Research in the Maghreb countries on date palm, arid plant biology, camel husbandry, pasture and forest resources
81.	Réseau international de traitement de données de sols	RITDS	ACCT	Soil analysis and enhancement of soil fertility
82.	Seeds Action Network	SAN	Rural Advancement Fund International; International Coalition for Development Action	Action 'watchdog' on the 'seeds' issue world-wide Patenting of plant varieties Conservation of genetic diversity Concerned with concentration of the genetic supply industry

No.	Network	Organization	Activities
83.	Soil–Water Processes	European Science Foundation (ESF)	Research workshops on degradation of chemicals in soil, soil-rhizosphere interactions, flux measurements in the vadose zone
84.	Southeast Asian Network for the Microbiology and Chemistry of Natural Products	Government of Japan, UNESCO	Symposia, fellowships, workshops, courses, conferences on regional basis
85.	Third World Network	Established in Malaysia	Monitors biotechnological activities, amongst others, of transnational and international governmental and non-governmental organizations
86.	Tropical Land Clearing for Sustainable Agriculture Network	International Board for Soil Research and Management	Promotion of appropriate technologies for land clearing for sustainable agriculture; Rehabilitation of poor farmers and degraded lands; Soil management and cropping systems
87.	Wastes Network WASTENET	UNESCO Regional Office for Science and Technology for Southeast Asia, UNDP, Institute of Advanced Studies, Malaysia	Management and Utilization of Industrial and Agricultural Wastes
88.	Worldwide Rhizobial Ecology Network WREN	University of Hawaii; National Science Foundation (US); US AID Office of Agriculture	Research on production and performance of introduced *Rhizobium* in tropical farming systems

Table 9.5. (*cont.*)

Network title	Common name	Sponsor	Remarks
89. Womens' Global Network on Reproduction Rights		Coalition of Women Activists	Safe and effective contraception Freedom from sterilization *abuse* Ethical issues and reproduction
90. UNDP/UNESCO/ UNIDO Regional network in Latin America and the Caribbean		UNDP, UNESCO, UNIDO, participating govts of Argentina, Brazil, Bolivia, Colombia, Costa Rica, Chile, Cuba, Ecuador, Guatemala, Mexico, Peru, Uruguay and Venezuela	High-level training courses, fellowships, symposia, inter-country research projects and seminars

[a]Restriction Fragment Length Polymorphism
[b]International Federation for Institutes of Advanced Study

Appendix 9.1. *The UNESCO world network microbiological resources centres (MIRCEN)*

Speciality	Location	Place and country
Rhizobium	Department of Soil Science and Botany, University of Nairobi	Nairobi, Kenya
Rhizobium	Instituto de Pesquisas Agronomicas	Porto Alegre, Brazil
Fermentation, food and waste recycling	Thailand Institute of Scientific and Technological Research	Bangkok, Thailand
Biotechnology	Ain Shams University	Cairo, Egypt
Biotechnology	Central American Research Institute for Industry	Guatemala City, Guatemala
Rhizobium	NifTAL Project, College of Tropical Agriculture, University of Hawaii	Hawaii, USA
Biotechnology	Karolinska Institutet	Stockholm, Sweden
World Data Centre	Life Science Research Information Section, RIKEN	Saitama, Japan
Rhizobium	Centre National de Recherches Agronomiques	Bambey, Senegal
Biotechnology	Planta Piloto de Procesos Industriales Microbiologicos (PROIMI)	Tucuman, Argentina
Rhizobium	Cell Culture and Nitrogen-Fixation Laboratory	Maryland, USA
Fermentation technology	Institute of Biotechnology, University of Osaka	Osaka, Japan
Biotechnology	Biological Laboratory, University of Kent and Canterbury	Kent, UK
Mycology	C.A.B. International, International Mycological Institute	Surrey, UK
Biotechnology and agriculture	University of Waterloo	Waterloo, Ontario, Canada

Appendix 9.1. (*cont.*)

Speciality	Location	Place and country
Marine biotechnology	Department of Microbiology, University of Maryland	Maryland, USA
Biotechnology	Centre de Transfert[a]	Toulouse, France
Biotechnology	University of Queensland	Brisbane, Australia
Microbial technology	Institute of Microbiology, Academia Sinica	Beijing, China
Microbial biotechnology	Caribbean Industrial, Research Institute	Tunapuna, Trinidad and Tobago
Culture collections and patents	German Collection of Microorganisms and Cell Culture	Braunschweig, Germany
Culture collections	Department of Microbiology, University of Horticulture and Food Industry	Budapest, Hungary
Biotechnology Information Exchange System (BITES)	International Centre for Chemical Stuides	Ljubljana, Yugoslavia
Bioconversion Technology	Department of Biology Chinese University of Hong Kong	Shatiu, Hong Kong

[a]Participants: Université de Technologie (Compiègne), INSBANA (Dijon), Centre d'Immunologie INSERM-CNRS (Marseille), Laboratoire de Chimie bactérienne CNRS (Marseille), INRA (Montpellier), Institut Pasteur (Paris), INSA (Toulouse).

10

Joint microbial biotechnological ventures in developing countries: social promises and economic considerations

HORST W. DOELLE AND E. GUMBIRA-SA'ID

Introduction

Biotechnology today is a frontier area offering a new technological basis for the provision of solutions to the problems of all countries, whether they consider themselves to be in the developed or still in the developing stage. The ever-increasing urbanization, pollution in the air (the so-called greenhouse effect) and of waterways, de-forestation and other ecological destructions call for drastic action and industrial re-thinking (Doelle, 1989b).

Biotechnology, in particular the applications of microbiology, can make a significant and immediate contribution to the socio-cultural, economic and technological aspects to the development of the developing countries with applications in both developing and developed countries. There is no doubt that the application of microbiology, and thus the newly developing areas in biotechnology, are regarded as the most recent major technological (DaSilva, 1986) or socio-economical revolution (Doelle, 1989a) following the industrial and green revolutions.

In the fields of energy, animal feed, food production, aquaculture and pharmacy, the production of biofuels and chemical feedstocks, Single Cell Protein and microbial biomass products together with the development of nitrogen-fixing bacteria, bioinsecticides, biocatalysts and other living systems are considered important indices of already fast-growing biotechnologies (OECD, 1979).

As commercial biotechnology grows in the USA, for example, state governments are perceiving this new industry as an important component of economic development (Blakeley & Nishikawa, 1989). This survey further indicated that the individual states operate almost as separate nations in pursuing their own economic strategies to improve their own economic position. It is therefore of interest to realize that biotechnological efforts are directed depending upon the existing industrial, educational and resources base as well as the philosophy concerning the role of state government. In crafting economic development they are developing commercial, innovative bio-industries, using state resources to facilitate the process. In contrast to Japan and United Kingdom, however, the US Government itself is not as yet prepared to play a highly active role in direct support of biotechnology commercialization, leaving the development to the competitiveness between biotechnology companies (Oxender & Fox, 1989) and between states (Blakeley & Nishikawa, 1989). It is, however, very encouraging to see that joint ventures are developing strongly in developed countries on economic considerations which may or may not show social promises.

Present situation in developing countries
In order to be able to develop joint ventures in developing countries, one has to know the situation in those countries. Despite their social and political diversity, the less-developed countries of Asia share a number of common characteristics.

(1)   They are densely populated: while these countries represent only approximately 13% of the land area, their combined population in 1980 accounted for 50% of the world population;
(2)   they are characterized by low-income economies;
(3)   they have predominantly agrarian economies in which 50–75% of the population depends on agriculture;
(4)   agriculture generates 33–50% of the domestic products;
(5)   their level of literacy as well as technical capability is very low;
(6)   with some exceptions, the economies of these countries are growing at a much slower rate compared to the world economy (Islam & Kaya, 1985).

These common characteristics, many of which are also common to those in the African, Latin American, South American and Pacific Region, stress the importance of applied microbiology in these developing countries particularly in the fields as diverse as agriculture, public health, water supply and sanitation, environmental conservation and resource management, as well as the production of food, fodder and energy (DaSilva, 1986). In many of the developing countries, indigenous fermented foods are very important, but they are socio-culturally bound (Doelle, Olguin & Prasertsan, 1987), especially in rural household and village community traditions.

Many of the developing countries base their diets on low-protein staple foodstuffs such as cassava, plantains, yams and taro. These roots, tubers and fruits are rich in starch and suitable for microbial protein enrichment. Cassava particularly is an abundant root crop in tropical areas with possibilities of being transformed into a high protein feed (Carrizales & Jaffe, 1986; Sukara & Doelle, 1989*a*).

The disposal of sewage wastes is one of the priority needs of less developed countries. Only about one-third of the population of the developing countries has adequate sanitation services. Due to a constant rural-to-urban migration, large low-cost urban areas have developed where less than 50% of the urban poor have suitable waste disposal facilities (Biswas, Sanchez & Warnock, 1985).

Technology transfer

Technology transfer could form a basis for joint ventures and has been, and still is, a rather popular slogan in both developed and developing countries. Under this term, one understands that a biotechnology process developed in one country is transferred as a whole to another country, which then will modify the process according to its own condition (Doelle, 1982). It is not surprising that in most cases governments of developing countries have had frustrating experience of failure in assimilating such imported technology (Islam & Kaya, 1985), because

(1) the developed countries have a biotechnology-oriented programme which is more toward industrial, business and economical advances and contain little or no socio-economical or socio-ecological orientation (Doelle, 1989*a*; Bunders, Sarink & DeBruin, 1989);

(2) most of the technologies are high-capital technologies in contrast to low-capital technology requirement (DaSilva, 1981);

(3) the lack of sufficient national scientific and technological infrastructure to assimilate any imported technology;

(4) the lack of units capable of advanced research and development in biotechnology whether at universities, national laboratories or industries (Zilinskas, 1988; Chakravarty, 1988);

(5) legal trends preventing the Third World researcher from access to important information sources (Barton, 1989);

(6) the relatively high expenditure required for the transfer with the existence of a lack of hard currency (Lamptey & Moo-Young, 1987; Stolp & Bunders, 1989).

In some developing countries a new technology has been diffused to farmers on a large scale without adequate investigations of its effect on the socio-cultural, economic and physical-biological environment. A large-scale adoption may adversely affect the social and cultural system or have unwanted economic effects such as input shortages or surplus product (Wilson, Philipp & Shauer, 1986).

The vast majority of the populations of less-developed countries live in villages and the importance of rural technology development in those countries cannot be overstated (DeBruin & DeBoer, 1986). In the context of technological development it is generally considered imperative to see that such developments are of benefit to their lives as well. It certainly is recognized that rural life is affected by many factors, such as political and social institutions, rural economic structures, communication, education and technology. An initial step, therefore, is that building up the rural technology capacity is one of the tools for development. Another step is the recognition that the technology employed or developed should suit locally available resources and skills and be in harmony with local cultures (DeBruin & DeBoer, 1986; Doelle et al., 1987). A gradual development of technology with little dependence on imported technology, skills and managerial support would be a good starting objective. Developed countries should act more in an advisory capacity rather than selling their technology at all cost.

A joint microbial biotechnological venture in developing countries has therefore to come from within the country. The motivation for any joint venture development effort must be based on either satisfying basic needs, such as food, shelter and human life conditions or improving standards by providing more material or intellectual goods, by improving working conditions or by increasing public participation in decision-making and discussions of long range social planning (Doelle, 1982; Ul Haq, 1988). Future development depends on proper planning and optimal utilization of local talents and resources. Judicious selection is required to determine those biotechnological processes that will provide net-positive socio-economic returns from the investment (Lamptey & Moo-Young, 1987).

Microbial biotechnological joint ventures

Infrastructure

There is no doubt that any joint venture with promises of social advances and economic benefits will have to be rural-based in most of the developing countries. Small farmers (2.5–5 acres or 1–2 ha) account for 19% of the cultivated holdings and 12% of the cultivated area in South East Asia with larger farmers making up the rest (Stolp & Bunders, 1989). It is therefore necessary that frequent communication occurs among the farming community, the government representatives and the biotechnologist (Bunders *et al.*, 1989) to discuss and establish joint ventures between all three and convince industry and entrepreneurs to join in the venture towards social advance and national economic benefits. It has to be the aim of these bodies, in particular the researcher, to convince society that biotechnology is not a threat to family or to morality (Fleising, 1989), but can bring enormous social and economic advances for the individual as well as the country. The local or national cooperative joint venture group should then seek cooperation or joint venture groups from the developed countries to help achieve their goal(s). An example of such development has recently been reported from Hungary (Dibner & Burrill, 1988) and Taiwan (Chang & Tein, 1989). A further advantage for such a development is the fact that developing countries are not bound by tradition in regard to research in the natural sciences as are the developed countries (Scheidegger, 1988). A suggested scheme for joint microbial biotechnological ventures for developing countries is outlined in Fig. 10.1.

In order to instigate rural technology in a particular developing country, national authorities have to set their priorities in regard to social, economical and ecological development. Such an authority (e.g. a Board of Development) should consist of farmers, farmer cooperatives, researchers, the appropriate government agencies and financiers (e.g. bankers, industry, entrepreneurs etc.). In co-opting consultants in biotechnology, a national programme should be established. This communication link between farmers, government and researchers is vital for any success in the establishment of rural industries (Bunders, 1988; Bunders *et al.*, 1989). Major consideration should be given to the raw material available, the local market demand to increase living standards, e.g. feed, food, fertilizer, fuel and energy. The savings which could be obtained through less imports could be significant to the national or communal economies, whereas the replacement of wood for energy could stop de-forestation, which is of considerable ecological importance.

Since every joint microbial biotechnological venture system depends on the availability of raw materials, such as agricultural products or agricultural, human and animal wastes, a Centre of Development may well be confronted additionally with the tasks of improving farm practices (Arua & Obidiegwu, 1988), soil denitrification (Biswas *et al.*, 1985), rhizobacterial plant growth promotion (Lambert & Joos, 1989; Kloepper, Lifshitz & Zablotowicz, 1989), plant disease-resistant breeding (Katz & Steck, 1989) and future planning and development of arable agriculture (Gotsch & Rieder, 1989) with the goal of new microbial biotechnological joint ventures for the improvement of society and economics. Such new development must always take care that it does

240   *H.W. Doelle and E. Gumbira-Sa'id*

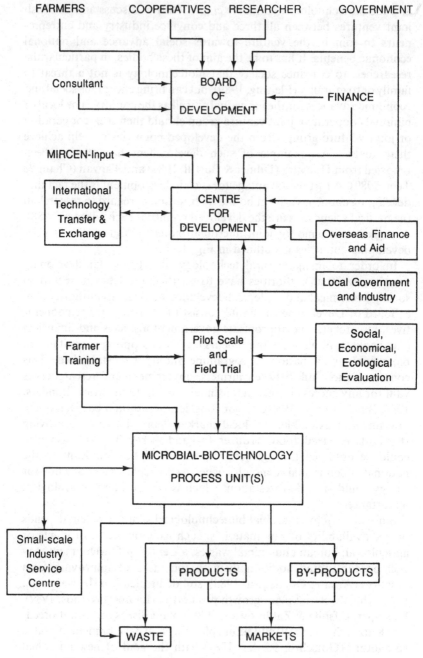

Fig. 10.1. Suggested scheme for joint microbial biotechnological ventures for developing countries.

not affect local traditional culture, although it should and can improve the conditions of the society within its traditional culture (Doelle *et al.*, 1987).

The suggested Board of Development would give its final instructions or recommendations to a Centre of Development. This centre should be a Biotechnology Research Centre devoted entirely to the development of rural biotechnology with the largest component centred on microbial technology. Basic and fundamental research should be contracted to university or other research institutes. Each developing nation should have one such Centre, which not only has a close link to the Regional MIRCEN-Network (DaSilva, 1989), but is also responsible for the development of an appropriate biotechnological system using, if possible, established technologies as a whole or in part for adaptation to the local conditions (Doelle, 1982). Such a Centre should attract overseas finance through aid programmes in addition to the input from the national government, local governments and financiers. One of the major goals should be an Exchange Programme, whereby local researchers are sent to specific laboratories (e.g. laboratories registered by the International Organization for Biochemical Engineering and Biotechnology, IOBB) and vice versa to learn techniques vital for the rural process development. The Centre should also be linked with teaching institutions such as universities and technical colleges in their own country and overseas, giving young researchers the chance of applied science and technology research projects, which in turn secures the manpower required. This certainly does not mean the creation of a so-called 'Science Park' (Russell & Moss, 1989), which could easily be a development in the wrong direction and fail in their infancy as so many have done in the developed countries. It is of great importance to ensure that the social and economic capacity of rural communities is increased through the application of science and technology (DeBruin & DeBoer, 1986), which is best served through a Centre of Development.

Any system developed in the proposed Centre of Development, whether it is a simple or integrated rural technology system, must go through pilot-scale and field trials. It is the trial outside protective laboratory conditions that has to withstand rigorous social, economical and ecological evaluation. No process should be acceptable that produces a product but simultaneously causes severe pollution of air, soil or waterways. These field trials must be able to exhibit to the farmer and the national and local governments the social, economical and ecological benefits and promises for the farmer, the region and the nation as a whole.

The successful field trials make the process available to the farming community. Depending upon the quantity of raw material available and the local market demand, the Biotechnology Process Unit has to be tailored to these requirements. It is certain that different locations may require different capacity sizes. It would therefore be of great benefit if each Biotechnology Process Unit has an Industry Service Centre (DeBruin & DeBoer, 1986) attached for direct and indirect support activities. Whereas it is the goal of the Process Unit to deliver the products from the available raw materials, the Service Centre could have a number of aims, such as:

(1) to help in the construction of the Process Unit;
(2) to maintain continuously the equipment etc. required in the Process Unit;
(3) to train the farmers in the area;
(4) to carry out extension work, which may lead to new methods of production, equipment and cost-saving repairs.

The Industry Service Centres should have a close communication link with the Centre of Development. The establishment of both the Process Unit and the Industry Service Centre brings to the local society and local government further employment and education, social advances and promises otherwise not available. This type of decentralization of services may stem the tide of migration from the rural to the urbanized cities.

Existing joint venture problems
Joint ventures in developing countries are at present few and relatively restricted to certain aspects of development. Most of these joint ventures suffer under so-called 'economic' or 'management' problems. Many of these projects never leave the research establishments and thus do not find their way into the applied field (Zilinskas, 1988). Other projects mainly financed by International Agencies to address possible food shortages (Brady, 1982; Swaminathan, 1982; Plucknett & Smith, 1982) led to improved crop production through the creation of higher yielding strains (e.g. HYV rice). These crops, however, required, in turn, a significantly higher quantity of fertilizer that the low-income farmer could not afford (Slesser *et al.*, unpublished report to UNESCO). A third type of example is the Indian Biogas Programme (Lichtman, 1987; Lalita & Sharada, 1988; Sen & Bhattacharya, 1989), where an imbalance between 'technology-focussed' and 'people-focussed' development assistance made success doubtful.

The problems faced in each of the above joint venture cases are created by a lack of socio-economic thinking together with a project analysis orientated more towards a single purpose rather than being multi-purpose projects with several outputs, the economist has to attempt to establish the best mix of resource disposal, resource use and resource recycling involving the translation of technical contraints into economic values (BOSTID, 1981). Output values must be realistic within a given socio-economic environment and alternative technologies must be available to satisfy changeable socio-economic development.

The concept of agribusiness (Schroder & Pollard, 1989) and agribusiness research (Hanf & Wright, 1989) should be linked with the newly established International Centre for Genetic Engineering and Biotechnology (UNIDO), the 18 different MIRCEN Regional Networks set up by UNESCO (Kamel, 1986; DaSilva, 1986) and other existing worldwide genetic resources (Bower, 1989), to establish expertise ranging from the crop availability and improvement to the actual dissemination through the MIRCENs to the Region, individual State or National Development Boards. Such close cooperation, interchange and training unfortunately does not yet exist owing to conflicts of interest (Zimmerman, 1983) and a distinct lack of coordination. International Agencies dealing with food production and crop improvement should seek tighter cooperation with those in the process technology and genetic resource development.

It is time that International and National Agencies start to realize that joint ventures in biotechnologies in developing countries can only be successful and socio-economically useful if multi-purpose projects in the form of integrated systems are considered (Little & Muir, 1987; Buttel, Kenney & Kloppenburg, 1985; Doelle, 1989*a*) and analysed by the economist. These multi-purpose projects start from the natural resource crop improvement to its use and conversion to multiple products. Such projects should be carried through to supply the rural and urban population with food, feed, fertilizer and fuel.

It is the aim of the authors to develop such a multi-purpose project for possible joint ventures for a socio-economic rural environment in the South East Asian and Pacific Region.

Multi-purpose project plan for joint microbiology biotechnology venture

In order to become self-efficient, which means supply and demand for domestic consumption is guaranteed (Maamun & Sarasutha, 1987), each government must strive and direct all its efforts towards increasing numbers of production and maintaining or reducing its demand by diversification of the staple food. In South East Asia and the Pacific, rice, cassava (manihot or tapioca) and sago are the main staple food crops used by the population. Of the three crops, rice undoubtedly

Table 10.1. *Estimate of area covered with good quality sago palm stands*

Country	Wild (ha)	Cultivated (ha)	Total (%)
Indonesia	1 000 000	128 000	51.22
Papua New Guinea	1 000 000	20 000	46.36
Malaysia	—	33 000	1.50
Pacific Islands	—	10 000	0.46
Philippines	—	5 000	0.23
Thailand	—	5 000	0.23
TOTAL	2 000 000	201 000	100.00

From Flach (1983).

outstrips by far the other two crops, making the latter an inexpensive starch source for diversification. Of the two, sago palm cultivation shows great prospects as an inexpensive substrate for diversification.

There exist at present an estimated two million hectares of natural or wild stands of sago palm compared to only 200 000 ha of cultivated sago palm. The production capacity of the wild and naturally occurring sago palm is about 2–5 tonnes moisture-free starch per hectare compared with 10–25 tonnes depending on the intensity of cultivation. Table 10.1 exhibits the major countries with good quality sago palm (Flach, 1983). It becomes clear from this table that Indonesia and Papua New Guinea are the favoured climatic regions for sago palm. For an economic development of both countries, sago palm could thus be a very important crop. As sago palm has also been successfully cultivated in Malaysia, Thailand, Philippines and the Pacific Islands, it becomes a very important agricultural product in this region.

Agronomically, the sago palm is unique compared to other starch-based agricultural crops (Flach, 1983). The palm grows well in swampy areas, which can only be developed for other crops at high cost. It is perennial, very suitable for humid tropical lowlands and is already available in areas which are in urgent need of economic development.

The sago palm belongs to the *Lepidocaryoid* subfamily of the *Arecaceae* (Palmae) with the most economically important species in the genus *Metroxylon*. However, many more palms are capable of producing sago starch (Soerjono, 1980; Tan, 1980), such as *Arenga pinnata*, *Egeissoma utilis*, *E. insiguis* etc. A comparison of the composition of the

Table 10.2. *Composition of several kinds of sago starch*

Components	Peters (1957)	Wilbert (1976)	Brautlecht (1953)	Gumbira-Sa'id (1983)
Water (%)	27.0	63.51	12–18	11.81
Protein (%)	0.2	1.62	0.1–0.3	0.28
Fat (%)	—	—	0.1–0.3	0.36
Carbohydrate (%)	71.0	9.64	81–87	86.78
Fibre (%)	0.3	24.68	0.1–0.5	0.77

several kinds of sago starch (Ruddle *et al.*, 1978; Gumbira-Sa'id, 1983) are given in Table 10.2.

Since the consumer demand for sago starch is very low compared to its natural abundance, many suggestions have been made for using this starch. One of the proposals is outlined in Fig. 10.2 (Flach, 1983). It is now the function of the Board of Development to give the Centre for Development its National Priority with farmer and cooperative representatives leading the way for a socio-economic rural development.

It has often been argued that such development should be the result of close university–government–industry interaction, as these were responsible for the great expansion of biotechnology and biotechnology industries. However, the past has shown that industrial research contracts often perturb the academic principles of free and open exchange of information and in particular independent research (Hardy, 1985). Such frictions develop because the majority of academia prefers pure over applied or industrially oriented research. Although pure research is vital for biotechnological development, it does not perpetuate joint ventures and often restricts rather than fosters a socio-economic rural development. In order to overcome possible frictions, conflicts and controversy, all applied orientated research is better carried out in the suggested Centre of Development with the help of academia, industry and government, but outside the individual environments. The National Priorities must be dominated by the Board of Development and not by any partner.

The Board of Development has set its priorities to increase the supply of food, feed, fuel and fertilizer. The term 'food' is explained as plant productivity improvement including new varieties, cultivation, farming and crop harvesting; the term 'feed' asks for the supply of protein-enriched animal and aquaculture feed; the term 'fuel' makes provision

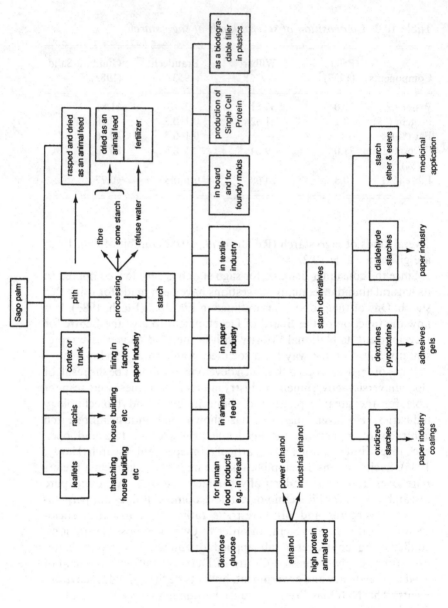

Fig. 10.2. The innumerable uses of the sago palm (Flach, 1983).

for energy supply and 'fertilizer' the replacement or part replacement of nitrogen fertilizer to avoid soil erosion and soil nutrient deficiency.

The proposed Centre of Development designed the integrated system outlined in Fig. 10.3 and subdivided its work into a number of areas of development in order to be able

(1) to seek help from International Agencies, e.g. Centre of Genetic Engineering and Biotechnology for plant cell cultivation and engineering etc.;
(2) to explore international technology transfer and exchange, e.g. in the field of food and fermentation process technology;
(3) to attract overseas finance and aid;
(4) to seek interest and participation from local government, industry, universities and research institutes in parts or the whole concept;

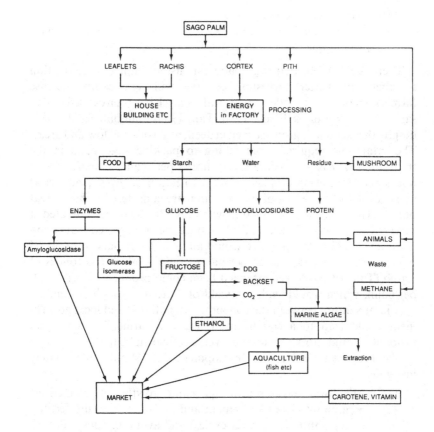

Fig. 10.3. Integrated system for the utilization of sago palm.

(5) to employ the local farming community in training and re-training.

Sago palm production

The National Guidelines of Indonesia for development mentions that the distribution aspect of income should be the first goal in the national development followed by economic growth (Nataatmadja, 1987). Serious efforts have already been made in this direction with the development of cooperative systems and so-called 'Nucleus Estate Smallholder' (NES) programmes. The main constraints related to the NES program have been recognized as:

(1) provision of land and land right;
(2) budget planning;
(3) recruitment of professional and skilled manpower;
(4) provision of plant material;
(5) infrastructure quality; and
(6) cooperation in cross sectoral and multi-disciplinary programme.

There is no doubt that sago palm expansion, improved cultivation together with better harvesting facilities will significantly increase farmers' income. Very little agricultural research has been carried out on sago palm (Stanton & Flach, 1980; Tan, 1983; Gumbira-Sa'id, 1983) despite the fact that it grows so well in deep, peat soils and lowland areas. The total time required from felling to packing sago palm in the traditional way is approximately 78 hours per plant compared to 32 hours per plant using processing mills. In South Sulawesi (Indonesia) alone a total of 61 981 ha of swampy area are considered to have great potential for sago palm production with only 3460 ha being cultivated at present (Maamun & Sarasutha, 1987). It has been suggested that clump densities of 593 palms per acre would allow a yearly harvest of 50–55 palms, which at 160 kg starch per palm would result in 6–9 tonnes of starch (Tan, 1983). A well-attended farm could produce 175 kg starch per palm, which would lead to a yield of 25 tonnes starch per ha.

A joint venture between the cooperatives, national and local government could lead to a significant increase in farmers' income and probably would attract local and overseas financial support.

The proposed Centre for Development thus should immediately instigate:

(1) agricultural research into sago palm growth and production;
(2) research into soil requirement and nutrition to secure fertility for replanting (8–10 year cycles) and avoid any possibility of soild erosion and de-forestation;

(3) research into harvesting methods, facilities and locations of processing mills; and

(4) extensive farmer training programme in the various local communities to demonstrate the greater benefits arising from more intensive cultivation and improved processing. Experienced local farmers should preferably be used in the teaching and demonstration courses.

A more intensive and greater expansion of sago palm cultivation would demand a significant increase in manpower and number of farmers. The increased income arising from the improved production would allow the cooperatives to purchase centralized processing mills, which in turn increases the time for the individual farmer to handle a greater number of sago palms. It may also prevent the accelerating demand for imported food which could have a detrimental effect on traditional culture and society (Doelle *et al.*, 1987; Townsend, 1982; Moranta, 1982; Ulijaszek, 1982) and the economics of the particular country.

Such a programme for increased food production should attract finance from International Agencies concerned with increased food production. At the same time the Centre for Development must form a link with the International Centre for Genetic Engineering and Biotechnology to learn and train staff to improve the quality of sago palm in general using the now available plant cell engineering techniques, such as cell fusion and disease resistant breeding.

Sago palm processing

Starch extraction After the removal of the cortex etc. from the pith, starch has to be extracted from the pith, which is probably one of the most laborious and labour intensive parts of the sago palm processing. Because of the difficulties in transportation of sago palm trunks, it must be the aim of the Centre for Development, in close cooperation with the local cooperatives and authorities, to develop small-scale extraction plants in the regions. It may be necessary to cut the trunks into 1–1.5 m lengths for transportation as is done in the sugarcane industry.

After the separation of the pith from the rest of the trunk, transportation becomes more convenient. The non-pith parts of the sago palm trunk form excellent building materials for local houses, a further reason for locating these processing plants more frequently throughout the regions.

Technology transfer experience can be gained from an information exchange with the small-scale processing plants in West Malaysia and

Sabah (Flach, 1983) and a joint venture for a Regional Technology Development should be explored.

The residue from the sago palm processing is a very strong pollutant consisting mainly of cellulosic fibrous material, which can either be used as an animal feed additive (Flach, 1983) or can form the basis for a mushroom industry, since the cultivation of edible fungi from lignocellulosic residues is well-known and represents the only current large-scale controlled application of microbial technology for the profitable conversion of waste lignocellulosic residues from agriculture and forestry (Wood, 1984; 1985; 1989; Wood & Smith, 1987).

The Centre for Development should instigate an immediate technology transfer to the pilot-scale and field trial section (see Fig. 10.1) which, together with farmer training and social, economical and ecological evaluation, would lead to an early cash-flow, attracting local investment and joint ventures.

A third application for the removal of the residue is the addition to a bio-gas plant, producing an additional source for energy required in the processing plant (see below).

The flexibility, simplicity and low-cost alternate re-usage of the residue not only removes a severe health hazard to the community but, more importantly, increases the self-efficiency of the processing plant using the cortex and/or bio-gas as energy source and increases the farmers' income through mushroom production.

Starch processing. The starch obtained from the sago palm processing unit can easily be transported to regional centres (e.g. Biotechnology Processing Unit) for further processing. A tremendous amount of research has been conducted over the past decades in the field of starch processing owing to the large and diverse starch-based agricultural crops available in the world. Although starch is a polymer of α-D-glucose, the qualities vary according to their amylose and amylopectin content ratio. The amylograph (Fig. 10.4; from Kainuma, 1977) shows that the amylose content of sago palm starch is comparable to that of corn starch (Ito, Arai & Hisazima, 1979).

The starch flour or meal can either be used by the local population for breadmaking or as staple food with the surplus being channelled into further processing, which all involve enzymatic plus microbiological conversion technologies. Most of these technologies are available through a technology transfer and exchange programme, although it should be realized that these technologies would have to be adapted to the sago palm starch conditions.

Enzyme production

The conversion of starch into marketing products requires the conversion of the polymer starch into glucose, which can only be done economically using two enzymes, α-amylase, to loosen the structure of the molecule and thus lower its viscosity, and amyloglucosidase for the final formation of glucose. Furthermore, the subsequent production of fructose from glucose, which may be desirable, is also an enzymatic process requiring the enzyme glucose isomerase.

Although all these enzymes are commercially available in the developed countries, it would be desirable for developing countries to produce their own enzymes to save foreign currency exchange (Aunstrup, 1979). This decision has to be made, of course, by the Board for Development and subsequently by the government of the particular country. It is anticipated that a joint venture between the Centre of

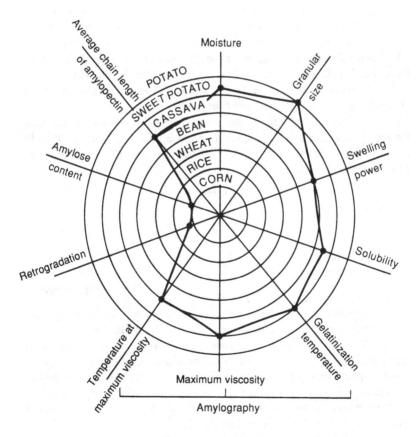

Fig. 10.4. Amylograph of sago starch (Kainuma, 1977).

Development and the corresponding industry could be of advantage for the establishment of an enzyme production industry in the developing country.

Amylase and amyloglucosidase production Amylase and amyloglucosidase are produced extracellularly by several genera of moulds and yeast (Pazur & Ando, 1959; Fogarty & Benson, 1983; McAllister, 1979). For commercial production, fungi belonging to the *Aspergillus* and *Rhizopus* genera are preferred (Saha & Zeikus, 1989; Fogarty & Benson, 1983; Kassim, 1983; Mitsue, Saha & Ueda, 1979). Of the two genera, *Aspergillus* is at present the favourite owing to the thermostability of its enzyme.

For the production of these enzymes, two methods are in general use (Aunstrup, 1979), a semi-solid and a submerged cultivation technique.

Amyloglucosidase plus Single Cell Protein production In order to improve the economics of enzyme production, a new technology was developed to allow a greater flexibility in the starch conversion process. The fungus *Rhizopus oligosporus* is well known in the Indonesian staple food diet for its use in the production of tempeh (Djien, 1982).

The fermentation pattern of the fungus (Sukara & Doelle, 1988) showed that with cassava tuber as substrate, a change in mineral addition shifts the product formation from high valued Single Cell Protein (Sukara & Doelle, 1989*a*) to glucose (Garg & Doelle, 1989*a,b*) or amyloglucosidase plus Single Cell Protein production (Sukara & Doelle, 1989*b*).

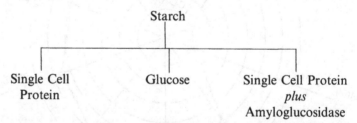

Such flexibility could be of great advantage to a local or regional community in regard to domestic market demand. It has been calculated from 100 litre pilot plant experiments that the one-step process of enzyme plus Single Cell Protein would produce from 65 tonnes cassava tubers approximately 3500 kg of Single Cell Protein and a highly productive enzyme in a quantity sufficient to convert approximately 39 000 tonnes of grain or cassava tuber into glucose. This process would require further exploration on large scale.

It is therefore up to the Centre for Development to obtain a technology transfer and exchange and explore the possibilities of using sago palm starch instead of cassava or corn. Preliminary research (Doelle & Gumbira-Sa'id, unpublished work) on solid-state fermentation of sago palm starch indicates that *Rhizopus oligosporus* grows very well on this starch substrate.

Single Cell Protein and, to a certain extent, the enzyme could be income-producing products on the local and export markets and an attractive proposition to joint ventures.

Glucose isomerase The enzyme glucose (or xylose) isomerase catalyses the reversible isomerization of glucose to fructose. The amount of enzyme used, principally in the USA, in 1983 was approximately 1750 tonnes of pure enzyme. Its commercial availability stresses again the importance to the Centre of Development for a decision as to an own production, joint venture with an existing overseas enzyme producing company or simple importation. Such a decision depends entirely on the demand for fructose syrup in the country or surrounding region.

Production of fructose

The conversion of glucose syrup to fructose was first developed and introduced in the USA in the 1970s, when the price of corn dropped to an alarmingly low level and society started to demand a lower-calorie sweetener. The process involves running glucose syrup through a column containing immobilized glucose isomerase so establishing approximate equilibrium concentrations of glucose and fructose. This process has also been found to work successfully with sago starch (Ito *et al.*, 1979) with a yield of 52% glucose, 42% fructose and 6% oligosaccharides.

Fructose production is a very successful commercial enterprise in the USA and the Centre of Development should seek a joint venture with one of the experienced companies to set up a fructose production plant.

Production of ethanol

Ethanol is gaining an ever-increasing importance as a fuel additive or even conventional non-renewable fuel replacement. Ethanol is able to reduce significantly the oil import into developing countries or can replace the present fuel allowing the government to save large import costs or increasing the export market of their own oil, both of which will contribute significantly towards a strengthening of foreign currency exchange.

It has frequently been argued that the energy balance from a starch-to-ethanol conversion is zero (Ham, de Loor & Flach, 1983), unless the normal fuel can be replaced. The only starch-based crop that possesses such an additional energy source is the sago palm. The Department of Minerals and Energy in Papua New Guinea considers sago palm to be the most potentially useful natural resource for the reduction or even replacement of petroleum imports into the country (Holmes & Newcombe, 1980; Newcombe & Holmes, 1982; Newcombe, Holmes & Paivoke, 1980; Flach, 1983). In addition, owing to its growing pattern, sago can be harvested throughout the year without any harmful effects on the present ecological pattern or disruption of the traditional life pattern.

The Government of Papua New Guinea chose the Sepik area to establish an ethanol industry because of the availability of sago palm in the wild and land suitable for further sago palm cultivation. It has been estimated that ethanol production could reach 0.56 l/kg of dry starch, which is probably a theoretical estimation since the US ethanol industry claims only an average of 0.35–0.37 l/kg corn starch (Lawford, 1986; Millichip & Doelle, 1989) using yeast technology. Higher yields, however, have been obtained from sago using *Zymomonas* technology (Rhee *et al.*, 1984; Kim *et al.*, 1988).

For ethanol production from starchy materials two technologies are now available: the traditional *Saccharomyces cerevisiae* yeast fermentation and a newly developed bacterial *Zymomonas* technology (Doelle & Doelle, 1989; Doelle & Wells, 1989; Millichip & Doelle, 1989; Doelle, Millichip & Doelle, 1989).

This particular product formation should attract significant joint venture capital as its technology has been proven viable in developed countries. The Centre for Development must make certain of its applicability to sago. The solid residual material from the process can be used as animal feed supplement as is the case with corn and milo in the USA (Distillers Dried Grain) and the thin stillage can be partly recycled or concentrated to a syrup then added to the solid residue to give an enriched animal feed.

Microalgae production

The application of modern biotechnology to the problem of efficient exploitation of algal resources (macroalgae and microalgae) presents developing countries with opportunities to expand existing and develop new markets. The potential of marine algae is unlimited (Singleton & Kramer, 1988; Borowitzka & Borowitzka, 1988). The cultivation of microalgae is becoming important not only for food and feed production, but also for chemicals and a 'clean environment' (Shelef & Soeder, 1980; Shelef *et al.*, 1980). The potential of microalgae includes production of Single Cell Protein, polyunsaturated fatty acids, essential fatty acids, glycerol, pigments, therapeutic agents, antibiotics, vitamins, energy, oxygen, hydrogen, fish feed etc. Although designs for large-scale algal cultures are well advanced, the processing of algae to obtain special products is still in its infancy. Only a few species, namely *Spirulina*, *Dunaliella*, *Chlorella* and *Porphyridium* have so far been cultivated on a large scale (Chen & Chi, 1981; Richmond, 1986; 1988; Vonshak, 1988).

Since most algae are photosynthetic autotrophs, they can use carbon dioxide as their sole carbon source and are able to take their nutrient requirement from wastes of all kinds (Taiganides, 1979; Taiganides, Chou & Lee, 1979) and carry out natural oxygenation of water systems. Both carbon dioxide and nutrients are by-products and thus wastes of ethanol production plants. This is a very important aspect as carbon dioxide from ethanol plants could contribute to the greenhouse effect through its release into the atmosphere (Doelle, 1989*b*).

An algal waste treatment process can therefore be converted into a production plant for high-quality protein (Becker & Venkataraman, 1980; Durand-Chastel, 1980; Richmond, 1988; Becker, 1988) and in the case of blue-green algae (Cyanobacteria) can be made into a biofertilizer production unit to provide nitrogen for rice paddies (Roger & Kulasooriya, 1980; Fontes *et al.*, 1982; Venkataraman *et al.*, 1980; 1982; Zimmerman, 1987; DePauw & Persoone, 1988). The production of special products would be a logical expansion of this technology in the future (Trevan & Mak, 1988; Borowitzka, 1988). Algae are also excellent feed supplements for the important and ever-increasing aquaculture (fish production).

Developing countries, in particular the proposed Centres for Development, should endeavour to form partnerships with industrialized countries to speed up the development in marine biotechnology (Singleton & Kramer, 1988). The impact of farming marine algae on a nation's economy and the individual farmer's or cooperative's income can be analogous to the cultivation of some crops in conventional agriculture.

Waste treatment and methane production

Any further by-product or residual waste of the above described multi-product process scheme should not be allowed to burden or pollute the natural environment. Waste recycling must be developed into a science if it is to survive the onslaught of modern, scientific agricultural production operations (Taiganides, 1979). The disposal of wastes must be done in such a way and at such a rate that nature will assimilate the wastes and recycle them into resources.

It has been demonstrated earlier how such recycling can be effective and contribute new income resources, e.g. algae or protein, or help in the conservation of natural resources, e.g. water recycling.

However, every industry requires a source of energy input but although the sago palm is able to produce such an energy source through its trunk or cortex, it may not be enough to sustain a multi-product process system.

An additional energy production system is required to avoid deforestation, reuse of the ethanol produced or energy importation. The gas methane is such an additional energy source and can be readily produced from any type of agricultural, human or animal waste. Since methane is a contributor to the greenhouse effect, about 10–20 times more potent than the same volume of carbon dioxide, and thus an environment polluter, care should be taken in its production and usage.

There is no doubt that bio-gas production systems have their origin in India, which therefore has already some experience with a number of joint venture systems. The model for recycling nutrients in crop, animal and bio-gas system (Mehla et al., 1986) gives an example of such considerations. However, problems have arisen in joint ventures for bio-gas development that should be avoidable and therefore must be carefully evaluated (Sen & Bhattacharya, 1989; Lichtman, 1987; Lahita & Sharada, 1988; Singh, 1988).

In this respect it is of great interest to follow the new development in the People's Republic of China of a non-waste technology and production (Zhong-Xian & Yi, 1986) together with their success in the use of digesters to produce bio-gas for energy and to conserve plant nutrients for field fertilization in the rural areas (Shian et al., 1979).

It is of further interest to recognize the aim of some molecular biologists to apply the modern tools of genetics and molecular biology (Konisky, 1989) to expand the application of the methanogens as a source of pharmaceuticals, vitamins etc., besides the production of methane.

The technology for bio-gas production is available and should be instigated by the Centre for Development as to its applicability to the wastes of the sago palm multi-product industry.

Conclusions

It has to be realized by all concerned that without an active and progressive farmer or rural household participation there will be little chance for a joint biotechnology venture in the developing countries. The existing gross imbalance between 'technology-focussed' and 'people-focussed' development assistance from international, national and other developed countries' agencies makes joint biotechnology ventures in developing countries difficult and very prone to failure. It is encouraging to see the start in the establishment of a farming systems research and development approach (Wilson *et al.*, 1986), resource management for bioproduction systems (Shah, Kutz & Bender, 1986) and rural development models (Lassey & Lovrich, 1985).

In order to help developing countries to become self-efficient and create better living standards for the low-income-earning farmer, joint biotechnology ventures into waste treatment and utilization are not the sole answer, although even their success is coming into doubt despite the fact that they are regarded as 'economical' by the developed countries owing to the cheaper resource material.

We have to change our approach and economic evaluation system. It is true that the biggest problems in the economic analysis of a biotechnology industry concerns how to define both the costs and benefits to the society. The reason for this problem lies with the economist, who at present is able to evaluate an industry *defined* by products but has great difficulties with an industry which is a *means* of production (Hacking, 1986).

In renewable-resource industries, the main resource will always be an agricultural product or the wastes of a product. A balance has to be found between its use as staple food and its use in bioprocessing. Never should it be allowed that these basic requirements for society compete with each other. This in itself requires a significant change in our attitudes towards bioprocessing and the economics for joint biotechnology ventures. First we have to succeed in obtaining better and more disease-resistant crops affordable to each farmer. In parallel we have to achieve an expansion and improvement in cultivation techniques making certain that soil fertility and replenishment is guaranteed. The surplus obtained, as a result from above achievements, or lower-quality grade, caused through adverse climatic conditions, will lead towards increased bioprocessing into products using microbial technology, which are of benefit to the rural community and society at large.

This review hopefully will have demonstrated that a well-planned, renewable-resource industry should have no or only minimal by-products or wastes to avoid ecological and environmental changes. This automatically highlights the need for a multi-product in place of the traditional single-product industry. The economist has to learn to assess not only the benefits to society but also a multi-product industry.

The review has further stressed on various occasions that such a multi-product industry can and should attract a number of individual joint biotechnology ventures. Each venture must realize, however, that their original resource is the same and the primary benefactor for the products is society. Individual marketing product processing therefore depends on the society or rural community demand rather than solely the individual profit margin. Some concept should be developed whereby the total profit from the multi-product bioprocessing is benefiting society as well as the participants in the joint biotechnological ventures.

Apart from the attitude of the economist and the prospective joint biotechnology venture participant, all developing agencies have to change their attitudes somewhat in order to be successful. How good is a higher yield crop if it requires larger amounts of fertilizer or has a lower disease resistance or is so expensive that a low-income farmer cannot afford the seeds? How good is a genetically engineered microorganism if it is a potential pathogen to mankind?

Professional societies and international agencies have to make a greater effort to understand the multidisciplinary nature of biotechnology and foster the development of a more 'people-focussed' assistance programmes to help bring a better balance between the 'technology-focussed' and 'people-focussed' programmes. We are still forging ahead in our individual disciplines and then try to merge the results, a concept which has not brought out the success in joint biotechnology ventures in developing countries as it did in some areas in the developed countries.

If this review catalyses a change in attitude within the national and, in particular, the international agencies whereby the present dominant emphasis towards technology and research is balanced with an increased rural development and training programme, we will have succeeded in our aim towards an increased future participation and development of joint biotechnology ventures in developing countries.

References

Arua, E.O. & Obidiegwu, N.W. (1988). Socio-economic assessment of the World Bank Rice Project in Eastern Nigeria. *Agricult. Systems*, **27**, 99–115.

Aunstrup, K. (1979). Production, isolation and economics of extracellular enzymes. *Appl. Biochem. Bioeng.*, **2**, 57–63.

Barton, J.H. (1989). Legal trends and agricultural biotechnology. *Trends Biotechnol.*, **7**, 264–8.

Becker, E.W. (1988). Microalgae for human and animal consumption. In *Microalgal Biotechnology*, M.A. Borowitzka & Borowitzka, L.J. (eds), pp. 222–49. Cambridge University Press.

Becker, E.W. & Venkataraman, L.V. (1980). Production and processing of algae in pilot plant scale experiences of the Indo-German project. In *Algae Biomass Production and Use*, G. Shelef & Soeder, C.J. (eds), pp. 35–50. Elsevier–North Holland, Amsterdam.

Biswas, N., Sanchez, O.A. & Warnock, R.G. (1985). Biological denitrification in on-site sewage disposal systems. *Int. J. Devel. Technol.*, 3, 173–83.

Blakeley, E.J. & Nishikawa, N. (1989). US states competitive strategies for the biotechnology industry. *Trends Biotechnol.*, 7, 222–6.

Borowitzka, M.A. (1988). Vitamins and fine chemicals from microalgae. In *Microalgal Biotechnology*, M.A. Borowitzka & Borowitzka, L.J. (eds), pp. 153–96. Cambridge University Press.

Borowitzka, M.A. & Borowitzka, L.J. (eds) (1988). *Microalgal Biotechnology*. Cambridge University Press.

BOSTID (1981). Non-technical considerations. In *Food, Fuel, and Fertilizer from Organic Wastes*, ed Advisory Committee on Technology Innovation, pp. 133–42, National Academy Press, Washington, DC.

Bower, D.J. (1989). Genetic resources worldwide. *Trends Biotechnol.*, 7, 111–16.

Brady, N.C. (1982). Chemistry and world food supplies. Science, *Wash.*, 218, 847–53.

Brautlecht, C.A. (1953). *Starch, its Sources, Production and Uses*. Reinhold Publ. Co., New York.

Bunders, J. (1988). Appropriate biotechnology for sustainable agriculture in developing countries. *Trends Biotechnol.*, 6, 173–80.

Bunders, J., Sarink, H. & DeBruin, J. (1989). Seeking a common language. *Trends Biotechnol.*, 7, S5–S7.

Buttel, F.H., Kenney, M. & Kloppenburg, J. (1985). From green revolution to biorevolution: Some observations on the changing technological bases of economic transformation in the Third World. *Econ. Dev. Cult. Change*, 34, 31–56.

Carrizales, V. & Jaffe, W. (1986). Solid state fermentation: An appropriate biotechnology for developing countries. *Interscienca*, 11, 9–14.

Chakravarty, S. (1988). Market mechanism versus balanced growth. *Development*, 1988, 34–6.

Chang, W.T.H. & Tein, W. (1989). Biotechnology in Taiwan: domestic markets and beyond. *Trends Biotechnol.* 7, 201–5.

Chen, B.J. & Chi, C.H. (1981). Process development and evaluation for algal glycerol production. *Biotech. Bioeng.*, 23, 1267–87.

DaSilva, E.J. (1981). The renaissance of biotechnology: man, microbe, biomass and industry. *Acta Biotechnol.*, 1, 207–46.

DaSilva, E.J. (1986). Applied microbiology and biotechnology: international co-operation between developed and developing countries. In *Perspectives in Biotechnology and Applied Microbiology*, D.I. Alani & M. Moo-Young, (eds), pp. 355–68, Elsevier Appl. Sci. Publ, London.

DaSilva, E.J. (1989) MIRCEN-Network in environmental, applied microbiological and biotechnolgical research. *MIRCEN-News*, 11, 1–3.

DeBruin, E.J. & DeBoer, S.J. (1986). A review of rural technology development through small-scale industry service centres. *Int. J. Devel. Technol.*, 4, 21–35.

DePauw, N. & Persoone, G. (1988). Microalgae for agriculture. In

Microalgal Biotechnology, M.A. Borowitzka & L.J. Borowitzka (eds), pp. 197–213. Cambridge University Press.

Dibner, M.D. & Burrill, G.S. (1988). Commercial biotechnology in Hungary: beyond small potatoes. *Trends Biotechnol.*, **6**, 180–4.

Djien, K.S. (1982). Indigenous fermented foods. *Econ. Microbiol.*, **7**, 15–37.

Doelle, H.W. (1982). Appropriate Biotechnology in Less Developed Countries. *Conserv. Recycl.* **5**, 75–7.

Doelle, H.W. (1989a). Socio-economic biotechnology development for developing countries. *MIRCEN J. Appl. Microbiol. Biotechnol.*, **5** (in press).

Doelle, H.W. (1989b). Microbial Technology and the Greenhouse Effect. *Proc. Austral.–New Zealand Solar Energy Conf., Brisbane*, pp. 69–1 – 69–6.

Doelle, H.W. & Doelle, M.B. (1989). *Zymomonas* ethanol technology: present state and development. *Aust. J. Biotechnol.*, **3**, 218–22.

Doelle, M.B., Millichip, R.J. & Doelle, H.W. (1989). Production of ethanol from corn using inoculum cascading of *Zymomonas mobilis*. *Process Biochem.*, **24**, 137–40.

Doelle, H.W., Olguin, E.J. & Prasertsan, P. (1987). Fermentation technology and its impact on culture and society. In *Microbial Technology in the Developing World*, E.J. DaSilva, Y.R. Dommergues, E.J. Nyns & C. Ratledge (eds), pp. 209–25. Oxford University Press.

Doelle, H.W. & Wells III, W. (1989). The Glucotech Process. In *Wheat is Unique*, Y. Pomeranz (ed.), *Amer. Assoc. Cereal Chem.*, **38**, 640–52.

Durand-Chastel, H. (1980). Production and use of *Spirulina* in Mexico. In *Algae Biomass Production and Use*, G. Shelef & C.J. Soeder (eds), pp. 51–80. Elsevier, North Holland.

Flach, M. (1983). The sago palm. *FAO Plant Production and Protection Paper*, **47**, 1–85.

Fleising, U. (1989). Risk and culture in biotechnology. *Trends Biotechnol.*, **7**, 52–7.

Fogarty, W.M. & Benson, C.P. (1983). Purification and properties of a thermophilic amyloglucosidase from *Aspergillus niger*. *Eur. J. Appl. Microbiol. Biotechnol.*, **18**, 271–8.

Fontes, A.G., Rivas, J., Guerrero, M.G. & Losada, M. (1982). Production of high quality biomass by nitrogen-fixing blue gree algae. In *Energy from Biomass*, A. Sturb, P. Chartier & G. Schleser (eds), pp. 265–9. Applied Sci. Publications, London.

Garg, S.K. & Doelle, H.W. (1989a). Optimization of physiological factors for direct saccharification of cassava starch to glucose by *Rhizopus oligosporus* 145F. *Biotech. Bioeng.*, **33**, 948–54.

Garg, S.K. & Doelle, H.W. (1989b). Cassava starch conversion to glucose by *Rhizopus oligosporus*. *MIRCEN J. Appl. Microbiol. Biotechnol.*, **5**, 297–305.

Gotsch, N. & Rieder, P. (1989). Future importance of biotechnology in arable farming. *Trends Biotechnol.*, **7**, 29–34.

Gumbira-Sa'id, E. (1983). Study of chemical and enzyme hydrolysis of starch of sagopalm (*Arenga pinnata*, MERR). M. Sc. thesis, Rijksuniversiteit Gent, Belgium.

Hacking, A.J. (1986). *Economic Aspects of Biotechnology*. Cambridge University Press.

Ham, J. van der, de Loor, J.P.B. & Flach, M. (1983). A comparison of crop for fluid energy in the tropics (as cited by Flach, 1983).

Hanf, C.H. & Wright, V. (1989). Agribusiness research. *Agri. Sci.*, **2**, 21–4.

Hardy, R.W.F. (1985). Roles of academe, government, and industry for agriculture in a changing world. In *Biotechnology in Plant Science Relevance to Agriculture in the 80's*, M. Zaitlin, P. Daynard & A. Hollander (eds), pp. 339–45. Academic Press Inc., San Diego.

Holmes, E.B. & Newcombe, K. (1980). Potential and proposed development of sago as a source of power alcohol in Papua New Guinea. In *Sago, the Equatorial Swamp as a Natural Resource*, W.R. Stanton & M. Flach (eds), pp. 164–74. Martinus Nijhoff Publications, The Hague.

Islam, N. & Kaya, Y. (1985). Technology assimilation in the less developed countries of Asia: lessons from Japan. *Int. J. Devel. Technol.*, **3**, 261–78.

Ito, T., Arai, Y. & Hisazima, S. (1979). Utilization of sago starch. *Jap. J. Trop. Agric.*, **23**, 48–56.

Kainuma, K. (1977). Present status of starch utilization in Japan. In *Sago '76'*, K. Tan (ed.), 1st Int. Sago Symp., Kuala Lumpur, pp. 224–9.

Kamel, W. (1986). The potential of biotechnology for the Gulf Region and the role of the International Centre for Genetic Engineering and Biotechnology. In *Perspectives in Biotechnology and Applied Microbiology*, D.I. Alani & M. Moo-Young (eds), pp. 369–77. Elsevier Appl. Sci. Publication, London.

Kassim, E.A. (1983). Effect of nutritional and physiological condition on the production of alpha amylase and glucoamylase by a selected strain *Aspergillus oryzae*. *Microbiologiya (USSR)*, **52**, 330–4.

Katz, J.S. & Steck, W. (1989). Canadian survey highlights plant biotechnology requirements for the 1990s. *Trends Biotechnol.*, **7**, 135–7.

Kim, C.H., Lee, G.M., Abidin, Z., Han, M.H. & Rhee, S.K. (1988). Immobilization of *Zymomonas mobilis* and amyloglucosidase for ethanol production from sago starch. *Enzyme Microb. Technol.*, **10**, 426–30.

Kloepper, J.W., Lifshitz, R. & Zablotowicz, R.M. (1989). Free-living bacterial inocula for enhancing crop productivity. *Trends Biotechnol.*, **7**, 39–44.

Konisky, J. (1989). Methanogens for biotechnology: application of genetics and molecular biology. *Trends Biotechnol.*, **7**, 88–91.

Lahita, K. & Sharada, D. (1988). Socio-economic and living conditions of farm labourers. *J. Rural Dev.*, **7**, 343–50.

Lambert, B. & Joos, H. (1989). Fundamental aspects of rhizobacterial plant growth promotion research. *Trends Biotechnol.*, **7**, 215–19.

Lamptey, J. & Moo-Young, M. (1987). Biotechnology: principles and options for developing countries. In *Microbial Technology in the*

Developing World, E.J. DaSilva, Y.R. Dommergues, E.J. Nyns & C. Ratledge (eds), pp. 335–75. Oxford University Press.

Lassey, W.R. & Lovrich Jr, N.P. (1985). A rural development model with potential international applications. *J. Rural Studies*, 1, 267–77.

Lawford, H.G. (1986). *Zymomonas, an alternative to yeast in alcohol production*. ALLTECH Sixth Ann. Nat. Course, ALLTECH Biotechnol. Centre, Nicholasville, Kentucky.

Lichtman, R. (1987). Toward the diffusion of rural energy technologies: Some lessons from the Indian Biogas Program. *World Dev.*, 15, 347–74.

Little, D. & Muir, J. (1987). Complete integrated systems. In *A Guide to Integrated Water Aquaculture*. Inst. Aquaculture Publ., Univ. Stirling, Scotland.

Maamun, Y. & Sarasutha, I.G.P. (1987). Prospect of palm sago in Indonesia: South Sulawesi Case Study. *Indonesian Agric. Res. Dev. J.*, 9, 52–6.

McAllister, R.V. (1979). Nutritive sweetners made from starch. *Adv. Carbohydrate Chem. Biochem.*, 36, 15–56.

Mehla, R.K., Srivastava, A., Manik, R.S. & Mudgal, V.D. (1986). A model for recycling of feed nutrients in a crop, animal and biogas system in India. *Agric. Systems*, 21, 159–69.

Millichip, R.J. & Doelle, H.W. (1989). Large scale ethanol production from milo (sorghum) using *Zymomonas mobilis*. *Process Biochem.*, 24, 141–5.

Mitsue, T., Saha, B.C. & Ueda, S. (1979). Glucoamylase of *Aspergillus oryzae* cultured on steamed rice. *J. Appl. Biochem.*, 1, 410–22.

Moranta, L. (1982). Sago dor food in a changing economy. In *Sago Research in Papua New Guinea*, Discussion Paper, Inst. Appl. Sci. and Economic Res., Boroko, Papua New Guinea.

Nataatmadja, H. (1987). Nucleus estate smallholder program: a bold social engineering experiment. *Indonesian Agric. Res. Dev. J.*, 9, 47–51.

Newcombe, K.J. & Holmes, E.B. (1982). *Implementation of alternative fuels in developing countries: alcohol fuels in Papua New Guinea*. Report no. 7/82, Energy Planning Unit, Department of Minerals and Energy, Konedoby, PNG, 18 pp. (as cited by Flach, 1983).

Newcombe, K.J., Holmes, E.B. & Paivoke, A. (1980). *Palm energy-alcohol fuel from the sago and nipa palms of Papua New Guinea. The development plans*. Report no. 6/80, Energy Planning Unit, Department of Minerals and Energy, Konedobu, PNG: 73 pp (as cited by Flach, 1983).

OECD (1979). *Facing the future – mastering the probable and managing the unpredictable*. Paris, France (as cited by DaSilva, 1981).

Oxender, D.L. & Fox, C.F. (1989). Barriers to US industrial biotechnology research consortia. *Trends Biotechnol.*, 7, 227–9.

Pazur, J.H. & Ando, T. (1959). The action of an amyloglucosidase of *Aspergillus niger* on starch and malto-oligosaccharides. *J. Biol. Chem.*, 234, 1966–70.

Peters, F.E. (1957). *Chemical composition of South Pacific Foods. An annotated bibliography*. South Pacific Commission Technical Paper 100, Naumea (as cited by Gumbira-Sa'id, 1983).

Plucknett, D.L. & Smith, N.J.H. (1982). Agricultural research and Third World food production. *Science, Wash.*, **217**, 215–20.

Rhee, S.K., Lee, G.M., Han, Y.T., Zainal, A., Han, M.H. & Lee, K.J. (1984). Ethanol production from cassava and sago starch using *Zymomonas mobilis*. *Biotech. Lett.*, **6**, 615–20.

Richmond, A.E. (1986). Microalgae culture. *CRC Crit. Rev. Biotechnol.*, **4**, 369–440.

Richmond, A.E. (1988). *Spirulina*. In *Microalgal Biotechnology*, M.A. Borowitzka & L.J. Borowitzka (eds), pp. 85–121. Cambridge University Press.

Roger, P.A. & Kulasooriya, S.A. (1980). *Blue-green Algae and Rice*. International Rice Research Institute, Manila.

Ruddle, K., John, D., Townsend, P.K. & Reed, J.D. (1978). *Palm Sago, a Tropical Starch from Marginal Lands*. The University Press of Hawaii, Honolulu.

Russell, M.G. & Moss, D.J. (1989). Science Parks and Economic Development. *Interdisc. Sci. Rev.*, **14**, 54–63.

Saha, B.C. & Zeikus, J.G. (1989). Microbial glucoamylase: biochemical and biotechnological features. *Starke/Starch*, **41**, 57–61.

Scheidegger, A. (1988). Biotechnology in Japan: a lesson in logistic? *Trends Biotechnol.*, **6**, 7–15; 47–53.

Schroder, B. & Pollard, V. (1989). The concept of Agribusiness. *Agric. Sci.*, **2**, 13–17.

Sen, D. & Bhattacharya, B. (1989). Managing Rural Energy Technologies: Some lessons from Gopanpalla Tanda. *J. Rural Dev.*, **8**, 117–24.

Shah, S.A., Kutz, L.J. & Bender, D.A. (1986). Optimal energy and resource management in bio-production systems. *Agric. Systems*, **20**, 161–74.

Shelef, G., Azof, Y., Moraine, R. & Oron, G. (1980). Algal mass production as an integral part of a wastewater treatment and reclamation. In *Algae Biomass Production and Use*, G. Shelef & C.J. Soeder (eds), pp. 163–89. Elsevier–North Holland, Amsterdam.

Shelef, G. & Soeder, C.J. (eds) (1980). *Algae Biomass Production and Use*. Elsevier–North Holland, Amsterdam.

Shian, S., Chang, M., Ye, Y. & Chang, W. (1979). The construction of single biogas digesters in the Province of Szechwan, China. *Agric. Waste*, **1**, 247–58.

Singh, A. (1988). Socio-economic problems of community biogas plants in Punjab. *J. Rural Dev.*, **7**, 591–9.

Singleton, F.L. & Kramer, J.G. (1988). Biotechnology of marine algae: opportunities for developing countries. *UNIDO Gen. Eng. Biotech. Monitor*, **25**, 83–90.

Soerjono, R. (1980). Potency of sago as a food-energy source in Indonesia. In *Sago, the Equatorial Swamp as a Natural Resource*, W.R. Stanton & M. Flach (eds), pp. 35–8. Martinus Nijhoff Publ., London.

Stanton, W.R. & Flach, M. (eds) (1980). *Sago, the Equatorial Swamp as a Natural Resource*. Martinus Nijhoff Publ., London.

264   H.W. Doelle and E. Gumbira-Sa'id

Stolp, A. & Bunders, J. (1989). Biotechnology: wedge or bridge? *Trends Biotechnol.*, **7**, S2–S4.

Sukara, E. & Doelle, H.W. (1988). Cassava starch fermentation pattern of *Rhizopus oligosporus. MIRCEN J. Appl. Microbiol. Biotechnol.*, **4**, 463–71.

Sukara, E. & Doelle, H.W. (1989a). Optimization of single cell proteion production from cassava starch (*Rhizopus oligosporus*). *Acta Biotechnol.*, **9**, 99–110.

Sukara, E. & Doelle, H.W. (1989b). A one-step process for the production of single cell protein and amyloglucosidase. *Appl. Microbiol. Biotechnol.*, **30**, 135–40.

Swaminathan, M.S. (1982). Biotechnology Research and Third World agriculture. *Science, Wash.*, **218**, 967–72.

Taiganides, E.P. (1979). Wastes are . . . resources out of place. *Agric. Waste*, **1**, 1–10.

Taiganides, E.P., Chou, K.C. & Lee, B.Y. (1979). Animal waste management and utilization in Singapore. *Agric. Waste*, **1**, 129–41.

Tan, K. (1980). Sago production in Southwest Peninsular Malaysia. In *Sago, the Equatorial Swamp as a Natural Resource*, W.R. Stanton & M. Flach (eds), pp. 56–83, Martinus Nijhoff Publ., London.

Tan, K. (1983). *The Swamp-Sago Industry in Malaysia*, Institute for Southeast Asia Studies, Singapore.

Trevan, M.D. & Mak, A.L. (1988). Immobilized algae and their potential for use as biocatalysts. *Trends Biotechnol.*, **6**, 68–73.

Townsend, P.K. (1982). A review of recent and needed sago research. In *Sago Research in Papua New Guinea, Discussion Paper*, Inst. Appl. Sci and Economic Res., Boroko, Papua New Guinea.

Ul Haq, M. (1988). People in development. *Development*, **1988**, 41–5.

Ulijaszek, S.J. (1982). Nutritional status of a sago-eating community in the Purari delta, Gulf Province. In *Sago Research in Papua New Guinea, Discussion Paper*, Inst. Appl. Sci. and Economic Res., Boroko, Papua New Guinea.

Venkataraman, A.N., Devi, K.M., Mahadevaswamy, M. & Kunhi, A.A.M. (1982). Utilization of rural wastes for algal biomass production with *Scenedesmus acutus* and *Spirulina platensis* in India. *Agric. Wastes*, **4**, 117–30.

Venkataraman, L.V., Nigam, B.P. & Ramanthan, P.K. (1980). Rural oriented fresh water cultivation and production of algae in India. In *Algal Biomass Production and Use*, G. Shelef & C.J. Soeder (eds), pp. 81–95. Elsevier-North Holland, Amsterdam.

Vonshak, A. (1988). Algae-derived biogas as fire wood substitute in tropical countries. In *Energy from Biomass*, A. Strub, P. Chartier & G. Schleser (eds), pp. 754–6. Applied Sci. Publ., London.

Wilbert, J. (1976). Manicaria saccifera and its cultural significance among the Warao Indians of Venezuela. *Bot. Leaflets*, **24**, 275–335. Harvard University, Cambridge (as cited by Ruddle *et al. loc. cit.*, 1978).

Wilson, K.K., Philipp, P.F. & Shauer, W.W. (1986). Socio-cultural effects on the farming systems research and development approach. *Agric. Systems*, **19**, 83–110.

Wood, D.A. (1984). Microbial processes in mushroom cultivation; a large scale solid substrate fermentation. *J. Chem. Tech. Biotechnol.*, **34B**, 232–40.

Wood, D.A. (1985). Useful biodegradation of lignocellulose. In *Plant Products and the New Technology*, K.W. Fuller & J.R. Gallon (eds), pp. 295–309, Clarendon Press, Oxford.

Wood, D.A. (1989). Mushroom biotechnology. *Int. Indust. Biotechnol.*, **9**, 1–8.

Wood, D.A. & Smith, J.F. (1987). The cultivation of mushrooms. In *Essays in Agricultural and Food Microbiology*, J.R. Norris & G.L. Pettipher (eds), pp. 309–43 (cited in Wood, 1989).

Zhong-Xian, Z. & Yi, Q. (1986). Development of non-waste technology and production in the People's Republic of China. *Int. J. Devel. Technol.*, **4**, 49–54.

Zilinskas, R. (1988). Biotechnology and the Third World: the missing link between research and applications. *Gen. Eng. Biotech. Monitor*, **24**, 105–15.

Zimmerman, B.K. (1983). Conflicts pervade Third World biotech proposal. *Bio/Technol.*, March, p. 132.

Zimmerman, W.J. (1987). Growth, nitrogen fixation and mass culture of isolated *Anabaena azollae. Biotechnol. Lett.*, **9**, 31–6.

11

The economic and social implications of gene technology to developing countries

BURKE K. ZIMMERMAN

Introduction

The spectacular advances in molecular and cell biology that have fuelled the Biotechnology Revolution in industrially advanced countries can without doubt also have an enormous effect on public health, agriculture and industrial development in developing countries. There is, of course, a continuum of what is defined as biotechnology, ranging from the traditional applications of microbial fermentation to food preservation, mushroom culture, cheese making and beer production, to intricate genetic strategies to design and produce new macromolecules with new pharmacological or enzymatic activities.

For what would seem to be purely practical reasons, the most successful programmes initiated by developed countries and international organizations have concentrated on the 'low' end of biotechnology – that is, the older, traditional and proven technologies – as instruments for the improvement of the health, the standard of living and economic conditions of the Third World.

In order that even these basic technologies will positively influence the economics and social conditions of a given region, its is primarily a matter of creating the environment suitable for their effective application and commercial development. This means facilitating local entrepreneurism, creating the availability of investment capital, strengthening and updating the educational system (which more often than not is usually critical), and redesigning government bureaucracies so that they help rather than hinder the application of technology, etc. The current catchword is 'infrastructure'. Without it, even the best technology would flounder helplessly and benefit no-one. Because it is this basic support environment that is deficient to some degree in the developing countries (essentially by definition – if it were not deficient, then a country wouldn't be 'developing' in the usual euphemistic usage), the focus of the practically minded is to 'keep it simple' and not launch overly ambitious programmes that will have a high probability of failure.

The importance of advanced biotechnology to developing countries

It is against this background that the development and use of the most advanced technologies in molecular and cell biology (in addition to the effective use of the traditional modes) are of critical importance to the economic and social development of the Third World. The need for undertaking such development becomes particularly compelling when one considers the rate of scientific advancement in the developed world, where the newest and most complex techniques to manipulate the genes of living cells and organisms are being exploited for all they are worth. To put it another way, if applications of biotechnology in developing countries remain confined to the standard and the traditional, while the most advanced technology is in full use elsewhere, then the infamous 'Gap' will only widen, and widen rather rapidly.

Unfortunately, many well-intentioned development programmes, facing the practical realities that exist in the Third World, in emphasizing the need for immediately effective and workable solutions to specific problems, exclude from the planning process and definition of long-term goals the vision that much of the developing world can and should aspire to the level of economic and social conditions enjoyed by the most advanced countries. Although not explicitly articulated, such a policy is effectively to treat the Third World in a condescending and patronizing way, suggesting that it is incapable of using effectively any but the simplest of technology, not only in the present (which may be the case), but *forever*. That approach can only be compared to telling a child, bright and full of the thirst to learn and to grow to adulthood, that he or she may not aspire to the goals attained by his already well-educated and accomplished parent, but must be content in the future only with what the undeveloped skills that youth allow him to do at present.

There are, then, two important, and quite interdependent, aspects to the case for a high degree of importance to advanced gene technology to the Third World.

> *(1) All of the people of the earth should, as a principle of basic justice, be entitled to the direct benefit of new technologies, where ever they are developed.*

When one applies the above principle to the implications of advanced gene technologies, it is implied that such technology will uniquely influence the economics and social conditions of any area where they are applied. Or, in other words, if the primary focus of biotechnology in developing countries is limited to traditional biotechnology, however successful such enterprises may be, there will be a level of attainment that will remain unreachable – that the traditional methods simply won't provide the gains in economic efficiency and the standard of living that could be achieved by the use of cutting-edge technology.

Of course, the proper application and management of traditional technology can bring about major gains in economic development and the standard of living overall. But is that really enough? As long as the knowledge exists that somewhere in the world, a better way has been developed and exists, or that new techniques have been devised to solve problems heretofore intractable by traditional approaches, then it is clearly not enough. That is, if policies were to limit the Third World to traditional and immediately 'doable' technologies, whether invoked by the aid agencies of the advanced countries or the developing countries themselves, it would be a tragic error. It would be a denial of the human potential of the Third World and its desire to be as good as anyone else, and indeed a devaluation of the need for the most efficient technology possible.

If one accepts, as a fundamental principle of justice, that everyone should have equal access to any available technology that can improve their lives, then a direct corollary is that all peoples of the world are entitled to the benefits of any and all technology that mankind has created.

> *(2) The goals of the Third World, in* research and development *as well as the use of technology, should be no less than those of any advanced country, even if realistic planning and a timetable for implementation means that it will take some years to catch up.*

In order to benefit from the present world standard of scientific and technological achievement, the developing countries of the world must take part in the research and development relevant to the applications appropriate to their specific environments and problems. Applied research in the advanced countries of the world, that directed to the development of new pharmaceuticals, improved crop varieties, biological pesticides or industrial processes, will inevitably be overwhelmingly aimed toward products and methods of direct relevance to the economies and the health and agricultural problems of the wealthiest countries, with little activity directed toward solutions to the problems of the poorest nations.

This is a simple corollary of the driving forces of commercialization and market economics. This should provide a powerful incentive for the developing nations to give a high priority to the development of their capacities to conduct advanced research and technological development, and in a few countries of the Third World, it seems that they have done so. That is, no country can sit idle waiting for a national aid programme, a United Nations agency, or an altruistic commercial organization to solve such problems for them. They must take the initiative themselves, availing themselves of all the human, financial and scientific resources they can muster.

This means that developing countries must make a commitment in time and money and people. It means hiring experts from abroad as consultants, and here there are often advantages in hiring their bright and successful compatriots who, earlier in their careers, emigrated to countries where their opportunities to employ their talents were greater (China has followed this pattern, with some success). It means careful planning that leaves out no piece of the complex puzzle needed to make a functional whole.

This contention does not, of course, mean to imply that it would be useful or appropriate to set up, today, an advanced protein design and computer modelling lab in Mauritania, to study the abstractions of protein folding and function. It does mean that a workable course of planning and development be followed that will allow the Mauritanians to hold a realistic vision that someday they will be as qualified as anyone to operate such a laboratory.

But enough of such abstractions. Can the principles set forth above be regarded as more than starry-eyed idealism? What does an application of such principles really mean with regard to the Third World enjoying all of the benefits of advanced gene technology? First, it is necessary to examine some (but by no means all) of the areas in which direct use of advanced molecular methods will have a unique and profound effect on the human condition.

Human health and veterinary medicine

Vaccines

The most common infectious disease of the temperate zones are, for the most part, amenable to the 'traditional' mode of prevention by vaccination, first developed by Louis Pasteur more than a century ago. That is, a weakened strain of a bacterium or virus, or a preparation made directly from the infectious agent containing the correct surface antigens, can serve to immunize people against the virulent forms of the disease. In recent years, the design of safe vaccines has been improved – in some cases – by the expression of the protein antigen using gene-splicing techniques in an efficient heterologous production system. But the basic principle of design of such vaccines is still fundamentally pasteurian.

However, there is a large class of parasitic and other diseases indigenous to the warm and tropical regions of the world, for which the straightforward approach of Pasteur simply does not always work. Often, both the organisms and their life cycles are complex. The propagation of the organisms may involve several different host organisms. The natural immune system is less effective in combatting complex parasitic organisms than it is in dealing with the simpler bacteria and viruses. For example, some organisms have evolved mechanisms of shuffling the genes of their surface proteins (e.g. forms of the spirochete *Borrelia*, keeping a step ahead of the immune response for weeks, while the condition of the afflicted continues to deteriorate). Others are too big and complex for circulating antibodies to inactivate them effectively, or for directed macrophages to be effective.

Only by a thorough understanding of the life cycle of such parasites, and subsequent identification of the critical and vulnerable point, can effective control of such diseases be possible. And does a mechanism exist to improve the efficiency of the human immune response? If so, it means a careful dissection of all of the elements of the human immune system, and the mechanisms by which the body's defences are marshalled. The rapid gains in understanding of the human immune response that have accrued during the past decade could only have come about through the use of the methods of advanced gene technology and analysis.

At present, the AIDS virus, an extraordinary example of evolution designed to outwit the ingenuity of the human immune system, is still essentially out of control world-wide. Nevertheless, it is receiving the most intensive attention around the world that any infectious agent has ever received in human history. Eventually, it will yield to human craft and advanced moleuclar biology. But here is a clear example where classical pasteurian immunology simply doesn't work.

The techniques of the computer modelling of protein structure and the design of new and modified biological properties is just now beginning to revolutionize many areas of health care technology. The challenge now before the immunologist is to design or redesign the natural molecules presented by pathogens so that the natural immune response will be more effective. There are several strategies that are being pursued, and it is beyond the scope of this contribution to go into them in detail. Though it seems to be that the Third World has inherited the lion's share of difficult diseases, the conclusion is clear that *only* through the use of advanced methods, including those to be discovered, will a lasting victory over the diseases that have afflicted people for millenia eventually be gained.

Diagnosis of disease

Effective prevention is, of course, better than curing diseases. An enormous amount of human death and disability could be prevented simply by early and accurate diagnosis of the infectious microbe. Here again, the methods of gene manipulation allow for the isolation of disease-specific antigens and their production in quantity by expressing them in a non-pathogenic production strain. Such antigens can thus be used for diagnostic tests, by monitoring for the presence of serum antibodies for many diseases common in the tropical countries (e.g. pneumonia, diarrhoea) so that the correct treatment be given quickly.

For more rapid tests, assays that positively identify the causal agent itself, based on poly- or monoclonal antibodies specific to the antigen, are badly needed. This technology goes hand-in-hand with the isolation and production of unique antigens.

The new DNA probe assays, a direct result of recombinant DNA methods, are now being used for the very precise identification of specific DNA base sequences, which means that both the presence of infectious agents and certain human genes can be detected with high sensitivity. The rate of the development of such methods is such that for many diseases, such tests will be preferred over immunoassays for antigen detection. Moreover, the presence of carriers of genetic diseases, undetectable by any other means is now possible as is the detection of genes implicated in the susceptibility to a variety of serious disorders. Such information, as important to the Third World as to the advanced countries, will greatly aid in the prevention of such pathological development and in counselling prospective parents who may be carrying genes that pose a risk to their future children.

Therapeutics

The design of novel therapeutic agents, or the making available of natural products of therapeutic value in large quantities, have been a valuable legacy of the development of modern gene technology. New classes of therapeutic agents including the use of natural or modified immune modulators to help fight cancer or infectious diseases have been made possible now. Even the application of genetic manipulation to microorganisms can greatly improve the yield and lower the cost of manufacture of known antibiotics, (e.g. the cephalosporins).

A new development concerns the design and production of specific fragments (natural or modified) of human antibodies. Such agents can serve as targetted carriers for indicating the presence of the antigens for which they are specific, such as cancer cells, or to carry a toxin or radioactive isotope to specifically locate and destroy such cells.

The design of therapeutics for viral and parasitic diseases of course represents a major challenge to science. Few agents have been found that may be effective to some degree, for example, the quinine derivatives used to treat and prevent malaria. Agents that specifically kill or prevent the growth of these infectious entities without accompanying side-effects are rare. This is where molecular design methods need to be deployed to create specifically targetted agents that can identify, bind and inactivate the pathogens of concern. The precise control of molecular topography needed to create the hand-and-glove fits needed for new pharmaceuticals is a science still in its infancy. Nevertheless, it could be a route to the control of parasitic diseases where the conventional and expensive random approach to pharmaceutical development has failed.

The latest novel approach to therapeutics is the concept of antisense pharmaceuticals, agents that recognize and bind a blocking function to the antisense strand of DNA. The application of such compounds has only begun to be explored.

The human genome sequencing project

The world-wide megaproject to determine the entire base sequence of the human genome, including the range of all of its variants is a new approach to understanding the genetic malfunctions encountered in hereditary diseases. It is estimated that there are at least 5000 base pair differences between any two individuals, and that with some 3 billion base pairs to deal with, many believe that this number may be vastly underestimated.

But what could this project possibly have to do with the Third World? It is not even generally accepted as being of value in the advanced countries, at least as an expensive, high priority endeavour. The reason why the project should receive a high priority is that it will provide a body of data on the organization of the human genome that can be obtained in no other way than by such a *tour de force*. Although the interpretation of the function of the total sequence will certainly not be immediately obvious, at least the data will be available to allow an interpretation of genetic disorders. There is no doubt that the coded genetic information will eventually be unravelled by human ingenuity. In addition to clarifying the structural–functional relationships between genetic sequence and the control of gene expression, or cellular differentiation, and of the organization and function of the central nervous system, it will also reveal in time a far more complete picture of genetic pathology than is now available.

Coupled with the DNA probe technology described above, it will soon be possible to identify the presence of overt and potentially disabling genetic defects as well as the presence of genetic factors that may predispose carrying individuals to certain kinds of pathology at some point in their lives. For example, a large class of auto-immune disorders, such as renal failure, certain forms of arthritis, and onset of adult diabetes, is related to the distribution of certain human leukocyte antigens (HLA). Although some worry about the risks of misuse of too complete a picture of an individual's genetic make-up, such as, for example, job discrimination against those susceptible to certain toxic substances, the benefit of the knowledge of such sensitivities and susceptibilities could be of great service to medical practitioners the world over. However, there are growing risks and worries that the availability of an individual's complete genetic make-up would be a discriminatory factor in the labour market. For example, the possibility that preference could be accorded to individuals non-susceptible to certain toxic substances over those that carry a predisposed susceptibility clearly exists.

Population genetics and genetically related diseases

It is well-known that individuals differ genetically and, therefore, phenotypically from one another. Today, the distribution of predominant genotypes and certain types of genetic disorders that vary considerably amongst different global populations is an important factor in the proper diagnosis, treatment and prevention of disease. This finding is now becoming more and more appreciated in the study of population genetics. The increased presence of *Tay-Sachs* syndrome among Ashkenazi Jews and sickle-cell disease in people with ancestors from certain African regions is a well-known illustration of this principle. More subtle is the genetic disposition of perhaps 30% of the population of southeast Finland to a genetically based disorder in lipid metabolism that greatly increases the risk of hyperlipidemia and arteriosclerosis. No doubt a large number of similar phenomena will be uncovered in time, dictating that certain preventive measures such as a low-risk diet, immunization against sensitizing infections, etc. be taken among the carriers of such genes. The extent to which detailed knowledge of the genetics of specific populations will be important in determining their susceptibility to certain tropical diseases remains unclear at present. However, such knowledge would certainly prevent grand commercial fiascos such as providing surplus milk to populations lacking the enzyme needed to digest lactose.

274   *B.K. Zimmerman*

Agriculture

The classical topic for discussion of the application of biotechnology to developing countries is agriculture. To be sure, much of the Third World is still bound by low-efficiency agrarian economies. As populations increase and climate plays tricks at random with the growing season in regions without an organized system of food distribution, major food shortages can and do still occur, with the predictable human toll.

Of course, as demonstrated by the Green Revolution, the application of classical plant breeding methods resulted in the distribution of many strains of rice and wheat that resisted common plant diseases and doubled and tripled the output per hectare. Furthermore, additional improvements in irrigation, simple crop rotation, and the judicious use of fertilizers and pesticides, have increased yields and continue to do so. However, in principle, advanced genetic techniques can do much more.

Enhanced productivity

When agricultural planners in United Nations agencies or developing countries are asked what is the most important application of biotechnology to agriculture, nitrogen fixation is often placed at the top of the list. Indeed, for certain legumes, the enhancement of the production of available nitrogen by mutation-selection techniques with rhizobium is realistic at present. Other improved N-fixing soil bacteria can be similarly selected for. The development of nitrogen-fixing plants, thereby eliminating or reducing the need for exogenous nitrogen, by inserting the family of genes controlling the bacterial N-fixing pathway directly into the plant genes, is sometimes discussed as though it were a straightforward application of gene splicing techniques. It is not, of course. Even if the correct set of microbial enzymes could be produced in plant cells, there are structural and physical barriers to the efficient uptake of atmospheric nitrogen. Nevertheless, however, such a concept should not be casually dismissed as forever impossible. In time, it will probably be done.

There are, however, more immediate ways in which gene technology can enhance agricultural productivity. The genetic control of the plant's basic physiology is probably a somewhat easier problem than the engineering of a family of 17 nitrogen fixing genes into plant tissue. This means beginning with the genes controlling the production of auxins, kinetins and gibberillins, which govern the basic growth rate and the production of the flowers, seeds and fruit. It may also be possible to enhance photosynthetic efficiency, although, for example, if one were to attempt to engineer into green plants the accessory pigments common in some blue-green algae in order to increase light utilization across the visible spectrum, the problem involving a great many genes could be formidably complex and difficult.

In any case, the goal with highly productive crop plants is to reduce the amount of plant growth and production of non-edible parts, whilst increasing number and size of the edible parts. Now that plant cell culture methods allow for the propagation of whole plants from single cells for most species, and vectors exist for manipulating and selecting the genes of the single cells/protoplasts, there is no theoretical limit to what may be done. As more is discerned about structural functional relationships in plants, the ability to manipulate the genes accordingly will also increase.

Biological pest control

The overuse of chemical pesticides, resulting in an undesirable environmental burden of toxic agents, adversely affecting both humans and animals, and the selection and evolution of resistant insect pests, are compelling reasons why healthier alternatives are required to chemical pesticides. Different strategies are being considered. Some target the insects themselves, others are designed to make the plant unpalatable or toxic to its principal insect enemies. Success has been limited so far. However, the progress made indicates that a combination of biological strategies will truly eliminate the need for the use of toxic chemicals.

Developing countries, much more than the agriculturally advanced countries of the world, are the main consumers of powerful toxic agents long since banned for use in Europe and America in large quantities in agriculture. The bugs of the tropics may indeed be more varied and voracious than their northern cousins, so the need is acute. But here is a good example of where the needed research and development, applied to the crops and the insects of the developing countries, is not likely to be carried out in the laboratories of the Northern Hemisphere. There is simply little incentive to do so.

Environmental pollution

There are many forms of environmental pollution. These include the toxic chemicals sprayed on crops, the atmospheric burden of particulates, oxidants, and heavy metals resulting from the burning of fossil fuels, and the result of burning *anything* other than pure hydrogen. The ratio of carbon dioxide to oxygen in the atmosphere continues to increase at an alarming rate. While experts may argue over the reality of the greenhouse effect, it is an inevitable result should the ratio continue to rise uncontrolled. Certainly, a long-range environmentally sound approach to industrialization and its given adjuncts to a high standard of living such as cars could greatly reduce and perhaps even reverse the rate at which the planet earth is slowly yet surely becoming an unfit habitat for life of any sort. Even if such an ideal could be realized, it is probably not enough. Again, the biological revolution can at least provide the technological tools with which to prevent and cure the destructive effects of pollution.

Microbes that degrade or detoxify pollutants

Over the past decade, there has been increasing attention to biological methods to detoxify contaminated soil and water, and to break down industrial wastes before their discharge into the environment. By simple screening and selecting natural microbes, organisms have been found that break down a wide variety of organic compounds, including polychlorinated biphenyls (PCBs), previously thought to be resistant to microbial degradation.

The first patent application for a genetically manipulated organism for degrading petroleum and petroleum-spills was issued in 1979. Four different plasmids had been inserted into the bacterium so that a complete enzyme pathway was present, not normally found in the strain of *Pseudomonas* in question.

This precedent-setting organism never really had the stamina to enable it to compete and survive in a real environment where there was a need to degrade oil spills. However, it publicized the need to pay more attention to the possibility of engineering organisms to combat what have become severe toxic burdens in many parts of the world. Although bacteria can evolve relatively rapidly to enable them to utilize new substrates, the process is still slow. In comparison, the synthetic ingenuity of organic chemists often would require several new enzymatic activities to appear at once in an organism to endow it with the capacity to attack the compound. It is here where the genetic and protein engineers can probably win the race with Mother Nature.

Alternatives to polluting technologies

Of course, with an eye to the future, the winning strategy is obviously not to create toxic compounds that require a clever strategy to get rid of them, but to accomplish the same goals without resorting to the use of undesirable chemicals in the first place. This is not to say that chemistry, *per se*, should be phased out. Environmentally damaging compounds such as petroleum are in use for many useful purposes, and accidents will happen. But certainly there are many unnecessary deliberate uses of toxic compounds. CFC propellants in spray cans are a passing and, in retrospect, unneeded novelty of the last half of this century. The dependence on agricultural pesticides discussed earlier demands an alternative strategy and is another case in point.

Energy

One area where the environmental burden of toxics could be reduced considerably is that of energy production. Advance industrial societies tend to waste energy for all sorts of unneeded applications as long as the cost is relatively low. Thus, while the cost of petroleum-based fuels remains a relatively small fraction of an individual's personal income, their use will probably continue to be extravagant in the industrialized nations. However, while solutions based on cultural engineering may fail there are other strategies. The development of alternative energy sources such as solar, geothermal and tidal will become much more popular as the supply of cheap fuels diminishes as it certainly must. However, it should be noted that it is not the contaminants of fossil fuels or esoteric toxics that are the only problem. The simple excess carbon dioxide resulting from the combustion of carbon compounds, today, can perhaps also be classified as a pollutant.

Moreover, the destruction of the forests of the tropics and of the temperate regions has been of the slash and burn type to gain more arable land. In many areas, e.g. northern Pakistan, trees have been burned for fuel. In the Philippines, the rain forests were cut down as fuel exports for the short-term profit of a few industries.

But where does biotechnology come in, and is it of significant potential to provide new energy strategies? On the one hand, relatively simple microbial technologies have been devised to generate combustible fuels, such as methane, from manure. On the other hand, strategies are being developed to engineer microbes to enhance the recovery of petroleum from oil shale, where most of the highly viscous and waxy crude oil remains trapped. Still other strategies focus on the generation of combustible alcohol fuels from cellulose and starch. These all, however, rely on combustion of carbon compounds to generate energy.

However, there is one simple fuel that is produced by a number of different microbes and that can be burned without the generation of any undesirable substances. This is molecular hydrogen, which burns to generate only water. Enhancing microbes to increase their efficiency of hydrogen production, while at the same time, producing other useful substances such as protein for animal feed is a potentially winning strategy. However, as long as conventional fuel is cheap there is little incentive for investment in the development of such technology. It is here where an excellent strategic opportunity may exist.

Industrial production of commodities

The applications of advanced genetic techniques to the production of foods, pharmaceuticals, and chemicals are slowly but surely beginning to replace conventional, energy-intensive and expensive production methods. Genetically engineered fungi, yeast, and bacteria are now used routinely for the production of industrial enzymes, and the commodities that require them. Soon cheese will be made with synthetic chymosin and rennet thus eliminating the need for producing the enzymes from newborn calves. A genetically engineered yeast developed in Finland can produce a fully mature beer in less than two days. The production of high fructose syrup, a universal sweetener, is already enhanced by the production of enzymes from genetically modified microbes. Many enzymatic industrial processes are now a reality on account of the use of heat-stable enzymes which enable production to be run at higher temperatures and greater efficiency. While a number of such enzymes have been found in nature, the techniques of protein engineering are now beginning to be applied to the design of such superior catalysts.

The case for the profound and unique implications of advanced methods in genetic manipulation and cell biology has been amply made through a general discussion of some of the important ways in which such techniques can and are being used. The obvious corollary is that if such technology is not employed in the service of developing countries, either by themselves or others, then these countries will continue to advance relatively more slowly than the advanced industrialized regions. And this can *only* mean that the differential in economic and social standards will increase, not decrease.

The challenge

Acknowledging the need for a complete infrastructure and an environment conducive for both the development and application of advanced technologies is not the same as creating the proper environment where the odds seem overwhelmingly against it.

Clearly, this is where the challenge to us all lies. The answers and solutions will be neither easy nor quick in coming. However, some important lessons have been learnt. One cannot depend upon the dynamics of international commerce to drive technological development toward the needs of developing countries. Though commercial interest exists, there has not been an economic incentive for substantial investment in the development of vaccines for diseases such as malaria that afflict primarily the countries of the South. Vaccines for malaria and hepatitis B, and the Chiron hepatitis vaccine are a case in point.

However, private entrepreneurial ventures, the driving force of biotechnology in the economically advanced countries is a rare phenomenon in the Third World. Yet abundant data show that, overall, it has been private, profit-driven business that has directed massive investment in the development of new technology and, by consequence, in advantageous gains for the consumer. The economic and scientific stagnation of the socialist countries of East Europe during the 40 years following World War II has shown us the result of well-intentioned planned programmes that lack and ignore the basis for human motivation. The overwhelming rejection of this way of life by those peoples during the past year is an adequate and eloquent testimony to its level of success.

There have been a number of initiatives to bring biotechnology to bear on the specific needs of developing countries. These have taken the form of aid programmes initiated by agencies in a few of the advanced countries, by international organizations such as the World Bank and several of the United Nations agencies, by philanthropic foundations, by initiatives in a number of developing countries themselves, or by some combination of the above. These have enjoyed varying degrees of success in meeting their objectives. Often cited at the top of the list is the development of more productive strains of staple seed crops known as the 'Green Revolution', as exemplified by the significant gains made in well-funded, focussed efforts coming from the application of traditional plant breeding techniques employing 'classical' genetics in the network of the international agricultural research institution of the Consultative Group on International Agricultural Research (CGIAR).

Some of these efforts have addressed one or more of the necessary components of functional biotechnology-based industries, medicine and agriculture. In general, however, these efforts have

(1) lacked sufficient funds to make significant strides in needed areas,
(2) often, not used the available resources efficiently when managed by large bureaucratic organizations,
(3) been plagued by the domination of political values in deference to scientific and economic criteria, and
(4) generally failed to address the requirements for a complete system.

For example, there have been a number of new programmes designed to promote biotechnology as a means of development that consist of the creation only of a new advanced research centre. Some of these are succeeding in enhancing the capacity of a country to conduct 'relevant' applied research. However, such centres alone are not sufficient to create the 'whole system' needed to have a significant positive effect on economic development and living standards.

It is not the purpose of this essay to present a compendium and critique of all of the major programmes in development for the Third World that are based on biotechnology. For the record, some of these have succeeded and are making a difference. Ironically and predictably, the programmes that have the most success are those that have focussed either on biotechnology at a level below that which may be considered advanced gene technology or on various elements of the 'infrastructure', such as providing advanced specialized training for scientists and technologists from developing countries. Overly ambitious programmes that have claimed to bring the most advanced technology to the Third World have generally not been very successful. Taken together, and as important as all these programmes are and have been, the gulf is still widening between the industrial countries and the non-technically advanced societies with very few exceptions. However, there *are* exceptions. The planners of tomorrow must ask what it is that is really different about these exceptions. Are they really too culturally idiosyncratic to provide any general principles upon which to base new initiatives. Or can they provide us with the key to imaginative new strategies?

For example, South Korea has moved in developmental status from a war-torn underdeveloped country of the mid-1950s to a highly competitive industrial nation. Its standard of living as measured by indices such as literacy, educational achievement, health and longevity, personal income, per capita GNP, etc. has risen steadily to levels that compare favourably, if not equally, with that of its neighbour Japan. And this has been accomplished in spite of the political turmoil and student revolt that dominate the international media.

The key to success is that the political and national environment has been conducive to and for aggressive private entrepreneurism. Whatever the problems of government, it has encouraged this kind of development rather than stifle the ambitious with a burden of legal and economic disincentives and oppressive taxation, a situation that, unfortunately, prevails today in many European countries and virtually throughout the Third World. Help for developing countries resides in the promotion of local entrepreneurism in high technology inclusive of advanced biotechnology. Consequently, the most successful programmes will be those in which the driving impetus comes from the country itself. This means that assistance should take the form of the availability of expert advice, risk capital, and equal, non-exploitive partnerships with successful corporations in the North.

There are at present several independent programmes in place or being organized that recognize this need and try to stimulate indigenous entrepreneurism. The Resources Development Foundation (RDF), founded in the mid-1980s in the United States by the Rockefeller Brothers Fund, began by concentrating on agricultural projects in South Asia. The scope of their operations is now being expanded to Africa and other regions.

The RDF approach includes the means to share and distribute technical and market information, the protection of intellectual property, and a number of tangentially related areas. However, the principal element of the RDF operating strategy is the creation of the means to couple 'foreign' investors, entrepreneurs and companies with appropriate partners and opportunities in developing countries, in a fair and mutually beneficial manner. In general the RDF has not pushed enterprises based on new advanced biotechnology where the business and technical risks may be high, but on traditional technology with relatively short development times to profitability.

A similar initiative is to be found in the Bioresource Development Corporation (BRDC), which has been the vision of Professor Carl-Göran Hedén, Professor Emeritus from the Karolinska Institutet in Stockholm. Briefly, the BRDC, organized as a project of the World Academy of Art and Science in collaboration with UNESCO's network of Microbial Resources Centres (MIRCENS) and, funded by private donation, is designed to be an organization to promote well-planned, commercially oriented business ventures in developing countries in co-operation with and financed by private capital. The BRDC, in a modus operandi similar to that used by the RDF, would, in the beginning, assume much of the role of the entrepreneur, in locating capital and suitable business partners. However, the ultimate goal would be to establish locally managed companies and to help individuals in the target country to become successful entrepreneurs. Perhaps the significant difference between the planned strategy of the BRDC and the RDF is the attempt to create the means to use the advanced and unique applications of genetic manipulation and cell biology to work in developing countries, and to identify the resources for projects that would sometimes be relatively long-term and high-risk.

The classical model of investment by large companies in the Third World has been exploitive in nature. That is, ventures have been designed and aimed at the markets in wealthier countries through the use of relatively cheap resources or labour. The BRDC, however, operates on the principles of fairness and ethical conduct on the part of all concerned. It invites the establishment of investments in and through the formation of joint ventures with companies or other organizations in Third World countries applying biotechnology to new products and methods that address market demands in the Third World as well as those in the economically developed countries. It is an 'everybody wins' strategy, as opposed to the traditional 'I win, you lose' approach.

There are other initiatives based in Europe and America with similar objectives. But these are only a beginning. In general, these organizations either depend on non-profit foundations or donations, or on relatively meagre amounts of private investment. The challenge of designing an organization along the lines of a for-profit business that can attract significant sums of venture capital or corporate investment is still to be met.

An obvious criticism to the above approach is the observation that cultural attitudes differ greatly among the countries and peoples of the world. The highly driven commitments of the Japanese and Koreans may simply be an indigenous cultural feature, without which successful entrepreneurism may be much more difficult to promote. One cannot easily and quickly change human attitudes and the basic approach to life. Therefore, the design and selection of appropriate ventures, and where to promote them is highly non-trivial. It may, unfortunately, be an approach that is not for everyone.

Finally, although it is acknowledged that the application of advanced biotechnology to new enterprises will certainly enhance the standard of living and have positive economic effects, it is also true that the implantation of revolutionary technology and rapid economic development will have a social and economic down side or negative aspect.

For example, there has been some strong criticism of the Green Revolution on account of the sociological perturbations it has had on rural agriculture. Using classical plant breeding techniques, the CGIAR institutions have made available varieties that can double and treble the yield of rice and other staples. At the same time, the use of this relatively small number of high-yield varieties has also dramatically altered agricultural practices in many areas, with a shift from labour-intensive peasant farming to larger, mechanized farms coupled to the use of more fertilizer and pesticides.

Some have argued that it is terrible and immoral to disrupt the centuries-old peasant farmer economy and to encourage large and efficient mechanized farms run by a much smaller number of people. It should be pointed out that these same changes have occurred throughout the world and are still occurring even in the most advanced countries (like the United States), in attempts to make agriculture more efficient. Although the transition periods of the industrial and agricultural 'revolutions' can and will be difficult and painful especially for farmers and workers in traditional endeavours who will be displaced by modern techniques, the standard of living, nevertheless, of peoples everywhere has increased at all levels of society. Change is inevitable, and change in one part of society invariably affects all other parts. There is certainly nothing sacred about the old ways, especially when this meant hunger and sickness, and indenturing a majority of the population to the production of food for subsistence.

The experience with the Green Revolution illustrates a very important point. One must be cognizant of the potential for dramatic sociological effects when applying new technologies and means of production, such as those made possible by many areas of biotechnology, in societies for which the current way of life is simply not suited to the new technology. That is, that the 'model', or the ideal planning process that one would like to introduce these ultimately beneficial technologies must take into account the ways these technologies will affect the social and economic order, and hence, politics. The greater the change in the technology introduced, the greater will be the challenge of ensuring that its introduction will proceed smoothly.

Conclusion

The case for the inclusion of the advanced methods in molecular and cell biology, including the full range of methods for genetic manipulation, in any programme for development in the Third World, has been made. Without the benefits of such technology and the capacity to develop such technology, any country will be at an increasing disadvantage.

While there are those who maintain that one should stick to the simple and proven methods when facing the multitude of problems in developing countries, i.e. doing only the doable, it seems that to follow such a path would be ultimately a losing strategy which would only maintain and probably intensify the 'Third World' label. Only if the goals of the entire world are uniformly high, can one then expect to see a just world in harmony with itself.

12

Making biotechnology appropriate – and environmentally sound

ROBERT WALGATE

Biotechnology, of which microbial technology is a crucial component, promises massive new interventions in health and agriculture in developing countries (Walgate, 1990).

For example, vaccines are now being developed for 28 diseases, including scourges such as malaria, which kills a million people – mostly children – every year in Africa alone. Yet since Louis Pasteur developed his vaccine against rabies in 1885, just 21 other vaccines have been produced. Just nine of the 22 are now used routinely against childhood diseases. The average rate of invention of routinely used vaccines has thus been less than one per decade. With biotechnology – using genes of the pathogenic microorganisms spliced into genomes of other, relatively benign bacteria and virusus – vaccine development rates are thus increased more than 20-fold.

In agriculture, virus-free cassava – produced by tissue culture, or by the engineering in of viral genes expressing the coat protein of cassava mosaic viruses – could doubly secure rural African calorie production; and hybrid rice, new wide crosses and perhaps engineered pest-resistant rice – and rice with new endophytic bacteria engineered to kill pests – could provide the extra 45 per cent rice production that Asia needs by the year 2000. Or so biotechnologists claim. What is needed is a more sober, human context for such claims. At the political level, the target should not be to build a capability in biotechnology at all costs but to alleviate poverty – which is surely the principal goal of development – and to see where biotechnology might help.

However, in practice, even where the interests of donors are clearly in favour of effective biotechnical aid, it is by no means easy to determine what aid would be appropriate. So what of the conditions in the countries where these technologies might be applied? How could better, more appropriate applications be developed?

Here I have collected and report views, including my own, which aim to help in reaching three goals: appropriate agricultural biotechnology; appropriate medical biotechnology; and more objective environmental thinking.

Appropriate agricultural biotechnology

The fundamental danger of much current biotechnology, the most advanced of which is in private, Northern hands, is that it could force resource-poor tropical farmers to take up inappropriate biotechnology products – ones developed basically for Northern markets – or quit, because no other options have been considered.

Paul Richards of the School of Oriental and African Studies, University of London, the agricultural anthropologist, argues (personal communication) that 'a strong, continuing commitment to public sector research *might* compensate' for the existing private, Northern emphasis of biotechnology. But he doubts whether that commitment will be forthcoming, as few public research institutes in the South have really demonstrated that they can reach out to and meet client requirements: even they tend to work in near-isolation, preferring to deliver research *ex cathedra* rather than respond directly to expressed grass roots demands. In Richards's view, if the public sector is to deliver truly relevant products, researchers need to find new attitudes of respect for rural need – and local knowledge – and new structures to identify appropriate research priorities. 'Short of such a new beginning, I cannot see biotechnology being harnessed to the needs of the poorest and most needy groups'.

The real need lies in the marginal lands, the drier and more risk-prone environments of Asia and Africa where farmers are poorer, and the 'Green Revolution' varieties of rice and wheat, which require high inputs of water, fertilizers and pesticides, are not appropriate. So what are the key issues that researchers must bear in mind if such areas are to be aided? Richards, writing from Sierra Leone, says that there

> no-one is asking for high-yielding varieties – all they want is to be able to buy or borrow enough to plant the land they have cleared with tried and test varieties (rice for men, groundnuts for women). Their main problem – bird damage – is intractable. Their main experiments are new social strategies for mobilizing timely labour. Scientists busy doing biotechnology must recognize the urgent need to provide farmers scope to solve these other kinds of managerial and combinatorial problems.

However, even where researchers actually want to respond to the needs and priorities of the poorest and most vulnerable groups it is often especially difficult to figure out what these needs actually are.

The popular buzz-words are 'consultation' and 'participation' – but committees do not design effective farming systems. In the village or the field, conventions of politeness may result in farmers saying what the researcher wants to hear; local power structures may mean that the poor will only say what the ruling elites – usually male – want them to say. 'The only way round this' says Richards 'is to look at what the farmers *do* as much as what they say.'

In Sierra Leone, farmers may say they want assistance to develop swamp farms (because they perceive the Ministry of Agriculture to have had a long-standing interest in that sort of thing), but in reality they may spend much of their time and effort trying to locate short-duration rices, or open up groundnut and cassava farms.

'Even though much further work is needed to assess whether what they are driving towards will, in the end, add up to a coherent sustainable strategy, the experiments that farmers undertake for themselves give some clue as to what directions are, for them, currently feasible and attractive', Richards argues. Richards is not optimistic for biotechnology in Sierra Leone, because as yet 'no research reaches this sector and impacts on these farmers' lives, for good or ill.' But if there are to be biotechnology applications, the most appropriate for the poor in Sierra Leone would be 'anything that will continue to yield in poor soils with "low management" (i.e. in conditions of labour shortage), and that would accelerate the breeding process as a means of combining desired characteristics.'

According to Donald Duvick, research director of the US-based multinational Plant Hi-Bred International, one of the world's largest seed companies, the new plant biotechnologies most likely to be of immediate use in developing countries are tissue culture (micropropagation and cloning of useful plants, embryo rescue for wide crossing, anther culture for speeding breeding programmes) and new precise disease diagnosis (Walgate, 1990). Nevertheless, compared with the 'Green Revolution', whose high-yield varieties averted famine in Asia and boosted cereal production in South America (but left Africa out), the new plant biotechnology will offer greater capacity to respond to precise user needs in matters of soil deficiency, drought, salinification, pests and diseases, which particularly affect African farmers. However, while such new plant biotechnology could reduce poverty among consumers and farmers, it threatens other groups, particularly those who might be affected by changes in relative agricultural efficiency – for example smallholder outgrowers of commercial crops (such as cocoa producers in West Africa), and agricultural labourers.

In developing appropriate research programmes, the following key points stand out.

(1) Marginal environments are often extremely fragile.

(2) In introducing new species and technologies to marginal environments, only the most flexible and responsive strategies for improvement will succeed.

(3) Historically, indigenous agriculture was often well-adapted to those environments. Remnants of such practices remain and can be learned from. Amazingly, when scientists with the International Board for the Protection of Genetic Resources collect species to conserve germplasm, no corresponding information is gathered on local uses of those plants. Much useful information may thus be being lost.

(4) In good times, even the poorest farmers and food preparers experiment with new methods, inoculants and new seeds from corners of their plots and from neighbours and travellers. Much can be learned from these 'informal' experiments.

(5) However, every farm and every farmer is different from place to place and year to year. So there are very few consistent patterns in the data. Too many factors are in play at once.

(6) Moreover, in present economic conditions in Africa, according to Richards, 'landless, debt-ridden, seasonally hungry farmers do not have much room for initiatives'.

(7) Data should be assembled on smallholder crop production from place to place and year to year, to identify leader and laggard crops and areas, candidates for research, and information on the success or failure of innovations.

(8) There must be positive efforts to identify real (and often diverse) end-user needs. For example, in Sierra Leone, a common farmers' preference is for lots of variability in the germplasm 'because that promises an escape route when the unexpected happens, as it always does' (P. Richards, personal communication).

(9) It would seem obvious that poor farmers in Africa need innovations that reduce risks from sporadic droughts and pest invasions, and that require few inputs. However, research planners should be aware that listening to farmers might lead to unexpected research requirements: for example, to provide snake serum to enable women to cut brushwood in greater safety.

(10) Research should aim to make local food compete in price with internationally traded grain.

(11)   Researchers must learn how improved varieties that they develop might or might not fit in to farmers' systems and seasons of production, work and consumption.

(12)   Labour and other input requirements of each potential technology must be taken into account. For example, in areas of rural under-employment (most of Asia), it must provide rural jobs to increase the numbers of people winning entitlement to food. But in areas of labour shortage (as in parts of Africa) it must reduce women's work load. It has been estimated that maize yield in Swaziland could be raised 50% if women farmers had the labour to plant and weed on time.

(13)   Attention must be paid to the distribution of any economic returns.

(14)   Farmers must be allowed to test out innovations before wholesale introduction.

(15)   Ideally, there should be strong local control of any resulting technology.

(16)   Environmental sustainability, including any danger of soil erosion, reduced fertility, or susceptibility to pests must not be ignored.

(17)   Provision must be made to avoid the genetic erosion of useful old land races and wild species by the widespread introduction of a 'superior' crop.

(18)   Research personnel and management must be adequate. For example in Africa, applications will be affected by the poor condition of African national research bodies, and their lack of farmer participation.

(19)   Professional researchers often ignore the linkages between their disciplines on the farm. Effective agricultural research must include at least breeders, pathologists, physiologists and food scientists.

(20)   There must be open, effective advance planning, policy-making and budgeting at ministries of agriculture and research.

(21)   While private biotechnology aims at profit, there may be no 'economic' use for marginal regions, other than as conservation and amenity areas managed by local peoples. Such uses are indeed encouraged in the North – for example, in the support of sheep farming on North-temperate uplands to preserve 'areas of natural beauty' for city leisure.

Short of real surveys of need, the present 'best estimates' of sympathetic experts are that smallholder technologies are required in Africa which will keep national food outputs growing at least as fast as populations, provide food cheap enough for the poor of the country to afford adequate diets, and, in some areas, employ people to generate rural incomes and to fill in seasonal gaps in productive work.

In Asia and elsewhere, those who failed to benefit from the 'Green Revolution' were mostly the rural poor in areas where the high-yielding varieties of crops were not used, because of a lack of reliable water supplies, poor climate, little access to necessary inputs, or poorly developed infrastructure to deliver inputs and sell surpluses. In South East Asia, 86.5 million hectares of poor soil are unsuitable for the new high-yielding crops because of poor soil conditions. In fact many in such areas were impoverished, as production increases in better-off regions led to reductions in world and local prices of rice and wheat. Biotechnology must help people farming these soils make a better living. However, while vitally important work on smallholder crops is relatively starved of funds, research on established crops is stretching the environmental limits of those crops further and further into marginal lands. This could push farmers into even worse conditions than they presently suffer if it proves they are unable to afford the new varieties.

Agricultural research in Africa needs to take more account of farmers' old-established agro-ecological practices and then to improve on them. Half the farmed land of Africa is under shifting cultivation – which was successful in the past. But population pressure, and the increases in estate cash cropping, which are pushing more and more farmers onto marginal lands, mean that these lands cannot be left fallow for long enough to regenerate. This leads to decreasing productivity and soil erosion. Biotechnology could be applied to reducing cultivation pressure and speeding up the fallowing recovery. Fast-growing leguminous trees could be developed for revitalizing the land; appropriate improved nitrogen-fixing bacterial inoculants could be developed; and mixed farming and alley cropping could be improved to reduce the impact of cultivation. Such research should closely involve farmers, to help identify essential and often localized constraints that research could break through.

Appropriate medical biotechnology

Much ill-health, in what statesmen Willi Brandt (Germany) and Edward Heath (UK) described, with some violence to geography, as 'the South' – the mass of developing countries – in contrast to the industrialized 'North', is the result of microbial and parasitic infections. Almost all biotechnological attempts to deal with them involve the cloning of relevant genes in bacteria. So how can biotechnology help to improve health in the South?

Medical biotechnology has developed in the rich North to a very high degree. For example, after an expensive race between US and British groups, scientists last August pin-pointed the gene for cystic fibrosis, the most common and eventually fatal genetic disorder in industrialized countries. The discovery may lead to new treatments or to the abortion of embryos carrying double copies of the gene – the condition that leads to the disease.

Some 35 000 children are born with cystic fibrosis each year throughout Europe and the USA. Research was right not to abandon them – and possible future unborn sufferers – to their fate. Yet approaching 20 million children are dying every year in the developing world from many other diseases. 'Rich countries must transfer technology, health manpower and power, because the poorest countries cannot help themselves' said the WHO director-general, Hiroshi Nakajima (WHO 1989a).

Ten million children are dying each year from respiratory diseases. Four million die from diarrhoea; and another two million from measles. Some 2.5 billion people suffer from episodic malaria, and 1.5 million – mostly children – die of the disease each year. A billion are affected by tuberculosis, which kills nearly a million people a year. Another million die from hepatitis B, according to Julia Walsh of the Harvard School of Public Health (Walsh, 1988). Many of these deaths are preventable, and in other cases research – usually requiring biotechnology – would provide better treatments or new vaccines.

Some may ask why more children should be saved when world populations are rising so unsustainably fast, particularly in the poorest of developing countries. In fact, better care for infants and mothers leads to smaller families – as has been seen clearly in the southern Indian state of Karnataka and in Columbia in South America. People act rationally. Where there is no state welfare, they have enough children that some will survive to look after them and to provide family income through their labour. Apart from its obvious simple humanity, health provision and child survival must be seen as part of a philosophy of improved welfare and development which will ultimately reduce population growth, just as it has in the rich North.

Simple diagnostic tests are also important, to ensure that patients are given appropriate treatments. Meanwhile, however, mothers should be listened to more carefully: in a recent health survey in a village in Gambia, mothers' diagnoses of basic disease categories in their children proved to be highly accurate, in a situation where early diagnosis of malaria complications can be essential to avoid death (B.M. Greenwood, *Malaria: killer of African children*, unpublished technical presentation to the 12th Joint Coordinating Board of the UNDP/World Bank/WHO Special Programme of Research and Training in Tropical

Diseases, 1989). Of course, safe water, sanitation, personal hygiene, nutrition, immunization – and the effective communication of simple, basic disease-prevention messages – could do a great deal to improve health in developing countries and reduce these tolls, as did similar measures a century ago in the industrialized world.

A hundred years ago in London, many died regularly of malaria along the marshy banks of the Thames; the mosquito that carried the malaria parasite can still be found in London's central green area, Hyde Park (C.J. Schofield, personal communication). Only decades of hygiene and development eventually rid the capital of the disease.

The same could happen in developing countries. But how soon? Many of the necessary public health interventions (such as safe water and clean sanitation for all) are very expensive and still a long way off. They will only come as fast as economic development – which seems a very distant prospect in the face of current debts being repaid by the poor nations to the rich. (Brazil alone paid Northern public and private lenders and banks a net US$56 billion in excess of debt repayments over aid in 1984–9.)

Some cheap interventions are already possible, however. According to Nakajima (see WHO, 1989*a*) the rate of disease and disablement in developing countries is 'a preventable tragedy – because the developed world has the resources and technology to end common diseases worldwide'. Oral re-hydration therapy salts for treating children with diarrhoea cost just 10 US cents a pack. As little as US$50 million a year could prevent two million child deaths, says Nakajima. And existing cheap vaccines against polio, tetanus, measles, diphtheria, whooping cough and tuberculosis, which can be delivered for around US$10 a head, could save another three million child deaths a year. Nevertheless, while in principle much can be done in this way, success is still far off. 'Despite massive, creative educational efforts (in promoting oral rehydration therapy), diarrhoeal disease mortality has not declined substantially' Walsh (1988). Furthermore, the vaccines currently available cannot tackle the major tropical parasitic diseases, such as malaria or Chagas disease.

Biotechnology would appear to be even further upstream. Certainly, it offers no immediate cure-all for diseases which have so many complex economic, environmental and social causes, as well as medical ones.

'A medical friend' writes Paul Richards from Sierra Leone (personal communication) 'reckons that in the tropics we now know most of what we need to know to make life very much more secure and healthy for the great majority. The remaining problems are either intractable or are luxuries. But the research juggernaut rolls on – no-one wins a Nobel Prize, or whatever, for making effective use of existing knowledge.' But, on the other hand, biotechnology does promise new interventions – particularly in vaccines (for example against bacteria causing diarrhoea, and against parasites) and drugs – which may offer new short cuts to health in developing countries. If well-designed, taking account of real conditions in the South, they could be of great use.

According to Walsh (1988)

> . . . the biotechnology revolution provides an extraordinary opportunity to identify unique immunogens for vaccines, antigens for diagnosis and surveillance, and drugs. Rapid methods exist for analysing the metabolic pathways peculiar to invading organisms and synthesising new drugs or vector control chemicals . . . The new biotechnology research techniques offer a historic opportunity for . . . treatment of the endemic diseases of the tropics.

New or improved vaccines are expected to be ready within five years for pertussis (whooping cough), *Hemophilus influenza* type B, influenza virus A and B, hepatitis A, *Herpes simplex, Neisseria meningitidis,* parainfluenza virus, rabies virus, respiratory syncytial virus, rotavirus (a major cause of child death from diarrhoea), *Salmonella typhi, Streptococcus pneumoniae,* and *Vibrio cholerae;* and within 10 years for Dengue, enterotoxigenic *Escherichia coli,* HIV, Japanese B encephalitis, *Mycobacterium leprae, Neisseria gonorrhoeae,* Plasmodium species (malaria), and Streptococcus groups A and B. An antipregnancy vaccine and a male anti-fertility vaccine should also be available within 10 years (Walsh, 1988).

Biotechnology is being applied to the many diseases in the Third World that are still not effectively curable or preventable, or where present treatments are difficult to deliver to those who need them. Here, biotechnology is rapidly accelerating the research and development of effective cures, preventative measures and delivery mechanisms. But how are research priorities to be set? Walsh (1988) argues for a rational health and research programme based on the actual burden of the various diseases and causes of death, and the present estimates of the costs of intervention and research. Also, researchers must know about local conditions, where a new health measure will be used. Clearly, a good health measure must be medically effective – but that is not all. It must be applicable through the primary health care system (for example, vaccines must not degrade if warmed, and should be easy to administer hygienically); and assured of full compliance by the patients.

Vaccines, in particular, must be delivered in a single dose. The personal immunity induced by the vaccine will prevent carriage and transmission of the pathogen (producing what doctors call 'herd immunity'). The vaccines will be stable at tropical temperatures for long periods. They will be easy to administer through a cheap disposable device not requiring on-site sterilization. They will cost much less than US$ 1 per dose. They will work on the new-born or early infant. They will have minimal side effects. They will be combinable with other vaccines in a single shot. They will not 'cross-react' – one vaccine will not cause a reaction against another (mainly a matter of ensuring purity). Immunity will be established shortly after vaccination (to stop epidemics quickly). It will be easy to discover what proportion of a population has received the vaccine (smallpox vaccine, for example, left a small scar on the arm).

Diagnostic and surveillance tools must be developed for effective diagnosis, for epidemiology, and for monitoring of treatment effectiveness. The vectors (such as mosquitoes) of diseases must be effectively controlled, now that attempts to eliminate them with DDT and other insecticides have faltered. Micronutrient dietary supplements (for example iodine) must be supplied to areas where they are deficient.

For pharmaceuticals, as with vaccines, the objective of research should be to find a drug which is effective in a single dose, has few adverse reactions, is cheap, is easily administered in primary health care. 'Vaccines are the most important health measure' says Walsh (1988), because they are triply effective – against sickness, death and (disease) transmission. Drugs and diagnostic tools have a slightly lower priority as 'usually the patient must have some degree of ill-health before seeking therapy'. After vaccines must come improvements in environmental health (sanitation and detoxification) and be accompanied by improvements in agriculture.

Vaccines also have another spin-off – a stimulus to the health system. Speaking of the campaign begun in 1988 to eradicate poliomyelitis, Ciro de Quadros, Latin American regional director of the Pan American Health Organisation (PAHO), said (personal communication) 'polio is a vehicle. It will help us deliver a whole health structure'.

De Quadros's experience is that programmes like the World Health Organization's Extended Programme of Immunization, which has delivered six cheap existing vaccines to half the world's children, can, if properly managed, raise the competence, standing, and morale of local health personnel, and of the whole health service. Health workers have 'a new sense of service' as a result of vaccination campaigns, de Quadros believes. 'They can see that when they are well-organised and well-supported they get results.' Children don't get polio any more. 'So their morale is very high' and confidence and support for the whole primary health care system improves.

Carlos Castillho, representative of the United Nations Children's Fund (UNICEF) in Haiti, felt the same about the first successful vaccination days in Haiti in 1988. 'Haiti had the lowest level of child immunization in the Americas. It was very sad' said Castillho (personal communication). But the vaccination days had been 'a tremendous victory – a miracle'. 'It was a victory for ordinary people' reported The Panos Institute (Walgate, 1988). Such victories are very rare in Haiti. According to Xavier Leus of the World Health Organization 'for the first time ever in Haiti they are taking services to the people, rather than waiting for them to come and ask. We know we won't reach 100% but just setting the objective has been highly significant . . . It's a re-orientation' (Walgate, 1988).

However, for such successes, the organization of vaccination campaigns has to be excellent, sensitive to local need and designed to leave not just vaccines behind – but also structures and new social and political attitudes and demands.

Moreover, partly for lack of research, but also because of technical difficulties, some important diseases have no prospect of an effective vaccine within a decade. Second only to malaria, tuberculosis (TB) kills probably three million people a year out of 20 million sufferers. Some 50–100 million people are at risk of the disease (Grange, 1989). The present 60-year-old 'BCG' vaccine against TB has only very variable degrees of success.

Research is needed on creating immunity to *Mycobacteria tuberculosis*, the active organism of tuberculosis. A mycobacterium also causes leprosy: *M. leprae*. A leprosy vaccine, produced through the culture of *M. leprae* in armadillos, is now on lengthy trial; but the difficulties of production will limit its usefulness, and biotechnology will help develop more practical and widely available substitutes.

Vaccines must be developed for the respiratory pathogens *Mycoplasma pneumoniae* and *Staphylococcus aureus*. Respiratory diseases kill 10 million people a year, most of them children. Vaccines must be developed for killer diarrhoeal disease caused by *Shigella, Campylobacter* and enteropathogenic *Escherichia coli*. Other than malaria, many of the parasitic diseases such as amoebiasis, hookworm, trypanosomiasis, onchocerciasis, ascariasis and leishmaniasis demand more intensive immunological research and vaccine development.

Effective means of controlling sexually transmitted diseases are also urgent, particularly in Africa where rapid change has disrupted traditional societies and resulted in greater transmission, probably also carrying with it greater transmission of the HIV (AIDS) viruses.

Walsh (1988) selects eight vaccine areas where research should be increased: tuberculosis vaccine; respiratory vaccines; group B Streptococcus (a major cause of maternal and infant mortality in the Third World); syphilis; amoebiasis; immunoadjuvants (chemicals given with the simpler vaccines designed to stimulate the immune system into action: they are particularly needed for the very young); improving the temperature stability of old and new vaccines; and family planning vaccines for men and women.

Vaccine development costs are, unfortunately, high and success is not always assured. After identifying an effective immunogen in animal and preliminary human trials, it will cost US$ 20–30 million and 7–10 years of development to arrive at a vaccine available and usable by ordinary paramedics in the field. The funding of development work on potential new vaccines for tropical diseases – much more expensive than the basic research which led up to them – may prove difficult. For example, the US Biotechnology company, Genentech, had agreed to develop a promising New York University vaccine against the sporozoite stage of the malaria parasite, but backed out when it calculated there was little profit to be made. The small British biotechnology agency, Rural Investment Overseas Ltd (RIO), considered developing vaccines against tropical diseases in the Philippines, in collaboration with the biotechnology group of Los Banos University in that country. However, the project was abandoned 'because the market size was too small'. Other plans are afoot, however, to help developers cover the costs of the development work through direct grants from outside donors (such as UNDP). The vaccine producers would then sell the vaccine to WHO at production cost only.

There can be technical setbacks along the way. Ty21a is a disabled typhoid bacillus discovered in 1975. Trials using the bacillus as a vaccine in Egypt produced high levels of protection. But later trials in Chile with a modified dose regime produced much lower protection, and new trials are underway in Chile and Indonesia.

The greatest hurdle may be clinical trials of new drugs and vaccines since they require large, carefully followable populations and experienced field study teams that sometimes must work in poorly accessible areas. (In pursuing such trials it will be essential to have the willing compliance of the population and the active help of the local health, media and political forces.) Full-scale trials are already needed to test ivermectin for filariasis, new anti-malarials, and difluoro-methyl-orthinine against African trypanosomiasis. Several places are conducting excellent field epidemiologic studies and can serve as models for others, such as the International Centre of Diarrhoeal Disease Research in Bangladesh; the British Medical Research Laboratory in Gambia; the respiratory disease and malaria field sites in Papua New Guinea; and the Kasongo Primary Health Care Project in Zaire.

Antibiotics are very erratically available in developing countries. A project developed by Biotics Ltd for approval by the European

Commission called the 'Regional Antibiotics Manufacturing Project' (RAMP) envisages joint antibiotic-making ventures between regional groups of less-developed countries (LDCs), established pharmaceutical companies and international donors. The manufacturing plants would be built in developing countries at the donors' cost. The LDC would provide labour, raw materials (fermentation feedstocks) and a guaranteed local market. They would gain health care improvements, jobs and a technology; the pharmaceutical company would gain a new source of supply at zero capital cost.

Few good diagnostic tests are available in Third World primary health care. Different pathogens, requiring different treatments, can cause similar symptoms – but a more precise diagnosis will distinguish them. Ovulation tests could provide an accurate means for some couples to plan families without contraceptives, important for Catholic communities. In public health, accurate tests will improve the assessment of existing disease control programmes and aid the planning of new ones. Nucleic acid hybridization tests have already been developed – at least in the laboratory – for enterotoxic *E. coli*, gonorrhoea, *Leishmania mexicana*, *Plasmodium falciparum* and *P. vivax* (the main malarial parasites), some *Salmonella* species, some *Shigella* species, cytomegalovirus, adenovirus, hepatitis B and some enteroviruses. Many require commercialization and/or field testing to prove their efficacy. Diagnostic equipment for primary health care in the Third World should be simple to use, cheap, fast, accurate, stable, and need minimal instrumentation.

In diagnosis, says Walsh (1988), quick, cheap and simple diagnostic tests are needed to measure haemoglobin levels, test water quality, test concentrations of ORT salts, identify different malaria parasites and their drug resistance, and identify different respiratory pathogens.

Applied research should aim for cheaper vaccines and drug production processes that are needed so the materials can be prepared in the Third World; improved storage and administration equipment; systems which will simultaneously administer several antigens; and better public health data.

In epidemiology, investigation is needed into the connection between infections in pregnancy and low-birth-weight babies. Eliminating low birth-weight should save 5 million lives annually. Similarly, the causes of maternal mortality (500 000 deaths annually, with serious consequences for whole families) should be investigated. In both cases, better scientific understanding of the causes should lead to more effective health strategies and treatments. Thorough field evaluations are also needed of the health impact of the World Health Organisation's present Extended Programme of Immunization and the Diarrhoeal Disease Control Programme.

Vector control will be improved by an integrated approach using all the tools of modern biology and public education – from filling in puddles and turning over cans (to prevent the growth of mosquito larvae), and other environmental management techniques including the use of larva-eating fishes in rice paddies, to the selection, possibly by the genetic engineering and release of bacteria, viruses and other organisms that will prey on disease vectors (and other pests). New less toxic but more effective chemical insecticides and control strategies may also be developed using detailed understanding of specific insect metabolisms and behaviour – such as the use of ox-breath substitutes to attract tsetse flies to insecticidal traps over kilometre ranges in Africa.

Of course, it is naive to suppose that the world will apply such a rational, cost-effective approach to reducing developing country diseases. Political and economic priorities turn heads in other directions. Nevertheless rational work is going on, particularly through the UNDP/World Bank/WHO Special Programme for Research and Training in Tropical Diseases (TDR). This specializes in seven main disease groups where the burden is high, and where industrialized world scientists could be persuaded to do work (by virtue of the mere scientific interest of the problem posed): these are malaria, schistosomiasis, the filariases, African trypanosomiasis, Chagas disease, the leishmaniases, and leprosy.

Also, many Northern scientists have turned to looking at tropical diseases simply because they offer a great scientific challenge. For example, the organisms that cause sleeping sickness (African trypanosomiasis), *Trypanosoma brucei brucei* and *T. brucei rhodesiense*, change their protein coats with bewildering speed to defeat the body's defences, using a massive 10% of their genomes to perform these changes. Because of this, and the light it sheds on bodily defences, rather than because of the impact of the disease, many molecular biologists have studied sleeping sickness at the molecular level.

On the other side of the coin, the Latin American Chagas disease, caused by a related organism, *Trypanosoma cruzi*, is less well studied, arguably because it is less interesting to molecular biologists: *T. cruzi* does not change its coat. Even here, though, the parasite offers basic molecular biological research opportunities – so that, for example, in 1987, despite a very tight research budget, the UK Medical Research Council increased its funding of tropical disease research, and granted one London biologist the opportunity to study *T. cruzi*, not for its medical importance, but for the light it shed on molecular biology.

Leprosy also has fascinated some scientists, quite apart from its medical importance, because of its apparent ability to turn off the body's defence apparatus, the immune system. Barry Bloom, a leading leprosy researcher in New York, said when he started 'it was hard to find six people for a meeting. Now it's almost a cottage industry' (personal communication).

Developing country scientists are also at work. For example in malaria, Victor Nussenzweig, a malaria specialist at New York University, says his work would not have been possible without his collaborators at the University of São Paolo and elsewhere. Colombian researcher Professor Pattaroyo has developed his own trial malaria vaccine. Sri Lanka boasts excellent malaria research.

Because of such research, North and South, the impacts of molecular biology and biotechnology on tropical disease are not negligible, and are increasing rapidly. Historically, pharmaceutical development has long been somewhat random. Thousands of compounds are tested for effects. Chemical modifications are made to the more promising ones – adding and taking away small groups of atoms here and there – in an attempt to improve performance, and a few resulting compounds prove useful. With greater understanding of disease organisms, and the body's reaction to them, however, it is proving possible to indulge in 'rational' drug design – targeting the organisms' weak spots.

These weak spots are most likely to be fundamental chemical steps taken by pathogens during their life in the body – such as the molecular mechanism whereby a malaria merozoite invades a red blood cell, or the 'metabolic pathway' whereby it gains oxygen. If (cheap) drugs could be designed to block these processes, while leaving the human host unaffected, the parasites would be effectively controlled.

Since rational vaccines require the identification of antigens, and since antigens are usually on the surface of a pathogen for a purpose (for example, in order to grapple with and enter a target cell), the development of vaccines against antigens can go hand in hand with the development of drugs against the same pieces of antigenic apparatus. Indeed, some scientists feel that since critical parts of the immune system, principally cell-mediated (T-cell) immunity, are still not well-explained, the search for vaccines may well lead to new drugs before it leads to effective vaccines.

One class of drugs that shows promise is the interferons (α, β, γ-interferon), a group of polypeptides produced by the cell-mediated immune apparatus to stimulate other immune cells and to deal with viruses.

Interferons were one of the first classes of protein to be produced commercially – by the genetic engineering of the interferon genes into *Escherichia coli* – because of indications from the reaction of a few Scandinavian patients that they might have a revolutionary impact on cancer. This proved not to be the case, except for one rare cancer ('hairy-cell' leukaemia). But now, interferons may be showing their worth against tropical diseases, according to evidence presented at a conference on the drugs in Havana, Cuba, in April 1989, where French and Brazilian scientists presented 'dramatic success' in treating visceral leishmaniasis with γ-interferon. The drug re-activated a depressed T-cell immune response to the diseases in 17 patients, who appeared 'cured' after just 10 days of treatment (Bialey, 1989).

Interleukin 2, was another T-cell signal molecule like the interferons, was reported at the same meeting, in work from New York, Louisiana and Addis Abbaba, to re-activate cell-mediated immunity against advanced leprosy (Bialey, 1989).

The research editor of Bio/Technology, Harvey Bialey, wrote (1989): 'It is a bit ironic and a bit wonderful that now – when we know how to produce them so cheaply – the first glamour drugs of biotechnology are showing such promise in the treatment of . . . "the diseases of the poor". Let's hope that this time we're right'.

Among other promising new drugs available, difluoromethylornithine targets a precise metabolic pathway in African trypanosomiasis. Ivermectin has proved highly effective in single-dose clinical trials against onchocerciasis and is showing encouraging results against lymphatic filariasis in India. Single-dose praziquantel has proved the most valuable treatment for schistosomiasis, and is poised for large-scale use in control programmes. Encouraging trends are emerging in the control of leprosy, grown resistant to traditional dapsone, with rifampicin, clofazimine and dapsone as a multi-drug treatment. Chemical derivatives several times more active than artemisinin, the active principle 'qinghaosu' of the Chinese herb 'quinghao', are being developed and have appeared to be effective against drug-resistant malaria; and recently licensed mefloquine in combination with pyrimethamine and sulphadoxine is also effective, and several other anti-malarial drugs are under development (WHO, 1989b).

How can a barefoot doctor easily prescribe the right treatment for the right disease? It might be simple if he or she had new diagnostic aids using monoclonal antibody or nucleic acid hybridization tests. However, present tests, while allowing mass screening of many patients at once, take longer to develop than a single patient is likely to wait, and are more useful in epidemiology and public health planning than in treatment. However, even in this use they will affect treatment, by allowing the efficient use of meagre health resources through surveys to indicate the prevalence of different diseases in different areas.

If new diagnostics can be used quickly and routinely by relatively untrained staff, and are cheap enough to be widely distributed, they will also help authorities to identify and react to developing epidemic conditions. DNA probes, for example, can handle large numbers of tests in one batch, so whole populations can be scanned. In Thailand, 5000 finger-prick blood samples were scanned for malaria with a DNA probe in two days: the standard microscope-and-slide method would have taken many times as long.

'The short-term effects of biotechnology will be in diagnostics' says Tore Godal, director of the UNDP/World Bank/WHO Special Programme of Research and Training in Tropical Diseases (TDR) (personal communication). 'Malaria is already well-covered – and probes are being explored in all other diseases.' Biotechnology is producing potential diagnostic techniques much faster than any other medical product, partly because the problem of diagnosis is easier to tackle than that of cure or treatment, and partly because there is less need for lengthy trials of tests in animals and humans. (Such essential efficacy and safety trials for a new drug or vaccine may delay its introduction for many years.) TDR lists 22 such products in its 1989 biennial report (WHO, 1989b) which have emerged from its research programmes – ranging from a monoclonal antibody test for *Brugia malayi* (a cause of filariasis) in insect larvae to synthetic peptides to test for antibodies to *Plasmodium falciparum* (a cause of malaria), to DNA probes for *Trypanosoma cruzi*, the cause of Chagas disease.

But what about production? It is all very well developing a new test in the laboratory, but there may be a long way to go before it can be made robust enough for field use. One of TDR's answers has been to establish a 'biotechnology initiative', a programme which has been identifying indigenous researchers, laboratories and companies to develop and produce diagnostic kits practical enough to use in the field. Another has been to establish a 'product development unit' which will foster greater cooperation between TDR and industry, drawing on industry's expertise both upstream in screening new drugs, and downstream in selecting and developing those research ideas which will make real marketable products.

The biotechnology initiative – begun in 1989 – will format the research idea into kit form – perhaps taking six months to a year to work out what is practical in the field, and then move to a first level of 'scale-up' to produce milligram or gram amounts of the relevant biological agents (DNA probe etc.) for the production of say 10 000 kits for large-scale field testing. The final step – if the tests are successful – will be a full scaling-up of production, and an integration and use of the product in the control and monitoring programme for the disease. TDR's product development unit was to begin work in 1990.

Better systems are also needed to deliver micronutrients. Lack of vitamin A causes 500 000 cases of corneal blindness and 6–7 million cases of non-corneal xerophthalmia among pre-school children. Some 800 million people live in areas deficient in iodine. Iron deficiency is widespread among reproductive women and young children. Control of these deficiencies need not await further research, but research is showing the key role of vitamin A in diminishing mortality and occurrences of common tropical diseases and certain epithelial cancers, and indicating the importance of iodine for normal growth – particularly of the brain of the unborn child. The biotechnical route to the solution of these problems would be to develop food crops with improved take-up of micronutrients, or production of vitamins. Work is in progress on a rice with a higher content of vitamin A.

Putting environmental risks in context

Current biotechnology is a combination of power and ignorance – power over the genome but relative ignorance of biological interactions from the level of the cell to the whole organism and on to the surrounding ecosystem. So is biotechnology dangerous?

There are two main issues: laboratory safety, where most institutions have regulations approximating the once stringent, but increasingly relaxed (or ignored), US National Institutes of Health guidelines; and the deliberate release of genetically engineered organisms. Laboratory safety is ignored here, to concentrate attention on the potential environmental (and health) risks of the release of genetically engineered organisms: altered microbes, plants and animals. What are these risks? Arguably, none of them are radically new – for what is being done is to introduce genes from one biological environment into another. This is an old game, played whenever some species of creature, from a disease organism to a tree, or even rabbits or foxes, were moved from one continent to another.

Genetic engineers, introducing a single gene or two within a cell, are unlikely to introduce anything as dangerous as a whole organism can be: for example, Kariba weed, a Latin American water plant that grows by division, thus 'cloning' itself, became so prolific that it choked the Kariba dam on the Zambesi River and several other water courses until a predator beetle was discovered that would devour it. The beetle, though not genetically engineered, was, however, taken from its original location and deliberately released into the new environment of the Kariba dam.

Genetically engineered organisms sound more dangerous because of their unfamiliarity. In fact, genetic engineering is only an amplification of what farmers have long done and continue to do – to shuffle genes through breeding to create useful plants and animals.

So there is no fundamental new biological risk involved in the release of genetically engineered organisms where the genes have arisen from harmless organisms whether they be microbial, plant or animal in origin.

The real risks of deliberate release today arise from three causes.

(1)   The short timescale on which the genes are shuffled, compared with traditional breeding methods, allowing little time for testing or ecological adjustment.

(2)   The breadth of the gene pool which is being and will be shuffled, widening the range of 'farmers' experiments'.

(3)   The exotic mechanisms used to do the work – laboratory gene splicing and cloning – which inevitably separates researchers from the real conditions where their discoveries and products will be used.

The scale, speed and objectives of gene, genome and organism transfers are the matters that introduce new risks, not the biology of the process itself (though see below for a few special examples of potential risk).

And whether old or new, the risks must be taken seriously because of the following.

The general public perceives the technology to be risky: it has many of the hallmarks of 'radiation'. Its operations are invisible, microscopic, and in the hands of experts whom the public do not understand and therefore may not trust.

Of their nature, genetic systems – like the Kariba weed – multiply themselves. The risk of a replicating, dangerous genetic system is thus of a potentially different order than, say, the release of a finite amount of oil from a tanker.

Since human error will continue forever, since technology often proceeds by learning from audacious mistakes (consider the history of bridge building), and since more and more gene transfers are going to be done, over wider and wider species barriers, in more and more varied ecologies, with little knowledge of local conditions, it seems certain that there will one day be some mistake – some release that eventually will be regretted, even if it is no more dangerous than Kariba weed or the rabbit in Australia.

In developing countries, there are added complications.

The technology is often in the hands of an economically far stronger foreigner – usually a multinational company or a foreign government – whose motives may be suspect.

The lax or non-existent regulations controlling biotechnology experiments and releases in Third World countries are attractive to companies or institutions wishing to test products that cannot be tested in the tougher regulatory climate of their home country.

There are recent examples of both complications: India banned the testing of genetically engineered vaccines developed in the USA, even though the vaccines might prove useful in India (for example, they include potential vaccines against malaria), being suspicious of American motives; the Argentina government and public reacted strongly after an unauthorized test of a live, engineered rabies vaccine by a US institute on an Argentinian farm; and in the Philippines, public controversy halted a rice rust experiment and stopped the import of key gene mapping reagents to speed rice breeding.

Regulation on the release of genetically engineered organisms 'will be the pacing item' in the application of biotechnology to developing country crops, according to Ellen Messer of the World Hunger Programme, who has been studying these issues at Brown University, USA (personal communication). It is essential therefore to: make ecological and physiological studies of the risks of the genes 'escaping' from engineered varieties, and entering wild plants (the risk of herbicide resistance is the most obvious); to decide where it is safest to run trials; and to decide what studies should be done before allowing a particular release. The public will get to know what is happening – 'and if that knowledge comes by rumour, the reaction will be much worse' said Messer. 'The information must come from the scientists' she said. Moreover 'the public need the information to get the benefit from the science'. The information could be provided through national conferences and 'careful work with newspapers' Messer said.

But in the public perception 'the public trust of scientists vanished with Chernobyl and Bhopal – I saw it fall away – there's a big gulf to bridge' says Hubert Zandstra, research director of the International Rice Research Institute (IRRI) in the Philippines (personal communication). After a controversy over an IRRI experiment with rice blast fungus, the Philippines government banned the import of DNA probes etc. until proper regulations are in force. 'We can't import mapping probes from Cornell because of the restrictions' said Lesley Sitch, who runs the wide crossing programme at IRRI (personal communication).

Biosafety committees must be set up to judge upon – and where appropriate – approve, the movement of the materials of the trade. The lack of such assessment processes (and consequent *ad hoc* regulation) 'is beginning to be the major constraint on our work' Zandstra said (personal communication).

These reflections lead to four basic conclusions.

National and international regulations, and watchdog bodies – with public representation to recognize public concern – overseeing research institutes and production facilities are necessary, to minimize the number, and the consequences, of biotechnical mistakes. Such regulations and bodies will also clear what will otherwise be a tangled path for legitimate, safe, beneficial research.

Abstract arguments will not be enough to resolve the safety issues. Actual experiments and studies are also needed to measure – rather than simply estimate – the health and environmental risks of different kinds of manipulations and releases of engineered organisms in different environments. Such experiments, which should accompany each new introduction, will demand, and may produce, a better understanding of the gene and ecosystem interactions into which the engineered genes are placed.

National and international agreements should be reached, in awareness of the distribution of risks and benefits of any gene technology, about responsibility for paying for the consequences of any disaster with that technology: the genetic equivalent of the 'polluter pays' principle should be established.

Clear, unbiased public information and reporting of issues is essential.

Hamdallah Zedan, the United Nations Environment Programme (UNEP) officer concerned with regulations on the release of genetically engineered organisms, has detailed the issues that face any assessment of risk (personal communication). According to Zedan, present risk assessment procedure for a potentially dangerous chemical involves: identification of a possibly dangerous substance; assessment of effects of a given dose; estimate of likely exposure; and finally detailing of the whole risk. To this list could be added studies of how the chemical is to be used, and in what quantities; of quality and risk control in the production process; and of the safe disposal of wastes associated with the chemical. These components could form a crude basis for risk assessment for the release of genetically engineered organisms, but particular difficulties arise because of the following.

Lack of sufficient reliable data, particularly on long-term dangers.

Complete variation of type of risk, and experiments required to measure it, from one case to the next. (Assessments on gene A in rice have nothing to do with those on gene B in rice or gene C in tilapia, etc.)

Difficulty in predicting the fate of released organisms or genes. (Too little is known about gene and organism interactions.)

Secrecy associated with much private-interest genetic engineering.

Absence of any monitoring procedure.

Lack of researchers able or willing to make the assessments.

The first step towards quantitative risk assessment would be to conduct a detailed study of actual introductions of engineered species as they occur, to provide a bank of experience for later work and regulations. There is little sign yet of this occurring on any effective scale.

Although – as argued above – there are no fundamental new biological risks in biotechnology, and the real risks lie in the scaling-up and speed of the movement of genomes or parts of genomes into new environments, there are some unusual dangers that have been raised that are worth outlining: these are, perhaps, a few of the potential 'Kariba weeds' or 'rabbits in Australia' that regulations, safety experiments, and watchdog bodies should be set up to avoid.

> Herbicide tolerance. Some are concerned that a gene to protect a crop from a certain herbicide, to encourage farmers to use that particular product, could 'leak' through natural crossing of the engineered plants with weedy species, into the weeds – resulting in super-hardy weeds that could not be destroyed with weed-killer.

But, proponents of the genes argue that such 'leakage' would be very unlikely, as these species are very difficult to cross with agricultural crops even in the laboratory.

However, quantified risk assessment data – experiments to show how great or small the risk is – are needed, say unbiased scientists working on the problem.

> Insect resistance. As with herbicide resistance, it is conceivable that *Bacillus thuringiensis* genes engineered into a crop to induce resistance to insects could cross into weeds, this time producing insect-resistant super-weeds.

Again, studies are needed to assess the crossing risk.

> Virus resistance. The risks of introducing genes for vital coat proteins into plants – to produce resistance to that virus – are that some other virus might collect that coat from the plant –

a process known as 'transcapsulation'. That would give that virus the entry properties of that coat, so viruses might move into other crops than their usual hosts. However, this would not create a permanent new virus species, as the transcapsulated virus would not possess the genes needed to make its new coat; its new 'entry properties' would only last for one infection.

In the other main method of inducing virus resistance – transferring genes of viral 'satellites' that normally reduce the virulence of their partner viruses – there is a danger that mutations in the satellite DNA may induce the opposite effect: hypervirulence. This danger arises because some viral satellites do cause hypervirulence, and the real mechanisms of satellite action are unknown, so it is not impossible (though unlikely) that one form of satellite could mutate into another. It follows that it might be wise to establish an international research effort on the risks of non-conventional virus resistance techniques.

> Marginal ecologies. Much 'appropriate' biotechnology will be directed at marginal lands, in part because that is where the poorest communities live, in part because their land is needed to increase food production. What effect, say, will a new engineered variety of rice, or some biopesticide, have in a marginal environment where the balance of creatures, soil and weather is delicate? Some scientists are arguing that, for example, the Rockefeller Foundation (whose rice biotechnology programme is so well advanced) should encourage the development of national and international protocols to control and monitor the release of new engineered rice varieties in countries, in case of environmental risks.

> Live vaccinia vaccines. One of the most recommended, and most rejected, potential carriers for new vaccines is the vaccinia virus, the agent of cow-pox and in itself the very first vaccine. Vaccinia is so similar to the smallpox virus that it acts as a living vaccine against it, though is much less virulent in humans, and it was used by the World Health Organization in the 1970s to eliminate smallpox from the globe. Its attraction for new vaccines is that it can be engineered easily to contain the genes to express many extra proteins, which could be chosen to mimic and confer resistance to a host of other disease organisms. (Already there is a vaccinia vaccine for cattle against rinderpest – developed by an Ethiopian scientist, Dr. Daniel Yilma.)

There are unfortunately two risks associated with this strategy. Firstly, vaccinia itself causes a severe reaction in a minority of patients. Its use was justified in eliminating the more dangerous condition of smallpox but would have to be re-assessed for other diseases. Secondly, in wide-scale use, vaccinia might mutate to a smallpox form. If it did so mutate, now that disease has gone and youngsters are not vaccinated, an epidemic could arise.

Vaccinia vaccine proponents says the latter risk is very small, and the former risk negligible against the effective delivery of a vaccine, say, against malaria. But both risks clearly need independent assessment.

An informal UNIDO/WHO/UNEP working group on biotechnological safety established in 1985–6 has been attending to issues of special interest to the developing countries in the release of genetically engineered organisms. Individual UN organizations have also been developing their own guidelines, such as WHO's for the manufacture and preparation of vaccines in developing countries, or UNIDO's for the research work of its International Centre for Genetic Engineering and Biotechnology in Trieste and New Delhi.

Hamdallah Zedan, the UNEP officer concerned with biotechnology regulations, argues (personal communication) that although genetic engineering has been in full swing in laboratories for over a decade 'the fact that no single health incident has been reported . . . could be attributed to the guidelines developed at that time'. The guidelines – resulting from scientists whistle-blowing over possible dangers – led to strict controls and containment of experiments. But as none of the vaunted dangers materialized, the guidelines have been relaxed. Now a new situation is arising, in that genetically engineered organisms are not only not to be contained, but to be deliberately released. 'Such organisms will be engineered mainly to spread and perform in the environment... risks will have to be evaluated' says Zedan; and in fact it may prove difficult to write effective guidelines until risks are better assessed.

Meetings of the UNIDO/WHO/UNEP group have reviewed existing safety practices and regulations in biotechnology research and industry, and begun (but by July 1989 not completed) the preparation of guidelines – and training programmes – on the release of genetically engineered organisms in developing countries.

Presently, the general pattern in developing countries is that a group of scientists – without any other representatives of, say, the public – is defining regulations, leaving the system open to potential bias.

The most widely quoted existing basis for the international regulation of biotechnology is that published by the Organization for Economic

Cooperation and Development (the rich nations' think tank) (OECD, 1986).

On the release of genetically engineered organisms, a relatively novel issue in 1986, the OECD recommendations seem likely to be widely followed – as in recently planned legislation in The Philippines (Walgate, 1990). In summary, the OECD recommends the following.

> An independent review of the potential risks of any proposed release should be conducted, prior to release.
> The development of engineered organisms for release should move 'step-wise' from laboratory, to growth chamber, to limited field testing and finally to large-scale field testing.
> Risk assessment research should be encouraged. Meanwhile 'considerable' existing data on the health and environmental effects of living (non-engineered) organisms should be used to guide assessments of the effects of the release of engineered organisms.

If all these conditions were adequately met – and this is a question to be monitored by journalists and, where possible, democratic institutions, public fears would be allayed, and dangers reduced to a minimum – consistent, at least, with the inevitable risks of all development.

References

Bialey, H. (1989). Biotechnology takes aim at leishmaniasis. *Bio/Technol.*, 7 (6), 549.

Grange, J.M. (1989). Mycobacterial disease in the world: yesterday, today and tomorrow. In *The Biology of Mycobacteria* vol. 3, C. Ratledge, J. Stanford & J.M. Grange (eds), pp. 1–36. Academic Press, London.

OECD (1986). *Recombinant DNA Safety Considerations*. Organisation for Economic Cooperation and Development (OECD), Paris.

Walgate, R. (1988). Haiti gets a shot in the arm. *Panos Features*, 27 January. The Panos Institute, London.

Walgate, R. (1990). *Miracle or Menace? Biotechnology and the Third World*. The Panos Institute, London.

Walsh, J.A. (1988). *Establishing Health Priorities in the Developing World*, Adams Publishing Group Ltd., Boston, MA. (Published under the auspices of the United Nations Development Programme.)

WHO (1989a). *Report on World Health*, WHO Features no. 136, September. WHO Media Service, Geneva.

WHO (1989b). *Tropical Diseases: Progress in International Research, 1987–1988*, UNDP/World Bank/WHO Special Programme of Research and Training in Tropical Diseases (TDR). WHO, Geneva.

13

Information support for research and development in biotechnological applications

A. KORNHAUSER AND B. BOH

Introduction

The quality of contemporary research and development depends to a large extent on the efficiency of the international transfer of *scientific information*. Furthermore, the use of information methods and techniques is of significance in setting up research hypotheses, as well as in teaching and learning.

The importance of *technical information* for research continues to grow. In the past, science was characterized by objective observation, powerful methods and techniques, and ability for prediction. Today, these characteristics are increasingly combined with the transfer of results into production, environmental protection and decision-making processes. Patents, technical reports and know-how offers have found their place next to scientific papers and conference reports. In applied disciplines, patents are often published before scientific papers. Biotechnology is a typical example of such a field.

The introduction of scientific and technical information into education and research is of undeniable importance also for another reason. Most highly developed universities have their 'silicon valleys', often labelled as 'science parks' or 'university developmental enterprises', where new scientific achievements serve as the basis for small-scale *entrepreneurship*, with the hope of at least some production and/or environmental protection on a larger scale. These activities have to compete in the world market, i.e. they have to have access to and to use the newest scientific, technical and economic information. Such information cannot be found in textbooks only.

Internationally accessible databases for biotechnology

There is an explosion of information in the field of biotechnology. A brief resumé is given in Table 13.1. In addition, the importance of the

Table 13.1. *Main international databases in biotechnology and related disciplines*

Database name, (producer)	Main subjects covered	Sources	Time range	Approx. size (annual increase)	Accessible via hosts	Reference sources
AGRIBUSINESS USA (Agribusiness)	all aspects of agribusiness, incl.: crop and livestock industries, biotechnology, agricultural chemicals, agricultural marketing	industry-related trade journals (approx. 300), government publications	1985 to the present	171 000 records	DIALOG, Compu-Serve, Knowledge Index, InfoMaster	Bruce *et al.*, 1989; DIALOG, 1990
AGRICOLA (National Agricultural Library)	agriculture and related subjects, incl.: chemistry, biotechnology, hydroponics, fertilizers, food science	journals, monographs	1970 to the present	2 650 000 records	DIALOG, BRS, Compu-Serve, Knowledge Index, InfoMaster	Bruce *et al.*, 1989; DIALOG, 1990
AGRIS INTERNATIONAL (US National Agricultural Library)	agriculture and related subjects, incl.: food production, plant production, protection of plants, animal production, aquatic sciences, fisheries	world-wide agricultural literature	1975 to the present	1 127 000 records	DIALOG	DIALOG, 1990
AQUACULTURE (US Oceanic and Atmospheric Administration)	culture of marine, brackish and freshwater organisms, food and nutrition, engineering, economics	periodicals, monographs, conference proceedings	1970–84 (closed file)		DIALOG	DIALOG, 1990

Name	Subject	Coverage	Dates	Records	Online services	References
ARTHUR D. LITTLE/ONLINE (Arthur D. Little Decision Resources)	various fields, incl.: chemical industry, specialty chemicals, pharmaceuticals, biotechnology, medical equipment, diagnostic products, food processing, environment	industry forecasts, technology assessments, product and market overviews, public opinion surveys, management commentaries	1977 to the present	1885 records (full text or extensive summary)	DIALOG, CompuServe	Bruce et al., 1989; DIALOG, 1990
BIOBUSINESS (Biosis, Inc.)	agriculture, animal production, biomass conversion, biotechnology, crop production, diet and nutrition, fermentation, food technology, forestry, genetic engineering, health care, industrial microbiology, medical diagnostics, medical instrumentation, occupational health, pesticides, pharmaceuticals, protein production, toxicology, veterinary science, waste treatment	world-wide technical and business journals, trade journals, magazines, newsletters, meeting proceedings, abstracts, books, US patents	1985 to the present	212 000 records (43 000 per year)	DIALOG, CompuServe, BRS, Knowledge Index, InfoMaster	Bruce et al., 1989; DIALOG, 1988; 1990
BIOCAS (Chemical Abstracts Service and Biosciences Information Service)	documents included in both the BIOSIS and CA File	see BIOSIS and CA	1969-85 (closed file)	1 200 000 records	STN International	STN International, 1986-90

Table 13.1. (*cont.*)

Database name, (producer)	Main subjects covered	Sources	Time range	Approx. size (annual increase)	Accessible via hosts	Reference sources
BIOCOMMERCE ABSTRACTS AND DIRECTORY (BioCommerce Data, Ltd.)	Technologies: biological control, biotransformations, cell hybridization, DNA probes, fermentation, genetic engineering, immunoassays, industrial enzymes, monoclonal antibodies, protein engineering, recombinant DNA, tissue culture. Applications in: agriculture, animal production, biochemistry, biomass conversion, brewing, chemical manufacture, crop protection, diagnostic tests, energy production, food technology, health care, horticulture, human genetics, medicine, microbiology,	more than 100 English-language core publications incl. newsletters, newspaper, trade journals, scientific magazines, technical periodicals	1981 to the present	54 000 abstracts referring over 130 000 articles (8400 abstracts and 1800 company profile records per year)	DIALOG, CompuServe, Knowledge Index, InfoMaster	Bruce *et al.*, 1989; DIALOG, 1990

molecular biology, pesticides, pharmaceuticals, veterinary sciences, waste treatment

Name	Subject coverage	Time span	Size	Host	References
BIOMASS (IEA Biomass Conversion Technical Information Service)	biomass production, harvesting, collection, processing, transportation and conversion techniques	1980 to the present	36 000 records (3600 per year)	STN International	STN International, 1986–90
BIOQUIP Deutsche Gesellschaft für Chemisches Apparatewesen, Chemische Technik und Biotechnologie – DECHEMA	biotechnology – manufacturers and suppliers of equipment, machinery, instruments and chemicals	permanently updated	400 companies, 1000 product groups	STN International	STN International, 1986–90
BIOSIS or BIOSIS PREVIEWS (Biosis, Inc.)	agriculture, anatomy, behaviour, biochemistry, bioengineering, biophysics, biotechnology, botany, cell biology, environmental biology, experimental/clinical medicine, genetics, immunology, microbiology, pathology, physiology, pharmacology, toxicology, zoology	1969 to the present	6 800 000 records (480 000 per year)	DIALOG, STN International, CompuServe, BRS, Knowledge Index, InfoMaster, MEAD, CAN/OLE, Data-Star, DIMDI, ESA-IRS, SDC	Bruce et al., 1989; Coombe & Alston, 1989; DIALOG, 1990; STN International, 1986–90

data provided by manufacturers and suppliers

journals, reports, conference proceedings, books, patents

journals (over 9000), US patents (1986–) technical reports, conference proceedings, reviews, books

Table 13.1. (*cont.*)

Database name, (producer)	Main subjects covered	Sources	Time range	Approx. size (annual increase)	Accessible via hosts	Reference sources
BIOTECHNOLOGY ABSTRACTS (Derwent Publications Ltd)	agriculture, animal and plant cell cultures, biocatalysts, biochemical engineering, biological control agents, chemical analysis and structure, downstream processing, energy and fuels, fermentation, food additives and SCP, fuels, genetics, industrial waste management, other chemicals, pharmaceuticals	journals (over 1000), patents, conference proceedings	1982 to the present	81 000 records, (12 000 per year)	DIALOG, ORBIT	DIALOG, 1990; ORBIT, 1989
BUSINESS DATALINE (UMI/Data Courier)	business data	full text of business publications in the USA	1985 to the present	225 000 records	DIALOG, CompuServe, BRS	Bruce *et al.*, 1989; DIALOG, 1990

Database	Subject coverage	Source materials	Dates	Number of records	Online hosts	References
CA – on STN International, CA Search – on DIALOG, Chemical Abstracts – on ORBIT (Chemical Abstracts Service)	biochemistry, organic chemistry, macromolecular chemistry, applied chemistry, chemical engineering, physical, inorganic and analytical chemistry	journals (over 12 000), patents, conference proceedings, technical reports, books, dissertations	1967 to the present	9 million records (400 000 per year)	STN International, DIALOG, ORBIT, BRS, CompuServe, InfoMaster, Data-Star, CAN/OLE, CNIC, VCH	Bruce et al., 1989; Coombs & Alston, 1989; DIALOG, 1990; ORBIT, 1989; STN International, 1986–90
CABA or CAB Abstracts (Commonwealth Agricultural Bureaux)	agriculture, animal science and reproduction, biotechnology, engineering, forestry, genetics, medicine (human, veterinary), nutrition	journals (over 10 000), books, monographs, technical reports, published theses, conference proceedings, patents, annual reports, bibliographies	1978 to the present	1 600 000 records (150 000 per year)	STN International, DIALOG, BRS, CompuServe, Knowledge Index, InfoMaster	
CABS – CURRENT AWARENESS IN BIOLOGICAL SCIENCES (Current Awareness in Biological Sciences)	information in the entire field of biological sciences, including: biochemistry, cell biology, genetics, microbiology, immunology, molecular biology	journals (3500)	1983 to the present	over 1 million records (190 000 per year)	ORBIT, Pergamon Infoline	Coombs & Alston, 1989; ORBIT, 1989; Pergamon Infoline, 1985–87
CHEMICAL ENGINEERING ABSTRACTS or CEA Database (The Royal Society of Chemistry)	chemical engineering and technology	journals (over 240)	1971 to the present	95 000 records	DIALOG, ORBIT, Data-STAR, Pergamon Infoline, ESA-IRS	Coombs & Alston, 1989; DIALOG, 1990; ORBIT, 1989; Pergamon Infoline, 1985–87

Table 13.1. (*cont.*)

Database name, (producer)	Main subjects covered	Sources	Time range	Approx. size (annual increase)	Accessible via hosts	Reference sources
CHEMICAL REACTIONS DOCUMENTATION SERVICE (Derwent Publications Ltd)	synthesis and chemical reaction in organic chemistry		1944 to the present	75 000 records	ORBIT	ORBIT, 1989
COMPENDEX PLUS (Engineering Information, Inc.)	technology and engineering, incl. bioengineering, medical equipment, chemical engineering, food technology, environmental technology	journals (4500), books, government reports	1970 to the present	2 520 000 records	DIALOG, BRS, CompuService, Knowledge Index, InfoMaster	Bruce *et al.*, 1989; DIALOG, 1990
CURRENT BIOTECHNOLOGY ABSTRACTS – on Dialog, CBA Database on Pergamon (The Royal Society of Chemistry)	main aspects of biotechnology, incl. genetic manipulation, monoclonal antibodies, immobilized cells and enzymes, Single-Cell Proteins, fermentation technology, pharmaceuticals, food, agriculture, chemical industry, fuels	journals (200), patents (EP, US, PCT, GB), conference proceedings, technical reports, announcements of books and meetings	1983 (April) to the present	34 000 records (5100 per year)	DIALOG, Pergamon Infoline, Data-Star, ESA-IRS	Coombs & Alston, 1989; DIALOG, 1990; Pergamon Infoline, 1985–87

Database	Subject coverage	Source types	Date range	Size	Host	References
DECHEMA – Dechema Chemical Engineering and Biotechnology Abstracts Data Bank (Deutsche Gesellschaft für Chemisches Apparatewesen, Chemische Technik und Biotechnologie – DECHEMA)	chemical technology, biotechnology, chemical equipment, pollution control, safety technology	journals, conference proceedings, books, dissertations	1975 to the present	120 000 records (10 000 per year)	STN International	Coombs & Alston, 1989; STN International, 1986–90
DEQUIP (DECHEMA)	manufacturers of apparatus and technical equipment in the fields of chemical engineering and biotechnology	current data provided by manufacturers and suppliers	permanently updated	3000 companies, 8000 product groups	STN International	Coombs & Alston, 1989; STN International, 1986–90
DIOGENES (Diogenes)	information relating to the Food and Drug Administration regulation for drugs and devices, incl.: pharmaceuticals, biotechnology, chemistry, medical devices	news, unpublished documents, incl. listings of approved products, experience reports, recall and regulatory action documentation	1976 to the present	486 000 records	DIALOG, CompuServe, Knowledge Index, InfoMaster	Bruce et al., 1989; DIALOG, 1990
EMBASE formerly EXCERPTA MEDICA (Excerpta Medica)	medical and pharmaceutical research, clinical practice	biomedical journals (over 4000)	1974 to the present	4 million records	DIALOG, BRS, CompuServe, Knowledge Index, InfoMaster	Bruce et al., 1989; DIALOG, 1990
FOOD SCIENCE AND TECHNOLOGY ABSTRACTS on Dialog, FSTA on STN International (Commonwealth Agricultural Bureaux)	food science and technology, agriculture, chemistry, biochemistry, engineering	journals (over 1200), patents, books, conference proceedings, technical reports	1969 to the present	380 000 records	DIALOG, STN International, ORBIT	DIALOG, 1990; ORBIT, 1989; STN International, 1986–90

Table 13.1. (cont.)

Database name, (producer)	Main subjects covered	Sources	Time range	Approx. size (annual increase)	Accessible via hosts	Reference sources
GENBANK (c/o Bolt Beranek & Newman Inc., Computer System Division)	nucleic acid sequences greater than 50 base pairs	data collected from scientific communities, journals	1989 to the present	over 40 million base pairs from over 33 000 entries	GenBank Online Service	Coombs & Alston, 1989; Gilna & Ryals, 1990
INPADOC (INPADOC International Patent Documentation Center)	all areas of science and technology	patents (INPADOC Patent, Gazette, INPADOC Legal Status Service)	patent citat.: 1968 to the present; legal status data: 1978 to the present	17 500 000 patent citations, 23 000 000 legal status data	STN International	STN International, 1986-90
INTERNATIONAL PHARMACEUTICAL ABSTRACTS (American Society of Hospital Pharmacists)	pharmaceutical industry, pharmacy, medicine	journals (over 650)	1970 to the present	162 000 records	DIALOG	Coombs & Alston, 1989; DIALOG, 1990
ISI BIOMED (Institute for Scientific Information)	biology, biochemistry, medicine	scientific literature			DIALOG, Data-Star	DIALOG, 1990
JICST-E (The Japan Information Center of Science and Technology)	scientific and technical information published in Japan, incl. biotechnology (English)	journals (4000), conference proceedings, technical reports		900 000 records (200 000 per year)	STN International	JIST-E, 1989; STN International, 1986-90
KIRK-OTHMER ONLINE (Wiley Electronic Publishing)	chemistry subject areas, incl. fermentation, drugs, food	Kirk-Othmer Encyclopedia of Chemical Technology (3rd Edition)		25 000 records representing 1200 chapters	DIALOG	DIALOG, 1990

Name	Subject/scope	Document types	Coverage	Records	Online availability	References
LIFESCIENCE COLLECTION (Cambridge Scientific Abstracts)	life sciences, including: biochemistry, biotechnology, genetics, immunology, microbiology, virology	journals, books, conference proceedings, reports	1978 to the present	1 200 000 records	DIALOG	DIALOG, 1990
MEDLINE or MEDLARS ONLINE (National Library of Medicine)	biomedical research, clinical medicine	journals (over 3900), books, conference proceedings	1972 to the present	6.2 million records (300 000 per year)	STN International, DIALOG, BRS, Knowledge Index, InfoMaster available online	Bruce et al., 1989; DIALOG, 1990; STN International, 1986–90
MiCIS – MICROBIAL CULTURE INFORMATION SERVICE (Department of Trade and Industry, UK)	culture collection – properties of individual strains: morphological, biochemical, genetic, industrial	culture collections				Coombs & Alston, 1989; Kirsop, 1988
MINE – Microbial Information Network Europe (database network)	culture collections	culture collections: Belgium, Germany, Netherlands, Portugal, UK (from 1988 also France, Greece, Italy, Spain)	1986–	150 000 strains	online network (access by using packet switching systems – PSS)	Aguilar, 1990
MSDN – MICROBIAL STRAIN DATA NETWORK (several regional databases)	culture collections – location of individual strains with specific properties	culture collections	1985 to the present		available online (DIALCOM, TELECOM GOLD network)	Kirsop, 1988
NTIS – NATIONAL TECHNICAL INFORMATION SERVICE (US Department of Commerce)	specialized scientific and technical documentation covering a wide spectrum of subjects, incl.: agriculture, food, chemistry, medicine, biology, business	reports of 250 agencies	1964 to the present	1 410 000 records	DIALOG, STN International, ORBIT	Coombs & Alston, 1989; DIALOG, 1990; ORBIT, 1989; STN International, 1988–90

Table 13.1. (*cont.*)

Database name, (producer)	Main subjects covered	Sources	Time range	Approx. size (annual increase)	Accessible via hosts	Reference sources
PASCAL (CNRS – Centre de Documentation Scientifique et Technique)	multidisciplinary database incl.: biology, medicine, biotechnology, chemistry, agriculture	journals, doctoral theses, reports, conference proceedings, books	1973 to the present	2 600 000 records	DIALOG	Coombs & Alston, 1989; DIALOG, 1990
PESTMAN – PESTICIDE DATABANK (The British Crop Protection Council, CAB International)	chemical and biological pesticides in the fields of agriculture, horticulture, animal health, industrial and domestic pest control (nomenclature, development, properties, uses, toxicology, analysis)		1989	approx. 1000 records	ORBIT	ORBIT, 1989
PNI – PHARMACEUTICAL NEWS INDEX (UMI/Data Courier)	research, industry, legislation and business news in pharmaceuticals, cosmetics, medical devices	journals, newspapers, reports, standards	1974 to the present	300 000 records	DIALOG, CompuServe, Knowledge Index, InfoMaster	Bruce *et al.*, 1989; DIALOG, 1990

Database (Producer)	Subject	Document types	Coverage	Size	Online services	References
PTS NEWSLETTER DATABASE (Predicasts, Inc.)	industrial information, incl. biotechnology	full texts of industrial publications, incl. Bioprocessing Technol., Genetic Technol. News, Japan Report: BT	1988 to the present	210 000 records	DIALOG, CompuServe, Knowledge Index, InfoMaster	Bruce et al., 1989; DIALOG, 1990
PTS PROMT – Predicasts Overview of Markets and Technology (Predicasts, Inc.)	business news, industrial information	newspapers, business magazines, government reports, trade journals, bank letters, special reports	1972 to the present	1.9 million records	DIALOG, BRS, CompuServe, Knowledge Index, InfoMaster	Bruce et al., 1989; DIALOG, 1990
SUPERTECH formerly TELEGEN (Bowker A. & I. Publishing)	biotechnology, genetic engineering, artificial intelligence, CAD/CAM, robotics, telecommunications	journals, conference proceedings, monographs, reports	subfile biotechnology from 1873 to the present	70 000 records	DIALOG, CompuServe, Knowledge Index, InfoMaster	Bruce et al., 1989; DIALOG, 1990
TROPAG – TROPICAL AGRICULTURE (Royal Tropical Institute)	tropical and sub-tropical agriculture, incl. crop production, crop protection, fertilizers, plant nutrition, crop processing and storage, farming systems	journals, monographs, theses, conference proceedings	1975 to the present	65 000 records	ORBIT	ORBIT, 1989

Table 13.1. (*cont.*)

Database name, (producer)	Main subjects covered	Sources	Time range	Approx. size (annual increase)	Accessible via hosts	Reference sources
WDC – WORLD DATA CENTER ON MICROORGANISMS: culture collections – CCINFO Database; their holdings – STRAIN Database; bibliographic Database IRIRS (Life Science Research Information Section of RIKEN)	culture collections, genera and species, services	culture collection, publications in the field of plant tissue and cell cultures	online from 1988	information on 350 culture collections	host computer Riken, Japan (access by using packet switching systems – PSS)	Kirsop, 1988; Takishima *et al.*, 1989
WORLD PATENTS INDEX (Derwent Publications Ltd)	inventions and patents in all subjects, incl.: pharmaceutical industry, biochemistry, organic and polymer chemistry, agriculture	patents	1963 to the present (all subjects covered from 1974)	6 million records	DIALOG	DIALOG, 1990
VtB – Verfahrenstechnische Berichte – Online (Bayer AG)	chemical and process engineering, biotechnology, material properties and handling, environmental protection, industrial safety and health, process control	journals, reports, books, dissertations, industrial publications	1966 to the present	168 000 records (7000 per year)	STN International	STN International, 1986–90

Table 13.2. *Examples of specialized biotech databases*

Database name (producer)	Main subject covered	Reference source
AMINO ACID SEQUENCES OF PROTEINS (Georgetown University Medical Center)	protein sequences	Cantley (1984)
BADGE DATABASE – Banque de Donnees pour le Genie Enzymatique (l'Universite Technologique de Compiegne)	enzymes: structure, activity, microorganisms, substrates, bibliographic references	Cantley (1984)
CarbBank – Carbohydrate Structure Database	molecular structures of carbohydrates	Johnson (1989)
CFISM (Institut National Agronomique)	microbial strains	Coombs & Alston (1989)
DDBJ – DNA Data Bank of Japan	nucleotide sequences	Johnson (1989)
EMBL, Heidelberg	nucleotide sequences	Johnson (1989)
HGML – Human Gene Mapping Library (Howard Hughes Medical Institute)	human genes	Johnson (1989)
HYBRIDOMAS and IMMUNOCLONES DATABANK (Pasteur Institute)	hybridomas and immunoclones	Cantley (1984)
IN VITRO CONSERVATION DATABASE (International Board for Plant Genetic Resources)	plant cell culture techniques	Coombs & Alston (1989)
MDS – Microbial Strains Database	microbial strains	Johnson (1989)
MIRDAB-MICROBIOLOGICAL RESOURCE DATABANK (Excerpta Medica)	available plant and animal cell lines and viruses	Coombs & Alston (1989)
NUCLEIC ACID DATA LIBRARY (European Molecular Biology Laboratory)	nucleotide sequences	Coombs & Alston (1989)
NUCLEOTIDE SEQUENCE BANK (US National Laboratory)	nucleotide sequences	Cantley (1984)

Table 13.2. (*cont.*)

Database name (producer)	Main subject covered	Reference source
NUCLEIC ACID SEQUENCE DATABASE (Georgetown University Medical Center)	nucleotide sequences	Cantley (1984)
PG-TRANS (Institute Pasteur, Computer Service Unit)	protein sequences	Coombs & Alston (1989)
PROTEIN DATABANK (Brookhaven; out-stations in Cambridge and Tokyo)	crystallographic coordinates of proteins, macromolecular structures	Cantley (1984); Johnson (1989)
PIR – Protein Identification Resource	amino acid sequence	Johnson (1989)
PRESEQDB – Protein Research Foundation Amino Acid Sequences Database, Japan	amino acid sequences	Johnson (1989)
PSD – Protein Sequence Database, Kyoto	protein sequences	Johnson (1989)

following databases (Table 13.2) in the challenging fields of amino acid sequence, enzyme kinetics, protein sequence and nucleic acids was stressed by Cantley (1984), Coombs & Alston (1989) and Johnson (1989).

Information base for problem solving

In most scientific disciplines, the amount of information is growing rapidly. Chemistry is often quoted as the field with an expontential growth of information (Fig. 13.1). As for biotechnology, most of the databases were launched only after the 1960s, which is a too recent period for reliable estimation of trends. However, an intensive growth of biotechnological information is evident in both the theoretical and commercial domains. The number of international online databases which included biotechnological information is increasing from year to year (Fig. 13.2).

The availability of large amounts of information alone does not ensure research of higher quality. On the contrary, the 'entropy' of information processing is higher, and many a researcher tends to avoid databases, relying more on information communication with selected research groups in the field. This contributes to the poor use of international databases, and turns many a national database into a scientific cemetery.

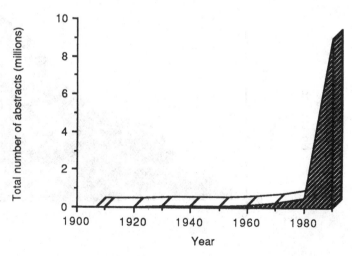

Fig. 13.1. The growth of the Chemical Abstracts database: millions of abstracts (DIALOG, 1990; Groves, 1984).

In order to cope with large amounts of information, 'filtering' is needed for research and decision making. *Problem solving and pattern recognition* methods should be introduced in both research and education. Skills for dealing with large sets of data, such as recognizing more important and reliable information, linking data into systems and patterns, i.e. transforming data into knowledge, need to be better developed.

The main steps, in general, towards solving a problem with information support include (Kornhauser, 1989) the following.

(1) Definition of the problem, its structure and sub-problems.
(2) *L'informatisation* of the problem, i.e. definition of types of information needed for its solution.
(3) Collection of data: use of available information sources, in particular specialized monographs, scientific papers, patents, know-how offers and other industrial information, market information; retrospective searches in international databases, constructing and optimizing profiles for regular processing of these databases; organization of primary documentation.
(4) Analysis of collected documentation, definition of parameters.
(5) Evaluation of selected parameters, their interactions and definition of their hierarchy.
(6) Structuring data, i.e. setting up hypothetical relations and

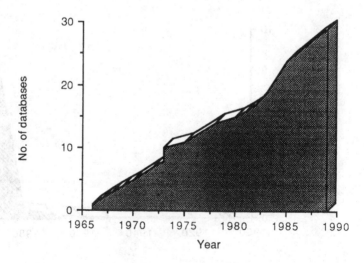

Fig. 13.2. The growth of the number of the main international online databases including biotechnological information.

patterns, evaluating and optimizing them on the basis of information density.

(7) Setting up hypotheses of higher (information) probability, and testing them in experimental work in the laboratory.

(8) Using the above approaches in the transfer of laboratory results into pilot-scale process.

Levels of information processing

Computerized scientific and technical information can provide support for both *memory* and *logic*, depending on the level of information processing (Fig. 13.3).

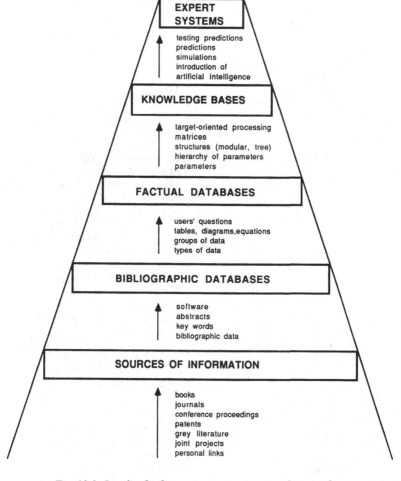

Fig. 13.3. Levels of information processing – with main characteristics.

Bibliographic databases
These databases offer brief information on publications that are
essential for the researcher in any research project. The examples below
are taken from specialized databases built since 1985 (Kornhauser &
Boh, 1990) from the Biotechnological Information Exchange System
(BITES) (Da Silva & Piuilla, 1988), which is a part of the UNDP/Unesco
Project 'Microbial Biotechnology and Bioengineering – Biotechnologi-
cal Applications (European Network)'.

```
Type of publication:    book
Title:                  THE BIOTECHNOLOGY
                        BUSINESS
Subtitle:               A strategic analysis
Authors:                Daly P.
Publisher:              Francis Pinter
                        Publishers; Rowman and
                        Allanheld Publishers
Publication year:       1985
Language:               Eng
Pages:                  155 pp.
Availability:           ICCS Ljubljana
Field:                  biotechnology
                        medicine
                        economy
Contents:               biotechnology
                        applications:
                        pharmaceuticals,
                        diagnostics,
                        speciality chemicals,
                        food, agriculture,
                        commodity chemicals;
                        biotechnology
                        business: companies in
                        USA, Japan, Europe,
                        industry, market;
                        science, government
                        policies; company case
                        studies: Genentech,
                        Genex, Cetus, Centocor,
                        Celltech, Eli-Lilly,
                        Monsanto; strategies,
                        management, financing
000093
Document type:          patent
Authors:                Weaver, M.O.; Bagley,
                        E.B.; Fanta, G.F.;
                        Doane, W.M.
Title:                  Immobilization of
                        enzymes with a starch-
                        graft copolymer
```

Institution(s):	United States Department of Agriculture
Location(s):	US, Washington, D.C.
Patent No.:	US 3985616, 761012, 12pp
Patent application(s):	US 611459, 750908
Patent class.:	C07G7/02
Publication year:	1976
Language:	Eng
Availability:	primary document
Internal No.:	00093
Key words:	modified starch, starch derivatives, alkali saponified gelatinized starch acrylonitrile graft copolymers, water insoluble aqueous fluid absorbing compositions, production, raw materials, gelatinized starch polyacrylonitrile graft polymer, GS-PAN, saponification, water soluble saponified GS-PAN, pH adjustment, isolation, drying, products: water soluble GS-PAN, GS-PAN amine salts, applications: food industry: enzymes immobilization, paper industry: paper galantery, disposable diapers, surgical pads, sheets, paper towels, agriculture: soil amendment, water holding capacity, seed germination, plant growth, chemical industry: jellied fuels, paint industry, waste waters: sewage sludge dewatering

Retrieval from bibliographic databases can also suggest trends, e.g. scientific paper vs. patents in biotechnology, as is given for Biotechnology Abstracts in Fig. 13.4.

The growth of the total number of publications per year is a good indicator of research intensity and spread, e.g. decrease on ethanol production (Fig. 13.5), and fermentation of antibiotics (Fig. 13.6) in comparison with an intensive growth of patents on monoclonal antibodies (Fig. 13.7). Fig. 13.8 is of special interest: the number of scientific papers in monoclonal antibodies per year is decreasing, while the number of patents is increasing. This means that the applications and investments in this field are growing.

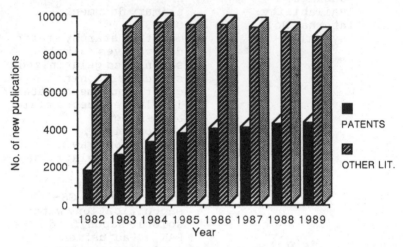

Fig. 13.4. Trends in biotechnological information: patents vs. papers (search on Biotechnology Abstracts).

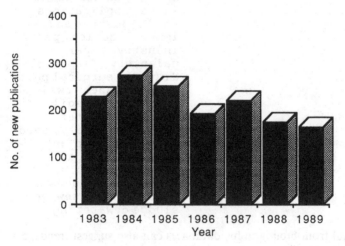

Fig. 13.5. Decreasing trend of publications on ethanol production (search on Biotechnology Abstracts).

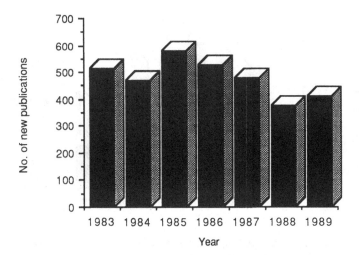

Fig. 13.6. Another decreasing trend of new publications on the fermentation of antibiotics (search on Biotechnology Abstracts).

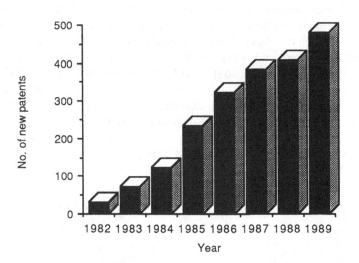

Fig. 13.7. Intensive growth of patents on monoclonal antibodies (search on Biotechnology Abstracts).

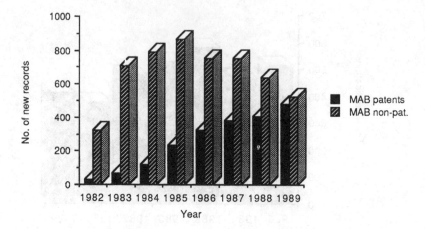

Fig. 13.8. Publications in the field of monoclonal antibodies: patent vs. non-patent literature (search on Biotechnology Abstracts).

Factual databases

These are usually built in connection with a defined problem, and are often open only to selected users. To increase an efficient building and use of such databases and to decrease the costs, international networks of researchers and users are formed, with a coordinating institution responsible for input and standards. An example of such a network is the already-cited BITES, for which the following fields were selected: biotechnology application domain, company, product, commercial name(s), use, scale of production, technology, organisms and substrates. References in the factual database are linked with the numbers in the primary document collection. An example is given below (Kornhauser & Boh, 1990).

```
Company:              Sankyo
                      Rohm and Haas
                      Takamine Lab.
                      Farbenind I.G.
Field:                speciality chemicals
Product:              enzymes
                      pectinase
Use:                  food industry:
                      clarification of fruit
                      juice, removal of
                      pectin, coffee
                      concentration
Scale:                industrial scale
Technology:           fermentation
```

```
Organisms:                    Solorotina libertina
                              Coniothyrium
                              diplodiella
                              Aspergillus oryzae
                              Aspergillus niger
                              Aspergillus flavus
Reference:                    Internal No. 390
```

Learning by doing

Efficient processing of international databases requires well-developed skills for quick online adaptation of the search profile. This skill can be developed best by learning how to build and use local databases developed for the needs of a project.

Highly specialized, research-problem-oriented databases are not only an opportunity for learning, but also the means to save funds. Most research institutions and universities in the world are facing the problem of limited funds for international database retrieval and purchasing literature. On the other hand, the researcher needs *complete information* to be able to produce research results acceptable for the international scientific community.

Such a situation imposes the need for selection of strategic fields for which complete information will be provided. These fields are usually the main research projects for which specialized bibliographic databases have to be built first and combined with the gathering of *primary documentation*. In such a way, even a poor university with international links can provide full information to the researcher.

This approach demands modest requirements: an IBM-compatible PC and efficient software.

UNESCO has developed the *CDS/ISIS software package* (Computerized Documentation System/Integrated Set of Information Systems, version 2.3, Copyright by UNESCO 1989) which is available free-of-charge to all UNESCO partners worldwide for either IBM-compatible PC or micro-vax computer. Its characteristics are as follows.

> Optional formatting of input document: optional number of fields, variable field length, repeatable fields, division of fields into subfields;
> optional definition of fields selected for searching;
> searching in one field or in several fields at the same time;
> optional printout formatting;
> preparation of sorted printouts, indexes and search terms dictionary;
> changing conditions for database processing in a premade database.

Table 13.3. *Some software packages and systems*

Application	Software	Producer	Computer
Bibliographic databases	CDS/ISIS ver. 1.0	UNESCO	IBM-compatible
	CDS/ISIS ver. 2.0	UNESCO	IBM-compatible
	CDS/ISIS ver. 2.3	UNESCO	IBM-compatible
	Allegro-C	Universitätsbibliothek Braunschweig	IBM-compatible
Factual databases	dBase III +	Ashton-Tate	IBM-compatible
	MacBusiness Database	Systematics International	Macintosh
Relational databases	Paradox	Borland	IBM-compatible
	Omnis 3 plus	Blyth Software	Macintosh
	Informix-SQL	Informix Software	IBM-compatible
	Informix-4GL	Informix Software	IBM-compatible
Expert system shells	KES	Software Architecture & Engineering, Inc.	IBM-compatible
	VPX	Paperback Software International	IBM-compatible
	1st-Class	Programs in Motion, Inc.	IBM-compatible
	PcPlus	Texas	IBM-compatible
	Acquaint	Lithp Systems BV	IBM-compatible
	MicroExpert	McGraw-Hill Book Company	IBM-compatible
Desk-top publishing	PageMaker	Aldus	Macintosh
Statistics	SPSS PC +	SPSS Inc.	IBM-compatible
Computer graphics	Cricket Graph	Cricket Software	Macintosh
	Mac Paint	Apple Computer	Macintosh
	Full Paint	Ann Arbor Softworks	Macintosh
	Mac Draw	Apple Computer	Macintosh
	Chem Draw	Cambridge Scientific Co.	Macintosh
	Jazz	Lotus	Macintosh
	Excell	Microsoft Corporation	Macintosh
	Lotus 123	Lotus	IBM-compatible
	Chemintosh Desk	SoftShell International	Macintosh

Table 13.3. (*cont.*)

Application	Software	Producer	Computer
Molecular design/ modelling and simulation	SYBIL	Tripos Associates	DEC, VAX
	NITRO	Tripos Associates	IBM-compatible, Macintosh-II
	Alchemy II	Tripos Associates	IBM-compatible, Macintosh
	Concord	Tripos Associates	DEC, VAX
	CoMFA	Tripos Associates	DEC, VAX
	CHARMm	Polygen	
	DelPhi	Blosym Technologies	
	QUANTA	Polygen	
	BioEngine (system)	Proteus Biotechnology	
	QSAR	Polygen, Chemical Design, Biodesign	
	Chemistry Viewer	Stardent	
	Max 3D	Molecular design	
	Topcat	Health Designs	
	AMF	Merck	
Nucleic acid/ Protein sequence analysis	IBI Pustell	IBI Kodak	IBM-compatible
	MacVector	IBI Kodak	Macintosh
	DNASIS	Pharmacia LKB	IBM-compatible
	DNA Sequence Analysis	International Biotechnologies	
Image analysers	OMNICON 3600	Dynatech Laboratories Inc.	IBM-compatible
	Java	RJA Handelsgesellschaft	IBM-compatible
	Cue (system)	Olympus	

Sources: Blackwell Scientific Publications (1990); Dixon (1989); Dynatech Laboratories (1990); Knight (1989; 1990); Kornhauser & Boh (1989); Ratner (1989); Tripos Associates (1990); UNESCO (1989).

A survey of this software package, as well as of software for higher levels of information processing in BITES testing and evaluation plan is given in the Table 13.3.

Applications of CD-ROM in biotechnology
CD-ROM (Compact Disc–Read Only Memory) offers enormous capacity – up to 600 MB of data and compact size (Mitchell, Harrison & Daum, 1990). It supports the cost-efficient distribution of parts of, or even entire, databases.

On a single CD-ROM, over a quarter of a million pages of text can be stored. Retrieval is faster than on a hard disc drive.

Once the CD-ROM has been pressed, it cannot be written to, or amended. In addition to the computer, a CD-ROM drive and retrieval software are needed; these are not cheap. CD-ROM drives can be used with different computers, e.g. Apple, DEC, HP, IBM and PC compatibles in constructing CD-ROM databases relevant to biotechnology (Table 13.4).

Higher levels of information processing

Who needs higher levels of information processing, including information analysis, synthesis, recognition of knowledge patterns, their evaluation and application in solving problems? First, the *researcher* for his comparative analysis of results of other researchers, followed by the synthesis of relevant data needed for developing new research hypotheses. The danger of unnecessary duplication of research can be avoided and the probability of good research hypotheses increased, if larger sets of information sources and research data are taken into consideration.

Second, the *engineer*, as an assistance in searching for appropriate equipment and technologies to be implemented in specific conditions, in evaluating them, and in stimulating development of new technological applications and products (Fig. 13.9).

Fig. 13.9. 'How to turn this upside-down?'

Table 13.4. *CD–ROM databases in biotechnology*

CD-ROM database	Producer	Type of information	Periodicity (1st issue)	Price
AGRIBUSINESS USA	Dialog Information Services, Inc.	bibliographic, data/statistics	quarterly (1988)	$2000
AGRICOLA	OCLC	bibliographic	quarterly	$300–350
AGRICOLA/CRIS	SilverPlatter Information, Inc.	bibliographic	quarterly	$1000
AGRIS	SilverPlatter Information, Inc.	bibliographic	quarterly	
BIOLOGICAL ABSTRACTS ON DISC	SilverPlatter Information, Inc.	bibliographic	quarterly (1989)	
BIOLOGICAL AND AGRICULTURAL INDEX	H.W. Wilson Co.	bibliographic	quarterly	$1495
BIOROM (corresponds to Biotechnology Abst.)	Derwent Publications Ltd	text, bibliographic, images	in preparation	
CAB ABSTRACTS	SilverPlatter Information, Inc.	text	annual	
CASSIS	NISC, US Patent & Trademark Office	text	six issues per annum (1989)	$465
CD-CHROM	Preston Publications	bibliographic, data/statistics (chromatography)	annual (1989)	$1295
CD-GENE	Hitachi America	data/statistics (DNA and protein sequences)	biannual (1987)	$950

Table 13.4. (*cont.*)

CD-ROM database	Producer	Type of information	Periodicity (1st issue)	Price
CD PLUS MEDLINE	CD Plus, Inc.	bibliographic	monthly (1988)	$3495
COMPREHENSIVE MEDLINE	EBSCO Electronic Information	bibliographic	monthly (1988)	$900
EMBL SEQUENCE DATABASE	European Molecular Biology Laboratory Data Library	text, data/statistics (DNA and protein sequences)	quarterly (1989)	DM 200–500
ESPACE	European Patent Office	text, bibliographic (European patent applications)	weekly	DM 4900
EXCERPTA MEDICA LIBRARY SERVICE	SilverPlatter Information, Inc., Elsevier Science Publishers	bibliographic	annual (1989)	Dfl 36,808
FINE CHEMICALS DATABASE	Chemron, Inc.	bibliographic, data/statistics, addresses, catalogue, product information	biannual (1989)	$495
FOOD, AGRICULTURE AND SCIENCE	CGIAR	text, graphics	(1989)	$99
LIFE SCIENCES COLLECTION	Cambridge Scientific Abstracts	bibliographic	semi-annual	$1000
KIRK-OTHMER ENCYCLOPAEDIA OF CHEMICAL TECHNOLOGY	John Wiley & Sons, Inc.	text	(1987)	£620

Name	Provider	Type	Frequency	Price
MEDLINE	SilverPlatter Information, Inc.	text, bibliographic	quarterly	$760–1250
MEDLINE	Dialog Information Services, Inc.	bibliographic	quarterly (1987)	$1250
NBS CRYSTAL DATA IDENTIFICATION FILE	International Centre for Diffraction Data	data/statistics (crystallographic and chemical data)	annual (1989)	$2000
PASCAL	INIST	bibliographic	annual (1989)	FRF 13 000
PEST-BANK	SilverPlatter Information, Inc.	bibliographic, product information (pesticides)	quarterly (1988)	£1800
The PESTICIDES DISC	Pergamon Compact Solution	text, graphics (pesticides)	biannual (1989)	$1600
PHARMAROM	Pharmarom Institute	text, product information	quarterly (1988)	
PHARMAROM	OFAC	text	semi-annual (1989)	
POWDER DIFFRACTION FILE	International Centre for Diffraction Data	data/statistics (X-ray diffraction patterns)	annual (1987)	$1400–5900
REGISTRY OF MASS SPECTRAL DATA	John Wiley and Sons, Inc.	Test (spectra records)	(1987)	£1995

Third, *teachers and students* should have better information support for the international exchange of knowledge, including know-how.

Last, but not least, journalists and the *general public* need objective information. Biotechnology is often distorted, either by inflated promises, or by dark pictures about pollution. Special files with accurate and relevant data, offered to the mass media, could contribute to the man in the street being better informed.

The main approach towards higher levels of information processing is based on structuring information into networks, if possible into trees with defined hierarchical data structure, and recognition of patterns (Kornhauser, 1989). For computer support, these have to be defined in the form of rules. By application of such rules, factual databases are developed into *knowledge bases*, which together with powerful programs, form *expert systems*.

The higher the level of information processing, the higher the logical support, but also the narrower is the field which can be considered. While bibliographic databases cover more or less the whole domain, the highest level, i.e. expert systems, can only be developed for specialized problems.

Structuring data into systems

Over one thousand documents were studied in the framework of BITES in order to define those biotechnological applications that have lead to marketable products (Kornhauser & Boh, 1988; 1989). This analysis was followed by studies of selected branches of the Biotechnology tree using the method of structuring data into systems (Figs 13.10–13.15).

It is hoped that BITES will be attractive to many institutions through active usage thereby allowing for the development of a more complete information system which will be of value and support to researchers and decision makers in the use of the resources available (UNDP, 1989).

Such cooperation is also needed for further development of methodological approaches towards *building structured databases*, which include in particular (Kornhauser, 1989) the following.

(1) *Recognition of main branches of a tree system.* The reliability of the tree structure strongly depends on the number of documents studied. By increasing this number, the structure is amended and refined. Such a database must be regarded as a self-improving system.

(2) *Selection of priority branches.* It is essential that branches grow to the top, i.e. to the product at the market. However, this is, due to limited availability of technical and commercial information, not easy to achieve and therefore all branches normally

cannot be followed completely. The selection of a specific branch is usually linked with on-going projects or priorities of users.

A comprehensive information system can be efficiently (including cost-efficiency) developed only if it has many users. If this is not the case, priority application branches have to be selected carefully, and always supported by a solid fundamental basis. Without the latter, the research usually ends in a blind alley.

(3) *Building a priority branch.* This should be linked with both information processing for setting up hypotheses of high probability, and checking them in the laboratory. In such an interaction, both can be improved: viz., the information

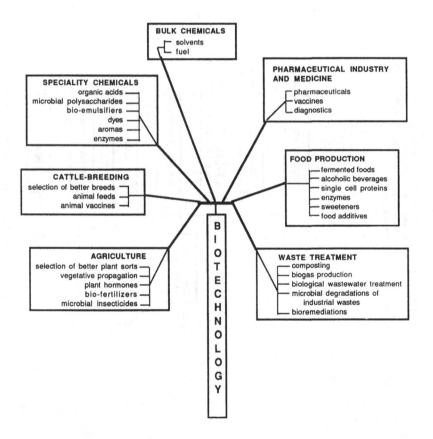

Fig. 13.10. Example of searching for the main structure of application fields in biotechnology.

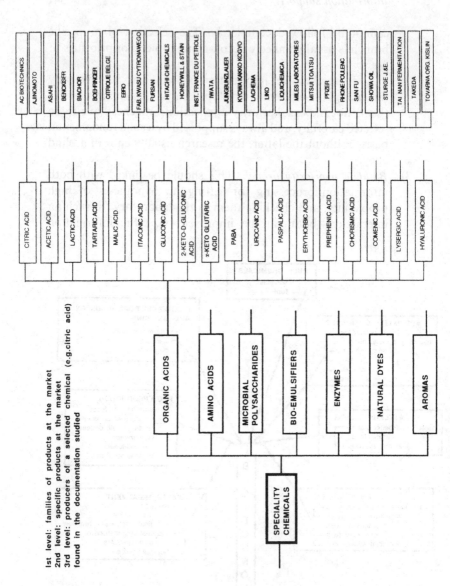

1st level: families of products at the market
2nd level: specific products at the market
3rd level: producers of a selected chemical (e.g. citric acid) found in the documentation studied

Fig. 13.11. Further branching of the speciality chemicals branch at three levels.

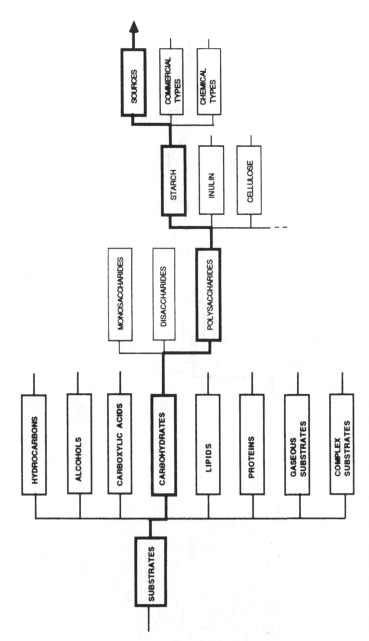

Fig. 13.12. Following a selected branch of substrates.

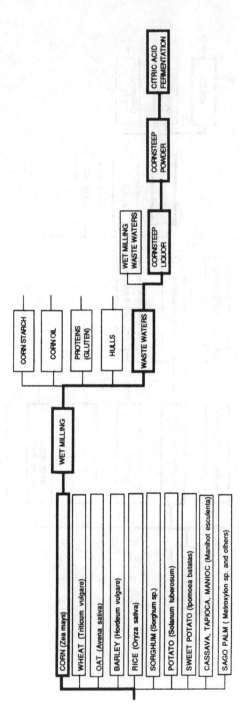

Fig. 13.13. Continuation of the starch branch in Fig. 13.12.

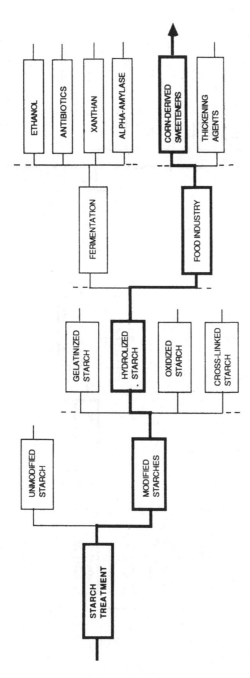

Fig. 13.14. Combination of chemical and biotechnological processes for the development of new products.

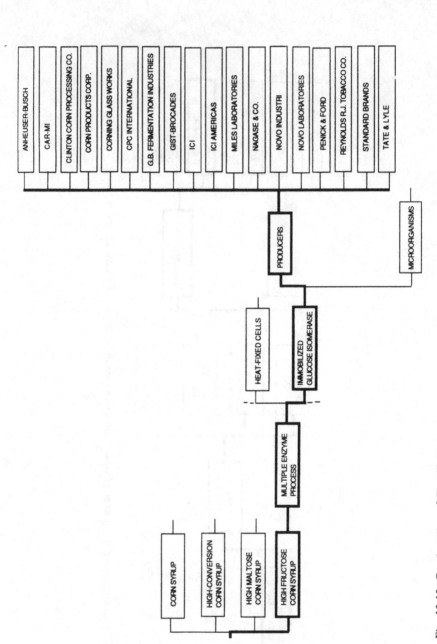

Fig. 13.15. Continuation of Fig. 13.14.

analysis and synthesis. The efficiency of the experimental work in the laboratory i.e. *the quality of the database structure must be evaluated according to its contribution to the time- and cost-efficiency of the laboratory research and pilot production.*

(4) *Higher levels of structuring data into systems.* These include studies of specific parameters, their relations, recognition of patterns leading to the mapping of concepts. Concept maps contribute to further development of basic knowledge, as well as to better teaching and learning.

Knowledge bases, expert systems

Expert systems are usually described as powerful computer programs for the presentation and application of factual knowledge in specific areas of expertise, oriented toward problem solving. They are products of the joint efforts of experts in a field and knowledge engineers (system developers).

An expert system consists of two main parts: a powerful computer program and a knowledge base that contains facts and rules. In building the knowledge base, in addition to data acquisition, higher levels of information processing must be incorporated, such as problem definition, conceptualization (definition of key concepts and their relationships), formalization (mapping of key concepts), implementation (formulating rules) and testing with the analysis of failures.

Opinions as to the utility and cost-efficiency of expert systems differ. Artificial intelligence groups often claim that an expert system not only autonomously applies human expertise, but also independently generates new knowledge. Experts in the field are usually more moderate and consider expert systems as tools that can replicate rare and/or expensive human knowledge. Next to this proven characteristic of expert systems, another important one has recently been developed: the reduction of parameters and/or measurements linked with selected processes, without reducing the reliability of tests (i.e. in monitoring pollution, selected production processes, diagnosis of selected diseases etc.). This new achievement greatly increases the economic potential of expert systems.

The *education system* often ignores the need for introduction of scientific and technical information into curricula at all levels. Computerized databases can be a very good teaching tool in schools, encouraging teachers and students to collect and store data, to compare and check their reliability, and to search for trends and predictions in research and development.

At the tertiary level, the use of international databases, and the building of specific information support for every project (at least a

Table 13.5. *Some examples of expert systems relevant to biotechnology*

Expert system, application	Developer or user	Reference source, publication year
CASCADE – control of nonlinear bacterial growth systems	Wang, Moore, Birdwell	search: DECHEMA, 1989
Expert system for the analysis and synthesis of metabolic pathways (enzyme, substrates, products)	California Inst. of Technology, CA, USA	search: COMPENDEX, 1988
Expert systems, applications to biotechnology	Intelligenetics, Inc.	search: BIOSIS, 1986
Expert Systems for biocatalytic conversion processes (sucrose inversion by Immobilized whole cell yeast invertase)	Helsinki Univ. of technology, Helsinki, Finland	search: COMPENDEX, 1985; DECHEMA, 1985; CHEM ENG & BIOTECH ABSTRACTS
Expert systems for biotechnology and food engineering	Lab. Teknillinen Korkeakoulu, Espoo, Finland	search: COMPENDEX, 1986; CHEM & BIOTECH ABSTRACTS
Expert system for the computer-assisted selection of bacterial strains for bioconversions	Ecole natl. Superieure de Chimie, Montpellier, France	search: COMPENDEX, 1987
Expert system for the control of space bioreactors	NASA	search: COMPENDEX, 1990

Expert system	Institution	Search source
Expert system to diagnose metabolic state of cells	Dep. Chem. Eng., Univ. Delaware, USA	search: BIOSIS, 1986
Expert system for fermentation bioreactor design	Lab. Biotechnol, and Food Eng., Helsinki Univ. Technol., Finland	search: BIOSIS, 1989
Expert system for fermentation control and process development	Mass. Inst. Technol., Cambridge, Mass., USA	search: BIOSIS, 1986
Expert system for fermentation process optimization	United Engineers and Constructors, Inc., Philadelphia, PA, USA	search: BIOBUSINESS, 1990
Expert system for modelling in biotechnology: sucrose conversion using immobilized β-fructifuranosidase		search: BIOTECHNOLOGY ABSTRACTS
Expert system for molecular structure determinations	Intelligenetics, California	search: BIOSIS, 1986
Expert systems to monitor large-scale formations and production-mode biotechnology	Intelligenetics, California	search: SUPERTECH
Expert systems in the operation and control of activated sludge plants	Dep. Civil Eng., Univ. Leeds, UK	search: BIOBUSINESS, 1986; BIOSIS, 1986
Expert system for pesticide residue analysis	Shell Agricultural Chemical Co., California, USA	search: CAB ABSTRACTS
Expert system for production management in agriculture and horticulture	Chiba Univ., Matsudo, Japan	search: COMPENDEX, 1990
Expert system for the rational design of large scale protein separation sequences	Biochem. Eng. Lab., Univ. Reading, UK	search: BIOSIS, 1988

Table 13.5. (*cont.*)

Expert system, application	Developer or user	Reference source, publication year
Expert system for selection and synthesis of protein purification processes	Biochem. Engineering Lab., Univ. Reading, Uk	search: BIOBUSINESS, 1989; BIOSIS, 1989
Expert system for species identification	Manchester Polytechnic, UK	search: COMPENDEX, 1987
Export system for stabilizing blood glucose (human insulin drug delivery system)	Biomed. Res. Div., Hosp. Sick Child., Toronto, Canada	search: BIOSIS, 1989
Expert system for timber harvesting system selection	Purdue Univ., West Lafayette, IN, USA	search: CAB ABSTRACTS
SPHINX – expert system for computer-aided decision in diabetes therapeutics	Service Biomathematiques, Statistiques Med. et Epidemiol., Marseille, France	search: BIOSIS, 1985
STRATEGENE – expert system for cloning SIMULATION		search: BIOTECHNOLOGY ABSTRACTS
SUPERVISOR – process control in biotechnology	Inst. Tech. Chem. Univ. Hannover	search: CHEMICAL ABSTRACTS, 1989

bibliographic database) is an imperative. Students should not only collect and store data, but must also learn how to transfer such data into comprehensive information, and then into knowledge with a logical structure.

Such an approach not only requires an effort to use the computer in dealing with information. It also demands another way of thinking, i.e. the transition: from dealing with separate data into operation with large sets of data; from studying a small number of isolated parameters towards building multiparameter systems of information (knowledge); from 'publish or perish' approach towards the transfer of knowledge to those who will use it in their research and decision making, and provide feed-back to the research team.

The first target for changing the way of thinking is the teacher (Fig. 13.16).

Fig. 13.16. 'Think! If you have five microcomputers and I take two away – how many have you left?'

References

Aguilar, A. (ed.) (1990). MINE, the Microbial Information Network Europe, Commission of the European Communities – European Laboratory Without Walls (ELWW), Biotechnology Action Programme, CFC brochure, 19 pp. Brussels, Belgium.

Blackwell Scientific Publications (1990). Blackwell Scientific Software: The New IBI Pustell for IBM-PC and MacVector for Macintosh, Commercial Publication.

Bruce, N.G., Arnette, S.L. & Dibner, M.D. (1989). Finding biotech information: databases and vendors, *Bio/Technol.*, 7, 455–8.

Cantley, M.F. (1984). Bio-Informatics in Europe: foundations and visions. *Swiss Biotechnol.*, 2(4), 7–14.

Coombs, J. & Alston, Y.R. (1989). *The International Biotechnology Directory 1989*, Information Services, Macmillan Publishers Ltd., pp. 11–34.

Da Silva, E. & Pinilla, A. (1988). Origins and justification for a UNDP/UNESCO European network on biotechnological applications: *Microbial Biotechnology and Bioengineering (Biotechnological Applications)*, European Network Symposium, Ljubljana, 3–8 October 1988 – Final Report, 1988, 4 pp.

DIALOG Database Catalog (1990). Dialog Information Services, Inc., 108 pp.

DIALOG Information Retrieval Service (1988–9). Blue Sheets No. 285, (1988), No. 286 (1989), No. 357 (1988), No. 358 (1988).

Dixon, B. (1989). Of bioprogramming, and a new program. *Bio/Technol.*, 7, 654.

Dynatech Laboratories Inc. (1990). Imaging Products: OMNICON 2000 Image Analysis; OMNICON 3600 Image Analyzer, Commercial Publications.

Gilna, P. & Ryals, J. (1990). Moving data from the laboratory to GenBank. *News from GenBank*, 3(1), 1–2.

Groves, P. (ed.) (1984). Using Chemical Abstracts – Chemistry Casette, The Royal Society of Chemistry, Educational Techniques Group, London, p. 5.

JICST-E, The Japan Information Center of Science and Technology (1989). Japanese Database on STN: The JICST-E File; Search Examples; User Aids, Commercial Publication, Tokyo, Japan, 8 pp.

Johnson, L.M. (1989). End-user searching of biotech databases. *Bio/Technol.*, 7, 378–9.

Kirsop, B. (1988). Microbial strain data network: a service to biotechnology, *Int. Indust. Biotechnol.*, 8(5), 24–7.

Knight, P. (1989). Innovations in image analysis, *Bio/Technol.*, 7, 954–6.

Knight, P. (1990). Non-protein engineering: small drug design. *Bio/Technol.*, 8, 105–7.

Kornhauser, A. (1989). Searching for patterns of knowledge, new information technologies in higher education. *CEPES* 1989, pp. 155–68.

Kornhauser, A. & Boh, B. (1988). Information Processing for Research, Development and Education in Biotechnology, *UNESCO/UNDP Seminar Microbial Biotechnology and Bioengineering (Biotechnological Applications) – European Network Symposium, Ljubljana, 3–8 October 1988.*

Kornhauser, A. & Boh, B. (1989). *Biotechnological Information Exchange System – BITES*, Unesco Report, Paris, France, 34 pp.

Kornhauser, A. & Boh, B. (1990). Bibliographic and Factual Database on Biotechnological Applications, IBM-compatible PC, CDS/ISIS2.3 Unesco Software, International Centre For Chemical Studies, Ljubljana, Yugoslavia.

Mitchell, J., Harrison, J. & Daum, A. (eds) (1990). *The CD-ROM Directory 1990*, 4th edition, TFPL Publishing, London, 450 pp.

ORBIT Database Catalog (1989). Orbit Search Service, A Division of Maxwell Online, 78 pp.

Pergamon Infoline User Guide – Databases, 1985–1987, Pergamon Infoline Ltd., London, UK.

Ratner, M. (1989). Dynamic market emerging for molecular modeling. *Bio/Technol.*, **7**, 43–7.

STN International, The Scientific and Technical Information Network: Summary Sheets, years 1986–1990.

Takishima, Y., Shimura, J., Ugava, Y. & Sugawara, H. (eds) (1989). WFCC World Data Center on Microorganisms, Guide to World Data Center on Microorganisms with List of Culture Collections in the World, First Edition, RIKEN, Wako, Saitama, Japan, pp. 1–9.

Tripos Associates (1990). ALCHEMY II Molecular Modelling Software for the Desktop; Comparative Molecular Field Analysis (CoMFA): User's Experience; CONCORD – A Powerful New Software Tool for Molecular Design; NITRO-Sybyl Graphics Emulation on the IBM PC or Mac II; SYBYL Integrating Scientific Strategies and Systems Solutions for Chemical Research, Commercial Publications.

UNDP – United Nations Development Programme (1989). Regional Project of the Governments of Europe: Microbial Biotechnology and Bioengineering (Biotechnological Applications) – European Network; Project Document, New York, USA, 34 pp.

UNESCO – United Nations Educational, Scientific and Cultural Organization (1989). Mini-micro CDS/ISIS Reference Manual (Version 2.3), Division of Software Development and Applications, Office of Information Programmes and Services. Paris, France.

14

The effects of emerging biotechnologies on plant and animal agriculture – a viewpoint

DARRELL L. HUETH, SHAIN-DOW KUNG
AND RITA R. COLWELL

Introduction

The development and adoption of new agricultural technologies have made North American agricultural producers and processors among the most productive in the world. As a result, North American households spend a smaller percentage of their income on food than households in other countries. However, concern has been expressed about whether the record of increasing productivity gains in agriculture can be sustained. The mechanization of agriculture is now virtually complete, and the use of chemical inputs developed for agriculture following World War II is widespread. Fortunately, scientists agree that another major technological revolution has started – a biotechnology revolution. It is argued that biotechnology has the potential to allow some countries in Europe and the United States to increase their industrial and agricultural productivity and hence maintain their competitiveness in world markets.

Biotechnology has two characteristics that are significantly different from previous agricultural technologies. First, biotechnology can be used to enhance product quality by improving characteristics of plants or animals. Second, biotechnology has the potential for conserving natural resources and improving environmental quality by use of genetically engineered organisms for degradation of toxic chemicals in the environment and by the development of insect and disease resistant plant varieties.

Current status and prospects of agricultural biotechnology

Biotechnology has its roots in agriculture and presents important opportunities for mankind. Powerful tools have been created to carry out the purpose of agriculture, i.e. to use intelligently natural resources for the production of more and better food and fibre products. The tools of biotechnology differ from traditional methods primarily in their speed, precision and reliability. All biotechnical developments must stem from naturally occurring genetic materials but rearrangements can be produced which nature is not capable of, namely, the development of transgenic plants and animals.

The use of technologies based on biological systems and living organisms includes recombinant DNA, gene transfer, embryo manipulation, embryo transfer, plant regeneration, cell culture, monoclonal antibodies, and bioprocess engineering (Board on Agriculture, 1987). These techniques are now being employed to discover information in elucidating gene structures, functions and regulations characterizing photosynthesis, diagnosing diseases, developing and using growth hormones, and clarifying the process of nitrogen fixation.

In the United States, over 300 companies are attempting to develop a variety of agricultural products using biotechnical techniques. Some of these companies are small and entrepreneurial in nature and others are *Fortune* 500 companies. Large agricultural chemical companies have shown significant interest in biotechnology because many of the products envisioned are potential substitutes and in some cases complements to products that are already in the production line.

At present, there are developments involving animals that are closer to the market than those involving plants (Table 14.1). For example, scientists have been able to genetically engineer bacteria to produce the growth hormone bovine somatrotrophin (BST) which is expected to be on the market soon. When administered to lactating cows under experimental conditions, BST causes an increase in milk production up to 40%. A growth hormone also has been engineered for swine that increases their ratio of muscle to fat and elevates their growth rates. This technology is somewhat further from the market. Other technologies currently being developed include those that produce multiple offspring and vaccines for disease prevention and control, as well as those that enhance aquacultural production. Researchers in veterinary medicine at the University of Maryland and the Maryland Biotechnology Institute have produced monoclonal antibodies against neutralization sites on infectious bursal disease viruses (IBD) and Newcastle disease viruses (NDV). The new IBD vaccine is effective and safe, and therefore dominates the market at the present time. Examples of technologies that are 'over the horizon' include those that can provide protection from multiple diseases using the vaccinia virus as a carrier and engineered microorganisms for increased feed efficiency.

There are many more transgenic plant species than animal species. Since 1985, more than 30 transgenic plants have been engineered for

Table 14.1. *Emerging biotechnologies*

Product or process	Biotechnology	Years to develop
Animal		
Enhanced dairy Production	Engineered growth hormone (BGH)	0
Enhanced growth rates for swine	Engineered growth hormone (PGH)	2
Pregnancy and oestrus testing	Monoclonal antibodies	1
Multiple offspring	Gene mapping – booroola gene	2–5
Disease prevention and control	Monoclonal antibodies	1–5
Enhanced aquaculture production	Engineered growth hormones – cold tolerance	3–5
Disease protection multiple diseases	Vaccinia virus	5–10
Increased feed efficiency	Engineering of intestinal organisms	5–10
Plant		
Herbicide resistance	Genetic transfer	0
Frost resistance	Genetic transfer	0
Plant regeneration	Cell culture	0
Insect resistance and control	Pheromones, juvenile hormones, genetic engineering	0
Disease detection and control	DNA probes and genetic transfer	0
Protein enhancement	Genetic transfer	2–5
Enhanced nitrogen fixation	Symbiotic rhizobium	5–10
Direct nitrogen fixation	Genetic engineering	10–20
Heat tolerance	Genetic transfer	5–10
Salinity tolerance	Genetic transfer	5–10

Table 14.2. *Transgenic plants produced*

	Monocotyledonous plants	
Asparagus	Millet	
Corn	Rice	

Dicotyledonous plants

Legumes		*Special crop*
Alfalfa	Cotton	
Clover	Flax	
Peas	Lotus	
Soybean	Sugar Beet	
	Sunflower	

Solanaceae		*Woody plants*
Eggplant	Pear	
Petunia	Poplar	
Potato	Walnut	
Tobacco		
Tomato		

Vegetable crop		*Special plant*
Cabbage	Arabidopsis	
Carrot		
Celery		
Cucumber		
Lettuce		
Rape		

Sources: Ratner (1989); Kung & Wu (1991).

conducting basic research and crop improvement. Table 14.2 lists the plant species in which transgenic plants have been successfully produced. The list is growing rapidly because the technology for inserting and expressing genes in plants is at hand, and more and more genes are being identified, together with the traits they control. In addition, no socio-ethical roadblocks exist which are equivalent to those encountered in patenting transgenic animals. Consequently, the potential developments in plant biotechnology are, in fact, more numerous than those in animal biotechnology.

A great part of plant biotechnology research has so far focused on developing plants that reduce losses caused by insects and diseases, resist frost damage, and tolerate certain herbicides. Insect-resistance research has centred on inserting a gene into plants or bacteria obtained from the bacterium *Bacillus thuringiensis* (BT). The gene produces a toxin that is fatal to insects. Efforts have concentrated on the use of BT because it has been used commercially in agriculture for 25 years and dissipates rapidly in the environment. Field trials were conducted recently in Maryland using this technology to protect corn against the European corn borer. Transgenic plant biotechnologies which reduce crop losses can significantly increase harvests without increasing the yield capability of the variety. This is in sharp contrast with the demands on transgenic animal research which must result in species which have greater inherent market capability.

Herbicide-resistance research has focused on developing tomato and tobacco cultivars that are resistant to herbicides such as glyphosate (Roundup Brand-name, Monsanto, St Louis, MO). Environmental groups have expressed concern about the benefits from this research since it is not clear whether it will lead to increased or decreased use of herbicides. The commercialization of these plant technologies may be 5 to 10 years away as a result of economic incentives, environmental regulation, and public acceptance. For example, a major economic consideration will be whether or not the cultivars produce fruit that meet the standards of the processors.

Plant technologies that involve multigenic traits such as nitrogen fixation and stress tolerance are even further away. Researchers are concerned because plants that are engineered to produce nitrogen may use so much energy in doing so that yields may fall dramatically. Much more needs to be learned about genetic structure, gene function, and gene regulation before these goods are achievable and marketable.

Potential impacts of agricultural biotechnology

Biotechnology can have significant impacts on agriculture. Four areas are particularly relevant. These are (1) production levels, (2) industry structure, (3) income distribution, and (4) environmental quality.

Production levels

BST is the only biotechnical development that has been subject to intensive evaluation thus far. Early estimates were that production per cow would increase by 40%. More recent estimates (Fallert *et al.*, 1987) have been in the 10–20% range for typical dairy herds and dairy managers. Also, there have been some production problems encountered with cows coming off a BST lactation and in some cases the width of the cows does not seem adequate to support the size of the udder. Still, there is a significant increase in productivity expected. The dairy industry, however, has had significant increases in productivity even without BST. From 1960 to 1982, milk output per cow increased 2.6%

per annum. Thus, it is likely that BST will accelerate, but not dramatically, dairy production.

Experimental studies of the use of growth hormones in meat production have shown that weight gain by hogs can be increased from 6 to 20% and a single study for beef cattle found a gain rate of 25% during a period of 18 weeks. Feed efficiency also has been shown to increase from 10 to 30%. However, it is unlikely that these gains in efficiency can be achieved in cattle feedlots and hog pens. Moreover, since swine and beef cattle generally are less confined than dairy cows, the labour and management required for daily injections could substantially increase costs and adversely affect technology adoption rates. Significant increases, nevertheless, in animal productivity are expected in the next 5 years.

Plant technologies that increase productivity are not likely to enter the market early. A study by the US Office of Technology Assessment (1986) indicates that plant biotechnologies will not have a major effect on aggregate agricultural productivity until the late 1990s or early twenty-first century and that annual increases in yields are not projected to differ significantly from historical averages between now and the year 2000.

The only previous plant technological change that compares in magnitude to the projections for BST in dairy production is the adoption of hybrid seed in corn. Corn yields, in the USA, increased 52.4% from 1935–9 when adoption was below 10% to 1949–53 when adoption was over 80% (Hueth & Just, 1987). In the hybrid corns case, however, drastic market adjustments were avoided because of the coincidental expansion of demand associated with the war years.

Although biotechnologies are expected to have major effects on production in specific commodities at the farm level, the effects on consumer prices and aggregate agricultural production are expected to be moderate for several reasons. An apt scenario is the situation in the USA. Firstly, the farm commodity component of food costs has witnessed a steady decline. As a consequence, farm level commodity price decreases have smaller effects on consumer food prices. Secondly, biotechnologies directed at reducing cost by eliminating the use of farm chemicals are directed at a segment of production costs that are already low. For example, fertilizer costs are 4% of production costs. Therefore, the elimination of expenditure on farm chemicals will not significantly reduce production costs and food prices. Again, from a similar economic view, advances in the development of a food ingredient in the food processing industry will have a small effect on food prices because the purchased food input cost component in food processing is only a small part of total costs.

Finally, unlike previous biological technical changes in agriculture such as hybrid corn and the Green Revolution which were developed in the public domain by public research universities or international agricultural research centres the world over, the locus of current research has moved into the private sector (Kenney & Buttel, 1985). Patents, proprietary information, trade secrets, and the necessity to price products sufficiently high to recover their research and development costs will impede the free flow of information and technology to potential users and thus will reduce the potential impacts and benefits from these emerging technologies.

In summary, therefore, the impact of agricultural biotechnologies on production levels is expected to be significant, non-dramatic and gradual.

Industry structure

The effect of agricultural biotechnology on the structure of agriculture is not clear. The technology revolution in farm machinery resulted in the largest farms becoming the most efficient farms whereas the chemical revolution tended to be scale neutral. Agricultural biotechnology generally increases the complexity of farming even though some developments such as pest-resistant cultivars make crop production less complex. On balance, increased complexity of management tends to favour larger farms over smaller farms.

Also, the major beneficiaries of these technologies will be the early adopters. These producers will expand their scale of operations to take advantage of the technology. The increased output from this group will depress prices and reduce profits for non-users. Some non-adopting producers will eventually be forced out of business.

In the long run, greater changes in the structure of agriculture are possible through biotechnology. The control of genetic characteristics has been a major factor in the vertical integrations of several agricultural industries, for example, the Perdue chicken. It has been pointed out (Phillips, 1988) that the greater control of genetic factors through novel biotechniques could lead to the integration of other industries such as pork, beef, vegetable, and fruit industries.

However, biotechnologies can be developed which are appropriate for small-scale low-input sustainable agriculture. For example, nitrogen-fixing legumes can be genetically engineered to be used effectively in crop-rotation production programmes in regions where they currently cannot survive.

The important point about agricultural biotechnologies is that they can in fact be targeted or directed to increase the efficiency of small-scale agriculture relative to large-scale agriculture if society so chooses. They are not inherently biased toward large- or small-scale agriculture. It really depends on how biotechnology is used.

Income distribution

Income distributional impacts of biotechnology are important between consumers and producers and between developed and developing countries.

Insofar as the technical change is either productivity increasing or cost reducing, the effect on consumers will be positive. That is, increased supplies will lead to lower prices and consumers will be better off. This of course holds true whether the consumers are households or are agribusiness firms who use farm products as inputs. For example, a study (Fallert *et al.*, 1987) by the US Department of Agriculture (USDA) shows that even under the price supports provided by the 1985 Farm Bill the overall milk prices are estimated to fall by 9% with the introduction of BST. Milk prices would fall even further were it not for the government purchases of dairy outputs.

The demand for most agricultural products is highly inelastic. This means that without governmental intervention small increases in supplies result in proportionally larger price decreases. The gains producers make by being able to sell a larger quantity are offset by the reduced prices they receive for their products. Even the early adopters of the new biotechnical tools may not be better off as the market effects of their decisions are realized. Again, governments can cushion these adverse effects on growers, but the current concern about budget deficits suggest this will not continue indefinitely. This is the case, for example, with the USA.

Biotechnology differs most significantly from previous technologies in its distributional impacts because the quality of agricultural products is frequently improved. A recent paper by Stevens (1988) reports that consumers are willing to pay more for food products which look better, taste better, are safer, i.e. contain less pesticide residues, and are more nutritious. Biotechnology, often called the 'designer' technology, is now being directed toward all of these ends. Successful research in this direction will mean that growers can produce more and still demand higher prices for their products. The primary beneficiaries from increased food quality will be farmers. However, consumers can be no worse off as food products of improved quality are introduced. The only possible losers are producers of products for which these new food products will be substitutes. Thus, research directed toward improving food quality can make both consumers and producers better off.

Although international impacts of plant biotechnologies have not been studied at this time, it is possible to speculate. Current work on these technologies is directed toward reducing crop losses. Thus, it would seem that the regions that have the greatest potential to gain are those that are currently experiencing the greatest losses from insects, weeds and diseases. This suggests that the developing world could be a major benefactor of plant technology.

Biotechnology research currently is concentrated in developed countries, but developing countries undoubtedly will require biotechnical developments to increase their agricultural self-sufficiency. The creation of plants that are drought resistant may enable African nations to produce far more food than currently is possible. Also, the USSR, which traditionally has been a large grain importer, may, in the near future, be able to grow crops in far colder regions and thus reduce imports. If biotechnical developments in the United States and Europe do not keep pace with those elsewhere, several industrialized countries will become less competitive in world markets.

The major constraints foreseen on the development and application of biotechnology in the developing world are as follows.

(1)   The lack of a free flow of scientific information among scientists and from laboratories in developed countries to developing countries on account of the proprietary nature of this information.

(2)   The possibilities that the multinational corporations will develop technologies that will not be appropriate for developing countries; for example, the development of reproductively unstable seed varieties will force farmers in a developing country into the market each year.

(3)   The lack of scientists and trained personnel in these countries to build research institutions where appropriate technologies can be developed. A large number of the most able molecular and cellular biologists in the developing world have relocated to industrial countries; and, many remaining scientists have financial linkages to multinational corporations.

(4)   The shortage of the skills required by labour and management to employ many biotechnologies. Future farm managers and workers will have to be able to inject hormones, carefully balance rations, identify insects and diseases, transfer embryos and carefully monitor environmental conditions. Computers also will be widely used to monitor plant and animal performance and for farm financial analysis. It is difficult to visualize farm managers in the developing world with these characteristics at the current time.

If developing countries are going to share fully in the benefits for the biotechnology revolution they must act either independently or collectively through some international organizations. The World Bank and the United Nations Agencies have provided funding for biotechnology research in developing countries and are expected to do more in the future. The developing world imperative is to direct this research toward goals that take into account the available resources that are unique to these societies.

The impact of agricultural biotechnology on international trade is unpredictable at this time. Biotechnology in primary agricultural commodities could increase the food self-sufficiency capabilities of importing countries and hence reduce the trade in primary commodities. But, it is also possible that biotechnology will increase the comparative advantage of traditional exporting countries such as the US, Canada and Australia. Since at the present time research and development is concentrated in these developed countries, the early effect of biotechnology likely will be increased market penetration by these countries.

The developed countries have recognized the potential gains from mutual reductions in agricultural trade barriers and elimination of subsidies to their agricultural sectors, as evidenced by current GATT negotiations. Concerns have been raised, however, that as tariff barriers are reduced they will be replaced with non-tariff barriers, many of which are related to biotechnology. The European Economic Community, for example, has refused to allow imports of BST-produced milk on the grounds that it presents a hazard to human health. This action, in turn, has been vigorously protested by the United States in particular.

Developed countries can be expected to increase their emphasis on the production of new and improved food products for the export market through biotechnology, particularly if opportunities for exports of basic commodities diminishes. Sixty-two per cent of large established firms, using biotechnology were involved in food processing in 1988 (Reilly, 1989). Thus, trade in value added biotechnical products is expected to increase in the future.

Environmental quality

Biotechnology is expected to reduce the land and water resources required for agricultural production. It also is expected, on balance, to reduce the use of chemical inputs. Thus, biotechnology can enhance surface and groundwater quality, soil productivity, and wildlife habitats, and reduce the health risks associated with agricultural chemicals.

Use of microorganisms engineered specifically for the degradation of toxic chemicals, pesticides, and spilled oil in the environment offer an application of major significance. Results of enhancement of microbially mediated degradation of oil spilled in Valdez, Alaska, suggest that directed microbial degradation of the spilled oil may be effective in the future.

Concern has been expressed, however, that genetically engineered organisms released into the environment may have unforeseen impacts. Weeds, for example, may acquire the genetic material from herbicide-resistant plant cultivars. Also, ecological systems may be disrupted by introducing an organism with no known predators or parasites into the environment. Currently, several governments are conducting open lease discussions and tests concerning regulations and risk assessment. The Federal government in the United States is regulating the testing and approval of biotechnology products under a coordinated framework, that includes the Environmental Protection Agency, USDA, and the Food and Drug Administration. At present, there is no generally accepted methodology for assessing the benefits and risks of agricultural biotechnology products.

In some cases, biotechnology has blurred the line between chemical agriculture and organic approaches, which has created unexpected complications for the regulatory process. For example, Ames & Gold (1988) review studies that have found some naturally occurring pesticides found in vegetables to be carcinogenic in laboratory animals under high exposures. Biotechnology can be used to enhance the levels of these naturally occurring substances to hazardous levels. Such changes in plants are not subject to the same degree of review as are pesticides.

The procedures for the regulation of field testing have become much clearer since the first tests were performed but the regulatory processes will be confronted by new and difficult decisions as they continue to evolve and attempts to balance the need for environmental and food safety with the need for affordable food supplies.

A research base – the United States: a case example

Biotechnology is on the verge of ushering in a new era of scientific research which will move us from hybrid organisms and the green revolution to transgenic organism and the gene revolution. Agricultural biotechnology research at both the basic and applied levels is growing rapidly and in the United States is currently focussed on reducing food costs, improving food quality and reducing environmental degradation. Agricultural biotechnology research will continue to move from university laboratories to industrial companies. Some insight can be given about new directions of US biotechnology, by a close examination of the research programme of one of the larger agricultural biotechnology units, the Center of Agricultural Biotechnology (CAB) at the University of Maryland.

There are biotechnology centres located on the campuses of universities in over 30 states. The State of Maryland, which has six centres associated with the Maryland Biotechnology Institute (MBI) includes CAB. A Task Force on Agricultural Biotechnology proposed the formation of CAB at The University of Maryland to invest in research that will benefit Maryland food consumers and agricultural producers, and enhance Maryland's natural resources. CAB was foreseen as a means of propelling Maryland into a national and international leadership role in agricultural biotechnology. To accomplish these goals, CAB was established on 1 July 1987 under the jurisdiction of the Maryland Biotechnology Institute. At present there are 20 scientists being funded by this programme, of which seven are in new positions on the College Park campus. Ten more positions will be filled in the next few years. The principal guideline used in formulating the research programmes is to capitalize on existing strengths, available talents, and projects of importance to Maryland.

One area that has been identified is plant protection through biological control. Both the Entomology and Botany Departments at College Park campus of the University of Maryland System have strengths in this area. The development of crops that are more resistant to diseases and insect pests, and the development of beneficial insects that are more antagonistic to pests can reduce the growers' reliance on chemicals and improve the quality of the water and soil resources in Maryland.

At the present time researchers are actively engaged in the study of plant–pathogen interactions including the viroid replication and pathogenesis and the factors which govern host specificity, fungal and bacterial pathogenicity and plant resistance. The interaction of host (plant) and pathogen is one of the most important and least understood problems in modern plant biology. Elucidation of the mechanisms which promote host resistance are critical to development of biological control techniques for plant protection. Biological control strategies promise to be more economical, less toxic and, ultimately, more stable than conventional chemical control methods.

In the field of Entomology, CAB scientists study insects as a model system on biological control. Insects are infinitely adaptable organisms that have become, or are in the process of becoming, resistant to a plethora of chemicals designed to control their reproduction. Despite our ever increasing need to control insects, chemically based methods of the past are becoming less and less acceptable. In search for long-term solutions attention is focussed on: (1) the role of insect vectors in the transmission of pathogenic viruses; (2) the effect of novel neuropeptides is disrupting normal insect development; (3) the transposable elements for introducing foreign genes into insects; and (4) the molecular/developmental mechanisms that generate morphological diversity.

Disease protection in poultry is a second area that has been targeted. The poultry industry is Maryland's largest agricultural industry. One of the highest priorities in that industry is to find vaccines that are safe, economical, predictable and effective. CAB has researchers who prepare antibodies against neutralization sites on infectious bursal disease virus (IBD) and Newcastle disease virus (NDV). Should the IBD and NDV vaccines under development in the School of Veterinary Medicine prove satisfactory, considerable potential exists to cover all economically important poultry diseases. Currently the first IBD vaccine developed dominates the market.

Marine biotechnology has flourished in recent years with the production of transgenic fish by MBI scientists in 1988. The future prospects for aquaculture appear highly promising.

Bioprocessing is another area where the University of Maryland has an established record of excellence. The Chemical Engineering Department has a component in bioprocessing, which is developing engineering techniques for large-scale fermentation with modern control strategies. Using recombinant DNA technology, it is now possible to produce a wide range of antibiotics, protein and other valuable substances. CAB members are developing theoretical and experimental approaches in these areas, in collaboration with researchers from many other disciplines.

Finally, it is clear that applied research stems from basic research. CAB is currently pursuing studies that include the chemistry of enzyme and drug action, molecular genetics of transposable elements, light-responsive elements in higher plants, regulation of glycosylation, and mechanisms of mitosis.

Conclusions

Biotechnology has the potential to allow countries like the United States to sustain their historical agricultural productivity growth. Currently biotechnology products in animals appear to be closer to the marketplace than plants, but the thrust in transgenic species appears to favour the potential in plants over animals principally because of a significantly larger pool of genetic resources. Also, transgenic biotechnology in plants can significantly increase harvests through reducing insect and disease losses from existing varieties whereas animal biotechnology faces the more difficult task of increasing the productive capability of the animal.

Because biotechnology can be used to improve product quality, farmers can receive higher prices for their products. This is in contrast with previous technical changes which resulted in increasing yields, but even lower prices and hence decreased revenues for agricultural producers.

The developing world has much to gain from emerging biotechnologies but substantial support from international organizations and institution building in these countries will be necessary before these gains can be realized. Perhaps governments in developing countries will have to form joint ventures with the private sector or international firms to insure that scientific manpower can be retained in those countries and so that technology appropriate for these countries will be developed.

Biotechnology can contribute significantly to improved environmental quality and reduce natural resource depletion; but again, policy decisions must provide the proper incentives to achieve these goals. Biotechnology is not inherently environmentally beneficial or detrimental; it must be directed toward society's best uses.

References

Ames, B.N. & Gold, L.S. (1988). Carcinogenic risk estimation: response, *Science, Wash.*, **240**, 1045–7.

Board on Agriculture, National Research Council (1987). *Agricultural Biotechnology*. National Academy Press, Washington, DC.

Fallert, R., McGucesin, T., Betts, C. & Bruner, G. (1987). *bst and the dairy industry – A national, regional and farm level analysis.* Economic Research Service, United States Department of Agriculture, Agricultural Economic Report Number 579.

Hueth, D.L. & Just, R.E. (1987). Policy implications of agricultural biotechnology. *Am. J. Agricult. Econ.*, **69**(2).

Kenney, M. & Buttel, F. (1985). Biotechnology: prospects and dilemmas for Third World development. *Develop. Change*, **16**, 61–91.

Kung, S.D. & Wu, R. (eds) (1991). *Transgenic Plants*. Butterworths, Boston.

Phillips, M.J. (1988). *A new technological era: How will it affect crop production on your farm?* Paper presented at Commercial Agricultural Institute Program on Crop Production, Columbia, Missouri.

Ratner, M. (1989). Crop Biotech '89: research efforts are market driven. *Biotechnology*, **7**(4), 338–41.

Reilly, J.M. (1989). *Consumer Effects of Biotechnology*. Economic Research Service, United States Department of Agriculture, Agriculture Information Bulletin, Number 581.

368   *D.L. Hueth, S.-D. Kung and R.R. Colwell*

Stevens, M.A. (1988). *Food quality, biotechnology, and the food company.* Paper presented at UM–USDA–DuPont International Symposium on Biotechnology and Food Quality.
US Congress, Office of Technology Assessment (1986). *Technology, Public Policy, and the Changing Structure of Agriculture.* US Government Printing Office, Washington, DC.

Index